200 Best Jobs™ for College Graduates

Third Edition

Part of JIST's Best Jobs™ Series

Michael Farr
With Database Work by Laurence Shatkin, Ph.D.

Also in JIST's Best Jobs Series

- *Best Jobs for the 21st Century*
- *300 Best Jobs Without a Four-Year Degree*
- *250 Best Jobs Through Apprenticeships*
- *50 Best Jobs for Your Personality*

JIST *Works*
America's Career Publisher

200 Best Jobs for College Graduates, Third Edition

© 2006 by JIST Publishing, Inc.

Published by JIST Works, an imprint of JIST Publishing, Inc.
8902 Otis Avenue
Indianapolis, IN 46216-1033

Phone: 1-800-648-JIST   Fax: 1-800-JIST-FAX
E-mail: info@jist.com   Web site: www.jist.com

Some Other Books by the Authors

Michael Farr
Seven Steps to Getting a Job Fast
The Quick Resume & Cover Letter Book
Getting the Job You Really Want
The Very Quick Job Search

Laurence Shatkin
Quick Guide to College Majors and Careers
Quick Guide to Career Training in Two Years or Less

Quantity discounts are available for JIST products. Please call 1-800-648-JIST or visit www.jist.com for a free catalog and more information.

Visit www.jist.com for information on JIST, free job search information, book excerpts, and ordering information on our many products. For free information on 14,000 job titles, visit www.careeroink.com.

Acquisitions Editor: Susan Pines
Development Editor: Stephanie Koutek
Cover and Interior Designer: Aleata Howard
Interior Layout: Carolyn J. Newland
Proofreaders: Jeanne Clark, Paula Lowell
Indexer: Kelly D. Henthorne

Printed in Canada

10 09 08 07 06 05   9 8 7 6 5 4 3 2 1

Library of Congress Cataloging-in-Publication Data

Farr, J. Michael.
    200 best jobs for college graduates / Michael Farr, with database work by
Laurence Shatkin.— 3rd ed.
        p. cm. — (JIST'S best jobs series)
    Includes index.
    ISBN 1-59357-241-7 (alk. paper)
  1. Vocational guidance. 2. College graduates—Employment. 3.
  Occupations—Forecasting. I. Title: Two hundred best jobs for college
graduates. II. Shatkin, Laurence. III. Title. IV. Series.
    HF5381.F4563 2006
    331.7'0235—dc22

                        2005012155

ISBN 1-59357-241-7

This Is a Big Book, But It Is Very Easy to Use

This book is for the many people who have or are considering getting a two- or four-year college degree or more and want to change or move ahead in their careers. It covers all the jobs in the U.S. Department of Labor's O*NET (Occupational Information Network) database that require a two-year associate's degree, a four-year bachelor's degree, or higher.

We decided to create this book after the success of another book we did called *Best Jobs for the 21st Century.* That book covers all major jobs at all levels of education and training that met our criteria for earnings, projected growth rate, and number of job openings. It has information on about 500 jobs. But covering that many jobs required nearly 700 pages, and the book includes many jobs that would not be of interest to people having or considering a college education.

So this book, *200 Best Jobs for College Graduates,* covers only those jobs that require a college degree. This approach allowed us to create a book that is less expensive, includes more-targeted lists, and has more useful information in the descriptions.

The nice thing about this book is that you don't have to read it all. Instead, we designed it to allow you to browse and find information that most interests you. The Table of Contents will give you a good idea of what's inside and how to use the book, so we suggest you start there. Part I of the book is made up of interesting lists that will help you explore jobs based on pay, interests, education level, personality type, and many other criteria. Part II provides descriptions for all major jobs that require a two-year associate's degree, a bachelor's degree, or higher. Just find a job that interests you in one of the lists in Part I and look up its description in Part II. Simple.

Some Things You Can Do with This Book

- Identify more-interesting or better-paying jobs that don't require additional training or education.
- Develop long-term plans that may require additional training, education, or experience.
- Explore and select a college major or a training or educational program that relates to a career objective.
- Find reliable earnings information to negotiate pay.
- Prepare for interviews.

(continued)

(continued)

These are a few of the many ways you can use this book. We hope you find it as interesting to browse as we did to put together. We have tried to make it easy to use and as interesting as occupational information can be.

When you are done with this book, pass it along or tell someone else about it. We wish you well in your career and in your life.

Credits and Acknowledgments: While the authors created this book, it is based on the work of many others. The occupational information is based on data obtained from the U.S. Department of Labor and the U.S. Census Bureau. These sources provide the most authoritative occupational information available. The job titles and their related descriptions are from the O*NET database, which was developed by researchers and developers under the direction of the U.S. Department of Labor. They, in turn, were assisted by thousands of employers who provided details on the nature of work in the many thousands of job samplings used in the database's development. We used the most recent version of the O*NET database, release 7.0. We appreciate and thank the staff of the U.S. Department of Labor for their efforts and expertise in providing such a rich source of data.

Table of Contents

Summary of Major Sections

Introduction. A short overview to help you better understand and use the book. *Starts on page 1.*

Part I—The Best Jobs Lists: Jobs That Require a Two- or Four-Year College Degree or More. Very useful for exploring career options! Lists are arranged into easy-to-use groups. The first group of lists presents the best overall jobs that require a college degree as well as jobs with the highest earnings, projected growth, and number of openings. More-specialized lists follow, presenting the best jobs for graduates age 20–24, graduates 55 and older, part-time graduates, self-employed graduates, women graduates, and men graduates. Other lists present the best jobs at various levels of education, by interest, and by personality type. The column starting at right presents all the list titles within the groups. *Starts on page 13.*

Part II—The Job Descriptions. Provides complete descriptions of all major jobs that require a college degree. *Starts on page 95.*

Detailed Table of Contents

Introduction

We kept this introduction as short as possible to encourage you to scan it. For this reason, we won't provide many details on the technical issues involved in creating the job lists or descriptions. Instead, we give you short explanations to help you understand and use the information the book provides for career exploration or planning.

How We Selected the 200 Best Jobs for College Graduates

Deciding on the "best" job is a choice that only you can make, but objective criteria can help you identify jobs that are, for example, better paying than other jobs with similar duties. We have sorted through the data for *all* major jobs and selected only those jobs that meet the following criteria:

1. We began by creating our own database of information from the O*NET, Census Bureau, and other sources to include the information we wanted. This database covered about 1,000 job titles at all levels of education and training.

2. The U.S. Department of Labor assigns a minimum level of training or education for entry into each job it tracks. We cut our initial list to include only those jobs requiring a two-year associate's degree or higher. A total of 346 jobs met this criterion at education/experience levels of two-year associate's degree, four-year bachelor's degree, work experience plus degree, master's degree, doctoral degree, or first professional degree. Among these 346 jobs are 35 specialized postsecondary education jobs that we combined into one job titled Postsecondary Teachers. We use this one job title throughout the lists but provide descriptions for all 35 of these specialized postsecondary jobs in Part II. (A list of these specialized job titles is provided in the introduction to Part II.) We also eliminated 43 jobs for which very little information is available. These are either catch-all titles (such as "Financial Specialists, All Other") that make the O*NET as comprehensive as possible or dummy occupations that help the O*NET match up better with occupational information from other government agencies. Census Bureau data is available for some of them, but no O*NET data is available for them, so we dropped them from consideration.

3. We obtained the core economic information about the remaining 268 jobs and decided that four of them—Mathematicians; Marine Architects; Marine Engineers; and Mining and Geological Engineers, Including Mining Safety Engineers—cannot be considered "best jobs" because they employ fewer than 500 workers per year and are expected to shrink rather than grow in workforce size. We then created three lists that ranked the remaining 264 jobs based on three major criteria: median annual earnings, projected growth through 2012, and number of job openings projected per year. Each of these lists was then sorted from highest to lowest and assigned a number score of from 264 (highest pay, for example) to 1 (lowest pay, for example).

4. We then created a new list that added the number scores for all three lists and arranged all 264 jobs in order from highest to lowest total score. We selected the 200 with the highest total score to be our 200 Best Jobs for College Graduates. For example, the job of Computer Software Engineers, Applications has the highest total combined score for earnings, growth, and number of job openings, so Computer Software Engineers, Applications is listed first in our 200 Best Jobs for College Graduates list, even though this job is not the highest-paying job (which is a tie between Anesthesiologists and some other physician jobs), the fastest-growing job (which is Network Systems and Data Communications Analysts), or the job with the most openings (which is General and Operations Managers).

You can find descriptions for the 200 best jobs in Part II, along with descriptions of the various specialized postsecondary teaching jobs, for a total of 234 descriptions in all.

We are not suggesting that the 200 jobs with the highest overall scores for earnings, growth, and number of openings are all good ones for you to consider—some will not be. But the 200 jobs that met our criteria encompass such a wide range that you are likely to find one or more that will interest you. The jobs that met our "best jobs" criteria are also more likely than average to have higher pay, faster projected growth, and a larger number of openings than other jobs at similar levels of education and training.

Where the Information Comes From

The information we used in creating this book comes from three major government sources:

◉ **The U.S. Department of Labor:** We used a variety of data sources to construct the information we used in this book. Most of the data comes from various databases of information provided by the U.S. Department of Labor. We started with the jobs included in the O*NET database. The O*NET includes information on more than 1,100 occupations and is now the primary source of detailed information on occupations. The Labor Department updates the O*NET on a regular basis, and we used the most recent one available—version 7.

- **The U.S. Census Bureau:** Because we wanted to include earnings, growth, number of openings, and other data not included in the O*NET, we used information on earnings from the U.S. Bureau of Labor Statistics (BLS). Some of this data came from the Current Population Survey, conducted by the U.S. Census Bureau, and other data came from the BLS's own Occupational Employment Statistics survey. The information on earnings is the most reliable information we could obtain. The BLS uses a slightly different system of job titles than the O*NET does, but we were able to link the BLS data to most of the O*NET job titles we used to develop this book. The Current Population Survey also provided information about the proportion of workers in each job who are self employed or work part time.

- **The U.S. Department of Education:** We used the Classification of Instructional Programs, a system developed by the U.S. Department of Education, to cross-reference the education or training programs related to each job.

The Data Complexities

For those of you who like details, we present some of the complexities inherent in our sources of information and what we did to make sense of them here. You don't need to know this to use the book, so jump to the next section of the Introduction if you are bored with details.

Earnings, Growth, and Number of Openings

We include information on earnings, projected growth, and number of job openings for each job throughout this book.

Earnings

The employment security agency of each state gathers information on earnings for various jobs and forwards it to the U.S. Bureau of Labor Statistics. This information is organized in standardized ways by a BLS program called Occupational Employment Statistics, or OES. To keep the earnings for the various jobs and regions comparable, the OES screens out certain types of earnings and includes others, so the OES earnings we use in this book represent straight-time gross pay exclusive of premium pay. More specifically, the OES earnings include the job's base rate; cost-of-living allowances; guaranteed pay; hazardous-duty pay; incentive pay, including commissions and production bonuses; on-call pay; and tips but do not include back pay, jury duty pay, overtime pay, severance pay, shift differentials, non-production bonuses, or tuition reimbursements. Also, self-employed workers are not included in the estimates, and they can be a significant segment in certain occupations.

The OES earnings data uses a system of job titles called the Standard Occupational Classification system, or SOC. Most of these jobs can be cross-referenced to the O*NET job titles we use in this book, so we can attach earnings information to most job titles and descriptions. But some of the O*NET jobs simply do not have earnings data available for them from the sources we used, so some jobs in the book have no earnings data presented for them. In some other cases, an SOC title cross-references to more than one O*NET job title. For example, the O*NET has separate information for Accountants and for Auditors, but the SOC reports earnings for a single occupation called Accountants and Auditors. Therefore you may notice that the salary we report for Accountants ($49,770) is identical to the salary we report for Auditors. In reality there probably is a difference, but this is the best information that is available.

Projected Growth and Number of Job Openings

This information comes from the Office of Occupational Statistics and Employment Projections, a program within the Bureau of Labor Statistics that develops information about projected trends in the nation's labor market for the next ten years. The most recent projections available cover the years from 2002 to 2012. The projections are based on information about people moving into and out of occupations. The BLS uses data from various sources in projecting the growth through 2012 and annual number of openings for each job title— some data comes from the Census Bureau's Current Population Survey and some comes from an OES survey. The projections assume that there will be no major war, depression, or other economic upheaval.

Like the earnings figures, the figures on projected growth and job openings are reported according to the SOC classification, so again you will find that a few jobs in this book do not include this information. As with earnings, some of the SOC jobs crosswalk to more than one O*NET job. To continue the example we used earlier, the SOC reports growth (19.5%) and openings (119,000) for one occupation called Accountants and Auditors, but in this book we report these figures separately for the occupation Accountants and for the occupation Auditors. When you see Accountants with 19.5% projected growth and 119,000 projected job openings, and Auditors with the same two numbers, you should realize that the 19.5% rate of projected growth represents the *average* of these two occupations—one may actually experience higher growth than the other—and that these two occupations will *share* the 119,000 projected openings.

While salary figures are fairly straightforward, you may not know what to make of job-growth figures. For example, is projected growth of 15% good or bad? You should keep in mind that the average (mean) growth projected for all occupations in the OES survey is 14.8%. One-quarter of the occupations have a growth projection of 4.7% or lower. Growth of 12.4% is the median, meaning that half of the occupations have more, half less. Only one-quarter of the occupations have growth projected at more than 19.4%.

Remember, however, that the jobs in this book are a distinguished set—they all require college and were selected as "best" partly on the basis of high growth, so their mean growth is a lofty 20.9%. Among these 200 high-powered jobs, the job ranked 50th by projected growth has a figure of 27.3%, the job ranked 100th (the median) has a projected growth of 19.5%, and the job ranked 150th has a projected growth of 13.2%.

Information in the Job Descriptions

- **Job Title:** We use the job titles as presented in the O*NET database as maintained by the U.S. Department of Labor.

- **Earnings, Percent Growth, Annual Job Openings, Percent Self-Employed, Percent Part-Time:** The source of the earnings, growth, and number of openings information is the same as described in this section and as used in the lists in Part I. The data on percentage of self-employed and part-time workers comes from the U.S. Census Bureau's Current Population Survey.

- **Summary Description and Tasks:** This information comes from the O*NET database.

- **Skills:** This information is also from the O*NET database. Data is provided on many skills for each job, so we listed a skill for a job only if the rating for the skill was higher than the average rating for that skill for all jobs. If there were more than eight high-rated skills, we included only those eight with the highest ratings, and we present them from highest to lowest score (that is, in terms of by how much its score exceeds the average score). We include up to 10 skills if scores were tied for eighth place.

- **GOE Information:** We used the newest interest areas and work groups as presented in the *New Guide for Occupational Exploration,* Fourth Edition (JIST Publishing). The GOE groupings allow you to explore all major jobs in the O*NET database based on your interests. The process we used to cross-reference the O*NET jobs to the GOE interest groupings is explained in the book itself, should you want to know more about how this was done. Looking at jobs based on your interests is a very useful approach because it introduces you to a variety of related jobs you may not consider otherwise.

- **Personality Type:** We used a field in the O*NET database that assigns each job to its most closely related personality type.

- **Education/Training Programs:** We linked the O*NET job titles we use in this book to related educational and training programs listed in another database called the Classification of Instructional Programs, or CIP. To do this, we used a "crosswalk" (a type of cross-reference system) created by the National Crosswalk Service Center, part of the Iowa Department of Education. Because this crosswalk was based on SOC rather than O*NET job titles, we made various changes to connect the O*NET job titles to the education or training programs related to them. We also modified the names of some education and training programs so they would be more easily understood.

- **Related Knowledge/Courses:** The information we used for this section of each job description comes from the O*NET database. We went through a process similar to the one we used for Skills (earlier in this list) to determine which entries were most important for each job. In this case, however, we listed at least two knowledge areas for each job, even if the ratings for those knowledge areas were lower than the average for all jobs. In many cases, these knowledge areas will help you identify specific courses or learning programs to take to best prepare for entry into the jobs that interest you.

Getting all the data to connect in a useful way was not a simple process, and it is not always perfect. Even so, we used the best and most recent sources of data we could find and think that our efforts will be helpful to many people.

The Data in This Book Can Be Misleading

We use the most reliable data we can obtain for the earnings, projected growth, number of openings, and other information to create this book, but keep in mind that this information may or may not be accurate for your situation.

As you look at the data, it is important to remember that the statistics are averages that may or may not relate to your situation. They give you a general idea about the number of workers employed, annual earnings, rate of job growth, and annual job openings. Understand, however, that this information is true on the average. But just as there is no precisely average person, there is no such thing as a statistically average example of a particular job. We say this because data, while helpful, can also be misleading.

Take, for example, the yearly earnings information in this book. This is highly reliable data obtained from a very large U.S. working population sample by the Bureau of Labor Statistics. It tells us the median annual pay received by people in various job titles. This sounds great, except that half of all people in that occupation earned less than that amount, and half earn more. (We often use "average" instead of "median" elsewhere in this book for ease of explanation).

For example, people just entering the occupation or with a few years of work experience will often earn much less than the average. People who live in rural areas or who work for smaller employers typically earn less than those who do similar work in cities, where the cost of living is higher, or for larger employers.

Information about job growth can also be deceptive. For example, for the 200 best jobs listed in this book, the average job growth between 2002 and 2012 is 20.9%. (This compares to an average job growth of 14.8% for all occupations.) The occupation Biomedical Engineers is expected to grow by 26.1%—a bit above average—but does that mean there will plenty of jobs going begging for applicants? Not really, because the workforce of this occupation is tiny: Fewer than 500 jobs per year are expected to open for Biomedical Engineers. For comparison, consider General and Operations Managers. Expected job growth is not as good—18.4%—but the workforce of this occupation is so much bigger that it will create 260,000 job openings per year.

But wait, there's still another caution: Even the number of job openings doesn't tell you the whole story about how easy it will be to find work. Remember that in economics, everything depends on the balance of supply and demand. The number of job openings merely tells you the *demand* for workers; it doesn't tell you about the *supply* of job applicants. The occupation General and Operations Managers does not have a lot of formal requirements, and people tend to stay in it for a long time because it combines high financial rewards with low physical demands. Therefore, as these jobs open up, a lot of people can be expected to apply—some of them lower-level managers, some of them experienced General and Operations Managers who want to move around or even come out of retirement. Competition for jobs will be keen. By comparison, the occupation Registered Nurses is expected to offer 215,000 job openings per year—not quite as many as for General and Operations Managers—but the most common entry route is a four-year college nursing program, which limits the number of qualified applicants. In addition, the job can be physically demanding, so job applicants are much less likely to come out of retirement. As a result, the market for job-seekers will be excellent.

So, in reviewing the information in this book, please understand the limitations of the data it presents. You need to use common sense in career decision-making as in most other things in life. Even so, we hope that you find the information helpful and interesting.

Part I—The Best Jobs Lists: Jobs That Require a Two- or Four-Year College Degree or More

There are 62 separate lists in Part I of this book—look in the Table of Contents for a complete list of them. The lists are not difficult to understand because they have clear titles and are organized into groupings of related lists.

Depending on your situation, some of the jobs lists in Part I will interest you more than others. For example, if you are young, you may be interested to learn the highest-paying jobs that employ high percentages of college graduates age 20–24. Other lists show jobs within interest groupings, personality types, levels of education, or other ways that you might find helpful in exploring your career options.

Whatever your situation, we suggest you use the lists that make sense for you to help explore career options. Following are the names of each group of lists along with short comments on each group. You will find additional information in a brief introduction provided at the beginning of each group of lists in Part I.

Here is an overview of each major group of lists you will find in Part I.

Best Jobs Overall: Lists of Jobs for College Graduates with the Highest Pay, Fastest Growth, and Most Openings

Four lists are in this group, and they are the ones that most people want to see first. The first list presents the top 200 job titles in order of their combined scores for earnings, growth, and number of job openings. Three more lists in this group are extracted from the 200 best and present the 100 jobs with the highest earnings, the 100 jobs projected to grow most rapidly, and the 100 jobs with the most openings.

Best Jobs Lists with High Percentages of Workers Age 20–24, Workers Age 55 and Over, Part-Time Workers, Self-Employed Workers, Women, and Men

This group of lists presents interesting information for a variety of types of people based on data from the U.S. Census Bureau. The lists are arranged into groups for workers age 20–24, workers 55 and older, part-time workers, self-employed workers, women, and men. We created five lists for each group, basing the last four on the information in the first list:

- The jobs having the highest percentage of people of each type
- The 25 jobs with the highest combined scores for earnings, growth, and number of openings
- The 25 jobs with the highest earnings
- The 25 jobs with the highest growth rates
- The 25 jobs with the largest number of openings

Best Jobs Lists Based on Levels of Education and Experience

We created separate lists for each level of college education and training as defined by the U.S. Department of Labor. We put each of the top 200 job titles into one of the lists based on the education and training required for entry. Jobs within these lists are presented in order of their total combined scores for earnings, growth, and number of openings. The lists include jobs in these groupings:

- Associate's degree
- Bachelor's degree
- Work experience plus degree
- Master's degree
- Doctoral degree
- First professional degree

Best Jobs Lists for College Graduates Based on Interests

These lists organize the 200 best jobs into groups based on interests. Within each list, jobs are presented in order of their total scores for earnings, growth, and number of openings. Here are the 16 interest areas used in these lists: Agriculture and Natural Resources; Architecture and Construction; Arts and Communication; Business and Administration; Education and Training; Finance and Insurance; Government and Public Administration; Health Science; Hospitality, Tourism, and Recreation; Human Service; Information Technology; Law and Public Safety; Manufacturing; Retail and Wholesale Sales and Service; Scientific Research, Engineering, and Mathematics; Transportation, Distribution, and Logistics.

Best Jobs Lists for College Graduates Based on Personality Types

These lists organize the 200 best jobs into six personality types described in the introduction to the lists: Realistic, Investigative, Artistic, Social, Enterprising, and Conventional. The jobs within each list are presented in order of their total scores for earnings, growth, and number of openings.

Part II—The Job Descriptions

This part of the book provides a brief but information-packed description for each of the 234 jobs that met our criteria for this book (that is, the 200 best plus all the specialized postsecondary teaching jobs). The descriptions are presented in alphabetical order, which makes it easy to look up a job you've identified in a list from Part I that you want to learn more about.

We used the most current information from a variety of government sources to create the descriptions. We designed the descriptions to be easy to understand, but the sample that follows, with an explanation of each of its component parts, may help you better understand and use the descriptions.

Here are details for each of the major parts of the job descriptions in Part II:

- **Job Title:** This is the job title for the job as defined by the U.S. Department of Labor and used in its O*NET database.
- **Data Elements:** The information on earnings, growth, annual openings, percent self-employed workers, and percent part-time workers comes from various government databases for this occupation, as we explain earlier in this Introduction.
- **Summary Description and Tasks:** The sentences in bold provide a summary description of the occupation. It is followed by a listing of tasks that are generally performed by people who work in the job. This information comes from the O*NET database.

◎ **Skills:** The O*NET database provides data on 35 skills, so we decided to list only those that were most important for each job rather than list pages of unhelpful details. For each job, we identified any skill with a rating that was higher than the average rating for this skill for all jobs. We ordered the skills by the amount by which their ratings exceeded the average rating for all occupations, from highest to lowest. If there were more than eight such skills, we included only those eight with the highest ratings. We included up to 10 skills if scores were tied for eighth place. If no skill had a rating higher than the average for all jobs, we noted that none met the criteria. Each listed skill is followed by a brief description of that skill.

◎ **GOE Information:** This information cross-references the Guide for Occupational Exploration (or the GOE), a system originally developed by the U.S. Department of Labor that organizes jobs based on interests. We used the groups from the fourth edition of the *New Guide for Occupational Exploration,* as published by JIST. This edition employs interest fields based on the 16 career clusters developed by the U.S. Department of Education and used in a variety of career information systems. The description includes the major Interest Area the job fits into, its more-specific Work Group, and a list of related O*NET job titles that are in this same GOE Work Group. This information will help you identify other job titles that have similar interests or require similar skills. You can find more information on the GOE and its Interest Areas in the introduction to the lists of jobs based on interests in Part I.

◎ **Personality Type:** This part gives the name of the personality type that most closely matches each job, as well as a brief definition of this personality type. You can find more information on the personality types in the introduction to the lists of jobs based on personality types in Part I.

◎ **Education/Training Programs:** This entry provides the name of the educational or training program or programs listed for the job in a related government data source called the Classification of Instruction Programs (CIP). This information will help you identify sources of formal or informal training for a job that interests you.

◎ **Related Knowledge/Courses:** This entry will help you understand the most important knowledge areas that are required for the job and the types of courses or programs you will likely need to take to prepare for it. We used information in the Department of Labor's O*NET database for this entry. We went through a process similar to the one described for the skills noted above to end up with entries that are most important for each job.

Job Title →

Landscape Architects

Data Elements →

- ◎ Education/Training Required: Bachelor's degree
- ◎ Annual Earnings: $50,780
- ◎ Growth: 22.2%
- ◎ Annual Job Openings: 2,000
- ◎ Self-Employed: 23.4%
- ◎ Part-Time: 5.5%

Summary Description and Tasks →

Plan and design land areas for such projects as parks and other recreational facilities, airports, highways, hospitals, schools, land subdivisions, and commercial, industrial, and residential sites. Prepare site plans, specifications, and cost estimates for land development, coordinating arrangement of existing and proposed land features and structures. Confer with clients, engineering personnel, and architects on overall program. Compile and analyze data on conditions, such as location, drainage, and location of structures for environmental reports and landscaping plans. Inspect landscape work to ensure compliance with specifications, approve quality of materials and work, and advise client and construction personnel.

Skills →

SKILLS—Coordination: Adjusting actions in relation to others' actions. **Operations Analysis:** Analyzing needs and product requirements to create a design. **Management of Financial Resources:** Determining how money will be spent to get the work done and accounting for these expenditures. **Persuasion:** Persuading others to change their minds or behavior. **Social Perceptiveness:** Being aware of others' reactions and understanding why they react as they do. **Time Management:** Managing one's own time and the time of others. **Instructing:** Teaching others how to do something. **Complex Problem Solving:** Identifying complex problems and reviewing related information to develop and evaluate options and implement solutions.

GOE Information →

GOE—Interest Area: 02. Architecture and Construction. **Work Group:** 02.02. Architectural Design. **Other Jobs in This Work Group:** Architects, Except Landscape and Naval. **PERSONALITY TYPE:** Artistic. Artistic occupations frequently involve working with forms, designs, and patterns. They often require self-expression, and the work can be done without following a clear set of rules.

Education/ Training Program(s) →

EDUCATION/TRAINING PROGRAM(S)— Environmental Design/Architecture; Landscape Architecture (BS, BSLA, BLA, MSLA, MLA, PhD).

Related Knowledge/Courses →

RELATED KNOWLEDGE/COURSES—Design: Knowledge of design techniques, tools, and principles involved in production of precision technical plans, blueprints, drawings, and models. **Building and Construction:** Knowledge of the materials, methods, and tools involved in the construction or repair of houses, buildings, or other structures such as highways and roads. **Geography:** Knowledge of principles and methods for describing the features of land, sea, and air masses, including their physical characteristics; locations; interrelationships; and distribution of plant, animal, and human life. **Engineering and Technology:** Knowledge of the practical application of engineering science and technology. This includes applying principles, techniques, procedures, and equipment to the design and production of various goods and services. **Biology:** Knowledge of plant and animal organisms and their tissues, cells, functions, interdependencies, and interactions with each other and the environment. **Sales and Marketing:** Knowledge of principles and methods for showing, promoting, and selling products or services. This includes marketing strategy and tactics, product demonstration, sales techniques, and sales control systems.

Sources of Additional Information

Hundreds of sources of career information exist, so here are a few we consider most helpful in getting additional information on the jobs listed in this book.

Print References

- *O*NET Dictionary of Occupational Titles:* Revised on a regular basis, this book provides good descriptions for all jobs listed in the U.S. Department of Labor's O*NET database. There are more than 1,100 job descriptions at all levels of education and training, plus lists of related job titles in other major career information sources, educational programs, and other information. Published by JIST.

- *New Guide for Occupational Exploration,* **Fourth Edition:** The new edition is cross-referenced in the descriptions in Part II. The book provides helpful information to consider on each of the interest areas and work groups, descriptions of all O*NET jobs within each GOE group, and many other features useful for exploring career options. Published by JIST.

- *Enhanced Occupational Outlook Handbook:* Updated regularly, this book provides thorough descriptions for more than 270 major jobs in the *Occupational Outlook Handbook,* brief descriptions for the O*NET jobs that are related to each, brief descriptions of thousands of more-specialized jobs from the *Dictionary of Occupational Titles,* and other information. Published by JIST.

Internet Resources

- **The U.S. Department of Labor Web site:** The Department of Labor Bureau of Labor Statistics Web site (http://www.bls.gov) provides a lot of career information, including links to other pages that provide information on the jobs covered in this book. The Web site is a bit formal and, well, confusing, but it will take you to the major sources of government career information if you explore its options.

- **O*NET site:** Go to http://www.onetcenter.org for a variety of information on the O*NET database, including links to sites that provide detailed information on the O*NET job titles presented in Part II of this book.

- **CareerOINK.com:** This site (at http://www.careeroink.com) is operated by JIST and includes free information on thousands of jobs, easy-to-use crosswalks between major career information systems, links from military to civilian jobs, sample resumes, and many other features. A link at http://www.jist.com will also take you to the CareerOINK Web site.

Thanks

Thanks for reading this introduction. You are surely a more thorough person than those who jumped into the book without reading it, and you will probably get more out of the book as a result.

We wish you a satisfying career and, more importantly, a good life.

PART I

The Best Jobs Lists: Jobs That Require a Two- or Four-Year College Degree or More

Tips on Using These Lists

We've tried to make the Best Jobs lists in this section both fun to use and informative. You can use the Table of Contents at the front of the book to find a complete listing of all the list titles in this section. You can then review the lists that most interest you or simply browse the lists in this section. Most, such as the list of jobs with the highest pay, are easy to understand and require little explanation. We provide comments on each group of related lists to inform you of the selection criteria or other details we think you may want to know.

As you review the lists, mark job titles that appeal to you (or, if someone else will be using this book, write them on a separate sheet of paper) so that you can look up their descriptions later in Part II.

Understand the Limitations of the Information

Most of the lists emphasize jobs with high pay, high growth, or large numbers of openings. Many people consider these factors important in selecting a desirable job, and they are also easily quantifiable. While these measures are important, we think you should also think about other factors in considering your career options. For example, location, liking the people you work with, having an opportunity to serve others, and enjoying your work are just a few of the many factors that may define the ideal job for you. These measures are difficult or impossible to objectively quantify based on the data we have available and are not, therefore, presented in this book. For this reason, we suggest that you consider the importance of these issues yourself and that you thoroughly research any job before making a firm decision.

For example, of the 200 jobs that require a college degree or more in our Best Jobs Overall list, the job with the lowest combined score for earnings, growth, and number of openings is Nuclear Engineer. It has annual earnings of $83,260, a slightly-below-zero percent growth rate, and 1,000 job openings per year. Is this a bad job, one you should avoid? No, of course not. It all depends on what you like or want to do. Another example is the job that had the very best overall score for earnings, growth, and number of openings: Computer Software Engineer, Applications. Is this job a great job to consider? Many people (the authors included) would not want to work in this job or may not have the skills or interest needed to do it well. It would be a great job for someone who was good at it and who would enjoy doing it, but it would simply not be right for someone else. On the other hand, the perfect job for some people would be Nuclear Engineer because they enjoy it and are good at it.

So, as you look at the lists that follow, keep in mind that earnings, growth, and number of openings are just some things to consider. Also consider that half of all people in a given job earn more than the earnings you will see in this book—and half earn less. If a job really appeals to you, you should consider it even if it is not among the highest paying. And you should also consider jobs not among the fastest growing and jobs with few openings for similar reasons, because openings are always available, even for jobs with slow or negative growth projections or with small numbers of openings.

Some Details on the Lists

The sources of the information we used in constructing these lists are presented in this book's Introduction. Here are some additional details on how we created the lists:

- **We collapsed a number of specialized postsecondary education jobs into one title.** The government database we used for the job titles and descriptions included more than 30 job titles for postsecondary educators, yet the data source we used for growth and number of openings provided data only for the more general job of Postsecondary Teacher. To make our lists more useful, we included only one listing, Postsecondary Teacher, rather than separate listings for each specialized job. We did, however, include descriptions for all the specific postsecondary teaching jobs in Part II. Should you wonder, here are the more specialized titles: Agricultural Sciences Teachers, Postsecondary; Anthropology and Archeology Teachers, Postsecondary; Architecture Teachers, Postsecondary; Area, Ethnic, and Cultural Studies Teachers, Postsecondary; Art, Drama, and Music Teachers, Postsecondary; Atmospheric, Earth, Marine, and Space Sciences Teachers, Postsecondary; Biological Science Teachers, Postsecondary; Business Teachers, Postsecondary; Chemistry Teachers, Postsecondary; Communications Teachers, Postsecondary; Computer Science Teachers, Postsecondary; Criminal Justice and Law Enforcement Teachers, Postsecondary; Economics Teachers, Postsecondary; Education

Teachers, Postsecondary; Engineering Teachers, Postsecondary; English Language and Literature Teachers, Postsecondary; Environmental Science Teachers, Postsecondary; Foreign Language and Literature Teachers, Postsecondary; Forestry and Conservation Science Teachers, Postsecondary; Geography Teachers, Postsecondary; Graduate Teaching Assistants; Health Specialties Teachers, Postsecondary; History Teachers, Postsecondary; Home Economics Teachers, Postsecondary; Law Teachers, Postsecondary; Library Science Teachers, Postsecondary; Mathematical Science Teachers, Postsecondary; Nursing Instructors and Teachers, Postsecondary; Philosophy and Religion Teachers, Postsecondary; Physics Teachers, Postsecondary; Political Science Teachers, Postsecondary; Psychology Teachers, Postsecondary; Recreation and Fitness Studies Teachers, Postsecondary; Social Work Teachers, Postsecondary; and Sociology Teachers, Postsecondary.

◎ **Many jobs have tied scores.** Many jobs have the same scores for one or more data elements. For example, in the listing of the best 200 jobs, four medical specializations—Anesthesiologists; Internists, General; Obstetricians and Gynecologists; and Surgeons—are listed in a row. You might think that Anesthesiologists is listed first because it has a higher rating, but that is not the case. The only data available applied to all four jobs, so they all have tied scores and are listed in alphabetical order. There was no way to avoid these issues, so simply understand that the difference of several positions on a list may not mean as much as it seems.

Best Jobs Overall: Lists of Jobs for College Graduates with the Highest Pay, Fastest Growth, and Most Openings

We consider the four lists that follow to be our premier lists. They are the lists that are most often mentioned in the media and the ones that most readers want to see. To create these lists, we first identified 264 jobs that typically require a two- or four-year college degree or more for entry and for which we had a full set of information. We then ordered these jobs according to their combined rankings for pay, growth, and number of openings and extracted the top 200 jobs to create the first list that appears on the next page. This is a very popular list because it represents jobs from the labor market according to quantifiable measures. We also ranked the top 200 jobs on three separate measures—annual earnings, projected percentage growth through 2012, and number of annual openings—and produced a list of the top 100 jobs for each of these measures. Descriptions for all the jobs in these lists are included in Part II.

The 200 Best Jobs Overall for College Graduates—Jobs with the Best Combination of Pay, Growth, and Openings

This list is the basis for all the lists in this book. To obtain this list, we sorted the 264 jobs that require a two- or four-year college degree or more into three lists based on pay, growth, and number of openings. We sorted each of these lists from highest to lowest and then assigned a number to each entry. For example, the job with the highest pay was given a score of 264, the one with the next highest pay was given a score of 263, and so on. This scoring process was continued for each job on each of the three lists, and we combined the three scores for each job to create a new list ranked by the total score for all three measures.

This list presents the top 200 jobs in order of their total scores. The job with the best overall score was Computer Software Engineers, Applications. Other jobs follow in order of their total scores for pay, growth, and openings. (When scores are tied, alphabetical ordering is used.) You can find descriptions for all of these jobs in Part II of this book.

The 200 Best Jobs for College Graduates

Job	Annual Earnings	Percent Growth	Annual Openings
1. Computer Software Engineers, Applications	$73,410	45.5%	55,000
2. Computer and Information Systems Managers	$90,490	36.1%	39,000
3. Computer Software Engineers, Systems Software	$77,250	45.5%	39,000
4. Sales Managers	$81,970	30.5%	54,000
5. Computer Systems Analysts	$65,050	39.4%	68,000
6. Management Analysts	$63,090	30.4%	78,000
7. Pharmacists	$82,520	30.1%	23,000
8. Anesthesiologists	more than $145,000	19.5%	38,000
9. Internists, General	more than $145,000	19.5%	38,000
10. Obstetricians and Gynecologists	more than $145,000	19.5%	38,000
11. Surgeons	more than $145,000	19.5%	38,000
12. Family and General Practitioners	$137,670	19.5%	38,000
13. Pediatricians, General	$136,490	19.5%	38,000
14. Postsecondary Teachers	$51,815	38.1%	216,000
15. Psychiatrists	$135,440	19.5%	38,000
16. Network Systems and Data Communications Analysts	$59,300	57.0%	29,000
17. Medical and Health Services Managers	$66,360	29.3%	33,000
18. Computer Security Specialists	$57,060	37.4%	35,000
19. Network and Computer Systems Administrators	$57,060	37.4%	35,000
20. General and Operations Managers	$74,600	18.4%	260,000
21. Chief Executives	$136,400	16.7%	63,000

The 200 Best Jobs for College Graduates

Job	Annual Earnings	Percent Growth	Annual Openings
22. Government Service Executives	$136,400	16.7%	63,000
23. Private Sector Executives	$136,400	16.7%	63,000
24. Marketing Managers	$85,220	21.3%	30,000
25. Financial Managers, Branch or Department	$79,090	18.3%	71,000
26. Treasurers, Controllers, and Chief Financial Officers	$79,090	18.3%	71,000
27. Lawyers	$92,730	17.0%	53,000
28. Education Administrators, Elementary and Secondary School	$73,960	20.7%	31,000
29. Registered Nurses	$51,020	27.3%	215,000
30. Personal Financial Advisors	$60,230	34.6%	18,000
31. Database Administrators	$59,150	44.2%	16,000
32. Education Administrators, Postsecondary	$67,760	25.9%	19,000
33. Logisticians	$49,740	27.5%	162,000
34. Physician Assistants	$68,200	48.9%	7,000
35. Physical Therapists	$58,700	35.3%	16,000
36. Compensation and Benefits Managers	$72,180	19.4%	21,000
37. Training and Development Managers	$72,180	19.4%	21,000
38. Special Education Teachers, Secondary School	$44,920	30.0%	59,000
39. Administrative Services Managers	$58,130	19.8%	40,000
40. Human Resources Managers	$70,350	19.4%	21,000
41. Special Education Teachers, Middle School	$43,260	30.0%	59,000
42. Dental Hygienists	$56,680	43.1%	9,000
43. Special Education Teachers, Preschool, Kindergarten, and Elementary School	$42,630	30.0%	59,000
44. Environmental Engineers	$64,040	38.2%	6,000
45. Public Relations Managers	$67,810	23.4%	10,000
46. Accountants	$49,770	19.5%	119,000
47. Auditors	$49,770	19.5%	119,000
48. Occupational Therapists	$53,320	35.2%	10,000
49. Computer Support Specialists	$39,900	30.3%	71,000
50. Advertising and Promotions Managers	$61,400	25.0%	13,000
51. Construction Managers	$67,620	12.0%	47,000
52. Training and Development Specialists	$44,270	27.9%	35,000
53. Market Research Analysts	$54,830	23.4%	18,000
54. Computer Programmers	$61,730	14.6%	45,000
55. Public Relations Specialists	$43,050	32.9%	28,000

(continued)

(continued)

The 200 Best Jobs for College Graduates

Job	Annual Earnings	Percent Growth	Annual Openings
56. Clinical Psychologists	$53,230	24.4%	17,000
57. Counseling Psychologists	$53,230	24.4%	17,000
58. Educational Psychologists	$53,230	24.4%	17,000
59. Financial Analysts	$61,130	18.7%	22,000
60. Sales Agents, Financial Services	$62,680	13.0%	39,000
61. Sales Agents, Securities and Commodities	$62,680	13.0%	39,000
62. Airline Pilots, Copilots, and Flight Engineers	$128,140	18.5%	6,000
63. Social and Community Service Managers	$46,200	27.7%	19,000
64. Sales Engineers	$68,510	19.9%	7,000
65. Instructional Coordinators	$47,550	25.4%	18,000
66. Preschool Teachers, Except Special Education	$20,450	36.2%	88,000
67. Kindergarten Teachers, Except Special Education	$40,980	27.2%	34,000
68. Medical Scientists, Except Epidemiologists	$60,200	26.9%	6,000
69. Compensation, Benefits, and Job Analysis Specialists	$46,890	28.0%	15,000
70. Speech-Language Pathologists	$50,890	27.2%	10,000
71. Secondary School Teachers, Except Special and Vocational Education	$45,180	18.2%	118,000
72. Employment Interviewers, Private or Public Employment Service	$40,970	27.3%	29,000
73. Personnel Recruiters	$40,970	27.3%	29,000
74. Veterinarians	$65,290	25.1%	4,000
75. Paralegals and Legal Assistants	$38,440	28.7%	29,000
76. Engineering Managers	$95,630	9.2%	16,000
77. Chiropractors	$66,610	23.3%	3,000
78. Loan Officers	$47,530	18.8%	30,000
79. Cost Estimators	$49,220	18.6%	25,000
80. Medical Records and Health Information Technicians	$24,920	46.8%	24,000
81. Respiratory Therapists	$42,050	34.8%	10,000
82. Technical Writers	$52,160	27.1%	6,000
83. Medical and Public Health Social Workers	$39,160	28.6%	18,000
84. Biologists	$64,390	22.3%	3,000
85. Elementary School Teachers, Except Special Education	$42,590	15.2%	183,000
86. Industrial Production Managers	$71,650	7.9%	18,000
87. Radiologic Technicians	$41,850	22.9%	21,000
88. Radiologic Technologists	$41,850	22.9%	21,000
89. Child, Family, and School Social Workers	$34,300	23.2%	45,000
90. Biochemists	$64,390	22.9%	2,000

The 200 Best Jobs for College Graduates

Job	Annual Earnings	Percent Growth	Annual Openings
91. Biophysicists	$64,390	22.9%	2,000
92. Physical Therapist Assistants	$37,280	44.6%	10,000
93. Electronics Engineers, Except Computer	$73,470	9.4%	11,000
94. Agents and Business Managers of Artists, Performers, and Athletes	$55,700	27.8%	2,000
95. Mental Health and Substance Abuse Social Workers	$33,650	34.5%	17,000
96. Optometrists	$87,340	17.1%	2,000
97. Industrial Engineers	$64,050	10.6%	16,000
98. Medical and Clinical Laboratory Technologists	$44,460	19.3%	21,000
99. Environmental Scientists and Specialists, Including Health	$50,070	23.7%	6,000
100. Architects, Except Landscape and Naval	$58,630	17.3%	8,000
101. City Planning Aides	$48,660	17.5%	18,000
102. Directors—Stage, Motion Pictures, Television, and Radio	$51,870	18.3%	10,000
103. Producers	$51,870	18.3%	10,000
104. Program Directors	$51,870	18.3%	10,000
105. Social Science Research Assistants	$48,660	17.5%	18,000
106. Graphic Designers	$36,930	21.9%	29,000
107. Radiation Therapists	$55,550	31.6%	1,000
108. Rehabilitation Counselors	$27,410	33.8%	19,000
109. Educational, Vocational, and School Counselors	$44,990	15.0%	32,000
110. Diagnostic Medical Sonographers	$50,980	24.0%	4,000
111. Natural Sciences Managers	$86,910	11.3%	5,000
112. Civil Engineers	$62,840	8.0%	17,000
113. Nuclear Medicine Technologists	$53,680	23.6%	2,000
114. Copy Writers	$43,340	16.1%	23,000
115. Creative Writers	$43,340	16.1%	23,000
116. Poets and Lyricists	$43,340	16.1%	23,000
117. Art Directors	$63,170	11.4%	8,000
118. Biomedical Engineers	$64,780	26.1%	fewer than 500
119. Recreation Workers	$18,950	20.5%	56,000
120. Veterinary Technologists and Technicians	$24,190	44.1%	11,000
121. Actuaries	$75,280	14.9%	2,000
122. Education Administrators, Preschool and Child Care Center/Program	$35,240	32.0%	9,000
123. Purchasing Agents, Except Wholesale, Retail, and Farm Products	$47,250	11.2%	29,000
124. Budget Analysts	$55,090	14.0%	8,000

(continued)

(continued)

The 200 Best Jobs for College Graduates

Job	Annual Earnings	Percent Growth	Annual Openings
125. Podiatrists	$95,550	15.0%	1,000
126. Dentists, General	$120,420	4.1%	7,000
127. Oral and Maxillofacial Surgeons	$120,420	4.1%	7,000
128. Orthodontists	$120,420	4.1%	7,000
129. Prosthodontists	$120,420	4.1%	7,000
130. Epidemiologists	$53,660	32.5%	fewer than 500
131. Cardiovascular Technologists and Technicians	$37,800	33.5%	6,000
132. Credit Analysts	$46,640	18.7%	9,000
133. Mechanical Engineers	$65,210	4.8%	14,000
134. Middle School Teachers, Except Special and Vocational Education	$42,960	9.0%	69,000
135. Physical Therapist Aides	$21,070	46.4%	8,000
136. Audiologists	$50,000	29.0%	1,000
137. Economists	$70,520	13.4%	2,000
138. Hydrologists	$59,010	21.0%	1,000
139. Computer Hardware Engineers	$79,090	6.1%	6,000
140. Electrical Engineers	$70,830	2.5%	11,000
141. Multi-Media Artists and Animators	$46,770	15.8%	12,000
142. Mental Health Counselors	$32,040	26.7%	13,000
143. Purchasing Managers	$67,830	4.8%	9,000
144. Occupational Therapist Assistants	$38,120	39.2%	3,000
145. Adult Literacy, Remedial Education, and GED Teachers and Instructors	$37,910	20.4%	14,000
146. Calibration and Instrumentation Technicians	$45,390	10.0%	24,000
147. Commercial and Industrial Designers	$52,080	14.7%	7,000
148. Directors, Religious Activities and Education	$29,240	24.1%	16,000
149. Electrical Engineering Technicians	$45,390	10.0%	24,000
150. Electronics Engineering Technicians	$45,390	10.0%	24,000
151. Landscape Architects	$50,780	22.2%	2,000
152. Chemists	$54,960	12.7%	7,000
153. Medical Transcriptionists	$27,790	22.6%	18,000
154. Property, Real Estate, and Community Association Managers	$38,750	12.8%	35,000
155. Interior Designers	$40,420	21.7%	8,000
156. Environmental Science and Protection Technicians, Including Health	$35,790	36.8%	4,000
157. Geologists	$68,570	11.5%	2,000
158. Judges, Magistrate Judges, and Magistrates	$91,230	8.7%	2,000

The 200 Best Jobs for College Graduates

Job	Annual Earnings	Percent Growth	Annual Openings
159. Atmospheric and Space Scientists	$65,400	16.2%	1,000
160. Clergy	$34,930	15.5%	34,000
161. Health Educators	$38,100	21.9%	8,000
162. Medical and Clinical Laboratory Technicians	$30,140	19.4%	21,000
163. Film and Video Editors	$41,820	26.4%	3,000
164. Meeting and Convention Planners	$39,070	21.3%	7,000
165. Substance Abuse and Behavioral Disorder Counselors	$31,510	23.3%	10,000
166. Dietitians and Nutritionists	$42,630	17.8%	8,000
167. Microbiologists	$52,100	20.0%	1,000
168. Insurance Sales Agents	$40,370	8.4%	52,000
169. Environmental Engineering Technicians	$38,180	28.4%	3,000
170. Insurance Underwriters	$48,370	10.0%	12,000
171. Geographers	$56,290	19.5%	fewer than 500
172. Industrial-Organizational Psychologists	$67,740	16.0%	fewer than 500
173. Librarians	$44,730	10.1%	15,000
174. Probation Officers and Correctional Treatment Specialists	$39,200	14.7%	15,000
175. Editors	$42,450	11.8%	14,000
176. Occupational Health and Safety Specialists	$48,330	13.2%	6,000
177. Aerospace Engineers	$77,340	–5.2%	5,000
178. Operations Research Analysts	$59,090	6.2%	6,000
179. Fire-Prevention and Protection Engineers	$61,430	7.9%	4,000
180. Industrial Safety and Health Engineers	$61,430	7.9%	4,000
181. Product Safety Engineers	$61,430	7.9%	4,000
182. Survey Researchers	$26,990	33.6%	3,000
183. Physicists	$83,570	6.9%	1,000
184. Urban and Regional Planners	$52,680	10.7%	5,000
185. Orthotists and Prosthetists	$49,860	18.9%	1,000
186. Marriage and Family Therapists	$38,210	22.4%	3,000
187. Vocational Education Teachers, Secondary School	$45,140	9.0%	12,000
188. Materials Scientists	$71,090	8.5%	1,000
189. Athletic Trainers	$32,990	29.9%	2,000
190. Political Scientists	$81,670	5.9%	1,000
191. Financial Examiners	$59,050	8.9%	3,000
192. Wholesale and Retail Buyers, Except Farm Products	$42,200	4.3%	24,000
193. Biological Technicians	$33,360	19.4%	7,000
194. Chemical Engineers	$75,310	0.4%	2,000
195. Gaming Managers	$57,930	12.4%	1,000

(continued)

(continued)

The 200 Best Jobs for College Graduates

Job	Annual Earnings	Percent Growth	Annual Openings
196. Fashion Designers	$54,530	10.6%	2,000
197. Statisticians	$64,320	4.8%	2,000
198. Materials Engineers	$65,010	4.1%	2,000
199. Astronomers	$85,910	4.9%	fewer than 500
200. Nuclear Engineers	$83,260	–0.1%	1,000

The 100 Best-Paying Jobs for College Graduates

We sorted the 200 best jobs that require a college degree or more based on their annual median earnings from highest to lowest. *Median earnings* means that half of all workers in these jobs earn more than that amount and half earn less. We then selected the 100 jobs with the highest earnings to create the list that follows.

It shouldn't be a big surprise to learn that most of the highest-paying jobs require advanced levels of education, training, and experience. For example, most of the 20 jobs with the highest earnings require a doctoral or professional degree, and others—such as Chief Executives and Airline Pilots, Copilots, and Flight Engineers—require extensive training and experience. Although the top 20 jobs may not appeal to you for a variety of reasons, you are likely to find others that will among the top 100 jobs with the highest earnings. Keep in mind that the earnings reflect the national average for all workers in the occupation. This is an important consideration because starting pay in the job is usually a lot less than the pay that workers can earn with several years of experience. Earnings also vary significantly by region of the country, so actual pay in your area could be substantially different.

The 100 Best-Paying Jobs for College Graduates

Job	Annual Earnings
1. Anesthesiologists	more than $145,000
2. Internists, General	more than $145,000
3. Obstetricians and Gynecologists	more than $145,000
4. Surgeons	more than $145,000
5. Family and General Practitioners	$137,670
6. Pediatricians, General	$136,490
7. Chief Executives	$136,400
8. Government Service Executives	$136,400

The 100 Best-Paying Jobs for College Graduates

Job	Annual Earnings
9. Private Sector Executives	$136,400
10. Psychiatrists	$135,440
11. Airline Pilots, Copilots, and Flight Engineers	$128,140
12. Dentists, General	$120,420
13. Oral and Maxillofacial Surgeons	$120,420
14. Orthodontists	$120,420
15. Prosthodontists	$120,420
16. Engineering Managers	$95,630
17. Podiatrists	$95,550
18. Lawyers	$92,730
19. Judges, Magistrate Judges, and Magistrates	$91,230
20. Computer and Information Systems Managers	$90,490
21. Optometrists	$87,340
22. Natural Sciences Managers	$86,910
23. Astronomers	$85,910
24. Marketing Managers	$85,220
25. Physicists	$83,570
26. Nuclear Engineers	$83,260
27. Pharmacists	$82,520
28. Sales Managers	$81,970
29. Political Scientists	$81,670
30. Computer Hardware Engineers	$79,090
31. Financial Managers, Branch or Department	$79,090
32. Treasurers, Controllers, and Chief Financial Officers	$79,090
33. Aerospace Engineers	$77,340
34. Computer Software Engineers, Systems Software	$77,250
35. Chemical Engineers	$75,310
36. Actuaries	$75,280
37. General and Operations Managers	$74,600
38. Education Administrators, Elementary and Secondary School	$73,960
39. Electronics Engineers, Except Computer	$73,470
40. Computer Software Engineers, Applications	$73,410
41. Compensation and Benefits Managers	$72,180
42. Training and Development Managers	$72,180
43. Industrial Production Managers	$71,650
44. Materials Scientists	$71,090

(continued)

(continued)

The 100 Best-Paying Jobs for College Graduates

Job	Annual Earnings
45. Electrical Engineers	$70,830
46. Economists	$70,520
47. Human Resources Managers	$70,350
48. Geologists	$68,570
49. Sales Engineers	$68,510
50. Physician Assistants	$68,200
51. Purchasing Managers	$67,830
52. Public Relations Managers	$67,810
53. Education Administrators, Postsecondary	$67,760
54. Industrial-Organizational Psychologists	$67,740
55. Construction Managers	$67,620
56. Chiropractors	$66,610
57. Medical and Health Services Managers	$66,360
58. Atmospheric and Space Scientists	$65,400
59. Veterinarians	$65,290
60. Mechanical Engineers	$65,210
61. Computer Systems Analysts	$65,050
62. Materials Engineers	$65,010
63. Biomedical Engineers	$64,780
64. Biochemists	$64,390
65. Biologists	$64,390
66. Biophysicists	$64,390
67. Statisticians	$64,320
68. Industrial Engineers	$64,050
69. Environmental Engineers	$64,040
70. Art Directors	$63,170
71. Management Analysts	$63,090
72. Civil Engineers	$62,840
73. Sales Agents, Financial Services	$62,680
74. Sales Agents, Securities and Commodities	$62,680
75. Computer Programmers	$61,730
76. Fire-Prevention and Protection Engineers	$61,430
77. Industrial Safety and Health Engineers	$61,430
78. Product Safety Engineers	$61,430
79. Advertising and Promotions Managers	$61,400
80. Financial Analysts	$61,130

The 100 Best-Paying Jobs for College Graduates

Job	Annual Earnings
81. Personal Financial Advisors	$60,230
82. Medical Scientists, Except Epidemiologists	$60,200
83. Network Systems and Data Communications Analysts	$59,300
84. Database Administrators	$59,150
85. Operations Research Analysts	$59,090
86. Financial Examiners	$59,050
87. Hydrologists	$59,010
88. Physical Therapists	$58,700
89. Architects, Except Landscape and Naval	$58,630
90. Administrative Services Managers	$58,130
91. Gaming Managers	$57,930
92. Computer Security Specialists	$57,060
93. Network and Computer Systems Administrators	$57,060
94. Dental Hygienists	$56,680
95. Geographers	$56,290
96. Agents and Business Managers of Artists, Performers, and Athletes	$55,700
97. Radiation Therapists	$55,550
98. Budget Analysts	$55,090
99. Chemists	$54,960
100. Market Research Analysts	$54,830

The 100 Fastest-Growing Jobs for College Graduates

We created this list by sorting the 200 best jobs that require a college degree or more by their projected growth over a ten-year period. Growth rates are one measure to consider in exploring career options, as jobs with higher growth rates tend to provide more job opportunities.

Jobs in the computer and medical fields dominate the 20 fastest-growing jobs. Network Systems and Data Communications Analysts is the job with the highest growth rate—the number employed is projected to grow by a bit more than half during this time. You can find a wide range of rapidly growing jobs in a variety of fields and at different levels of training and education among the jobs on this list.

The 100 Fastest-Growing Jobs for College Graduates

Job	Percent Growth
1. Network Systems and Data Communications Analysts	57.0%
2. Physician Assistants	48.9%
3. Medical Records and Health Information Technicians	46.8%
4. Physical Therapist Aides	46.4%
5. Computer Software Engineers, Applications	45.5%
6. Computer Software Engineers, Systems Software	45.5%
7. Physical Therapist Assistants	44.6%
8. Database Administrators	44.2%
9. Veterinary Technologists and Technicians	44.1%
10. Dental Hygienists	43.1%
11. Computer Systems Analysts	39.4%
12. Occupational Therapist Assistants	39.2%
13. Environmental Engineers	38.2%
14. Postsecondary Teachers	38.1%
15. Computer Security Specialists	37.4%
16. Network and Computer Systems Administrators	37.4%
17. Environmental Science and Protection Technicians, Including Health	36.8%
18. Preschool Teachers, Except Special Education	36.2%
19. Computer and Information Systems Managers	36.1%
20. Physical Therapists	35.3%
21. Occupational Therapists	35.2%
22. Respiratory Therapists	34.8%
23. Personal Financial Advisors	34.6%
24. Mental Health and Substance Abuse Social Workers	34.5%
25. Rehabilitation Counselors	33.8%
26. Survey Researchers	33.6%
27. Cardiovascular Technologists and Technicians	33.5%
28. Public Relations Specialists	32.9%
29. Epidemiologists	32.5%
30. Education Administrators, Preschool and Child Care Center/Program	32.0%
31. Radiation Therapists	31.6%
32. Sales Managers	30.5%
33. Management Analysts	30.4%
34. Computer Support Specialists	30.3%
35. Pharmacists	30.1%
36. Special Education Teachers, Middle School	30.0%
37. Special Education Teachers, Preschool, Kindergarten, and Elementary School	30.0%

The 100 Fastest-Growing Jobs for College Graduates

Job	Percent Growth
38. Special Education Teachers, Secondary School	30.0%
39. Athletic Trainers	29.9%
40. Medical and Health Services Managers	29.3%
41. Audiologists	29.0%
42. Paralegals and Legal Assistants	28.7%
43. Medical and Public Health Social Workers	28.6%
44. Environmental Engineering Technicians	28.4%
45. Compensation, Benefits, and Job Analysis Specialists	28.0%
46. Training and Development Specialists	27.9%
47. Agents and Business Managers of Artists, Performers, and Athletes	27.8%
48. Social and Community Service Managers	27.7%
49. Logisticians	27.5%
50. Employment Interviewers, Private or Public Employment Service	27.3%
51. Personnel Recruiters	27.3%
52. Registered Nurses	27.3%
53. Kindergarten Teachers, Except Special Education	27.2%
54. Speech-Language Pathologists	27.2%
55. Technical Writers	27.1%
56. Medical Scientists, Except Epidemiologists	26.9%
57. Mental Health Counselors	26.7%
58. Film and Video Editors	26.4%
59. Biomedical Engineers	26.1%
60. Education Administrators, Postsecondary	25.9%
61. Instructional Coordinators	25.4%
62. Veterinarians	25.1%
63. Advertising and Promotions Managers	25.0%
64. Clinical Psychologists	24.4%
65. Counseling Psychologists	24.4%
66. Educational Psychologists	24.4%
67. Directors, Religious Activities and Education	24.1%
68. Diagnostic Medical Sonographers	24.0%
69. Environmental Scientists and Specialists, Including Health	23.7%
70. Nuclear Medicine Technologists	23.6%
71. Market Research Analysts	23.4%
72. Public Relations Managers	23.4%
73. Chiropractors	23.3%
74. Substance Abuse and Behavioral Disorder Counselors	23.3%

(continued)

(continued)

The 100 Fastest-Growing Jobs for College Graduates

Job	Percent Growth
75. Child, Family, and School Social Workers	23.2%
76. Biochemists	22.9%
77. Biophysicists	22.9%
78. Radiologic Technicians	22.9%
79. Radiologic Technologists	22.9%
80. Medical Transcriptionists	22.6%
81. Marriage and Family Therapists	22.4%
82. Biologists	22.3%
83. Landscape Architects	22.2%
84. Graphic Designers	21.9%
85. Health Educators	21.9%
86. Interior Designers	21.7%
87. Marketing Managers	21.3%
88. Meeting and Convention Planners	21.3%
89. Hydrologists	21.0%
90. Education Administrators, Elementary and Secondary School	20.7%
91. Recreation Workers	20.5%
92. Adult Literacy, Remedial Education, and GED Teachers and Instructors	20.4%
93. Microbiologists	20.0%
94. Sales Engineers	19.9%
95. Administrative Services Managers	19.8%
96. Accountants	19.5%
97. Anesthesiologists	19.5%
98. Auditors	19.5%
99. Family and General Practitioners	19.5%
100. Geographers	19.5%

The 100 Jobs with the Most Openings for College Graduates

We created this list by sorting the 200 best jobs that require a college degree or more by the number of job openings that each is expected to have per year. It makes sense that jobs that employ large numbers of people are likely to have more job openings in a given year. Jobs with the most annual openings often provide easier entry for new workers or make it easier to move from one position to another. Some of these jobs may also be attractive to people re-entering the labor market, part-time workers, and workers who want to move from one employer to another.

The 100 Jobs with the Most Openings for College Graduates

Job	Annual Openings
1. General and Operations Managers	260,000
2. Postsecondary Teachers	216,000
3. Registered Nurses	215,000
4. Elementary School Teachers, Except Special Education	183,000
5. Logisticians	162,000
6. Accountants	119,000
7. Auditors	119,000
8. Secondary School Teachers, Except Special and Vocational Education	118,000
9. Preschool Teachers, Except Special Education	88,000
10. Management Analysts	78,000
11. Computer Support Specialists	71,000
12. Financial Managers, Branch or Department	71,000
13. Treasurers, Controllers, and Chief Financial Officers	71,000
14. Middle School Teachers, Except Special and Vocational Education	69,000
15. Computer Systems Analysts	68,000
16. Chief Executives	63,000
17. Government Service Executives	63,000
18. Private Sector Executives	63,000
19. Special Education Teachers, Middle School	59,000
20. Special Education Teachers, Preschool, Kindergarten, and Elementary School	59,000
21. Special Education Teachers, Secondary School	59,000
22. Recreation Workers	56,000
23. Computer Software Engineers, Applications	55,000
24. Sales Managers	54,000
25. Lawyers	53,000
26. Insurance Sales Agents	52,000
27. Construction Managers	47,000
28. Child, Family, and School Social Workers	45,000
29. Computer Programmers	45,000
30. Administrative Services Managers	40,000
31. Computer and Information Systems Managers	39,000
32. Computer Software Engineers, Systems Software	39,000
33. Sales Agents, Financial Services	39,000
34. Sales Agents, Securities and Commodities	39,000
35. Anesthesiologists	38,000
36. Family and General Practitioners	38,000

(continued)

(continued)

The 100 Jobs with the Most Openings for College Graduates

Job	Annual Openings
37. Internists, General	38,000
38. Obstetricians and Gynecologists	38,000
39. Pediatricians, General	38,000
40. Psychiatrists	38,000
41. Surgeons	38,000
42. Computer Security Specialists	35,000
43. Network and Computer Systems Administrators	35,000
44. Property, Real Estate, and Community Association Managers	35,000
45. Training and Development Specialists	35,000
46. Clergy	34,000
47. Kindergarten Teachers, Except Special Education	34,000
48. Medical and Health Services Managers	33,000
49. Educational, Vocational, and School Counselors	32,000
50. Education Administrators, Elementary and Secondary School	31,000
51. Loan Officers	30,000
52. Marketing Managers	30,000
53. Employment Interviewers, Private or Public Employment Service	29,000
54. Graphic Designers	29,000
55. Network Systems and Data Communications Analysts	29,000
56. Paralegals and Legal Assistants	29,000
57. Personnel Recruiters	29,000
58. Purchasing Agents, Except Wholesale, Retail, and Farm Products	29,000
59. Public Relations Specialists	28,000
60. Cost Estimators	25,000
61. Calibration and Instrumentation Technicians	24,000
62. Electrical Engineering Technicians	24,000
63. Electronics Engineering Technicians	24,000
64. Medical Records and Health Information Technicians	24,000
65. Wholesale and Retail Buyers, Except Farm Products	24,000
66. Copy Writers	23,000
67. Creative Writers	23,000
68. Pharmacists	23,000
69. Poets and Lyricists	23,000
70. Financial Analysts	22,000
71. Compensation and Benefits Managers	21,000
72. Human Resources Managers	21,000

The 100 Jobs with the Most Openings for College Graduates

Job	Annual Openings
73. Medical and Clinical Laboratory Technicians	21,000
74. Medical and Clinical Laboratory Technologists	21,000
75. Radiologic Technicians	21,000
76. Radiologic Technologists	21,000
77. Training and Development Managers	21,000
78. Education Administrators, Postsecondary	19,000
79. Rehabilitation Counselors	19,000
80. Social and Community Service Managers	19,000
81. City Planning Aides	18,000
82. Industrial Production Managers	18,000
83. Instructional Coordinators	18,000
84. Market Research Analysts	18,000
85. Medical and Public Health Social Workers	18,000
86. Medical Transcriptionists	18,000
87. Personal Financial Advisors	18,000
88. Social Science Research Assistants	18,000
89. Civil Engineers	17,000
90. Clinical Psychologists	17,000
91. Counseling Psychologists	17,000
92. Educational Psychologists	17,000
93. Mental Health and Substance Abuse Social Workers	17,000
94. Database Administrators	16,000
95. Directors, Religious Activities and Education	16,000
96. Engineering Managers	16,000
97. Industrial Engineers	16,000
98. Physical Therapists	16,000
99. Compensation, Benefits, and Job Analysis Specialists	15,000
100. Librarians	15,000

Best Jobs Lists with High Percentages of Workers Age 20–24, Workers Age 55 and Over, Part-Time Workers, Self-Employed Workers, Women, and Men

We decided it would be interesting to include lists in this section that show what sorts of jobs different types of people are most likely to have. For example, what jobs have the highest percentage of men college graduates or recent college graduates? We're not saying that men or recent grads should consider these jobs over others, but it is interesting information to know.

In some cases, the lists can give you ideas for jobs to consider that you might otherwise overlook. For example, perhaps women should consider some jobs that traditionally have high percentages of men in them. Or older workers might consider some jobs typically held by recent graduates. Although these are not obvious ways of using these lists, the lists may give you some good ideas on jobs to consider. The lists may also help you identify jobs that work well for others in your situation (for example, jobs with plentiful opportunities for part-time work, if that is something you want to do).

All of the lists in this section were created using a similar process. We began with the 200 best jobs that require a two- or four-year college degree or more. Next, we sorted those jobs in order of the primary criteria for each set of lists. For example, we sorted the 200 jobs based on the percentage of workers age 20 to 24 from highest to lowest percentage. We then selected the jobs with a high percentage of workers age 20 to 24 (the 28 jobs with a percentage greater than 10 percent) and listed them in order of that percentage along with their earnings, growth, and number of openings data. From this list of jobs with a high percentage of each type of worker, we created four more-specialized lists:

- 25 Best Jobs Overall (the subset of jobs that have the highest combined scores for earnings, growth rate, and number of openings)
- 25 Best-Paying Jobs
- 25 Fastest-Growing Jobs
- 25 Jobs with the Most Openings

Again, each of these four lists includes only jobs that have high percentages of each type of worker. The same basic process was used to create all the lists in this section. The lists are very interesting, and we hope you find them helpful.

Best Jobs with a High Percentage of College Graduates Age 20–24

These jobs have higher percentages (more than 10 percent) of recent college graduates. Recent grads are found in all jobs, but those with higher percentages of recent grads may present more opportunities for initial entry or upward mobility. Many jobs with the highest percentages of recent grads are those requiring technical training lasting two years, though there is a wide variety of jobs in different fields among the top 100.

Best Jobs with the Highest Percentage of College Graduates Age 20–24

Job	Percent Age 20–24	Annual Earnings	Percent Growth	Annual Openings
1. City Planning Aides	26.3%	$48,660	17.5%	18,000
2. Environmental Science and Protection Technicians, Including Health	26.3%	$35,790	36.8%	4,000
3. Social Science Research Assistants	26.3%	$48,660	17.5%	18,000
4. Veterinary Technologists and Technicians	20.1%	$24,190	44.1%	11,000
5. Credit Analysts	20.0%	$46,640	18.7%	9,000
6. Medical Records and Health Information Technicians	18.7%	$24,920	46.8%	24,000
7. Recreation Workers	17.7%	$18,950	20.5%	56,000
8. Biological Technicians	17.4%	$33,360	19.4%	7,000
9. Medical Transcriptionists	16.5%	$27,790	22.6%	18,000
10. Film and Video Editors	15.4%	$41,820	26.4%	3,000
11. Agents and Business Managers of Artists, Performers, and Athletes	15.0%	$55,700	27.8%	2,000
12. Orthotists and Prosthetists	14.4%	$49,860	18.9%	1,000
13. Occupational Therapist Assistants	14.3%	$38,120	39.2%	3,000
14. Adult Literacy, Remedial Education, and GED Teachers and Instructors	12.1%	$37,910	20.4%	14,000
15. Cost Estimators	12.0%	$49,220	18.6%	25,000
16. Dietitians and Nutritionists	11.8%	$42,630	17.8%	8,000
17. Computer Support Specialists	11.2%	$39,900	30.3%	71,000
18. Kindergarten Teachers, Except Special Education	11.1%	$40,980	27.2%	34,000
19. Preschool Teachers, Except Special Education	11.1%	$20,450	36.2%	88,000
20. Market Research Analysts	10.5%	$54,830	23.4%	18,000
21. Survey Researchers	10.5%	$26,990	33.6%	3,000
22. Financial Analysts	10.4%	$61,130	18.7%	22,000
23. Directors, Religious Activities and Education	10.3%	$29,240	24.1%	16,000

(continued)

(continued)

Best Jobs with the Highest Percentage of College Graduates Age 20–24

Job	Percent Age 20–24	Annual Earnings	Percent Growth	Annual Openings
24. Physical Therapist Aides	10.3%	$21,070	46.4%	8,000
25. Physical Therapist Assistants	10.3%	$37,280	44.6%	10,000
26. Network Systems and Data Communications Analysts	10.3%	$59,300	57.0%	29,000
27. Meeting and Convention Planners	10.3%	$39,070	21.3%	7,000
28. Advertising and Promotions Managers	10.1%	$61,400	25.0%	13,000

25 Best Jobs Overall with a High Percentage of College Graduates Age 20–24

Job	Percent Age 20–24	Annual Earnings	Percent Growth	Annual Openings
1. Network Systems and Data Communications Analysts	10.3%	$59,300	57.0%	29,000
2. Computer Support Specialists	11.2%	$39,900	30.3%	71,000
3. Advertising and Promotions Managers	10.1%	$61,400	25.0%	13,000
4. Market Research Analysts	10.5%	$54,830	23.4%	18,000
5. Financial Analysts	10.4%	$61,130	18.7%	22,000
6. Preschool Teachers, Except Special Education	11.1%	$20,450	36.2%	88,000
7. Kindergarten Teachers, Except Special Education	11.1%	$40,980	27.2%	34,000
8. Cost Estimators	12.0%	$49,220	18.6%	25,000
9. Medical Records and Health Information Technicians	18.7%	$24,920	46.8%	24,000
10. Physical Therapist Assistants	10.3%	$37,280	44.6%	10,000
11. Agents and Business Managers of Artists, Performers, and Athletes	15.0%	$55,700	27.8%	2,000
12. City Planning Aides	26.3%	$48,660	17.5%	18,000
13. Social Science Research Assistants	26.3%	$48,660	17.5%	18,000
14. Recreation Workers	17.7%	$18,950	20.5%	56,000
15. Veterinary Technologists and Technicians	20.1%	$24,190	44.1%	11,000
16. Credit Analysts	20.0%	$46,640	18.7%	9,000
17. Physical Therapist Aides	10.3%	$21,070	46.4%	8,000
18. Occupational Therapist Assistants	14.3%	$38,120	39.2%	3,000
19. Adult Literacy, Remedial Education, and GED Teachers and Instructors	12.1%	$37,910	20.4%	14,000

25 Best Jobs Overall with a High Percentage of College Graduates Age 20–24

Job	Percent Age 20–24	Annual Earnings	Percent Growth	Annual Openings
20. Directors, Religious Activities and Education	10.3%	$29,240	24.1%	16,000
21. Medical Transcriptionists	16.5%	$27,790	22.6%	18,000
22. Environmental Science and Protection Technicians, Including Health	26.3%	$35,790	36.8%	4,000
23. Film and Video Editors	15.4%	$41,820	26.4%	3,000
24. Meeting and Convention Planners	10.3%	$39,070	21.3%	7,000
25. Dietitians and Nutritionists	11.8%	$42,630	17.8%	8,000

25 Best-Paying Jobs with a High Percentage of College Graduates Age 20–24

Job	Percent Age 20–24	Annual Earnings
1. Advertising and Promotions Managers	10.1%	$61,400
2. Financial Analysts	10.4%	$61,130
3. Network Systems and Data Communications Analysts	10.3%	$59,300
4. Agents and Business Managers of Artists, Performers, and Athletes	15.0%	$55,700
5. Market Research Analysts	10.5%	$54,830
6. Orthotists and Prosthetists	14.4%	$49,860
7. Cost Estimators	12.0%	$49,220
8. City Planning Aides	26.3%	$48,660
9. Social Science Research Assistants	26.3%	$48,660
10. Credit Analysts	20.0%	$46,640
11. Dietitians and Nutritionists	11.8%	$42,630
12. Film and Video Editors	15.4%	$41,820
13. Kindergarten Teachers, Except Special Education	11.1%	$40,980
14. Computer Support Specialists	11.2%	$39,900
15. Meeting and Convention Planners	10.3%	$39,070
16. Occupational Therapist Assistants	14.3%	$38,120
17. Adult Literacy, Remedial Education, and GED Teachers and Instructors	12.1%	$37,910
18. Physical Therapist Assistants	10.3%	$37,280
19. Environmental Science and Protection Technicians, Including Health	26.3%	$35,790
20. Biological Technicians	17.4%	$33,360
21. Directors, Religious Activities and Education	10.3%	$29,240

(continued)

(continued)

25 Best-Paying Jobs with a High Percentage of College Graduates Age 20–24

Job	Percent Age 20–24	Annual Earnings
22. Medical Transcriptionists	16.5%	$27,790
23. Survey Researchers	10.5%	$26,990
24. Medical Records and Health Information Technicians	18.7%	$24,920
25. Veterinary Technologists and Technicians	20.1%	$24,190

25 Fastest-Growing Jobs with a High Percentage of College Graduates Age 20–24

Job	Percent Age 20–24	Percent Growth
1. Network Systems and Data Communications Analysts	10.3%	57.0%
2. Medical Records and Health Information Technicians	18.7%	46.8%
3. Physical Therapist Aides	10.3%	46.4%
4. Physical Therapist Assistants	10.3%	44.6%
5. Veterinary Technologists and Technicians	20.1%	44.1%
6. Occupational Therapist Assistants	14.3%	39.2%
7. Environmental Science and Protection Technicians, Including Health	26.3%	36.8%
8. Preschool Teachers, Except Special Education	11.1%	36.2%
9. Survey Researchers	10.5%	33.6%
10. Computer Support Specialists	11.2%	30.3%
11. Agents and Business Managers of Artists, Performers, and Athletes	15.0%	27.8%
12. Kindergarten Teachers, Except Special Education	11.1%	27.2%
13. Film and Video Editors	15.4%	26.4%
14. Advertising and Promotions Managers	10.1%	25.0%
15. Directors, Religious Activities and Education	10.3%	24.1%
16. Market Research Analysts	10.5%	23.4%
17. Medical Transcriptionists	16.5%	22.6%
18. Meeting and Convention Planners	10.3%	21.3%
19. Recreation Workers	17.7%	20.5%
20. Adult Literacy, Remedial Education, and GED Teachers and Instructors	12.1%	20.4%
21. Biological Technicians	17.4%	19.4%
22. Orthotists and Prosthetists	14.4%	18.9%
23. Credit Analysts	20.0%	18.7%
24. Financial Analysts	10.4%	18.7%
25. Cost Estimators	12.0%	18.6%

25 Jobs with the Most Openings with a High Percentage of College Graduates Age 20–24

Job	Percent Age 20–24	Annual Openings
1. Preschool Teachers, Except Special Education	11.1%	88,000
2. Computer Support Specialists	11.2%	71,000
3. Recreation Workers	17.7%	56,000
4. Kindergarten Teachers, Except Special Education	11.1%	34,000
5. Network Systems and Data Communications Analysts	10.3%	29,000
6. Cost Estimators	12.0%	25,000
7. Medical Records and Health Information Technicians	18.7%	24,000
8. Financial Analysts	10.4%	22,000
9. City Planning Aides	26.3%	18,000
10. Market Research Analysts	10.5%	18,000
11. Medical Transcriptionists	16.5%	18,000
12. Social Science Research Assistants	26.3%	18,000
13. Directors, Religious Activities and Education	10.3%	16,000
14. Adult Literacy, Remedial Education, and GED Teachers and Instructors	12.1%	14,000
15. Advertising and Promotions Managers	10.1%	13,000
16. Veterinary Technologists and Technicians	20.1%	11,000
17. Physical Therapist Assistants	10.3%	10,000
18. Credit Analysts	20.0%	9,000
19. Dietitians and Nutritionists	11.8%	8,000
20. Physical Therapist Aides	10.3%	8,000
21. Biological Technicians	17.4%	7,000
22. Meeting and Convention Planners	10.3%	7,000
23. Environmental Science and Protection Technicians, Including Health	26.3%	4,000
24. Film and Video Editors	15.4%	3,000
25. Occupational Therapist Assistants	14.3%	3,000

Best Jobs with a High Percentage of College Graduates Age 55 and Over

Older workers don't change careers as often as younger ones do and, on the average, they tend to have been in their jobs for quite some time. Many of the jobs with the highest percentages of college graduates age 55 and over—and those with the highest earnings—require considerable preparation, either through experience or through education and training. These are not the sort of jobs most young graduates could easily get just out of college. That should not come as a big surprise, as many of these folks would have been in the workforce for a long time and would therefore have lots of experience.

But go down the list of jobs with more than 20 percent older workers and you will find a variety of jobs that many older workers could more easily enter if they were changing careers. Some would make good "retirement" jobs, particularly if they allowed for part-time work or self-employment.

Best Jobs with the Highest Percentage of College Graduates Age 55 and Over

Job	Percentage Age 55 and Over	Annual Earnings	Percent Growth	Annual Openings
1. Astronomers	44.4%	$85,910	4.9%	fewer than 500
2. Physicists	44.4%	$83,570	6.9%	1,000
3. Judges, Magistrate Judges, and Magistrates	42.4%	$91,230	8.7%	2,000
4. Clergy	32.7%	$34,930	15.5%	34,000
5. Property, Real Estate, and Community Association Managers	32.0%	$38,750	12.8%	35,000
6. Clinical Psychologists	31.4%	$53,230	24.4%	17,000
7. Counseling Psychologists	31.4%	$53,230	24.4%	17,000
8. Educational Psychologists	31.4%	$53,230	24.4%	17,000
9. Industrial-Organizational Psychologists	31.4%	$67,740	16.0%	fewer than 500
10. Librarians	28.9%	$44,730	10.1%	15,000
11. Management Analysts	27.4%	$63,090	30.4%	78,000
12. Dentists, General	26.1%	$120,420	4.1%	7,000
13. Oral and Maxillofacial Surgeons	26.1%	$120,420	4.1%	7,000
14. Orthodontists	26.1%	$120,420	4.1%	7,000
15. Prosthodontists	26.1%	$120,420	4.1%	7,000
16. Education Administrators, Elementary and Secondary School	25.9%	$73,960	20.7%	31,000
17. Education Administrators, Postsecondary	25.9%	$67,760	25.9%	19,000
18. Education Administrators, Preschool and Child Care Center/Program	25.9%	$35,240	32.0%	9,000
19. Chief Executives	25.5%	$136,400	16.7%	63,000
20. Government Service Executives	25.5%	$136,400	16.7%	63,000
21. Private Sector Executives	25.5%	$136,400	16.7%	63,000
22. Postsecondary Teachers	24.5%	$51,815	38.1%	216,000
23. Directors, Religious Activities and Education	24.1%	$29,240	24.1%	16,000
24. Social and Community Service Managers	23.8%	$46,200	27.7%	19,000
25. Copy Writers	23.7%	$43,340	16.1%	23,000
26. Creative Writers	23.7%	$43,340	16.1%	23,000
27. Poets and Lyricists	23.7%	$43,340	16.1%	23,000
28. Audiologists	23.1%	$50,000	29.0%	1,000

Best Jobs with the Highest Percentage of College Graduates Age 55 and Over

Job	Percentage Age 55 and Over	Annual Earnings	Percent Growth	Annual Openings
29. Meeting and Convention Planners	23.1%	$39,070	21.3%	7,000
30. Urban and Regional Planners	22.7%	$52,680	10.7%	5,000
31. Art Directors	22.6%	$63,170	11.4%	8,000
32. Multi-Media Artists and Animators	22.6%	$46,770	15.8%	12,000
33. Pharmacists	22.4%	$82,520	30.1%	23,000
34. Nuclear Engineers	22.2%	$83,260	–0.1%	1,000
35. Veterinarians	22.0%	$65,290	25.1%	4,000
36. Lawyers	21.8%	$92,730	17.0%	53,000
37. Insurance Sales Agents	21.4%	$40,370	8.4%	52,000
38. Cost Estimators	21.0%	$49,220	18.6%	25,000
39. Instructional Coordinators	20.9%	$47,550	25.4%	18,000
40. Economists	20.6%	$70,520	13.4%	2,000

25 Best Jobs Overall with a High Percentage of College Graduates Age 55 and Over

Job	Percentage Age 55 and Over	Annual Earnings	Percent Growth	Annual Openings
1. Management Analysts	27.4%	$63,090	30.4%	78,000
2. Pharmacists	22.4%	$82,520	30.1%	23,000
3. Postsecondary Teachers	24.5%	$51,815	38.1%	216,000
4. Chief Executives	25.5%	$136,400	16.7%	63,000
5. Government Service Executives	25.5%	$136,400	16.7%	63,000
6. Private Sector Executives	25.5%	$136,400	16.7%	63,000
7. Lawyers	21.8%	$92,730	17.0%	53,000
8. Education Administrators, Elementary and Secondary School	25.9%	$73,960	20.7%	31,000
9. Education Administrators, Postsecondary	25.9%	$67,760	25.9%	19,000
10. Clinical Psychologists	31.4%	$53,230	24.4%	17,000
11. Counseling Psychologists	31.4%	$53,230	24.4%	17,000
12. Educational Psychologists	31.4%	$53,230	24.4%	17,000
13. Social and Community Service Managers	23.8%	$46,200	27.7%	19,000
14. Instructional Coordinators	20.9%	$47,550	25.4%	18,000
15. Veterinarians	22.0%	$65,290	25.1%	4,000

(continued)

(continued)

25 Best Jobs Overall with a High Percentage of College Graduates Age 55 and Over

Job	Percentage Age 55 and Over	Annual Earnings	Percent Growth	Annual Openings
16. Cost Estimators	21.0%	$49,220	18.6%	25,000
17. Copy Writers	23.7%	$43,340	16.1%	23,000
18. Creative Writers	23.7%	$43,340	16.1%	23,000
19. Poets and Lyricists	23.7%	$43,340	16.1%	23,000
20. Art Directors	22.6%	$63,170	11.4%	8,000
21. Education Administrators, Preschool and Child Care Center/Program	25.9%	$35,240	32.0%	9,000
22. Dentists, General	26.1%	$120,420	4.1%	7,000
23. Oral and Maxillofacial Surgeons	26.1%	$120,420	4.1%	7,000
24. Orthodontists	26.1%	$120,420	4.1%	7,000
25. Prosthodontists	26.1%	$120,420	4.1%	7,000

25 Best-Paying Jobs with a High Percentage of College Graduates Age 55 and Over

Job	Percent Age 55 and Over	Annual Earnings
1. Chief Executives	25.5%	$136,400
2. Government Service Executives	25.5%	$136,400
3. Private Sector Executives	25.5%	$136,400
4. Dentists, General	26.1%	$120,420
5. Oral and Maxillofacial Surgeons	26.1%	$120,420
6. Orthodontists	26.1%	$120,420
7. Prosthodontists	26.1%	$120,420
8. Lawyers	21.8%	$92,730
9. Judges, Magistrate Judges, and Magistrates	42.4%	$91,230
10. Astronomers	44.4%	$85,910
11. Physicists	44.4%	$83,570
12. Nuclear Engineers	22.2%	$83,260
13. Pharmacists	22.4%	$82,520
14. Education Administrators, Elementary and Secondary School	25.9%	$73,960
15. Economists	20.6%	$70,520
16. Education Administrators, Postsecondary	25.9%	$67,760
17. Industrial-Organizational Psychologists	31.4%	$67,740
18. Veterinarians	22.0%	$65,290
19. Art Directors	22.6%	$63,170

25 Best-Paying Jobs with a High Percentage of College Graduates Age 55 and Over

Job	Percent Age 55 and Over	Annual Earnings
20. Management Analysts	27.4%	$63,090
21. Clinical Psychologists	31.4%	$53,230
22. Counseling Psychologists	31.4%	$53,230
23. Educational Psychologists	31.4%	$53,230
24. Urban and Regional Planners	22.7%	$52,680
25. Postsecondary Teachers	24.5%	$51,815

25 Fastest-Growing Jobs with a High Percentage of College Graduates Age 55 and Over

Job	Percent Age 55 and Over	Percent Growth
1. Postsecondary Teachers	24.5%	38.1%
2. Education Administrators, Preschool and Child Care Center/Program	25.9%	32.0%
3. Management Analysts	27.4%	30.4%
4. Pharmacists	22.4%	30.1%
5. Audiologists	23.1%	29.0%
6. Social and Community Service Managers	23.8%	27.7%
7. Education Administrators, Postsecondary	25.9%	25.9%
8. Instructional Coordinators	20.9%	25.4%
9. Veterinarians	22.0%	25.1%
10. Clinical Psychologists	31.4%	24.4%
11. Counseling Psychologists	31.4%	24.4%
12. Educational Psychologists	31.4%	24.4%
13. Directors, Religious Activities and Education	24.1%	24.1%
14. Meeting and Convention Planners	23.1%	21.3%
15. Education Administrators, Elementary and Secondary School	25.9%	20.7%
16. Cost Estimators	21.0%	18.6%
17. Lawyers	21.8%	17.0%
18. Chief Executives	25.5%	16.7%
19. Government Service Executives	25.5%	16.7%
20. Private Sector Executives	25.5%	16.7%
21. Copy Writers	23.7%	16.1%
22. Creative Writers	23.7%	16.1%
23. Poets and Lyricists	23.7%	16.1%
24. Industrial-Organizational Psychologists	31.4%	16.0%
25. Multi-Media Artists and Animators	22.6%	15.8%

25 Jobs with the Most Openings with a High Percentage of College Graduates Age 55 and Over

Job	Percent Age 55 and Over	Annual Openings
1. Postsecondary Teachers	24.5%	216,000
2. Management Analysts	27.4%	78,000
3. Chief Executives	25.5%	63,000
4. Government Service Executives	25.5%	63,000
5. Private Sector Executives	25.5%	63,000
6. Lawyers	21.8%	53,000
7. Insurance Sales Agents	21.4%	52,000
8. Property, Real Estate, and Community Association Managers	32.0%	35,000
9. Clergy	32.7%	34,000
10. Education Administrators, Elementary and Secondary School	25.9%	31,000
11. Cost Estimators	21.0%	25,000
12. Copy Writers	23.7%	23,000
13. Creative Writers	23.7%	23,000
14. Pharmacists	22.4%	23,000
15. Poets and Lyricists	23.7%	23,000
16. Education Administrators, Postsecondary	25.9%	19,000
17. Social and Community Service Managers	23.8%	19,000
18. Instructional Coordinators	20.9%	18,000
19. Clinical Psychologists	31.4%	17,000
20. Counseling Psychologists	31.4%	17,000
21. Educational Psychologists	31.4%	17,000
22. Directors, Religious Activities and Education	24.1%	16,000
23. Librarians	28.9%	15,000
24. Multi-Media Artists and Animators	22.6%	12,000
25. Education Administrators, Preschool and Child Care Center/Program	25.9%	9,000

Best Jobs for College Graduates with a High Percentage of Part-Time Workers

These lists show jobs typically requiring a college degree or more that had a percentage of part-time workers higher than 20 percent. Look over the list of jobs with high percentages of part-time college grads and you will find some interesting things. For example, many of the jobs near the top involve health care. Some of these workers may want the freedom of time that a part-time job can provide, but others may do so because they can't find full-time employment in these areas. These folks may work in other full- or part-time jobs to make ends meet. If you want to work part time now or in the future, these lists will help you identify jobs that are more likely to provide that opportunity. If you want full-time work, the lists may also help you identify jobs that may make such opportunities more difficult to find. In either case, it's good information to know in advance.

Best Jobs for College Graduates with the Highest Percentage of Part-Time Workers

Job	Percent Part-Time Workers	Annual Earnings	Percent Growth	Annual Openings
1. Dental Hygienists	57.8%	$56,680	43.1%	9,000
2. Adult Literacy, Remedial Education, and GED Teachers and Instructors	41.0%	$37,910	20.4%	14,000
3. Recreation Workers	35.6%	$18,950	20.5%	56,000
4. Occupational Therapists	31.1%	$53,320	35.2%	10,000
5. Directors, Religious Activities and Education	28.2%	$29,240	24.1%	16,000
6. Speech-Language Pathologists	28.1%	$50,890	27.2%	10,000
7. Postsecondary Teachers	27.7%	$51,815	38.1%	216,000
8. Clinical Psychologists	27.2%	$53,230	24.4%	17,000
9. Counseling Psychologists	27.2%	$53,230	24.4%	17,000
10. Educational Psychologists	27.2%	$53,230	24.4%	17,000
11. Industrial-Organizational Psychologists	27.2%	$67,740	16.0%	fewer than 500
12. Occupational Therapist Assistants	25.5%	$38,120	39.2%	3,000
13. Medical Transcriptionists	25.3%	$27,790	22.6%	18,000
14. Optometrists	25.1%	$87,340	17.1%	2,000
15. Kindergarten Teachers, Except Special Education	24.9%	$40,980	27.2%	34,000
16. Preschool Teachers, Except Special Education	24.9%	$20,450	36.2%	88,000
17. Dietitians and Nutritionists	24.3%	$42,630	17.8%	8,000
18. Copy Writers	24.2%	$43,340	16.1%	23,000
19. Creative Writers	24.2%	$43,340	16.1%	23,000
20. Poets and Lyricists	24.2%	$43,340	16.1%	23,000
21. Physical Therapists	23.8%	$58,700	35.3%	16,000
22. Art Directors	23.1%	$63,170	11.4%	8,000
23. Librarians	23.1%	$44,730	10.1%	15,000
24. Veterinary Technologists and Technicians	23.0%	$24,190	44.1%	11,000
25. Physical Therapist Assistants	22.8%	$37,280	44.6%	10,000
26. Physical Therapist Aides	22.8%	$21,070	46.4%	8,000
27. Audiologists	22.7%	$50,000	29.0%	1,000
28. Dentists, General	22.3%	$120,420	4.1%	7,000

(continued)

Best Jobs for College Graduates with the Highest Percentage of Part-Time Workers

Job	Percent Part-Time Workers	Annual Earnings	Percent Growth	Annual Openings
29. Oral and Maxillofacial Surgeons	22.3%	$120,420	4.1%	7,000
30. Orthodontists	22.3%	$120,420	4.1%	7,000
31. Prosthodontists	22.3%	$120,420	4.1%	7,000
32. Chiropractors	22.2%	$66,610	23.3%	3,000
33. Registered Nurses	22.0%	$51,020	27.3%	215,000
34. Film and Video Editors	20.4%	$41,820	26.4%	3,000
35. City Planning Aides	20.2%	$48,660	17.5%	18,000
36. Environmental Science and Protection Technicians, Including Health	20.2%	$35,790	36.8%	4,000
37. Social Science Research Assistants	20.2%	$48,660	17.5%	18,000

25 Best Jobs Overall for College Graduates with a High Percentage of Part-Time Workers

Job	Percent Part-Time Workers	Annual Earnings	Percent Growth	Annual Openings
1. Postsecondary Teachers	27.7%	$51,815	38.1%	216,000
2. Registered Nurses	22.0%	$51,020	27.3%	215,000
3. Physical Therapists	23.8%	$58,700	35.3%	16,000
4. Dental Hygienists	57.8%	$56,680	43.1%	9,000
5. Occupational Therapists	31.1%	$53,320	35.2%	10,000
6. Clinical Psychologists	27.2%	$53,230	24.4%	17,000
7. Counseling Psychologists	27.2%	$53,230	24.4%	17,000
8. Educational Psychologists	27.2%	$53,230	24.4%	17,000
9. Preschool Teachers, Except Special Education	24.9%	$20,450	36.2%	88,000
10. Kindergarten Teachers, Except Special Education	24.9%	$40,980	27.2%	34,000
11. Speech-Language Pathologists	28.1%	$50,890	27.2%	10,000
12. Chiropractors	22.2%	$66,610	23.3%	3,000
13. Physical Therapist Assistants	22.8%	$37,280	44.6%	10,000
14. Optometrists	25.1%	$87,340	17.1%	2,000
15. City Planning Aides	20.2%	$48,660	17.5%	18,000
16. Social Science Research Assistants	20.2%	$48,660	17.5%	18,000
17. Copy Writers	24.2%	$43,340	16.1%	23,000
18. Creative Writers	24.2%	$43,340	16.1%	23,000

25 Best Jobs Overall for College Graduates with a High Percentage of Part-Time Workers

Job	Percent Part-Time Workers	Annual Earnings	Percent Growth	Annual Openings
19. Poets and Lyricists	24.2%	$43,340	16.1%	23,000
20. Art Directors	23.1%	$63,170	11.4%	8,000
21. Recreation Workers	35.6%	$18,950	20.5%	56,000
22. Veterinary Technologists and Technicians	23.0%	$24,190	44.1%	11,000
23. Dentists, General	22.3%	$120,420	4.1%	7,000
24. Oral and Maxillofacial Surgeons	22.3%	$120,420	4.1%	7,000
25. Orthodontists	22.3%	$120,420	4.1%	7,000

25 Best-Paying Jobs for College Graduates with a High Percentage of Part-Time Workers

Job	Percent Part-Time Workers	Annual Earnings
1. Dentists, General	22.3%	$120,420
2. Oral and Maxillofacial Surgeons	22.3%	$120,420
3. Orthodontists	22.3%	$120,420
4. Prosthodontists	22.3%	$120,420
5. Optometrists	25.1%	$87,340
6. Industrial-Organizational Psychologists	27.2%	$67,740
7. Chiropractors	22.2%	$66,610
8. Art Directors	23.1%	$63,170
9. Physical Therapists	23.8%	$58,700
10. Dental Hygienists	57.8%	$56,680
11. Occupational Therapists	31.1%	$53,320
12. Clinical Psychologists	27.2%	$53,230
13. Counseling Psychologists	27.2%	$53,230
14. Educational Psychologists	27.2%	$53,230
15. Postsecondary Teachers	27.7%	$51,815
16. Registered Nurses	22.0%	$51,020
17. Speech-Language Pathologists	28.1%	$50,890
18. Audiologists	22.7%	$50,000
19. City Planning Aides	20.2%	$48,660
20. Social Science Research Assistants	20.2%	$48,660
21. Librarians	23.1%	$44,730

(continued)

(continued)

25 Best-Paying Jobs for College Graduates with a High Percentage of Part-Time Workers

Job	Percent Part-Time Workers	Annual Earnings
22. Copy Writers	24.2%	$43,340
23. Creative Writers	24.2%	$43,340
24. Poets and Lyricists	24.2%	$43,340
25. Dietitians and Nutritionists	24.3%	$42,630

25 Fastest-Growing Jobs for College Graduates with a High Percentage of Part-Time Workers

Job	Percent Part-Time Workers	Percent Growth
1. Physical Therapist Aides	22.8%	46.4%
2. Physical Therapist Assistants	22.8%	44.6%
3. Veterinary Technologists and Technicians	23.0%	44.1%
4. Dental Hygienists	57.8%	43.1%
5. Occupational Therapist Assistants	25.5%	39.2%
6. Postsecondary Teachers	27.7%	38.1%
7. Environmental Science and Protection Technicians, Including Health	20.2%	36.8%
8. Preschool Teachers, Except Special Education	24.9%	36.2%
9. Physical Therapists	23.8%	35.3%
10. Occupational Therapists	31.1%	35.2%
11. Audiologists	22.7%	29.0%
12. Registered Nurses	22.0%	27.3%
13. Kindergarten Teachers, Except Special Education	24.9%	27.2%
14. Speech-Language Pathologists	28.1%	27.2%
15. Film and Video Editors	20.4%	26.4%
16. Clinical Psychologists	27.2%	24.4%
17. Counseling Psychologists	27.2%	24.4%
18. Educational Psychologists	27.2%	24.4%
19. Directors, Religious Activities and Education	28.2%	24.1%
20. Chiropractors	22.2%	23.3%
21. Medical Transcriptionists	25.3%	22.6%
22. Recreation Workers	35.6%	20.5%
23. Adult Literacy, Remedial Education, and GED Teachers and Instructors	41.0%	20.4%
24. Dietitians and Nutritionists	24.3%	17.8%
25. City Planning Aides	20.2%	17.5%

25 Jobs with the Most Openings for College Graduates with a High Percentage of Part-Time Workers

Job	Percent Part-Time Workers	Annual Openings
1. Postsecondary Teachers	27.7%	216,000
2. Registered Nurses	22.0%	215,000
3. Preschool Teachers, Except Special Education	24.9%	88,000
4. Recreation Workers	35.6%	56,000
5. Kindergarten Teachers, Except Special Education	24.9%	34,000
6. Copy Writers	24.2%	23,000
7. Creative Writers	24.2%	23,000
8. Poets and Lyricists	24.2%	23,000
9. City Planning Aides	20.2%	18,000
10. Medical Transcriptionists	25.3%	18,000
11. Social Science Research Assistants	20.2%	18,000
12. Clinical Psychologists	27.2%	17,000
13. Counseling Psychologists	27.2%	17,000
14. Educational Psychologists	27.2%	17,000
15. Directors, Religious Activities and Education	28.2%	16,000
16. Physical Therapists	23.8%	16,000
17. Librarians	23.1%	15,000
18. Adult Literacy, Remedial Education, and GED Teachers and Instructors	41.0%	14,000
19. Veterinary Technologists and Technicians	23.0%	11,000
20. Occupational Therapists	31.1%	10,000
21. Physical Therapist Assistants	22.8%	10,000
22. Speech-Language Pathologists	28.1%	10,000
23. Dental Hygienists	57.8%	9,000
24. Art Directors	23.1%	8,000
25. Dietitians and Nutritionists	24.3%	8,000

Best Jobs for College Graduates with a High Percentage of Self-Employed Workers

More than 10 percent of the workforce is self-employed. Although you may think of the self-employed as having similar jobs, they actually work in an enormous range of situations, fields, and work environments that you may not have considered.

Among the self-employed are people who own small or large businesses; professionals such as lawyers, psychologists, and medical doctors; part-time workers; people working on a contract basis for one or more employers; people running home consulting or other businesses; and people in other situations. They may go to the same office every day, as an attorney might; visit multiple employers during the course of a week; or do most of their work from home. Some work part time, others full time, some as a way to have fun, some so they can spend time with their kids or go to school.

The point is that there is an enormous range of situations, and one of them could make sense for you now or in the future. Although people are self-employed in many jobs, these lists focus on the jobs that normally require a college degree or more and have more than 25 percent of self-employed workers. So browse these lists if they interest you, and think creatively about the opportunities they might offer.

Best Jobs with the Highest Percentage of Self-Employed College Graduates

Job	Percent Self-Employed Workers	Annual Earnings	Percent Growth	Annual Openings
1. Copy Writers	67.9%	$43,340	16.1%	23,000
2. Creative Writers	67.9%	$43,340	16.1%	23,000
3. Poets and Lyricists	67.9%	$43,340	16.1%	23,000
4. Chiropractors	58.5%	$66,610	23.3%	3,000
5. Art Directors	53.6%	$63,170	11.4%	8,000
6. Multi-Media Artists and Animators	53.5%	$46,770	15.8%	12,000
7. Construction Managers	46.9%	$67,620	12.0%	47,000
8. Property, Real Estate, and Community Association Managers	46.0%	$38,750	12.8%	35,000
9. Podiatrists	44.4%	$95,550	15.0%	1,000
10. Dentists, General	39.9%	$120,420	4.1%	7,000
11. Oral and Maxillofacial Surgeons	39.9%	$120,420	4.1%	7,000
12. Orthodontists	39.9%	$120,420	4.1%	7,000
13. Prosthodontists	39.9%	$120,420	4.1%	7,000
14. Gaming Managers	38.6%	$57,930	12.4%	1,000
15. Personal Financial Advisors	37.7%	$60,230	34.6%	18,000
16. Directors—Stage, Motion Pictures, Television, and Radio	32.8%	$51,870	18.3%	10,000
17. Producers	32.8%	$51,870	18.3%	10,000
18. Program Directors	32.8%	$51,870	18.3%	10,000
19. Interior Designers	32.2%	$40,420	21.7%	8,000
20. Graphic Designers	31.8%	$36,930	21.9%	29,000
21. Commercial and Industrial Designers	31.0%	$52,080	14.7%	7,000

Best Jobs with the Highest Percentage of Self-Employed College Graduates

Job	Percent Self-Employed Workers	Annual Earnings	Percent Growth	Annual Openings
22. Management Analysts	29.8%	$63,090	30.4%	78,000
23. Fashion Designers	29.3%	$54,530	10.6%	2,000
24. Optometrists	29.2%	$87,340	17.1%	2,000
25. Veterinarians	27.7%	$65,290	25.1%	4,000
26. Agents and Business Managers of Artists, Performers, and Athletes	27.0%	$55,700	27.8%	2,000
27. Industrial-Organizational Psychologists	26.8%	$67,740	16.0%	fewer than 500
28. Lawyers	26.8%	$92,730	17.0%	53,000
29. Insurance Sales Agents	26.2%	$40,370	8.4%	52,000
30. Clinical Psychologists	25.4%	$53,230	24.4%	17,000
31. Counseling Psychologists	25.4%	$53,230	24.4%	17,000
32. Educational Psychologists	25.4%	$53,230	24.4%	17,000

25 Best Jobs Overall with a High Percentage of Self-Employed College Graduates

Job	Percent Self-Employed Workers	Annual Earnings	Percent Growth	Annual Openings
1. Management Analysts	29.8%	$63,090	30.4%	78,000
2. Lawyers	26.8%	$92,730	17.0%	53,000
3. Personal Financial Advisors	37.7%	$60,230	34.6%	18,000
4. Construction Managers	46.9%	$67,620	12.0%	47,000
5. Clinical Psychologists	25.4%	$53,230	24.4%	17,000
6. Counseling Psychologists	25.4%	$53,230	24.4%	17,000
7. Educational Psychologists	25.4%	$53,230	24.4%	17,000
8. Veterinarians	27.7%	$65,290	25.1%	4,000
9. Chiropractors	58.5%	$66,610	23.3%	3,000
10. Agents and Business Managers of Artists, Performers, and Athletes	27.0%	$55,700	27.8%	2,000
11. Optometrists	29.2%	$87,340	17.1%	2,000
12. Directors—Stage, Motion Pictures, Television, and Radio	32.8%	$51,870	18.3%	10,000
13. Producers	32.8%	$51,870	18.3%	10,000
14. Program Directors	32.8%	$51,870	18.3%	10,000

(continued)

(continued)

25 Best Jobs Overall with a High Percentage of Self-Employed College Graduates

Job	Percent Self-Employed Workers	Annual Earnings	Percent Growth	Annual Openings
15. Graphic Designers	31.8%	$36,930	21.9%	29,000
16. Copy Writers	67.9%	$43,340	16.1%	23,000
17. Creative Writers	67.9%	$43,340	16.1%	23,000
18. Poets and Lyricists	67.9%	$43,340	16.1%	23,000
19. Art Directors	53.6%	$63,170	11.4%	8,000
20. Podiatrists	44.4%	$95,550	15.0%	1,000
21. Dentists, General	39.9%	$120,420	4.1%	7,000
22. Oral and Maxillofacial Surgeons	39.9%	$120,420	4.1%	7,000
23. Orthodontists	39.9%	$120,420	4.1%	7,000
24. Prosthodontists	39.9%	$120,420	4.1%	7,000
25. Multi-Media Artists and Animators	53.5%	$46,770	15.8%	12,000

25 Best-Paying Jobs with a High Percentage of Self-Employed College Graduates

Job	Percent Self-Employed Workers	Annual Earnings
1. Dentists, General	39.9%	$120,420
2. Oral and Maxillofacial Surgeons	39.9%	$120,420
3. Orthodontists	39.9%	$120,420
4. Prosthodontists	39.9%	$120,420
5. Podiatrists	44.4%	$95,550
6. Lawyers	26.8%	$92,730
7. Optometrists	29.2%	$87,340
8. Industrial-Organizational Psychologists	26.8%	$67,740
9. Construction Managers	46.9%	$67,620
10. Chiropractors	58.5%	$66,610
11. Veterinarians	27.7%	$65,290
12. Art Directors	53.6%	$63,170
13. Management Analysts	29.8%	$63,090
14. Personal Financial Advisors	37.7%	$60,230
15. Gaming Managers	38.6%	$57,930
16. Agents and Business Managers of Artists, Performers, and Athletes	27.0%	$55,700

25 Best-Paying Jobs with a High Percentage of Self-Employed College Graduates

Job	Percent Self-Employed Workers	Annual Earnings
17. Fashion Designers	29.3%	$54,530
18. Clinical Psychologists	25.4%	$53,230
19. Counseling Psychologists	25.4%	$53,230
20. Educational Psychologists	25.4%	$53,230
21. Commercial and Industrial Designers	31.0%	$52,080
22. Directors—Stage, Motion Pictures, Television, and Radio	32.8%	$51,870
23. Producers	32.8%	$51,870
24. Program Directors	32.8%	$51,870
25. Multi-Media Artists and Animators	53.5%	$46,770

25 Fastest-Growing Jobs with a High Percentage of Self-Employed College Graduates

Job	Percent Self-Employed Workers	Percent Growth
1. Personal Financial Advisors	37.7%	34.6%
2. Management Analysts	29.8%	30.4%
3. Agents and Business Managers of Artists, Performers, and Athletes	27.0%	27.8%
4. Veterinarians	27.7%	25.1%
5. Clinical Psychologists	25.4%	24.4%
6. Counseling Psychologists	25.4%	24.4%
7. Educational Psychologists	25.4%	24.4%
8. Chiropractors	58.5%	23.3%
9. Graphic Designers	31.8%	21.9%
10. Interior Designers	32.2%	21.7%
11. Directors—Stage, Motion Pictures, Television, and Radio	32.8%	18.3%
12. Producers	32.8%	18.3%
13. Program Directors	32.8%	18.3%
14. Optometrists	29.2%	17.1%
15. Lawyers	26.8%	17.0%
16. Copy Writers	67.9%	16.1%
17. Creative Writers	67.9%	16.1%
18. Poets and Lyricists	67.9%	16.1%

(continued)

(continued)

25 Fastest-Growing Jobs with a High Percentage of Self-Employed College Graduates

Job	Percent Self-Employed Workers	Percent Growth
19. Industrial-Organizational Psychologists	26.8%	16.0%
20. Multi-Media Artists and Animators	53.5%	15.8%
21. Podiatrists	44.4%	15.0%
22. Commercial and Industrial Designers	31.0%	14.7%
23. Property, Real Estate, and Community Association Managers	46.0%	12.8%
24. Gaming Managers	38.6%	12.4%
25. Construction Managers	46.9%	12.0%

25 Jobs with the Most Openings with a High Percentage of Self-Employed College Graduates

Job	Percent Self-Employed Workers	Annual Openings
1. Management Analysts	29.8%	78,000
2. Lawyers	26.8%	53,000
3. Insurance Sales Agents	26.2%	52,000
4. Construction Managers	46.9%	47,000
5. Property, Real Estate, and Community Association Managers	46.0%	35,000
6. Graphic Designers	31.8%	29,000
7. Copy Writers	67.9%	23,000
8. Creative Writers	67.9%	23,000
9. Poets and Lyricists	67.9%	23,000
10. Personal Financial Advisors	37.7%	18,000
11. Clinical Psychologists	25.4%	17,000
12. Counseling Psychologists	25.4%	17,000
13. Educational Psychologists	25.4%	17,000
14. Multi-Media Artists and Animators	53.5%	12,000
15. Directors—Stage, Motion Pictures, Television, and Radio	32.8%	10,000
16. Producers	32.8%	10,000
17. Program Directors	32.8%	10,000
18. Art Directors	53.6%	8,000
19. Interior Designers	32.2%	8,000
20. Commercial and Industrial Designers	31.0%	7,000

25 Jobs with the Most Openings with a High Percentage of Self-Employed College Graduates

Job	Percent Self-Employed Workers	Annual Openings
21. Dentists, General	39.9%	7,000
22. Oral and Maxillofacial Surgeons	39.9%	7,000
23. Orthodontists	39.9%	7,000
24. Prosthodontists	39.9%	7,000
25. Veterinarians	27.7%	4,000

Best Jobs with a High Percentage of Women College Graduates

To create the four lists that follow, we sorted the 200 best jobs requiring a two- or four-year college degree or more according to the percentages of women and men in the workforce. These are our most controversial lists, and we knew we would create some controversy when we first included the best jobs lists with high percentages (more than 70 percent) of men and women. But these lists are not meant to restrict women or men from considering job options—our reason for including these lists is exactly the opposite. We hope the lists help people see possibilities that they might not otherwise have considered.

The fact is that jobs with high percentages of women or high percentages of men offer good opportunities for both men and women if they want to do one of these jobs. So we suggest that women browse the lists of jobs that employ high percentages of men and that men browse the lists of jobs with high percentages of women. There are jobs among both lists that pay well, and women or men who are interested in them and who have or can obtain the necessary education and training should consider them. Some employers are seeking female recruits to counterbalance a traditional male dominance.

An interesting and unfortunate tidbit to bring up at your next party is that the average earnings for the 100 jobs with the highest percentage of women college grads is $46,835, compared to average earnings of $74,247 for the 100 jobs with the highest percentage of men college grads. But earnings don't tell the whole story. We computed the average growth and job openings of the 100 jobs with the highest percentage of women college grads and found statistics of 23.9% growth and 26,320 openings, compared to 17.9% growth and 24,420 openings for the 100 jobs with the highest percentage of men college grads. This discrepancy reinforces the idea that men have had more problems than women in adapting to an economy dominated by service and information-based jobs. Many women may simply be better prepared for these jobs, possessing more appropriate skills for the jobs that are now growing rapidly and have more job openings.

Best Jobs for College Graduates with the Highest Percentage of Women

Job	Percent Women	Annual Earnings	Percent Growth	Annual Openings
1. Kindergarten Teachers, Except Special Education	97.8%	$40,980	27.2%	34,000
2. Preschool Teachers, Except Special Education	97.8%	$20,450	36.2%	88,000
3. Dental Hygienists	97.7%	$56,680	43.1%	9,000
4. Speech-Language Pathologists	95.1%	$50,890	27.2%	10,000
5. Registered Nurses	92.4%	$51,020	27.3%	215,000
6. Medical Records and Health Information Technicians	91.0%	$24,920	46.8%	24,000
7. Dietitians and Nutritionists	90.5%	$42,630	17.8%	8,000
8. Occupational Therapists	90.0%	$53,320	35.2%	10,000
9. Medical Transcriptionists	88.0%	$27,790	22.6%	18,000
10. Occupational Therapist Assistants	87.2%	$38,120	39.2%	3,000
11. Special Education Teachers, Middle School	86.6%	$43,260	30.0%	59,000
12. Special Education Teachers, Preschool, Kindergarten, and Elementary School	86.6%	$42,630	30.0%	59,000
13. Special Education Teachers, Secondary School	86.6%	$44,920	30.0%	59,000
14. Paralegals and Legal Assistants	86.1%	$38,440	28.7%	29,000
15. Librarians	82.6%	$44,730	10.1%	15,000
16. Veterinary Technologists and Technicians	80.7%	$24,190	44.1%	11,000
17. Elementary School Teachers, Except Special Education	79.0%	$42,590	15.2%	183,000
18. Middle School Teachers, Except Special and Vocational Education	79.0%	$42,960	9.0%	69,000
19. Child, Family, and School Social Workers	78.5%	$34,300	23.2%	45,000
20. Medical and Public Health Social Workers	78.5%	$39,160	28.6%	18,000
21. Mental Health and Substance Abuse Social Workers	78.5%	$33,650	34.5%	17,000
22. Audiologists	76.7%	$50,000	29.0%	1,000
23. Physical Therapist Aides	76.0%	$21,070	46.4%	8,000
24. Physical Therapist Assistants	76.0%	$37,280	44.6%	10,000
25. Meeting and Convention Planners	75.4%	$39,070	21.3%	7,000
26. Medical and Clinical Laboratory Technicians	73.9%	$30,140	19.4%	21,000
27. Medical and Clinical Laboratory Technologists	73.9%	$44,460	19.3%	21,000

Best Jobs for College Graduates with the Highest Percentage of Women

Job	Percent Women	Annual Earnings	Percent Growth	Annual Openings
28. Cardiovascular Technologists and Technicians	71.7%	$37,800	33.5%	6,000
29. Diagnostic Medical Sonographers	71.7%	$50,980	24.0%	4,000
30. Nuclear Medicine Technologists	71.7%	$53,680	23.6%	2,000
31. Radiologic Technicians	71.7%	$41,850	22.9%	21,000
32. Radiologic Technologists	71.7%	$41,850	22.9%	21,000
33. Physical Therapists	70.4%	$58,700	35.3%	16,000

25 Best Jobs Overall for College Graduates with a High Percentage of Women

Job	Percent Women	Annual Earnings	Percent Growth	Annual Openings
1. Registered Nurses	92.4%	$51,020	27.3%	215,000
2. Physical Therapists	70.4%	$58,700	35.3%	16,000
3. Special Education Teachers, Secondary School	86.6%	$44,920	30.0%	59,000
4. Special Education Teachers, Middle School	86.6%	$43,260	30.0%	59,000
5. Dental Hygienists	97.7%	$56,680	43.1%	9,000
6. Special Education Teachers, Preschool, Kindergarten, and Elementary School	86.6%	$42,630	30.0%	59,000
7. Occupational Therapists	90.0%	$53,320	35.2%	10,000
8. Preschool Teachers, Except Special Education	97.8%	$20,450	36.2%	88,000
9. Kindergarten Teachers, Except Special Education	97.8%	$40,980	27.2%	34,000
10. Speech-Language Pathologists	95.1%	$50,890	27.2%	10,000
11. Paralegals and Legal Assistants	86.1%	$38,440	28.7%	29,000
12. Medical Records and Health Information Technicians	91.0%	$24,920	46.8%	24,000
13. Medical and Public Health Social Workers	78.5%	$39,160	28.6%	18,000
14. Elementary School Teachers, Except Special Education	79.0%	$42,590	15.2%	183,000
15. Radiologic Technicians	71.7%	$41,850	22.9%	21,000
16. Radiologic Technologists	71.7%	$41,850	22.9%	21,000
17. Child, Family, and School Social Workers	78.5%	$34,300	23.2%	45,000
18. Physical Therapist Assistants	76.0%	$37,280	44.6%	10,000

(continued)

(continued)

25 Best Jobs Overall for College Graduates with a High Percentage of Women

Job	Percent Women	Annual Earnings	Percent Growth	Annual Openings
19. Mental Health and Substance Abuse Social Workers	78.5%	$33,650	34.5%	17,000
20. Medical and Clinical Laboratory Technologists	73.9%	$44,460	19.3%	21,000
21. Diagnostic Medical Sonographers	71.7%	$50,980	24.0%	4,000
22. Nuclear Medicine Technologists	71.7%	$53,680	23.6%	2,000
23. Veterinary Technologists and Technicians	80.7%	$24,190	44.1%	11,000
24. Cardiovascular Technologists and Technicians	71.7%	$37,800	33.5%	6,000
25. Middle School Teachers, Except Special and Vocational Education	79.0%	$42,960	9.0%	69,000

25 Best-Paying Jobs for College Graduates with a High Percentage of Women

Job	Percent Women	Annual Earnings
1. Physical Therapists	70.4%	$58,700
2. Dental Hygienists	97.7%	$56,680
3. Nuclear Medicine Technologists	71.7%	$53,680
4. Occupational Therapists	90.0%	$53,320
5. Registered Nurses	92.4%	$51,020
6. Diagnostic Medical Sonographers	71.7%	$50,980
7. Speech-Language Pathologists	95.1%	$50,890
8. Audiologists	76.7%	$50,000
9. Special Education Teachers, Secondary School	86.6%	$44,920
10. Librarians	82.6%	$44,730
11. Medical and Clinical Laboratory Technologists	73.9%	$44,460
12. Special Education Teachers, Middle School	86.6%	$43,260
13. Middle School Teachers, Except Special and Vocational Education	79.0%	$42,960
14. Dietitians and Nutritionists	90.5%	$42,630
15. Special Education Teachers, Preschool, Kindergarten, and Elementary School	86.6%	$42,630
16. Elementary School Teachers, Except Special Education	79.0%	$42,590
17. Radiologic Technicians	71.7%	$41,850
18. Radiologic Technologists	71.7%	$41,850
19. Kindergarten Teachers, Except Special Education	97.8%	$40,980
20. Medical and Public Health Social Workers	78.5%	$39,160

25 Best-Paying Jobs for College Graduates with a High Percentage of Women

Job	Percent Women	Annual Earnings
21. Meeting and Convention Planners	75.4%	$39,070
22. Paralegals and Legal Assistants	86.1%	$38,440
23. Occupational Therapist Assistants	87.2%	$38,120
24. Cardiovascular Technologists and Technicians	71.7%	$37,800
25. Physical Therapist Assistants	76.0%	$37,280

25 Fastest-Growing Jobs for College Graduates with a High Percentage of Women

Job	Percent Women	Percent Growth
1. Medical Records and Health Information Technicians	91.0%	46.8%
2. Physical Therapist Aides	76.0%	46.4%
3. Physical Therapist Assistants	76.0%	44.6%
4. Veterinary Technologists and Technicians	80.7%	44.1%
5. Dental Hygienists	97.7%	43.1%
6. Occupational Therapist Assistants	87.2%	39.2%
7. Preschool Teachers, Except Special Education	97.8%	36.2%
8. Physical Therapists	70.4%	35.3%
9. Occupational Therapists	90.0%	35.2%
10. Mental Health and Substance Abuse Social Workers	78.5%	34.5%
11. Cardiovascular Technologists and Technicians	71.7%	33.5%
12. Special Education Teachers, Middle School	86.6%	30.0%
13. Special Education Teachers, Preschool, Kindergarten, and Elementary School	86.6%	30.0%
14. Special Education Teachers, Secondary School	86.6%	30.0%
15. Audiologists	76.7%	29.0%
16. Paralegals and Legal Assistants	86.1%	28.7%
17. Medical and Public Health Social Workers	78.5%	28.6%
18. Registered Nurses	92.4%	27.3%
19. Kindergarten Teachers, Except Special Education	97.8%	27.2%
20. Speech-Language Pathologists	95.1%	27.2%
21. Diagnostic Medical Sonographers	71.7%	24.0%
22. Nuclear Medicine Technologists	71.7%	23.6%
23. Child, Family, and School Social Workers	78.5%	23.2%
24. Radiologic Technicians	71.7%	22.9%
25. Radiologic Technologists	71.7%	22.9%

25 Jobs with the Most Openings for College Graduates with a High Percentage of Women

Job	Percent Women	Annual Openings
1. Registered Nurses	92.4%	215,000
2. Elementary School Teachers, Except Special Education	79.0%	183,000
3. Preschool Teachers, Except Special Education	97.8%	88,000
4. Middle School Teachers, Except Special and Vocational Education	79.0%	69,000
5. Special Education Teachers, Middle School	86.6%	59,000
6. Special Education Teachers, Preschool, Kindergarten, and Elementary School	86.6%	59,000
7. Special Education Teachers, Secondary School	86.6%	59,000
8. Child, Family, and School Social Workers	78.5%	45,000
9. Kindergarten Teachers, Except Special Education	97.8%	34,000
10. Paralegals and Legal Assistants	86.1%	29,000
11. Medical Records and Health Information Technicians	91.0%	24,000
12. Medical and Clinical Laboratory Technicians	73.9%	21,000
13. Medical and Clinical Laboratory Technologists	73.9%	21,000
14. Radiologic Technicians	71.7%	21,000
15. Radiologic Technologists	71.7%	21,000
16. Medical and Public Health Social Workers	78.5%	18,000
17. Medical Transcriptionists	88.0%	18,000
18. Mental Health and Substance Abuse Social Workers	78.5%	17,000
19. Physical Therapists	70.4%	16,000
20. Librarians	82.6%	15,000
21. Veterinary Technologists and Technicians	80.7%	11,000
22. Occupational Therapists	90.0%	10,000
23. Physical Therapist Assistants	76.0%	10,000
24. Speech-Language Pathologists	95.1%	10,000
25. Dental Hygienists	97.7%	9,000

Best Jobs with a High Percentage of Men College Graduates

If you have not already read the intro to the previous group of lists, jobs with high percentages of women college graduates, consider doing so. Much of the content there applies to these lists as well.

We did not include these groups of lists with the assumption that men college grads should consider jobs with high percentages of men college grads or that women should consider jobs with high percentages of women. Instead, these lists are here because we think they are interesting and perhaps helpful in considering nontraditional career options. For example, some men college graduates would do very well in and enjoy some of the jobs with high percentages of women college graduates but may not have considered them seriously. In a similar way, some women college graduates would very much enjoy and do well in some jobs that have traditionally been held by high percentages of men college graduates. We hope that these lists help you consider options that you simply did not seriously consider because of gender stereotypes.

Best Jobs for College Graduates with the Highest Percentage of Men

Job	Percent Men	Annual Earnings	Percent Growth	Annual Openings
1. Airline Pilots, Copilots, and Flight Engineers	96.0%	$128,140	18.5%	6,000
2. Sales Engineers	94.0%	$68,510	19.9%	7,000
3. Mechanical Engineers	93.5%	$65,210	4.8%	14,000
4. Engineering Managers	93.4%	$95,630	9.2%	16,000
5. Construction Managers	93.2%	$67,620	12.0%	47,000
6. Nuclear Engineers	91.6%	$83,260	–0.1%	1,000
7. Electrical Engineers	91.3%	$70,830	2.5%	11,000
8. Electronics Engineers, Except Computer	91.3%	$73,470	9.4%	11,000
9. Aerospace Engineers	90.9%	$77,340	–5.2%	5,000
10. Civil Engineers	89.9%	$62,840	8.0%	17,000
11. Biomedical Engineers	89.6%	$64,780	26.1%	fewer than 500
12. Cost Estimators	88.0%	$49,220	18.6%	25,000
13. Materials Engineers	88.0%	$65,010	4.1%	2,000
14. Atmospheric and Space Scientists	87.1%	$65,400	16.2%	1,000
15. Astronomers	86.1%	$85,910	4.9%	fewer than 500
16. Physicists	86.1%	$83,570	6.9%	1,000
17. Clergy	85.7%	$34,930	15.5%	34,000
18. Chemical Engineers	85.6%	$75,310	0.4%	2,000
19. Podiatrists	84.3%	$95,550	15.0%	1,000
20. Computer Hardware Engineers	83.7%	$79,090	6.1%	6,000
21. Fire-Prevention and Protection Engineers	83.4%	$61,430	7.9%	4,000
22. Industrial Engineers	83.4%	$64,050	10.6%	16,000
23. Industrial Production Managers	83.4%	$71,650	7.9%	18,000
24. Industrial Safety and Health Engineers	83.4%	$61,430	7.9%	4,000
25. Product Safety Engineers	83.4%	$61,430	7.9%	4,000
26. Dentists, General	82.1%	$120,420	4.1%	7,000

(continued)

(continued)

Best Jobs for College Graduates with the Highest Percentage of Men

Job	Percent Men	Annual Earnings	Percent Growth	Annual Openings
27. Oral and Maxillofacial Surgeons	82.1%	$120,420	4.1%	7,000
28. Orthodontists	82.1%	$120,420	4.1%	7,000
29. Prosthodontists	82.1%	$120,420	4.1%	7,000
30. Chief Executives	81.2%	$136,400	16.7%	63,000
31. Government Service Executives	81.2%	$136,400	16.7%	63,000
32. Private Sector Executives	81.2%	$136,400	16.7%	63,000
33. Film and Video Editors	81.1%	$41,820	26.4%	3,000
34. Calibration and Instrumentation Technicians	80.9%	$45,390	10.0%	24,000
35. Electrical Engineering Technicians	80.9%	$45,390	10.0%	24,000
36. Electronics Engineering Technicians	80.9%	$45,390	10.0%	24,000
37. Environmental Engineering Technicians	80.9%	$38,180	28.4%	3,000
38. Architects, Except Landscape and Naval	79.7%	$58,630	17.3%	8,000
39. Landscape Architects	79.7%	$50,780	22.2%	2,000
40. Chiropractors	77.8%	$66,610	23.3%	3,000
41. Environmental Engineers	77.8%	$64,040	38.2%	6,000
42. Computer Security Specialists	76.7%	$57,060	37.4%	35,000
43. Network and Computer Systems Administrators	76.7%	$57,060	37.4%	35,000
44. Environmental Scientists and Specialists, Including Health	75.9%	$50,070	23.7%	6,000
45. Geologists	75.9%	$68,570	11.5%	2,000
46. Hydrologists	75.9%	$59,010	21.0%	1,000
47. Computer Software Engineers, Applications	75.3%	$73,410	45.5%	55,000
48. Computer Software Engineers, Systems Software	75.3%	$77,250	45.5%	39,000
49. General and Operations Managers	73.7%	$74,600	18.4%	260,000
50. Network Systems and Data Communications Analysts	73.5%	$59,300	57.0%	29,000
51. Anesthesiologists	73.2% more than	$145,000	19.5%	38,000
52. Family and General Practitioners	73.2%	$137,670	19.5%	38,000
53. Internists, General	73.2% more than	$145,000	19.5%	38,000
54. Obstetricians and Gynecologists	73.2% more than	$145,000	19.5%	38,000
55. Pediatricians, General	73.2%	$136,490	19.5%	38,000
56. Psychiatrists	73.2%	$135,440	19.5%	38,000
57. Surgeons	73.2% more than	$145,000	19.5%	38,000
58. Computer Programmers	72.5%	$61,730	14.6%	45,000
59. Optometrists	72.4%	$87,340	17.1%	2,000
60. Lawyers	71.3%	$92,730	17.0%	53,000
61. Computer and Information Systems Managers	70.3%	$90,490	36.1%	39,000

25 Best Jobs Overall for College Graduates with a High Percentage of Men

Job	Percent Men	Annual Earnings	Percent Growth	Annual Openings
1. Computer Software Engineers, Applications	75.3%	$73,410	45.5%	55,000
2. Computer and Information Systems Managers	70.3%	$90,490	36.1%	39,000
3. Computer Software Engineers, Systems Software	75.3%	$77,250	45.5%	39,000
4. Anesthesiologists	73.2%	more than $145,000	19.5%	38,000
5. Internists, General	73.2%	more than $145,000	19.5%	38,000
6. Obstetricians and Gynecologists	73.2%	more than $145,000	19.5%	38,000
7. Surgeons	73.2%	more than $145,000	19.5%	38,000
8. Family and General Practitioners	73.2%	$137,670	19.5%	38,000
9. Pediatricians, General	73.2%	$136,490	19.5%	38,000
10. Psychiatrists	73.2%	$135,440	19.5%	38,000
11. Network Systems and Data Communications Analysts	73.5%	$59,300	57.0%	29,000
12. Computer Security Specialists	76.7%	$57,060	37.4%	35,000
13. Network and Computer Systems Administrators	76.7%	$57,060	37.4%	35,000
14. General and Operations Managers	73.7%	$74,600	18.4%	260,000
15. Chief Executives	81.2%	$136,400	16.7%	63,000
16. Government Service Executives	81.2%	$136,400	16.7%	63,000
17. Private Sector Executives	81.2%	$136,400	16.7%	63,000
18. Lawyers	71.3%	$92,730	17.0%	53,000
19. Environmental Engineers	77.8%	$64,040	38.2%	6,000
20. Construction Managers	93.2%	$67,620	12.0%	47,000
21. Computer Programmers	72.5%	$61,730	14.6%	45,000
22. Airline Pilots, Copilots, and Flight Engineers	96.0%	$128,140	18.5%	6,000
23. Sales Engineers	94.0%	$68,510	19.9%	7,000
24. Engineering Managers	93.4%	$95,630	9.2%	16,000
25. Chiropractors	77.8%	$66,610	23.3%	3,000

25 Best-Paying Jobs for College Graduates with a High Percentage of Men

Job	Percent Men	Annual Earnings
1. Anesthesiologists	73.2%	more than $145,000
2. Internists, General	73.2%	more than $145,000
3. Obstetricians and Gynecologists	73.2%	more than $145,000
4. Surgeons	73.2%	more than $145,000
5. Family and General Practitioners	73.2%	$137,670
6. Pediatricians, General	73.2%	$136,490
7. Chief Executives	81.2%	$136,400
8. Government Service Executives	81.2%	$136,400
9. Private Sector Executives	81.2%	$136,400
10. Psychiatrists	73.2%	$135,440
11. Airline Pilots, Copilots, and Flight Engineers	96.0%	$128,140
12. Dentists, General	82.1%	$120,420
13. Oral and Maxillofacial Surgeons	82.1%	$120,420
14. Orthodontists	82.1%	$120,420
15. Prosthodontists	82.1%	$120,420
16. Engineering Managers	93.4%	$95,630
17. Podiatrists	84.3%	$95,550
18. Lawyers	71.3%	$92,730
19. Computer and Information Systems Managers	70.3%	$90,490
20. Optometrists	72.4%	$87,340
21. Astronomers	86.1%	$85,910
22. Physicists	86.1%	$83,570
23. Nuclear Engineers	91.6%	$83,260
24. Computer Hardware Engineers	83.7%	$79,090
25. Aerospace Engineers	90.9%	$77,340

25 Fastest-Growing Jobs for College Graduates with a High Percentage of Men

Job	Percent Men	Percent Growth
1. Network Systems and Data Communications Analysts	73.5%	57.0%
2. Computer Software Engineers, Applications	75.3%	45.5%
3. Computer Software Engineers, Systems Software	75.3%	45.5%
4. Environmental Engineers	77.8%	38.2%

25 Fastest-Growing Jobs for College Graduates with a High Percentage of Men

Job	Percent Men	Percent Growth
5. Computer Security Specialists	76.7%	37.4%
6. Network and Computer Systems Administrators	76.7%	37.4%
7. Computer and Information Systems Managers	70.3%	36.1%
8. Environmental Engineering Technicians	80.9%	28.4%
9. Film and Video Editors	81.1%	26.4%
10. Biomedical Engineers	89.6%	26.1%
11. Environmental Scientists and Specialists, Including Health	75.9%	23.7%
12. Chiropractors	77.8%	23.3%
13. Landscape Architects	79.7%	22.2%
14. Hydrologists	75.9%	21.0%
15. Sales Engineers	94.0%	19.9%
16. Anesthesiologists	73.2%	19.5%
17. Family and General Practitioners	73.2%	19.5%
18. Internists, General	73.2%	19.5%
19. Obstetricians and Gynecologists	73.2%	19.5%
20. Pediatricians, General	73.2%	19.5%
21. Psychiatrists	73.2%	19.5%
22. Surgeons	73.2%	19.5%
23. Cost Estimators	88.0%	18.6%
24. Airline Pilots, Copilots, and Flight Engineers	96.0%	18.5%
25. General and Operations Managers	73.7%	18.4%

25 Jobs with the Most Openings for College Graduates with a High Percentage of Men

Job	Percent Men	Annual Openings
1. General and Operations Managers	73.7%	260,000
2. Chief Executives	81.2%	63,000
3. Government Service Executives	81.2%	63,000
4. Private Sector Executives	81.2%	63,000
5. Computer Software Engineers, Applications	75.3%	55,000
6. Lawyers	71.3%	53,000
7. Construction Managers	93.2%	47,000

(continued)

(continued)

25 Jobs with the Most Openings for College Graduates with a High Percentage of Men

Job	Percent Men	Annual Openings
8. Computer Programmers	72.5%	45,000
9. Computer and Information Systems Managers	70.3%	39,000
10. Computer Software Engineers, Systems Software	75.3%	39,000
11. Anesthesiologists	73.2%	38,000
12. Family and General Practitioners	73.2%	38,000
13. Internists, General	73.2%	38,000
14. Obstetricians and Gynecologists	73.2%	38,000
15. Pediatricians, General	73.2%	38,000
16. Psychiatrists	73.2%	38,000
17. Surgeons	73.2%	38,000
18. Computer Security Specialists	76.7%	35,000
19. Network and Computer Systems Administrators	76.7%	35,000
20. Clergy	85.7%	34,000
21. Network Systems and Data Communications Analysts	73.5%	29,000
22. Cost Estimators	88.0%	25,000
23. Calibration and Instrumentation Technicians	80.9%	24,000
24. Electrical Engineering Technicians	80.9%	24,000
25. Electronics Engineering Technicians	80.9%	24,000

Best Jobs Lists Based on Levels of Education and Experience

The lists in this section organize the 200 best jobs requiring a two- or four-year college degree or more into groups based on the education or training typically required for entry. Unlike many of the previous sections, here we do not include separate lists for highest pay, growth, or number of openings. Instead, for each of the education levels we provide one list for the occupations at that level, ranking them by their total combined score for earnings, growth, and number of openings.

These lists can help you identify a job with higher earnings or upward mobility but with a similar level of education to the job you now hold. For example, you will find jobs within the same level of education that require similar skills, yet one pays significantly better than the other, is projected to grow more rapidly, or has significantly more job openings per year. This information can help you leverage your present skills and experience into jobs that might be better for you.

You can also use these lists to explore possible job options if you were to get additional training, education, or work experience. For example, students can use these lists to identify occupations that offer high potential, and graduates can use them to identify degrees that could improve their employment options.

The lists can also help you when you plan your education. For example, you might be thinking about a particular college major because the pay is very good, but the lists may help you identify a college major that interests you more and offers even better potential for the same general educational requirements.

The Education Levels

College degrees have no universal standards. Each college or university determines the number of credit hours and courses that are required for a specific degree. For example, the requirements for a major in anthropology varied at three universities from 27 to 36 semester hours, and the total hours required to get the bachelor's degree varied from 120 to 126 hours. Also, there can be a wide difference in degree requirements depending on the type of major. At one university, a Bachelor of Architecture degree requires 160 semester hours while a Bachelor of Arts in History requires 126 hours. Thus, when a job indicates that a bachelor's degree is required, additional research is needed to determine the investment in years and courses required for the specific degree necessary for that occupation.

There are, however, guidelines that can help you understand what is generally required to earn a specific degree. The following definitions are used by the federal government to classify jobs based on the minimum level of education typically required for entry and are the definitions we use for constructing the lists in this section.

- **Associate's degree:** The associate's degree usually requires 60 to 63 semester hours to complete. A normal course load for a full-time student each semester is 15 hours. This means that it typically takes two years to complete an associate's degree.

- **Bachelor's degree:** A bachelor's degree usually requires 120 to 130 semester hours to complete. A full-time student usually takes four to five years to complete a bachelor's degree, depending on the complexity of courses. Traditionally, people have thought of the bachelor's degree as a four-year degree. There are some bachelor's degrees—like the Bachelor of Architecture degree we previously mentioned—that are considered a first professional degree and take five or more years to complete.

- **Work experience plus degree:** Some jobs require work experience in a related job in addition to a degree. For example, almost all managers have worked in a related job before being promoted into a management position. Most of the jobs in this group require a four-year bachelor's degree, although some require an associate's degree or a master's degree.

- **Master's degree:** This degree usually requires 33 to 60 semester hours beyond the bachelor's degree. The academic master's degrees—like a Master of Arts in Political Science—usually require 33 to 36 hours. A first professional degree at the master's level—like a Master of Social Work—requires almost two years of full-time work.

⬡ **Doctoral degree:** The doctoral degree prepares students for careers that consist primarily of theory development, research, and/or college teaching. This type of degree is typically the Doctor of Philosophy (Ph.D.) or Doctor of Education (Ed.D.). Normally, a requirement for a doctoral degree is the completion of a master's degree plus an additional two to three years of full-time coursework and a one- to two-semester research project and paper called the dissertation. It usually takes four to five years beyond the bachelor's degree to complete a doctoral degree.

⬡ **First professional degree:** Some professional degrees require three or more years of full-time academic study beyond the bachelor's degree. A professional degree prepares students for a specific profession. It uses theory and research to teach practical applications in a professional occupation. Examples of this type of degree are Doctor of Medicine (M.D.) for physicians, Doctor of Ministry (D.Min.) for clergy, and Juris Doctor (J.D.) for attorneys.

Another Warning About the Data

We warned you in the Introduction to this book to use caution in interpreting the data we use, and we want to do it again here. The occupational data we use is the most accurate available anywhere, but it has limitations. For example, a four-year degree in accounting, finance, or a related area is typically required for entry into the accounting profession. But some people working as accountants don't have such a degree, and others have much more education than the "minimum" required for entry.

In a similar way, people with a graduate degree will typically earn considerably more than someone with an associate's or bachelor's degree. However, some people with an associate's degree earn considerably more than the average for those with higher levels of education. In a similar way, new entrants to any job will typically earn less than the average, and some areas of the country have lower wages overall (but may also have lower costs of living).

So as you browse the lists that follow, please use them as a way to be encouraged rather than discouraged. Education and training are very important for success in the labor market of the future, but so are ability, drive, initiative, and, yes, luck.

Having said this, we encourage you to get as much education and training as you can. It used to be that you got your schooling and never went back, but this is not a good attitude to have now. You will probably need to continue learning new things throughout your working life. This can be done by going to school, which is a good thing for many people to do. But there are also many other ways to learn, such as workshops, adult education programs, certification programs, employer training, professional conferences, Internet training, reading related books and magazines, and many others. Upgrading your computer skills—and other technical skills—is particularly important in our rapidly changing workplace, and you avoid doing so at your peril.

Best Jobs Requiring an Associate's Degree

Job	Annual Earnings	Percent Growth	Annual Openings
1. Registered Nurses	$51,020	27.3%	215,000
2. Dental Hygienists	$56,680	43.1%	9,000
3. Computer Support Specialists	$39,900	30.3%	71,000
4. Paralegals and Legal Assistants	$38,440	28.7%	29,000
5. Medical Records and Health Information Technicians	$24,920	46.8%	24,000
6. Respiratory Therapists	$42,050	34.8%	10,000
7. Radiologic Technicians	$41,850	22.9%	21,000
8. Radiologic Technologists	$41,850	22.9%	21,000
9. Physical Therapist Assistants	$37,280	44.6%	10,000
10. City Planning Aides	$48,660	17.5%	18,000
11. Social Science Research Assistants	$48,660	17.5%	18,000
12. Radiation Therapists	$55,550	31.6%	1,000
13. Diagnostic Medical Sonographers	$50,980	24.0%	4,000
14. Nuclear Medicine Technologists	$53,680	23.6%	2,000
15. Veterinary Technologists and Technicians	$24,190	44.1%	11,000
16. Cardiovascular Technologists and Technicians	$37,800	33.5%	6,000
17. Physical Therapist Aides	$21,070	46.4%	8,000
18. Occupational Therapist Assistants	$38,120	39.2%	3,000
19. Calibration and Instrumentation Technicians	$45,390	10.0%	24,000
20. Electrical Engineering Technicians	$45,390	10.0%	24,000
21. Electronics Engineering Technicians	$45,390	10.0%	24,000
22. Medical Transcriptionists	$27,790	22.6%	18,000
23. Environmental Science and Protection Technicians, Including Health	$35,790	36.8%	4,000
24. Medical and Clinical Laboratory Technicians	$30,140	19.4%	21,000
25. Environmental Engineering Technicians	$38,180	28.4%	3,000
26. Biological Technicians	$33,360	19.4%	7,000

Best Jobs Requiring a Bachelor's Degree

Job	Annual Earnings	Percent Growth	Annual Openings
1. Computer Software Engineers, Applications	$73,410	45.5%	55,000
2. Computer Software Engineers, Systems Software	$77,250	45.5%	39,000
3. Computer Systems Analysts	$65,050	39.4%	68,000

(continued)

(continued)

Best Jobs Requiring a Bachelor's Degree

Job	Annual Earnings	Percent Growth	Annual Openings
4. Network Systems and Data Communications Analysts	$59,300	57.0%	29,000
5. Computer Security Specialists	$57,060	37.4%	35,000
6. Network and Computer Systems Administrators	$57,060	37.4%	35,000
7. Personal Financial Advisors	$60,230	34.6%	18,000
8. Database Administrators	$59,150	44.2%	16,000
9. Logisticians	$49,740	27.5%	162,000
10. Physician Assistants	$68,200	48.9%	7,000
11. Special Education Teachers, Secondary School	$44,920	30.0%	59,000
12. Special Education Teachers, Middle School	$43,260	30.0%	59,000
13. Special Education Teachers, Preschool, Kindergarten, and Elementary School	$42,630	30.0%	59,000
14. Environmental Engineers	$64,040	38.2%	6,000
15. Accountants	$49,770	19.5%	119,000
16. Auditors	$49,770	19.5%	119,000
17. Occupational Therapists	$53,320	35.2%	10,000
18. Construction Managers	$67,620	12.0%	47,000
19. Training and Development Specialists	$44,270	27.9%	35,000
20. Market Research Analysts	$54,830	23.4%	18,000
21. Computer Programmers	$61,730	14.6%	45,000
22. Public Relations Specialists	$43,050	32.9%	28,000
23. Financial Analysts	$61,130	18.7%	22,000
24. Sales Agents, Financial Services	$62,680	13.0%	39,000
25. Sales Agents, Securities and Commodities	$62,680	13.0%	39,000
26. Airline Pilots, Copilots, and Flight Engineers	$128,140	18.5%	6,000
27. Social and Community Service Managers	$46,200	27.7%	19,000
28. Sales Engineers	$68,510	19.9%	7,000
29. Preschool Teachers, Except Special Education	$20,450	36.2%	88,000
30. Kindergarten Teachers, Except Special Education	$40,980	27.2%	34,000
31. Compensation, Benefits, and Job Analysis Specialists	$46,890	28.0%	15,000
32. Secondary School Teachers, Except Special and Vocational Education	$45,180	18.2%	118,000
33. Employment Interviewers, Private or Public Employment Service	$40,970	27.3%	29,000
34. Personnel Recruiters	$40,970	27.3%	29,000
35. Loan Officers	$47,530	18.8%	30,000
36. Cost Estimators	$49,220	18.6%	25,000
37. Technical Writers	$52,160	27.1%	6,000

Best Jobs Requiring a Bachelor's Degree

Job	Annual Earnings	Percent Growth	Annual Openings
38. Medical and Public Health Social Workers	$39,160	28.6%	18,000
39. Elementary School Teachers, Except Special Education	$42,590	15.2%	183,000
40. Industrial Production Managers	$71,650	7.9%	18,000
41. Child, Family, and School Social Workers	$34,300	23.2%	45,000
42. Electronics Engineers, Except Computer	$73,470	9.4%	11,000
43. Industrial Engineers	$64,050	10.6%	16,000
44. Medical and Clinical Laboratory Technologists	$44,460	19.3%	21,000
45. Environmental Scientists and Specialists, Including Health	$50,070	23.7%	6,000
46. Architects, Except Landscape and Naval	$58,630	17.3%	8,000
47. Graphic Designers	$36,930	21.9%	29,000
48. Rehabilitation Counselors	$27,410	33.8%	19,000
49. Civil Engineers	$62,840	8.0%	17,000
50. Copy Writers	$43,340	16.1%	23,000
51. Creative Writers	$43,340	16.1%	23,000
52. Poets and Lyricists	$43,340	16.1%	23,000
53. Biomedical Engineers	$64,780	26.1%	fewer than 500
54. Recreation Workers	$18,950	20.5%	56,000
55. Purchasing Agents, Except Wholesale, Retail, and Farm Products	$47,250	11.2%	29,000
56. Budget Analysts	$55,090	14.0%	8,000
57. Credit Analysts	$46,640	18.7%	9,000
58. Mechanical Engineers	$65,210	4.8%	14,000
59. Middle School Teachers, Except Special and Vocational Education	$42,960	9.0%	69,000
60. Economists	$70,520	13.4%	2,000
61. Hydrologists	$59,010	21.0%	1,000
62. Computer Hardware Engineers	$79,090	6.1%	6,000
63. Electrical Engineers	$70,830	2.5%	11,000
64. Multi-Media Artists and Animators	$46,770	15.8%	12,000
65. Adult Literacy, Remedial Education, and GED Teachers and Instructors	$37,910	20.4%	14,000
66. Commercial and Industrial Designers	$52,080	14.7%	7,000
67. Directors, Religious Activities and Education	$29,240	24.1%	16,000
68. Landscape Architects	$50,780	22.2%	2,000
69. Chemists	$54,960	12.7%	7,000
70. Property, Real Estate, and Community Association Managers	$38,750	12.8%	35,000

(continued)

(continued)

Best Jobs Requiring a Bachelor's Degree

Job	Annual Earnings	Percent Growth	Annual Openings
71. Interior Designers	$40,420	21.7%	8,000
72. Geologists	$68,570	11.5%	2,000
73. Atmospheric and Space Scientists	$65,400	16.2%	1,000
74. Film and Video Editors	$41,820	26.4%	3,000
75. Meeting and Convention Planners	$39,070	21.3%	7,000
76. Dietitians and Nutritionists	$42,630	17.8%	8,000
77. Insurance Sales Agents	$40,370	8.4%	52,000
78. Insurance Underwriters	$48,370	10.0%	12,000
79. Geographers	$56,290	19.5%	fewer than 500
80. Probation Officers and Correctional Treatment Specialists	$39,200	14.7%	15,000
81. Editors	$42,450	11.8%	14,000
82. Aerospace Engineers	$77,340	–5.2%	5,000
83. Fire-Prevention and Protection Engineers	$61,430	7.9%	4,000
84. Industrial Safety and Health Engineers	$61,430	7.9%	4,000
85. Product Safety Engineers	$61,430	7.9%	4,000
86. Survey Researchers	$26,990	33.6%	3,000
87. Orthotists and Prosthetists	$49,860	18.9%	1,000
88. Vocational Education Teachers, Secondary School	$45,140	9.0%	12,000
89. Materials Scientists	$71,090	8.5%	1,000
90. Athletic Trainers	$32,990	29.9%	2,000
91. Financial Examiners	$59,050	8.9%	3,000
92. Wholesale and Retail Buyers, Except Farm Products	$42,200	4.3%	24,000
93. Chemical Engineers	$75,310	0.4%	2,000
94. Fashion Designers	$54,530	10.6%	2,000
95. Materials Engineers	$65,010	4.1%	2,000
96. Nuclear Engineers	$83,260	–0.1%	1,000

Best Jobs Requiring Work Experience Plus Degree

Job	Annual Earnings	Percent Growth	Annual Openings
1. Computer and Information Systems Managers	$90,490	36.1%	39,000
2. Sales Managers	$81,970	30.5%	54,000
3. Management Analysts	$63,090	30.4%	78,000
4. Medical and Health Services Managers	$66,360	29.3%	33,000

Best Jobs Requiring Work Experience Plus Degree

Job	Annual Earnings	Percent Growth	Annual Openings
5. General and Operations Managers	$74,600	18.4%	260,000
6. Chief Executives	$136,400	16.7%	63,000
7. Government Service Executives	$136,400	16.7%	63,000
8. Private Sector Executives	$136,400	16.7%	63,000
9. Marketing Managers	$85,220	21.3%	30,000
10. Financial Managers, Branch or Department	$79,090	18.3%	71,000
11. Treasurers, Controllers, and Chief Financial Officers	$79,090	18.3%	71,000
12. Education Administrators, Elementary and Secondary School	$73,960	20.7%	31,000
13. Education Administrators, Postsecondary	$67,760	25.9%	19,000
14. Compensation and Benefits Managers	$72,180	19.4%	21,000
15. Training and Development Managers	$72,180	19.4%	21,000
16. Administrative Services Managers	$58,130	19.8%	40,000
17. Human Resources Managers	$70,350	19.4%	21,000
18. Public Relations Managers	$67,810	23.4%	10,000
19. Advertising and Promotions Managers	$61,400	25.0%	13,000
20. Engineering Managers	$95,630	9.2%	16,000
21. Agents and Business Managers of Artists, Performers, and Athletes	$55,700	27.8%	2,000
22. Directors—Stage, Motion Pictures, Television, and Radio	$51,870	18.3%	10,000
23. Producers	$51,870	18.3%	10,000
24. Program Directors	$51,870	18.3%	10,000
25. Natural Sciences Managers	$86,910	11.3%	5,000
26. Art Directors	$63,170	11.4%	8,000
27. Actuaries	$75,280	14.9%	2,000
28. Education Administrators, Preschool and Child Care Center/Program	$35,240	32.0%	9,000
29. Purchasing Managers	$67,830	4.8%	9,000
30. Judges, Magistrate Judges, and Magistrates	$91,230	8.7%	2,000
31. Gaming Managers	$57,930	12.4%	1,000

Best Jobs Requiring a Master's Degree

Job	Annual Earnings	Percent Growth	Annual Openings
1. Postsecondary Teachers	$51,815	38.1%	216,000
2. Physical Therapists	$58,700	35.3%	16,000
3. Clinical Psychologists	$53,230	24.4%	17,000

(continued)

(continued)

Best Jobs Requiring a Master's Degree

Job	Annual Earnings	Percent Growth	Annual Openings
4. Counseling Psychologists	$53,230	24.4%	17,000
5. Educational Psychologists	$53,230	24.4%	17,000
6. Instructional Coordinators	$47,550	25.4%	18,000
7. Speech-Language Pathologists	$50,890	27.2%	10,000
8. Mental Health and Substance Abuse Social Workers	$33,650	34.5%	17,000
9. Educational, Vocational, and School Counselors	$44,990	15.0%	32,000
10. Audiologists	$50,000	29.0%	1,000
11. Mental Health Counselors	$32,040	26.7%	13,000
12. Health Educators	$38,100	21.9%	8,000
13. Substance Abuse and Behavioral Disorder Counselors	$31,510	23.3%	10,000
14. Industrial-Organizational Psychologists	$67,740	16.0%	fewer than 500
15. Librarians	$44,730	10.1%	15,000
16. Occupational Health and Safety Specialists	$48,330	13.2%	6,000
17. Operations Research Analysts	$59,090	6.2%	6,000
18. Urban and Regional Planners	$52,680	10.7%	5,000
19. Marriage and Family Therapists	$38,210	22.4%	3,000
20. Political Scientists	$81,670	5.9%	1,000
21. Statisticians	$64,320	4.8%	2,000

Best Jobs Requiring a Doctoral Degree

Job	Annual Earnings	Percent Growth	Annual Openings
1. Medical Scientists, Except Epidemiologists	$60,200	26.9%	6,000
2. Biologists	$64,390	22.3%	3,000
3. Biochemists	$64,390	22.9%	2,000
4. Biophysicists	$64,390	22.9%	2,000
5. Epidemiologists	$53,660	32.5%	fewer than 500
6. Microbiologists	$52,100	20.0%	1,000
7. Physicists	$83,570	6.9%	1,000
8. Astronomers	$85,910	4.9%	fewer than 500

Best Jobs Requiring a First Professional Degree

Job	Annual Earnings	Percent Growth	Annual Openings
1. Pharmacists	$82,520	30.1%	23,000
2. Anesthesiologists	more than $145,000	19.5%	38,000
3. Internists, General	more than $145,000	19.5%	38,000
4. Obstetricians and Gynecologists	more than $145,000	19.5%	38,000
5. Surgeons	more than $145,000	19.5%	38,000
6. Family and General Practitioners	$137,670	19.5%	38,000
7. Pediatricians, General	$136,490	19.5%	38,000
8. Psychiatrists	$135,440	19.5%	38,000
9. Lawyers	$92,730	17.0%	53,000
10. Veterinarians	$65,290	25.1%	4,000
11. Chiropractors	$66,610	23.3%	3,000
12. Optometrists	$87,340	17.1%	2,000
13. Podiatrists	$95,550	15.0%	1,000
14. Dentists, General	$120,420	4.1%	7,000
15. Oral and Maxillofacial Surgeons	$120,420	4.1%	7,000
16. Orthodontists	$120,420	4.1%	7,000
17. Prosthodontists	$120,420	4.1%	7,000
18. Clergy	$34,930	15.5%	34,000

Best Jobs Lists for College Graduates Based on Interests

This group of lists organizes the 200 best jobs that typically require a college degree or more into 16 interest areas. These interest areas are used in a variety of career exploration systems and can help you to quickly identify jobs based on your interests.

Simply find the area or areas that interest you most. Then review the jobs in those areas to identify jobs you want to explore in more detail and look up their descriptions in Part II. You can also review interest areas where you have had past experience, education, or training to see whether other jobs in those areas would meet your current requirements.

Within each interest area, jobs are listed in order of their total combined scores based on earnings, growth, and number of openings.

Some of the interest areas will have just a few jobs listed in them. This is because few jobs in those interest areas typically require a college degree. Even so, if one of those areas interests you most, you can often come up with a creative way to use your education and training in that interest area. For example, you might start or manage a business in an area that interests you or work in an industry that involves your interest area.

Note: The 16 interest areas used in these lists are based on those developed by the U.S. Department of Education as a way to assist in career exploration and planning. This is the same classification scheme used in the New Guide for Occupational Exploration, *Fourth Edition, published by JIST.*

Descriptions for the 16 Interest Areas

Brief descriptions for the 16 interest areas we use in the lists follow. Note that the descriptions are as they appear in the *New Guide for Occupational Exploration*, Fourth Edition, and include some job titles that differ from those used in our lists.

Also note that we put each job into only one interest area list, the one it fit into best. However, many jobs could be included in more than one list, so consider reviewing a variety of these interest areas to find jobs that you might otherwise overlook.

- **Agriculture and Natural Resources:** *An interest in working with plants, animals, forests, or mineral resources for agriculture, horticulture, conservation, extraction, and other purposes.* You can satisfy this interest by working in farming, landscaping, forestry, fishing, mining, and related fields. You may like doing physical work outdoors, such as on a farm or ranch, in a forest, or on a drilling rig. If you have scientific curiosity, you could study plants and animals or analyze biological or rock samples in a lab. If you have management ability, you could own, operate, or manage a fish hatchery, a landscaping business, or a greenhouse.

- **Architecture and Construction:** *An interest in designing, assembling, and maintaining components of buildings and other structures.* You may want to be part of the team of architects, drafters, and others who design buildings and render the plans. If construction interests you, you can find fulfillment in the many building projects that are being undertaken at all times. If you like to organize and plan, you can find careers in managing these projects. Or you can play a more direct role in putting up and finishing buildings by doing jobs such as plumbing, carpentry, masonry, painting, or roofing, either as a skilled craftsworker or as a helper. You can prepare the building site by operating heavy equipment or install, maintain, and repair vital building equipment and systems such as electricity and heating.

- **Arts and Communication:** *An interest in creatively expressing feelings or ideas, in communicating news or information, or in performing.* You can satisfy this interest in creative, verbal, or performing activities. For example, if you enjoy literature, perhaps writing or editing would appeal to you. Journalism and public relations are other fields for people who like to use their writing or speaking skills. Do you prefer to work in the performing arts? If so, you could direct or perform in drama, music, or dance. If you especially enjoy the visual arts, you could create paintings, sculpture, or ceramics or design products or visual displays. A flair for technology might lead you to specialize in photography, broadcast production, or dispatching.

◉ **Business and Administration:** *An interest in making a business organization or function run smoothly.* You can satisfy this interest by working in a position of leadership or by specializing in a function that contributes to the overall effort in a business, nonprofit organization, or government agency. If you especially enjoy working with people, you may find fulfillment from working in human resources. An interest in numbers may lead you to consider accounting, finance, budgeting, billing, or financial record-keeping. A job as an administrative assistant may interest you if you like a variety of work in a busy environment. If you are good with details and word processing, you may enjoy a job as a secretary or data-entry keyer. Or perhaps you would do well as the manager of a business.

◉ **Education and Training:** *An interest in helping people learn.* You can satisfy this interest by teaching students, who may be preschoolers, retirees, or any age in between. You may specialize in a particular academic field or work with learners of a particular age, with a particular interest, or with a particular learning problem. Working in a library or museum may give you an opportunity to expand people's understanding of the world.

◉ **Finance and Insurance:** *An interest in helping businesses and people be assured of a financially secure future.* You can satisfy this interest by working in a financial or insurance business in a leadership or support role. If you like gathering and analyzing information, you may find fulfillment as an insurance adjuster or financial analyst. Or you may deal with information at the clerical level as a financial or insurance clerk or in person-to-person situations providing customer service. Another way to interact with people is to sell financial or insurance services that will meet their needs.

◉ **Government and Public Administration:** *An interest in helping a government agency serve the needs of the public.* You can satisfy this interest by working in a position of leadership or by specializing in a function that contributes to the role of government. You may help protect the public by working as an inspector or examiner to enforce standards. If you enjoy using clerical skills, you may work as a clerk in a law court or government office. Or perhaps you prefer the top-down perspective of a government executive or city planner.

◉ **Health Science:** *An interest in helping people and animals be healthy.* You can satisfy this interest by working in a health-care team as a doctor, therapist, or nurse. You might specialize in one of the many different parts of the body (such as the teeth or eyes) or in one of the many different types of care. Or you may wish to be a generalist who deals with the whole patient. If you like technology, you might find satisfaction working with X rays or new methods of diagnosis. You might work with healthy people, helping them eat right. If you enjoy working with animals, you might care for them and keep them healthy.

◉ **Hospitality, Tourism, and Recreation:** *An interest in catering to the personal wishes and needs of others so that they may enjoy a clean environment, good food and drink, comfortable lodging away from home, and recreation.* You can satisfy this interest by providing services for the convenience, care, and pampering of others in hotels, restaurants, airplanes, and so on. You may wish to use your love of cooking as a chef. If you like working with people, you may wish to provide personal services by being a travel guide, a flight attendant, a concierge, or a waiter. You may wish to work in cleaning and building services if you like a clean environment. If you enjoy sports or games, you may work for an athletic team or casino.

- ◎ **Human Service:** *An interest in improving people's social, mental, emotional, or spiritual well-being.* You can satisfy this interest as a counselor, social worker, or religious worker who helps people sort out their complicated lives or solve personal problems. You may work as a caretaker for very young people or the elderly. Or you may interview people to help identify the social services they need.

- ◎ **Information Technology:** *An interest in designing, developing, managing, and supporting information systems.* You can satisfy this interest by working with hardware, software, multimedia, or integrated systems. If you like to use your organizational skills, you might work as an administrator of a system or database. Or you can solve complex problems as a software engineer or systems analyst. If you enjoy getting your hands on the hardware, you might find work servicing computers, peripherals, and information-intense machines such as cash registers and ATMs.

- ◎ **Law and Public Safety:** *An interest in upholding people's rights or in protecting people and property by using authority, inspecting, or investigating.* You can satisfy this interest by working in law, law enforcement, fire fighting, the military, and related fields. For example, if you enjoy mental challenge and intrigue, you could investigate crimes or fires for a living. If you enjoy working with verbal skills and research skills, you may want to defend citizens in court or research deeds, wills, and other legal documents. If you want to help people in critical situations, you may want to fight fires, work as a police officer, or become a paramedic. Or, if you want more routine work in public safety, perhaps a job in guarding, patrolling, or inspecting would appeal to you. If you have management ability, you could seek a leadership position in law enforcement and the protective services. Work in the military gives you a chance to use technical and leadership skills while serving your country.

- ◎ **Manufacturing:** *An interest in processing materials into intermediate or final products or maintaining and repairing products by using machines or hand tools.* You can satisfy this interest by working in one of many industries that mass-produce goods or by working for a utility that distributes electric power or other resources. You may enjoy manual work, using your hands or hand tools in highly skilled jobs such as assembling engines or electronic equipment. If you enjoy making machines run efficiently or fixing them when they break down, you could seek a job installing or repairing such devices as copiers, aircraft engines, cars, or watches. Perhaps you prefer to set up or operate machines that are used to manufacture products made of food, glass, or paper. You may enjoy cutting and grinding metal and plastic parts to desired shapes and measurements. Or you may wish to operate equipment in systems that provide water and process wastewater. You may like inspecting, sorting, counting, or weighing products. Another option is to work with your hands and machinery to move boxes and freight in a warehouse. If leadership appeals to you, you could manage people engaged in production and repair.

◎ **Retail and Wholesale Sales and Service:** *An interest in bringing others to a particular point of view by personal persuasion and by sales and promotional techniques.* You can satisfy this interest in a variety of jobs that involve persuasion and selling. If you like using knowledge of science, you may enjoy selling pharmaceutical, medical, or electronic products or services. Real estate offers several kinds of sales jobs as well. If you like speaking on the phone, you could work as a telemarketer. Or you may enjoy selling apparel and other merchandise in a retail setting. If you prefer to help people, you may want a job in customer service or want to help people in a hands-on way by styling their hair.

◎ **Scientific Research, Engineering, and Mathematics:** *An interest in discovering, collecting, and analyzing information about the natural world; in applying scientific research findings to problems in medicine, the life sciences, human behavior, and the natural sciences; in imagining and manipulating quantitative data; and in applying technology to manufacturing, transportation, and other economic activities.* You can satisfy this interest by working with the knowledge and processes of the sciences. You may enjoy researching and developing new knowledge in mathematics, or perhaps solving problems in the physical, life, or social sciences would appeal to you. You may wish to study engineering and help create new machines, processes, and structures. If you want to work with scientific equipment and procedures, you could seek a job in a research or testing laboratory.

◎ **Transportation, Distribution, and Logistics:** *An interest in operations that move people or materials.* You can satisfy this interest by managing a transportation service, by helping vehicles keep on their assigned schedules and routes, or by driving or piloting a vehicle. If you enjoy taking responsibility, perhaps managing a rail line would appeal to you. If you work well with details and can take pressure on the job, you might consider being an air traffic controller. Or would you rather get out on the highway, on the water, or up in the air? If so, then you could drive a truck from state to state, be employed on a ship, or fly a crop duster over a cornfield. If you prefer to stay closer to home, you could drive a delivery van, taxi, or school bus. You can use your physical strength to load freight and arrange it so it gets to its destination in one piece.

Best Jobs for College Graduates Interested in Agriculture and Natural Resources

Job	Annual Earnings	Percent Growth	Annual Openings
1. Environmental Engineers	$64,040	38.2%	6,000
2. Environmental Science and Protection Technicians, Including Health	$35,790	36.8%	4,000

Only two jobs are listed here because most jobs in this interest area do not typically require a college degree to enter, although many people with college degrees do work in these jobs.

Best Jobs for College Graduates Interested in Architecture and Construction

Job	Annual Earnings	Percent Growth	Annual Openings
1. Construction Managers	$67,620	12.0%	47,000
2. Architects, Except Landscape and Naval	$58,630	17.3%	8,000
3. Landscape Architects	$50,780	22.2%	2,000

Only three jobs are listed here because most jobs in this interest area do not typically require a college degree to enter, although many people with college degrees do work in these jobs.

Best Jobs for College Graduates Interested in Arts and Communication

Job	Annual Earnings	Percent Growth	Annual Openings
1. Public Relations Managers	$67,810	23.4%	10,000
2. Public Relations Specialists	$43,050	32.9%	28,000
3. Technical Writers	$52,160	27.1%	6,000
4. Agents and Business Managers of Artists, Performers, and Athletes	$55,700	27.8%	2,000
5. Directors—Stage, Motion Pictures, Television, and Radio	$51,870	18.3%	10,000
6. Producers	$51,870	18.3%	10,000
7. Program Directors	$51,870	18.3%	10,000
8. Graphic Designers	$36,930	21.9%	29,000
9. Copy Writers	$43,340	16.1%	23,000
10. Creative Writers	$43,340	16.1%	23,000
11. Poets and Lyricists	$43,340	16.1%	23,000
12. Art Directors	$63,170	11.4%	8,000
13. Multi-Media Artists and Animators	$46,770	15.8%	12,000
14. Commercial and Industrial Designers	$52,080	14.7%	7,000
15. Interior Designers	$40,420	21.7%	8,000
16. Film and Video Editors	$41,820	26.4%	3,000
17. Editors	$42,450	11.8%	14,000
18. Fashion Designers	$54,530	10.6%	2,000

Best Jobs for College Graduates Interested in Business and Administration

Job	Annual Earnings	Percent Growth	Annual Openings
1. Management Analysts	$63,090	30.4%	78,000
2. General and Operations Managers	$74,600	18.4%	260,000
3. Chief Executives	$136,400	16.7%	63,000
4. Private Sector Executives	$136,400	16.7%	63,000
5. Logisticians	$49,740	27.5%	162,000
6. Compensation and Benefits Managers	$72,180	19.4%	21,000
7. Training and Development Managers	$72,180	19.4%	21,000
8. Administrative Services Managers	$58,130	19.8%	40,000
9. Human Resources Managers	$70,350	19.4%	21,000
10. Accountants	$49,770	19.5%	119,000
11. Auditors	$49,770	19.5%	119,000
12. Training and Development Specialists	$44,270	27.9%	35,000
13. Compensation, Benefits, and Job Analysis Specialists	$46,890	28.0%	15,000
14. Employment Interviewers, Private or Public Employment Service	$40,970	27.3%	29,000
15. Personnel Recruiters	$40,970	27.3%	29,000
16. Budget Analysts	$55,090	14.0%	8,000
17. Meeting and Convention Planners	$39,070	21.3%	7,000
18. Operations Research Analysts	$59,090	6.2%	6,000

Best Jobs for College Graduates Interested in Education and Training

Job	Annual Earnings	Percent Growth	Annual Openings
1. Postsecondary Teachers	$51,815	38.1%	216,000
2. Education Administrators, Elementary and Secondary School	$73,960	20.7%	31,000
3. Education Administrators, Postsecondary	$67,760	25.9%	19,000
4. Special Education Teachers, Secondary School	$44,920	30.0%	59,000
5. Special Education Teachers, Middle School	$43,260	30.0%	59,000
6. Special Education Teachers, Preschool, Kindergarten, and Elementary School	$42,630	30.0%	59,000
7. Instructional Coordinators	$47,550	25.4%	18,000
8. Preschool Teachers, Except Special Education	$20,450	36.2%	88,000

(continued)

(continued)

Best Jobs for College Graduates Interested in Education and Training

Job	Annual Earnings	Percent Growth	Annual Openings
9. Kindergarten Teachers, Except Special Education	$40,980	27.2%	34,000
10. Secondary School Teachers, Except Special and Vocational Education	$45,180	18.2%	118,000
11. Elementary School Teachers, Except Special Education	$42,590	15.2%	183,000
12. Educational, Vocational, and School Counselors	$44,990	15.0%	32,000
13. Education Administrators, Preschool and Child Care Center/Program	$35,240	32.0%	9,000
14. Middle School Teachers, Except Special and Vocational Education	$42,960	9.0%	69,000
15. Adult Literacy, Remedial Education, and GED Teachers and Instructors	$37,910	20.4%	14,000
16. Health Educators	$38,100	21.9%	8,000
17. Librarians	$44,730	10.1%	15,000
18. Vocational Education Teachers, Secondary School	$45,140	9.0%	12,000

Best Jobs for College Graduates Interested in Finance and Insurance

Job	Annual Earnings	Percent Growth	Annual Openings
1. Financial Managers, Branch or Department	$79,090	18.3%	71,000
2. Treasurers, Controllers, and Chief Financial Officers	$79,090	18.3%	71,000
3. Personal Financial Advisors	$60,230	34.6%	18,000
4. Market Research Analysts	$54,830	23.4%	18,000
5. Financial Analysts	$61,130	18.7%	22,000
6. Sales Agents, Financial Services	$62,680	13.0%	39,000
7. Sales Agents, Securities and Commodities	$62,680	13.0%	39,000
8. Loan Officers	$47,530	18.8%	30,000
9. Cost Estimators	$49,220	18.6%	25,000
10. Credit Analysts	$46,640	18.7%	9,000
11. Insurance Sales Agents	$40,370	8.4%	52,000
12. Insurance Underwriters	$48,370	10.0%	12,000
13. Survey Researchers	$26,990	33.6%	3,000

Best Jobs for College Graduates Interested in Government and Public Administration

Job	Annual Earnings	Percent Growth	Annual Openings
1. Government Service Executives	$136,400	16.7%	63,000
2. Social and Community Service Managers	$46,200	27.7%	19,000
3. City Planning Aides	$48,660	17.5%	18,000
4. Occupational Health and Safety Specialists	$48,330	13.2%	6,000
5. Urban and Regional Planners	$52,680	10.7%	5,000
6. Financial Examiners	$59,050	8.9%	3,000

Best Jobs for College Graduates Interested in Health Science

Job	Annual Earnings	Percent Growth	Annual Openings
1. Pharmacists	$82,520	30.1%	23,000
2. Anesthesiologists	more than $145,000	19.5%	38,000
3. Internists, General	more than $145,000	19.5%	38,000
4. Obstetricians and Gynecologists	more than $145,000	19.5%	38,000
5. Surgeons	more than $145,000	19.5%	38,000
6. Family and General Practitioners	$137,670	19.5%	38,000
7. Pediatricians, General	$136,490	19.5%	38,000
8. Psychiatrists	$135,440	19.5%	38,000
9. Medical and Health Services Managers	$66,360	29.3%	33,000
10. Registered Nurses	$51,020	27.3%	215,000
11. Physician Assistants	$68,200	48.9%	7,000
12. Physical Therapists	$58,700	35.3%	16,000
13. Dental Hygienists	$56,680	43.1%	9,000
14. Occupational Therapists	$53,320	35.2%	10,000
15. Speech-Language Pathologists	$50,890	27.2%	10,000
16. Veterinarians	$65,290	25.1%	4,000
17. Chiropractors	$66,610	23.3%	3,000
18. Medical Records and Health Information Technicians	$24,920	46.8%	24,000
19. Respiratory Therapists	$42,050	34.8%	10,000
20. Radiologic Technicians	$41,850	22.9%	21,000
21. Radiologic Technologists	$41,850	22.9%	21,000
22. Physical Therapist Assistants	$37,280	44.6%	10,000
23. Optometrists	$87,340	17.1%	2,000

(continued)

(continued)

Best Jobs for College Graduates Interested in Health Science

Job	Annual Earnings	Percent Growth	Annual Openings
24. Medical and Clinical Laboratory Technologists	$44,460	19.3%	21,000
25. Radiation Therapists	$55,550	31.6%	1,000
26. Diagnostic Medical Sonographers	$50,980	24.0%	4,000
27. Nuclear Medicine Technologists	$53,680	23.6%	2,000
28. Veterinary Technologists and Technicians	$24,190	44.1%	11,000
29. Podiatrists	$95,550	15.0%	1,000
30. Dentists, General	$120,420	4.1%	7,000
31. Oral and Maxillofacial Surgeons	$120,420	4.1%	7,000
32. Orthodontists	$120,420	4.1%	7,000
33. Prosthodontists	$120,420	4.1%	7,000
34. Cardiovascular Technologists and Technicians	$37,800	33.5%	6,000
35. Physical Therapist Aides	$21,070	46.4%	8,000
36. Audiologists	$50,000	29.0%	1,000
37. Occupational Therapist Assistants	$38,120	39.2%	3,000
38. Medical Transcriptionists	$27,790	22.6%	18,000
39. Medical and Clinical Laboratory Technicians	$30,140	19.4%	21,000
40. Dietitians and Nutritionists	$42,630	17.8%	8,000
41. Orthotists and Prosthetists	$49,860	18.9%	1,000
42. Athletic Trainers	$32,990	29.9%	2,000
43. Biological Technicians	$33,360	19.4%	7,000

Best Jobs for College Graduates Interested in Hospitality, Tourism, and Recreation

Job	Annual Earnings	Percent Growth	Annual Openings
1. Recreation Workers	$18,950	20.5%	56,000
2. Gaming Managers	$57,930	12.4%	1,000

Only two jobs are listed here because most jobs in this interest area do not typically require a college degree to enter, although many people with college degrees do work in these jobs.

Best Jobs for College Graduates Interested in Human Service

Job	Annual Earnings	Percent Growth	Annual Openings
1. Clinical Psychologists	$53,230	24.4%	17,000
2. Counseling Psychologists	$53,230	24.4%	17,000
3. Medical and Public Health Social Workers	$39,160	28.6%	18,000
4. Child, Family, and School Social Workers	$34,300	23.2%	45,000
5. Mental Health and Substance Abuse Social Workers	$33,650	34.5%	17,000
6. Rehabilitation Counselors	$27,410	33.8%	19,000
7. Mental Health Counselors	$32,040	26.7%	13,000
8. Directors, Religious Activities and Education	$29,240	24.1%	16,000
9. Clergy	$34,930	15.5%	34,000
10. Substance Abuse and Behavioral Disorder Counselors	$31,510	23.3%	10,000
11. Probation Officers and Correctional Treatment Specialists	$39,200	14.7%	15,000
12. Marriage and Family Therapists	$38,210	22.4%	3,000

Best Jobs for College Graduates Interested in Information Technology

Job	Annual Earnings	Percent Growth	Annual Openings
1. Computer Software Engineers, Applications	$73,410	45.5%	55,000
2. Computer and Information Systems Managers	$90,490	36.1%	39,000
3. Computer Software Engineers, Systems Software	$77,250	45.5%	39,000
4. Computer Systems Analysts	$65,050	39.4%	68,000
5. Network Systems and Data Communications Analysts	$59,300	57.0%	29,000
6. Computer Security Specialists	$57,060	37.4%	35,000
7. Network and Computer Systems Administrators	$57,060	37.4%	35,000
8. Database Administrators	$59,150	44.2%	16,000
9. Computer Support Specialists	$39,900	30.3%	71,000
10. Computer Programmers	$61,730	14.6%	45,000

Best Jobs for College Graduates Interested in Law and Public Safety

Job	Annual Earnings	Percent Growth	Annual Openings
1. Lawyers	$92,730	17.0%	53,000
2. Paralegals and Legal Assistants	$38,440	28.7%	29,000
3. Judges, Magistrate Judges, and Magistrates	$91,230	8.7%	2,000

Only three jobs are listed here because most jobs in this interest area do not typically require a college degree to enter, although many people with college degrees do work in these jobs.

Best Jobs for College Graduates Interested in Manufacturing

Job	Annual Earnings	Percent Growth	Annual Openings
1. Industrial Production Managers	$71,650	7.9%	18,000

Only one job is listed here because most jobs in this interest area do not typically require a college degree to enter, although many people with college degrees do work in these jobs.

Best Jobs for College Graduates Interested in Retail and Wholesale Sales and Service

Job	Annual Earnings	Percent Growth	Annual Openings
1. Sales Managers	$81,970	30.5%	54,000
2. Marketing Managers	$85,220	21.3%	30,000
3. Advertising and Promotions Managers	$61,400	25.0%	13,000
4. Sales Engineers	$68,510	19.9%	7,000
5. Purchasing Agents, Except Wholesale, Retail, and Farm Products	$47,250	11.2%	29,000
6. Purchasing Managers	$67,830	4.8%	9,000
7. Property, Real Estate, and Community Association Managers	$38,750	12.8%	35,000
8. Wholesale and Retail Buyers, Except Farm Products	$42,200	4.3%	24,000

Best Jobs for College Graduates Interested in Scientific Research, Engineering, and Mathematics

Job	Annual Earnings	Percent Growth	Annual Openings
1. Educational Psychologists	$53,230	24.4%	17,000
2. Medical Scientists, Except Epidemiologists	$60,200	26.9%	6,000
3. Engineering Managers	$95,630	9.2%	16,000
4. Biologists	$64,390	22.3%	3,000
5. Biochemists	$64,390	22.9%	2,000
6. Biophysicists	$64,390	22.9%	2,000
7. Electronics Engineers, Except Computer	$73,470	9.4%	11,000
8. Industrial Engineers	$64,050	10.6%	16,000
9. Environmental Scientists and Specialists, Including Health	$50,070	23.7%	6,000

Best Jobs for College Graduates Interested in Scientific Research, Engineering, and Mathematics

Job	Annual Earnings	Percent Growth	Annual Openings
10. Social Science Research Assistants	$48,660	17.5%	18,000
11. Natural Sciences Managers	$86,910	11.3%	5,000
12. Civil Engineers	$62,840	8.0%	17,000
13. Biomedical Engineers	$64,780	26.1%	fewer than 500
14. Actuaries	$75,280	14.9%	2,000
15. Epidemiologists	$53,660	32.5%	fewer than 500
16. Mechanical Engineers	$65,210	4.8%	14,000
17. Economists	$70,520	13.4%	2,000
18. Hydrologists	$59,010	21.0%	1,000
19. Computer Hardware Engineers	$79,090	6.1%	6,000
20. Electrical Engineers	$70,830	2.5%	11,000
21. Calibration and Instrumentation Technicians	$45,390	10.0%	24,000
22. Electrical Engineering Technicians	$45,390	10.0%	24,000
23. Electronics Engineering Technicians	$45,390	10.0%	24,000
24. Chemists	$54,960	12.7%	7,000
25. Geologists	$68,570	11.5%	2,000
26. Atmospheric and Space Scientists	$65,400	16.2%	1,000
27. Microbiologists	$52,100	20.0%	1,000
28. Environmental Engineering Technicians	$38,180	28.4%	3,000
29. Geographers	$56,290	19.5%	fewer than 500
30. Industrial-Organizational Psychologists	$67,740	16.0%	fewer than 500
31. Aerospace Engineers	$77,340	−5.2%	5,000
32. Fire-Prevention and Protection Engineers	$61,430	7.9%	4,000
33. Industrial Safety and Health Engineers	$61,430	7.9%	4,000
34. Product Safety Engineers	$61,430	7.9%	4,000
35. Physicists	$83,570	6.9%	1,000
36. Materials Scientists	$71,090	8.5%	1,000
37. Political Scientists	$81,670	5.9%	1,000
38. Chemical Engineers	$75,310	0.4%	2,000
39. Statisticians	$64,320	4.8%	2,000
40. Materials Engineers	$65,010	4.1%	2,000
41. Astronomers	$85,910	4.9%	fewer than 500
42. Nuclear Engineers	$83,260	−0.1%	1,000

Best Jobs for College Graduates Interested in Transportation, Distribution, and Logistics			
Job	Annual Earnings	Percent Growth	Annual Openings
1. Airline Pilots, Copilots, and Flight Engineers	$128,140	18.5%	6,000

Only one job is listed here because most jobs in this interest area do not typically require a college degree to enter, although many people with college degrees do work in these jobs.

Best Jobs Lists for College Graduates Based on Personality Types

These lists organize the 200 best jobs requiring a college degree into groups matching six personality types. The personality types are Realistic, Investigative, Artistic, Social, Enterprising, and Conventional. This system was developed by John Holland and is used in the Self-Directed Search (SDS) and other career assessment inventories and information systems.

If you have used one of these career inventories or systems, the lists will help you identify jobs that most closely match these personality types. Even if you have not used one of these systems, the concept of personality types and the jobs that are related to them can help you identify jobs that most closely match the type of person you are.

We've ranked the jobs within each personality type based on their total combined scores for earnings, growth, and annual job openings. Like the job lists for education levels, there is only one list for each personality type. Note that each of the 200 jobs is listed in the one personality type it most closely matches, even though it might also fit into others. (The only exception is Postsecondary Teachers, which is included in several lists because the various postsecondary teaching occupations fall into several personality types. A footnote lists the specific postsecondary teaching occupations for each personality type.) Consider reviewing the jobs for more than one personality type so you don't overlook possible jobs that would interest you.

Following are brief descriptions for each of the six personality types used in the lists. Select the two or three descriptions that most closely describe you and then use the lists to identify jobs that best fit these personality types.

Descriptions of the Six Personality Types

◎ **Realistic:** These occupations frequently involve work activities that include practical, hands-on problems and solutions. They often deal with plants, animals, and real-world materials like wood, tools, and machinery. Many of the occupations require working outside and do not involve a lot of paperwork or working closely with others.

◎ **Investigative:** These occupations frequently involve working with ideas and require an extensive amount of thinking. These occupations can involve searching for facts and figuring out problems mentally.

◎ **Artistic:** These occupations frequently involve working with forms, designs, and patterns. They often require self-expression, and the work can be done without following a clear set of rules.

◎ **Social:** These occupations frequently involve working with, communicating with, and teaching people. These occupations often involve helping or providing service to others.

◎ **Enterprising:** These occupations frequently involve starting up and carrying out projects. These occupations can involve leading people and making many decisions. They sometimes require risk taking and often deal with business.

◎ **Conventional:** These occupations frequently involve following set procedures and routines. These occupations can include working with data and details more than with ideas. Usually there is a clear line of authority to follow.

Best Jobs for College Graduates with a Realistic Personality Type

Job	Annual Earnings	Percent Growth	Annual Openings
1. Airline Pilots, Copilots, and Flight Engineers	$128,140	18.5%	6,000
2. Radiologic Technicians	$41,850	22.9%	21,000
3. Radiologic Technologists	$41,850	22.9%	21,000
4. Civil Engineers	$62,840	8.0%	17,000
5. Mechanical Engineers	$65,210	4.8%	14,000
6. Calibration and Instrumentation Technicians	$45,390	10.0%	24,000
7. Electrical Engineering Technicians	$45,390	10.0%	24,000
8. Electronics Engineering Technicians	$45,390	10.0%	24,000
9. Medical and Clinical Laboratory Technicians	$30,140	19.4%	21,000
10. Biological Technicians	$33,360	19.4%	7,000

Best Jobs for College Graduates with an Investigative Personality Type

Job	Annual Earnings	Percent Growth	Annual Openings
1. Computer Software Engineers, Applications	$73,410	45.5%	55,000
2. Computer Software Engineers, Systems Software	$77,250	45.5%	39,000
3. Computer Systems Analysts	$65,050	39.4%	68,000
4. Pharmacists	$82,520	30.1%	23,000
5. Anesthesiologists	more than $145,000	19.5%	38,000
6. Internists, General	more than $145,000	19.5%	38,000
7. Obstetricians and Gynecologists	more than $145,000	19.5%	38,000
8. Surgeons	more than $145,000	19.5%	38,000
9. Family and General Practitioners	$137,670	19.5%	38,000
10. Pediatricians, General	$136,490	19.5%	38,000
11. Postsecondary Teachers	$51,815	38.1%	216,000
12. Psychiatrists	$135,440	19.5%	38,000
13. Network Systems and Data Communications Analysts	$59,300	57.0%	29,000
14. Computer Security Specialists	$57,060	37.4%	35,000
15. Database Administrators	$59,150	44.2%	16,000
16. Physician Assistants	$68,200	48.9%	7,000
17. Computer Support Specialists	$39,900	30.3%	71,000
18. Market Research Analysts	$54,830	23.4%	18,000
19. Computer Programmers	$61,730	14.6%	45,000
20. Clinical Psychologists	$53,230	24.4%	17,000
21. Educational Psychologists	$53,230	24.4%	17,000
22. Financial Analysts	$61,130	18.7%	22,000
23. Medical Scientists, Except Epidemiologists	$60,200	26.9%	6,000
24. Compensation, Benefits, and Job Analysis Specialists	$46,890	28.0%	15,000
25. Veterinarians	$65,290	25.1%	4,000
26. Chiropractors	$66,610	23.3%	3,000
27. Respiratory Therapists	$42,050	34.8%	10,000
28. Biologists	$64,390	22.3%	3,000
29. Biochemists	$64,390	22.9%	2,000
30. Biophysicists	$64,390	22.9%	2,000
31. Electronics Engineers, Except Computer	$73,470	9.4%	11,000
32. Optometrists	$87,340	17.1%	2,000
33. Medical and Clinical Laboratory Technologists	$44,460	19.3%	21,000
34. Environmental Scientists and Specialists, Including Health	$50,070	23.7%	6,000
35. Natural Sciences Managers	$86,910	11.3%	5,000
36. Nuclear Medicine Technologists	$53,680	23.6%	2,000
37. Dentists, General	$120,420	4.1%	7,000

Best Jobs for College Graduates with an Investigative Personality Type

Job	Annual Earnings	Percent Growth	Annual Openings
38. Oral and Maxillofacial Surgeons	$120,420	4.1%	7,000
39. Orthodontists	$120,420	4.1%	7,000
40. Prosthodontists	$120,420	4.1%	7,000
41. Epidemiologists	$53,660	32.5%	fewer than 500
42. Cardiovascular Technologists and Technicians	$37,800	33.5%	6,000
43. Economists	$70,520	13.4%	2,000
44. Hydrologists	$59,010	21.0%	1,000
45. Computer Hardware Engineers	$79,090	6.1%	6,000
46. Electrical Engineers	$70,830	2.5%	11,000
47. Chemists	$54,960	12.7%	7,000
48. Environmental Science and Protection Technicians, Including Health	$35,790	36.8%	4,000
49. Geologists	$68,570	11.5%	2,000
50. Atmospheric and Space Scientists	$65,400	16.2%	1,000
51. Dietitians and Nutritionists	$42,630	17.8%	8,000
52. Microbiologists	$52,100	20.0%	1,000
53. Geographers	$56,290	19.5%	fewer than 500
54. Industrial-Organizational Psychologists	$67,740	16.0%	fewer than 500
55. Aerospace Engineers	$77,340	−5.2%	5,000
56. Operations Research Analysts	$59,090	6.2%	6,000
57. Fire-Prevention and Protection Engineers	$61,430	7.9%	4,000
58. Industrial Safety and Health Engineers	$61,430	7.9%	4,000
59. Product Safety Engineers	$61,430	7.9%	4,000
60. Physicists	$83,570	6.9%	1,000
61. Urban and Regional Planners	$52,680	10.7%	5,000
62. Materials Scientists	$71,090	8.5%	1,000
63. Political Scientists	$81,670	5.9%	1,000
64. Chemical Engineers	$75,310	0.4%	2,000
65. Statisticians	$64,320	4.8%	2,000
66. Materials Engineers	$65,010	4.1%	2,000
67. Astronomers	$85,910	4.9%	fewer than 500
68. Nuclear Engineers	$83,260	−0.1%	1,000

Postsecondary Teachers is listed here because the following jobs are associated with the Investigative personality type: Agricultural Sciences Teachers, Postsecondary; Biological Science Teachers, Postsecondary; Chemistry Teachers, Postsecondary; Computer Science Teachers, Postsecondary; Engineering Teachers, Postsecondary; Forestry and Conservation Science Teachers, Postsecondary; Health Specialties Teachers, Postsecondary; Mathematical Science Teachers, Postsecondary; and Physics Teachers, Postsecondary.

Best Jobs for College Graduates with an Artistic Personality Type

Job	Annual Earnings	Percent Growth	Annual Openings
1. Postsecondary Teachers	$51,815	38.1%	216,000
2. Advertising and Promotions Managers	$61,400	25.0%	13,000
3. Technical Writers	$52,160	27.1%	6,000
4. Architects, Except Landscape and Naval	$58,630	17.3%	8,000
5. Directors—Stage, Motion Pictures, Television, and Radio	$51,870	18.3%	10,000
6. Producers	$51,870	18.3%	10,000
7. Graphic Designers	$36,930	21.9%	29,000
8. Copy Writers	$43,340	16.1%	23,000
9. Creative Writers	$43,340	16.1%	23,000
10. Poets and Lyricists	$43,340	16.1%	23,000
11. Art Directors	$63,170	11.4%	8,000
12. Commercial and Industrial Designers	$52,080	14.7%	7,000
13. Landscape Architects	$50,780	22.2%	2,000
14. Interior Designers	$40,420	21.7%	8,000
15. Film and Video Editors	$41,820	26.4%	3,000
16. Librarians	$44,730	10.1%	15,000
17. Editors	$42,450	11.8%	14,000
18. Fashion Designers	$54,530	10.6%	2,000

Postsecondary Teachers is listed here because the following jobs are associated with the Artistic personality type: Art, Drama, and Music Teachers, Postsecondary; English Language and Literature Teachers, Postsecondary; and Foreign Language and Literature Teachers, Postsecondary.

Best Jobs for College Graduates with a Social Personality Type

Job	Annual Earnings	Percent Growth	Annual Openings
1. Postsecondary Teachers	$51,815	38.1%	216,000
2. Education Administrators, Elementary and Secondary School	$73,960	20.7%	31,000
3. Registered Nurses	$51,020	27.3%	215,000
4. Personal Financial Advisors	$60,230	34.6%	18,000
5. Physical Therapists	$58,700	35.3%	16,000
6. Special Education Teachers, Secondary School	$44,920	30.0%	59,000
7. Special Education Teachers, Middle School	$43,260	30.0%	59,000
8. Dental Hygienists	$56,680	43.1%	9,000
9. Special Education Teachers, Preschool, Kindergarten, and Elementary School	$42,630	30.0%	59,000

Best Jobs for College Graduates with a Social Personality Type

Job	Annual Earnings	Percent Growth	Annual Openings
10. Occupational Therapists	$53,320	35.2%	10,000
11. Training and Development Specialists	$44,270	27.9%	35,000
12. Counseling Psychologists	$53,230	24.4%	17,000
13. Social and Community Service Managers	$46,200	27.7%	19,000
14. Instructional Coordinators	$47,550	25.4%	18,000
15. Preschool Teachers, Except Special Education	$20,450	36.2%	88,000
16. Kindergarten Teachers, Except Special Education	$40,980	27.2%	34,000
17. Speech-Language Pathologists	$50,890	27.2%	10,000
18. Secondary School Teachers, Except Special and Vocational Education	$45,180	18.2%	118,000
19. Employment Interviewers, Private or Public Employment Service	$40,970	27.3%	29,000
20. Medical and Public Health Social Workers	$39,160	28.6%	18,000
21. Elementary School Teachers, Except Special Education	$42,590	15.2%	183,000
22. Child, Family, and School Social Workers	$34,300	23.2%	45,000
23. Physical Therapist Assistants	$37,280	44.6%	10,000
24. Mental Health and Substance Abuse Social Workers	$33,650	34.5%	17,000
25. Radiation Therapists	$55,550	31.6%	1,000
26. Educational, Vocational, and School Counselors	$44,990	15.0%	32,000
27. Recreation Workers	$18,950	20.5%	56,000
28. Education Administrators, Preschool and Child Care Center/Program	$35,240	32.0%	9,000
29. Podiatrists	$95,550	15.0%	1,000
30. Middle School Teachers, Except Special and Vocational Education	$42,960	9.0%	69,000
31. Physical Therapist Aides	$21,070	46.4%	8,000
32. Audiologists	$50,000	29.0%	1,000
33. Mental Health Counselors	$32,040	26.7%	13,000
34. Occupational Therapist Assistants	$38,120	39.2%	3,000
35. Adult Literacy, Remedial Education, and GED Teachers and Instructors	$37,910	20.4%	14,000
36. Directors, Religious Activities and Education	$29,240	24.1%	16,000
37. Clergy	$34,930	15.5%	34,000
38. Health Educators	$38,100	21.9%	8,000
39. Substance Abuse and Behavioral Disorder Counselors	$31,510	23.3%	10,000
40. Probation Officers and Correctional Treatment Specialists	$39,200	14.7%	15,000
41. Occupational Health and Safety Specialists	$48,330	13.2%	6,000

(continued)

Best Jobs for College Graduates with a Social Personality Type

Job	Annual Earnings	Percent Growth	Annual Openings
42. Orthotists and Prosthetists	$49,860	18.9%	1,000
43. Vocational Education Teachers, Secondary School	$45,140	9.0%	12,000
44. Athletic Trainers	$32,990	29.9%	2,000

Postsecondary Teachers is listed here because the following jobs are associated with the Social personality type: Anthropology and Archeology Teachers, Postsecondary; Area, Ethnic, and Cultural Studies Teachers, Postsecondary; Economics Teachers, Postsecondary; History Teachers, Postsecondary; Nursing Instructors and Teachers, Postsecondary; Political Science Teachers, Postsecondary; Psychology Teachers, Postsecondary; and Sociology Teachers, Postsecondary.

Best Jobs for College Graduates with an Enterprising Personality Type

Job	Annual Earnings	Percent Growth	Annual Openings
1. Computer and Information Systems Managers	$90,490	36.1%	39,000
2. Sales Managers	$81,970	30.5%	54,000
3. Management Analysts	$63,090	30.4%	78,000
4. Medical and Health Services Managers	$66,360	29.3%	33,000
5. Government Service Executives	$136,400	16.7%	63,000
6. Private Sector Executives	$136,400	16.7%	63,000
7. Marketing Managers	$85,220	21.3%	30,000
8. Financial Managers, Branch or Department	$79,090	18.3%	71,000
9. Treasurers, Controllers, and Chief Financial Officers	$79,090	18.3%	71,000
10. Lawyers	$92,730	17.0%	53,000
11. Education Administrators, Postsecondary	$67,760	25.9%	19,000
12. Compensation and Benefits Managers	$72,180	19.4%	21,000
13. Training and Development Managers	$72,180	19.4%	21,000
14. Administrative Services Managers	$58,130	19.8%	40,000
15. Human Resources Managers	$70,350	19.4%	21,000
16. Construction Managers	$67,620	12.0%	47,000
17. Public Relations Specialists	$43,050	32.9%	28,000
18. Sales Agents, Financial Services	$62,680	13.0%	39,000
19. Sales Agents, Securities and Commodities	$62,680	13.0%	39,000
20. Sales Engineers	$68,510	19.9%	7,000
21. Personnel Recruiters	$40,970	27.3%	29,000
22. Paralegals and Legal Assistants	$38,440	28.7%	29,000
23. Engineering Managers	$95,630	9.2%	16,000
24. Loan Officers	$47,530	18.8%	30,000

Best Jobs for College Graduates with an Enterprising Personality Type

Job	Annual Earnings	Percent Growth	Annual Openings
25. Industrial Production Managers	$71,650	7.9%	18,000
26. Agents and Business Managers of Artists, Performers, and Athletes	$55,700	27.8%	2,000
27. Industrial Engineers	$64,050	10.6%	16,000
28. Program Directors	$51,870	18.3%	10,000
29. Purchasing Agents, Except Wholesale, Retail, and Farm Products	$47,250	11.2%	29,000
30. Purchasing Managers	$67,830	4.8%	9,000
31. Property, Real Estate, and Community Association Managers	$38,750	12.8%	35,000
32. Judges, Magistrate Judges, and Magistrates	$91,230	8.7%	2,000
33. Meeting and Convention Planners	$39,070	21.3%	7,000
34. Insurance Sales Agents	$40,370	8.4%	52,000
35. Financial Examiners	$59,050	8.9%	3,000
36. Wholesale and Retail Buyers, Except Farm Products	$42,200	4.3%	24,000
37. Gaming Managers	$57,930	12.4%	1,000

Best Jobs for College Graduates with a Conventional Personality Type

Job	Annual Earnings	Percent Growth	Annual Openings
1. Accountants	$49,770	19.5%	119,000
2. Auditors	$49,770	19.5%	119,000
3. Cost Estimators	$49,220	18.6%	25,000
4. Medical Records and Health Information Technicians	$24,920	46.8%	24,000
5. City Planning Aides	$48,660	17.5%	18,000
6. Actuaries	$75,280	14.9%	2,000
7. Budget Analysts	$55,090	14.0%	8,000
8. Credit Analysts	$46,640	18.7%	9,000
9. Insurance Underwriters	$48,370	10.0%	12,000

PART II

The Job Descriptions

This part provides descriptions for all the jobs included in one or more of the lists in Part I. The Introduction gives more details on how to use and interpret the job descriptions, but here is some additional information:

◎ Job descriptions are arranged in alphabetical order by job title. This approach allows you to quickly find a description if you know its correct title from one of the lists in Part I.

◎ If you are using this section to browse for interesting options, we suggest you begin with the Table of Contents. Part I features many interesting lists that will help you identify job titles to explore in more detail. If you have not browsed the lists in Part I, consider spending some time there. The lists are interesting and will help you identify job titles you can find described in the material that follows. The job titles in Part II are also listed in the Table of Contents.

◎ We include descriptions for the many specific jobs that we included under the single job title of Postsecondary Teachers in the lists in Part I. These more-specific job titles are also cross-referenced under the Postsecondary Teachers job title in Part II and include Agricultural Sciences Teachers, Postsecondary; Anthropology and Archeology Teachers, Postsecondary; Architecture Teachers, Postsecondary; Area, Ethnic, and Cultural Studies Teachers, Postsecondary; Art, Drama, and Music Teachers, Postsecondary; Atmospheric, Earth, Marine, and Space Sciences Teachers, Postsecondary; Biological Science Teachers, Postsecondary; Business Teachers, Postsecondary; Chemistry Teachers, Postsecondary; Communications Teachers, Postsecondary; Computer Science Teachers, Postsecondary; Criminal Justice and Law Enforcement Teachers, Postsecondary; Economics Teachers, Postsecondary; Education Teachers, Postsecondary; Engineering Teachers, Postsecondary; English Language and Literature Teachers, Postsecondary; Environmental

Science Teachers, Postsecondary; Foreign Language and Literature Teachers, Postsecondary; Forestry and Conservation Science Teachers, Postsecondary; Geography Teachers, Postsecondary; Graduate Teaching Assistants; Health Specialties Teachers, Postsecondary; History Teachers, Postsecondary; Home Economics Teachers, Postsecondary; Law Teachers, Postsecondary; Library Science Teachers, Postsecondary; Mathematical Science Teachers, Postsecondary; Nursing Instructors and Teachers, Postsecondary; Philosophy and Religion Teachers, Postsecondary; Physics Teachers, Postsecondary; Political Science Teachers, Postsecondary; Psychology Teachers, Postsecondary; Recreation and Fitness Studies Teachers, Postsecondary; Social Work Teachers, Postsecondary; and Sociology Teachers, Postsecondary.

Accountants

- Education/Training Required: Bachelor's degree
- Annual Earnings: $49,770
- Growth: 19.5%
- Annual Job Openings: 119,000
- Self-Employed: 10.6%
- Part-Time: 8.8%

Analyze financial information and prepare financial reports to determine or maintain record of assets, liabilities, profit and loss, tax liability, or other financial activities within an organization. Prepare, examine, and analyze accounting records, financial statements, and other financial reports to assess accuracy, completeness, and conformance to reporting and procedural standards. Compute taxes owed and prepare tax returns, ensuring compliance with payment, reporting, and other tax requirements. Analyze business operations, trends, costs, revenues, financial commitments, and obligations to project future revenues and expenses or to provide advice. Report to management regarding the finances of establishment. Establish tables of accounts and assign entries to proper accounts. Develop, maintain, and analyze budgets, preparing periodic reports that compare budgeted costs to actual costs. Develop, implement, modify, and document record-keeping and accounting systems, making use of current computer technology. Prepare forms and manuals for accounting and bookkeeping personnel and direct their work activities. Survey operations to ascertain accounting needs and to recommend, develop, and maintain solutions to business and financial problems. Work as Internal Revenue Service agents. Advise management about issues such as resource utilization, tax strategies, and the assumptions underlying budget forecasts. Provide internal and external auditing services for businesses and individuals. Advise clients in areas such as compensation, employee health-care benefits, the design of accounting and data processing systems, and long-range tax and estate plans. Investigate bankruptcies and other complex financial transactions and prepare reports summarizing the findings. Represent clients before taxing authorities and provide support during litigation involving financial issues. Appraise, evaluate, and inventory real property and equipment, recording information such as the property's description, value, and location. Maintain and examine the records of government agencies. **SKILLS—Management of Financial Resources:** Determining how money will be spent to get the work done and accounting for these expenditures. **Systems Evaluation:** Identifying measures or indicators of system performance and the actions needed to improve or correct performance relative to the goals of the system. **Systems Analysis:** Determining how a system should work and how changes in conditions, operations, and the environment will affect outcomes. **Operations Analysis:** Analyzing needs and product requirements to create a design. **Judgment and Decision Making:** Considering the relative costs and benefits of potential actions to choose the most appropriate one. **Time Management:** Managing one's own time and the time of others. **Monitoring:** Monitoring or assessing your performance or that of other individuals or organizations to make improvements or take corrective action. **Negotiation:** Bringing others together and trying to reconcile differences.

GOE—Interest Area: 04. Business and Administration. **Work Group:** 04.05. Accounting, Auditing, and Analytical Support. **Other Jobs in This Work Group:** Auditors; Budget Analysts; Industrial Engineering Technicians; Logisticians; Management Analysts; Operations Research Analysts. **PERSONALITY TYPE:** Conventional. Conventional occupations frequently involve following set procedures and routines. These occupations can include working with data and details more than with ideas. Usually there is a clear line of authority to follow.

EDUCATION/TRAINING PROGRAM(S)— Accounting; Accounting and Business/Management; Accounting and Computer Science; Accounting and Finance; Auditing; Taxation.

RELATED KNOWLEDGE/COURSES—Economics and Accounting: Knowledge of economic and accounting principles and practices, the financial markets, banking, and the analysis and reporting of financial data. Clerical Practices: Knowledge of administrative and clerical procedures and systems such as word processing, managing files and records, stenography and transcription, designing forms, and other office procedures and terminology. Mathematics: Knowledge of arithmetic, algebra, geometry, calculus, and statistics and their applications. Law and Government: Knowledge of laws, legal codes, court procedures, precedents, government regulations, executive orders, agency rules, and the democratic political process. Customer and Personal Service: Knowledge of principles and processes for providing customer and personal services. This includes customer needs assessment, meeting quality standards for services, and evaluation of customer satisfaction. Computers and Electronics: Knowledge of circuit boards, processors, chips, electronic equipment, and computer hardware and software, including applications and programming.

Actuaries

- ◎ Education/Training Required: Work experience plus degree
- ◎ Annual Earnings: $75,280
- ◎ Growth: 14.9%
- ◎ Annual Job Openings: 2,000
- ◎ Self-Employed: 1.4%
- ◎ Part-Time: 6.4%

Analyze statistical data, such as mortality, accident, sickness, disability, and retirement rates, and construct probability tables to forecast risk and liability for payment of future benefits. May ascertain premium rates required and cash reserves necessary to ensure payment of future benefits. Ascertain premium rates required and cash reserves and liabilities necessary to ensure payment of future benefits. Analyze statistical information to estimate mortality, accident, sickness, disability, and retirement rates. Design, review, and help administer insurance, annuity, and pension plans, determining financial soundness and calculating premiums. Collaborate with programmers, underwriters, accounts, claims experts, and senior management to help companies develop plans for new lines of business or improving existing business. Determine or help determine company policy and explain complex technical matters to company executives, government officials, shareholders, policyholders, and/or the public. Testify before public agencies on proposed legislation affecting businesses. Provide advice to clients on a contract basis, working as a consultant. Testify in court as expert witness or to provide legal evidence on matters such as the value of potential lifetime earnings of a person who is disabled or killed in an accident. Construct probability tables for events such as fires, natural disasters, and unemployment based on analysis of statistical data and other pertinent information. Determine policy contract provisions for each type of insurance. SKILLS—Mathematics: Using mathematics to solve problems. Programming: Writing computer programs for various purposes. Active Learning: Understanding the implications of new information for both current and future problem-solving and decision-making. Complex Problem Solving: Identifying complex problems and reviewing related information to develop and evaluate options and implement solutions. Critical Thinking: Using logic and reasoning to identify the strengths and weaknesses of alternative solutions, conclusions, or approaches to problems. Operations Analysis: Analyzing needs and product requirements to create a design. Monitoring: Monitoring or assessing your performance or that of other individuals or organizations to make improvements or take corrective action. Instructing: Teaching others how to do something.

GOE—**Interest Area:** 15. Scientific Research, Engineering, and Mathematics. **Work Group:** 15.06. Mathematics and Data Analysis. **Other Jobs in This Work Group:** Mathematical Technicians; Mathematicians; Social Science Research Assistants; Statistical Assistants; Statisticians. **PERSONALITY TYPE:** Conventional. Conventional occupations frequently involve following set procedures and routines. These occupations can include working with data and details more than with ideas. Usually there is a clear line of authority to follow.

EDUCATION/TRAINING PROGRAM(S)—Actuarial Science. **RELATED KNOWLEDGE/ COURSES—Mathematics:** Knowledge of arithmetic, algebra, geometry, calculus, and statistics and their applications. **Economics and Accounting:** Knowledge of economic and accounting principles and practices, the financial markets, banking, and the analysis and reporting of financial data. **Computers and Electronics:** Knowledge of circuit boards, processors, chips, electronic equipment, and computer hardware and software, including applications and programming. **Sales and Marketing:** Knowledge of principles and methods for showing, promoting, and selling products or services. This includes marketing strategy and tactics, product demonstration, sales techniques, and sales control systems. **English Language:** Knowledge of the structure and content of the English language, including the meaning and spelling of words, rules of composition, and grammar. **Personnel and Human Resources:** Knowledge of principles and procedures for personnel recruitment, selection, training, compensation and benefits, labor relations and negotiation, and personnel information systems.

Administrative Services Managers

- Education/Training Required: Work experience plus degree
- Annual Earnings: $58,130
- Growth: 19.8%
- Annual Job Openings: 40,000
- Self-Employed: 0.2%
- Part-Time: 4.6%

Plan, direct, or coordinate supportive services of an organization, such as record-keeping, mail distribution, telephone operator/receptionist, and other office support services. May oversee facilities planning and maintenance and custodial operations. Monitor the facility to ensure that it remains safe, secure, and well-maintained. Direct or coordinate the supportive services department of a business, agency, or organization. Set goals and deadlines for the department. Prepare and review operational reports and schedules to ensure accuracy and efficiency. Analyze internal processes and recommend and implement procedural or policy changes to improve operations, such as supply changes or the disposal of records. Acquire, distribute, and store supplies. Plan, administer, and control budgets for contracts, equipment, and supplies. Oversee construction and renovation projects to improve efficiency and to ensure that facilities meet environmental, health, and security standards and comply with government regulations. Hire and terminate clerical and administrative personnel. Oversee the maintenance and repair of machinery, equipment, and electrical and mechanical systems. Manage leasing of facility space. **SKILLS—Management of Personnel Resources:** Motivating, developing, and directing people as they work, identifying the best people for the job. **Service Orientation:** Actively looking for ways to help people. **Coordination:** Adjusting actions in relation to others' actions. **Management of Financial Resources:**

Determining how money will be spent to get the work done and accounting for these expenditures. **Monitoring:** Monitoring or assessing your performance or that of other individuals or organizations to make improvements or take corrective action. **Social Perceptiveness:** Being aware of others' reactions and understanding why they react as they do. **Speaking:** Talking to others to convey information effectively. **Time Management:** Managing one's own time and the time of others.

GOE—Interest Area: 04. Business and Administration. **Work Group:** 04.02. Managerial Work in Business Detail. **Other Jobs in This Work Group:** First-Line Supervisors, Administrative Support; First-Line Supervisors, Customer Service; Housekeeping Supervisors; Janitorial Supervisors; Meeting and Convention Planners. **PERSONALITY TYPE:** Enterprising. Enterprising occupations frequently involve starting up and carrying out projects. These occupations can involve leading people and making many decisions. They sometimes require risk taking and often deal with business.

EDUCATION/TRAINING PROGRAM(S)— Business Administration and Management, General; Business/Commerce, General; Medical/Health Management and Clinical Assistant/Specialist; Public Administration; Purchasing, Procurement/ Acquisitions, and Contracts Management. **RELATED KNOWLEDGE/COURSES—Personnel and Human Resources:** Knowledge of principles and procedures for personnel recruitment, selection, training, compensation and benefits, labor relations and negotiation, and personnel information systems. **Clerical Practices:** Knowledge of administrative and clerical procedures and systems such as word processing, managing files and records, stenography and transcription, designing forms, and other office procedures and terminology. **Customer and Personal Service:** Knowledge of principles and processes for providing customer and personal services. This includes customer needs assessment, meeting quality standards for services, and evaluation of customer satisfaction. **Economics and**

Accounting: Knowledge of economic and accounting principles and practices, the financial markets, banking, and the analysis and reporting of financial data. **Administration and Management:** Knowledge of business and management principles involved in strategic planning, resource allocation, human resources modeling, leadership technique, production methods, and coordination of people and resources. **Public Safety and Security:** Knowledge of relevant equipment, policies, procedures, and strategies to promote effective local, state, or national security operations for the protection of people, data, property, and institutions. **Law and Government:** Knowledge of laws, legal codes, court procedures, precedents, government regulations, executive orders, agency rules, and the democratic political process.

Adult Literacy, Remedial Education, and GED Teachers and Instructors

- Education/Training Required: Bachelor's degree
- Annual Earnings: $37,910
- Growth: 20.4%
- Annual Job Openings: 14,000
- Self-Employed: 19.5%
- Part-Time: 41.0%

Teach or instruct out-of-school youths and adults in remedial education classes, preparatory classes for the General Educational Development test, literacy, or English as a Second Language. Teaching may or may not take place in a traditional educational institution. Adapt teaching methods and instructional materials to meet students' varying needs, abilities, and interests. Confer with other staff members to plan and schedule lessons that promote learning, following approved curricula. Enforce administration policies and rules governing students. Establish and enforce rules for behavior and procedures for maintaining order among the students for whom they are responsible. Establish clear objectives for all lessons, units, and projects and communicate those objectives to students. Guide and counsel students with adjustment and/or academic problems or special academic interests. Maintain accurate and complete student records as required by laws or administrative policies. Meet with other professionals to discuss individual students' needs and progress. Observe and evaluate students' work to determine progress and make suggestions for improvement. Observe students to determine qualifications, limitations, abilities, interests, and other individual characteristics. Plan and conduct activities for a balanced program of instruction, demonstration, and work time that provides students with opportunities to observe, question, and investigate. Conduct classes, workshops, and demonstrations to teach principles, techniques, or methods in subjects such as basic English language skills, life skills, and workforce entry skills. Instruct students individually and in groups, using various teaching methods such as lectures, discussions, and demonstrations. Assign and grade class work and homework. Plan and supervise class projects, field trips, visits by guest speakers, contests, or other experiential activities and guide students in learning from those activities. Prepare and administer written, oral, and performance tests and issue grades in accordance with performance. Prepare and implement remedial programs for students requiring extra help. Prepare for assigned classes and show written evidence of preparation upon request of immediate supervisors. Prepare materials and classrooms for class activities. Prepare objectives and outlines for courses of study, following curriculum guidelines or requirements of states and schools. **SKILLS— Instructing:** Teaching others how to do something. **Writing:** Communicating effectively in writing as appropriate for the needs of the audience. **Speaking:** Talking to others to convey information effectively. **Learning Strategies:** Selecting and using training/instructional methods and procedures appropriate for the situation when learning or teaching new things. **Service Orientation:** Actively looking for ways to help people. **Systems Evaluation:** Identifying measures or indicators of system performance and the actions needed to improve or correct performance relative to the goals of the system. **Reading Comprehension:** Understanding written sentences and paragraphs in work-related documents. **Active Listening:** Giving full attention to what other people are saying, taking time to understand the points being made, asking questions as appropriate, and not interrupting at inappropriate times. **Judgment and Decision Making:** Considering the relative costs and benefits of potential actions to choose the most appropriate one. **Management of Material Resources:** Obtaining and seeing to the appropriate use of equipment, facilities, and materials needed to do certain work.

GOE—Interest Area: 05. Education and Training. **Work Group:** 05.03. Postsecondary and Adult Teaching and Instructing. **Other Jobs in This Work Group:** Agricultural Sciences Teachers, Postsecondary; Anthropology and Archeology Teachers, Postsecondary; Architecture Teachers, Postsecondary; Area, Ethnic, and Cultural Studies Teachers, Postsecondary; Art, Drama, and Music Teachers, Postsecondary; Atmospheric, Earth, Marine, and Space Sciences Teachers, Postsecondary; Biological Science Teachers, Postsecondary; Business Teachers, Postsecondary; Chemistry Teachers, Postsecondary; Communications Teachers, Postsecondary; Computer Science Teachers, Postsecondary; Criminal Justice and Law Enforcement Teachers, Postsecondary; Economics Teachers, Postsecondary; Education Teachers, Postsecondary; Engineering Teachers, Postsecondary; English Language and Literature Teachers, Postsecondary; Environmental Science Teachers, Postsecondary; Farm and Home Management Advisors; Foreign Language and Literature Teachers, Postsecondary;

Forestry and Conservation Science Teachers, Post-secondary; Geography Teachers, Postsecondary; Graduate Teaching Assistants; Health Specialties Teachers, Postsecondary; History Teachers, Postsecondary; Home Economics Teachers, Postsecondary; Law Teachers, Postsecondary; Library Science Teachers, Postsecondary; Mathematical Science Teachers, Postsecondary; Nursing Instructors and Teachers, Postsecondary; Philosophy and Religion Teachers, Postsecondary; Physics Teachers, Postsecondary; Political Science Teachers, Postsecondary; Psychology Teachers, Postsecondary; Recreation and Fitness Studies Teachers, Postsecondary; Self-Enrichment Education Teachers; Social Work Teachers, Postsecondary; Sociology Teachers, Postsecondary; Vocational Education Teachers, Postsecondary. **PERSONALITY TYPE:** Social. Social occupations frequently involve working with, communicating with, and teaching people. These occupations often involve helping or providing service to others.

EDUCATION/TRAINING PROGRAM(S)— Adult and Continuing Education and Teaching; Adult Literacy Tutor/Instructor; Bilingual and Multilingual Education; Multicultural Education; Teaching English as a Second or Foreign Language/ESL Language Instructor. **RELATED KNOWLEDGE/COURSES—Education and Training:** Knowledge of principles and methods for curriculum and training design, teaching and instruction for individuals and groups, and the measurement of training effects. **English Language:** Knowledge of the structure and content of the English language, including the meaning and spelling of words, rules of composition, and grammar. **Philosophy and Theology:** Knowledge of different philosophical systems and religions. This includes their basic principles, values, ethics, ways of thinking, customs, and practices and their impact on human culture. **Sociology and Anthropology:** Knowledge of group behavior and dynamics, societal trends and influences, human migrations, ethnicity, and cultures and their history and origins. **History and Archeology:** Knowledge of historical events and

their causes, indicators, and effects on civilizations and cultures. **Economics and Accounting:** Knowledge of economic and accounting principles and practices, the financial markets, banking, and the analysis and reporting of financial data.

Advertising and Promotions Managers

◎ Education/Training Required: Work experience plus degree
◎ Annual Earnings: $61,400
◎ Growth: 25.0%
◎ Annual Job Openings: 13,000
◎ Self-Employed: 2.4%
◎ Part-Time: 7.5%

Plan and direct advertising policies and programs or produce collateral materials, such as posters, contests, coupons, or give-aways, to create extra interest in the purchase of a product or service for a department or an entire organization or on an account basis. Prepare budgets and submit estimates for program costs as part of campaign plan development. Plan and prepare advertising and promotional material to increase sales of products or services, working with customers, company officials, sales departments, and advertising agencies. Assist with annual budget development. Inspect layouts and advertising copy and edit scripts, audio tapes and videotapes, and other promotional material for adherence to specifications. Coordinate activities of departments, such as sales, graphic arts, media, finance, and research. Prepare and negotiate advertising and sales contracts. Identify and develop contacts for promotional campaigns and industry programs that meet identified buyer targets such as dealers, distributors, or consumers. Gather and organize information to plan advertising campaigns. Confer with department heads and/or staff to discuss topics such as contracts, selection of advertising media, or product to be advertised. Confer with clients to provide marketing or technical advice. Monitor and analyze sales promotion results to determine cost-effectiveness of promotion campaigns. Read trade journals and professional literature to stay informed on trends, innovations, and changes that affect media planning. Formulate plans to extend business with established accounts and to transact business as agent for advertising accounts. Provide presentation and product demonstration support during the introduction of new products and services to field staff and customers. Direct, motivate, and monitor the mobilization of a campaign team to advance campaign goals. Plan and execute advertising policies and strategies for organizations. Track program budgets and expenses and campaign response rates to evaluate each campaign based on program objectives and industry norms. Assemble and communicate with a strong, diverse coalition of organizations and/or public figures, securing their cooperation, support, and action to further campaign goals. Train and direct workers engaged in developing and producing advertisements. Coordinate with the media to disseminate advertising. **SKILLS—Service Orientation:** Actively looking for ways to help people. **Management of Financial Resources:** Determining how money will be spent to get the work done and accounting for these expenditures. **Persuasion:** Persuading others to change their minds or behavior. **Negotiation:** Bringing others together and trying to reconcile differences. **Time Management:** Managing one's own time and the time of others. **Coordination:** Adjusting actions in relation to others' actions. **Management of Personnel Resources:** Motivating, developing, and directing people as they work, identifying the best people for the job. **Monitoring:** Monitoring or assessing your performance or that of other individuals or organizations to make improvements or take corrective action.

GOE—Interest Area: 14. Retail and Wholesale Sales and Service. **Work Group:** 14.01. Managerial Work in Retail/Wholesale Sales and Service.

Other Jobs in This Work Group: First-Line Supervisors/Managers of Non-Retail Sales Workers; First-Line Supervisors/Managers of Retail Sales Workers; Funeral Directors; Marketing Managers; Property, Real Estate, and Community Association Managers; Purchasing Managers; Sales Managers. **PERSONALITY TYPE:** Artistic. Artistic occupations frequently involve working with forms, designs, and patterns. They often require self-expression, and the work can be done without following a clear set of rules.

EDUCATION/TRAINING PROGRAM(S)— Advertising; Marketing/Marketing Management, General; Public Relations/Image Management. **RELATED KNOWLEDGE/COURSES—Sales and Marketing:** Knowledge of principles and methods for showing, promoting, and selling products or services. This includes marketing strategy and tactics, product demonstration, sales techniques, and sales control systems. **Customer and Personal Service:** Knowledge of principles and processes for providing customer and personal services. This includes customer needs assessment, meeting quality standards for services, and evaluation of customer satisfaction. **Communications and Media:** Knowledge of media production, communication, and dissemination techniques and methods. This includes alternative ways to inform and entertain via written, oral, and visual media. **Production and Processing:** Knowledge of raw materials, production processes, quality control, costs, and other techniques for maximizing the effective manufacture and distribution of goods. **Design:** Knowledge of design techniques, tools, and principles involved in production of precision technical plans, blueprints, drawings, and models. **Clerical Practices:** Knowledge of administrative and clerical procedures and systems such as word processing, managing files and records, stenography and transcription, designing forms, and other office procedures and terminology.

Aerospace Engineers

- Education/Training Required: Bachelor's degree
- Annual Earnings: $77,340
- Growth: –5.2%
- Annual Job Openings: 5,000
- Self-Employed: 1.6%
- Part-Time: 2.7%

Perform a variety of engineering work in designing, constructing, and testing aircraft, missiles, and spacecraft. May conduct basic and applied research to evaluate adaptability of materials and equipment to aircraft design and manufacture. May recommend improvements in testing equipment and techniques. Formulate conceptual design of aeronautical or aerospace products or systems to meet customer requirements. Direct and coordinate activities of engineering or technical personnel designing, fabricating, modifying, or testing aircraft or aerospace products. Develop design criteria for aeronautical or aerospace products or systems, including testing methods, production costs, quality standards, and completion dates. Plan and conduct experimental, environmental, operational, and stress tests on models and prototypes of aircraft and aerospace systems and equipment. Evaluate product data and design from inspections and reports for conformance to engineering principles, customer requirements, and quality standards. Formulate mathematical models or other methods of computer analysis to develop, evaluate, or modify design according to customer engineering requirements. Write technical reports and other documentation, such as handbooks and bulletins, for use by engineering staff, management, and customers. Analyze project requests and proposals and engineering data to determine feasibility, producibility, cost, and production time of aerospace or aeronautical product. Review performance reports and documentation from customers and field engineers and inspect malfunctioning or damaged products to determine problem. Direct research and development programs. Evaluate and approve selection of vendors by study of past performance and new advertisements. Plan and coordinate activities concerned with investigating and resolving customers' reports of technical problems with aircraft or aerospace vehicles. Maintain records of performance reports for future reference. **SKILLS—Systems Evaluation:** Identifying measures or indicators of system performance and the actions needed to improve or correct performance relative to the goals of the system. **Systems Analysis:** Determining how a system should work and how changes in conditions, operations, and the environment will affect outcomes. **Science:** Using scientific rules and methods to solve problems. **Persuasion:** Persuading others to change their minds or behavior. **Judgment and Decision Making:** Considering the relative costs and benefits of potential actions to choose the most appropriate one. **Time Management:** Managing one's own time and the time of others. **Management of Personnel Resources:** Motivating, developing, and directing people as they work, identifying the best people for the job. **Technology Design:** Generating or adapting equipment and technology to serve user needs.

GOE—Interest Area: 15. Scientific Research, Engineering, and Mathematics. **Work Group:** 15.07. Research and Design Engineering. **Other Jobs in This Work Group:** Biomedical Engineers; Chemical Engineers; Civil Engineers; Computer Hardware Engineers; Electrical Engineers; Electronics Engineers, Except Computer; Marine Architects; Marine Engineers; Materials Engineers; Mechanical Engineers; Nuclear Engineers. **PERSONALITY TYPE:** Investigative. Investigative occupations frequently involve working with ideas and require an extensive amount of thinking. These occupations can involve searching for facts and figuring out problems mentally.

EDUCATION/TRAINING PROGRAM(S)— Aerospace, Aeronautical, and Astronautical Engineering. **RELATED KNOWLEDGE/COURSES —Engineering and Technology:** Knowledge of the practical application of engineering science and technology. This includes applying principles, techniques, procedures, and equipment to the design and production of various goods and services. **Design:** Knowledge of design techniques, tools, and principles involved in production of precision technical plans, blueprints, drawings, and models. **Physics:** Knowledge and prediction of physical principles and laws and their interrelationships and applications to understanding fluid, material, and atmospheric dynamics and mechanical, electrical, atomic, and subatomic structures and processes. **Mechanical Devices:** Knowledge of machines and tools, including their designs, uses, repair, and maintenance. **Computers and Electronics:** Knowledge of circuit boards, processors, chips, electronic equipment, and computer hardware and software, including applications and programming. **Mathematics:** Knowledge of arithmetic, algebra, geometry, calculus, and statistics and their applications.

Agents and Business Managers of Artists, Performers, and Athletes

- ◎ Education/Training Required: Work experience plus degree
- ◎ Annual Earnings: $55,700
- ◎ Growth: 27.8%
- ◎ Annual Job Openings: 2,000
- ◎ Self-Employed: 27.0%
- ◎ Part-Time: 15.2%

Represent and promote artists, performers, and athletes to prospective employers. May handle contract negotiation and other business matters for clients. Arrange meetings concerning issues involving their clients. Collect fees, commissions, or other payments according to contract terms. Conduct auditions or interviews in order to evaluate potential clients. Confer with clients to develop strategies for their careers and to explain actions taken on their behalf. Develop contacts with individuals and organizations and apply effective strategies and techniques to ensure their clients' success. Keep informed of industry trends and deals. Manage business and financial affairs for clients, such as arranging travel and lodging, selling tickets, and directing marketing and advertising activities. Negotiate with managers, promoters, union officials, and other persons regarding clients' contractual rights and obligations. Obtain information about and/or inspect performance facilities, equipment, and accommodations to ensure that they meet specifications. Schedule promotional or performance engagements for clients. Advise clients on financial and legal matters such as investments and taxes. Hire trainers or coaches to advise clients on performance matters such as training techniques or performance presentations. Prepare periodic accounting statements for clients. **SKILLS—Negotiation:** Bringing others together and trying to reconcile differences. **Management of Financial Resources:** Determining how money will be spent to get the work done and accounting for these expenditures. **Management of Personnel Resources:** Motivating, developing, and directing people as they work, identifying the best people for the job. **Time Management:** Managing one's own time and the time of others. **Service Orientation:** Actively looking for ways to help people. **Speaking:** Talking to others to convey information effectively. **Coordination:** Adjusting actions in relation to others' actions. **Persuasion:** Persuading others to change their minds or behavior.

GOE—Interest Area: 03. Arts and Communication. **Work Group:** 03.01. Managerial Work in Arts and Communication. **Other Jobs in This Work Group:** Art Directors; Producers; Program Directors; Public Relations Managers; Technical Directors/Managers. **PERSONALITY TYPE:**

Enterprising. Enterprising occupations frequently involve starting up and carrying out projects. These occupations can involve leading people and making many decisions. They sometimes require risk taking and often deal with business.

EDUCATION/TRAINING PROGRAM(S)— Arts Management; Purchasing, Procurement/ Acquisitions, and Contracts Management. **RELATED KNOWLEDGE/COURSES—Sales and Marketing:** Knowledge of principles and methods for showing, promoting, and selling products or services. This includes marketing strategy and tactics, product demonstration, sales techniques, and sales control systems. **Economics and Accounting:** Knowledge of economic and accounting principles and practices, the financial markets, banking, and the analysis and reporting of financial data. **Personnel and Human Resources:** Knowledge of principles and procedures for personnel recruitment, selection, training, compensation and benefits, labor relations and negotiation, and personnel information systems. **Administration and Management:** Knowledge of business and management principles involved in strategic planning, resource allocation, human resources modeling, leadership technique, production methods, and coordination of people and resources. **Fine Arts:** Knowledge of the theory and techniques required to compose, produce, and perform works of music, dance, visual arts, drama, and sculpture. **Law and Government:** Knowledge of laws, legal codes, court procedures, precedents, government regulations, executive orders, agency rules, and the democratic political process.

Agricultural Sciences Teachers, Postsecondary

- ⚙ Education/Training Required: Master's degree
- ⚙ Annual Earnings: $64,970
- ⚙ Growth: 38.1% for all Postsecondary Teachers
- ⚙ Annual Job Openings: 216,000 for all Postsecondary Teachers
- ⚙ Self-Employed: 0.3% for all Postsecondary Teachers
- ⚙ Part-Time: 27.7% for all Postsecondary Teachers

Teach courses in the agricultural sciences. Includes teachers of agronomy, dairy sciences, fisheries management, horticultural sciences, poultry sciences, range management, and agricultural soil conservation. Evaluate and grade students' class work, laboratory work, assignments, and papers. Prepare and deliver lectures to undergraduate and/or graduate students on topics such as crop production, plant genetics, and soil chemistry. Advise students on academic and vocational curricula and on career issues. Compile, administer, and grade examinations or assign this work to others. Compile bibliographies of specialized materials for outside reading assignments. Initiate, facilitate, and moderate classroom discussions. Keep abreast of developments in their field by reading current literature, talking with colleagues, and participating in professional conferences. Maintain regularly scheduled office hours in order to advise and assist students. Maintain student attendance records, grades, and other required records. Plan, evaluate, and revise curricula, course content, and course materials and methods of instruction. Prepare course materials such as syllabi, homework assignments, and handouts. Select and obtain materials and supplies such as textbooks and laboratory equipment. Supervise laboratory sessions and field work and coordinate laboratory operations. Supervise undergraduate and/or graduate teaching, internship, and research work. Act as advisers to student organizations. Collaborate with colleagues to address teaching and research issues. Conduct research in a particular field of knowledge and publish findings in professional journals, books, and/or electronic media. Participate in campus and community events. Participate in student recruitment, registration, and placement activities. Perform administrative duties such as serving as department head. Provide professional consulting services to government and/or industry. Serve on academic or administrative committees that deal with institutional policies, departmental matters, and academic issues. Write grant proposals to procure external research funding. **SKILLS—Science:** Using scientific rules and methods to solve problems. **Instructing:** Teaching others how to do something. **Learning Strategies:** Selecting and using training/instructional methods and procedures appropriate for the situation when learning or teaching new things. **Reading Comprehension:** Understanding written sentences and paragraphs in work-related documents. **Active Learning:** Understanding the implications of new information for both current and future problem-solving and decision-making. **Writing:** Communicating effectively in writing as appropriate for the needs of the audience. **Critical Thinking:** Using logic and reasoning to identify the strengths and weaknesses of alternative solutions, conclusions, or approaches to problems. **Mathematics:** Using mathematics to solve problems.

GOE—Interest Area: 05. Education and Training. **Work Group:** 05.03. Postsecondary and Adult Teaching and Instructing. **Other Jobs in This Work Group:** Adult Literacy, Remedial Education, and GED Teachers and Instructors; Anthropology and Archeology Teachers, Postsecondary; Architecture Teachers, Postsecondary; Area, Ethnic, and Cultural Studies Teachers, Postsecondary; Art, Drama, and Music Teachers, Postsecondary; Atmospheric, Earth, Marine, and Space Sciences Teachers, Postsecondary; Biological Science Teachers, Postsecondary; Business Teachers, Postsecondary; Chemistry Teachers, Postsecondary; Communications Teachers, Postsecondary; Computer Science Teachers, Postsecondary; Criminal Justice and Law Enforcement Teachers, Postsecondary; Economics Teachers, Postsecondary; Education Teachers, Postsecondary; Engineering Teachers, Postsecondary; English Language and Literature Teachers, Postsecondary; Environmental Science Teachers, Postsecondary; Farm and Home Management Advisors; Foreign Language and Literature Teachers, Postsecondary; Forestry and Conservation Science Teachers, Postsecondary; Geography Teachers, Postsecondary; Graduate Teaching Assistants; Health Specialties Teachers, Postsecondary; History Teachers, Postsecondary; Home Economics Teachers, Postsecondary; Law Teachers, Postsecondary; Library Science Teachers, Postsecondary; Mathematical Science Teachers, Postsecondary; Nursing Instructors and Teachers, Postsecondary; Philosophy and Religion Teachers, Postsecondary; Physics Teachers, Postsecondary; Political Science Teachers, Postsecondary; Psychology Teachers, Postsecondary; Recreation and Fitness Studies Teachers, Postsecondary; Self-Enrichment Education Teachers; Social Work Teachers, Postsecondary; Sociology Teachers, Postsecondary; Vocational Education Teachers, Postsecondary. **PERSONALITY TYPE:** Investigative. Investigative occupations frequently involve working with ideas and require an extensive amount of thinking. These occupations can involve searching for facts and figuring out problems mentally.

EDUCATION/TRAINING PROGRAM(S)— Agribusiness/Agricultural Business Operations; Agricultural and Domestic Animal Services, Other; Agricultural and Food Products Processing; Agricultural and Horticultural Plant Breeding; Agricultural Animal Breeding; Agricultural Business and Management, General; Agricultural Business and Management, Other; Agricultural Economics; Agricultural Mechanization, General; Agricultural Mechanization, Other; Agricultural Power

Machinery Operation; Agricultural Production Operations, General; Agricultural Production Operations, Other; Agricultural Teacher Education; Agricultural/Farm Supplies Retailing and Wholesaling; Agriculture, Agriculture Operations, and Related Sciences, Other; Agriculture, General; Agronomy and Crop Science; Animal Health; Animal Nutrition; Animal Sciences, General; Animal Sciences, Other; Animal Training; Animal/Livestock Husbandry and Production; Applied Horticulture/Horticultural Business Services, Other; Applied Horticulture/Horticultural Operations, General; Aquaculture; Crop Production; Dairy Science; Equestrian/Equine Studies; Farm/Farm and Ranch Management; Food Science; Greenhouse Operations and Management; Horticultural Science; International Agriculture; Landscaping and Groundskeeping; Livestock Management; Ornamental Horticulture; Plant Nursery Operations and Management; Plant Protection and Integrated Pest Management; Plant Sciences, General; Plant Sciences, Other; Poultry Science; Range Science and Management; Soil Science and Agronomy, General; Turf and Turfgrass Management. **RELATED KNOWLEDGE/COURSES—Biology:** Knowledge of plant and animal organisms and their tissues, cells, functions, interdependencies, and interactions with each other and the environment. **Education and Training:** Knowledge of principles and methods for curriculum and training design, teaching and instruction for individuals and groups, and the measurement of training effects. **Medicine and Dentistry:** Knowledge of the information and techniques needed to diagnose and treat human injuries, diseases, and deformities. This includes symptoms, treatment alternatives, drug properties and interactions, and preventive health-care measures. **Chemistry:** Knowledge of the chemical composition, structure, and properties of substances and of the chemical processes and transformations that they undergo. This includes uses of chemicals and their danger signs, production techniques, and disposal methods. **Therapy and Counseling:** Knowledge of principles, methods, and procedures for diagnosis, treatment, and

rehabilitation of physical and mental dysfunctions and for career counseling and guidance. **Psychology:** Knowledge of human behavior and performance; individual differences in ability, personality, and interests; learning and motivation; psychological research methods; and the assessment and treatment of behavioral and affective disorders.

Airline Pilots, Copilots, and Flight Engineers

◎ Education/Training Required: Bachelor's degree

◎ Annual Earnings: $128,140

◎ Growth: 18.5%

◎ Annual Job Openings: 6,000

◎ Self-Employed: 0%

◎ Part-Time: 12.9%

Pilot and navigate the flight of multi-engine aircraft in regularly scheduled service for the transport of passengers and cargo. Requires Federal Air Transport rating and certification in specific aircraft type used. File instrument flight plans with air traffic control to ensure that flights are coordinated with other air traffic. Inspect aircraft for defects and malfunctions according to pre-flight checklists. Make announcements regarding flights, using public address systems. Monitor engine operation, fuel consumption, and functioning of aircraft systems during flights. Monitor gauges, warning devices, and control panels to verify aircraft performance and to regulate engine speed. Order changes in fuel supplies, loads, routes, or schedules to ensure safety of flights. Plan and formulate flight activities and test schedules; prepare flight evaluation reports. Respond to and report in-flight emergencies and malfunctions. Start engines, operate controls, and pilot airplanes to transport passengers, mail, or freight while adhering to flight plans, regulations, and procedures. Steer aircraft along planned routes with the assistance of autopilot and flight management computers. Work as part of a flight team with other crew members, especially during takeoffs and landings. Brief crews about flight details such as destinations, duties, and responsibilities. Check passenger and cargo distributions and fuel amounts to ensure that weight and balance specifications are met. Choose routes, altitudes, and speeds that will provide the fastest, safest, and smoothest flights. Confer with flight dispatchers and weather forecasters to keep abreast of flight conditions. Contact control towers for takeoff clearances, arrival instructions, and other information, using radio equipment. Coordinate flight activities with ground crews and air-traffic control and inform crew members of flight and test procedures. Direct activities of aircraft crews during flights. Conduct in-flight tests and evaluations at specified altitudes and in all types of weather in order to determine the receptivity and other characteristics of equipment and systems. Evaluate other pilots or pilot-license applicants for proficiency. Instruct other pilots and student pilots in aircraft operations and the principles of flight. Load smaller aircraft, handling passenger luggage and supervising refueling. **SKILLS—Operation and Control:** Controlling operations of equipment or systems. **Operation Monitoring:** Watching gauges, dials, or other indicators to make sure a machine is working properly. **Instructing:** Teaching others how to do something. **Science:** Using scientific rules and methods to solve problems. **Coordination:** Adjusting actions in relation to others' actions. **Systems Evaluation:** Identifying measures or indicators of system performance and the actions needed to improve or correct performance relative to the goals of the system. **Judgment and Decision Making:** Considering the relative costs and benefits of potential actions to choose the most appropriate one. **Systems Analysis:** Determining how a system should work and how changes in conditions, operations, and the environment will affect outcomes.

GOE—Interest Area: 16. Transportation, Distribution, and Logistics. **Work Group:** 16.02. Air Vehicle Operation. **Other Jobs in This Work Group:** Commercial Pilots. **PERSONALITY TYPE:** Realistic. Realistic occupations frequently involve work activities that include practical, hands-on problems and solutions. They often deal with plants, animals, and real-world materials like wood, tools, and machinery. Many of the occupations require working outside and do not involve a lot of paperwork or working closely with others.

EDUCATION/TRAINING PROGRAM(S)— Airline/Commercial/Professional Pilot and Flight Crew; Flight Instructor. **RELATED KNOWLEDGE/COURSES—Transportation:** Knowledge of principles and methods for moving people or goods by air, rail, sea, or road, including the relative costs and benefits. **Geography:** Knowledge of principles and methods for describing the features of land, sea, and air masses, including their physical characteristics; locations; interrelationships; and distribution of plant, animal, and human life. **Public Safety and Security:** Knowledge of relevant equipment, policies, procedures, and strategies to promote effective local, state, or national security operations for the protection of people, data, property, and institutions. **Education and Training:** Knowledge of principles and methods for curriculum and training design, teaching and instruction for individuals and groups, and the measurement of training effects. **Mechanical Devices:** Knowledge of machines and tools, including their designs, uses, repair, and maintenance. **Physics:** Knowledge and prediction of physical principles and laws and their interrelationships and applications to understanding fluid, material, and atmospheric dynamics and mechanical, electrical, atomic, and subatomic structures and processes.

Anesthesiologists

◎ Education/Training Required: First professional degree

◎ Annual Earnings: More than $145,000

◎ Growth: 19.5%

◎ Annual Job Openings: 38,000

◎ Self-Employed: 16.9%

◎ Part-Time: 8.1%

Administer anesthetics during surgery or other medical procedures. Administer anesthetic or sedation during medical procedures, using local, intravenous, spinal, or caudal methods. Confer with other medical professionals to determine type and method of anesthetic or sedation to render patient insensible to pain. Coordinate administration of anesthetics with surgeons during operation. Decide when patients have recovered or stabilized enough to be sent to another room or ward or to be sent home following outpatient surgery. Examine patient, obtain medical history, and use diagnostic tests to determine risk during surgical, obstetrical, and other medical procedures. Monitor patient before, during, and after anesthesia and counteract adverse reactions or complications. Record type and amount of anesthesia and patient condition throughout procedure. Conduct medical research to aid in controlling and curing disease, to investigate new medications, and to develop and test new medical techniques. Coordinate and direct work of nurses, medical technicians, and other health-care providers. Diagnose illnesses, using examinations, tests, and reports. Inform students and staff of types and methods of anesthesia administration, signs of complications, and emergency methods to counteract reactions. Manage anesthesiological services, coordinating them with other medical activities and formulating plans and procedures. Order laboratory tests, X rays, and other diagnostic procedures. Position patient on operating table to maximize patient comfort and surgical accessibility. Provide and maintain life support and airway management and help prepare patients for emergency surgery. Provide medical care and consultation in many settings, prescribing medication and treatment and referring patients for surgery. Instruct individuals and groups on ways to preserve health and prevent disease. Schedule and maintain use of surgical suite, including operating, wash-up, waiting rooms, and anesthetic and sterilizing equipment. **SKILLS —Operation Monitoring:** Watching gauges, dials, or other indicators to make sure a machine is working properly. **Judgment and Decision Making:** Considering the relative costs and benefits of potential actions to choose the most appropriate one. **Reading Comprehension:** Understanding written sentences and paragraphs in work-related documents. **Instructing:** Teaching others how to do something. **Critical Thinking:** Using logic and reasoning to identify the strengths and weaknesses of alternative solutions, conclusions, or approaches to problems. **Coordination:** Adjusting actions in relation to others' actions. **Systems Evaluation:** Identifying measures or indicators of system performance and the actions needed to improve or correct performance relative to the goals of the system. **Active Learning:** Understanding the implications of new information for both current and future problem-solving and decision-making. **Monitoring:** Monitoring or assessing your performance or that of other individuals or organizations to make improvements or take corrective action.

GOE—**Interest Area:** 08. Health Science. **Work Group:** 08.02. Medicine and Surgery. **Other Jobs in This Work Group:** Family and General Practitioners; Internists, General; Medical Assistants; Medical Transcriptionists; Obstetricians and Gynecologists; Pediatricians, General; Pharmacists; Pharmacy Aides; Pharmacy Technicians; Physician Assistants; Psychiatrists; Registered Nurses; Surgeons; Surgical Technologists. **PERSONALITY TYPE:** Investigative. Investigative occupations frequently involve working with ideas and require an extensive amount of thinking. These occupations can involve searching for facts and figuring out problems mentally.

EDUCATION/TRAINING PROGRAM(S)— Anesthesiology; Critical Care Anesthesiology. RELATED KNOWLEDGE/COURSES—**Medicine and Dentistry:** Knowledge of the information and techniques needed to diagnose and treat human injuries, diseases, and deformities. This includes symptoms, treatment alternatives, drug properties and interactions, and preventive health-care measures. **Biology:** Knowledge of plant and animal organisms and their tissues, cells, functions, interdependencies, and interactions with each other and the environment. **Chemistry:** Knowledge of the chemical composition, structure, and properties of substances and of the chemical processes and transformations that they undergo. This includes uses of chemicals and their danger signs, production techniques, and disposal methods. **English Language:** Knowledge of the structure and content of the English language, including the meaning and spelling of words, rules of composition, and grammar. **Mathematics:** Knowledge of arithmetic, algebra, geometry, calculus, and statistics and their applications. **Physics:** Knowledge and prediction of physical principles and laws and their interrelationships and applications to understanding fluid, material, and atmospheric dynamics and mechanical, electrical, atomic, and subatomic structures and processes.

Anthropology and Archeology Teachers, Postsecondary

- Education/Training Required: Master's degree
- Annual Earnings: $60,290
- Growth: 38.1% for all Postsecondary Teachers
- Annual Job Openings: 216,000 for all Postsecondary Teachers
- Self-Employed: 0.3% for all Postsecondary Teachers
- Part-Time: 27.7% for all Postsecondary Teachers

Teach courses in anthropology or archeology. Participate in student recruitment, registration, and placement activities. Perform administrative duties such as serving as department head. Provide professional consulting services to government and/or industry. Serve on academic or administrative committees that deal with institutional policies, departmental matters, and academic issues. Write grant proposals to procure external research funding. Evaluate and grade students' class work, assignments, and papers. Prepare and deliver lectures to undergraduate and/or graduate students on topics such as research methods, urban anthropology, and language and culture. Advise students on academic and vocational curricula, career issues, and laboratory and field research. Compile, administer, and grade examinations or assign this work to others. Compile bibliographies of specialized materials for outside reading assignments. Initiate, facilitate, and moderate classroom discussions. Keep abreast of developments in their field by reading current literature, talking with colleagues, and participating in professional conferences. Maintain regularly scheduled office hours in order to advise and assist students. Maintain student attendance records, grades, and other required records. Plan, evaluate, and revise curricula, course content, and course materials and methods of instruction. Prepare course materials such as syllabi, homework assignments, and handouts. Select and obtain materials and supplies such as textbooks and laboratory equipment. Supervise students' laboratory or field work. Supervise undergraduate and/or graduate teaching, internship, and research work. Act as advisers to student organizations. Collaborate with colleagues to address teaching and research issues. Conduct research in a particular field of knowledge and publish findings in professional journals, books, and/or electronic media. Participate in campus and community events. **SKILLS—Instructing:** Teaching others how to do something. **Learning Strategies:** Selecting and using training/instructional methods and procedures appropriate for the situation when learning or teaching new things. **Reading Comprehension:** Understanding written sentences and paragraphs in work-related documents. **Active Learning:** Understanding the implications of new information for both current and future problem-solving and decision-making. **Speaking:** Talking to others to convey information effectively. **Writing:** Communicating effectively in writing as appropriate for the needs of the audience. **Science:** Using scientific rules and methods to solve problems. **Active Listening:** Giving full attention to what other people are saying, taking time to understand the points being made, asking questions as appropriate, and not interrupting at inappropriate times. **Critical Thinking:** Using logic and reasoning to identify the strengths and weaknesses of alternative solutions, conclusions, or approaches to problems.

GOE—Interest Area: 05. Education and Training. **Work Group:** 05.03. Postsecondary and Adult Teaching and Instructing. **Other Jobs in This Work Group:** Adult Literacy, Remedial Education, and GED Teachers and Instructors; Agricultural Sciences Teachers, Postsecondary; Architecture Teachers, Postsecondary; Area, Ethnic, and Cultural Studies Teachers, Postsecondary; Art, Drama, and Music Teachers, Postsecondary; Atmospheric,

Earth, Marine, and Space Sciences Teachers, Post-secondary; Biological Science Teachers, Postsecondary; Business Teachers, Postsecondary; Chemistry Teachers, Postsecondary; Communications Teachers, Postsecondary; Computer Science Teachers, Postsecondary; Criminal Justice and Law Enforcement Teachers, Postsecondary; Economics Teachers, Postsecondary; Education Teachers, Postsecondary; Engineering Teachers, Postsecondary; English Language and Literature Teachers, Postsecondary; Environmental Science Teachers, Postsecondary; Farm and Home Management Advisors; Foreign Language and Literature Teachers, Postsecondary; Forestry and Conservation Science Teachers, Postsecondary; Geography Teachers, Postsecondary; Graduate Teaching Assistants; Health Specialties Teachers, Postsecondary; History Teachers, Postsecondary; Home Economics Teachers, Postsecondary; Law Teachers, Postsecondary; Library Science Teachers, Postsecondary; Mathematical Science Teachers, Postsecondary; Nursing Instructors and Teachers, Postsecondary; Philosophy and Religion Teachers, Postsecondary; Physics Teachers, Postsecondary; Political Science Teachers, Postsecondary; Psychology Teachers, Postsecondary; Recreation and Fitness Studies Teachers, Postsecondary; Self-Enrichment Education Teachers; Social Work Teachers, Postsecondary; Sociology Teachers, Postsecondary; Vocational Education Teachers, Postsecondary. **PERSONALITY TYPE:** Social. Social occupations frequently involve working with, communicating with, and teaching people. These occupations often involve helping or providing service to others.

EDUCATION/TRAINING PROGRAM(S)— Anthropology; Archeology; Physical Anthropology; Social Science Teacher Education. **RELATED KNOWLEDGE/COURSES—Sociology and Anthropology:** Knowledge of group behavior and dynamics, societal trends and influences, human migrations, ethnicity, and cultures and their history and origins. **History and Archeology:** Knowledge of historical events and their causes, indicators, and effects on civilizations and cultures. **Education and**

Training: Knowledge of principles and methods for curriculum and training design, teaching and instruction for individuals and groups, and the measurement of training effects. **Psychology:** Knowledge of human behavior and performance; individual differences in ability, personality, and interests; learning and motivation; psychological research methods; and the assessment and treatment of behavioral and affective disorders. **Economics and Accounting:** Knowledge of economic and accounting principles and practices, the financial markets, banking, and the analysis and reporting of financial data. **English Language:** Knowledge of the structure and content of the English language, including the meaning and spelling of words, rules of composition, and grammar.

Architects, Except Landscape and Naval

- Education/Training Required: Bachelor's degree
- Annual Earnings: $58,630
- Growth: 17.3%
- Annual Job Openings: 8,000
- Self-Employed: 21.4%
- Part-Time: 5.5%

Plan and design structures, such as private residences, office buildings, theaters, factories, and other structural property. Prepare information regarding design, structure specifications, materials, color, equipment, estimated costs, and construction time. Consult with client to determine functional and spatial requirements of structure. Direct activities of workers engaged in preparing drawings and specification documents. Plan layout of project. Prepare contract documents for building contractors. Prepare scale drawings. Integrate engineering element into unified design. Conduct periodic on-site observation of work during construction to monitor compliance with plans. Administer construction contracts. Represent client in obtaining bids and awarding construction contracts. **SKILLS—Operations Analysis:** Analyzing needs and product requirements to create a design. **Management of Financial Resources:** Determining how money will be spent to get the work done and accounting for these expenditures. **Coordination:** Adjusting actions in relation to others' actions. **Management of Personnel Resources:** Motivating, developing, and directing people as they work, identifying the best people for the job. **Negotiation:** Bringing others together and trying to reconcile differences. **Complex Problem Solving:** Identifying complex problems and reviewing related information to develop and evaluate options and implement solutions. **Persuasion:** Persuading others to change their minds or behavior. **Active Learning:** Understanding the implications of new information for both current and future problem-solving and decision-making.

GOE—Interest Area: 02. Architecture and Construction. **Work Group:** 02.02. Architectural Design. **Other Jobs in This Work Group:** Landscape Architects. **PERSONALITY TYPE:** Artistic. Artistic occupations frequently involve working with forms, designs, and patterns. They often require self-expression, and the work can be done without following a clear set of rules.

EDUCATION/TRAINING PROGRAM(S)— Architectural History and Criticism, General; Architecture (BArch, BA/BS, MArch, MA/MS, PhD); Architecture and Related Services, Other; Environmental Design/Architecture. **RELATED KNOWLEDGE/COURSES—Building and Construction:** Knowledge of the materials, methods, and tools involved in the construction or repair of houses, buildings, or other structures such as highways and roads. **Design:** Knowledge of design techniques, tools, and principles involved in production of precision technical plans, blueprints, drawings, and models. **Engineering and Technology:** Knowledge of the practical application of engineering science and technology. This includes applying principles, techniques, procedures, and equipment to the design and production of various goods and services. **Law and Government:** Knowledge of laws, legal codes, court procedures, precedents, government regulations, executive orders, agency rules, and the democratic political process. **Public Safety and Security:** Knowledge of relevant equipment, policies, procedures, and strategies to promote effective local, state, or national security operations for the protection of people, data, property, and institutions. **Fine Arts:** Knowledge of the theory and techniques required to compose, produce, and perform works of music, dance, visual arts, drama, and sculpture.

Architecture Teachers, Postsecondary

- ◎ Education/Training Required: Master's degree
- ◎ Annual Earnings: $59,120
- ◎ Growth: 38.1% for all Postsecondary Teachers
- ◎ Annual Job Openings: 216,000 for all Postsecondary Teachers
- ◎ Self-Employed: 0.3% for all Postsecondary Teachers
- ◎ Part-Time: 27.7% for all Postsecondary Teachers

Teach courses in architecture and architectural design, such as architectural environmental design, interior architecture/design, and landscape architecture. Evaluate and grade students' work, including work performed in design studios. Prepare and deliver lectures to undergraduate and/or graduate students on topics such as architectural design methods, aesthetics and design, and structures and materials. Advise students on academic and vocational curricula and on career issues. Compile, administer, and grade examinations or assign this work to others. Compile bibliographies of specialized materials for outside reading assignments. Initiate, facilitate, and moderate classroom discussions. Keep abreast of developments in their field by reading current literature, talking with colleagues, and participating in professional conferences. Maintain regularly scheduled office hours in order to advise and assist students. Maintain student attendance records, grades, and other required records. Plan, evaluate, and revise curricula, course content, and course materials and methods of instruction. Prepare course materials such as syllabi, homework assignments, and handouts. Select and obtain materials and supplies such as textbooks and laboratory equipment. Supervise undergraduate and/or graduate teaching, internship, and research work. Act as advisers to student organizations. Collaborate with colleagues to address teaching and research issues. Conduct research in a particular field of knowledge and publish findings in professional journals, books, and/or electronic media. Participate in campus and community events. Participate in student recruitment, registration, and placement activities. Perform administrative duties such as serving as department head. Provide professional consulting services to government and/or industry. Serve on academic or administrative committees that deal with institutional policies, departmental matters, and academic issues. Write grant proposals to procure external research funding. **SKILLS**—No data available.

GOE—Interest Area: 05. Education and Training. **Work Group:** 05.03. Postsecondary and Adult Teaching and Instructing. **Other Jobs in This Work Group:** Adult Literacy, Remedial Education, and GED Teachers and Instructors; Agricultural Sciences Teachers, Postsecondary; Anthropology and Archeology Teachers, Postsecondary; Area, Ethnic, and Cultural Studies Teachers, Postsecondary; Art, Drama, and Music Teachers, Postsecondary; Atmospheric, Earth, Marine, and Space Sciences Teachers, Postsecondary; Biological Science Teachers, Postsecondary; Business Teachers, Postsecondary;

Chemistry Teachers, Postsecondary; Communications Teachers, Postsecondary; Computer Science Teachers, Postsecondary; Criminal Justice and Law Enforcement Teachers, Postsecondary; Economics Teachers, Postsecondary; Education Teachers, Postsecondary; Engineering Teachers, Postsecondary; English Language and Literature Teachers, Postsecondary; Environmental Science Teachers, Postsecondary; Farm and Home Management Advisors; Foreign Language and Literature Teachers, Postsecondary; Forestry and Conservation Science Teachers, Postsecondary; Geography Teachers, Postsecondary; Graduate Teaching Assistants; Health Specialties Teachers, Postsecondary; History Teachers, Postsecondary; Home Economics Teachers, Postsecondary; Law Teachers, Postsecondary; Library Science Teachers, Postsecondary; Mathematical Science Teachers, Postsecondary; Nursing Instructors and Teachers, Postsecondary; Philosophy and Religion Teachers, Postsecondary; Physics Teachers, Postsecondary; Political Science Teachers, Postsecondary; Psychology Teachers, Postsecondary; Recreation and Fitness Studies Teachers, Postsecondary; Self-Enrichment Education Teachers; Social Work Teachers, Postsecondary; Sociology Teachers, Postsecondary; Vocational Education Teachers, Postsecondary. **PERSONALITY TYPE:** No data available.

EDUCATION/TRAINING PROGRAM(S)—Architectural Engineering; Architecture (BArch, BA/BS, MArch, MA/MS, PhD); City/Urban, Community, and Regional Planning; Environmental Design/Architecture; Interior Architecture; Landscape Architecture (BS, BSLA, BLA, MSLA, MLA, PhD); Teacher Education and Professional Development, Specific Subject Areas, Other. **RELATED KNOWLEDGE/COURSES—**No data available.

Area, Ethnic, and Cultural Studies Teachers, Postsecondary

- Education/Training Required: Master's degree
- Annual Earnings: $55,760
- Growth: 38.1% for all Postsecondary Teachers
- Annual Job Openings: 216,000 for all Postsecondary Teachers
- Self-Employed: 0.3% for all Postsecondary Teachers
- Part-Time: 27.7% for all Postsecondary Teachers

Teach courses pertaining to the culture and development of an area (e.g., Latin America), an ethnic group, or any other group (e.g., women's studies, urban affairs). Evaluate and grade students' class work, assignments, and papers. Prepare and deliver lectures to undergraduate and/or graduate students on topics such as race and ethnic relations, gender studies, and cross-cultural perspectives. Advise students on academic and vocational curricula and on career issues. Compile, administer, and grade examinations or assign this work to others. Compile bibliographies of specialized materials for outside reading assignments. Incorporate experiential/site visit components into courses. Initiate, facilitate, and moderate classroom discussions. Keep abreast of developments in their field by reading current literature, talking with colleagues, and participating in professional conferences. Maintain regularly scheduled office hours in order to advise and assist students. Maintain student attendance records, grades, and other required records. Plan, evaluate, and revise curricula, course content, and course materials and methods of instruction. Prepare course materials such as syllabi, homework assignments, and handouts. Select and obtain materials and supplies such as textbooks. Supervise undergraduate and/or graduate teaching, internship, and research work. Act as advisers to student organizations. Collaborate with colleagues to address teaching and research issues. Conduct research in a particular field of knowledge and publish findings in professional journals, books, and/or electronic media. Participate in campus and community events. Participate in student recruitment, registration, and placement activities. Perform administrative duties such as serving as department head. Provide professional consulting services to government and/or industry. Serve on academic or administrative committees that deal with institutional policies, departmental matters, and academic issues. Write grant proposals to procure external research funding. **SKILLS—Instructing:** Teaching others how to do something. **Learning Strategies:** Selecting and using training/instructional methods and procedures appropriate for the situation when learning or teaching new things. **Reading Comprehension:** Understanding written sentences and paragraphs in work-related documents. **Active Learning:** Understanding the implications of new information for both current and future problem-solving and decision-making. **Speaking:** Talking to others to convey information effectively. **Writing:** Communicating effectively in writing as appropriate for the needs of the audience. **Science:** Using scientific rules and methods to solve problems. **Active Listening:** Giving full attention to what other people are saying, taking time to understand the points being made, asking questions as appropriate, and not interrupting at inappropriate times. **Critical Thinking:** Using logic and reasoning to identify the strengths and weaknesses of alternative solutions, conclusions, or approaches to problems.

GOE—Interest Area: 05. Education and Training. **Work Group:** 05.03. Postsecondary and Adult Teaching and Instructing. **Other Jobs in This Work Group:** Adult Literacy, Remedial Education, and GED Teachers and Instructors; Agricultural Sciences Teachers, Postsecondary; Anthropology and Archeology Teachers, Postsecondary; Architecture Teachers, Postsecondary; Art, Drama, and Music Teachers, Postsecondary; Atmospheric, Earth, Marine, and Space Sciences Teachers, Postsecondary; Biological Science Teachers, Postsecondary; Business Teachers, Postsecondary; Chemistry Teachers, Postsecondary; Communications Teachers, Postsecondary; Computer Science Teachers, Postsecondary; Criminal Justice and Law Enforcement Teachers, Postsecondary; Economics Teachers, Postsecondary; Education Teachers, Postsecondary; Engineering Teachers, Postsecondary; English Language and Literature Teachers, Postsecondary; Environmental Science Teachers, Postsecondary; Farm and Home Management Advisors; Foreign Language and Literature Teachers, Postsecondary; Forestry and Conservation Science Teachers, Postsecondary; Geography Teachers, Postsecondary; Graduate Teaching Assistants; Health Specialties Teachers, Postsecondary; History Teachers, Postsecondary; Home Economics Teachers, Postsecondary; Law Teachers, Postsecondary; Library Science Teachers, Postsecondary; Mathematical Science Teachers, Postsecondary; Nursing Instructors and Teachers, Postsecondary; Philosophy and Religion Teachers, Postsecondary; Physics Teachers, Postsecondary; Political Science Teachers, Postsecondary; Psychology Teachers, Postsecondary; Recreation and Fitness Studies Teachers, Postsecondary; Self-Enrichment Education Teachers; Social Work Teachers, Postsecondary; Sociology Teachers, Postsecondary; Vocational Education Teachers, Postsecondary. **PERSONALITY TYPE:** Social. Social occupations frequently involve working with, communicating with, and teaching people. These occupations often involve helping or providing service to others.

EDUCATION/TRAINING PROGRAM(S)— African Studies; African-American/Black Studies; American Indian/Native American Studies; American/United States Studies/Civilization; Area Studies, Other; Area, Ethnic, Cultural, and Gender Studies, Other; Asian Studies/Civilization; Asian-American Studies; Balkans Studies; Baltic Studies;

Canadian Studies; Caribbean Studies; Central/Middle and Eastern European Studies; Chinese Studies; Commonwealth Studies; East Asian Studies; Ethnic, Cultural Minority, and Gender Studies, Other; European Studies/Civilization; French Studies; Gay/Lesbian Studies; German Studies; Hispanic-American, Puerto Rican, and Mexican-American/Chicano Studies; Intercultural/Multicultural and Diversity Studies; Islamic Studies; Italian Studies; Japanese Studies; Jewish/Judaic Studies; Korean Studies; Latin American Studies; Near and Middle Eastern Studies; Pacific Area/Pacific Rim Studies; Polish Studies; Regional Studies (U.S., Canadian, Foreign); Religion/Religious Studies, Other; Russian Studies; Scandinavian Studies; Slavic Studies; Social Studies Teacher Education; South Asian Studies; Southeast Asian Studies; Spanish and Iberian Studies; Tibetan Studies; Ukraine Studies; Ural-Altaic and Central Asian Studies; Western European Studies; Women's Studies. **RELATED KNOWLEDGE/COURSES—Sociology and Anthropology:** Knowledge of group behavior and dynamics, societal trends and influences, human migrations, ethnicity, and cultures and their history and origins. **History and Archeology:** Knowledge of historical events and their causes, indicators, and effects on civilizations and cultures. **Education and Training:** Knowledge of principles and methods for curriculum and training design, teaching and instruction for individuals and groups, and the measurement of training effects. **Psychology:** Knowledge of human behavior and performance; individual differences in ability, personality, and interests; learning and motivation; psychological research methods; and the assessment and treatment of behavioral and affective disorders. **Economics and Accounting:** Knowledge of economic and accounting principles and practices, the financial markets, banking, and the analysis and reporting of financial data. **English Language:** Knowledge of the structure and content of the English language, including the meaning and spelling of words, rules of composition, and grammar.

Art Directors

- ◎ Education/Training Required: Work experience plus degree
- ◎ Annual Earnings: $63,170
- ◎ Growth: 11.4%
- ◎ Annual Job Openings: 8,000
- ◎ Self-Employed: 53.6%
- ◎ Part-Time: 23.1%

Formulate design concepts and presentation approaches and direct workers engaged in art work, layout design, and copy writing for visual communications media such as magazines, books, newspapers, and packaging. Formulate basic layout design or presentation approach and specify material details such as style and size of type, photographs, graphics, animation, video, and sound. Review and approve proofs of printed copy and art and copy materials developed by staff members. Manage own accounts and projects, working within budget and scheduling requirements. Confer with creative, art, copy-writing, or production department heads to discuss client requirements and presentation concepts and to coordinate creative activities. Present final layouts to clients for approval. Confer with clients to determine objectives; budget; background information; and presentation approaches, styles, and techniques. Hire, train, and direct staff members who develop design concepts into art layouts or who prepare layouts for printing. Work with creative directors to develop design solutions. Review illustrative material to determine if it conforms to standards and specifications. Attend photo shoots and printing sessions to ensure that the products needed are obtained. Create custom illustrations or other graphic elements. Mark up, paste, and complete layouts and write typography instructions to prepare materials for typesetting or printing. Negotiate with printers and estimators to determine what services will be performed. Conceptualize and help design interfaces for multimedia games, products, and devices. **SKILLS—Coordination:** Adjusting actions in relation to others' actions. **Negotiation:** Bringing others together and trying to reconcile differences. **Persuasion:** Persuading others to change their minds or behavior. **Service Orientation:** Actively looking for ways to help people. **Management of Financial Resources:** Determining how money will be spent to get the work done and accounting for these expenditures. **Instructing:** Teaching others how to do something. **Time Management:** Managing one's own time and the time of others. **Operations Analysis:** Analyzing needs and product requirements to create a design.

GOE—Interest Area: 03. Arts and Communication. **Work Group:** 03.01. Managerial Work in Arts and Communication. **Other Jobs in This Work Group:** Agents and Business Managers of Artists, Performers, and Athletes; Producers; Program Directors; Public Relations Managers; Technical Directors/Managers. **PERSONALITY TYPE:** Artistic. Artistic occupations frequently involve working with forms, designs, and patterns. They often require self-expression, and the work can be done without following a clear set of rules.

EDUCATION/TRAINING PROGRAM(S)— Graphic Design; Intermedia/Multimedia. **RELATED KNOWLEDGE/COURSES— Design:** Knowledge of design techniques, tools, and principles involved in production of precision technical plans, blueprints, drawings, and models. **Fine Arts:** Knowledge of the theory and techniques required to compose, produce, and perform works of music, dance, visual arts, drama, and sculpture. **Computers and Electronics:** Knowledge of circuit boards, processors, chips, electronic equipment, and computer hardware and software, including applications and programming. **Communications and Media:** Knowledge of media production, communication, and dissemination techniques and methods. This includes alternative ways to inform and entertain via written, oral, and visual media. **Production and Processing:** Knowledge of raw materials, production processes, quality control, costs, and other techniques for maximizing the effective manufacture and distribution of goods. **Customer and**

Personal Service: Knowledge of principles and processes for providing customer and personal services. This includes customer needs assessment, meeting quality standards for services, and evaluation of customer satisfaction. **Education and Training:** Knowledge of principles and methods for curriculum and training design, teaching and instruction for individuals and groups, and the measurement of training effects.

Art, Drama, and Music Teachers, Postsecondary

- ◎ Education/Training Required: Master's degree
- ◎ Annual Earnings: $48,150
- ◎ Growth: 38.1% for all Postsecondary Teachers
- ◎ Annual Job Openings: 216,000 for all Postsecondary Teachers
- ◎ Self-Employed: 0.3% for all Postsecondary Teachers
- ◎ Part-Time: 27.7% for all Postsecondary Teachers

Teach courses in drama, music, and the arts, including fine and applied art, such as painting and sculpture, or design and crafts. Serve on academic or administrative committees that deal with institutional policies, departmental matters, and academic issues. Write grant proposals to procure external research funding. Evaluate and grade students' class work, performances, projects, assignments, and papers. Prepare and deliver lectures to undergraduate and/or graduate students on topics such as acting techniques, fundamentals of music, and art history. Advise students on academic and vocational curricula and on career issues. Compile, administer, and grade examinations or assign this work to others. Compile bibliographies of specialized materials for outside reading assignments. Explain and demonstrate artistic techniques. Initiate, facilitate, and moderate classroom discussions. Keep abreast of developments in their field by reading current literature, talking with colleagues, and participating in professional conferences. Maintain regularly scheduled office hours in order to advise and assist students. Maintain student attendance records, grades, and other required records. Plan, evaluate, and revise curricula, course content, and course materials and methods of instruction. Prepare course materials such as syllabi, homework assignments, and handouts. Prepare students for performances, exams, or assessments. Select and obtain materials and supplies such as textbooks and performance pieces. Supervise undergraduate and/or graduate teaching, internship, and research work. Act as advisers to student organizations. Collaborate with colleagues to address teaching and research issues. Conduct research in a particular field of knowledge and publish findings in professional journals, books, and/or electronic media. Display students' work in schools, galleries, and exhibitions. Keep students informed of community events such as plays and concerts. Organize performance groups and direct their rehearsals. Participate in campus and community events. Participate in student recruitment, registration, and placement activities. Perform administrative duties such as serving as department head. Provide professional consulting services to government and/or industry. **SKILLS—Instructing:** Teaching others how to do something. **Learning Strategies:** Selecting and using training/instructional methods and procedures appropriate for the situation when learning or teaching new things. **Writing:** Communicating effectively in writing as appropriate for the needs of the audience. **Speaking:** Talking to others to convey information effectively. **Reading Comprehension:** Understanding written sentences and paragraphs in work-related documents. **Complex Problem Solving:** Identifying complex problems and reviewing related information to develop and evaluate options and implement solutions. **Time Management:**

Managing one's own time and the time of others. **Active Learning:** Understanding the implications of new information for both current and future problem-solving and decision-making.

GOE—Interest Area: 05. Education and Training. **Work Group:** 05.03. Postsecondary and Adult Teaching and Instructing. **Other Jobs in This Work Group:** Adult Literacy, Remedial Education, and GED Teachers and Instructors; Agricultural Sciences Teachers, Postsecondary; Anthropology and Archeology Teachers, Postsecondary; Architecture Teachers, Postsecondary; Area, Ethnic, and Cultural Studies Teachers, Postsecondary; Atmospheric, Earth, Marine, and Space Sciences Teachers, Postsecondary; Biological Science Teachers, Postsecondary; Business Teachers, Postsecondary; Chemistry Teachers, Postsecondary; Communications Teachers, Postsecondary; Computer Science Teachers, Postsecondary; Criminal Justice and Law Enforcement Teachers, Postsecondary; Economics Teachers, Postsecondary; Education Teachers, Postsecondary; Engineering Teachers, Postsecondary; English Language and Literature Teachers, Postsecondary; Environmental Science Teachers, Postsecondary; Farm and Home Management Advisors; Foreign Language and Literature Teachers, Postsecondary; Forestry and Conservation Science Teachers, Postsecondary; Geography Teachers, Postsecondary; Graduate Teaching Assistants; Health Specialties Teachers, Postsecondary; History Teachers, Postsecondary; Home Economics Teachers, Postsecondary; Law Teachers, Postsecondary; Library Science Teachers, Postsecondary; Mathematical Science Teachers, Postsecondary; Nursing Instructors and Teachers, Postsecondary; Philosophy and Religion Teachers, Postsecondary; Physics Teachers, Postsecondary; Political Science Teachers, Postsecondary; Psychology Teachers, Postsecondary; Recreation and Fitness Studies Teachers, Postsecondary; Self-Enrichment Education Teachers; Social Work Teachers, Postsecondary; Sociology Teachers, Postsecondary; Vocational Education Teachers, Postsecondary. **PERSONALITY TYPE:** Artistic. Artistic occupations frequently involve working

A

with forms, designs, and patterns. They often require self-expression, and the work can be done without following a clear set of rules.

EDUCATION/TRAINING PROGRAM(S)— Art History, Criticism, and Conservation; Art/Art Studies, General; Arts Management; Ceramic Arts and Ceramics; Cinematography and Film/Video Production; Commercial Photography; Conducting; Crafts/Craft Design, Folk Art, and Artisanry; Dance, General; Design and Applied Arts, Other; Design and Visual Communications, General; Directing and Theatrical Production; Drama and Dramatics/Theatre Arts, General; Dramatic/Theatre Arts and Stagecraft, Other; Fashion/Apparel Design; Fiber, Textile, and Weaving Arts; Film/Cinema Studies; Film/Video and Photographic Arts, Other; Fine Arts and Art Studies, Other; Fine/Studio Arts, General; Graphic Design; Industrial Design; Interior Design; Intermedia/Multimedia; Jazz/Jazz Studies; Metal and Jewelry Arts; Music History, Literature, and Theory; Music Management and Merchandising; Music Pedagogy; Music Performance, General; Music Theory and Composition; Music, Other; Musicology and Ethnomusicology; Painting; Photography; Piano and Organ; Playwriting and Screenwriting; Printmaking; Sculpture; Technical Theatre/Theatre Design and Technology; Theatre Literature, History, and Criticism; Theatre/Theatre Arts Management; Violin, Viola, Guitar, and Other Stringed Instruments; Visual and Performing Arts, General; Visual and Performing Arts, Other; Voice and Opera. RELATED KNOWLEDGE/COURSES—Fine Arts: Knowledge of the theory and techniques required to compose, produce, and perform works of music, dance, visual arts, drama, and sculpture. Education and Training: Knowledge of principles and methods for curriculum and training design, teaching and instruction for individuals and groups, and the measurement of training effects. English Language: Knowledge of the structure and content of the English language, including the meaning and spelling of words, rules of composition, and grammar. Communications and Media: Knowledge of media pro-duction, communication, and dissemination techniques and methods. This includes alternative ways to inform and entertain via written, oral, and visual media. Administration and Management: Knowledge of business and management principles involved in strategic planning, resource allocation, human resources modeling, leadership technique, production methods, and coordination of people and resources. Clerical Practices: Knowledge of administrative and clerical procedures and systems such as word processing, managing files and records, stenography and transcription, designing forms, and other office procedures and terminology.

Astronomers

- ◎ Education/Training Required: Doctoral degree
- ◎ Annual Earnings: $85,910
- ◎ Growth: 4.9%
- ◎ Annual Job Openings: Fewer than 500
- ◎ Self-Employed: 2.1%
- ◎ Part-Time: 2.4%

Observe, research, and interpret celestial and astronomical phenomena to increase basic knowledge and apply such information to practical problems. Studies celestial phenomena from ground or above atmosphere, using various optical devices such as telescopes situated on ground or attached to satellites. Designs optical, mechanical, and electronic instruments for astronomical research. Develops mathematical tables giving positions of sun, moon, planets, and stars at given times for use by air and sea navigators. Analyzes wave lengths of radiation from celestial bodies as observed in all ranges of spectrum. Determines exact time by celestial observations and conducts research into relationships between time and space. Studies history, structure, extent, and evolution of stars, stellar systems, and universe. Computes positions of sun, moon, planets, stars, nebulae, and galaxies. Calculates orbits and determines sizes, shapes, brightness, and motions of different celestial bodies. **SKILLS—Science:** Using scientific rules and methods to solve problems. **Technology Design:** Generating or adapting equipment and technology to serve user needs. **Mathematics:** Using mathematics to solve problems. **Active Learning:** Understanding the implications of new information for both current and future problem-solving and decision-making. **Programming:** Writing computer programs for various purposes. **Critical Thinking:** Using logic and reasoning to identify the strengths and weaknesses of alternative solutions, conclusions, or approaches to problems. **Operations Analysis:** Analyzing needs and product requirements to create a design. **Reading Comprehension:** Understanding written sentences and paragraphs in work-related documents.

GOE—Interest Area: 15. Scientific Research, Engineering, and Mathematics. **Work Group:** 15.02. Physical Sciences. **Other Jobs in This Work Group:** Atmospheric and Space Scientists; Chemists; Geographers; Geologists; Hydrologists; Materials Scientists; Physicists. **PERSONALITY TYPE:** Investigative. Investigative occupations frequently involve working with ideas and require an extensive amount of thinking. These occupations can involve searching for facts and figuring out problems mentally.

EDUCATION/TRAINING PROGRAM(S)— Astronomy; Astronomy and Astrophysics, Other; Astrophysics; Planetary Astronomy and Science. **RELATED KNOWLEDGE/COURSES—** **Physics:** Knowledge and prediction of physical principles and laws and their interrelationships and applications to understanding fluid, material, and atmospheric dynamics and mechanical, electrical, atomic, and subatomic structures and processes. **Mathematics:** Knowledge of arithmetic, algebra, geometry, calculus, and statistics and their applications. **History and Archeology:** Knowledge of historical events and their causes, indicators, and effects on civilizations and cultures. **Design:** Knowledge of design techniques, tools, and principles

involved in production of precision technical plans, blueprints, drawings, and models. **Engineering and Technology:** Knowledge of the practical application of engineering science and technology. This includes applying principles, techniques, procedures, and equipment to the design and production of various goods and services. **Geography:** Knowledge of principles and methods for describing the features of land, sea, and air masses, including their physical characteristics; locations; interrelationships; and distribution of plant, animal, and human life.

Athletic Trainers

- Education/Training Required: Bachelor's degree
- Annual Earnings: $32,990
- Growth: 29.9%
- Annual Job Openings: 2,000
- Self-Employed: 0.1%
- Part-Time: 6.5%

Evaluate, advise, and treat athletes to assist recovery from injury, avoid injury, or maintain peak physical fitness. Conduct an initial assessment of an athlete's injury or illness in order to provide emergency or continued care and to determine whether they should be referred to physicians for definitive diagnosis and treatment. Care for athletic injuries using physical therapy equipment, techniques, and medication. Evaluate athletes' readiness to play and provide participation clearances when necessary and warranted. Apply protective or injury preventive devices such as tape, bandages, or braces to body parts such as ankles, fingers, or wrists. Assess and report the progress of recovering athletes to coaches and physicians. Collaborate with physicians in order to develop and implement comprehensive rehabilitation programs for athletic injuries. Advise athletes on the proper use of equipment. Plan and implement comprehensive athletic injury and illness prevention programs. Develop training programs and routines designed to improve athletic performance. Travel with athletic teams in order to be available at sporting events. Instruct coaches, athletes, parents, medical personnel, and community members in the care and prevention of athletic injuries. Inspect playing fields in order to locate any items that could injure players. Conduct research and provide instruction on subject matter related to athletic training or sports medicine. Recommend special diets in order to improve athletes' health, increase their stamina, and/or alter their weight. Massage body parts in order to relieve soreness, strains, and bruises. Confer with coaches in order to select protective equipment. Accompany injured athletes to hospitals. Perform team-support duties such as running errands, maintaining equipment, and stocking supplies. Lead stretching exercises for team members prior to games and practices. **SKILLS—Social Perceptiveness:** Being aware of others' reactions and understanding why they react as they do. **Time Management:** Managing one's own time and the time of others. **Service Orientation:** Actively looking for ways to help people. **Instructing:** Teaching others how to do something. **Management of Material Resources:** Obtaining and seeing to the appropriate use of equipment, facilities, and materials needed to do certain work. **Coordination:** Adjusting actions in relation to others' actions. **Management of Personnel Resources:** Motivating, developing, and directing people as they work, identifying the best people for the job. **Management of Financial Resources:** Determining how money will be spent to get the work done and accounting for these expenditures.

GOE—Interest Area: 08. Health Science. **Work Group:** 08.09. Health Protection and Promotion. **Other Jobs in This Work Group:** Dietetic Technicians; Dietitians and Nutritionists; Embalmers. **PERSONALITY TYPE:** Social. Social occupations frequently involve working with, communicating with, and teaching people. These occupations often involve helping or providing service to others.

EDUCATION/TRAINING PROGRAM(S)— Athletic Training/Trainer. **RELATED KNOWLEDGE/COURSES—Therapy and Counseling:** Knowledge of principles, methods, and procedures for diagnosis, treatment, and rehabilitation of physical and mental dysfunctions and for career counseling and guidance. **Medicine and Dentistry:** Knowledge of the information and techniques needed to diagnose and treat human injuries, diseases, and deformities. This includes symptoms, treatment alternatives, drug properties and interactions, and preventive health-care measures. **Psychology:** Knowledge of human behavior and performance; individual differences in ability, personality, and interests; learning and motivation; psychological research methods; and the assessment and treatment of behavioral and affective disorders. **Customer and Personal Service:** Knowledge of principles and processes for providing customer and personal services. This includes customer needs assessment, meeting quality standards for services, and evaluation of customer satisfaction. **Biology:** Knowledge of plant and animal organisms and their tissues, cells, functions, interdependencies, and interactions with each other and the environment. **Education and Training:** Knowledge of principles and methods for curriculum and training design, teaching and instruction for individuals and groups, and the measurement of training effects.

Atmospheric and Space Scientists

- ◉ Education/Training Required: Bachelor's degree
- ◉ Annual Earnings: $65,400
- ◉ Growth: 16.2%
- ◉ Annual Job Openings: 1,000
- ◉ Self-Employed: 2.1%
- ◉ Part-Time: 4.3%

Investigate atmospheric phenomena and interpret meteorological data gathered by surface and air stations, satellites, and radar to prepare reports and forecasts for public and other uses. Collect and analyze historical climate information such as precipitation and temperature records in order to help predict future weather and climate trends. Conduct basic or applied meteorological research into the processes and determinants of atmospheric phenomena, weather, and climate. Conduct numerical simulations of climate conditions in order to understand and predict global and regional weather patterns. Gather data from sources such as surface and upper air stations, satellites, weather bureaus, and radar for use in meteorological reports and forecasts. Operate computer graphic equipment to produce weather reports and maps for analysis, distribution, or use in weather broadcasts. Prepare forecasts and briefings to meet the needs of industry, business, government, and other groups. Study and interpret data, reports, maps, photographs, and charts to predict long- and short-range weather conditions, using computer models and knowledge of climate theory, physics, and mathematics. Apply meteorological knowledge to problems in areas including agriculture, pollution control, and water management and to issues such as global warming or ozone depletion. Broadcast weather conditions, forecasts, and severe weather warnings to the public via television, radio, and the Internet and/or provide this information to the news media. Collect air samples from planes and ships over land and sea to study atmospheric composition. Consult with agencies, professionals, or researchers regarding the use and interpretation of climatological information. Design and develop new equipment and methods for meteorological data collection, remote sensing, or related applications. Develop and use weather forecasting tools such as mathematical and computer models. Measure wind, temperature, and humidity in the upper atmosphere, using weather balloons. Research and analyze the impact of industrial projects and pollution on climate, air quality, and weather phenomena. Direct forecasting services at weather stations or at radio or television broadcasting facilities. Make scientific presentations and publish reports, articles, or texts. **SKILLS—Science:** Using scientific rules and methods to solve problems. **Active Learning:** Understanding the implications of new information for both current and future problem-solving and decision-making. **Management of Personnel Resources:** Motivating, developing, and directing people as they work, identifying the best people for the job. **Critical Thinking:** Using logic and reasoning to identify the strengths and weaknesses of alternative solutions, conclusions, or approaches to problems. **Speaking:** Talking to others to convey information effectively. **Judgment and Decision Making:** Considering the relative costs and benefits of potential actions to choose the most appropriate one. **Systems Analysis:** Determining how a system should work and how changes in conditions, operations, and the environment will affect outcomes. **Complex Problem Solving:** Identifying complex problems and reviewing related information to develop and evaluate options and implement solutions.

GOE—Interest Area: 15. Scientific Research, Engineering, and Mathematics. **Work Group:** 15.02. Physical Sciences. **Other Jobs in This Work Group:** Astronomers; Chemists; Geographers; Geologists; Hydrologists; Materials Scientists; Physicists. **PERSONALITY TYPE:** Investigative. Investigative occupations frequently involve working with ideas and require an extensive amount of thinking. These occupations can involve searching for facts and figuring out problems mentally.

EDUCATION/TRAINING PROGRAM(S)—Atmospheric Chemistry and Climatology; Atmospheric Physics and Dynamics; Atmospheric Sciences and Meteorology, General; Atmospheric Sciences and Meteorology, Other; Meteorology.
RELATED KNOWLEDGE/COURSES—
Physics: Knowledge and prediction of physical principles and laws and their interrelationships and applications to understanding fluid, material, and atmospheric dynamics and mechanical, electrical, atomic, and subatomic structures and processes. **Geography:** Knowledge of principles and methods for describing the features of land, sea, and air masses, including their physical characteristics; locations; interrelationships; and distribution of plant, animal, and human life. **Communications and Media:** Knowledge of media production, communication, and dissemination techniques and methods. This includes alternative ways to inform and entertain via written, oral, and visual media. **Telecommunications:** Knowledge of transmission, broadcasting, switching, control, and operation of telecommunications systems. **Administration and Management:** Knowledge of business and management principles involved in strategic planning, resource allocation, human resources modeling, leadership technique, production methods, and coordination of people and resources. **Mathematics:** Knowledge of arithmetic, algebra, geometry, calculus, and statistics and their applications.

Atmospheric, Earth, Marine, and Space Sciences Teachers, Postsecondary

- ◉ Education/Training Required: Master's degree
- ◉ Annual Earnings: $64,080
- ◉ Growth: 38.1% for all Postsecondary Teachers
- ◉ Annual Job Openings: 216,000 for all Postsecondary Teachers
- ◉ Self-Employed: 0.3% for all Postsecondary Teachers
- ◉ Part-Time: 27.7% for all Postsecondary Teachers

Teach courses in the physical sciences, except chemistry and physics. Evaluate and grade students' class work, assignments, and papers. Prepare and deliver lectures to undergraduate and/or graduate students on topics such as structural geology, micrometeorology, and atmospheric thermodynamics. Advise students on academic and vocational curricula and on career issues. Compile, administer, and grade examinations or assign this work to others. Compile bibliographies of specialized materials for outside reading assignments. Initiate, facilitate, and moderate classroom discussions. Keep abreast of developments in their field by reading current literature, talking with colleagues, and participating in professional conferences. Maintain regularly scheduled office hours in order to advise and assist students. Maintain student attendance records, grades, and other required records. Plan, evaluate, and revise curricula, course content, and course materials and methods of instruction. Prepare course materials such as syllabi, homework assignments, and handouts. Select and obtain materials and supplies such as textbooks and laboratory equipment. Supervise laboratory work and field work. Supervise undergraduate and/or graduate teaching, internship, and research work. Act as advisers to student organizations. Collaborate with colleagues to address teaching and research issues. Conduct research in a particular field of knowledge and publish findings in professional journals, books, and/or electronic media. Participate in campus and community events. Participate in student recruitment, registration, and placement activities. Perform administrative duties such as serving as department head. Provide professional consulting services to government and/or industry. Serve on academic or administrative committees that deal with institutional policies, departmental matters, and academic issues. Write grant proposals to procure external research funding. **SKILLS**—No data available.

GOE—**Interest Area:** 05. Education and Training. **Work Group:** 05.03. Postsecondary and Adult Teaching and Instructing. **Other Jobs in This Work Group:** Adult Literacy, Remedial Education, and GED Teachers and Instructors; Agricultural Sciences Teachers, Postsecondary; Anthropology and Archeology Teachers, Postsecondary; Architecture Teachers, Postsecondary; Area, Ethnic, and Cultural Studies Teachers, Postsecondary; Art, Drama, and Music Teachers, Postsecondary; Biological Science Teachers, Postsecondary; Business Teachers, Postsecondary; Chemistry Teachers, Postsecondary; Communications Teachers, Postsecondary; Computer Science Teachers, Postsecondary; Criminal Justice and Law Enforcement Teachers, Postsecondary; Economics Teachers, Postsecondary; Education Teachers, Postsecondary; Engineering Teachers, Postsecondary; English Language and Literature Teachers, Postsecondary; Environmental Science Teachers, Postsecondary; Farm and Home Management Advisors; Foreign Language and Literature Teachers, Postsecondary; Forestry and Conservation Science Teachers, Postsecondary; Geography Teachers, Postsecondary; Graduate Teaching Assistants; Health Specialties Teachers, Postsecondary; History Teachers, Postsecondary; Home Economics Teachers, Postsecondary; Law Teachers, Postsecondary; Library Science Teachers, Postsecondary; Mathematical Science Teachers, Postsecondary; Nursing Instructors and Teachers, Postsecondary; Philosophy and Religion Teachers, Postsecondary; Physics Teachers, Postsecondary; Political Science Teachers, Postsecondary; Psychology Teachers, Postsecondary; Recreation and Fitness Studies Teachers, Postsecondary; Self-Enrichment Education Teachers; Social Work Teachers, Postsecondary; Sociology Teachers, Postsecondary; Vocational Education Teachers, Postsecondary. **PERSONALITY TYPE:** No data available.

EDUCATION/TRAINING PROGRAM(S)—Acoustics; Astronomy; Astrophysics; Atmospheric Chemistry and Climatology; Atmospheric Physics and Dynamics; Atmospheric Sciences and Meteorology, General; Atmospheric Sciences and Meteorology, Other; Atomic/Molecular Physics; Elementary Particle Physics; Geochemistry; Geochemistry and Petrology; Geological and Earth Sciences/Geosciences, Other; Geology/Earth Science, General; Geophysics and Seismology; Hydrology and Water Resources Science; Meteorology; Nuclear Physics; Oceanography, Chemical and Physical; Optics/Optical Sciences; Paleontology; Physics Teacher Education; Physics, Other; Planetary Astronomy and Science; Plasma and High-Temperature Physics; Science Teacher Education/General Science Teacher Education; Solid State and Low-Temperature Physics; Theoretical and Mathematical Physics. **RELATED KNOWLEDGE/COURSES**—No data available.

Audiologists

- ⊚ Education/Training Required: Master's degree
- ⊚ Annual Earnings: $50,000
- ⊚ Growth: 29.0%
- ⊚ Annual Job Openings: 1,000
- ⊚ Self-Employed: 7.1%
- ⊚ Part-Time: 22.7%

Assess and treat persons with hearing and related disorders. May fit hearing aids and provide auditory training. May perform research related to hearing problems. Administer hearing or speech/language evaluations, tests, or examinations to patients to collect information on type and degree of impairment, using specialized instruments and electronic equipment. Counsel and instruct clients in techniques to improve hearing or speech impairment, including sign language or lip-reading. Evaluate hearing and speech/language disorders to determine diagnoses and courses of treatment. Examine and clean patients' ear canals. Fit and dispense assistive devices, such as hearing aids. Maintain client records at all stages, including initial evaluation and discharge. Monitor clients' progress and discharge them from treatment when goals have been attained. Plan and conduct treatment programs for clients' hearing or speech problems, consulting with physicians, nurses, psychologists, and other health-care personnel as necessary. Recommend assistive devices according to clients' needs or nature of impairments. Refer clients to additional medical or educational services if needed. Advise educators or other medical staff on speech or hearing topics. Conduct or direct research on hearing or speech topics and report findings to help in the development of procedures, technology, or treatments. Develop and supervise hearing screening programs. Educate and supervise audiology students and health-care personnel. Fit and tune cochlear implants, providing rehabilitation for adjustment to listening with implant amplification systems. Instruct clients, parents, teachers, or employers in how to avoid behavior patterns that lead to miscommunication. Participate in conferences or training to update or share knowledge of new hearing or speech disorder treatment methods or technologies. Measure noise levels in workplaces and conduct hearing protection programs in industry, schools, and communities. Work with multi-disciplinary teams to assess and rehabilitate recipients of implanted hearing devices. **SKILLS—Instructing:** Teaching others how to do something. **Management of Personnel Resources:** Motivating, developing, and directing people as they work, identifying the best people for the job. **Management of Financial Resources:** Determining how money will be spent to get the work done and accounting for these expenditures. **Writing:** Communicating effectively in writing as appropriate for the needs of the audience. **Service Orientation:** Actively looking for ways to help people. **Learning Strategies:** Selecting and using training/instructional methods and procedures appropriate for the situation when learning or teaching new things. **Speaking:** Talking to others to convey information effectively. **Reading Comprehension:** Understanding written sentences and paragraphs in work-related documents. **Active Learning:** Understanding the implications of new information for both current and future problem-solving and decision-making. **Social Perceptiveness:** Being aware of others' reactions and understanding why they react as they do.

GOE—Interest Area: 08. Health Science. **Work Group:** 08.07. Medical Therapy. **Other Jobs in This Work Group:** Massage Therapists; Occupational Therapist Aides; Occupational Therapist Assistants; Occupational Therapists; Physical Therapist Aides; Physical Therapist Assistants; Physical Therapists; Radiation Therapists; Recreational Therapists; Respiratory Therapists; Respiratory Therapy Technicians; Speech-Language Pathologists. **PERSONALITY TYPE:** Social. Social occupations frequently involve working with, communicating with, and teaching people. These occupations often involve helping or providing service to others.

EDUCATION/TRAINING PROGRAM(S)— Audiology/Audiologist and Hearing Sciences; Audiology/Audiologist and Speech-Language Pathology/Pathologist; Communication Disorders Sciences and Services, Other; Communication Disorders, General. **RELATED KNOWLEDGE/COURSES—Therapy and Counseling:** Knowledge of principles, methods, and procedures for diagnosis, treatment, and rehabilitation of physical and mental dysfunctions and for career counseling and guidance. **Medicine and Dentistry:** Knowledge of the information and techniques needed to diagnose and treat human injuries, diseases, and deformities. This includes symptoms, treatment alternatives, drug properties and interactions, and preventive health-care measures. **Education and Training:** Knowledge of principles and methods for curriculum and training design, teaching and instruction for individuals and groups, and the measurement of training effects. **Personnel and Human Resources:** Knowledge of principles and procedures for personnel recruitment, selection, training, compensation and benefits, labor relations and negotiation, and personnel information systems. **Economics and Accounting:** Knowledge of economic and accounting principles and practices, the financial markets, banking, and the analysis and reporting of financial data. **Biology:** Knowledge of plant and animal organisms and their tissues, cells, functions, interdependencies, and interactions with each other and the environment.

Auditors

- Education/Training Required: Bachelor's degree
- Annual Earnings: $49,770
- Growth: 19.5%
- Annual Job Openings: 119,000
- Self-Employed: 10.6%
- Part-Time: 8.8%

Examine and analyze accounting records to determine financial status of establishment and prepare financial reports concerning operating procedures. Collect and analyze data to detect deficient controls; duplicated effort; extravagance; fraud; or non-compliance with laws, regulations, and management policies. Report to management about asset utilization and audit results and recommend changes in operations and financial activities. Prepare detailed reports on audit findings. Review data about material assets, net worth, liabilities, capital stock, surplus, income, and expenditures. Inspect account books and accounting systems for efficiency, effectiveness, and use of accepted accounting procedures to record transactions. Examine and evaluate financial and information systems, recommending controls to ensure system reliability and data integrity. Supervise auditing of establishments and determine scope of investigation required. Prepare, analyze, and verify annual reports, financial statements, and other records, using accepted accounting and statistical procedures to assess financial condition and facilitate financial planning. Confer with company officials about financial and regulatory matters. Inspect cash on hand, notes receivable and payable, negotiable securities, and canceled checks to confirm records are accurate. Examine inventory to verify journal and ledger entries. Examine whether the organization's objectives are reflected in its management activities and whether employees understand the objectives. Examine records and interview workers to ensure recording of transactions and compliance with laws and regulations. Direct activities of personnel engaged in filing, recording, compiling, and transmitting financial records. Produce up-to-the-minute information, using internal computer systems, to allow management to base decisions on actual, not historical, data. Conduct pre-implementation audits to determine if systems and programs under development will work as planned. **SKILLS—Management of Financial Resources:** Determining how money will be spent to get the work done and accounting for these expenditures. **Time Management:** Managing one's own time and the time of others. **Instructing:** Teaching others how to do something. **Negotiation:** Bringing others together and trying to reconcile differences. **Service Orientation:** Actively looking for ways to help people. **Writing:** Communicating effectively in writing as appropriate for the needs of the audience. **Critical Thinking:** Using logic and reasoning to identify the strengths and weaknesses of alternative solutions, conclusions, or approaches to problems. **Persuasion:** Persuading others to change their minds or behavior.

GOE—**Interest Area:** 04. Business and Administration. **Work Group:** 04.05. Accounting, Auditing, and Analytical Support. **Other Jobs in This Work Group:** Accountants; Budget Analysts; Industrial Engineering Technicians; Logisticians; Management Analysts; Operations Research Analysts. **PERSONALITY TYPE:** Conventional. Conventional occupations frequently involve following set procedures and routines. These occupations can include working with data and details more than with ideas. Usually there is a clear line of authority to follow.

EDUCATION/TRAINING PROGRAM(S)— Accounting; Accounting and Business/Management; Accounting and Computer Science; Accounting and Finance; Auditing; Taxation. **RELATED KNOWLEDGE/COURSES—Economics and Accounting:** Knowledge of economic and accounting principles and practices, the financial markets, banking, and the analysis and reporting of financial data. **Customer and Personal Service:** Knowledge of principles and processes for providing customer and personal services. This includes customer needs assessment, meeting quality standards for services, and evaluation of customer satisfaction. **Mathematics:** Knowledge of arithmetic, algebra, geometry, calculus, and statistics and their applications. **Sales and Marketing:** Knowledge of principles and methods for showing, promoting, and selling products or services. This includes marketing strategy and tactics, product demonstration, sales techniques, and sales control systems. **Law and Government:** Knowledge of laws, legal codes, court procedures, precedents, government regulations, executive orders, agency rules, and the democratic political process. **Computers and Electronics:** Knowledge of circuit boards, processors, chips, electronic equipment, and computer hardware and software, including applications and programming.

Biochemists

- Education/Training Required: Doctoral degree
- Annual Earnings: $64,390
- Growth: 22.9%
- Annual Job Openings: 2,000
- Self-Employed: 2.6%
- Part-Time: 7.1%

Research or study chemical composition and processes of living organisms that affect vital processes such as growth and aging to determine chemical actions and effects on organisms such as the action of foods, drugs, or other substances on body functions and tissues. Study chemistry of living processes, such as cell development, breathing, and digestion, and living energy changes, such as growth, aging, and death. Research methods of transferring characteristics, such as resistance to disease, from one organism to another. Examine chemical aspects of formation of antibodies and research chemistry of cells and blood corpuscles. Develop and execute tests to detect disease, genetic disorders, or other abnormalities. Develop and test new drugs and medications used for commercial distribution. Design and build laboratory equipment needed for special research projects. Analyze foods to determine nutritional value and effects of cooking, canning, and processing on this value. Clean, purify, refine, and otherwise prepare pharmaceutical compounds for commercial distribution. Prepare reports and recommendations based upon research outcomes. Develop methods to process, store, and use food, drugs, and chemical compounds. Isolate, analyze, and identify hormones, vitamins, allergens, minerals, and enzymes and determine their effects on body functions. Research and determine chemical action of substances such as drugs, serums, hormones, and food on tissues and vital processes. **SKILLS—Science:** Using scientific rules and methods to solve problems. **Writing:** Communicating effectively in writing as appropriate for the needs of the audience. **Reading Comprehension:** Understanding written sentences and paragraphs in work-related documents. **Active Learning:** Understanding the implications of new information for both current and future problem-solving and decision-making. **Programming:** Writing computer programs for various purposes. **Critical Thinking:** Using logic and reasoning to identify the strengths and weaknesses of alternative solutions, conclusions, or approaches to problems. **Mathematics:** Using mathematics to solve problems. **Equipment Selection:** Determining the kind of tools and equipment needed to do a job.

GOE—Interest Area: 15. Scientific Research, Engineering, and Mathematics. **Work Group:** 15.03. Life Sciences. **Other Jobs in This Work Group:** Biologists; Biophysicists; Environmental Scientists and Specialists, Including Health; Epidemiologists; Medical Scientists, Except Epidemiologists; Microbiologists. **PERSONALITY TYPE:** Investigative. Investigative occupations frequently involve working with ideas and require an extensive amount of thinking. These occupations can involve searching for facts and figuring out problems mentally.

EDUCATION/TRAINING PROGRAM(S)— Biochemistry; Biochemistry/Biophysics and Molecular Biology; Biophysics; Cell/Cellular Biology and Anatomical Sciences, Other; Molecular Biochemistry; Molecular Biophysics; Soil Chemistry and Physics; Soil Microbiology. **RELATED KNOWLEDGE/COURSES—Biology:** Knowledge of plant and animal organisms and their tissues, cells, functions, interdependencies, and interactions with each other and the environment. **Chemistry:** Knowledge of the chemical composition, structure, and properties of substances and of the chemical processes and transformations that they undergo. This includes uses of chemicals and their danger signs, production techniques, and disposal methods. **Mathematics:** Knowledge of arithmetic, algebra, geometry, calculus, and statistics and their applications. **Building and Construction:** Knowledge of the materials, methods, and tools involved in the construction or repair of houses, buildings, or other structures such as highways and roads. **Engineering and Technolo-**

gy: Knowledge of the practical application of engineering science and technology. This includes applying principles, techniques, procedures, and equipment to the design and production of various goods and services. **English Language:** Knowledge of the structure and content of the English language, including the meaning and spelling of words, rules of composition, and grammar.

Biological Science Teachers, Postsecondary

- ◎ Education/Training Required: Master's degree
- ◎ Annual Earnings: $60,850
- ◎ Growth: 38.1% for all Postsecondary Teachers
- ◎ Annual Job Openings: 216,000 for all Postsecondary Teachers
- ◎ Self-Employed: 0.3% for all Postsecondary Teachers
- ◎ Part-Time: 27.7% for all Postsecondary Teachers

Teach courses in biological sciences. Evaluate and grade students' class work, laboratory work, assignments, and papers. Prepare and deliver lectures to undergraduate and/or graduate students on topics such as molecular biology, marine biology, and botany. Advise students on academic and vocational curricula and on career issues. Compile, administer, and grade examinations or assign this work to others. Compile bibliographies of specialized materials for outside reading assignments. Initiate, facilitate, and moderate classroom discussions. Keep abreast of developments in their field by reading current literature, talking with colleagues, and participating in professional conferences. Maintain regularly scheduled office hours in order to advise and assist students. Maintain student attendance records, grades, and other required records. Plan, evaluate, and revise curricula, course content, and course materials and methods of instruction. Prepare course materials such as syllabi, homework assignments, and handouts. Select and obtain materials and supplies such as textbooks and laboratory equipment. Supervise students' laboratory work. Supervise undergraduate and/or graduate teaching, internship, and research work. Act as advisers to student organizations. Collaborate with colleagues to address teaching and research issues. Conduct research in a particular field of knowledge and publish findings in professional journals, books, and/or electronic media. Participate in campus and community events. Participate in student recruitment, registration, and placement activities. Perform administrative duties such as serving as department head. Provide professional consulting services to government and/or industry. Serve on academic or administrative committees that deal with institutional policies, departmental matters, and academic issues. Write grant proposals to procure external research funding. **SKILLS—Science:** Using scientific rules and methods to solve problems. **Instructing:** Teaching others how to do something. **Learning Strategies:** Selecting and using training/instructional methods and procedures appropriate for the situation when learning or teaching new things. **Reading Comprehension:** Understanding written sentences and paragraphs in work-related documents. **Active Learning:** Understanding the implications of new information for both current and future problem-solving and decision-making. **Writing:** Communicating effectively in writing as appropriate for the needs of the audience. **Critical Thinking:** Using logic and reasoning to identify the strengths and weaknesses of alternative solutions, conclusions, or approaches to problems. **Mathematics:** Using mathematics to solve problems.

GOE—Interest Area: 05. Education and Training. **Work Group:** 05.03. Postsecondary and Adult Teaching and Instructing. **Other Jobs in This Work Group:** Adult Literacy, Remedial Education, and

GED Teachers and Instructors; Agricultural Sciences Teachers, Postsecondary; Anthropology and Archeology Teachers, Postsecondary; Architecture Teachers, Postsecondary; Area, Ethnic, and Cultural Studies Teachers, Postsecondary; Art, Drama, and Music Teachers, Postsecondary; Atmospheric, Earth, Marine, and Space Sciences Teachers, Postsecondary; Business Teachers, Postsecondary; Chemistry Teachers, Postsecondary; Communications Teachers, Postsecondary; Computer Science Teachers, Postsecondary; Criminal Justice and Law Enforcement Teachers, Postsecondary; Economics Teachers, Postsecondary; Education Teachers, Postsecondary; Engineering Teachers, Postsecondary; English Language and Literature Teachers, Postsecondary; Environmental Science Teachers, Postsecondary; Farm and Home Management Advisors; Foreign Language and Literature Teachers, Postsecondary; Forestry and Conservation Science Teachers, Postsecondary; Geography Teachers, Postsecondary; Graduate Teaching Assistants; Health Specialties Teachers, Postsecondary; History Teachers, Postsecondary; Home Economics Teachers, Postsecondary; Law Teachers, Postsecondary; Library Science Teachers, Postsecondary; Mathematical Science Teachers, Postsecondary; Nursing Instructors and Teachers, Postsecondary; Philosophy and Religion Teachers, Postsecondary; Physics Teachers, Postsecondary; Political Science Teachers, Postsecondary; Psychology Teachers, Postsecondary; Recreation and Fitness Studies Teachers, Postsecondary; Self-Enrichment Education Teachers; Social Work Teachers, Postsecondary; Sociology Teachers, Postsecondary; Vocational Education Teachers, Postsecondary. **PERSONALITY TYPE:** Investigative. Investigative occupations frequently involve working with ideas and require an extensive amount of thinking. These occupations can involve searching for facts and figuring out problems mentally.

EDUCATION/TRAINING PROGRAM(S)— Anatomy; Animal Physiology; Biochemistry; Biological and Biomedical Sciences, Other; Biology/Biological Sciences, General; Biometry/Biometrics; Biophysics; Biotechnology; Botany/

Plant Biology; Cell/Cellular Biology and Histology; Ecology; Ecology, Evolution, Systematics, and Population Biology, Other; Entomology; Evolutionary Biology; Immunology; Marine Biology and Biological Oceanography; Microbiology, General; Molecular Biology; Neuroscience; Nutrition Sciences; Parasitology; Pathology/Experimental Pathology; Pharmacology; Plant Genetics; Plant Pathology/Phytopathology; Plant Physiology; Radiation Biology/Radiobiology; Toxicology; Virology; Zoology/Animal Biology. **RELATED KNOWLEDGE/COURSES—Biology:** Knowledge of plant and animal organisms and their tissues, cells, functions, interdependencies, and interactions with each other and the environment. **Education and Training:** Knowledge of principles and methods for curriculum and training design, teaching and instruction for individuals and groups, and the measurement of training effects. **Medicine and Dentistry:** Knowledge of the information and techniques needed to diagnose and treat human injuries, diseases, and deformities. This includes symptoms, treatment alternatives, drug properties and interactions, and preventive health-care measures. **Chemistry:** Knowledge of the chemical composition, structure, and properties of substances and of the chemical processes and transformations that they undergo. This includes uses of chemicals and their danger signs, production techniques, and disposal methods. **Therapy and Counseling:** Knowledge of principles, methods, and procedures for diagnosis, treatment, and rehabilitation of physical and mental dysfunctions and for career counseling and guidance. **Psychology:** Knowledge of human behavior and performance; individual differences in ability, personality, and interests; learning and motivation; psychological research methods; and the assessment and treatment of behavioral and affective disorders.

Biological Technicians

- Education/Training Required: Associate's degree
- Annual Earnings: $33,360
- Growth: 19.4%
- Annual Job Openings: 7,000
- Self-Employed: 0.1%
- Part-Time: 9.7%

Assist biological and medical scientists in laboratories. Set up, operate, and maintain laboratory instruments and equipment, monitor experiments, make observations, and calculate and record results. May analyze organic substances, such as blood, food, and drugs. Keep detailed logs of all work-related activities. Monitor laboratory work to ensure compliance with set standards. Isolate, identify, and prepare specimens for examination. Use computers, computer-interfaced equipment, robotics, and high-technology industrial applications to perform work duties. Conduct, or assist in conducting, research, including the collection of information and samples such as blood, water, soil, plants, and animals. Set up, adjust, calibrate, clean, maintain, and troubleshoot laboratory and field equipment. Provide technical support and services for scientists and engineers working in fields such as agriculture, environmental science, resource management, biology, and health sciences. Clean, maintain, and prepare supplies and work areas. Participate in the research, development, and manufacturing of medicinal and pharmaceutical preparations. Conduct standardized biological, microbiological, and biochemical tests and laboratory analyses to evaluate the quantity or quality of physical or chemical substances in food and other products. Analyze experimental data and interpret results to write reports and summaries of findings. Measure or weigh compounds and solutions for use in testing or animal feed. Monitor and observe experiments, recording production and test data for evaluation by research personnel. Examine animals and specimens to detect the presence of disease or other problems. Conduct or supervise operational programs such as fish hatcheries, greenhouses, and livestock production programs. **SKILLS—Science:** Using scientific rules and methods to solve problems. **Active Learning:** Understanding the implications of new information for both current and future problem-solving and decision-making. **Instructing:** Teaching others how to do something. **Learning Strategies:** Selecting and using training/instructional methods and procedures appropriate for the situation when learning or teaching new things. **Equipment Maintenance:** Performing routine maintenance on equipment and determining when and what kind of maintenance is needed. **Troubleshooting:** Determining causes of operating errors and deciding what to do about them. **Technology Design:** Generating or adapting equipment and technology to serve user needs. **Service Orientation:** Actively looking for ways to help people. **Quality Control Analysis:** Conducting tests and inspections of products, services, or processes to evaluate quality or performance.

GOE—Interest Area: 08. Health Science. **Work Group:** 08.06. Medical Technology. **Other Jobs in This Work Group:** Cardiovascular Technologists and Technicians; Diagnostic Medical Sonographers; Medical and Clinical Laboratory Technicians; Medical and Clinical Laboratory Technologists; Medical Equipment Preparers; Medical Records and Health Information Technicians; Nuclear Medicine Technologists; Opticians, Dispensing; Orthotists and Prosthetists; Radiologic Technicians; Radiologic Technologists. **PERSONALITY TYPE:** Realistic. Realistic occupations frequently involve work activities that include practical, hands-on problems and solutions. They often deal with plants, animals, and real-world materials like wood, tools, and machinery. Many of the occupations require working outside and do not involve a lot of paperwork or working closely with others.

EDUCATION/TRAINING PROGRAM(S)— Biology Technician/Biotechnology Laboratory Technician. **RELATED KNOWLEDGE/**

COURSES—Chemistry: Knowledge of the chemical composition, structure, and properties of substances and of the chemical processes and transformations that they undergo. This includes uses of chemicals and their danger signs, production techniques, and disposal methods. **Biology:** Knowledge of plant and animal organisms and their tissues, cells, functions, interdependencies, and interactions with each other and the environment. **Mathematics:** Knowledge of arithmetic, algebra, geometry, calculus, and statistics and their applications. **English Language:** Knowledge of the structure and content of the English language, including the meaning and spelling of words, rules of composition, and grammar. **Production and Processing:** Knowledge of raw materials, production processes, quality control, costs, and other techniques for maximizing the effective manufacture and distribution of goods. **Geography:** Knowledge of principles and methods for describing the features of land, sea, and air masses, including their physical characteristics; locations; interrelationships; and distribution of plant, animal, and human life.

Biologists

- Education/Training Required: Doctoral degree
- Annual Earnings: $64,390
- Growth: 22.3%
- Annual Job Openings: 3,000
- Self-Employed: 2.7%
- Part-Time: 7.1%

Research or study basic principles of plant and animal life, such as origin, relationship, development, anatomy, and functions. Develop and maintain liaisons and effective working relations with groups and individuals, agencies, and the public to encourage cooperative management strategies or to develop information and interpret findings. Program and use computers to store, process, and analyze data. Collect and analyze biological data about relationships among and between organisms and their environment. Study aquatic plants and animals and environmental conditions affecting them, such as radioactivity or pollution. Communicate test results to state and federal representatives and general public. Identify, classify, and study structure, behavior, ecology, physiology, nutrition, culture, and distribution of plant and animal species. Prepare environmental impact reports for industry, government, or publication. Represent employer in a technical capacity at conferences. Plan and administer biological research programs for government, research firms, medical industries, or manufacturing firms. Research environmental effects of present and potential uses of land and water areas, determining methods of improving environmental conditions or such outputs as crop yields. Review reports such as those relating to land use classifications and recreational development for accuracy and adequacy. Measure salinity, acidity, light, oxygen content, and other physical conditions of water to determine their relationship to aquatic life. Teach, supervise students, and perform research at universities and colleges. Supervise biological technicians and technologists and other scientists. Study basic principles of plant and animal life, such as origin, relationship, development, anatomy, and functions. Study and manage wild animal populations. Prepare requests for proposals or statements of work. Cultivate, breed, and grow aquatic life, such as lobsters, clams, or fish. Prepare plans for management of renewable resources. **SKILLS—Negotiation:** Bringing others together and trying to reconcile differences. **Persuasion:** Persuading others to change their minds or behavior. **Management of Financial Resources:** Determining how money will be spent to get the work done and accounting for these expenditures. **Science:** Using scientific rules and methods to solve problems. **Judgment and Decision Making:** Considering the relative costs and benefits of potential actions to choose the most appropriate one. **Active Learning:** Understanding the implications of new information for both current and future problem-solving and decision-making. **Management of Material Resources:** Obtaining and seeing to the appropriate use of equipment, facilities, and materials needed to do certain work. **Critical Thinking:** Using logic and reasoning to identify the strengths and weaknesses of alternative solutions, conclusions, or approaches to problems.

GOE—Interest Area: 15. Scientific Research, Engineering, and Mathematics. **Work Group:** 15.03. Life Sciences. **Other Jobs in This Work Group:** Biochemists; Biophysicists; Environmental Scientists and Specialists, Including Health; Epidemiologists; Medical Scientists, Except Epidemiologists; Microbiologists. **PERSONALITY TYPE:** Investigative. Investigative occupations frequently involve working with ideas and require an extensive amount of thinking. These occupations can involve searching for facts and figuring out problems mentally.

EDUCATION/TRAINING PROGRAM(S)— Biochemistry; Biochemistry/Biophysics and Molecular Biology; Biology/Biological Sciences, General; Biophysics; Cell/Cellular Biology, and Anatomical Sciences, Other; Molecular Biochemistry; Soil Microbiology. **RELATED KNOWLEDGE/COURSES—Biology:** Knowledge of plant and animal organisms and their tissues, cells, functions, interdependencies, and interactions with each other and the environment. **Law and Government:** Knowledge of laws, legal codes, court procedures, precedents, government regulations, executive orders, agency rules, and the democratic political process. **Chemistry:** Knowledge of the chemical composition, structure, and properties of substances and of the chemical processes and transformations that they undergo. This includes uses of chemicals and their danger signs, production techniques, and disposal methods. **Geography:** Knowledge of principles and methods for describing the features of land, sea, and air masses, including their physical characteristics; locations; interrelationships; and distribution of plant, animal, and human life. **Computers and Electronics:** Knowledge of circuit boards, processors, chips, electronic equipment, and computer hardware and software, including applications and programming. **Physics:** Knowledge and prediction of physical principles and laws and their interrelationships and applications to understanding fluid, material, and atmospheric dynamics and mechanical, electrical, atomic, and subatomic structures and processes. **Public Safety and Security:** Knowledge of relevant equipment, policies, procedures, and strategies to promote effective local, state, or national security operations for the protection of people, data, property, and institutions.

Biomedical Engineers

- ◎ Education/Training Required: Bachelor's degree
- ◎ Annual Earnings: $64,780
- ◎ Growth: 26.1%
- ◎ Annual Job Openings: Fewer than 500
- ◎ Self-Employed: 4.9%
- ◎ Part-Time: 2.8%

Apply knowledge of engineering, biology, and biomechanical principles to the design, development, and evaluation of biological and health systems and products, such as artificial organs, prostheses, instrumentation, medical information systems, and health management and care delivery systems. Develop new applications for energy sources, such as using nuclear power for biomedical implants. Diagnose and interpret bioelectric data, using signal processing techniques. Teach biomedical engineering or disseminate knowledge about field through writing or consulting. Advise and assist in the application of instrumentation in clinical environments. Conduct research, along with life scientists, chemists, and medical scientists, on the engineering aspects of the biological systems of humans and animals. Design and develop medical diagnostic and clinical instrumentation, equipment, and procedures, utilizing the principles of engineering and bio-behavioral sciences. Develop models or computer simulations of human bio-behavioral systems in order to obtain data for measuring or controlling life processes. Evaluate the safety, efficiency, and effectiveness of biomedical equipment. Install, adjust, maintain, and/or repair biomedical equipment. Research new materials to be used for products such as implanted artificial organs. Adapt or design computer hardware or software for medical science uses. Advise hospital administrators on the planning, acquisition, and use of medical equipment. Analyze new medical procedures in order to forecast likely outcomes. Design and deliver technology to assist people with disabilities. **SKILLS—** No data available.

GOE—Interest Area: 15. Scientific Research, Engineering, and Mathematics. **Work Group:** 15.07. Research and Design Engineering. **Other Jobs in This Work Group:** Aerospace Engineers; Chemical Engineers; Civil Engineers; Computer Hardware Engineers; Electrical Engineers; Electronics Engineers, Except Computer; Marine Architects; Marine Engineers; Materials Engineers; Mechanical Engineers; Nuclear Engineers. **PERSONALITY TYPE:** No data available.

EDUCATION/TRAINING PROGRAM(S)— Biomedical/Medical Engineering. **RELATED KNOWLEDGE/COURSES—**No data available.

Biophysicists

- ◎ Education/Training Required: Doctoral degree
- ◎ Annual Earnings: $64,390
- ◎ Growth: 22.9%
- ◎ Annual Job Openings: 2,000
- ◎ Self-Employed: 2.6%
- ◎ Part-Time: 7.1%

Research or study physical principles of living cells and organisms, their electrical and mechanical

energy, and related phenomena. Researches transformation of substances in cells, using atomic isotopes. Studies physical principles of living cells and organisms and their electrical and mechanical energy. Investigates transmission of electrical impulses along nerves and muscles. Studies absorption of light by chlorophyll in photosynthesis or by pigments of eye involved in vision. Researches cancer treatment, using radiation and nuclear particles. Analyzes functions of electronic and human brains, such as learning, thinking, and memory. Investigates dynamics of seeing and hearing. Studies spatial configuration of submicroscopic molecules, such as proteins, using X-ray and electron microscope. Researches manner in which characteristics of plants and animals are carried through successive generations. Investigates damage to cells and tissues caused by X rays and nuclear particles. **SKILLS—Science:** Using scientific rules and methods to solve problems. **Reading Comprehension:** Understanding written sentences and paragraphs in work-related documents. **Writing:** Communicating effectively in writing as appropriate for the needs of the audience. **Mathematics:** Using mathematics to solve problems. **Active Learning:** Understanding the implications of new information for both current and future problem-solving and decision-making. **Critical Thinking:** Using logic and reasoning to identify the strengths and weaknesses of alternative solutions, conclusions, or approaches to problems. **Complex Problem Solving:** Identifying complex problems and reviewing related information to develop and evaluate options and implement solutions. **Programming:** Writing computer programs for various purposes.

GOE—Interest Area: 15. Scientific Research, Engineering, and Mathematics. **Work Group:** 15.03. Life Sciences. **Other Jobs in This Work Group:** Biochemists; Biologists; Environmental Scientists and Specialists, Including Health; Epidemiologists; Medical Scientists, Except Epidemiologists; Microbiologists. **PERSONALITY TYPE:** Investigative. Investigative occupations frequently involve working with ideas and require an extensive amount of thinking. These occupations can involve searching for facts and figuring out problems mentally.

EDUCATION/TRAINING PROGRAM(S)— Biochemistry; Biochemistry/Biophysics and Molecular Biology; Biophysics; Cell/Cellular Biology and Anatomical Sciences, Other; Molecular Biochemistry; Molecular Biophysics; Soil Chemistry and Physics; Soil Microbiology. **RELATED KNOWLEDGE/COURSES—Biology:** Knowledge of plant and animal organisms and their tissues, cells, functions, interdependencies, and interactions with each other and the environment. **Physics:** Knowledge and prediction of physical principles and laws and their interrelationships and applications to understanding fluid, material, and atmospheric dynamics and mechanical, electrical, atomic, and subatomic structures and processes. **Mathematics:** Knowledge of arithmetic, algebra, geometry, calculus, and statistics and their applications. **Chemistry:** Knowledge of the chemical composition, structure, and properties of substances and of the chemical processes and transformations that they undergo. This includes uses of chemicals and their danger signs, production techniques, and disposal methods.

Budget Analysts

- ◎ Education/Training Required: Bachelor's degree
- ◎ Annual Earnings: $55,090
- ◎ Growth: 14.0%
- ◎ Annual Job Openings: 8,000
- ◎ Self-Employed: 0%
- ◎ Part-Time: 4.7%

Examine budget estimates for completeness, accuracy, and conformance with procedures and regulations. Analyze budgeting and accounting reports for the purpose of maintaining expenditure controls. Analyze monthly department budgeting and accounting reports to maintain expenditure controls. Direct the preparation of regular and special budget reports. Consult with managers to ensure that budget adjustments are made in accordance with program changes. Match appropriations for specific programs with appropriations for broader programs, including items for emergency funds. Provide advice and technical assistance with cost analysis, fiscal allocation, and budget preparation. Summarize budgets and submit recommendations for the approval or disapproval of funds requests. Seek new ways to improve efficiency and increase profits. Review operating budgets to analyze trends affecting budget needs. Examine budget estimates for completeness, accuracy, and conformance with procedures and regulations. Perform cost-benefits analyses to compare operating programs, review financial requests, and explore alternative financing methods. Interpret budget directives and establish policies for carrying out directives. Compile and analyze accounting records and other data to determine the financial resources required to implement a program. Testify before examining and fund-granting authorities, clarifying and promoting the proposed budgets. **SKILLS—Management of Financial Resources:** Determining how money will be spent to get the work done and accounting for these expenditures. **Operations Analysis:** Analyzing needs and product requirements to create a design. **Mathematics:** Using mathematics to solve problems. **Service Orientation:** Actively looking for ways to help people. **Negotiation:** Bringing others together and trying to reconcile differences. **Time Management:** Managing one's own time and the time of others. **Active Learning:** Understanding the implications of new information for both current and future problem-solving and decision-making. **Monitoring:** Monitoring or assessing your performance or that of other individuals or organizations to make improvements or take corrective action.

GOE—Interest Area: 04. Business and Administration. **Work Group:** 04.05. Accounting, Auditing, and Analytical Support. **Other Jobs in This Work Group:** Accountants; Auditors; Industrial Engineering Technicians; Logisticians; Management Analysts; Operations Research Analysts. **PERSONALITY TYPE:** Conventional. Conventional occupations frequently involve following set procedures and routines. These occupations can include working with data and details more than with ideas. Usually there is a clear line of authority to follow.

EDUCATION/TRAINING PROGRAM(S)— Accounting; Finance, General. **RELATED KNOWLEDGE/COURSES—Economics and Accounting:** Knowledge of economic and accounting principles and practices, the financial markets, banking, and the analysis and reporting of financial data. **Administration and Management:** Knowledge of business and management principles involved in strategic planning, resource allocation, human resources modeling, leadership technique, production methods, and coordination of people and resources. **Clerical Practices:** Knowledge of administrative and clerical procedures and systems such as word processing, managing files and records, stenography and transcription, designing forms, and other office procedures and terminology. **Computers and Electronics:** Knowledge of circuit boards, processors, chips, electronic equipment, and computer hardware and software, including applications and programming. **Mathematics:** Knowledge of arithmetic, algebra, geometry, calculus, and statistics and their applications. **English Language:** Knowledge of the structure and content of the English language, including the meaning and spelling of words, rules of composition, and grammar.

Business Teachers, Postsecondary

◉ Education/Training Required: Master's degree

◉ Annual Earnings: $56,560

◉ Growth: 38.1% for all Postsecondary Teachers

◉ Annual Job Openings: 216,000 for all Postsecondary Teachers

◉ Self-Employed: 0.3% for all Postsecondary Teachers

◉ Part-Time: 27.7% for all Postsecondary Teachers

Teach courses in business administration and management, such as accounting, finance, human resources, labor relations, marketing, and operations research. Prepare course materials such as syllabi, homework assignments, and handouts. Select and obtain materials and supplies such as textbooks. Supervise undergraduate and/or graduate teaching, internship, and research work. Act as advisers to student organizations. Collaborate with colleagues to address teaching and research issues. Collaborate with members of the business community to improve programs, to develop new programs, and to provide student access to learning opportunities such as internships. Conduct research in a particular field of knowledge and publish findings in professional journals, books, and/or electronic media. Participate in campus and community events. Participate in student recruitment, registration, and placement activities. Perform administrative duties such as serving as department head. Provide professional consulting services to government and/or industry. Serve on academic or administrative committees that deal with institutional policies, departmental matters, and academic issues. Write grant proposals to procure external research funding. Evaluate and grade students' class work, assignments, and papers. Prepare and deliver lectures to undergraduate and/or graduate students on topics such as financial accounting, principles of marketing, and operations management. Advise students on academic and vocational curricula and on career issues. Compile, administer, and grade examinations or assign this work to others. Compile bibliographies of specialized materials for outside reading assignments. Initiate, facilitate, and moderate classroom discussions. Keep abreast of developments in their field by reading current literature, talking with colleagues, and participating in professional organizations and conferences. Maintain regularly scheduled office hours in order to advise and assist students. Maintain student attendance records, grades, and other required records. Plan, evaluate, and revise curricula, course content, and course materials and methods of instruction. **SKILLS—** No data available.

GOE—Interest Area: 05. Education and Training. **Work Group:** 05.03. Postsecondary and Adult Teaching and Instructing. **Other Jobs in This Work Group:** Adult Literacy, Remedial Education, and GED Teachers and Instructors; Agricultural Sciences Teachers, Postsecondary; Anthropology and Archeology Teachers, Postsecondary; Architecture Teachers, Postsecondary; Area, Ethnic, and Cultural Studies Teachers, Postsecondary; Art, Drama, and Music Teachers, Postsecondary; Atmospheric, Earth, Marine, and Space Sciences Teachers, Postsecondary; Biological Science Teachers, Postsecondary; Chemistry Teachers, Postsecondary; Communications Teachers, Postsecondary; Computer Science Teachers, Postsecondary; Criminal Justice and Law Enforcement Teachers, Postsecondary; Economics Teachers, Postsecondary; Education Teachers, Postsecondary; Engineering Teachers, Postsecondary; English Language and Literature Teachers, Postsecondary; Environmental Science Teachers, Postsecondary; Farm and Home Management Advisors; Foreign Language and Literature Teachers, Postsecondary; Forestry and Conservation Science Teachers, Postsecondary; Geography Teachers, Postsecondary; Graduate Teaching Assistants; Health Specialties Teachers, Postsecondary;

B

History Teachers, Postsecondary; Home Economics Teachers, Postsecondary; Law Teachers, Postsecondary; Library Science Teachers, Postsecondary; Mathematical Science Teachers, Postsecondary; Nursing Instructors and Teachers, Postsecondary; Philosophy and Religion Teachers, Postsecondary; Physics Teachers, Postsecondary; Political Science Teachers, Postsecondary; Psychology Teachers, Postsecondary; Recreation and Fitness Studies Teachers, Postsecondary; Self-Enrichment Education Teachers; Social Work Teachers, Postsecondary; Sociology Teachers, Postsecondary; Vocational Education Teachers, Postsecondary. **PERSONALITY TYPE:** No data available.

EDUCATION/TRAINING PROGRAM(S)— Accounting; Actuarial Science; Business Administration and Management, General; Business Statistics; Business Teacher Education; Business/Commerce, General; Business/Corporate Communications; Entrepreneurship/Entrepreneurial Studies; Finance, General; Financial Planning and Services; Franchising and Franchise Operations; Human Resources Management/Personnel Administration, General; Insurance; International Business/Trade/Commerce; International Finance; International Marketing; Investments and Securities; Labor and Industrial Relations; Logistics and Materials Management; Management Science, General; Marketing Research; Marketing/Marketing Management, General; Operations Management and Supervision; Organizational Behavior Studies; Public Finance; Purchasing, Procurement/Acquisitions, and Contracts Management. **RELATED KNOWLEDGE/COURSES—**No data available.

Calibration and Instrumentation Technicians

- ◎ Education/Training Required: Associate's degree
- ◎ Annual Earnings: $45,390
- ◎ Growth: 10.0%
- ◎ Annual Job Openings: 24,000
- ◎ Self-Employed: 0.4%
- ◎ Part-Time: 5.0%

Develop, test, calibrate, operate, and repair electrical, mechanical, electromechanical, electrohydraulic, or electronic measuring and recording instruments, apparatus, and equipment. Plans sequence of testing and calibration program for instruments and equipment according to blueprints, schematics, technical manuals, and other specifications. Performs preventative and corrective maintenance of test apparatus and peripheral equipment. Confers with engineers, supervisor, and other technical workers to assist with equipment installation, maintenance, and repair techniques. Analyzes and converts test data, using mathematical formulas, and reports results and proposed modifications. Sets up test equipment and conducts tests on performance and reliability of mechanical, structural, or electromechanical equipment. Selects sensing, telemetering, and recording instrumentation and circuitry. Disassembles and reassembles instruments and equipment, using hand tools, and inspects instruments and equipment for defects. Sketches plans for developing jigs, fixtures, instruments, and related nonstandard apparatus. Modifies performance and operation of component parts and circuitry to specifications, using test equipment and precision instruments. **SKILLS—Technology Design:** Generating or adapting equipment and technology to serve user needs. **Equipment Maintenance:** Performing routine maintenance on equipment and determining when and what kind of maintenance is needed. **Quality Control Analysis:** Conducting tests and inspections of products, services, or processes to evaluate quality or performance. **Science:** Using scientific rules and methods to solve problems. **Equipment Selection:** Determining the kind of tools and equipment needed to do a job. **Troubleshooting:** Determining causes of operating errors and deciding what to do about them. **Installation:** Installing equipment, machines, wiring, or programs to meet specifications. **Operations Analysis:** Analyzing needs and product requirements to create a design.

GOE—Interest Area: 15. Scientific Research, Engineering, and Mathematics. **Work Group:** 15.09. Engineering Technology. **Other Jobs in This Work Group:** Aerospace Engineering and Operations Technicians; Cartographers and Photogrammetrists; Civil Engineering Technicians; Electrical Engineering Technicians; Electro-Mechanical Technicians; Electronic Drafters; Electronics Engineering Technicians; Environmental Engineering Technicians; Mapping Technicians; Mechanical Drafters; Mechanical Engineering Technicians; Surveying Technicians. **PERSONALITY TYPE:** Realistic. Realistic occupations frequently involve work activities that include practical, hands-on problems and solutions. They often deal with plants, animals, and real-world materials like wood, tools, and machinery. Many of the occupations require working outside and do not involve a lot of paperwork or working closely with others.

EDUCATION/TRAINING PROGRAM(S)— Computer Engineering Technology/Technician; Computer Technology/Computer Systems Technology; Electrical and Electronic Engineering Technologies/Technicians, Other; Electrical, Electronic, and Communications Engineering Technology/Technician; Telecommunications Technology/Technician. **RELATED KNOWLEDGE/COURSES—Design:** Knowledge of design techniques, tools, and principles involved in production of precision technical plans, blueprints, drawings, and models. **Mathematics:** Knowledge of arith-

metic, algebra, geometry, calculus, and statistics and their applications. **Computers and Electronics:** Knowledge of circuit boards, processors, chips, electronic equipment, and computer hardware and software, including applications and programming. **Engineering and Technology:** Knowledge of the practical application of engineering science and technology. This includes applying principles, techniques, procedures, and equipment to the design and production of various goods and services. **Mechanical Devices:** Knowledge of machines and tools, including their designs, uses, repair, and maintenance. **Physics:** Knowledge and prediction of physical principles and laws and their interrelationships and applications to understanding fluid, material, and atmospheric dynamics and mechanical, electrical, atomic, and subatomic structures and processes.

Cardiovascular Technologists and Technicians

- ◉ Education/Training Required: Associate's degree
- ◉ Annual Earnings: $37,800
- ◉ Growth: 33.5%
- ◉ Annual Job Openings: 6,000
- ◉ Self-Employed: 0.2%
- ◉ Part-Time: 17.5%

Conduct tests on pulmonary or cardiovascular systems of patients for diagnostic purposes. May conduct or assist in electrocardiograms, cardiac catheterizations, pulmonary-functions, lung capacity, and similar tests. Monitor patients' blood pressure and heart rate, using electrocardiogram (EKG) equipment during diagnostic and therapeutic procedures in order to notify the physician if something appears wrong. Monitor patients' comfort and safety during tests, alerting physicians to abnormalities or changes in patient responses. Explain testing procedures to patient to obtain cooperation and reduce anxiety. Prepare reports of diagnostic procedures for interpretation by physician. Observe gauges, recorder, and video screens of data analysis system during imaging of cardiovascular system. Conduct electrocardiogram, phonocardiogram, echocardiogram, stress testing, and other cardiovascular tests to record patients' cardiac activity, using specialized electronic test equipment, recording devices, and laboratory instruments. Prepare and position patients for testing. Obtain and record patient identification, medical history, and test results. Attach electrodes to the patients' chests, arms, and legs; connect electrodes to leads from the electrocardiogram (EKG) machine; and operate the EKG machine to obtain a reading. Adjust equipment and controls according to physicians' orders or established protocol. Check, test, and maintain cardiology equipment, making minor repairs when necessary, to ensure proper operation. Supervise and train other cardiology technologists and students. Assist physicians in diagnosis and treatment of cardiac and peripheral vascular treatments, for example, assisting with balloon angioplasties to treat blood vessel blockages. Operate diagnostic imaging equipment to produce contrast-enhanced radiographs of heart and cardiovascular system. Inject contrast medium into patients' blood vessels. Observe ultrasound display screen and listen to signals to record vascular information such as blood pressure, limb volume changes, oxygen saturation, and cerebral circulation. Assess cardiac physiology and calculate valve areas from blood flow velocity measurements. Compare measurements of heart wall thickness and chamber sizes to standard norms to identify abnormalities. Activate fluoroscope and camera to produce images used to guide catheter through cardiovascular system. **SKILLS—Instructing:** Teaching others how to do something. **Service Orientation:** Actively looking for ways to help people. **Active Learning:** Understanding the implications of new information for both current and future problem-solving and decision-making. **Oper-**ation Monitoring: Watching gauges, dials, or other indicators to make sure a machine is working properly. **Equipment Maintenance:** Performing routine maintenance on equipment and determining when and what kind of maintenance is needed. **Time Management:** Managing one's own time and the time of others. **Social Perceptiveness:** Being aware of others' reactions and understanding why they react as they do. **Learning Strategies:** Selecting and using training/instructional methods and procedures appropriate for the situation when learning or teaching new things.

GOE—Interest Area: 08. Health Science. **Work Group:** 08.06. Medical Technology. **Other Jobs in This Work Group:** Biological Technicians; Diagnostic Medical Sonographers; Medical and Clinical Laboratory Technicians; Medical and Clinical Laboratory Technologists; Medical Equipment Preparers; Medical Records and Health Information Technicians; Nuclear Medicine Technologists; Opticians, Dispensing; Orthotists and Prosthetists; Radiologic Technicians; Radiologic Technologists. **PERSONALITY TYPE:** Investigative. Investigative occupations frequently involve working with ideas and require an extensive amount of thinking. These occupations can involve searching for facts and figuring out problems mentally.

EDUCATION/TRAINING PROGRAM(S)— Cardiopulmonary Technology/Technologist; Cardiovascular Technology/Technologist; Electrocardiograph Technology/Technician; Perfusion Technology/Perfusionist. **RELATED KNOWLEDGE/COURSES—Customer and Personal Service:** Knowledge of principles and processes for providing customer and personal services. This includes customer needs assessment, meeting quality standards for services, and evaluation of customer satisfaction. **Medicine and Dentistry:** Knowledge of the information and techniques needed to diagnose and treat human injuries, diseases, and deformities. This includes symptoms, treatment alternatives, drug properties and interactions, and preventive health-care measures. **Psychology:** Knowledge of human behavior and performance; individual differences in ability, personality, and interests; learning and motivation; psychological research methods; and the assessment and treatment of behavioral and affective disorders. **Education and Training:** Knowledge of principles and methods for curriculum and training design, teaching and instruction for individuals and groups, and the measurement of training effects. **Physics:** Knowledge and prediction of physical principles and laws and their interrelationships and applications to understanding fluid, material, and atmospheric dynamics and mechanical, electrical, atomic, and subatomic structures and processes. **Computers and Electronics:** Knowledge of circuit boards, processors, chips, electronic equipment, and computer hardware and software, including applications and programming. **English Language:** Knowledge of the structure and content of the English language, including the meaning and spelling of words, rules of composition, and grammar.

Chemical Engineers

◎ Education/Training Required: Bachelor's degree

◎ Annual Earnings: $75,310

◎ Growth: 0.4%

◎ Annual Job Openings: 2,000

◎ Self-Employed: 0.6%

◎ Part-Time: 2.8%

Design chemical plant equipment and devise processes for manufacturing chemicals and products, such as gasoline, synthetic rubber, plastics, detergents, cement, paper, and pulp, by applying principles and technology of chemistry, physics, and engineering. Perform tests throughout stages of production to determine degree of control over variables, including temperature, density, specific gravity, and pressure. Develop safety procedures to be employed by workers operating equipment or work-

ing in close proximity to ongoing chemical reactions. Determine most effective arrangement of operations, such as mixing, crushing, heat transfer, distillation, and drying. Prepare estimate of production costs and production progress reports for management. Direct activities of workers who operate or who are engaged in constructing and improving absorption, evaporation, or electromagnetic equipment. Perform laboratory studies of steps in manufacture of new product and test proposed process in small-scale operation (pilot plant). Develop processes to separate components of liquids or gases or generate electrical currents, using controlled chemical processes. Conduct research to develop new and improved chemical manufacturing processes. Design measurement and control systems for chemical plants based on data collected in laboratory experiments and in pilot plant operations. **SKILLS—Science:** Using scientific rules and methods to solve problems. **Technology Design:** Generating or adapting equipment and technology to serve user needs. **Troubleshooting:** Determining causes of operating errors and deciding what to do about them. **Mathematics:** Using mathematics to solve problems. **Operations Analysis:** Analyzing needs and product requirements to create a design. **Systems Analysis:** Determining how a system should work and how changes in conditions, operations, and the environment will affect outcomes. **Active Learning:** Understanding the implications of new information for both current and future problem-solving and decision-making. **Installation:** Installing equipment, machines, wiring, or programs to meet specifications. **Systems Evaluation:** Identifying measures or indicators of system performance and the actions needed to improve or correct performance relative to the goals of the system.

GOE—Interest Area: 15. Scientific Research, Engineering, and Mathematics. **Work Group:** 15.07. Research and Design Engineering. **Other Jobs in This Work Group:** Aerospace Engineers; Biomedical Engineers; Civil Engineers; Computer Hardware Engineers; Electrical Engineers; Electronics Engineers, Except Computer; Marine Architects;

Marine Engineers; Materials Engineers; Mechanical Engineers; Nuclear Engineers. **PERSONALITY TYPE:** Investigative. Investigative occupations frequently involve working with ideas and require an extensive amount of thinking. These occupations can involve searching for facts and figuring out problems mentally.

EDUCATION/TRAINING PROGRAM(S)— Chemical Engineering. **RELATED KNOWLEDGE/COURSES—Engineering and Technology:** Knowledge of the practical application of engineering science and technology. This includes applying principles, techniques, procedures, and equipment to the design and production of various goods and services. **Chemistry:** Knowledge of the chemical composition, structure, and properties of substances and of the chemical processes and transformations that they undergo. This includes uses of chemicals and their danger signs, production techniques, and disposal methods. **Physics:** Knowledge and prediction of physical principles and laws and their interrelationships and applications to understanding fluid, material, and atmospheric dynamics and mechanical, electrical, atomic, and subatomic structures and processes. **Design:** Knowledge of design techniques, tools, and principles involved in production of precision technical plans, blueprints, drawings, and models. **Production and Processing:** Knowledge of raw materials, production processes, quality control, costs, and other techniques for maximizing the effective manufacture and distribution of goods. **Mathematics:** Knowledge of arithmetic, algebra, geometry, calculus, and statistics and their applications.

Chemistry Teachers, Postsecondary

- Education/Training Required: Master's degree
- Annual Earnings: $56,190
- Growth: 38.1% for all Postsecondary Teachers
- Annual Job Openings: 216,000 for all Postsecondary Teachers
- Self-Employed: 0.3% for all Postsecondary Teachers
- Part-Time: 27.7% for all Postsecondary Teachers

Teach courses pertaining to the chemical and physical properties and compositional changes of substances. Work may include instruction in the methods of qualitative and quantitative chemical analysis. Includes both teachers primarily engaged in teaching and those who do a combination of both teaching and research. Supervise undergraduate and/or graduate teaching, internship, and research work. Act as advisers to student organizations. Collaborate with colleagues to address teaching and research issues. Conduct research in a particular field of knowledge and publish findings in professional journals, books, and/or electronic media. Participate in campus and community events. Participate in student recruitment, registration, and placement activities. Perform administrative duties such as serving as department head. Provide professional consulting services to government and/or industry. Serve on academic or administrative committees that deal with institutional policies, departmental matters, and academic issues. Write grant proposals to procure external research funding. Perform administrative duties such as serving as a department head. Prepare and submit required reports related to instruction. Provide professional consulting services to government and/or industry. Evaluate and grade students' class work, laboratory performance, assignments, and papers. Prepare and deliver lectures to undergraduate and/or graduate students on topics such as organic chemistry, analytical chemistry, and chemical separation. Advise students on academic and vocational curricula and on career issues. Compile, administer, and grade examinations or assign this work to others. Compile bibliographies of specialized materials for outside reading assignments. Initiate, facilitate, and moderate classroom discussions. Keep abreast of developments in their field by reading current literature, talking with colleagues, and participating in professional conferences. Maintain regularly scheduled office hours in order to advise and assist students. Maintain student attendance records, grades, and other required records. Plan, evaluate, and revise curricula, course content, and course materials and methods of instruction. Prepare course materials such as syllabi, homework assignments, and handouts. Select and obtain materials and supplies such as textbooks and laboratory equipment. Supervise students' laboratory work. **SKILLS—Science:** Using scientific rules and methods to solve problems. **Instructing:** Teaching others how to do something. **Writing:** Communicating effectively in writing as appropriate for the needs of the audience. **Learning Strategies:** Selecting and using training/instructional methods and procedures appropriate for the situation when learning or teaching new things. **Reading Comprehension:** Understanding written sentences and paragraphs in work-related documents. **Active Learning:** Understanding the implications of new information for both current and future problem-solving and decision-making. **Speaking:** Talking to others to convey information effectively. **Management of Personnel Resources:** Motivating, developing, and directing people as they work, identifying the best people for the job.

GOE—Interest Area: 05. Education and Training. **Work Group:** 05.03. Postsecondary and Adult Teaching and Instructing. **Other Jobs in This Work Group:** Adult Literacy, Remedial Education, and GED Teachers and Instructors; Agricultural Sciences Teachers, Postsecondary; Anthropology and Archeology Teachers, Postsecondary; Architecture Teachers, Postsecondary; Area, Ethnic, and Cultural Studies Teachers, Postsecondary; Art, Drama, and Music Teachers, Postsecondary; Atmospheric, Earth, Marine, and Space Sciences Teachers, Postsecondary; Biological Science Teachers, Postsecondary; Business Teachers, Postsecondary; Communications Teachers, Postsecondary; Computer Science Teachers, Postsecondary; Criminal Justice and Law Enforcement Teachers, Postsecondary; Economics Teachers, Postsecondary; Education Teachers, Postsecondary; Engineering Teachers, Postsecondary; English Language and Literature Teachers, Postsecondary; Environmental Science Teachers, Postsecondary; Farm and Home Management Advisors; Foreign Language and Literature Teachers, Postsecondary; Forestry and Conservation Science Teachers, Postsecondary; Geography Teachers, Postsecondary; Graduate Teaching Assistants; Health Specialties Teachers, Postsecondary; History Teachers, Postsecondary; Home Economics Teachers, Postsecondary; Law Teachers, Postsecondary; Library Science Teachers, Postsecondary; Mathematical Science Teachers, Postsecondary; Nursing Instructors and Teachers, Postsecondary; Philosophy and Religion Teachers, Postsecondary; Physics Teachers, Postsecondary; Political Science Teachers, Postsecondary; Psychology Teachers, Postsecondary; Recreation and Fitness Studies Teachers, Postsecondary; Self-Enrichment Education Teachers; Social Work Teachers, Postsecondary; Sociology Teachers, Postsecondary; Vocational Education Teachers, Postsecondary. **PERSONALITY TYPE:** Investigative. Investigative occupations frequently involve working with ideas and require an extensive amount of thinking. These occupations can involve searching for facts and figuring out problems mentally.

EDUCATION/TRAINING PROGRAM(S)— Analytical Chemistry; Chemical Physics; Chemistry, General; Chemistry, Other; Geochemistry; Inorganic Chemistry; Organic Chemistry; Physical and Theoretical Chemistry; Polymer Chemistry.

RELATED KNOWLEDGE/COURSES—Chemistry: Knowledge of the chemical composition, structure, and properties of substances and of the chemical processes and transformations that they undergo. This includes uses of chemicals and their danger signs, production techniques, and disposal methods. **Mathematics:** Knowledge of arithmetic, algebra, geometry, calculus, and statistics and their applications. **Education and Training:** Knowledge of principles and methods for curriculum and training design, teaching and instruction for individuals and groups, and the measurement of training effects. **English Language:** Knowledge of the structure and content of the English language, including the meaning and spelling of words, rules of composition, and grammar. **Physics:** Knowledge and prediction of physical principles and laws and their interrelationships and applications to understanding fluid, material, and atmospheric dynamics and mechanical, electrical, atomic, and subatomic structures and processes. **Administration and Management:** Knowledge of business and management principles involved in strategic planning, resource allocation, human resources modeling, leadership technique, production methods, and coordination of people and resources.

Chemists

- Education/Training Required: Bachelor's degree
- Annual Earnings: $54,960
- Growth: 12.7%
- Annual Job Openings: 7,000
- Self-Employed: 0.2%
- Part-Time: 4.2%

Conduct qualitative and quantitative chemical analyses or chemical experiments in laboratories for quality or process control or to develop new products or knowledge. Analyze organic and inor-ganic compounds to determine chemical and physical properties, composition, structure, relationships, and reactions, utilizing chromatography, spectroscopy, and spectrophotometry techniques. Develop, improve, and customize products, equipment, formulas, processes, and analytical methods. Compile and analyze test information to determine process or equipment operating efficiency and to diagnose malfunctions. Confer with scientists and engineers to conduct analyses of research projects, interpret test results, or develop nonstandard tests. Direct, coordinate, and advise personnel in test procedures for analyzing components and physical properties of materials. Induce changes in composition of substances by introducing heat, light, energy, and chemical catalysts for quantitative and qualitative analysis. Write technical papers and reports; prepare standards and specifications for processes, facilities, products, and tests. Study effects of various methods of processing, preserving, and packaging on composition and properties of foods. Prepare test solutions, compounds, and reagents for laboratory personnel to conduct test. SKILLS—Science: Using scientific rules and methods to solve problems. **Quality Control Analysis:** Conducting tests and inspections of products, services, or processes to evaluate quality or performance. **Technology Design:** Generating or adapting equipment and technology to serve user needs. **Time Management:** Managing one's own time and the time of others. **Instructing:** Teaching others how to do something. **Management of Financial Resources:** Determining how money will be spent to get the work done and accounting for these expenditures. **Management of Material Resources:** Obtaining and seeing to the appropriate use of equipment, facilities, and materials needed to do certain work. **Equipment Selection:** Determining the kind of tools and equipment needed to do a job. **Operation Monitoring:** Watching gauges, dials, or other indicators to make sure a machine is working properly. **Troubleshooting:** Determining causes of operating errors and deciding what to do about them.

GOE—**Interest Area:** 15. Scientific Research, Engineering, and Mathematics. **Work Group:** 15.02. Physical Sciences. **Other Jobs in This Work Group:** Astronomers; Atmospheric and Space Scientists; Geographers; Geologists; Hydrologists; Materials Scientists; Physicists. **PERSONALITY TYPE:** Investigative. Investigative occupations frequently involve working with ideas and require an extensive amount of thinking. These occupations can involve searching for facts and figuring out problems mentally.

EDUCATION/TRAINING PROGRAM(S)—Analytical Chemistry; Chemical Physics; Chemistry, General; Chemistry, Other; Inorganic Chemistry; Organic Chemistry; Physical and Theoretical Chemistry; Polymer Chemistry. **RELATED KNOWLEDGE/COURSES—Chemistry:** Knowledge of the chemical composition, structure, and properties of substances and of the chemical processes and transformations that they undergo. This includes uses of chemicals and their danger signs, production techniques, and disposal methods. **Mathematics:** Knowledge of arithmetic, algebra, geometry, calculus, and statistics and their applications. **Engineering and Technology:** Knowledge of the practical application of engineering science and technology. This includes applying principles, techniques, procedures, and equipment to the design and production of various goods and services. **Computers and Electronics:** Knowledge of circuit boards, processors, chips, electronic equipment, and computer hardware and software, including applications and programming. **Education and Training:** Knowledge of principles and methods for curriculum and training design, teaching and instruction for individuals and groups, and the measurement of training effects. **English Language:** Knowledge of the structure and content of the English language, including the meaning and spelling of words, rules of composition, and grammar.

Chief Executives

- Education/Training Required: Work experience plus degree
- Annual Earnings: $136,400
- Growth: 16.7%
- Annual Job Openings: 63,000
- Self-Employed: 14.6%
- Part-Time: 5.3%

Determine and formulate policies and provide the overall direction of companies or private and public sector organizations within the guidelines set up by a board of directors or similar governing body. Plan, direct, or coordinate operational activities at the highest level of management with the help of subordinate executives and staff managers. Analyze operations to evaluate performance of a company and its staff in meeting objectives and to determine areas of potential cost reduction, program improvement, or policy change. Appoint department heads or managers and assign or delegate responsibilities to them. Confer with board members, organization officials, and staff members to discuss issues, coordinate activities, and resolve problems. Coordinate the development and implementation of budgetary control systems, record-keeping systems, and other administrative control processes. Direct and coordinate an organization's financial and budget activities in order to fund operations, maximize investments, and increase efficiency. Direct human resources activities, including the approval of human resource plans and activities, the selection of directors and other high-level staff, and the establishment and organization of major departments. Direct, plan, and implement policies, objectives, and activities of organizations or businesses to ensure continuing operations, to maximize returns on investments, and to increase productivity. Establish departmental responsibilities and coordinate functions among departments and sites. Implement corrective action plans to solve organizational or departmental problems. Prepare and present reports concerning activities, expenses, budgets, government statutes and rulings, and other items affecting businesses or program services. Preside over or serve on boards of directors, management committees, or other governing boards. Represent organizations and promote their objectives at official functions or delegate representatives to do so. Serve as liaisons between organizations, shareholders, and outside organizations. Administer programs for selection of sites, construction of buildings, and provision of equipment and supplies. Attend and participate in meetings of municipal councils and council committees. Deliver speeches, write articles, and present information at meetings or conventions in order to promote services, exchange ideas, and accomplish objectives. Direct and conduct studies and research on issues affecting areas of responsibility. **SKILLS—** No data available.

GOE—Interest Area: 04. Business and Administration. **Work Group:** 04.01. Managerial Work in General Business. **Other Jobs in This Work Group:** Compensation and Benefits Managers; General and Operations Managers; Human Resources Managers; Private Sector Executives; Training and Development Managers. **PERSONALITY TYPE:** No data available.

EDUCATION/TRAINING PROGRAM(S)— Business Administration and Management, General; Business/Commerce, General; Entrepreneurship/Entrepreneurial Studies; International Business/Trade/Commerce; Public Administration; Public Administration and Social Service Professions, Other; Public Policy Analysis. **RELATED KNOWLEDGE/COURSES—** No data available.

Child, Family, and School Social Workers

- Education/Training Required: Bachelor's degree
- Annual Earnings: $34,300
- Growth: 23.2%
- Annual Job Openings: 45,000
- Self-Employed: 1.7%
- Part-Time: 8.7%

Provide social services and assistance to improve the social and psychological functioning of children and their families and to maximize the family well-being and the academic functioning of children. May assist single parents, arrange adoptions, and find foster homes for abandoned or abused children. In schools, they address such problems as teenage pregnancy, misbehavior, and truancy. May also advise teachers on how to deal with problem children. Interview clients individually, in families, or in groups, assessing their situations, capabilities, and problems to determine what services are required to meet their needs. Counsel individuals, groups, families, or communities regarding issues including mental health, poverty, unemployment, substance abuse, physical abuse, rehabilitation, social adjustment, child care, and/or medical care. Maintain case history records and prepare reports. Counsel students whose behavior, school progress, or mental or physical impairment indicate a need for assistance, diagnosing students' problems and arranging for needed services. Consult with parents, teachers, and other school personnel to determine causes of problems such as truancy and misbehavior and to implement solutions. Counsel parents with child-rearing problems, interviewing the child and family to determine whether further action is required. Develop and review service plans in consultation with clients and perform follow-ups assessing the quantity and quality of services provided. Collect supplementary information needed to assist client, such as employment records, medical records, or school reports. Address legal issues such as child abuse and discipline, assisting with hearings and providing testimony to inform custody arrangements. Provide, find, or arrange for support services, such as child care, homemaker service, prenatal care, substance abuse treatment, job training, counseling, or parenting classes, to prevent more-serious problems from developing. Refer clients to community resources for services such as job placement, debt counseling, legal aid, housing, medical treatment, or financial assistance and provide concrete information, such as where to go and how to apply. Arrange for medical, psychiatric, and other tests that may disclose causes of difficulties and indicate remedial measures. Work in child and adolescent residential institutions. Administer welfare programs. Evaluate personal characteristics and home conditions of foster home or adoption applicants. Serve as liaisons between students, homes, schools, family services, child guidance clinics, courts, protective services, doctors, and other contacts to help children who face problems such as disabilities, abuse, or poverty. **SKILLS—Social Perceptiveness:** Being aware of others' reactions and understanding why they react as they do. **Service Orientation:** Actively looking for ways to help people. **Learning Strategies:** Selecting and using training/instructional methods and procedures appropriate for the situation when learning or teaching new things. **Negotiation:** Bringing others together and trying to reconcile differences. **Monitoring:** Monitoring or assessing your performance or that of other individuals or organizations to make improvements or take corrective action. **Speaking:** Talking to others to convey information effectively. **Active Listening:** Giving full attention to what other people are saying, taking time to understand the points being made, asking questions as appropriate, and not interrupting at inappropriate times. **Persuasion:** Persuading others to change their minds or behavior.

GOE—Interest Area: 10. Human Service. **Work Group:** 10.01. Counseling and Social Work. **Other**

Jobs in This Work Group: Clinical Psychologists; Counseling Psychologists; Marriage and Family Therapists; Medical and Public Health Social Workers; Mental Health and Substance Abuse Social Workers; Mental Health Counselors; Probation Officers and Correctional Treatment Specialists; Rehabilitation Counselors; Residential Advisors; Social and Human Service Assistants; Substance Abuse and Behavioral Disorder Counselors. **PERSONALITY TYPE:** Social. Social occupations frequently involve working with, communicating with, and teaching people. These occupations often involve helping or providing service to others.

EDUCATION/TRAINING PROGRAM(S)— Juvenile Corrections; Social Work; Youth Services/Administration. **RELATED KNOWLEDGE/ COURSES—Therapy and Counseling:** Knowledge of principles, methods, and procedures for diagnosis, treatment, and rehabilitation of physical and mental dysfunctions and for career counseling and guidance. **Psychology:** Knowledge of human behavior and performance; individual differences in ability, personality, and interests; learning and motivation; psychological research methods; and the assessment and treatment of behavioral and affective disorders. **Sociology and Anthropology:** Knowledge of group behavior and dynamics, societal trends and influences, human migrations, ethnicity, and cultures and their history and origins. **Customer and Personal Service:** Knowledge of principles and processes for providing customer and personal services. This includes customer needs assessment, meeting quality standards for services, and evaluation of customer satisfaction. **Law and Government:** Knowledge of laws, legal codes, court procedures, precedents, government regulations, executive orders, agency rules, and the democratic political process. **Philosophy and Theology:** Knowledge of different philosophical systems and religions. This includes their basic principles, values, ethics, ways of thinking, customs, and practices and their impact on human culture.

Chiropractors

- Education/Training Required: First professional degree
- Annual Earnings: $66,610
- Growth: 23.3%
- Annual Job Openings: 3,000
- Self-Employed: 58.5%
- Part-Time: 22.2%

Adjust spinal column and other articulations of the body to correct abnormalities of the human body believed to be caused by interference with the nervous system. Examine patient to determine nature and extent of disorder. Manipulate spine or other involved area. May utilize supplementary measures, such as exercise, rest, water, light, heat, and nutritional therapy. Advise patients about recommended courses of treatment. Consult with and refer patients to appropriate health practitioners when necessary. Counsel patients about nutrition, exercise, sleeping habits, stress management, and other matters. Diagnose health problems by reviewing patients' health and medical histories; questioning, observing, and examining patients; and interpreting X rays. Evaluate the functioning of the neuromuscularskeletal system and the spine, using systems of chiropractic diagnosis. Maintain accurate case histories of patients. Obtain and record patients' medical histories. Perform a series of manual adjustments to the spine, or other articulations of the body, in order to correct the musculoskeletal system. Suggest and apply the use of supports such as straps, tapes, bandages, and braces if necessary. Analyze X rays in order to locate the sources of patients' difficulties and to rule out fractures or diseases as sources of problems. Arrange for diagnostic X rays to be taken. **SKILLS—Science:** Using scientific rules and methods to solve problems. **Reading Comprehension:** Understanding written sentences and paragraphs in work-related documents. **Judgment and Decision Making:** Considering the relative costs and benefits of potential actions to choose

the most appropriate one. **Active Learning:** Understanding the implications of new information for both current and future problem-solving and decision-making. **Complex Problem Solving:** Identifying complex problems and reviewing related information to develop and evaluate options and implement solutions. **Social Perceptiveness:** Being aware of others' reactions and understanding why they react as they do. **Persuasion:** Persuading others to change their minds or behavior. **Systems Analysis:** Determining how a system should work and how changes in conditions, operations, and the environment will affect outcomes.

GOE—**Interest Area:** 08. Health Science. **Work Group:** 08.04. Health Specialties. **Other Jobs in This Work Group:** Optometrists; Podiatrists. **PERSONALITY TYPE:** Investigative. Investigative occupations frequently involve working with ideas and require an extensive amount of thinking. These occupations can involve searching for facts and figuring out problems mentally.

EDUCATION/TRAINING PROGRAM(S)—Chiropractic (DC). **RELATED KNOWLEDGE/COURSES—Medicine and Dentistry:** Knowledge of the information and techniques needed to diagnose and treat human injuries, diseases, and deformities. This includes symptoms, treatment alternatives, drug properties and interactions, and preventive health-care measures. **Biology:** Knowledge of plant and animal organisms and their tissues, cells, functions, interdependencies, and interactions with each other and the environment. **Therapy and Counseling:** Knowledge of principles, methods, and procedures for diagnosis, treatment, and rehabilitation of physical and mental dysfunctions and for career counseling and guidance. **English Language:** Knowledge of the structure and content of the English language, including the meaning and spelling of words, rules of composition, and grammar. **Customer and Personal Service:** Knowledge of principles and processes for providing customer and personal services. This includes customer needs assessment, meeting quality standards for services, and evaluation of customer satisfaction. **Chemistry:** Knowledge of the chemical composition, structure, and properties of substances and of the chemical processes and transformations that they undergo. This includes uses of chemicals and their danger signs, production techniques, and disposal methods.

City Planning Aides

- ◉ Education/Training Required: Associate's degree
- ◉ Annual Earnings: $48,660
- ◉ Growth: 17.5%
- ◉ Annual Job Openings: 18,000
- ◉ Self-Employed: 1.1%
- ◉ Part-Time: 20.2%

Compile data from various sources, such as maps, reports, and field and file investigations, for use by city planner in making planning studies. Perform clerical duties such as composing, typing, and proofreading documents; scheduling appointments and meetings; handling mail; and posting public notices. Perform code enforcement tasks. Prepare reports, using statistics, charts, and graphs, to illustrate planning studies in areas such as population, land use, or zoning. Provide and process zoning and project permits and applications. Participate in and support team planning efforts. Prepare, develop, and maintain maps and databases. Prepare, maintain, and update files and records, including land use data and statistics. Research, compile, analyze, and organize information from maps, reports, investigations, and books for use in reports and special projects. Respond to public inquiries and complaints. Serve as a liaison between planning department and other departments and agencies. Conduct interviews, surveys, and site inspections concerning factors that affect land usage, such as zoning, traffic flow, and housing. Inspect sites and review plans for minor development permit applications. **SKILLS—**

Writing: Communicating effectively in writing as appropriate for the needs of the audience. **Mathematics:** Using mathematics to solve problems. **Speaking:** Talking to others to convey information effectively. **Active Listening:** Giving full attention to what other people are saying, taking time to understand the points being made, asking questions as appropriate, and not interrupting at inappropriate times. **Reading Comprehension:** Understanding written sentences and paragraphs in work-related documents. **Critical Thinking:** Using logic and reasoning to identify the strengths and weaknesses of alternative solutions, conclusions, or approaches to problems.

GOE—Interest Area: 07. Government and Public Administration. **Work Group:** 07.02. Public Planning. **Other Jobs in This Work Group:** Urban and Regional Planners. **PERSONALITY TYPE:** Conventional. Conventional occupations frequently involve following set procedures and routines. These occupations can include working with data and details more than with ideas. Usually there is a clear line of authority to follow.

EDUCATION/TRAINING PROGRAM(S)— Social Sciences, General. **RELATED KNOWLEDGE/COURSES—Geography:** Knowledge of principles and methods for describing the features of land, sea, and air masses, including their physical characteristics; locations; interrelationships; and distribution of plant, animal, and human life. **Mathematics:** Knowledge of arithmetic, algebra, geometry, calculus, and statistics and their applications. **Clerical Practices:** Knowledge of administrative and clerical procedures and systems such as word processing, managing files and records, stenography and transcription, designing forms, and other office procedures and terminology. **Sociology and Anthropology:** Knowledge of group behavior and dynamics, societal trends and influences, human migrations, ethnicity, and cultures and their history and origins. **Law and Government:** Knowledge of laws, legal codes, court procedures, precedents, government regulations, executive orders, agency rules, and the democratic political process. **Communica-**

C

tions and Media: Knowledge of media production, communication, and dissemination techniques and methods. This includes alternative ways to inform and entertain via written, oral, and visual media.

Civil Engineers

- Education/Training Required: Bachelor's degree
- Annual Earnings: $62,840
- Growth: 8.0%
- Annual Job Openings: 17,000
- Self-Employed: 6.7%
- Part-Time: 3.3%

Perform engineering duties in planning, designing, and overseeing construction and maintenance of building structures and facilities, such as roads, railroads, airports, bridges, harbors, channels, dams, irrigation projects, pipelines, power plants, water and sewage systems, and waste disposal units. Includes architectural, structural, traffic, ocean, and geo-technical engineers. Analyze survey reports, maps, drawings, blueprints, aerial photography, and other topographical or geologic data to plan projects. Plan and design transportation or hydraulic systems and structures, following construction and government standards and using design software and drawing tools. Compute load and grade requirements, water flow rates, and material stress factors to determine design specifications. Inspect project sites to monitor progress and ensure conformance to design specifications and safety or sanitation standards. Direct construction, operations, and maintenance activities at project site. Direct or participate in surveying to lay out installations and establish reference points, grades, and elevations to guide construction. Estimate quantities and cost of materials, equipment, or labor to determine project feasibility. Prepare or present public reports, such as bid proposals, deeds, environmental

impact statements, and property and right-of-way descriptions. Test soils and materials to determine the adequacy and strength of foundations, concrete, asphalt, or steel. Provide technical advice regarding design, construction, or program modifications and structural repairs to industrial and managerial personnel. **SKILLS—Coordination:** Adjusting actions in relation to others' actions. **Science:** Using scientific rules and methods to solve problems. **Persuasion:** Persuading others to change their minds or behavior. **Negotiation:** Bringing others together and trying to reconcile differences. **Mathematics:** Using mathematics to solve problems. **Instructing:** Teaching others how to do something. **Operations Analysis:** Analyzing needs and product requirements to create a design. **Monitoring:** Monitoring or assessing your performance or that of other individuals or organizations to make improvements or take corrective action. **Service Orientation:** Actively looking for ways to help people. **Technology Design:** Generating or adapting equipment and technology to serve user needs.

GOE—Interest Area: 15. Scientific Research, Engineering, and Mathematics. **Work Group:** 15.07. Research and Design Engineering. **Other Jobs in This Work Group:** Aerospace Engineers; Biomedical Engineers; Chemical Engineers; Computer Hardware Engineers; Electrical Engineers; Electronics Engineers, Except Computer; Marine Architects; Marine Engineers; Materials Engineers; Mechanical Engineers; Nuclear Engineers. **PERSONALITY TYPE:** Realistic. Realistic occupations frequently involve work activities that include practical, hands-on problems and solutions. They often deal with plants, animals, and real-world materials like wood, tools, and machinery. Many of the occupations require working outside and do not involve a lot of paperwork or working closely with others.

EDUCATION/TRAINING PROGRAM(S)— Civil Engineering, General; Civil Engineering, Other; Transportation and Highway Engineering; Water Resources Engineering. **RELATED KNOWLEDGE/COURSES—Engineering and Technology:** Knowledge of the practical application of engineering science and technology. This includes applying principles, techniques, procedures, and equipment to the design and production of various goods and services. **Design:** Knowledge of design techniques, tools, and principles involved in production of precision technical plans, blueprints, drawings, and models. **Building and Construction:** Knowledge of the materials, methods, and tools involved in the construction or repair of houses, buildings, or other structures such as highways and roads. **Mathematics:** Knowledge of arithmetic, algebra, geometry, calculus, and statistics and their applications. **Customer and Personal Service:** Knowledge of principles and processes for providing customer and personal services. This includes customer needs assessment, meeting quality standards for services, and evaluation of customer satisfaction. **Transportation:** Knowledge of principles and methods for moving people or goods by air, rail, sea, or road, including the relative costs and benefits. **Physics:** Knowledge and prediction of physical principles and laws and their interrelationships and applications to understanding fluid, material, and atmospheric dynamics and mechanical, electrical, atomic, and subatomic structures and processes.

Clergy

- ◎ Education/Training Required: First professional degree
- ◎ Annual Earnings: $34,930
- ◎ Growth: 15.5%
- ◎ Annual Job Openings: 34,000
- ◎ Self-Employed: 0.3%
- ◎ Part-Time: 9.4%

Conduct religious worship and perform other spiritual functions associated with beliefs and practices of religious faith or denomination. Provide spiritual and moral guidance and assistance to members. Administer religious rites or ordinances. Study and interpret religious laws, doctrines, and/or traditions.

Counsel individuals and groups concerning their spiritual, emotional, and personal needs. Organize and lead regular religious services. Conduct special ceremonies such as weddings, funerals, and confirmations. Instruct people who seek conversion to a particular faith. Pray and promote spirituality. Prepare and deliver sermons and other talks. Prepare people for participation in religious ceremonies. Read from sacred texts such as the Bible, Torah, or Koran. Collaborate with committees and individuals to address financial and administrative issues pertaining to congregations. Devise ways in which congregation membership can be expanded. Organize and engage in interfaith, community, civic, educational, and recreational activities sponsored by or related to their religion. Participate in fundraising activities to support congregation activities and facilities. Perform administrative duties such as overseeing building management, ordering supplies, contracting for services and repairs, and supervising the work of staff members and volunteers. Plan and lead religious education programs for their congregations. Refer people to community support services, psychologists, and/or doctors as necessary. Respond to requests for assistance during emergencies or crises. Share information about religious issues by writing articles, giving speeches, or teaching. Train leaders of church, community, and youth groups. Visit people in homes, hospitals, and prisons to provide them with comfort and support. **SKILLS—Service Orientation:** Actively looking for ways to help people. **Social Perceptiveness:** Being aware of others' reactions and understanding why they react as they do. **Speaking:** Talking to others to convey information effectively. **Writing:** Communicating effectively in writing as appropriate for the needs of the audience. **Active Listening:** Giving full attention to what other people are saying, taking time to understand the points being made, asking questions as appropriate, and not interrupting at inappropriate times. **Reading Comprehension:** Understanding written sentences and paragraphs in work-related documents. **Persuasion:** Persuading others to change their minds or behavior. **Learning Strategies:** Selecting and using training/instructional methods and procedures appropriate for the situation when learning or teaching new things.

GOE—**Interest Area:** 10. Human Service. **Work Group:** 10.02. Religious Work. **Other Jobs in This Work Group:** Directors, Religious Activities and Education. **PERSONALITY TYPE:** Social. Social occupations frequently involve working with, communicating with, and teaching people. These occupations often involve helping or providing service to others.

EDUCATION/TRAINING PROGRAM(S)— Clinical Pastoral Counseling/Patient Counseling; Divinity/Ministry (BD, MDiv.); Pastoral Counseling and Specialized Ministries, Other; Pastoral Studies/Counseling; Pre-Theology/Pre-Ministerial Studies; Rabbinical Studies; Theological and Ministerial Studies, Other; Theology and Religious Vocations, Other; Theology/Theological Studies; Youth Ministry. **RELATED KNOWLEDGE/COURSES—Philosophy and Theology:** Knowledge of different philosophical systems and religions. This includes their basic principles, values, ethics, ways of thinking, customs, and practices and their impact on human culture. **Education and Training:** Knowledge of principles and methods for curriculum and training design, teaching and instruction for individuals and groups, and the measurement of training effects. **Therapy and Counseling:** Knowledge of principles, methods, and procedures for diagnosis, treatment, and rehabilitation of physical and mental dysfunctions and for career counseling and guidance. **Psychology:** Knowledge of human behavior and performance; individual differences in ability, personality, and interests; learning and motivation; psychological research methods; and the assessment and treatment of behavioral and affective disorders. **English Language:** Knowledge of the structure and content of the English language, including the meaning and spelling of words, rules of composition, and grammar. **Communications and Media:** Knowledge of media production, communication, and dissemination techniques and methods. This includes alternative ways to inform and entertain via written, oral, and visual media.

Clinical Psychologists

- Education/Training Required: Master's degree
- Annual Earnings: $53,230
- Growth: 24.4%
- Annual Job Openings: 17,000
- Self-Employed: 25.4%
- Part-Time: 27.2%

Diagnose or evaluate mental and emotional disorders of individuals through observation, interview, and psychological tests and formulate and administer programs of treatment. Consult reference material such as textbooks, manuals, and journals in order to identify symptoms, make diagnoses, and develop approaches to treatment. Counsel individuals and groups regarding problems such as stress, substance abuse, and family situations in order to modify behavior and/or improve personal, social, and vocational adjustment. Develop and implement individual treatment plans, specifying type, frequency, intensity, and duration of therapy. Discuss the treatment of problems with clients. Evaluate the effectiveness of counseling or treatments and the accuracy and completeness of diagnoses; then modify plans and diagnoses as necessary. Identify psychological, emotional, or behavioral issues and diagnose disorders, using information obtained from interviews, tests, records, and reference materials. Interact with clients to assist them in gaining insight, defining goals, and planning action to achieve effective personal, social, educational, and vocational development and adjustment. Observe individuals at play, in group interactions, or in other contexts to detect indications of mental deficiency, abnormal behavior, or maladjustment. Obtain and study medical, psychological, social, and family histories by interviewing individuals, couples, or families and by reviewing records. Provide occupational, educational, and other information to individuals so that they can make educational and vocational plans. Select, administer, score, and interpret psychological tests in order to obtain information on individuals' intelligence, achievements, interests, and personalities. Utilize a variety of treatment methods such as psychotherapy, hypnosis, behavior modification, stress reduction therapy, psychodrama, and play therapy. Maintain current knowledge of relevant research. Plan, supervise, and conduct psychological research and write papers describing research results. Refer clients to other specialists, institutions, or support services as necessary. Write reports on clients and maintain required paperwork. Develop, direct, and participate in training programs for staff and students. **SKILLS—Social Perceptiveness:** Being aware of others' reactions and understanding why they react as they do. **Active Listening:** Giving full attention to what other people are saying, taking time to understand the points being made, asking questions as appropriate, and not interrupting at inappropriate times. **Systems Evaluation:** Identifying measures or indicators of system performance and the actions needed to improve or correct performance relative to the goals of the system. **Persuasion:** Persuading others to change their minds or behavior. **Speaking:** Talking to others to convey information effectively. **Reading Comprehension:** Understanding written sentences and paragraphs in work-related documents. **Systems Analysis:** Determining how a system should work and how changes in conditions, operations, and the environment will affect outcomes. **Science:** Using scientific rules and methods to solve problems.

GOE—Interest Area: 10. Human Service. **Work Group:** 10.01. Counseling and Social Work. **Other Jobs in This Work Group:** Child, Family, and School Social Workers; Counseling Psychologists; Marriage and Family Therapists; Medical and Public Health Social Workers; Mental Health and Substance Abuse Social Workers; Mental Health Counselors; Probation Officers and Correctional Treatment Specialists; Rehabilitation Counselors; Residential Advisors; Social and Human Service

Assistants; Substance Abuse and Behavioral Disorder Counselors. **PERSONALITY TYPE:** Investigative. Investigative occupations frequently involve working with ideas and require an extensive amount of thinking. These occupations can involve searching for facts and figuring out problems mentally.

EDUCATION/TRAINING PROGRAM(S)— Clinical Child Psychology; Clinical Psychology; Counseling Psychology; Developmental and Child Psychology; Psychoanalysis and Psychotherapy; Psychology, General; School Psychology. **RELATED KNOWLEDGE/COURSES—Therapy and Counseling:** Knowledge of principles, methods, and procedures for diagnosis, treatment, and rehabilitation of physical and mental dysfunctions and for career counseling and guidance. **Psychology:** Knowledge of human behavior and performance; individual differences in ability, personality, and interests; learning and motivation; psychological research methods; and the assessment and treatment of behavioral and affective disorders. **Administration and Management:** Knowledge of business and management principles involved in strategic planning, resource allocation, human resources modeling, leadership technique, production methods, and coordination of people and resources. **Sociology and Anthropology:** Knowledge of group behavior and dynamics, societal trends and influences, human migrations, ethnicity, and cultures and their history and origins. **Customer and Personal Service:** Knowledge of principles and processes for providing customer and personal services. This includes customer needs assessment, meeting quality standards for services, and evaluation of customer satisfaction. **English Language:** Knowledge of the structure and content of the English language, including the meaning and spelling of words, rules of composition, and grammar.

Commercial and Industrial Designers

⊚ Education/Training Required: Bachelor's degree

⊚ Annual Earnings: $52,080

⊚ Growth: 14.7%

⊚ Annual Job Openings: 7,000

⊚ Self-Employed: 31.0%

⊚ Part-Time: 16.5%

Develop and design manufactured products, such as cars, home appliances, and children's toys. Combine artistic talent with research on product use, marketing, and materials to create the most functional and appealing product design. Direct and coordinate the fabrication of models or samples and the drafting of working drawings and specification sheets from sketches. Modify and refine designs, using working models, to conform with customer specifications, production limitations, or changes in design trends. Prepare sketches of ideas, detailed drawings, illustrations, artwork, and/or blueprints, using drafting instruments, paints and brushes, or computer-aided design equipment. Present designs and reports to customers or design committees for approval and discuss need for modification. Read publications, attend showings, and study competing products and design styles and motifs to obtain perspective and generate design concepts. Advise corporations on issues involving corporate image projects or problems. Evaluate feasibility of design ideas, based on factors such as appearance, safety, function, serviceability, budget, production costs/methods, and market characteristics. Fabricate models or samples in paper, wood, glass, fabric, plastic, metal, or other materials, using hand and/or power tools. Research production specifications, costs, production materials, and manufacturing methods and provide cost estimates and itemized production requirements. Supervise assistants' work throughout the design process. Develop industrial standards and regulatory guidelines. Confer with engineering, marketing, production, and/or sales departments or with customers to establish and evaluate design concepts for manufactured products. Coordinate the look and function of product lines. Design graphic material for use as ornamentation, illustration, or advertising on manufactured materials and packaging or containers. Develop manufacturing procedures and monitor the manufacture of their designs in a factory to improve operations and product quality. Investigate product characteristics such as the product's safety and handling qualities; its market appeal; how efficiently it can be produced; and ways of distributing, using, and maintaining it. Participate in new product planning or market research, including studying the potential need for new products. **SKILLS—Operations Analysis:** Analyzing needs and product requirements to create a design. **Management of Financial Resources:** Determining how money will be spent to get the work done and accounting for these expenditures. **Active Learning:** Understanding the implications of new information for both current and future problem-solving and decision-making. **Equipment Selection:** Determining the kind of tools and equipment needed to do a job. **Persuasion:** Persuading others to change their minds or behavior. **Systems Analysis:** Determining how a system should work and how changes in conditions, operations, and the environment will affect outcomes. **Systems Evaluation:** Identifying measures or indicators of system performance and the actions needed to improve or correct performance relative to the goals of the system. **Negotiation:** Bringing others together and trying to reconcile differences.

GOE—Interest Area: 03. Arts and Communication. **Work Group:** 03.05. Design. **Other Jobs in This Work Group:** Exhibit Designers; Fashion Designers; Floral Designers; Graphic Designers; Interior Designers; Merchandise Displayers and Window Trimmers; Set Designers. **PERSONALITY TYPE:** Artistic. Artistic occupations frequently involve working with forms, designs, and patterns.

They often require self-expression, and the work can be done without following a clear set of rules.

EDUCATION/TRAINING PROGRAM(S)— Commercial and Advertising Art; Design and Applied Arts, Other; Design and Visual Communications, General; Industrial Design. **RELATED KNOWLEDGE/COURSES—Design:** Knowledge of design techniques, tools, and principles involved in production of precision technical plans, blueprints, drawings, and models. **Fine Arts:** Knowledge of the theory and techniques required to compose, produce, and perform works of music, dance, visual arts, drama, and sculpture. **Production and Processing:** Knowledge of raw materials, production processes, quality control, costs, and other techniques for maximizing the effective manufacture and distribution of goods. **Sales and Marketing:** Knowledge of principles and methods for showing, promoting, and selling products or services. This includes marketing strategy and tactics, product demonstration, sales techniques, and sales control systems. **English Language:** Knowledge of the structure and content of the English language, including the meaning and spelling of words, rules of composition, and grammar. **Communications and Media:** Knowledge of media production, communication, and dissemination techniques and methods. This includes alternative ways to inform and entertain via written, oral, and visual media.

Communications Teachers, Postsecondary

- Education/Training Required: Master's degree
- Annual Earnings: $49,420
- Growth: 38.1% for all Postsecondary Teachers
- Annual Job Openings: 216,000 for all Postsecondary Teachers
- Self-Employed: 0.3% for all Postsecondary Teachers
- Part-Time: 27.7% for all Postsecondary Teachers

Teach courses in communications, such as organizational communications, public relations, radio/television broadcasting, and journalism. Evaluate and grade students' class work, assignments, and papers. Prepare and deliver lectures to undergraduate and/or graduate students on topics such as public speaking, media criticism, and oral traditions. Advise students on academic and vocational curricula and on career issues. Compile, administer, and grade examinations or assign this work to others. Compile bibliographies of specialized materials for outside reading assignments. Initiate, facilitate, and moderate classroom discussions. Keep abreast of developments in their field by reading current literature, talking with colleagues, and participating in professional conferences. Maintain regularly scheduled office hours in order to advise and assist students. Maintain student attendance records, grades, and other required records. Plan, evaluate, and revise curricula, course content, and course materials and methods of instruction. Prepare course materials such as syllabi, homework assignments, and handouts. Select and obtain materials and supplies such as textbooks. Supervise undergraduate and/or graduate teaching, internship, and research work. Act as advisers to student organizations. Collaborate with colleagues to address teaching and research issues. Conduct research in a particular field of knowledge and publish findings in professional journals, books, and/or electronic media. Participate in campus and community events. Participate in student recruitment, registration, and placement activities. Perform administrative duties such as serving as department head. Provide professional consulting services to government and/or industry. Serve on academic or administrative committees that deal with institutional policies, departmental matters, and academic issues. Write grant proposals to procure external research funding. **SKILLS**—No data available.

GOE—Interest Area: 05. Education and Training. **Work Group:** 05.03. Postsecondary and Adult Teaching and Instructing. **Other Jobs in This Work Group:** Adult Literacy, Remedial Education, and GED Teachers and Instructors; Agricultural Sciences Teachers, Postsecondary; Anthropology and Archeology Teachers, Postsecondary; Architecture Teachers, Postsecondary; Area, Ethnic, and Cultural Studies Teachers, Postsecondary; Art, Drama, and Music Teachers, Postsecondary; Atmospheric, Earth, Marine, and Space Sciences Teachers, Postsecondary; Biological Science Teachers, Postsecondary; Business Teachers, Postsecondary; Chemistry Teachers, Postsecondary; Computer Science Teachers, Postsecondary; Criminal Justice and Law Enforcement Teachers, Postsecondary; Economics Teachers, Postsecondary; Education Teachers, Postsecondary; Engineering Teachers, Postsecondary; English Language and Literature Teachers, Postsecondary; Environmental Science Teachers, Postsecondary; Farm and Home Management Advisors; Foreign Language and Literature Teachers, Postsecondary; Forestry and Conservation Science Teachers, Postsecondary; Geography Teachers, Postsecondary; Graduate Teaching Assistants; Health Specialties Teachers, Postsecondary; History Teachers, Postsecondary; Home Economics Teachers, Postsecondary; Law Teachers, Postsecondary;

Library Science Teachers, Postsecondary; Mathematical Science Teachers, Postsecondary; Nursing Instructors and Teachers, Postsecondary; Philosophy and Religion Teachers, Postsecondary; Physics Teachers, Postsecondary; Political Science Teachers, Postsecondary; Psychology Teachers, Postsecondary; Recreation and Fitness Studies Teachers, Postsecondary; Self-Enrichment Education Teachers; Social Work Teachers, Postsecondary; Sociology Teachers, Postsecondary; Vocational Education Teachers, Postsecondary. **PERSONALITY TYPE:** No data available.

EDUCATION/TRAINING PROGRAM(S)—Advertising; Broadcast Journalism; Communication Studies/Speech Communication and Rhetoric; Communication, Journalism, and Related Programs, Other; Digital Communication and Media/Multimedia; Health Communication; Journalism; Journalism, Other; Mass Communication/Media Studies; Political Communication; Public Relations/Image Management; Radio and Television. **RELATED KNOWLEDGE/COURSES**—No data available.

Compensation and Benefits Managers

◎ Education/Training Required: Work experience plus degree

◎ Annual Earnings: $72,180

◎ Growth: 19.4%

◎ Annual Job Openings: 21,000

◎ Self-Employed: 0%

◎ Part-Time: 3.7%

Plan, direct, or coordinate compensation and benefits activities and staff of an organization. Advise management on such matters as equal employment opportunity, sexual harassment, and discrimination. Direct preparation and distribution of written and verbal information to inform employees of benefits, compensation, and personnel policies. Administer, direct, and review employee benefit programs, including the integration of benefit programs following mergers and acquisitions. Plan and conduct new employee orientations to foster positive attitude toward organizational objectives. Plan, direct, supervise, and coordinate work activities of subordinates and staff relating to employment, compensation, labor relations, and employee relations. Identify and implement benefits to increase the quality of life for employees by working with brokers and researching benefits issues. Design, evaluate, and modify benefits policies to ensure that programs are current, competitive, and in compliance with legal requirements. Analyze compensation policies, government regulations, and prevailing wage rates to develop competitive compensation plan. Formulate policies, procedures, and programs for recruitment, testing, placement, classification, orientation, benefits and compensation, and labor and industrial relations. Mediate between benefits providers and employees, such as by assisting in handling employees' benefit-related questions or taking suggestions. Fulfill all reporting requirements of all relevant government rules and regulations, including the Employee Retirement Income Security Act (ERISA). Maintain records and compile statistical reports concerning personnel-related data such as hires, transfers, performance appraisals, and absenteeism rates. Analyze statistical data and reports to identify and determine causes of personnel problems and develop recommendations for improvement of organization's personnel policies and practices. Develop methods to improve employment policies, processes, and practices and recommend changes to management. Negotiate bargaining agreements. Investigate and report on industrial accidents for insurance carriers. Represent organization at personnel-related hearings and investigations. **SKILLS—Management of Personnel Resources:** Motivating, developing, and directing people as they work, identifying the best people for the job. **Management of Financial Resources:** Determining how money will be spent to get the work done and accounting for these expenditures. **Time Management:** Managing one's own time and the time of others. **Social Perceptiveness:** Being aware of others' reactions and understanding why they react as they do. **Monitoring:** Monitoring or assessing your performance or that of other individuals or organizations to make improvements or take corrective action. **Instructing:** Teaching others how to do something. **Management of Material Resources:** Obtaining and seeing to the appropriate use of equipment, facilities, and materials needed to do certain work. **Negotiation:** Bringing others together and trying to reconcile differences.

GOE—Interest Area: 04. Business and Administration. **Work Group:** 04.01. Managerial Work in General Business. **Other Jobs in This Work Group:** Chief Executives; General and Operations Managers; Human Resources Managers; Private Sector Executives; Training and Development Managers. **PERSONALITY TYPE:** Enterprising. Enterprising occupations frequently involve starting up and carrying out projects. These occupations can involve leading people and making many decisions. They sometimes require risk taking and often deal with business.

EDUCATION/TRAINING PROGRAM(S)— Human Resources Management/Personnel Administration, General; Labor and Industrial Relations. **RELATED KNOWLEDGE/COURSES—Personnel and Human Resources:** Knowledge of principles and procedures for personnel recruitment, selection, training, compensation and benefits, labor relations and negotiation, and personnel information systems. **Clerical Practices:** Knowledge of administrative and clerical procedures and systems such as word processing, managing files and records, stenography and transcription, designing forms, and other office procedures and terminology. **Administration and Management:** Knowledge of business and management principles involved in strategic planning, resource allocation, human resources modeling, leadership technique, production methods, and coordination of people and resources. **Economics and Accounting:** Knowledge of economic and accounting principles and practices, the financial markets, banking, and the analysis and reporting of financial data. **Law and Government:** Knowledge of laws, legal codes, court procedures, precedents, government regulations, executive orders, agency rules, and the democratic political process. **Education and Training:** Knowledge of principles and methods for curriculum and training design, teaching and instruction for individuals and groups, and the measurement of training effects.

Compensation, Benefits, and Job Analysis Specialists

- ◎ Education/Training Required: Bachelor's degree
- ◎ Annual Earnings: $46,890
- ◎ Growth: 28.0%
- ◎ Annual Job Openings: 15,000
- ◎ Self-Employed: 0.8%
- ◎ Part-Time: 7.7%

Conduct programs of compensation and benefits and job analysis for employer. May specialize in specific areas, such as position classification and pension programs. Evaluate job positions, determining classification, exempt or non-exempt status, and salary. Ensure company compliance with federal and state laws, including reporting requirements. Advise managers and employees on state and federal employment regulations, collective agreements, benefit and compensation policies, personnel procedures, and classification programs. Plan, develop, evaluate, improve, and communicate methods and techniques for selecting, promoting, compensating, evaluating, and training workers. Provide advice on the resolution of classification and salary complaints. Prepare occupational classifications, job descriptions, and salary scales. Assist in preparing and maintaining personnel records and handbooks. Prepare reports, such as organization and flow charts and career path reports, to summarize job analysis and evaluation and compensation analysis information. Administer employee insurance, pension, and savings plans, working with insurance brokers and plan carriers. Negotiate collective agreements on behalf of employers or workers and mediate labor disputes and grievances. Develop, implement, administer, and evaluate personnel and labor relations programs, including performance appraisal, affirmative action, and employment equity programs. Perform multifactor data and cost analyses that may be used in areas such as support of collective bargaining agreements. Research employee benefit and health and safety practices and recommend changes or modifications to existing policies. Analyze organizational, occupational, and industrial data to facilitate organizational functions and provide technical information to business, industry, and government. Advise staff of individuals' qualifications. Assess need for and develop job analysis instruments and materials. Review occupational data on Alien Employment Certification Applications to determine the appropriate occupational title and code and provide local offices with information about immigration and occupations. Research job and worker requirements, structural and functional relationships among jobs and occupations, and occupational trends. **SKILLS—Service Orientation:** Actively looking for ways to help people. **Persuasion:** Persuading others to change their minds or behavior. **Coordination:** Adjusting actions in relation to others' actions. **Negotiation:** Bringing others together and trying to reconcile differences. **Active Listening:** Giving full attention to what other people are saying, taking time to understand the points being made, asking questions as appropriate, and not interrupting at inappropriate times. **Critical Thinking:** Using logic and reasoning to identify the strengths and weaknesses of alternative solutions, conclusions, or approaches to problems. **Time Management:** Managing one's own time and the time of others. **Social Perceptiveness:** Being aware of others' reactions and understanding why they react as they do.

GOE—Interest Area: 04. Business and Administration. **Work Group:** 04.03. Human Resources Support. **Other Jobs in This Work Group:** Employment Interviewers, Private or Public Employment Service; Personnel Recruiters; Training and Development Specialists. **PERSONALITY TYPE:** Investigative. Investigative occupations frequently involve working with ideas and require an extensive amount of thinking. These occupations can involve searching for facts and figuring out problems mentally.

EDUCATION/TRAINING PROGRAM(S)— Human Resources Management/Personnel Administration, General; Labor and Industrial Relations. **RELATED KNOWLEDGE/COURSES—Personnel and Human Resources:** Knowledge of principles and procedures for personnel recruitment, selection, training, compensation and benefits, labor relations and negotiation, and personnel information systems. **Clerical Practices:** Knowledge of administrative and clerical procedures and systems such as word processing, managing files and records, stenography and transcription, designing forms, and other office procedures and terminology. **Customer and Personal Service:** Knowledge of principles and processes for providing customer and personal services. This includes customer needs assessment, meeting quality standards for services, and evaluation of customer satisfaction. **English Language:** Knowledge of the structure and content of the English language, including the meaning and spelling of words, rules of composition, and grammar. **Administration and Management:** Knowledge of business and management principles involved in strategic planning, resource allocation, human resources modeling, leadership technique, production methods, and coordination of people and resources. **Education and Training:** Knowledge of

principles and methods for curriculum and training design, teaching and instruction for individuals and groups, and the measurement of training effects.

Computer and Information Systems Managers

- ◎ Education/Training Required: Work experience plus degree
- ◎ Annual Earnings: $90,490
- ◎ Growth: 36.1%
- ◎ Annual Job Openings: 39,000
- ◎ Self-Employed: 1.1%
- ◎ Part-Time: 1.8%

Plan, direct, or coordinate activities in such fields as electronic data processing, information systems, systems analysis, and computer programming. Manage backup, security, and user help systems. Consult with users, management, vendors, and technicians to assess computing needs and system requirements. Direct daily operations of department, analyzing workflow, establishing priorities, developing standards, and setting deadlines. Assign and review the work of systems analysts, programmers, and other computer-related workers. Stay abreast of advances in technology. Develop computer information resources, providing for data security and control, strategic computing, and disaster recovery. Review and approve all systems charts and programs prior to their implementation. Evaluate the organization's technology use and needs and recommend improvements, such as hardware and software upgrades. Control operational budget and expenditures. Meet with department heads, managers, supervisors, vendors, and others to solicit cooperation and resolve problems. Develop and interpret organizational goals, policies, and procedures. Recruit, hire, train, and supervise staff and/or

C

participate in staffing decisions. Review project plans in order to plan and coordinate project activity. Evaluate data processing proposals to assess project feasibility and requirements. Prepare and review operational reports or project progress reports. Purchase necessary equipment. **SKILLS—Management of Financial Resources:** Determining how money will be spent to get the work done and accounting for these expenditures. **Negotiation:** Bringing others together and trying to reconcile differences. **Operations Analysis:** Analyzing needs and product requirements to create a design. **Persuasion:** Persuading others to change their minds or behavior. **Programming:** Writing computer programs for various purposes. **Management of Material Resources:** Obtaining and seeing to the appropriate use of equipment, facilities, and materials needed to do certain work. **Systems Analysis:** Determining how a system should work and how changes in conditions, operations, and the environment will affect outcomes. **Technology Design:** Generating or adapting equipment and technology to serve user needs. **Systems Evaluation:** Identifying measures or indicators of system performance and the actions needed to improve or correct performance relative to the goals of the system.

GOE—Interest Area: 11. Information Technology. **Work Group:** 11.01. Managerial Work in Information Technology . **Other Jobs in This Work Group:** Network and Computer Systems Administrators. **PERSONALITY TYPE:** Enterprising. Enterprising occupations frequently involve starting up and carrying out projects. These occupations can involve leading people and making many decisions. They sometimes require risk taking and often deal with business.

EDUCATION/TRAINING PROGRAM(S)— Computer and Information Sciences, General; Computer Science; Information Resources Management/CIO Training; Information Science/Studies; Knowledge Management; Management Information Systems, General; Operations Management and Supervision; System Administration/Administrator. **RELATED KNOWLEDGE/COURSES—**

Clerical Practices: Knowledge of administrative and clerical procedures and systems such as word processing, managing files and records, stenography and transcription, designing forms, and other office procedures and terminology. **Computers and Electronics:** Knowledge of circuit boards, processors, chips, electronic equipment, and computer hardware and software, including applications and programming. **Economics and Accounting:** Knowledge of economic and accounting principles and practices, the financial markets, banking, and the analysis and reporting of financial data. **Engineering and Technology:** Knowledge of the practical application of engineering science and technology. This includes applying principles, techniques, procedures, and equipment to the design and production of various goods and services. **Administration and Management:** Knowledge of business and management principles involved in strategic planning, resource allocation, human resources modeling, leadership technique, production methods, and coordination of people and resources. **Design:** Knowledge of design techniques, tools, and principles involved in production of precision technical plans, blueprints, drawings, and models.

Computer Hardware Engineers

- Education/Training Required: Bachelor's degree
- Annual Earnings: $79,090
- Growth: 6.1%
- Annual Job Openings: 6,000
- Self-Employed: 4.7%
- Part-Time: 3.4%

Research, design, develop, and test computer or computer-related equipment for commercial, industrial, military, or scientific use. May supervise

the manufacturing and installation of computer or computer-related equipment and components. Analyze information to determine, recommend, and plan layout, including type of computers and peripheral equipment modifications. Analyze user needs and recommend appropriate hardware. Build, test, and modify product prototypes, using working models or theoretical models constructed using computer simulation. Confer with engineering staff and consult specifications to evaluate interface between hardware and software and operational and performance requirements of overall system. Design and develop computer hardware and support peripherals, including central processing units (CPUs), support logic, microprocessors, custom integrated circuits, and printers and disk drives. Evaluate factors such as reporting formats required, cost constraints, and need for security restrictions to determine hardware configuration. Monitor functioning of equipment and make necessary modifications to ensure system operates in conformance with specifications. Specify power supply requirements and configuration, drawing on system performance expectations and design specifications. Store, retrieve, and manipulate data for analysis of system capabilities and requirements. Test and verify hardware and support peripherals to ensure that they meet specifications and requirements, analyzing and recording test data. Write detailed functional specifications that document the hardware development process and support hardware introduction. Assemble and modify existing pieces of equipment to meet special needs. Direct technicians, engineering designers, or other technical support personnel as needed. Provide technical support to designers, marketing and sales departments, suppliers, engineers, and other team members throughout the product development and implementation process. Provide training and support to system designers and users. Recommend purchase of equipment to control dust, temperature, and humidity in area of system installation. Select hardware and material, assuring compliance with specifications and product requirements. Update knowledge and skills to keep up with rapid advancements in computer technolo-

gy. **SKILLS—Programming:** Writing computer programs for various purposes. **Troubleshooting:** Determining causes of operating errors and deciding what to do about them. **Installation:** Installing equipment, machines, wiring, or programs to meet specifications. **Science:** Using scientific rules and methods to solve problems. **Operations Analysis:** Analyzing needs and product requirements to create a design. **Technology Design:** Generating or adapting equipment and technology to serve user needs. **Management of Material Resources:** Obtaining and seeing to the appropriate use of equipment, facilities, and materials needed to do certain work. **Active Learning:** Understanding the implications of new information for both current and future problem-solving and decision-making.

GOE—Interest Area: 15. Scientific Research, Engineering, and Mathematics. **Work Group:** 15.07. Research and Design Engineering. **Other Jobs in This Work Group:** Aerospace Engineers; Biomedical Engineers; Chemical Engineers; Civil Engineers; Electrical Engineers; Electronics Engineers, Except Computer; Marine Architects; Marine Engineers; Materials Engineers; Mechanical Engineers; Nuclear Engineers. **PERSONALITY TYPE:** Investigative. Investigative occupations frequently involve working with ideas and require an extensive amount of thinking. These occupations can involve searching for facts and figuring out problems mentally.

EDUCATION/TRAINING PROGRAM(S)— Computer Engineering, General; Computer Hardware Engineering. **RELATED KNOWLEDGE/ COURSES—Computers and Electronics:** Knowledge of circuit boards, processors, chips, electronic equipment, and computer hardware and software, including applications and programming. **Mathematics:** Knowledge of arithmetic, algebra, geometry, calculus, and statistics and their applications. **Engineering and Technology:** Knowledge of the practical application of engineering science and technology. This includes applying principles, techniques, procedures, and equipment to the design and production of various goods and services. **Design:** Knowledge of design techniques, tools, and principles involved in production of precision technical plans, blueprints, drawings, and models. **Telecommunications:** Knowledge of transmission, broadcasting, switching, control, and operation of telecommunications systems. **Education and Training:** Knowledge of principles and methods for curriculum and training design, teaching and instruction for individuals and groups, and the measurement of training effects.

Computer Programmers

- Education/Training Required: Bachelor's degree
- Annual Earnings: $61,730
- Growth: 14.6%
- Annual Job Openings: 45,000
- Self-Employed: 3.7%
- Part-Time: 4.6%

Convert project specifications and statements of problems and procedures to detailed logical flow charts for coding into computer language. Develop and write computer programs to store, locate, and retrieve specific documents, data, and information. May program Web sites. Correct errors by making appropriate changes and then rechecking the program to ensure that the desired results are produced. Conduct trial runs of programs and software applications to be sure that they will produce the desired information and that the instructions are correct. Compile and write documentation of program development and subsequent revisions, inserting comments in the coded instructions so others can understand the program. Write, update, and maintain computer programs or software packages to handle specific jobs, such as tracking inventory, storing or retrieving data, or controlling other equipment. Consult with managerial, engineering, and technical personnel to clarify program intent, identify problems, and suggest changes. Perform or direct revision, repair, or expansion of existing programs to increase operating efficiency or adapt to new requirements. Write, analyze, review, and rewrite programs, using workflow chart and diagram and applying knowledge of computer capabilities, subject matter, and symbolic logic. Write or contribute to instructions or manuals to guide end users. Investigate whether networks, workstations, the central processing unit of the system, and/or peripheral equipment are responding to a program's instructions. Prepare detailed workflow charts and diagrams that describe input, output, and logical operation and convert them into a series of instructions coded in a computer language. Perform systems analysis and programming tasks to maintain and control the use of computer systems software as a systems programmer. Consult with and assist computer operators or system analysts to define and resolve problems in running computer programs. Assign, coordinate, and review work and activities of programming personnel. **SKILLS—Programming:** Writing computer programs for various purposes. **Operations Analysis:** Analyzing needs and product requirements to create a design. **Technology Design:** Generating or adapting equipment and technology to serve user needs. **Troubleshooting:** Determining causes of operating errors and deciding what to do about them. **Critical Thinking:** Using logic and reasoning to identify the strengths and weaknesses of alternative solutions, conclusions, or approaches to problems. **Active Learning:** Understanding the implications of new information for both current and future problem-solving and decision-making. **Complex Problem Solving:** Identifying complex problems and reviewing related information to develop and evaluate options and implement solutions. **Systems Analysis:** Determining how a system should work and how changes in conditions, operations, and the environment will affect outcomes.

GOE—Interest Area: 11. Information Technology. **Work Group:** 11.02. Information Technology Specialties. **Other Jobs in This Work Group:** Computer Operators; Computer Security Specialists;

Computer Software Engineers, Applications; Computer Software Engineers, Systems Software; Computer Support Specialists; Computer Systems Analysts; Database Administrators; Network Systems and Data Communications Analysts. **PERSONALITY TYPE:** Investigative. Investigative occupations frequently involve working with ideas and require an extensive amount of thinking. These occupations can involve searching for facts and figuring out problems mentally.

EDUCATION/TRAINING PROGRAM(S)— Artificial Intelligence and Robotics; Bioinformatics; Computer Graphics; Computer Programming, Specific Applications; Computer Programming, Vendor/Product Certification; Computer Programming/Programmer, General; E-Commerce/Electronic Commerce; Management Information Systems, General; Medical Informatics; Medical Office Computer Specialist/Assistant; Web Page, Digital/Multimedia, and Information Resources Design; Web/Multimedia Management and Webmaster. **RELATED KNOWLEDGE/COURSES— Computers and Electronics:** Knowledge of circuit boards, processors, chips, electronic equipment, and computer hardware and software, including applications and programming. **Design:** Knowledge of design techniques, tools, and principles involved in production of precision technical plans, blueprints, drawings, and models. **Mathematics:** Knowledge of arithmetic, algebra, geometry, calculus, and statistics and their applications. **Telecommunications:** Knowledge of transmission, broadcasting, switching, control, and operation of telecommunications systems. **English Language:** Knowledge of the structure and content of the English language, including the meaning and spelling of words, rules of composition, and grammar. **Customer and Personal Service:** Knowledge of principles and processes for providing customer and personal services. This includes customer needs assessment, meeting quality standards for services, and evaluation of customer satisfaction.

Computer Science Teachers, Postsecondary

- Education/Training Required: Master's degree
- Annual Earnings: $52,040
- Growth: 38.1% for all Postsecondary Teachers
- Annual Job Openings: 216,000 for all Postsecondary Teachers
- Self-Employed: 0.3% for all Postsecondary Teachers
- Part-Time: 27.7% for all Postsecondary Teachers

Teach courses in computer science. May specialize in a field of computer science, such as the design and function of computers or operations and research analysis. Evaluate and grade students' class work, laboratory work, assignments, and papers. Prepare and deliver lectures to undergraduate and/or graduate students on topics such as programming, data structures, and software design. Advise students on academic and vocational curricula and on career issues. Compile, administer, and grade examinations or assign this work to others. Compile bibliographies of specialized materials for outside reading assignments. Initiate, facilitate, and moderate classroom discussions. Keep abreast of developments in their field by reading current literature, talking with colleagues, and participating in professional conferences. Maintain regularly scheduled office hours in order to advise and assist students. Maintain student attendance records, grades, and other required records. Plan, evaluate, and revise curricula, course content, and course materials and methods of instruction. Prepare course materials such as syllabi, homework assignments, and handouts. Select and obtain materials and supplies such as textbooks and laboratory equipment.

Supervise students' laboratory work. Supervise undergraduate and/or graduate teaching, internship, and research work. Act as advisers to student organizations. Collaborate with colleagues to address teaching and research issues. Conduct research in a particular field of knowledge and publish findings in professional journals, books, and/or electronic media. Direct research of other teachers or of graduate students working for advanced academic degrees. Participate in campus and community events. Participate in student recruitment, registration, and placement activities. Perform administrative duties such as serving as department head. Provide professional consulting services to government and/or industry. Serve on academic or administrative committees that deal with institutional policies, departmental matters, and academic issues. Write grant proposals to procure external research funding. **SKILLS—Programming:** Writing computer programs for various purposes. **Instructing:** Teaching others how to do something. **Writing:** Communicating effectively in writing as appropriate for the needs of the audience. **Learning Strategies:** Selecting and using training/instructional methods and procedures appropriate for the situation when learning or teaching new things. **Active Learning:** Understanding the implications of new information for both current and future problem-solving and decision-making. **Reading Comprehension:** Understanding written sentences and paragraphs in work-related documents. **Mathematics:** Using mathematics to solve problems. **Science:** Using scientific rules and methods to solve problems.

GOE—Interest Area: 05. Education and Training. **Work Group:** 05.03. Postsecondary and Adult Teaching and Instructing. **Other Jobs in This Work Group:** Adult Literacy, Remedial Education, and GED Teachers and Instructors; Agricultural Sciences Teachers, Postsecondary; Anthropology and Archeology Teachers, Postsecondary; Architecture Teachers, Postsecondary; Area, Ethnic, and Cultural Studies Teachers, Postsecondary; Art, Drama, and Music Teachers, Postsecondary; Atmospheric, Earth, Marine, and Space Sciences Teachers, Postsecondary; Biological Science Teachers, Postsecondary; Business Teachers, Postsecondary; Chemistry Teachers, Postsecondary; Communications Teachers, Postsecondary; Criminal Justice and Law Enforcement Teachers, Postsecondary; Economics Teachers, Postsecondary; Education Teachers, Postsecondary; Engineering Teachers, Postsecondary; English Language and Literature Teachers, Postsecondary; Environmental Science Teachers, Postsecondary; Farm and Home Management Advisors; Foreign Language and Literature Teachers, Postsecondary; Forestry and Conservation Science Teachers, Postsecondary; Geography Teachers, Postsecondary; Graduate Teaching Assistants; Health Specialties Teachers, Postsecondary; History Teachers, Postsecondary; Home Economics Teachers, Postsecondary; Law Teachers, Postsecondary; Library Science Teachers, Postsecondary; Mathematical Science Teachers, Postsecondary; Nursing Instructors and Teachers, Postsecondary; Philosophy and Religion Teachers, Postsecondary; Physics Teachers, Postsecondary; Political Science Teachers, Postsecondary; Psychology Teachers, Postsecondary; Recreation and Fitness Studies Teachers, Postsecondary; Self-Enrichment Education Teachers; Social Work Teachers, Postsecondary; Sociology Teachers, Postsecondary; Vocational Education Teachers, Postsecondary. **PERSONALITY TYPE:** Investigative. Investigative occupations frequently involve working with ideas and require an extensive amount of thinking. These occupations can involve searching for facts and figuring out problems mentally.

EDUCATION/TRAINING PROGRAM(S)— Computer and Information Sciences, General; Computer Programming/Programmer, General; Computer Science; Computer Systems Analysis/Analyst; Information Science/Studies. **RELATED KNOWLEDGE/COURSES—Computers and Electronics:** Knowledge of circuit boards, processors, chips, electronic equipment, and computer hardware and software, including applications and programming. **Education and Training:** Knowledge of principles and methods for curriculum and training design, teaching and instruction for individuals and groups, and the measurement of training effects. **Mathematics:** Knowledge of arithmetic, algebra, geometry, calculus, and statistics and their applications. **Physics:** Knowledge and prediction of physical principles and laws and their interrelationships and applications to understanding fluid, material, and atmospheric dynamics and mechanical, electrical, atomic, and subatomic structures and processes. **English Language:** Knowledge of the structure and content of the English language, including the meaning and spelling of words, rules of composition, and grammar. **Administration and Management:** Knowledge of business and management principles involved in strategic planning, resource allocation, human resources modeling, leadership technique, production methods, and coordination of people and resources. **Telecommunications:** Knowledge of transmission, broadcasting, switching, control, and operation of telecommunications systems.

Computer Security Specialists

- Education/Training Required: Bachelor's degree
- Annual Earnings: $57,060
- Growth: 37.4%
- Annual Job Openings: 35,000
- Self-Employed: 0.5%
- Part-Time: 3.9%

Plan, coordinate, and implement security measures for information systems to regulate access to computer data files and prevent unauthorized modification, destruction, or disclosure of information. Confer with users to discuss issues such as computer data access needs, security violations, and programming changes. Develop plans to safeguard computer files against accidental or unauthorized modification, destruction, or disclosure and to meet emergency data processing needs. Document computer security and emergency measures policies, procedures, and tests. Encrypt data transmissions and erect firewalls to conceal confidential information as it is being transmitted and to keep out tainted digital transfers. Modify computer security files to incorporate new software, correct errors, or change individual access status. Monitor current reports of computer viruses to determine when to update virus protection systems. Monitor use of data files and regulate access to safeguard information in computer files. Perform risk assessments and execute tests of data processing system to ensure functioning of data processing activities and security measures. Review violations of computer security procedures and discuss procedures with violators to ensure violations are not repeated. Coordinate implementation of computer system plan with establishment personnel and outside vendors. Train users and promote security awareness to ensure system security and to improve server and network efficiency. Maintain permanent fleet cryptologic and carry-on direct support systems required in special land, sea surface, and subsurface operations. SKILLS—**Programming:** Writing computer programs for various purposes. **Technology Design:** Generating or adapting equipment and technology to serve user needs. **Installation:** Installing equipment, machines, wiring, or programs to meet specifications. **Operations Analysis:** Analyzing needs and product requirements to create a design. **Management of Material Resources:** Obtaining and seeing to the appropriate use of equipment, facilities, and materials needed to do certain work. **Science:** Using scientific rules and methods to solve problems. **Writing:** Communicating effectively in writing as appropriate for the needs of the audience. **Mathematics:** Using mathematics to solve problems. **Quality Control Analysis:** Conducting tests and inspections of products, services, or processes to evaluate quality or performance.

GOE—**Interest Area:** 11. Information Technology. **Work Group:** 11.02. Information Technology Specialties. **Other Jobs in This Work Group:** Computer Operators; Computer Programmers; Computer Software Engineers, Applications; Computer Software Engineers, Systems Software; Computer Support Specialists; Computer Systems Analysts; Database Administrators; Network Systems and Data Communications Analysts. **PERSONALITY TYPE:** Investigative. Investigative occupations frequently involve working with ideas and require an extensive amount of thinking. These occupations can involve searching for facts and figuring out problems mentally.

EDUCATION/TRAINING PROGRAM(S)— Computer and Information Sciences and Support Services, Other; Computer and Information Sciences, General; Computer and Information Systems Security; Computer Systems Analysis/Analyst; Computer Systems Networking and Telecommunications; Information Science/Studies; System Administration/Administrator; System, Networking, and LAN/WAN Management/Manager. **RELATED KNOWLEDGE/COURSES—Computers and Electronics:** Knowledge of circuit boards, processors, chips, electronic equipment, and computer hardware and software, including applications and programming. **Public Safety and Security:** Knowledge of relevant equipment, policies, procedures, and strategies to promote effective local, state, or national security operations for the protection of people, data, property, and institutions. **Administration and Management:** Knowledge of business and management principles involved in strategic planning, resource allocation, human resources modeling, leadership technique, production methods, and coordination of people and resources. **Telecommunications:** Knowledge of transmission, broadcasting, switching, control, and operation of telecommunications systems.

Computer Software Engineers, Applications

- Education/Training Required: Bachelor's degree
- Annual Earnings: $73,410
- Growth: 45.5%
- Annual Job Openings: 55,000
- Self-Employed: 3.1%
- Part-Time: 2.4%

Develop, create, and modify general computer applications software or specialized utility programs. Analyze user needs and develop software solutions. Design software or customize software for client use with the aim of optimizing operational efficiency. May analyze and design databases within an application area, working individually or coordinating database development as part of a team. Confer with systems analysts, engineers, programmers, and others to design system and to obtain information on project limitations and capabilities, performance requirements, and interfaces. Modify existing software to correct errors, allow it to adapt to new hardware, or improve its performance. Analyze user needs and software requirements to determine feasibility of design within time and cost constraints. Consult with customers about software system design and maintenance. Coordinate software system installation and monitor equipment functioning to ensure specifications are met. Design, develop, and modify software systems, using scientific analysis and mathematical models to predict and measure outcome and consequences of design. Develop and direct software system testing and validation procedures, programming, and documentation. Analyze information to determine, recommend, and plan computer specifications and layouts and peripheral equipment modifications. Supervise the work of programmers, technologists and technicians, and other engineering and scientific personnel. Obtain and evaluate information on factors such as reporting formats required, costs, and security needs to determine hardware configuration. Determine system performance standards. Train users to use new or modified equipment. Store, retrieve, and manipulate data for analysis of system capabilities and requirements. **SKILLS— Programming:** Writing computer programs for various purposes. **Troubleshooting:** Determining causes of operating errors and deciding what to do about them. **Technology Design:** Generating or adapting equipment and technology to serve user needs. **Systems Analysis:** Determining how a system should work and how changes in conditions, operations, and the environment will affect outcomes. **Quality Control Analysis:** Conducting tests and inspections of products, services, or processes to evaluate quality or performance. **Operations Analysis:** Analyzing needs and product requirements to create a design. **Complex Problem Solving:** Identifying complex problems and reviewing related information to develop and evaluate options and implement solutions. **Critical Thinking:** Using logic and reasoning to identify the strengths and weaknesses of alternative solutions, conclusions, or approaches to problems.

GOE—Interest Area: 11. Information Technology. **Work Group:** 11.02. Information Technology Specialties. **Other Jobs in This Work Group:** Computer Operators; Computer Programmers; Computer Security Specialists; Computer Software Engineers, Systems Software; Computer Support Specialists; Computer Systems Analysts; Database Administrators; Network Systems and Data Communications Analysts. **PERSONALITY TYPE:** Investigative. Investigative occupations frequently involve working with ideas and require an extensive amount of thinking. These occupations can involve searching for facts and figuring out problems mentally.

EDUCATION/TRAINING PROGRAM(S)— Artificial Intelligence and Robotics; Bioinformatics; Computer Engineering Technologies/Technicians, Other; Computer Engineering, General; Computer Science; Computer Software Engineering; Informa-

tion Technology; Medical Illustration and Informatics, Other; Medical Informatics. **RELATED KNOWLEDGE/COURSES—Computers and Electronics:** Knowledge of circuit boards, processors, chips, electronic equipment, and computer hardware and software, including applications and programming. **Telecommunications:** Knowledge of transmission, broadcasting, switching, control, and operation of telecommunications systems. **Engineering and Technology:** Knowledge of the practical application of engineering science and technology. This includes applying principles, techniques, procedures, and equipment to the design and production of various goods and services. **Mathematics:** Knowledge of arithmetic, algebra, geometry, calculus, and statistics and their applications. **Design:** Knowledge of design techniques, tools, and principles involved in production of precision technical plans, blueprints, drawings, and models. **English Language:** Knowledge of the structure and content of the English language, including the meaning and spelling of words, rules of composition, and grammar.

Computer Software Engineers, Systems Software

- ◉ Education/Training Required: Bachelor's degree
- ◉ Annual Earnings: $77,250
- ◉ Growth: 45.5%
- ◉ Annual Job Openings: 39,000
- ◉ Self-Employed: 3.0%
- ◉ Part-Time: 2.4%

Research, design, develop, and test operating systems–level software, compilers, and network distribution software for medical, industrial, military,

C

communications, aerospace, business, scientific, and general computing applications. **Set operational specifications and formulate and analyze software requirements. Apply principles and techniques of computer science, engineering, and mathematical analysis.** Modify existing software to correct errors, to adapt it to new hardware, or to upgrade interfaces and improve performance. Design and develop software systems, using scientific analysis and mathematical models to predict and measure outcome and consequences of design. Consult with engineering staff to evaluate interface between hardware and software, develop specifications and performance requirements, and resolve customer problems. Analyze information to determine, recommend, and plan installation of a new system or modification of an existing system. Develop and direct software system testing and validation procedures. Direct software programming and development of documentation. Consult with customers and/or other departments on project status, proposals, and technical issues such as software system design and maintenance. Advise customer about, or perform, maintenance of software system. Coordinate installation of software system. Monitor functioning of equipment to ensure system operates in conformance with specifications. Store, retrieve, and manipulate data for analysis of system capabilities and requirements. Confer with data processing and project managers to obtain information on limitations and capabilities for data processing projects. Prepare reports and correspondence concerning project specifications, activities, and status. Evaluate factors such as reporting formats required, cost constraints, and need for security restrictions to determine hardware configuration. Supervise and assign work to programmers, designers, technologists and technicians, and other engineering and scientific personnel. Train users to use new or modified equipment. Utilize microcontrollers to develop control signals, implement control algorithms, and measure process variables such as temperatures, pressures, and positions. **SKILLS—Programming:** Writing computer programs for various purposes. **Technology Design:** Generating or adapting equipment and technology to serve user needs. **Troubleshooting:** Determining causes of operating errors and deciding what to do about them. **Systems Analysis:** Determining how a system should work and how changes in conditions, operations, and the environment will affect outcomes. **Complex Problem Solving:** Identifying complex problems and reviewing related information to develop and evaluate options and implement solutions. **Operations Analysis:** Analyzing needs and product requirements to create a design. **Active Learning:** Understanding the implications of new information for both current and future problem-solving and decision-making. **Critical Thinking:** Using logic and reasoning to identify the strengths and weaknesses of alternative solutions, conclusions, or approaches to problems.

GOE—Interest Area: 11. Information Technology. **Work Group:** 11.02. Information Technology Specialties. **Other Jobs in This Work Group:** Computer Operators; Computer Programmers; Computer Security Specialists; Computer Software Engineers, Applications; Computer Support Specialists; Computer Systems Analysts; Database Administrators; Network Systems and Data Communications Analysts. **PERSONALITY TYPE:** Investigative. Investigative occupations frequently involve working with ideas and require an extensive amount of thinking. These occupations can involve searching for facts and figuring out problems mentally.

EDUCATION/TRAINING PROGRAM(S)— Artificial Intelligence and Robotics; Computer Engineering Technologies/Technicians, Other; Computer Engineering, General; Computer Science; Information Science/Studies; Information Technology. **RELATED KNOWLEDGE/ COURSES—Computers and Electronics:** Knowledge of circuit boards, processors, chips, electronic equipment, and computer hardware and software, including applications and programming. **Design:** Knowledge of design techniques, tools, and principles involved in production of precision technical plans, blueprints, drawings, and models. **Engineering and Technology:** Knowledge of the practical application of engineering science and technology.

This includes applying principles, techniques, procedures, and equipment to the design and production of various goods and services. **Telecommunications:** Knowledge of transmission, broadcasting, switching, control, and operation of telecommunications systems. **Mathematics:** Knowledge of arithmetic, algebra, geometry, calculus, and statistics and their applications. **Education and Training:** Knowledge of principles and methods for curriculum and training design, teaching and instruction for individuals and groups, and the measurement of training effects.

Computer Support Specialists

⊚ Education/Training Required: Associate's degree
⊚ Annual Earnings: $39,900
⊚ Growth: 30.3%
⊚ Annual Job Openings: 71,000
⊚ Self-Employed: 0.6%
⊚ Part-Time: 6.8%

Provide technical assistance to computer system users. Answer questions or resolve computer problems for clients in person, via telephone, or from remote location. May provide assistance concerning the use of computer hardware and software, including printing, installation, word processing, electronic mail, and operating systems. Answer users' inquiries regarding computer software and hardware operation to resolve problems. Enter commands and observe system functioning to verify correct operations and detect errors. Install and perform minor repairs to hardware, software, and peripheral equipment, following design or installation specifications. Oversee the daily performance of computer systems. Set up equipment for employee use, performing or ensuring proper installation of cable, operating systems, and appropriate software. Maintain record of daily data communication transactions, problems and remedial action taken, and installation activities. Read technical manuals, confer with users, and conduct computer diagnostics to investigate and resolve problems and to provide technical assistance and support. Confer with staff, users, and management to establish requirements for new systems or modifications. Develop training materials and procedures and/or train users in the proper use of hardware and software. Refer major hardware or software problems or defective products to vendors or technicians for service. Prepare evaluations of software or hardware and recommend improvements or upgrades. Read trade magazines and technical manuals and attend conferences and seminars to maintain knowledge of hardware and software. Supervise and coordinate workers engaged in problem-solving, monitoring, and installing data communication equipment and software. Inspect equipment and read order sheets to prepare for delivery to users. Modify and customize commercial programs for internal needs. **SKILLS— Troubleshooting:** Determining causes of operating errors and deciding what to do about them. **Repairing:** Repairing machines or systems, using the needed tools. **Persuasion:** Persuading others to change their minds or behavior. **Social Perceptiveness:** Being aware of others' reactions and understanding why they react as they do. **Installation:** Installing equipment, machines, wiring, or programs to meet specifications. **Instructing:** Teaching others how to do something. **Equipment Maintenance:** Performing routine maintenance on equipment and determining when and what kind of maintenance is needed. **Writing:** Communicating effectively in writing as appropriate for the needs of the audience. **Service Orientation:** Actively looking for ways to help people.

GOE—Interest Area: 11. Information Technology. **Work Group:** 11.02. Information Technology Specialties. **Other Jobs in This Work Group:** Computer Operators; Computer Programmers; Computer Security Specialists; Computer Software Engineers,

Applications; Computer Software Engineers, Systems Software; Computer Systems Analysts; Database Administrators; Network Systems and Data Communications Analysts. **PERSONALITY TYPE:** Investigative. Investigative occupations frequently involve working with ideas and require an extensive amount of thinking. These occupations can involve searching for facts and figuring out problems mentally.

EDUCATION/TRAINING PROGRAM(S)— Accounting and Computer Science; Agricultural Business Technology; Computer Hardware Technology/Technician; Computer Software Technology/Technician; Data Processing and Data Processing Technology/Technician; Medical Office Computer Specialist/Assistant. **RELATED KNOWLEDGE/COURSES—Computers and Electronics:** Knowledge of circuit boards, processors, chips, electronic equipment, and computer hardware and software, including applications and programming. **Customer and Personal Service:** Knowledge of principles and processes for providing customer and personal services. This includes customer needs assessment, meeting quality standards for services, and evaluation of customer satisfaction. **Telecommunications:** Knowledge of transmission, broadcasting, switching, control, and operation of telecommunications systems. **Production and Processing:** Knowledge of raw materials, production processes, quality control, costs, and other techniques for maximizing the effective manufacture and distribution of goods. **Engineering and Technology:** Knowledge of the practical application of engineering science and technology. This includes applying principles, techniques, procedures, and equipment to the design and production of various goods and services. **Design:** Knowledge of design techniques, tools, and principles involved in production of precision technical plans, blueprints, drawings, and models.

Computer Systems Analysts

◎ Education/Training Required: Bachelor's degree

◎ Annual Earnings: $65,050

◎ Growth: 39.4%

◎ Annual Job Openings: 68,000

◎ Self-Employed: 6.4%

◎ Part-Time: 5.7%

Analyze science, engineering, business, and all other data processing problems for application to electronic data processing systems. Analyze user requirements, procedures, and problems to automate or improve existing systems and review computer system capabilities, workflow, and scheduling limitations. May analyze or recommend commercially available software. May supervise computer programmers. Provide staff and users with assistance solving computer-related problems, such as malfunctions and program problems. Test, maintain, and monitor computer programs and systems, including coordinating the installation of computer programs and systems. Use object-oriented programming languages, as well as client/server applications development processes and multimedia and Internet technology. Confer with clients regarding the nature of the information processing or computation needs a computer program is to address. Coordinate and link the computer systems within an organization to increase compatibility and so information can be shared. Consult with management to ensure agreement on system principles. Expand or modify system to serve new purposes or improve work flow. Interview or survey workers, observe job performance, and/or perform the job in order to determine what information is processed and how it is processed. Determine computer software or hardware needed to set up or alter system. Train staff and users to work with computer systems and programs. Analyze information processing or computation needs and plan and design computer systems, using techniques such as structured analysis, data modeling, and information engineering. Assess the usefulness of pre-developed application packages and adapt them to a user environment. Define the goals of the system and devise flow charts and diagrams describing logical operational steps of programs. Develop, document, and revise system design procedures, test procedures, and quality standards. Review and analyze computer printouts and performance indicators to locate code problems and correct errors by correcting codes. Recommend new equipment or software packages. Read manuals, periodicals, and technical reports to learn how to develop programs that meet staff and user requirements. Supervise computer programmers or other systems analysts or serve as project leaders for particular systems projects. Utilize the computer in the analysis and solution of business problems such as the development of integrated production and inventory control and cost analysis systems. **SKILLS—Quality Control Analysis:** Conducting tests and inspections of products, services, or processes to evaluate quality or performance. **Installation:** Installing equipment, machines, wiring, or programs to meet specifications. **Troubleshooting:** Determining causes of operating errors and deciding what to do about them. **Technology Design:** Generating or adapting equipment and technology to serve user needs. **Time Management:** Managing one's own time and the time of others. **Service Orientation:** Actively looking for ways to help people. **Systems Analysis:** Determining how a system should work and how changes in conditions, operations, and the environment will affect outcomes. **Operations Analysis:** Analyzing needs and product requirements to create a design.

GOE—Interest Area: 11. Information Technology. **Work Group:** 11.02. Information Technology Specialties. **Other Jobs in This Work Group:** Computer Operators; Computer Programmers; Computer Security Specialists; Computer Software Engineers, Applications; Computer Software Engineers, Systems Software; Computer Support Specialists; Data-base Administrators; Network Systems and Data Communications Analysts. **PERSONALITY TYPE:** Investigative. Investigative occupations frequently involve working with ideas and require an extensive amount of thinking. These occupations can involve searching for facts and figuring out problems mentally.

EDUCATION/TRAINING PROGRAM(S)— Computer and Information Sciences, General; Computer Systems Analysis/Analyst; Information Technology; Web/Multimedia Management and Webmaster. **RELATED KNOWLEDGE/COURSES—Computers and Electronics:** Knowledge of circuit boards, processors, chips, electronic equipment, and computer hardware and software, including applications and programming. **Customer and Personal Service:** Knowledge of principles and processes for providing customer and personal services. This includes customer needs assessment, meeting quality standards for services, and evaluation of customer satisfaction. **Telecommunications:** Knowledge of transmission, broadcasting, switching, control, and operation of telecommunications systems. **Design:** Knowledge of design techniques, tools, and principles involved in production of precision technical plans, blueprints, drawings, and models. **Education and Training:** Knowledge of principles and methods for curriculum and training design, teaching and instruction for individuals and groups, and the measurement of training effects. **English Language:** Knowledge of the structure and content of the English language, including the meaning and spelling of words, rules of composition, and grammar.

Construction Managers

- Education/Training Required: Bachelor's degree
- Annual Earnings: $67,620
- Growth: 12.0%
- Annual Job Openings: 47,000
- Self-Employed: 46.9%
- Part-Time: 3.6%

Plan, direct, coordinate, or budget, usually through subordinate supervisory personnel, activities concerned with the construction and maintenance of structures, facilities, and systems. Participate in the conceptual development of a construction project and oversee its organization, scheduling, and implementation. Confer with supervisory personnel, owners, contractors, and design professionals to discuss and resolve matters such as work procedures, complaints, and construction problems. Plan, organize, and direct activities concerned with the construction and maintenance of structures, facilities, and systems. Schedule the project in logical steps and budget time required to meet deadlines. Determine labor requirements and dispatch workers to construction sites. Inspect and review projects to monitor compliance with building and safety codes and other regulations. Interpret and explain plans and contract terms to administrative staff, workers, and clients, representing the owner or developer. Prepare contracts and negotiate revisions, changes, and additions to contractual agreements with architects, consultants, clients, suppliers, and subcontractors. Obtain all necessary permits and licenses. Direct and supervise workers. Study job specifications to determine appropriate construction methods. Select, contract, and oversee workers who complete specific pieces of the project, such as painting or plumbing. Requisition supplies and materials to complete construction projects. Prepare and submit budget estimates and progress and cost tracking reports. Develop and implement quality control programs. Take actions to deal with the results of delays, bad weather, or emergencies at construction site. Investigate damage, accidents, or delays at construction sites to ensure that proper procedures are being carried out. Evaluate construction methods and determine cost-effectiveness of plans, using computers. **SKILLS—Coordination:** Adjusting actions in relation to others' actions. **Negotiation:** Bringing others together and trying to reconcile differences. **Troubleshooting:** Determining causes of operating errors and deciding what to do about them. **Installation:** Installing equipment, machines, wiring, or programs to meet specifications. **Repairing:** Repairing machines or systems, using the needed tools. **Instructing:** Teaching others how to do something. **Management of Material Resources:** Obtaining and seeing to the appropriate use of equipment, facilities, and materials needed to do certain work. **Persuasion:** Persuading others to change their minds or behavior. **Management of Financial Resources:** Determining how money will be spent to get the work done and accounting for these expenditures.

GOE—Interest Area: 02. Architecture and Construction. **Work Group:** 02.01. Managerial Work in Architecture/Construction . **Other Jobs in This Work Group:** First-Line Supervisors and Manager/Supervisors—Construction Trades Workers. **PERSONALITY TYPE:** Enterprising. Enterprising occupations frequently involve starting up and carrying out projects. These occupations can involve leading people and making many decisions. They sometimes require risk taking and often deal with business.

EDUCATION/TRAINING PROGRAM(S)— Business Administration and Management, General; Business/Commerce, General; Construction Engineering Technology/Technician; Operations Management and Supervision. **RELATED KNOWLEDGE/COURSES—Building and Construction:** Knowledge of the materials, methods, and tools involved in the construction or repair of houses, buildings, or other structures such as highways and roads. **Design:** Knowledge of design techniques, tools, and principles involved in production of precision technical plans, blueprints, drawings, and models. **Administration and Management:** Knowledge of business and management principles involved in strategic planning, resource allocation, human resources modeling, leadership technique, production methods, and coordination of people and resources. **Public Safety and Security:** Knowledge of relevant equipment, policies, procedures, and strategies to promote effective local, state, or national security operations for the protection of people, data, property, and institutions. **Customer and Personal Service:** Knowledge of principles and processes for providing customer and personal services. This includes customer needs assessment, meeting quality standards for services, and evaluation of customer satisfaction. **Mechanical Devices:** Knowledge of machines and tools, including their designs, uses, repair, and maintenance.

Copy Writers

- Education/Training Required: Bachelor's degree
- Annual Earnings: $43,340
- Growth: 16.1%
- Annual Job Openings: 23,000
- Self-Employed: 67.9%
- Part-Time: 24.2%

Write advertising copy for use by publication or broadcast media to promote sale of goods and services. Write advertising copy for use by publication, broadcast, or Internet media to promote the sale of goods and services. Present drafts and ideas to clients. Discuss with the client the product, advertising themes and methods, and any changes that should be made in advertising copy. Vary language and tone of messages based on product and medium. Consult with sales, media, and marketing representatives to obtain information on product or service and discuss style and length of advertising copy. Edit or rewrite existing copy as necessary and submit copy for approval by supervisor. Write to customers in their terms and on their level so that the advertiser's sales message is more readily received. Write articles, bulletins, sales letters, speeches, and other related informative, marketing, and promotional material. Invent names for products and write the slogans that appear on packaging, brochures, and other promotional material. Review advertising trends, consumer surveys, and other data regarding marketing of goods and services to determine the best way to promote products. Develop advertising campaigns for a wide range of clients, working with an advertising agency's creative director and art director to determine the best way to present advertising information. Conduct research and interviews to determine which of a product's selling features should be promoted. **SKILLS—Persuasion:** Persuading others to change their minds or behavior. **Time Management:** Managing one's own time and the time of others. **Instructing:** Teaching others how to do something. **Coordination:** Adjusting actions in relation to others' actions. **Negotiation:** Bringing others together and trying to reconcile differences. **Technology Design:** Generating or adapting equipment and technology to serve user needs. **Critical Thinking:** Using logic and reasoning to identify the strengths and weaknesses of alternative solutions, conclusions, or approaches to problems. **Active Listening:** Giving full attention to what other people are saying, taking time to understand the points being made, asking questions as appropriate, and not interrupting at inappropriate times.

GOE—Interest Area: 03. Arts and Communication. **Work Group:** 03.02. Writing and Editing. **Other Jobs in This Work Group:** Creative Writers; Editors; Poets and Lyricists; Technical Writers. **PERSONALITY TYPE:** Artistic. Artistic occupations frequently involve working with forms, designs, and patterns. They often require self-expression, and the work can be done without following a clear set of rules.

C

EDUCATION/TRAINING PROGRAM(S)—Broadcast Journalism; Business/Corporate Communications; Communication Studies/Speech Communication and Rhetoric; Communication, Journalism, and Related Programs, Other; Creative Writing; English Composition; Family and Consumer Sciences/Human Sciences Communication; Journalism; Mass Communication/Media Studies; Playwriting and Screenwriting; Technical and Business Writing. **RELATED KNOWLEDGE/ COURSES—Sales and Marketing:** Knowledge of principles and methods for showing, promoting, and selling products or services. This includes marketing strategy and tactics, product demonstration, sales techniques, and sales control systems. **Communications and Media:** Knowledge of media production, communication, and dissemination techniques and methods. This includes alternative ways to inform and entertain via written, oral, and visual media. **Sociology and Anthropology:** Knowledge of group behavior and dynamics, societal trends and influences, human migrations, ethnicity, and cultures and their history and origins. **English Language:** Knowledge of the structure and content of the English language, including the meaning and spelling of words, rules of composition, and grammar. **Computers and Electronics:** Knowledge of circuit boards, processors, chips, electronic equipment, and computer hardware and software, including applications and programming. **Administration and Management:** Knowledge of business and management principles involved in strategic planning, resource allocation, human resources modeling, leadership technique, production methods, and coordination of people and resources.

Cost Estimators

- Education/Training Required: Bachelor's degree
- Annual Earnings: $49,220
- Growth: 18.6%
- Annual Job Openings: 25,000
- Self-Employed: 1.7%
- Part-Time: 5.9%

Prepare cost estimates for product manufacturing, construction projects, or services to aid management in bidding on or determining price of product or service. May specialize according to particular service performed or type of product manufactured. Analyze blueprints and other documentation to prepare time, cost, materials, and labor estimates. Assess cost effectiveness of products, projects, or services, tracking actual costs relative to bids as the project develops. Consult with clients, vendors, personnel in other departments, or construction foremen to discuss and formulate estimates and resolve issues. Confer with engineers, architects, owners, contractors, and subcontractors on changes and adjustments to cost estimates. Prepare estimates used by management for purposes such as planning, organizing, and scheduling work. Prepare estimates for use in selecting vendors or subcontractors. Review material and labor requirements to decide whether it is more cost-effective to produce or purchase components. Prepare cost and expenditure statements and other necessary documentation at regular intervals for the duration of the project. Prepare and maintain a directory of suppliers, contractors, and subcontractors. Set up cost monitoring and reporting systems and procedures. Establish and maintain tendering process and conduct negotiations. Conduct special studies to develop and establish standard hour and related cost data or to effect cost reduction. Visit site and record information about access, drainage and topography, and availability of services such as water and electricity. **SKILLS—Management of Financial**

Resources: Determining how money will be spent to get the work done and accounting for these expenditures. **Negotiation:** Bringing others together and trying to reconcile differences. **Coordination:** Adjusting actions in relation to others' actions. **Management of Personnel Resources:** Motivating, developing, and directing people as they work, identifying the best people for the job. **Persuasion:** Persuading others to change their minds or behavior. **Time Management:** Managing one's own time and the time of others. **Mathematics:** Using mathematics to solve problems. **Active Listening:** Giving full attention to what other people are saying, taking time to understand the points being made, asking questions as appropriate, and not interrupting at inappropriate times.

GOE—Interest Area: 06. Finance and Insurance. **Work Group:** 06.02. Finance/Insurance Investigation and Analysis. **Other Jobs in This Work Group:** Appraisers, Real Estate; Assessors; Claims Examiners, Property and Casualty Insurance; Credit Analysts; Financial Analysts; Insurance Adjusters, Examiners, and Investigators; Insurance Appraisers, Auto Damage; Insurance Underwriters; Loan Counselors; Loan Officers; Market Research Analysts; Survey Researchers. **PERSONALITY TYPE:** Conventional. Conventional occupations frequently involve following set procedures and routines. These occupations can include working with data and details more than with ideas. Usually there is a clear line of authority to follow.

EDUCATION/TRAINING PROGRAM(S)— Business Administration and Management, General; Business/Commerce, General; Construction Engineering; Construction Engineering Technology/Technician; Manufacturing Engineering; Materials Engineering; Mechanical Engineering. **RELATED KNOWLEDGE/COURSES—** **Administration and Management:** Knowledge of business and management principles involved in strategic planning, resource allocation, human resources modeling, leadership technique, production methods, and coordination of people and

resources. **Sales and Marketing:** Knowledge of principles and methods for showing, promoting, and selling products or services. This includes marketing strategy and tactics, product demonstration, sales techniques, and sales control systems. **Production and Processing:** Knowledge of raw materials, production processes, quality control, costs, and other techniques for maximizing the effective manufacture and distribution of goods. **Clerical Practices:** Knowledge of administrative and clerical procedures and systems such as word processing, managing files and records, stenography and transcription, designing forms, and other office procedures and terminology. **Economics and Accounting:** Knowledge of economic and accounting principles and practices, the financial markets, banking, and the analysis and reporting of financial data. **Personnel and Human Resources:** Knowledge of principles and procedures for personnel recruitment, selection, training, compensation and benefits, labor relations and negotiation, and personnel information systems. **Mathematics:** Knowledge of arithmetic, algebra, geometry, calculus, and statistics and their applications.

Counseling Psychologists

- ◎ Education/Training Required: Master's degree
- ◎ Annual Earnings: $53,230
- ◎ Growth: 24.4%
- ◎ Annual Job Openings: 17,000
- ◎ Self-Employed: 25.4%
- ◎ Part-Time: 27.2%

Assess and evaluate individuals' problems through the use of case history, interview, and observation and provide individual or group counseling services to assist individuals in achieving more-effective

personal, social, educational, and vocational development and adjustment. Provide consulting services to schools, social service agencies, and businesses. Advise clients on how they could be helped by counseling. Analyze data such as interview notes, test results, and reference manuals in order to identify symptoms and to diagnose the nature of clients' problems. Collect information about individuals or clients, using interviews, case histories, observational techniques, and other assessment methods. Counsel individuals, groups, or families to help them understand problems, define goals, and develop realistic action plans. Develop therapeutic and treatment plans based on clients' interests, abilities, and needs. Evaluate the results of counseling methods to determine the reliability and validity of treatments. Select, administer, and interpret psychological tests to assess intelligence, aptitudes, abilities, or interests. Consult with other professionals to discuss therapies, treatments, counseling resources, or techniques and to share occupational information. Refer clients to specialists or to other institutions for non-counseling treatment of problems. Conduct research to develop or improve diagnostic or therapeutic counseling techniques. **SKILLS—Social Perceptiveness:** Being aware of others' reactions and understanding why they react as they do. **Active Listening:** Giving full attention to what other people are saying, taking time to understand the points being made, asking questions as appropriate, and not interrupting at inappropriate times. **Learning Strategies:** Selecting and using training/instructional methods and procedures appropriate for the situation when learning or teaching new things. **Critical Thinking:** Using logic and reasoning to identify the strengths and weaknesses of alternative solutions, conclusions, or approaches to problems. **Persuasion:** Persuading others to change their minds or behavior. **Reading Comprehension:** Understanding written sentences and paragraphs in work-related documents. **Active Learning:** Understanding the implications of new information for both current and future problem-solving and decision-making. **Science:** Using scientific rules and methods to solve problems.

Monitoring: Monitoring or assessing your performance or that of other individuals or organizations to make improvements or take corrective action.

GOE—Interest Area: 10. Human Service. **Work Group:** 10.01. Counseling and Social Work. **Other Jobs in This Work Group:** Child, Family, and School Social Workers; Clinical Psychologists; Marriage and Family Therapists; Medical and Public Health Social Workers; Mental Health and Substance Abuse Social Workers; Mental Health Counselors; Probation Officers and Correctional Treatment Specialists; Rehabilitation Counselors; Residential Advisors; Social and Human Service Assistants; Substance Abuse and Behavioral Disorder Counselors. **PERSONALITY TYPE:** Social. Social occupations frequently involve working with, communicating with, and teaching people. These occupations often involve helping or providing service to others.

EDUCATION/TRAINING PROGRAM(S)— Clinical Child Psychology; Clinical Psychology; Counseling Psychology; Developmental and Child Psychology; Psychoanalysis and Psychotherapy; Psychology, General; School Psychology. **RELATED KNOWLEDGE/COURSES—Therapy and Counseling:** Knowledge of principles, methods, and procedures for diagnosis, treatment, and rehabilitation of physical and mental dysfunctions and for career counseling and guidance. **Psychology:** Knowledge of human behavior and performance; individual differences in ability, personality, and interests; learning and motivation; psychological research methods; and the assessment and treatment of behavioral and affective disorders. **Sociology and Anthropology:** Knowledge of group behavior and dynamics, societal trends and influences, human migrations, ethnicity, and cultures and their history and origins. **Philosophy and Theology:** Knowledge of different philosophical systems and religions. This includes their basic principles, values, ethics, ways of thinking, customs, and practices and their impact on human culture. **Mathematics:** Knowledge of arithmetic, algebra, geometry, calculus, and statistics and their applications. **Education and**

Training: Knowledge of principles and methods for curriculum and training design, teaching and instruction for individuals and groups, and the measurement of training effects.

Creative Writers

- Education/Training Required: Bachelor's degree
- Annual Earnings: $43,340
- Growth: 16.1%
- Annual Job Openings: 23,000
- Self-Employed: 67.9%
- Part-Time: 24.2%

Create original written works, such as plays or prose, for publication or performance. Writes fiction or nonfiction prose work, such as short story, novel, biography, article, descriptive or critical analysis, or essay. Writes play or script for moving pictures or television based on original ideas or adapted from fictional, historical, or narrative sources. Organizes material for project, plans arrangement or outline, and writes synopsis. Collaborates with other writers on specific projects. Confers with client, publisher, or producer to discuss development changes or revisions. Conducts research to obtain factual information and authentic detail, utilizing sources such as newspaper accounts, diaries, and interviews. Reviews, submits for approval, and revises written material to meet personal standards and satisfy needs of client, publisher, director, or producer. Selects subject or theme for writing project based on personal interest and writing specialty or assignment from publisher, client, producer, or director. Develops factors such as theme, plot, characterization, psychological analysis, historical environment, action, and dialogue to create material. Writes humorous material for publication or performance, such as comedy routines, gags, comedy shows, or scripts for entertainers.

SKILLS—Writing: Communicating effectively in writing as appropriate for the needs of the audience. **Reading Comprehension:** Understanding written sentences and paragraphs in work-related documents. **Coordination:** Adjusting actions in relation to others' actions. **Critical Thinking:** Using logic and reasoning to identify the strengths and weaknesses of alternative solutions, conclusions, or approaches to problems. **Complex Problem Solving:** Identifying complex problems and reviewing related information to develop and evaluate options and implement solutions. **Social Perceptiveness:** Being aware of others' reactions and understanding why they react as they do. **Monitoring:** Monitoring or assessing your performance or that of other individuals or organizations to make improvements or take corrective action. **Negotiation:** Bringing others together and trying to reconcile differences.

GOE—Interest Area: 03. Arts and Communication. **Work Group:** 03.02. Writing and Editing. **Other Jobs in This Work Group:** Copy Writers; Editors; Poets and Lyricists; Technical Writers. **PERSONALITY TYPE:** Artistic. Artistic occupations frequently involve working with forms, designs, and patterns. They often require self-expression, and the work can be done without following a clear set of rules.

EDUCATION/TRAINING PROGRAM(S)— Broadcast Journalism; Business/Corporate Communications; Communication Studies/Speech Communication and Rhetoric; Communication, Journalism, and Related Programs, Other; Creative Writing; English Composition; Family and Consumer Sciences/Human Sciences Communication; Journalism; Mass Communication/Media Studies; Playwriting and Screenwriting; Technical and Business Writing. **RELATED KNOWLEDGE/ COURSES—English Language:** Knowledge of the structure and content of the English language, including the meaning and spelling of words, rules of composition, and grammar. **Communications and Media:** Knowledge of media production, communication, and dissemination techniques and methods. This includes alternative ways to inform and entertain via written, oral, and visual media. **Fine Arts:** Knowledge of the theory and techniques required to compose, produce, and perform works of music, dance, visual arts, drama, and sculpture. **Sociology and Anthropology:** Knowledge of group behavior and dynamics, societal trends and influences, human migrations, ethnicity, and cultures and their history and origins. **Computers and Electronics:** Knowledge of circuit boards, processors, chips, electronic equipment, and computer hardware and software, including applications and programming.

Credit Analysts

- ◎ Education/Training Required: Bachelor's degree
- ◎ Annual Earnings: $46,640
- ◎ Growth: 18.7%
- ◎ Annual Job Openings: 9,000
- ◎ Self-Employed: 0%
- ◎ Part-Time: 4.1%

Analyze current credit data and financial statements of individuals or firms to determine the degree of risk involved in extending credit or lending money. Prepare reports with this credit information for use in decision-making. Analyze credit data and financial statements to determine the degree of risk involved in extending credit or lending money. Prepare reports that include the degree of risk involved in extending credit or lending money. Evaluate customer records and recommend payment plans based on earnings, savings data, payment history, and purchase activity. Confer with credit association and other business representatives to exchange credit information. Complete loan applications, including credit analyses and summaries of loan requests, and submit to loan committees for approval. Generate financial ratios, using computer programs, to evaluate customers' financial status. Review individual or commercial customer files to identify and select delinquent accounts for collection. Compare liquidity, profitability, and credit histories of establishments being evaluated with those of similar establishments in the same industries and geographic locations. Consult with customers to resolve complaints and verify financial and credit transactions. Analyze financial data such as income growth, quality of management, and market share to determine expected profitability of loans. **SKILLS—Speaking:** Talking to others to convey information effectively. **Negotiation:** Bringing others together and trying to reconcile differences. **Writing:** Communicating effectively in writing as appropriate for the needs of the audience. **Instructing:** Teaching others how to do something. **Social Perceptiveness:** Being aware of others' reactions and understanding why they react as they do. **Active Listening:** Giving full attention to what other people are saying, taking time to understand the points being made, asking questions as appropriate, and not interrupting at inappropriate times. **Monitoring:** Monitoring or assessing your performance or that of other individuals or organizations to make improvements or take corrective action. **Service Orientation:** Actively looking for ways to help people. **Operations Analysis:** Analyzing needs and product requirements to create a design. **Judgment and Decision Making:** Considering the relative costs and benefits of potential actions to choose the most appropriate one.

GOE—Interest Area: 06. Finance and Insurance. **Work Group:** 06.02. Finance/Insurance Investigation and Analysis. **Other Jobs in This Work Group:** Appraisers, Real Estate; Assessors; Claims Examiners, Property and Casualty Insurance; Cost Estimators; Financial Analysts; Insurance Adjusters, Examiners, and Investigators; Insurance Appraisers, Auto Damage; Insurance Underwriters; Loan Counselors; Loan Officers; Market Research Analysts; Survey Researchers. **PERSONALITY TYPE:** Conventional. Conventional occupations frequently involve following set procedures and routines. These occupations can include working with data and details more than with ideas. Usually there is a clear line of authority to follow.

EDUCATION/TRAINING PROGRAM(S)—Accounting; Credit Management; Finance, General. **RELATED KNOWLEDGE/COURSES—Economics and Accounting:** Knowledge of economic and accounting principles and practices, the financial markets, banking, and the analysis and reporting of financial data. **Clerical Practices:** Knowledge of administrative and clerical procedures and systems such as word processing, managing files and records, stenography and transcription, designing forms, and other office procedures and terminology. **Mathematics:** Knowledge of arithmetic, algebra, geometry, calculus, and statistics and their applications. **Customer and Personal Service:** Knowledge of principles and processes for providing customer and personal services. This includes customer needs assessment, meeting quality standards for services, and evaluation of customer satisfaction. **Administration and Management:** Knowledge of business and management principles involved in strategic planning, resource allocation, human resources modeling, leadership technique, production methods, and coordination of people and resources. **English Language:** Knowledge of the structure and content of the English language, including the meaning and spelling of words, rules of composition, and grammar. **Law and Government:** Knowledge of laws, legal codes, court procedures, precedents, government regulations, executive orders, agency rules, and the democratic political process.

Criminal Justice and Law Enforcement Teachers, Postsecondary

- Education/Training Required: Master's degree
- Annual Earnings: $46,030
- Growth: 38.1% for all Postsecondary Teachers
- Annual Job Openings: 216,000 for all Postsecondary Teachers
- Self-Employed: 0.3% for all Postsecondary Teachers
- Part-Time: 27.7% for all Postsecondary Teachers

Teach courses in criminal justice, corrections, and law enforcement administration. Evaluate and grade students' class work, assignments, and papers. Prepare and deliver lectures to undergraduate and/or graduate students on topics such as criminal law, defensive policing, and investigation techniques. Advise students on academic and vocational curricula and on career issues. Compile, administer, and grade examinations or assign this work to others. Compile bibliographies of specialized materials for outside reading assignments. Initiate, facilitate, and moderate classroom discussions. Keep abreast of developments in their field by reading current literature, talking with colleagues, and participating in professional conferences. Maintain regularly scheduled office hours in order to advise and assist students. Maintain student attendance records, grades, and other required records. Plan, evaluate, and revise curricula, course content, and course materials and methods of instruction. Prepare course materials such as syllabi, homework assignments, and handouts. Select and obtain materials and supplies such as textbooks. Supervise undergraduate

C

and/or graduate teaching, internship, and research work. Act as advisers to student organizations. Collaborate with colleagues to address teaching and research issues. Conduct research in a particular field of knowledge and publish findings in professional journals, books, and/or electronic media. Participate in campus and community events. Participate in student recruitment, registration, and placement activities. Perform administrative duties such as serving as department head. Provide professional consulting services to government and/or industry. Serve on academic or administrative committees that deal with institutional policies, departmental matters, and academic issues. Write grant proposals to procure external research funding. **SKILLS**—No data available.

GOE—Interest Area: 05. Education and Training. **Work Group:** 05.03. Postsecondary and Adult Teaching and Instructing. **Other Jobs in This Work Group:** Adult Literacy, Remedial Education, and GED Teachers and Instructors; Agricultural Sciences Teachers, Postsecondary; Anthropology and Archeology Teachers, Postsecondary; Architecture Teachers, Postsecondary; Area, Ethnic, and Cultural Studies Teachers, Postsecondary; Art, Drama, and Music Teachers, Postsecondary; Atmospheric, Earth, Marine, and Space Sciences Teachers, Postsecondary; Biological Science Teachers, Postsecondary; Business Teachers, Postsecondary; Chemistry Teachers, Postsecondary; Communications Teachers, Postsecondary; Computer Science Teachers, Postsecondary; Economics Teachers, Postsecondary; Education Teachers, Postsecondary; Engineering Teachers, Postsecondary; English Language and Literature Teachers, Postsecondary; Environmental Science Teachers, Postsecondary; Farm and Home Management Advisors; Foreign Language and Literature Teachers, Postsecondary; Forestry and Conservation Science Teachers, Postsecondary; Geography Teachers, Postsecondary; Graduate Teaching Assistants; Health Specialties Teachers, Postsecondary; History Teachers, Postsecondary; Home Economics Teachers, Postsecondary; Law Teachers, Postsecondary; Library Science Teachers, Postsecondary; Mathematical Science Teachers, Postsecondary; Nursing Instructors and Teachers, Postsecondary; Philosophy and Religion Teachers, Postsecondary; Physics Teachers, Postsecondary; Political Science Teachers, Postsecondary; Psychology Teachers, Postsecondary; Recreation and Fitness Studies Teachers, Postsecondary; Self-Enrichment Education Teachers; Social Work Teachers, Postsecondary; Sociology Teachers, Postsecondary; Vocational Education Teachers, Postsecondary. **PERSONALITY TYPE:** No data available.

EDUCATION/TRAINING PROGRAM(S)—Corrections; Corrections Administration; Corrections and Criminal Justice, Other; Criminal Justice/Law Enforcement Administration; Criminal Justice/Police Science; Criminal Justice/Safety Studies; Criminalistics and Criminal Science; Forensic Science and Technology; Juvenile Corrections; Security and Loss Prevention Services; Teacher Education and Professional Development, Specific Subject Areas, Other. **RELATED KNOWLEDGE/COURSES**—No data available.

Database Administrators

◎ Education/Training Required: Bachelor's degree
◎ Annual Earnings: $59,150
◎ Growth: 44.2%
◎ Annual Job Openings: 16,000
◎ Self-Employed: 0.6%
◎ Part-Time: 4.6%

Coordinate changes to computer databases; test and implement the database, applying knowledge of database management systems. May plan, coordinate, and implement security measures to safeguard computer databases. Develop standards and guidelines to guide the use and acquisition of software and to protect vulnerable information. Modify existing databases and database management systems or direct programmers and analysts to make changes. Test programs or databases, correct errors, and make necessary modifications. Plan, coordinate, and implement security measures to safeguard information in computer files against accidental or unauthorized damage, modification, or disclosure. Approve, schedule, plan, and supervise the installation and testing of new products and improvements to computer systems, such as the installation of new databases. Train users and answer questions. Establish and calculate optimum values for database parameters, using manuals and calculator. Specify users and user access levels for each segment of database. Develop data model describing data elements and how they are used, following procedures and using pen, template, or computer software. Develop methods for integrating different products so they work properly together, such as customizing commercial databases to fit specific needs. Review project requests describing database user needs to estimate time and cost required to accomplish project. Review procedures in database management system manuals for making changes to database. Work as part of a project team to coordinate database development and determine project scope and limitations. Select and enter codes to monitor database performance and to create production database. Identify and evaluate industry trends in database systems to serve as a source of information and advice for upper management. Write and code logical and physical database descriptions and specify identifiers of database to management system or direct others in coding descriptions. Review workflow charts developed by programmer analyst to understand tasks computer will perform, such as updating records. Revise company definition of data as defined in data dictionary. **SKILLS—Troubleshooting:** Determining causes of operating errors and deciding what to do about them. **Persuasion:** Persuading others to change their minds or behavior. **Operations Analysis:** Analyzing needs and product requirements to create a design. **Instructing:** Teaching others how to do something. **Systems**

Evaluation: Identifying measures or indicators of system performance and the actions needed to improve or correct performance relative to the goals of the system. **Management of Personnel Resources:** Motivating, developing, and directing people as they work, identifying the best people for the job. **Time Management:** Managing one's own time and the time of others. **Technology Design:** Generating or adapting equipment and technology to serve user needs.

GOE—Interest Area: 11. Information Technology. **Work Group:** 11.02. Information Technology Specialties. **Other Jobs in This Work Group:** Computer Operators; Computer Programmers; Computer Security Specialists; Computer Software Engineers, Applications; Computer Software Engineers, Systems Software; Computer Support Specialists; Computer Systems Analysts; Network Systems and Data Communications Analysts. **PERSONALITY TYPE:** Investigative. Investigative occupations frequently involve working with ideas and require an extensive amount of thinking. These occupations can involve searching for facts and figuring out problems mentally.

EDUCATION/TRAINING PROGRAM(S)— Computer and Information Sciences, General; Computer and Information Systems Security; Computer Systems Analysis/Analyst; Data Modeling/Warehousing and Database Administration; Management Information Systems, General. **RELATED KNOWLEDGE/COURSES—Computers and Electronics:** Knowledge of circuit boards, processors, chips, electronic equipment, and computer hardware and software, including applications and programming. **Clerical Practices:** Knowledge of administrative and clerical procedures and systems such as word processing, managing files and records, stenography and transcription, designing forms, and other office procedures and terminology. **Customer and Personal Service:** Knowledge of principles and processes for providing customer and personal services. This includes customer needs assessment, meeting quality standards for services, and evaluation of customer satisfaction. **Economics**

and **Accounting:** Knowledge of economic and accounting principles and practices, the financial markets, banking, and the analysis and reporting of financial data. **Administration and Management:** Knowledge of business and management principles involved in strategic planning, resource allocation, human resources modeling, leadership technique, production methods, and coordination of people and resources. **Mathematics:** Knowledge of arithmetic, algebra, geometry, calculus, and statistics and their applications.

Dental Hygienists

- ◉ Education/Training Required: Associate's degree
- ◉ Annual Earnings: $56,680
- ◉ Growth: 43.1%
- ◉ Annual Job Openings: 9,000
- ◉ Self-Employed: 0.7%
- ◉ Part-Time: 57.8%

Clean teeth and examine oral areas, head, and neck for signs of oral disease. May educate patients on oral hygiene, take and develop X rays, or apply fluoride or sealants. Clean calcareous deposits, accretions, and stains from teeth and beneath margins of gums, using dental instruments. Feel and visually examine gums for sores and signs of disease. Chart conditions of decay and disease for diagnosis and treatment by dentist. Feel lymph nodes under patient's chin to detect swelling or tenderness that could indicate presence of oral cancer. Apply fluorides and other cavity-preventing agents to arrest dental decay. Examine gums, using probes, to locate periodontal recessed gums and signs of gum disease. Expose and develop X ray film. Provide clinical services and health education to improve and maintain oral health of school children. Remove excess cement from coronal surfaces of teeth. Make impressions for study casts. Place, carve, and finish amalgam restorations. Administer local anesthetic

agents. Conduct dental health clinics for community groups to augment services of dentist. **SKILLS— Time Management:** Managing one's own time and the time of others. **Active Learning:** Understanding the implications of new information for both current and future problem-solving and decision-making. **Social Perceptiveness:** Being aware of others' reactions and understanding why they react as they do. **Instructing:** Teaching others how to do something. **Persuasion:** Persuading others to change their minds or behavior. **Learning Strategies:** Selecting and using training/instructional methods and procedures appropriate for the situation when learning or teaching new things. **Reading Comprehension:** Understanding written sentences and paragraphs in work-related documents. **Service Orientation:** Actively looking for ways to help people.

GOE—Interest Area: 08. Health Science. **Work Group:** 08.03. Dentistry. **Other Jobs in This Work Group:** Dental Assistants; Dentists, General; Oral and Maxillofacial Surgeons; Orthodontists; Prosthodontists. **PERSONALITY TYPE:** Social. Social occupations frequently involve working with, communicating with, and teaching people. These occupations often involve helping or providing service to others.

EDUCATION/TRAINING PROGRAM(S)— Dental Hygiene/Hygienist. **RELATED KNOWLEDGE/COURSES—Biology:** Knowledge of plant and animal organisms and their tissues, cells, functions, interdependencies, and interactions with each other and the environment. **Medicine and Dentistry:** Knowledge of the information and techniques needed to diagnose and treat human injuries, diseases, and deformities. This includes symptoms, treatment alternatives, drug properties and interactions, and preventive health-care measures. **Customer and Personal Service:** Knowledge of principles and processes for providing customer and personal services. This includes customer needs assessment, meeting quality standards for services, and evaluation of customer satisfaction. **Psychology:** Knowledge of human behavior and performance; individual differences in ability, personality, and interests; learning and motivation; psychological research methods; and the assessment and treatment of behavioral and affective disorders. **Chemistry:** Knowledge of the chemical composition, structure, and properties of substances and of the chemical processes and transformations that they undergo. This includes uses of chemicals and their danger signs, production techniques, and disposal methods. **Sales and Marketing:** Knowledge of principles and methods for showing, promoting, and selling products or services. This includes marketing strategy and tactics, product demonstration, sales techniques, and sales control systems.

Dentists, General

- Education/Training Required: First professional degree
- Annual Earnings: $120,420
- Growth: 4.1%
- Annual Job Openings: 7,000
- Self-Employed: 39.9%
- Part-Time: 22.3%

Diagnose and treat diseases, injuries, and malformations of teeth and gums and related oral structures. May treat diseases of nerve, pulp, and other dental tissues affecting vitality of teeth. Administer anesthetics to limit the amount of pain experienced by patients during procedures. Advise and instruct patients regarding preventive dental care, the causes and treatment of dental problems, and oral health-care services. Analyze and evaluate dental needs to determine changes and trends in patterns of dental disease. Apply fluoride and sealants to teeth. Bleach, clean, or polish teeth to restore natural color. Design, make, and fit prosthodontic appliances, such as space maintainers, bridges, and dentures, or write fabrication instructions or prescriptions for denturists and dental technicians. Diagnose and treat diseases, injuries, and malformations of teeth,

gums, and related oral structures and provide preventive and corrective services. Eliminate irritating margins of fillings and correct occlusions, using dental instruments. Examine teeth, gums, and related tissues, using dental instruments, X rays, and other diagnostic equipment, to evaluate dental health, diagnose diseases or abnormalities, and plan appropriate treatments. Fill pulp chamber and canal with endodontic materials. Formulate plan of treatment for patient's teeth and mouth tissue. Manage business, employing and supervising staff and handling paperwork and insurance claims. Perform oral and periodontal surgery on the jaw or mouth. Remove diseased tissue, using surgical instruments. Treat exposure of pulp by pulp capping, removal of pulp from pulp chamber, or root canal, using dental instruments. Plan, organize, and maintain dental health programs. Produce and evaluate dental health educational materials. Write prescriptions for antibiotics and other medications. Use air turbine and hand instruments, dental appliances, and surgical implements. Use masks, gloves, and safety glasses to protect themselves and their patients from infectious diseases. **SKILLS—Science:** Using scientific rules and methods to solve problems. **Reading Comprehension:** Understanding written sentences and paragraphs in work-related documents. **Active Learning:** Understanding the implications of new information for both current and future problem-solving and decision-making. **Service Orientation:** Actively looking for ways to help people. **Critical Thinking:** Using logic and reasoning to identify the strengths and weaknesses of alternative solutions, conclusions, or approaches to problems. **Judgment and Decision Making:** Considering the relative costs and benefits of potential actions to choose the most appropriate one. **Learning Strategies:** Selecting and using training/instructional methods and procedures appropriate for the situation when learning or teaching new things. **Writing:** Communicating effectively in writing as appropriate for the needs of the audience. **Monitoring:** Monitoring or assessing your performance or that of other individuals or organizations to make improvements or take corrective action. **Management of Financial Resources:**

D

Determining how money will be spent to get the work done and accounting for these expenditures.

GOE—Interest Area: 08. Health Science. **Work Group:** 08.03. Dentistry. **Other Jobs in This Work Group:** Dental Assistants; Dental Hygienists; Oral and Maxillofacial Surgeons; Orthodontists; Prosthodontists. **PERSONALITY TYPE:** Investigative. Investigative occupations frequently involve working with ideas and require an extensive amount of thinking. These occupations can involve searching for facts and figuring out problems mentally.

EDUCATION/TRAINING PROGRAM(S)— Advanced General Dentistry (Cert, MS, PhD); Dental Public Health and Education (Cert, MS/MPH, PhD/DPH); Dental Public Health Specialty; Dentistry (DDS, DMD); Pediatric Dentistry/Pedodontics (Cert, MS, PhD); Pedodontics Specialty. **RELATED KNOWLEDGE/COURSES—Medicine and Dentistry:** Knowledge of the information and techniques needed to diagnose and treat human injuries, diseases, and deformities. This includes symptoms, treatment alternatives, drug properties and interactions, and preventive healthcare measures. **Biology:** Knowledge of plant and animal organisms and their tissues, cells, functions, interdependencies, and interactions with each other and the environment. **Chemistry:** Knowledge of the chemical composition, structure, and properties of substances and of the chemical processes and transformations that they undergo. This includes uses of chemicals and their danger signs, production techniques, and disposal methods. **English Language:** Knowledge of the structure and content of the English language, including the meaning and spelling of words, rules of composition, and grammar. **Administration and Management:** Knowledge of business and management principles involved in strategic planning, resource allocation, human resources modeling, leadership technique, production methods, and coordination of people and resources. **Psychology:** Knowledge of human behavior and performance; individual differences in ability, personality, and interests; learning and motivation; psy-

chological research methods; and the assessment and treatment of behavioral and affective disorders.

Diagnostic Medical Sonographers

- Education/Training Required: Associate's degree
- Annual Earnings: $50,980
- Growth: 24.0%
- Annual Job Openings: 4,000
- Self-Employed: 0.2%
- Part-Time: 17.5%

Produce ultrasonic recordings of internal organs for use by physicians. Decide which images to include, looking for differences between healthy and pathological areas. Observe screen during scan to ensure that image produced is satisfactory for diagnostic purposes, making adjustments to equipment as required. Observe and care for patients throughout examinations to ensure their safety and comfort. Provide sonogram and oral or written summary of technical findings to physician for use in medical diagnosis. Operate ultrasound equipment to produce and record images of the motion, shape, and composition of blood, organs, tissues, and bodily masses such as fluid accumulations. Select appropriate equipment settings and adjust patient positions to obtain the best sites and angles. Determine whether scope of exam should be extended, based on findings. Process and code film from procedures and complete appropriate documentation. Obtain and record accurate patient history, including prior test results and information from physical examinations. Prepare patient for exam by explaining procedure, transferring them to ultrasound table, scrubbing skin and applying gel, and positioning them properly. Record and store suitable images, using camera unit connected to the ultrasound equipment. Coordinate work with physicians and other health-care team members, including providing assistance during invasive procedures. Maintain records that include patient information, sonographs and interpretations, files of correspondence, publications and regulations, and quality assurance records (e.g., pathology, biopsy, post-operative reports). Perform legal and ethical duties, including preparing safety and accident reports, obtaining written consent from patient to perform invasive procedures, and reporting symptoms of abuse and neglect. Supervise and train students and other medical sonographers. Maintain stock and supplies, preparing supplies for special examinations and ordering supplies when necessary. Clean, check, and maintain sonographic equipment, submitting maintenance requests or performing minor repairs as necessary. Perform clerical duties such as scheduling exams and special procedures, keeping records, and archiving computerized images. **SKILLS—Social Perceptiveness:** Being aware of others' reactions and understanding why they react as they do. **Reading Comprehension:** Understanding written sentences and paragraphs in work-related documents. **Instructing:** Teaching others how to do something. **Learning Strategies:** Selecting and using training/instructional methods and procedures appropriate for the situation when learning or teaching new things. **Active Learning:** Understanding the implications of new information for both current and future problem-solving and decision-making. **Service Orientation:** Actively looking for ways to help people. **Operation and Control:** Controlling operations of equipment or systems. **Active Listening:** Giving full attention to what other people are saying, taking time to understand the points being made, asking questions as appropriate, and not interrupting at inappropriate times.

GOE—Interest Area: 08. Health Science. **Work Group:** 08.06. Medical Technology. **Other Jobs in This Work Group:** Biological Technicians; Cardiovascular Technologists and Technicians; Medical and Clinical Laboratory Technicians; Medical and Clinical Laboratory Technologists; Medical Equip-

ment Preparers; Medical Records and Health Information Technicians; Nuclear Medicine Technologists; Opticians, Dispensing; Orthotists and Prosthetists; Radiologic Technicians; Radiologic Technologists. **PERSONALITY TYPE:** No data available.

EDUCATION/TRAINING PROGRAM(S)— Allied Health Diagnostic, Intervention, and Treatment Professions, Other; Diagnostic Medical Sonography/Sonographer and Ultrasound Technician. **RELATED KNOWLEDGE/COURSES—Medicine and Dentistry:** Knowledge of the information and techniques needed to diagnose and treat human injuries, diseases, and deformities. This includes symptoms, treatment alternatives, drug properties and interactions, and preventive health-care measures. **Biology:** Knowledge of plant and animal organisms and their tissues, cells, functions, interdependencies, and interactions with each other and the environment. **Physics:** Knowledge and prediction of physical principles and laws and their interrelationships and applications to understanding fluid, material, and atmospheric dynamics and mechanical, electrical, atomic, and subatomic structures and processes. **Customer and Personal Service:** Knowledge of principles and processes for providing customer and personal services. This includes customer needs assessment, meeting quality standards for services, and evaluation of customer satisfaction. **Education and Training:** Knowledge of principles and methods for curriculum and training design, teaching and instruction for individuals and groups, and the measurement of training effects. **Clerical Practices:** Knowledge of administrative and clerical procedures and systems such as word processing, managing files and records, stenography and transcription, designing forms, and other office procedures and terminology. **Psychology:** Knowledge of human behavior and performance; individual differences in ability, personality, and interests; learning and motivation; psychological research methods; and the assessment and treatment of behavioral and affective disorders.

D

Dietitians and Nutritionists

- Education/Training Required: Bachelor's degree
- Annual Earnings: $42,630
- Growth: 17.8%
- Annual Job Openings: 8,000
- Self-Employed: 6.3%
- Part-Time: 24.3%

Plan and conduct food service or nutritional programs to assist in the promotion of health and control of disease. May supervise activities of a department providing quantity food services, counsel individuals, or conduct nutritional research. Assess nutritional needs, diet restrictions, and current health plans to develop and implement dietary-care plans and provide nutritional counseling. Consult with physicians and health-care personnel to determine nutritional needs and diet restrictions of patient or client. Advise patients and their families on nutritional principles, dietary plans and diet modifications, and food selection and preparation. Counsel individuals and groups on basic rules of good nutrition, healthy eating habits, and nutrition monitoring to improve their quality of life. Monitor food service operations to ensure conformance to nutritional, safety, sanitation, and quality standards. Coordinate recipe development and standardization and develop new menus for independent food service operations. Develop policies for food service or nutritional programs to assist in health promotion and disease control. Inspect meals served for conformance to prescribed diets and standards of palatability and appearance. Develop curriculum and prepare manuals, visual aids, course outlines, and other materials used in teaching. Prepare and administer budgets for food, equipment, and supplies. Purchase food in accordance with health and safety codes. Select, train, and supervise workers who plan, prepare, and serve meals. Manage quantity food service departments or clinical and community nutrition services. Coordinate diet counseling services. Advise food service managers and organizations on sanitation, safety procedures, menu development, budgeting, and planning to assist with the establishment, operation, and evaluation of food service facilities and nutrition programs. Organize, develop, analyze, test, and prepare special meals such as low-fat, low-cholesterol and chemical-free meals. Plan, conduct, and evaluate dietary, nutritional, and epidemiological research. Plan and conduct training programs in dietetics, nutrition, and institutional management and administration for medical students, health-care personnel, and the general public. Make recommendations regarding public policy, such as nutrition labeling, food fortification, and nutrition standards for school programs. **SKILLS—Instructing:** Teaching others how to do something. **Social Perceptiveness:** Being aware of others' reactions and understanding why they react as they do. **Persuasion:** Persuading others to change their minds or behavior. **Learning Strategies:** Selecting and using training/instructional methods and procedures appropriate for the situation when learning or teaching new things. **Science:** Using scientific rules and methods to solve problems. **Writing:** Communicating effectively in writing as appropriate for the needs of the audience. **Service Orientation:** Actively looking for ways to help people. **Speaking:** Talking to others to convey information effectively. **Time Management:** Managing one's own time and the time of others.

GOE—Interest Area: 08. Health Science. **Work Group:** 08.09. Health Protection and Promotion. **Other Jobs in This Work Group:** Athletic Trainers; Dietetic Technicians; Embalmers. **PERSONALITY TYPE:** Investigative. Investigative occupations frequently involve working with ideas and require an extensive amount of thinking. These occupations can involve searching for facts and figuring out problems mentally.

EDUCATION/TRAINING PROGRAM(S)—Clinical Nutrition/Nutritionist; Dietetics and Clinical Nutrition Services, Other; Dietetics/Dietitian (RD); Foods, Nutrition, and Related Services, Other; Foods, Nutrition, and Wellness Studies, General; Foodservice Systems Administration/Management; Human Nutrition; Nutrition Sciences. **RELATED KNOWLEDGE/COURSES—Sociology and Anthropology:** Knowledge of group behavior and dynamics, societal trends and influences, human migrations, ethnicity, and cultures and their history and origins. **Food Production:** Knowledge of techniques and equipment for planting, growing, and harvesting food products (both plant and animal) for consumption, including storage/handling techniques. **Therapy and Counseling:** Knowledge of principles, methods, and procedures for diagnosis, treatment, and rehabilitation of physical and mental dysfunctions and for career counseling and guidance. **Psychology:** Knowledge of human behavior and performance; individual differences in ability, personality, and interests; learning and motivation; psychological research methods; and the assessment and treatment of behavioral and affective disorders. **Education and Training:** Knowledge of principles and methods for curriculum and training design, teaching and instruction for individuals and groups, and the measurement of training effects. **Customer and Personal Service:** Knowledge of principles and processes for providing customer and personal services. This includes customer needs assessment, meeting quality standards for services, and evaluation of customer satisfaction.

Directors—Stage, Motion Pictures, Television, and Radio

- ◉ Education/Training Required: Work experience plus degree
- ◉ Annual Earnings: $51,870
- ◉ Growth: 18.3%
- ◉ Annual Job Openings: 10,000
- ◉ Self-Employed: 32.8%
- ◉ Part-Time: 9.1%

Interpret script, conduct rehearsals, and direct activities of cast and technical crew for stage, motion pictures, television, or radio programs. Direct live broadcasts, films and recordings, or non-broadcast programming for public entertainment or education. Supervise and coordinate the work of camera, lighting, design, and sound crewmembers. Study and research scripts in order to determine how they should be directed. Cut and edit film or tape in order to integrate component parts into desired sequences. Collaborate with film and sound editors during the post-production process as films are edited and soundtracks are added. Confer with technical directors, managers, crew members, and writers to discuss details of production, such as photography, script, music, sets, and costumes. Plan details such as framing, composition, camera movement, sound, and actor movement for each shot or scene. Communicate to actors the approach, characterization, and movement needed for each scene in such a way that rehearsals and takes are minimized. Establish pace of programs and sequences of scenes according to time requirements and cast and set accessibility. Choose settings and locations for films and determine how scenes will be shot in these settings. Identify and approve equipment and elements required for productions, such as scenery, lights, props, costumes, choreography, and music. Compile scripts, program notes, and other material related to productions. Perform producers' duties, such as securing financial backing, establishing and administering budgets, and recruiting cast and crew. Select plays or scripts for production and determine how material should be interpreted and performed. Compile cue words and phrases and cue announcers, cast members, and technicians during performances. Consult with writers, producers, and/or actors about script changes or "workshop" scripts through rehearsal with writers and actors to create final drafts. Review film daily in order to check on work in progress and to plan for future filming. Collaborate with producers in order to hire crewmembers such as art directors, cinematographers, and costumer designers. Interpret stage-set diagrams to determine stage layouts and supervise placement of equipment and scenery. **SKILLS—Management of Personnel Resources:** Motivating, developing, and directing people as they work, identifying the best people for the job. **Time Management:** Managing one's own time and the time of others. **Judgment and Decision Making:** Considering the relative costs and benefits of potential actions to choose the most appropriate one. **Critical Thinking:** Using logic and reasoning to identify the strengths and weaknesses of alternative solutions, conclusions, or approaches to problems. **Active Listening:** Giving full attention to what other people are saying, taking time to understand the points being made, asking questions as appropriate, and not interrupting at inappropriate times. **Operations Analysis:** Analyzing needs and product requirements to create a design. **Speaking:** Talking to others to convey information effectively. **Active Learning:** Understanding the implications of new information for both current and future problem-solving and decision-making.

GOE—Interest Area: 03. Arts and Communication. **Work Group:** 03.06. Drama. **Other Jobs in This Work Group:** Actors; Costume Attendants; Makeup Artists, Theatrical and Performance; Public Address System and Other Announcers; Radio and Television Announcers. **PERSONALITY TYPE:** Artistic. Artistic occupations frequently involve working with forms, designs, and patterns. They often require self-expression, and the work can be done without following a clear set of rules.

EDUCATION/TRAINING PROGRAM(S)— Cinematography and Film/Video Production; Directing and Theatrical Production; Drama and Dramatics/Theatre Arts, General; Dramatic/Theatre Arts and Stagecraft, Other; Film/Cinema Studies; Radio and Television; Theatre/Theatre Arts Management. **RELATED KNOWLEDGE/COURSES—Communications and Media:** Knowledge of media production, communication, and dissemination techniques and methods. This includes alternative ways to inform and entertain via written, oral, and visual media. **Telecommunications:** Knowledge of transmission, broadcasting, switching, control, and operation of telecommunications systems. **Computers and Electronics:** Knowledge of circuit boards, processors, chips, electronic equipment, and computer hardware and software, including applications and programming. **Geography:** Knowledge of principles and methods for describing the features of land, sea, and air masses, including their physical characteristics; locations; interrelationships; and distribution of plant, animal, and human life. **Education and Training:** Knowledge of principles and methods for curriculum and training design, teaching and instruction for individuals and groups, and the measurement of training effects. **Fine Arts:** Knowledge of the theory and techniques required to compose, produce, and perform works of music, dance, visual arts, drama, and sculpture.

Directors, Religious Activities and Education

- Education/Training Required: Bachelor's degree
- Annual Earnings: $29,240
- Growth: 24.1%
- Annual Job Openings: 16,000
- Self-Employed: 0%
- Part-Time: 28.2%

Direct and coordinate activities of a denominational group to meet religious needs of students. Plan, direct, or coordinate church school programs designed to promote religious education among church membership. May provide counseling and guidance relative to marital, health, financial, and religious problems. Counsel individuals regarding interpersonal, health, financial, and religious problems. Interpret religious education activities to the public through speaking, leading discussions, and writing articles for local and national publications. Participate in denominational activities aimed at goals such as promoting interfaith understanding or providing aid to new or small congregations. Plan and conduct conferences dealing with the interpretation of religious ideas and convictions. Visit congregation members' homes or arrange for pastoral visits in order to provide information and resources regarding religious education programs. Analyze member participation and changes in congregation emphasis to determine needs for religious education. Collaborate with other ministry members to establish goals and objectives for religious education programs and to develop ways to encourage program participation. Confer with clergy members, congregation officials, and congregation organizations to encourage support of and participation in religious education activities. Develop and direct study courses and religious education programs within congregations. Identify and recruit potential volunteer workers. Implement program plans by ordering needed materials, scheduling speakers, reserving space, and handling other administrative details. Locate and distribute resources such as periodicals and curricula in order to enhance the effectiveness of educational programs. Publicize programs through sources such as newsletters, bulletins, and mailings. Schedule special events such as camps, conferences, meetings, seminars, and retreats. Select appropriate curricula and class structures for educational programs. Train and supervise religious education instructional staff. Analyze revenue and program cost data to determine budget priorities. Attend workshops, seminars, and conferences to obtain program ideas, information, and resources. **SKILLS—Management of Financial Resources:** Determining how money will be spent to get the work done and accounting for these expenditures. **Social Perceptiveness:** Being aware of others' reactions and understanding why they react as they do. **Management of Personnel Resources:** Motivating, developing, and directing people as they work, identifying the best people for the job. **Service Orientation:** Actively looking for ways to help people. **Management of Material Resources:** Obtaining and seeing to the appropriate use of equipment, facilities, and materials needed to do certain work. **Instructing:** Teaching others how to do something. **Systems Analysis:** Determining how a system should work and how changes in conditions, operations, and the environment will affect outcomes. **Coordination:** Adjusting actions in relation to others' actions. **Judgment and Decision Making:** Considering the relative costs and benefits of potential actions to choose the most appropriate one.

GOE—Interest Area: 10. Human Service. **Work Group:** 10.02. Religious Work. **Other Jobs in This Work Group:** Clergy. **PERSONALITY TYPE:** Social. Social occupations frequently involve working with, communicating with, and teaching people. These occupations often involve helping or providing service to others.

EDUCATION/TRAINING PROGRAM(S)—
Bible/Biblical Studies; Missions/Missionary Studies
and Missiology; Religious Education; Youth Ministry. **RELATED KNOWLEDGE/COURSES—**
Therapy and Counseling: Knowledge of principles,
methods, and procedures for diagnosis, treatment,
and rehabilitation of physical and mental dysfunctions and for career counseling and guidance. **Phi-**
losophy and Theology: Knowledge of different
philosophical systems and religions. This includes
their basic principles, values, ethics, ways of thinking, customs, and practices and their impact on
human culture. **Administration and Management:**
Knowledge of business and management principles
involved in strategic planning, resource allocation,
human resources modeling, leadership technique,
production methods, and coordination of people
and resources. **Sociology and Anthropology:**
Knowledge of group behavior and dynamics, societal trends and influences, human migrations, ethnicity, and cultures and their history and origins.
Psychology: Knowledge of human behavior and
performance; individual differences in ability, personality, and interests; learning and motivation; psychological research methods; and the assessment
and treatment of behavioral and affective disorders.
Education and Training: Knowledge of principles
and methods for curriculum and training design,
teaching and instruction for individuals and groups,
and the measurement of training effects.

Economics Teachers, Postsecondary

- Education/Training Required: Master's degree
- Annual Earnings: $66,300
- Growth: 38.1% for all Postsecondary Teachers
- Annual Job Openings: 216,000 for all Postsecondary Teachers
- Self-Employed: 0.3% for all Postsecondary Teachers
- Part-Time: 27.7% for all Postsecondary Teachers

Teach courses in economics. Participate in campus
and community events. Participate in student
recruitment, registration, and placement activities.
Perform administrative duties such as serving as
department head. Provide professional consulting
services to government and/or industry. Serve on
academic or administrative committees that deal
with institutional policies, departmental matters,
and academic issues. Write grant proposals to procure external research funding. Evaluate and grade
students' class work, assignments, and papers. Prepare and deliver lectures to undergraduate and/or
graduate students on topics such as econometrics,
price theory, and macroeconomics. Advise students
on academic and vocational curricula and on career
issues. Compile, administer, and grade examinations or assign this work to others. Compile bibliographies of specialized materials for outside reading
assignments. Initiate, facilitate, and moderate classroom discussions. Keep abreast of developments in
their field by reading current literature, talking with
colleagues, and participating in professional conferences. Maintain regularly scheduled office hours in
order to advise and assist students. Maintain student
attendance records, grades, and other required
records. Plan, evaluate, and revise curricula, course
content, and course materials and methods of

instruction. Prepare course materials such as syllabi, homework assignments, and handouts. Select and obtain materials and supplies such as textbooks. Supervise undergraduate and/or graduate teaching, internship, and research work. Act as advisers to student organizations. Collaborate with colleagues to address teaching and research issues. Conduct research in a particular field of knowledge and publish findings in professional journals, books, and/or electronic media. **SKILLS—Instructing:** Teaching others how to do something. **Learning Strategies:** Selecting and using training/instructional methods and procedures appropriate for the situation when learning or teaching new things. **Reading Comprehension:** Understanding written sentences and paragraphs in work-related documents. **Active Learning:** Understanding the implications of new information for both current and future problem-solving and decision-making. **Speaking:** Talking to others to convey information effectively. **Writing:** Communicating effectively in writing as appropriate for the needs of the audience. **Science:** Using scientific rules and methods to solve problems. **Active Listening:** Giving full attention to what other people are saying, taking time to understand the points being made, asking questions as appropriate, and not interrupting at inappropriate times. **Critical Thinking:** Using logic and reasoning to identify the strengths and weaknesses of alternative solutions, conclusions, or approaches to problems.

GOE—Interest Area: 05. Education and Training. **Work Group:** 05.03. Postsecondary and Adult Teaching and Instructing. **Other Jobs in This Work Group:** Adult Literacy, Remedial Education, and GED Teachers and Instructors; Agricultural Sciences Teachers, Postsecondary; Anthropology and Archeology Teachers, Postsecondary; Architecture Teachers, Postsecondary; Area, Ethnic, and Cultural Studies Teachers, Postsecondary; Art, Drama, and Music Teachers, Postsecondary; Atmospheric, Earth, Marine, and Space Sciences Teachers, Postsecondary; Biological Science Teachers, Postsecondary; Business Teachers, Postsecondary; Chemistry Teachers, Postsecondary; Communica-

tions Teachers, Postsecondary; Computer Science Teachers, Postsecondary; Criminal Justice and Law Enforcement Teachers, Postsecondary; Education Teachers, Postsecondary; Engineering Teachers, Postsecondary; English Language and Literature Teachers, Postsecondary; Environmental Science Teachers, Postsecondary; Farm and Home Management Advisors; Foreign Language and Literature Teachers, Postsecondary; Forestry and Conservation Science Teachers, Postsecondary; Geography Teachers, Postsecondary; Graduate Teaching Assistants; Health Specialties Teachers, Postsecondary; History Teachers, Postsecondary; Home Economics Teachers, Postsecondary; Law Teachers, Postsecondary; Library Science Teachers, Postsecondary; Mathematical Science Teachers, Postsecondary; Nursing Instructors and Teachers, Postsecondary; Philosophy and Religion Teachers, Postsecondary; Physics Teachers, Postsecondary; Political Science Teachers, Postsecondary; Psychology Teachers, Postsecondary; Recreation and Fitness Studies Teachers, Postsecondary; Self-Enrichment Education Teachers; Social Work Teachers, Postsecondary; Sociology Teachers, Postsecondary; Vocational Education Teachers, Postsecondary. **PERSONALITY TYPE:** Social. Social occupations frequently involve working with, communicating with, and teaching people. These occupations often involve helping or providing service to others.

EDUCATION/TRAINING PROGRAM(S)— Applied Economics; Business/Managerial Economics; Development Economics and International Development; Econometrics and Quantitative Economics; Economics, General; Economics, Other; International Economics; Social Science Teacher Education. **RELATED KNOWLEDGE/COURSES—Sociology and Anthropology:** Knowledge of group behavior and dynamics, societal trends and influences, human migrations, ethnicity, and cultures and their history and origins. **History and Archeology:** Knowledge of historical events and their causes, indicators, and effects on civilizations and cultures. **Education and Training:** Knowledge of principles and methods for curriculum and train-

E

ing design, teaching and instruction for individuals and groups, and the measurement of training effects. **Psychology:** Knowledge of human behavior and performance; individual differences in ability, personality, and interests; learning and motivation; psychological research methods; and the assessment and treatment of behavioral and affective disorders. **Economics and Accounting:** Knowledge of economic and accounting principles and practices, the financial markets, banking, and the analysis and reporting of financial data. **English Language:** Knowledge of the structure and content of the English language, including the meaning and spelling of words, rules of composition, and grammar.

Economists

- ◎ Education/Training Required: Bachelor's degree
- ◎ Annual Earnings: $70,520
- ◎ Growth: 13.4%
- ◎ Annual Job Openings: 2,000
- ◎ Self-Employed: 11.5%
- ◎ Part-Time: 8.3%

Conduct research, prepare reports, or formulate plans to aid in solution of economic problems arising from production and distribution of goods and services. May collect and process economic and statistical data using econometric and sampling techniques. Compile, analyze, and report data to explain economic phenomena and forecast market trends, applying mathematical models and statistical techniques. Develop economic guidelines and standards and prepare points of view used in forecasting trends and formulating economic policy. Forecast production and consumption of renewable resources and supply, consumption and depletion of non-renewable resources. Study economic and statistical data in area of specialization, such as finance, labor, or agriculture. Formulate recommendations,

policies, or plans to solve economic problems or to interpret markets. Provide advice and consultation on economic relationships to businesses, public and private agencies, and other employers. Supervise research projects and students' study projects. Teach theories, principles, and methods of economics. Testify at regulatory or legislative hearings concerning the estimated effects of changes in legislation or public policy and present recommendations based on cost-benefit analyses. **SKILLS—Systems Evaluation:** Identifying measures or indicators of system performance and the actions needed to improve or correct performance relative to the goals of the system. **Systems Analysis:** Determining how a system should work and how changes in conditions, operations, and the environment will affect outcomes. **Persuasion:** Persuading others to change their minds or behavior. **Judgment and Decision Making:** Considering the relative costs and benefits of potential actions to choose the most appropriate one. **Complex Problem Solving:** Identifying complex problems and reviewing related information to develop and evaluate options and implement solutions. **Instructing:** Teaching others how to do something. **Writing:** Communicating effectively in writing as appropriate for the needs of the audience. **Learning Strategies:** Selecting and using training/instructional methods and procedures appropriate for the situation when learning or teaching new things.

GOE—Interest Area: 15. Scientific Research, Engineering, and Mathematics. **Work Group:** 15.04. Social Sciences. **Other Jobs in This Work Group:** Anthropologists; Archeologists; Educational Psychologists; Historians; Industrial-Organizational Psychologists; Political Scientists; Sociologists. **PERSONALITY TYPE:** Investigative. Investigative occupations frequently involve working with ideas and require an extensive amount of thinking. These occupations can involve searching for facts and figuring out problems mentally.

EDUCATION/TRAINING PROGRAM(S)— Agricultural Economics; Applied Economics; Business/Managerial Economics; Development

Economics and International Development; Econometrics and Quantitative Economics; Economics, General; Economics, Other; International Economics. **RELATED KNOWLEDGE/COURSES— Economics and Accounting:** Knowledge of economic and accounting principles and practices, the financial markets, banking, and the analysis and reporting of financial data. **Mathematics:** Knowledge of arithmetic, algebra, geometry, calculus, and statistics and their applications. **Education and Training:** Knowledge of principles and methods for curriculum and training design, teaching and instruction for individuals and groups, and the measurement of training effects. **Personnel and Human Resources:** Knowledge of principles and procedures for personnel recruitment, selection, training, compensation and benefits, labor relations and negotiation, and personnel information systems. **Production and Processing:** Knowledge of raw materials, production processes, quality control, costs, and other techniques for maximizing the effective manufacture and distribution of goods. **Computers and Electronics:** Knowledge of circuit boards, processors, chips, electronic equipment, and computer hardware and software, including applications and programming.

Editors

- Education/Training Required: Bachelor's degree
- Annual Earnings: $42,450
- Growth: 11.8%
- Annual Job Openings: 14,000
- Self-Employed: 12.9%
- Part-Time: 13.0%

Perform variety of editorial duties, such as laying out, indexing, and revising content of written materials, in preparation for final publication. Prepare, rewrite and edit copy to improve readability, or supervise others who do this work. Read copy or proof to detect and correct errors in spelling, punctuation, and syntax. Allocate print space for story text, photos, and illustrations according to space parameters and copy significance, using knowledge of layout principles. Plan the contents of publications according to the publication's style, editorial policy, and publishing requirements. Verify facts, dates, and statistics, using standard reference sources. Review and approve proofs submitted by composing room prior to publication production. Develop story or content ideas, considering reader or audience appeal. Oversee publication production, including artwork, layout, computer typesetting, and printing, ensuring adherence to deadlines and budget requirements. Confer with management and editorial staff members regarding placement and emphasis of developing news stories. Assign topics, events and stories to individual writers or reporters for coverage. Read, evaluate and edit manuscripts or other materials submitted for publication and confer with authors regarding changes in content, style or organization, or publication. Monitor news-gathering operations to ensure utilization of all news sources, such as press releases, telephone contacts, radio, television, wire services, and other reporters. Meet frequently with artists, typesetters, layout personnel, marketing directors, and production managers to discuss projects and resolve problems. Supervise and coordinate work of reporters and other editors. Make manuscript acceptance or revision recommendations to the publisher. Select local, state, national, and international news items received from wire services, based on assessment of items' significance and interest value. Interview and hire writers and reporters or negotiate contracts, royalties, and payments for authors or freelancers. **SKILLS—Writing:** Communicating effectively in writing as appropriate for the needs of the audience. **Reading Comprehension:** Understanding written sentences and paragraphs in work-related documents. **Active Listening:** Giving full attention to what other people are saying, taking time to understand the points being made, asking questions as appropriate, and not interrupting at inappropriate times. **Time Management:** Managing one's own time and the time of others. **Persuasion:** Persuading others to change their minds or behavior. **Critical Thinking:** Using logic and reasoning to identify the strengths and weaknesses of alternative solutions, conclusions, or approaches to problems. **Active Learning:** Understanding the implications of new information for both current and future problem-solving and decision-making. **Social Perceptiveness:** Being aware of others' reactions and understanding why they react as they do.

GOE—Interest Area: 03. Arts and Communication. **Work Group:** 03.02. Writing and Editing. **Other Jobs in This Work Group:** Copy Writers; Creative Writers; Poets and Lyricists; Technical Writers. **PERSONALITY TYPE:** Artistic. Artistic occupations frequently involve working with forms, designs, and patterns. They often require self-expression, and the work can be done without following a clear set of rules.

EDUCATION/TRAINING PROGRAM(S)— Broadcast Journalism; Business/Corporate Communications; Communication, Journalism, and Related Programs, Other; Creative Writing; Journalism; Mass Communication/Media Studies; Publishing; Technical and Business Writing. **RELATED KNOWLEDGE/COURSES—Communications and Media:** Knowledge of media production, communication, and dissemination techniques and methods. This includes alternative ways to inform and entertain via written, oral, and visual media. **English Language:** Knowledge of the structure and content of the English language, including the meaning and spelling of words, rules of composition, and grammar. **Geography:** Knowledge of principles and methods for describing the features of land, sea, and air masses, including their physical characteristics; locations; interrelationships; and distribution of plant, animal, and human life. **History and Archeology:** Knowledge of historical events and their causes, indicators, and effects on civilizations and cultures. **Clerical Practices:** Knowledge of administrative and clerical procedures and systems such as word processing, managing files and records,

stenography and transcription, designing forms, and other office procedures and terminology. **Computers and Electronics:** Knowledge of circuit boards, processors, chips, electronic equipment, and computer hardware and software, including applications and programming.

Education Administrators, Elementary and Secondary School

- ◎ Education/Training Required: Work experience plus degree
- ◎ Annual Earnings: $73,960
- ◎ Growth: 20.7%
- ◎ Annual Job Openings: 31,000
- ◎ Self-Employed: 3.2%
- ◎ Part-Time: 7.2%

Plan, direct, or coordinate the academic, clerical, or auxiliary activities of public or private elementary or secondary level schools. Write articles, manuals, and other publications, and assist in the distribution of promotional literature about facilities and programs. Advocate for new schools to be built, or for existing facilities to be repaired or remodeled. Establish, coordinate, and oversee particular programs across school districts, such as programs to evaluate student academic achievement. Plan and develop instructional methods and content for educational, vocational, or student activity programs. Prepare and submit budget requests and recommendations, or grant proposals to solicit program funding. Prepare, maintain, or oversee the preparation/maintenance of attendance, activity, planning, or personnel reports and records. Recommend personnel actions related to programs and services. Recruit, hire, train, and evaluate primary and supplemental staff. Review and approve new programs, or recommend modifications to existing programs, submitting program proposals for school board approval as necessary. Set educational standards and goals, and help establish policies and procedures to carry them out. Collect and analyze survey data, regulatory information, and data on demographic and employment trends to forecast enrollment patterns and curriculum change needs. Confer with parents and staff to discuss educational activities, policies, and student behavioral or learning problems. Counsel and provide guidance to students regarding personal, academic, vocational, or behavioral issues. Develop partnerships with businesses, communities, and other organizations to help meet identified educational needs and to provide school-to-work programs. Direct and coordinate school maintenance services and the use of school facilities. Enforce discipline and attendance rules. Organize and direct committees of specialists, volunteers, and staff to provide technical and advisory assistance for programs. Review and interpret government codes, and develop programs to ensure adherence to codes and facility safety, security, and maintenance. Teach classes or courses to students. Direct and coordinate activities of teachers, administrators, and support staff at schools, public agencies, and institutions. **SKILLS—Management of Financial Resources:** Determining how money will be spent to get the work done and accounting for these expenditures. **Management of Personnel Resources:** Motivating, developing, and directing people as they work, identifying the best people for the job. **Management of Material Resources:** Obtaining and seeing to the appropriate use of equipment, facilities, and materials needed to do certain work. **Systems Analysis:** Determining how a system should work and how changes in conditions, operations, and the environment will affect outcomes. **Systems Evaluation:** Identifying measures or indicators of system performance and the actions needed to improve or correct performance relative to the goals of the system. **Coordination:** Adjusting actions in relation to others' actions. **Learning Strategies:** Selecting and using training/instructional

methods and procedures appropriate for the situation when learning or teaching new things. **Writing:** Communicating effectively in writing as appropriate for the needs of the audience.

GOE—Interest Area: 05. Education and Training. **Work Group:** 05.01. Managerial Work in Education. **Other Jobs in This Work Group:** Education Administrators, Postsecondary; Education Administrators, Preschool and Child Care Center/Program; Instructional Coordinators. **PERSONALITY TYPE:** Social. Social occupations frequently involve working with, communicating with, and teaching people. These occupations often involve helping or providing service to others.

EDUCATION/TRAINING PROGRAM(S)— Educational Administration and Supervision, Other; Educational Leadership and Administration, General; Educational, Instructional, and Curriculum Supervision; Elementary and Middle School Administration/Principalship; Secondary School Administration/Principalship. **RELATED KNOWLEDGE/COURSES—Education and Training:** Knowledge of principles and methods for curriculum and training design, teaching and instruction for individuals and groups, and the measurement of training effects. **Sales and Marketing:** Knowledge of principles and methods for showing, promoting, and selling products or services. This includes marketing strategy and tactics, product demonstration, sales techniques, and sales control systems. **Personnel and Human Resources:** Knowledge of principles and procedures for personnel recruitment, selection, training, compensation and benefits, labor relations and negotiation, and personnel information systems. **Administration and Management:** Knowledge of business and management principles involved in strategic planning, resource allocation, human resources modeling, leadership technique, production methods, and coordination of people and resources. **Economics and Accounting:** Knowledge of economic and accounting principles and practices, the financial markets, banking, and the analysis and reporting of financial data. **English Language:** Knowledge of the

E

structure and content of the English language, including the meaning and spelling of words, rules of composition, and grammar.

Education Administrators, Postsecondary

- ◎ Education/Training Required: Work experience plus degree
- ◎ Annual Earnings: $67,760
- ◎ Growth: 25.9%
- ◎ Annual Job Openings: 19,000
- ◎ Self-Employed: 2.6%
- ◎ Part-Time: 7.2%

Plan, direct, or coordinate research, instructional, student administration and services, and other educational activities at postsecondary institutions, including universities, colleges, and junior and community colleges. Direct activities of administrative departments such as admissions, registration, and career services. Direct, coordinate, and evaluate the activities of personnel engaged in administering academic institutions, departments, and/or alumni organizations. Establish operational policies and procedures and make any necessary modifications, based on analysis of operations, demographics, and other research information. Appoint individuals to faculty positions, and evaluate their performance. Confer with other academic staff to explain and formulate admission requirements and course credit policies. Develop curricula, and recommend curricula revisions and additions. Participate in faculty and college committee activities. Participate in student recruitment, selection, and admission, making admissions recommendations when required to do so. Plan, administer, and control budgets, maintain financial records, and produce financial reports. Provide assistance to fac-

ulty and staff in duties such as teaching classes, conducting orientation programs, issuing transcripts, and scheduling events. Recruit, hire, train, and terminate departmental personnel. Represent institutions at community and campus events, in meetings with other institution personnel, and during accreditation processes. Review registration statistics, and consult with faculty officials to develop registration policies. Audit the financial status of student organizations and facility accounts. Coordinate the production and dissemination of university publications such as course catalogs and class schedules. Determine course schedules, and coordinate teaching assignments and room assignments in order to ensure optimum use of buildings and equipment. Direct and participate in institutional fundraising activities, and encourage alumni participation in such activities. Direct scholarship, fellowship, and loan programs, performing activities such as selecting recipients and distributing aid. Plan and promote sporting events and social, cultural, and recreational activities. Review student misconduct reports requiring disciplinary action, and counsel students regarding such reports. **SKILLS—Management of Financial Resources:** Determining how money will be spent to get the work done and accounting for these expenditures. **Systems Evaluation:** Identifying measures or indicators of system performance and the actions needed to improve or correct performance relative to the goals of the system. **Management of Personnel Resources:** Motivating, developing, and directing people as they work, identifying the best people for the job. **Management of Material Resources:** Obtaining and seeing to the appropriate use of equipment, facilities, and materials needed to do certain work. **Coordination:** Adjusting actions in relation to others' actions. **Negotiation:** Bringing others together and trying to reconcile differences. **Systems Analysis:** Determining how a system should work and how changes in conditions, operations, and the environment will affect outcomes. **Judgment and Decision Making:** Considering the relative costs and benefits of potential actions to choose the most appropriate one.

GOE—**Interest Area:** 05. Education and Training. **Work Group:** 05.01. Managerial Work in Education. **Other Jobs in This Work Group:** Education Administrators, Elementary and Secondary School; Education Administrators, Preschool and Child Care Center/Program; Instructional Coordinators. **PERSONALITY TYPE:** Enterprising. Enterprising occupations frequently involve starting up and carrying out projects. These occupations can involve leading people and making many decisions. They sometimes require risk taking and often deal with business.

EDUCATION/TRAINING PROGRAM(S)— Community College Education; Educational Administration and Supervision, Other; Educational Leadership and Administration, General; Educational, Instructional, and Curriculum Supervision; Higher Education/Higher Education Administration. **RELATED KNOWLEDGE/COURSES— Education and Training:** Knowledge of principles and methods for curriculum and training design, teaching and instruction for individuals and groups, and the measurement of training effects. **Administration and Management:** Knowledge of business and management principles involved in strategic planning, resource allocation, human resources modeling, leadership technique, production methods, and coordination of people and resources. **Economics and Accounting:** Knowledge of economic and accounting principles and practices, the financial markets, banking, and the analysis and reporting of financial data. **Personnel and Human Resources:** Knowledge of principles and procedures for personnel recruitment, selection, training, compensation and benefits, labor relations and negotiation, and personnel information systems. **Law and Government:** Knowledge of laws, legal codes, court procedures, precedents, government regulations, executive orders, agency rules, and the democratic political process. **English Language:** Knowledge of the structure and content of the English language, including the meaning and spelling of words, rules of composition, and grammar.

Education Administrators, Preschool and Child Care Center/Program

- Education/Training Required: Work experience plus degree
- Annual Earnings: $35,240
- Growth: 32.0%
- Annual Job Openings: 9,000
- Self-Employed: 3.0%
- Part-Time: 7.2%

Plan, direct, or coordinate the academic and nonacademic activities of preschool and child care centers or programs. Direct and coordinate activities of teachers or administrators at daycare centers, schools, public agencies, and/or institutions. Plan, direct, and monitor instructional methods and content of educational, vocational, or student activity programs. Recruit, hire, train, and evaluate primary and supplemental staff, and recommend personnel actions for programs and services. Determine allocations of funds for staff, supplies, materials, and equipment, and authorize purchases. Determine the scope of educational program offerings, and prepare drafts of program schedules and descriptions, in order to estimate staffing and facility requirements. Organize and direct committees of specialists, volunteers, and staff to provide technical and advisory assistance for programs. Prepare and submit budget requests or grant proposals to solicit program funding. Prepare and maintain attendance, activity, planning, accounting, or personnel reports and records for officials and agencies, or direct preparation and maintenance activities. Review and evaluate new and current programs to determine their efficiency, effectiveness, and compliance with state, local, and federal regulations; recommend any necessary modifications. Review and interpret government codes,

E

and develop procedures to meet codes and to ensure facility safety, security, and maintenance. Set educational standards and goals, and help establish policies, procedures, and programs to carry them out. Collect and analyze survey data, regulatory information, and demographic and employment trends, in order to forecast enrollment patterns and the need for curriculum changes. Confer with parents and staff to discuss educational activities and policies, and students' behavioral or learning problems. Inform businesses, community groups, and governmental agencies about educational needs, available programs, and program policies. Monitor students' progress, and provide students and teachers with assistance in resolving any problems. Teach classes or courses, and/or provide direct care to children. Write articles, manuals, and other publications, and assist in the distribution of promotional literature about programs and facilities. **SKILLS—Management of Financial Resources:** Determining how money will be spent to get the work done and accounting for these expenditures. **Management of Personnel Resources:** Motivating, developing, and directing people as they work, identifying the best people for the job. **Management of Material Resources:** Obtaining and seeing to the appropriate use of equipment, facilities, and materials needed to do certain work. **Systems Analysis:** Determining how a system should work and how changes in conditions, operations, and the environment will affect outcomes. **Systems Evaluation:** Identifying measures or indicators of system performance and the actions needed to improve or correct performance relative to the goals of the system. **Coordination:** Adjusting actions in relation to others' actions. **Learning Strategies:** Selecting and using training/instructional methods and procedures appropriate for the situation when learning or teaching new things. **Writing:** Communicating effectively in writing as appropriate for the needs of the audience.

GOE—Interest Area: 05. Education and Training. **Work Group:** 05.01. Managerial Work in Education. **Other Jobs in This Work Group:** Education Administrators, Elementary and Secondary School; Education Administrators, Postsecondary; Instructional Coordinators. **PERSONALITY TYPE:** Social. Social occupations frequently involve working with, communicating with, and teaching people. These occupations often involve helping or providing service to others.

EDUCATION/TRAINING PROGRAM(S)— Educational Administration and Supervision, Other; Educational Leadership and Administration, General; Educational, Instructional, and Curriculum Supervision. **RELATED KNOWLEDGE/COURSES—Education and Training:** Knowledge of principles and methods for curriculum and training design, teaching and instruction for individuals and groups, and the measurement of training effects. **Sales and Marketing:** Knowledge of principles and methods for showing, promoting, and selling products or services. This includes marketing strategy and tactics, product demonstration, sales techniques, and sales control systems. **Personnel and Human Resources:** Knowledge of principles and procedures for personnel recruitment, selection, training, compensation and benefits, labor relations and negotiation, and personnel information systems. **Administration and Management:** Knowledge of business and management principles involved in strategic planning, resource allocation, human resources modeling, leadership technique, production methods, and coordination of people and resources. **Economics and Accounting:** Knowledge of economic and accounting principles and practices, the financial markets, banking, and the analysis and reporting of financial data. **English Language:** Knowledge of the structure and content of the English language, including the meaning and spelling of words, rules of composition, and grammar.

Education Teachers, Postsecondary

◎ Education/Training Required: Master's degree

◎ Annual Earnings: $48,180

◎ Growth: 38.1% for all Postsecondary Teachers

◎ Annual Job Openings: 216,000 for all Postsecondary Teachers

◎ Self-Employed: 0.3% for all Postsecondary Teachers

◎ Part-Time: 27.7% for all Postsecondary Teachers

Teach courses pertaining to education, such as counseling, curriculum, guidance, instruction, teacher education, and teaching English as a second language. Participate in student recruitment, registration, and placement activities. Perform administrative duties such as serving as department head. Provide professional consulting services to government and/or industry. Serve on academic or administrative committees that deal with institutional policies, departmental matters, and academic issues. Write grant proposals to procure external research funding. Advise and instruct teachers employed in school systems, by providing activities such as in-service seminars. Evaluate and grade students' class work, assignments, and papers. Prepare and deliver lectures to undergraduate and/or graduate students on topics such as children's literature, learning and development, and reading instruction. Advise students on academic and vocational curricula, and on career issues. Compile, administer, and grade examinations, or assign this work to others. Compile bibliographies of specialized materials for outside reading assignments. Initiate, facilitate, and moderate classroom discussions. Keep abreast of developments in their field by reading current literature, talking with colleagues, and participating in professional conferences. Maintain regularly sched-uled office hours in order to advise and assist students. Maintain student attendance records, grades, and other required records. Plan, evaluate, and revise curricula, course content, and course materials and methods of instruction. Prepare course materials such as syllabi, homework assignments, and handouts. Select and obtain materials and supplies such as textbooks. Supervise students' fieldwork, internship, and research work. Act as advisers to student organizations. Collaborate with colleagues to address teaching and research issues. Conduct research in a particular field of knowledge, and publish findings in professional journals, books, and/or electronic media. Participate in campus and community events. **SKILLS**—No data available.

GOE—Interest Area: 05. Education and Training. **Work Group:** 05.03. Postsecondary and Adult Teaching and Instructing. **Other Jobs in This Work Group:** Adult Literacy, Remedial Education, and GED Teachers and Instructors; Agricultural Sciences Teachers, Postsecondary; Anthropology and Archeology Teachers, Postsecondary; Architecture Teachers, Postsecondary; Area, Ethnic, and Cultural Studies Teachers, Postsecondary; Art, Drama, and Music Teachers, Postsecondary; Atmospheric, Earth, Marine, and Space Sciences Teachers, Postsecondary; Biological Science Teachers, Postsecondary; Business Teachers, Postsecondary; Chemistry Teachers, Postsecondary; Communications Teachers, Postsecondary; Computer Science Teachers, Postsecondary; Criminal Justice and Law Enforcement Teachers, Postsecondary; Economics Teachers, Postsecondary; Engineering Teachers, Postsecondary; English Language and Literature Teachers, Postsecondary; Environmental Science Teachers, Postsecondary; Farm and Home Management Advisors; Foreign Language and Literature Teachers, Postsecondary; Forestry and Conservation Science Teachers, Postsecondary; Geography Teachers, Postsecondary; Graduate Teaching Assistants; Health Specialties Teachers, Postsecondary; History Teachers, Postsecondary; Home Economics Teachers, Postsecondary; Law Teachers, Postsecondary; Library Science Teachers, Postsecondary; Mathematical Science Teachers, Postsecondary; Nursing Instructors and Teachers, Postsecondary; Philosophy and Religion Teachers, Postsecondary; Physics Teachers, Postsecondary; Political Science Teachers, Postsecondary; Psychology Teachers, Postsecondary; Recreation and Fitness Studies Teachers, Postsecondary; Self-Enrichment Education Teachers; Social Work Teachers, Postsecondary; Sociology Teachers, Postsecondary; Vocational Education Teachers, Postsecondary. **PERSONALITY TYPE:** No data available.

EDUCATION/TRAINING PROGRAM(S)— Agricultural Teacher Education; Art Teacher Education; Biology Teacher Education; Business Teacher Education; Chemistry Teacher Education; Computer Teacher Education; Drama and Dance Teacher Education; Driver and Safety Teacher Education; Education, General; English/Language Arts Teacher Education; Family and Consumer Sciences/Home Economics Teacher Education; Foreign Language Teacher Education; French Language Teacher Education; Geography Teacher Education; German Language Teacher Education; Health Occupations Teacher Education; Health Teacher Education; History Teacher Education; Mathematics Teacher Education; Music Teacher Education; Physical Education Teaching and Coaching; Physics Teacher Education; Reading Teacher Education; Sales and Marketing Operations/Marketing and Distribution Teacher Education; Science Teacher Education/General Science Teacher Education; Social Science Teacher Education; Social Studies Teacher Education; Spanish Language Teacher Education; Speech Teacher Education; Teacher Education and Professional Development, Specific Subject Areas, Other; Technical Teacher Education; Technology Teacher Education/Industrial Arts Teacher Education; Trade and Industrial Teacher Education. **RELATED KNOWLEDGE/COURSES—**No data available.

Educational Psychologists

- Education/Training Required: Master's degree
- Annual Earnings: $53,230
- Growth: 24.4%
- Annual Job Openings: 17,000
- Self-Employed: 25.4%
- Part-Time: 27.2%

Investigate processes of learning and teaching and develop psychological principles and techniques applicable to educational problems. Collect and analyze data to evaluate the effectiveness of academic programs and other services, such as behavioral management systems. Collaborate with other educational professionals to develop teaching strategies and school programs. Compile and interpret students' test results, along with information from teachers and parents, in order to diagnose conditions, and to help assess eligibility for special services. Design classes and programs to meet the needs of special students. Develop individualized educational plans in collaboration with teachers and other staff members. Promote an understanding of child development and its relationship to learning and behavior. Provide consultation to parents, teachers, administrators, and others on topics such as learning styles and behavior modification techniques. Provide educational programs on topics such as classroom management, teaching strategies, or parenting skills. Refer students and their families to appropriate community agencies for medical, vocational, or social services. Select, administer, and score psychological tests. Serve as a resource to help families and schools deal with crises, such as separation and loss. Attend workshops, seminars, and/or professional meetings in order to remain informed of new developments in school psychology. Conduct research to generate new knowledge that can be used to address learning and behavior issues. Initiate and direct efforts to foster tolerance, understanding, and appreciation of diversity in school communities. Maintain student records, including special education reports, confidential records, records of services provided, and behavioral data. Report any pertinent information to the proper authorities in cases of child endangerment, neglect, or abuse. Assess an individual child's needs, limitations, and potential, using observation, review of school records, and consultation with parents and school personnel. Counsel children and families to help solve conflicts and problems in learning and adjustment. **SKILLS—Social Perceptiveness:** Being aware of others' reactions and understanding why they react as they do. **Systems Evaluation:** Identifying measures or indicators of system performance and the actions needed to improve or correct performance relative to the goals of the system. **Science:** Using scientific rules and methods to solve problems. **Learning Strategies:** Selecting and using training/instructional methods and procedures appropriate for the situation when learning or teaching new things. **Systems Analysis:** Determining how a system should work and how changes in conditions, operations, and the environment will affect outcomes. **Writing:** Communicating effectively in writing as appropriate for the needs of the audience. **Complex Problem Solving:** Identifying complex problems and reviewing related information to develop and evaluate options and implement solutions. **Mathematics:** Using mathematics to solve problems. **Service Orientation:** Actively looking for ways to help people.

GOE—Interest Area: 15. Scientific Research, Engineering, and Mathematics. **Work Group:** 15.04. Social Sciences. **Other Jobs in This Work Group:** Anthropologists; Archeologists; Economists; Historians; Industrial-Organizational Psychologists; Political Scientists; Sociologists. **PERSONALITY TYPE:** Investigative. Investigative occupations frequently involve working with ideas and require an extensive amount of thinking. These occupations can involve searching for facts and figuring out problems mentally.

EDUCATION/TRAINING PROGRAM(S)— Clinical Child Psychology; Clinical Psychology; Counseling Psychology; Developmental and Child Psychology; Psychoanalysis and Psychotherapy; Psychology, General; School Psychology. **RELATED KNOWLEDGE/COURSES—Psychology:** Knowledge of human behavior and performance; individual differences in ability, personality, and interests; learning and motivation; psychological research methods; and the assessment and treatment of behavioral and affective disorders. **Education and Training:** Knowledge of principles and methods for curriculum and training design, teaching and instruction for individuals and groups, and the measurement of training effects. **Therapy and Counseling:** Knowledge of principles, methods, and procedures for diagnosis, treatment, and rehabilitation of physical and mental dysfunctions and for career counseling and guidance. **Sociology and Anthropology:** Knowledge of group behavior and dynamics, societal trends and influences, human migrations, ethnicity, and cultures and their history and origins. **Mathematics:** Knowledge of arithmetic, algebra, geometry, calculus, and statistics and their applications. **English Language:** Knowledge of the structure and content of the English language, including the meaning and spelling of words, rules of composition, and grammar.

Educational, Vocational, and School Counselors

- ◎ Education/Training Required: Master's degree
- ◎ Annual Earnings: $44,990
- ◎ Growth: 15.0%
- ◎ Annual Job Openings: 32,000
- ◎ Self-Employed: 4.4%
- ◎ Part-Time: 14.6%

Counsel individuals and provide group educational and vocational guidance services. Assess needs for assistance such as rehabilitation, financial aid, or additional vocational training, and refer clients to the appropriate services. Compile and study occupational, educational, and economic information to assist counselees in determining and carrying out vocational and educational objectives. Conduct follow-up interviews with counselees to determine if their needs have been met. Confer with parents or guardians, teachers, other counselors, and administrators to resolve students' behavioral, academic, and other problems. Enforce all administration policies and rules governing students. Establish and enforce behavioral rules and procedures to maintain order among students. Establish and supervise peer counseling and peer tutoring programs. Instruct individuals in career development techniques such as job search and application strategies, resume writing, and interview skills. Interview clients to obtain information about employment history, educational background, and career goals, and to identify barriers to employment. Maintain accurate and complete student records as required by laws, district policies, and administrative regulations. Meet with other professionals to discuss individual students' needs and progress. Counsel individuals to help them understand and overcome personal, social, or behavioral problems affecting their educational or vocational situations. Counsel students regarding educational issues such as course and program selection, class scheduling, school adjustment, truancy, study habits, and career planning. Evaluate individuals' abilities, interests, and personality characteristics using tests, records, interviews, and professional sources. Address community groups, faculty, and staff members to explain available counseling services. Meet with parents and guardians to discuss their children's progress, and to determine their priorities for their children and their resource needs. Observe and evaluate students' performance, behavior, social development, and physical health. Plan and conduct orientation programs and group conferences to promote the adjustment of individuals to new life experiences such as starting college. **SKILLS—Service Orientation:** Actively looking for ways to help people. **Social Perceptiveness:** Being aware of others' reactions and understanding why they react as they do. **Active Listening:** Giving full attention to what other people are saying, taking time to understand the points being made, asking questions as appropriate, and not interrupting at inappropriate times. **Speaking:** Talking to others to convey information effectively. **Systems Evaluation:** Identifying measures or indicators of system performance and the actions needed to improve or correct performance relative to the goals of the system. **Instructing:** Teaching others how to do something. **Reading Comprehension:** Understanding written sentences and paragraphs in work-related documents. **Active Learning:** Understanding the implications of new information for both current and future problem-solving and decision-making.

GOE—Interest Area: 05. Education and Training. **Work Group:** 05.06. Counseling, Health, and Fitness Education. **Other Jobs in This Work Group:** Fitness Trainers and Aerobics Instructors; Health Educators. **PERSONALITY TYPE:** Social. Social occupations frequently involve working with, communicating with, and teaching people. These occupations often involve helping or providing service to others.

EDUCATION/TRAINING PROGRAM(S)— College Student Counseling and Personnel Services; Counselor Education/School Counseling and Guidance Services. **RELATED KNOWLEDGE/ COURSES—Therapy and Counseling:** Knowledge of principles, methods, and procedures for diagnosis, treatment, and rehabilitation of physical and mental dysfunctions and for career counseling and guidance. **Psychology:** Knowledge of human behavior and performance; individual differences in ability, personality, and interests; learning and motivation; psychological research methods; and the assessment and treatment of behavioral and affective disorders. **Education and Training:** Knowledge of principles and methods for curriculum and training design, teaching and instruction for individuals and groups, and the measurement of training effects.

Sociology and Anthropology: Knowledge of group behavior and dynamics, societal trends and influences, human migrations, ethnicity, and cultures and their history and origins. **English Language:** Knowledge of the structure and content of the English language, including the meaning and spelling of words, rules of composition, and grammar. **Personnel and Human Resources:** Knowledge of principles and procedures for personnel recruitment, selection, training, compensation and benefits, labor relations and negotiation, and personnel information systems.

Electrical Engineering Technicians

◎ Education/Training Required: Associate's degree
◎ Annual Earnings: $45,390
◎ Growth: 10.0%
◎ Annual Job Openings: 24,000
◎ Self-Employed: 0.4%
◎ Part-Time: 5.0%

Apply electrical theory and related knowledge to test and modify developmental or operational electrical machinery and electrical control equipment and circuitry in industrial or commercial plants and laboratories. Usually work under direction of engineering staff. Provide technical assistance and resolution when electrical or engineering problems are encountered before, during, and after construction. Assemble electrical and electronic systems and prototypes according to engineering data and knowledge of electrical principles, using hand tools and measuring instruments. Install and maintain electrical control systems and solid state equipment. Modify electrical prototypes, parts, assemblies, and systems to correct functional deviations. Set up and operate test equipment to evaluate performance of developmental parts, assemblies, or systems under simulated operating conditions, and record results. Collaborate with electrical engineers and other personnel to identify, define, and solve developmental problems. Build, calibrate, maintain, troubleshoot and repair electrical instruments or testing equipment. Analyze and interpret test information to resolve design-related problems. Write commissioning procedures for electrical installations. Prepare project cost and work-time estimates. Evaluate engineering proposals, shop drawings and design comments for sound electrical engineering practice and conformance with established safety and design criteria, and recommend approval or disapproval. Draw or modify diagrams and write engineering specifications to clarify design details and functional criteria of experimental electronics units. Conduct inspections for quality control and assurance programs, reporting findings and recommendations. Prepare contracts and initiate, review and coordinate modifications to contract specifications and plans throughout the construction process. Plan, schedule and monitor work of support personnel to assist supervisor. Review existing electrical engineering criteria to identify necessary revisions, deletions or amendments to outdated material. Perform supervisory duties such as recommending work assignments, approving leaves and completing performance evaluations. Plan method and sequence of operations for developing and testing experimental electronic and electrical equipment. **SKILLS—Troubleshooting:** Determining causes of operating errors and deciding what to do about them. **Repairing:** Repairing machines or systems, using the needed tools. **Installation:** Installing equipment, machines, wiring, or programs to meet specifications. **Technology Design:** Generating or adapting equipment and technology to serve user needs. **Operations Analysis:** Analyzing needs and product requirements to create a design. **Equipment Maintenance:** Performing routine maintenance on equipment and determining when and what kind of maintenance is needed. **Mathematics:** Using mathematics to solve problems. **Science:** Using scientific rules and methods to solve problems.

E

GOE—**Interest Area:** 15. Scientific Research, Engineering, and Mathematics. **Work Group:** 15.09. Engineering Technology. **Other Jobs in This Work Group:** Aerospace Engineering and Operations Technicians; Calibration and Instrumentation Technicians; Cartographers and Photogrammetrists; Civil Engineering Technicians; Electro-Mechanical Technicians; Electronic Drafters; Electronics Engineering Technicians; Environmental Engineering Technicians; Mapping Technicians; Mechanical Drafters; Mechanical Engineering Technicians; Surveying Technicians. **PERSONALITY TYPE:** Realistic. Realistic occupations frequently involve work activities that include practical, hands-on problems and solutions. They often deal with plants, animals, and real-world materials like wood, tools, and machinery. Many of the occupations require working outside and do not involve a lot of paperwork or working closely with others.

EDUCATION/TRAINING PROGRAM(S)— Computer Engineering Technology/Technician; Computer Technology/Computer Systems Technology; Electrical and Electronic Engineering Technologies/Technicians, Other; Electrical, Electronic and Communications Engineering Technology/Technician; Telecommunications Technology/Technician. **RELATED KNOWLEDGE/COURSES—Engineering and Technology:** Knowledge of the practical application of engineering science and technology. This includes applying principles, techniques, procedures, and equipment to the design and production of various goods and services. **Design:** Knowledge of design techniques, tools, and principles involved in production of precision technical plans, blueprints, drawings, and models. **Computers and Electronics:** Knowledge of circuit boards, processors, chips, electronic equipment, and computer hardware and software, including applications and programming. **Physics:** Knowledge and prediction of physical principles and laws and their interrelationships and applications to understanding fluid, material, and atmospheric dynamics and mechanical, electrical, atomic, and subatomic structures and processes. **Mechanical**

Devices: Knowledge of machines and tools, including their designs, uses, repair, and maintenance. **Telecommunications:** Knowledge of transmission, broadcasting, switching, control, and operation of telecommunications systems.

Electrical Engineers

- ◎ Education/Training Required: Bachelor's degree
- ◎ Annual Earnings: $70,830
- ◎ Growth: 2.5%
- ◎ Annual Job Openings: 11,000
- ◎ Self-Employed: 3.3%
- ◎ Part-Time: 2.4%

Design, develop, test, or supervise the manufacturing and installation of electrical equipment, components, or systems for commercial, industrial, military, or scientific use. Confer with engineers, customers, and others to discuss existing or potential engineering projects and products. Design, implement, maintain, and improve electrical instruments, equipment, facilities, components, products, and systems for commercial, industrial, and domestic purposes. Operate computer-assisted engineering and design software and equipment to perform engineering tasks. Direct and coordinate manufacturing, construction, installation, maintenance, support, documentation, and testing activities to ensure compliance with specifications, codes, and customer requirements. Perform detailed calculations to compute and establish manufacturing, construction, and installation standards and specifications. Inspect completed installations and observe operations, to ensure conformance to design and equipment specifications and compliance with operational and safety standards. Plan and implement research methodology and procedures to apply principles of electrical theory to engineering projects. Prepare specifications for purchase of materials and equipment. Supervise and train project team members as necessary. Investigate and test vendors' and competitors' products. Oversee project production efforts to assure projects are completed satisfactorily, on time and within budget. Prepare and study technical drawings, specifications of electrical systems, and topographical maps to ensure that installation and operations conform to standards and customer requirements. Investigate customer or public complaints, determine nature and extent of problem, and recommend remedial measures. Plan layout of electric power generating plants and distribution lines and stations. Assist in developing capital project programs for new equipment and major repairs. Develop budgets, estimating labor, material, and construction costs. **SKILLS— Troubleshooting:** Determining causes of operating errors and deciding what to do about them. **Technology Design:** Generating or adapting equipment and technology to serve user needs. **Systems Analysis:** Determining how a system should work and how changes in conditions, operations, and the environment will affect outcomes. **Science:** Using scientific rules and methods to solve problems. **Systems Evaluation:** Identifying measures or indicators of system performance and the actions needed to improve or correct performance relative to the goals of the system. **Management of Material Resources:** Obtaining and seeing to the appropriate use of equipment, facilities, and materials needed to do certain work. **Complex Problem Solving:** Identifying complex problems and reviewing related information to develop and evaluate options and implement solutions. **Equipment Selection:** Determining the kind of tools and equipment needed to do a job.

GOE—Interest Area: 15. Scientific Research, Engineering, and Mathematics. **Work Group:** 15.07. Research and Design Engineering. **Other Jobs in This Work Group:** Aerospace Engineers; Biomedical Engineers; Chemical Engineers; Civil Engineers; Computer Hardware Engineers; Electronics Engineers, Except Computer; Marine Architects; Marine Engineers; Materials Engineers; Mechanical

Engineers; Nuclear Engineers. **PERSONALITY TYPE:** Investigative. Investigative occupations frequently involve working with ideas and require an extensive amount of thinking. These occupations can involve searching for facts and figuring out problems mentally.

EDUCATION/TRAINING PROGRAM(S)— Electrical, Electronics and Communications Engineering. **RELATED KNOWLEDGE/COURSES —Engineering and Technology:** Knowledge of the practical application of engineering science and technology. This includes applying principles, techniques, procedures, and equipment to the design and production of various goods and services. **Design:** Knowledge of design techniques, tools, and principles involved in production of precision technical plans, blueprints, drawings, and models. **Computers and Electronics:** Knowledge of circuit boards, processors, chips, electronic equipment, and computer hardware and software, including applications and programming. **Physics:** Knowledge and prediction of physical principles and laws and their interrelationships and applications to understanding fluid, material, and atmospheric dynamics and mechanical, electrical, atomic, and subatomic structures and processes. **Mathematics:** Knowledge of arithmetic, algebra, geometry, calculus, and statistics and their applications. **Telecommunications:** Knowledge of transmission, broadcasting, switching, control, and operation of telecommunications systems.

E

Electronics Engineering Technicians

◎ Education/Training Required: Associate's degree

◎ Annual Earnings: $45,390

◎ Growth: 10.0%

◎ Annual Job Openings: 24,000

◎ Self-Employed: 0.4%

◎ Part-Time: 5.0%

Lay out, build, test, troubleshoot, repair, and modify developmental and production electronic components, parts, equipment, and systems, such as computer equipment, missile control instrumentation, electron tubes, test equipment, and machine tool numerical controls, applying principles and theories of electronics, electrical circuitry, engineering mathematics, electronic and electrical testing, and physics. Usually work under direction of engineering staff. Test electronics units, using standard test equipment, and analyze results to evaluate performance and determine need for adjustment. Perform preventative maintenance and calibration of equipment and systems. Read blueprints, wiring diagrams, schematic drawings, and engineering instructions for assembling electronics units, applying knowledge of electronic theory and components. Identify and resolve equipment malfunctions, working with manufacturers and field representatives as necessary to procure replacement parts. Maintain system logs and manuals to document testing and operation of equipment. Assemble, test, and maintain circuitry or electronic components according to engineering instructions, technical manuals, and knowledge of electronics, using hand and power tools. Adjust and replace defective or improperly functioning circuitry and electronics components, using hand tools and soldering iron. Procure parts and maintain inventory and related documentation. Maintain working knowledge of state-of-the-art tools, software, etc., through reading and/or attending conferences, workshops or other training. Provide user applications and engineering support and recommendations for new and existing equipment with regard to installation, upgrades and enhancement. Write reports and record data on testing techniques, laboratory equipment, and specifications to assist engineers. Provide customer support and education, working with users to identify needs, determine sources of problems and to provide information on product use. Design basic circuitry and draft sketches for clarification of details and design documentation under engineers' direction, using drafting instruments and computer aided design equipment. Build prototypes from rough sketches or plans. Develop and upgrade preventative maintenance procedures for components, equipment, parts and systems. Fabricate parts, such as coils, terminal boards, and chassis, using bench lathes, drills, or other machine tools. Research equipment and component needs, sources, competitive prices, delivery times and ongoing operational costs. **SKILLS— Repairing:** Repairing machines or systems, using the needed tools. **Troubleshooting:** Determining causes of operating errors and deciding what to do about them. **Equipment Maintenance:** Performing routine maintenance on equipment and determining when and what kind of maintenance is needed. **Installation:** Installing equipment, machines, wiring, or programs to meet specifications. **Technology Design:** Generating or adapting equipment and technology to serve user needs. **Operation Monitoring:** Watching gauges, dials, or other indicators to make sure a machine is working properly. **Service Orientation:** Actively looking for ways to help people. **Systems Evaluation:** Identifying measures or indicators of system performance and the actions needed to improve or correct performance relative to the goals of the system.

GOE—Interest Area: 15. Scientific Research, Engineering, and Mathematics. **Work Group:** 15.09. Engineering Technology. **Other Jobs in This Work Group:** Aerospace Engineering and Operations Technicians; Calibration and Instrumentation Technicians; Cartographers and Photogrammetrists;

Civil Engineering Technicians; Electrical Engineering Technicians; Electro-Mechanical Technicians; Electronic Drafters; Environmental Engineering Technicians; Mapping Technicians; Mechanical Drafters; Mechanical Engineering Technicians; Surveying Technicians. **PERSONALITY TYPE:** Realistic. Realistic occupations frequently involve work activities that include practical, hands-on problems and solutions. They often deal with plants, animals, and real-world materials like wood, tools, and machinery. Many of the occupations require working outside and do not involve a lot of paperwork or working closely with others.

EDUCATION/TRAINING PROGRAM(S)— Computer Engineering Technology/Technician; Computer Technology/Computer Systems Technology; Electrical and Electronic Engineering Technologies/Technicians, Other; Electrical, Electronic and Communications Engineering Technology/ Technician; Telecommunications Technology/Technician. **RELATED KNOWLEDGE/COURSES— Engineering and Technology:** Knowledge of the practical application of engineering science and technology. This includes applying principles, techniques, procedures, and equipment to the design and production of various goods and services. **Computers and Electronics:** Knowledge of circuit boards, processors, chips, electronic equipment, and computer hardware and software, including applications and programming. **Mechanical Devices:** Knowledge of machines and tools, including their designs, uses, repair, and maintenance. **Mathematics:** Knowledge of arithmetic, algebra, geometry, calculus, and statistics and their applications. **Design:** Knowledge of design techniques, tools, and principles involved in production of precision technical plans, blueprints, drawings, and models. **Telecommunications:** Knowledge of transmission, broadcasting, switching, control, and operation of telecommunications systems.

Electronics Engineers, Except Computer

- Education/Training Required: Bachelor's degree
- Annual Earnings: $73,470
- Growth: 9.4%
- Annual Job Openings: 11,000
- Self-Employed: 3.1%
- Part-Time: 2.4%

Research, design, develop, and test electronic components and systems for commercial, industrial, military, or scientific use utilizing knowledge of electronic theory and materials properties. Design electronic circuits and components for use in fields such as telecommunications, aerospace guidance and propulsion control, acoustics, or instruments and controls. Analyze system requirements, capacity, cost, and customer needs to determine feasibility of project and develop system plan. Confer with engineers, customers, vendors and others to discuss existing and potential engineering projects or products. Design electronic components and software, products and systems for commercial, industrial, medical, military, and scientific applications. Develop and perform operational, maintenance, and testing procedures for electronic products, components, equipment, and systems. Direct and coordinate activities concerned with manufacture, construction, installation, maintenance, operation, and modification of electronic equipment, products, and systems. Evaluate operational systems, prototypes and proposals and recommend repair or design modifications based on factors such as environment, service, cost, and system capabilities. Inspect electronic equipment, instruments, products, and systems to ensure conformance to specifications, safety standards, and applicable codes and regulations. Plan and develop applications and modifications for electronic properties used in components, products, and systems, to improve technical performance. Plan and implement research, methodology, and procedures to apply principles of electronic theory to engineering projects. Prepare engineering sketches and specifications for construction, relocation, and installation of equipment, facilities, products, and systems. Determine material and equipment needs and order supplies. Prepare, review, and maintain maintenance schedules, design documentation and operational reports and charts. Provide technical support and instruction to staff and customers regarding equipment standards, and help solve specific, difficult in-service engineering problems. Review and evaluate work of others, inside and outside the organization, to ensure effectiveness, technical adequacy and compatibility in the resolution of complex engineering problems. Review or prepare budget and cost estimates for equipment, construction, and installation projects, and control expenditures. Operate computer-assisted engineering and design software and equipment to perform engineering tasks. **SKILLS—Science:** Using scientific rules and methods to solve problems. **Mathematics:** Using mathematics to solve problems. **Writing:** Communicating effectively in writing as appropriate for the needs of the audience. **Judgment and Decision Making:** Considering the relative costs and benefits of potential actions to choose the most appropriate one. **Management of Financial Resources:** Determining how money will be spent to get the work done and accounting for these expenditures. **Reading Comprehension:** Understanding written sentences and paragraphs in work-related documents. **Technology Design:** Generating or adapting equipment and technology to serve user needs. **Systems Analysis:** Determining how a system should work and how changes in conditions, operations, and the environment will affect outcomes.

GOE—Interest Area: 15. Scientific Research, Engineering, and Mathematics. **Work Group:** 15.07. Research and Design Engineering. **Other Jobs in This Work Group:** Aerospace Engineers; Biomedical Engineers; Chemical Engineers; Civil Engineers; Computer Hardware Engineers; Electrical Engineers; Marine Architects; Marine Engineers; Materials Engineers; Mechanical Engineers; Nuclear Engineers. **PERSONALITY TYPE:** Investigative. Investigative occupations frequently involve working with ideas and require an extensive amount of thinking. These occupations can involve searching for facts and figuring out problems mentally.

EDUCATION/TRAINING PROGRAM(S)— Electrical, Electronics and Communications Engineering. **RELATED KNOWLEDGE/COURSES —Engineering and Technology:** Knowledge of the practical application of engineering science and technology. This includes applying principles, techniques, procedures, and equipment to the design and production of various goods and services. **Design:** Knowledge of design techniques, tools, and principles involved in production of precision technical plans, blueprints, drawings, and models. **Computers and Electronics:** Knowledge of circuit boards, processors, chips, electronic equipment, and computer hardware and software, including applications and programming. **Telecommunications:** Knowledge of transmission, broadcasting, switching, control, and operation of telecommunications systems. **Production and Processing:** Knowledge of raw materials, production processes, quality control, costs, and other techniques for maximizing the effective manufacture and distribution of goods. **Mathematics:** Knowledge of arithmetic, algebra, geometry, calculus, and statistics and their applications.

Elementary School Teachers, Except Special Education

- Education/Training Required: Bachelor's degree
- Annual Earnings: $42,590
- Growth: 15.2%
- Annual Job Openings: 183,000
- Self-Employed: 0.1%
- Part-Time: 9.2%

Teach pupils in public or private schools at the elementary level basic academic, social, and other formative skills. Plan and conduct activities for a balanced program of instruction, demonstration, and work time that provides students with opportunities to observe, question, and investigate. Plan and supervise class projects, field trips, visits by guest speakers or other experiential activities, and guide students in learning from those activities. Prepare and implement remedial programs for students requiring extra help. Prepare for assigned classes, and show written evidence of preparation upon request of immediate supervisors. Prepare materials and classrooms for class activities. Prepare objectives and outlines for courses of study, following curriculum guidelines or requirements of states and schools. Prepare reports on students and activities as required by administration. Prepare students for later grades by encouraging them to explore learning opportunities and to persevere with challenging tasks. Provide a variety of materials and resources for children to explore, manipulate and use, both in learning activities and in imaginative play. Read books to entire classes or small groups. Supervise, evaluate, and plan assignments for teacher assistants and volunteers. Establish clear objectives for all lessons, units, and projects, and communicate those objectives to students. Instruct students individually and in groups, using various teaching methods such as lectures, discussions, and demonstrations. Prepare, administer, and grade tests and assignments in order to evaluate students' progress. Assign and grade class work and homework. Adapt teaching methods and instructional materials to meet students' varying needs and interests. Confer with other staff members to plan and schedule lessons promoting learning, following approved curricula. Confer with parents or guardians, teachers, counselors, and administrators in order to resolve students' behavioral and academic problems. Enforce administration policies and rules governing students. Establish and enforce rules for behavior and procedures for maintaining order among the students for whom they are responsible. Guide and counsel students with adjustment and/or academic problems, or special academic interests. **SKILLS— Learning Strategies:** Selecting and using training/instructional methods and procedures appropriate for the situation when learning or teaching new things. **Social Perceptiveness:** Being aware of others' reactions and understanding why they react as they do. **Instructing:** Teaching others how to do something. **Service Orientation:** Actively looking for ways to help people. **Science:** Using scientific rules and methods to solve problems. **Speaking:** Talking to others to convey information effectively. **Coordination:** Adjusting actions in relation to others' actions. **Time Management:** Managing one's own time and the time of others.

GOE—Interest Area: 05. Education and Training. **Work Group:** 05.02. Pre-school, Elementary, and Secondary Teaching and Instructing. **Other Jobs in This Work Group:** Kindergarten Teachers, Except Special Education; Middle School Teachers, Except Special and Vocational Education; Preschool Teachers, Except Special Education; Secondary School Teachers, Except Special and Vocational Education; Special Education Teachers, Middle School; Special Education Teachers, Preschool, Kindergarten, and Elementary School; Special Education Teachers, Secondary School; Teacher Assistants; Vocational Education Teachers, Middle School; Vocational Education Teachers, Secondary School. **PERSON-**

ALITY TYPE: Social. Social occupations frequently involve working with, communicating with, and teaching people. These occupations often involve helping or providing service to others.

EDUCATION/TRAINING PROGRAM(S)— Elementary Education and Teaching; Teacher Education, Multiple Levels. RELATED KNOWLEDGE/COURSES—Geography: Knowledge of principles and methods for describing the features of land, sea, and air masses, including their physical characteristics; locations; interrelationships; and distribution of plant, animal, and human life. History and Archeology: Knowledge of historical events and their causes, indicators, and effects on civilizations and cultures. Education and Training: Knowledge of principles and methods for curriculum and training design, teaching and instruction for individuals and groups, and the measurement of training effects. Sociology and Anthropology: Knowledge of group behavior and dynamics, societal trends and influences, human migrations, ethnicity, and cultures and their history and origins. Therapy and Counseling: Knowledge of principles, methods, and procedures for diagnosis, treatment, and rehabilitation of physical and mental dysfunctions and for career counseling and guidance. Psychology: Knowledge of human behavior and performance; individual differences in ability, personality, and interests; learning and motivation; psychological research methods; and the assessment and treatment of behavioral and affective disorders.

Employment Interviewers, Private or Public Employment Service

- Education/Training Required: Bachelor's degree
- Annual Earnings: $40,970
- Growth: 27.3%
- Annual Job Openings: 29,000
- Self-Employed: 0.8%
- Part-Time: 7.7%

Interview job applicants in employment office and refer them to prospective employers for consideration. Search application files, notify selected applicants of job openings, and refer qualified applicants to prospective employers. Contact employers to verify referral results. Record and evaluate various pertinent data. Inform applicants of job openings and details such as duties and responsibilities, compensation, benefits, schedules, working conditions, and promotion opportunities. Interview job applicants to match their qualifications with employers' needs, recording and evaluating applicant experience, education, training, and skills. Review employment applications and job orders to match applicants with job requirements, using manual or computerized file searches. Select qualified applicants or refer them to employers, according to organization policy. Perform reference and background checks on applicants. Maintain records of applicants not selected for employment. Instruct job applicants in presenting a positive image by providing help with resume writing, personal appearance, and interview techniques. Refer applicants to services such as vocational counseling, literacy or language instruction, transportation assistance, vocational training and child care. Contact employers to solicit orders for job vacancies, determining their requirements and recording relevant data such as job descriptions. Conduct workshops and demonstrate the use of job listings to assist applicants with skill building. Search for and recruit applicants for open positions through campus job fairs and advertisements. Provide background information on organizations with which interviews are scheduled. Administer assessment tests to identify skill building needs. Conduct or arrange for skill, intelligence, or psychological testing of applicants and current employees. Hire workers and place them with employers needing temporary help. Evaluate selection and testing techniques by conducting research or follow-up activities and conferring with management and supervisory personnel. **SKILLS— Service Orientation:** Actively looking for ways to help people. **Social Perceptiveness:** Being aware of others' reactions and understanding why they react as they do. **Persuasion:** Persuading others to change their minds or behavior. **Management of Personnel Resources:** Motivating, developing, and directing people as they work, identifying the best people for the job. **Negotiation:** Bringing others together and trying to reconcile differences. **Instructing:** Teaching others how to do something. **Speaking:** Talking to others to convey information effectively. **Time Management:** Managing one's own time and the time of others.

GOE—**Interest Area:** 04. Business and Administration. **Work Group:** 04.03. Human Resources Support. **Other Jobs in This Work Group:** Compensation, Benefits, and Job Analysis Specialists; Personnel Recruiters; Training and Development Specialists. **PERSONALITY TYPE:** Social. Social occupations frequently involve working with, communicating with, and teaching people. These occupations often involve helping or providing service to others.

EDUCATION/TRAINING PROGRAM(S)— Human Resources Management/Personnel Administration, General; Labor and Industrial Relations. **RELATED KNOWLEDGE/COURSES—Customer and Personal Service:** Knowledge of principles and processes for providing customer and personal services. This includes customer needs assessment, meeting quality standards for services, and evaluation of customer satisfaction. **Clerical Practices:** Knowledge of administrative and clerical procedures and systems such as word processing, managing files and records, stenography and transcription, designing forms, and other office procedures and terminology. **Foreign Language:** Knowledge of the structure and content of a foreign (non-English) language, including the meaning and spelling of words, rules of composition and grammar, and pronunciation. **Personnel and Human Resources:** Knowledge of principles and procedures for personnel recruitment, selection, training, compensation and benefits, labor relations and negotiation, and personnel information systems. **English Language:** Knowledge of the structure and content of the English language, including the meaning and spelling of words, rules of composition, and grammar. **Sales and Marketing:** Knowledge of principles and methods for showing, promoting, and selling products or services. This includes marketing strategy and tactics, product demonstration, sales techniques, and sales control systems.

Engineering Managers

- Education/Training Required: Work experience plus degree
- Annual Earnings: $95,630
- Growth: 9.2%
- Annual Job Openings: 16,000
- Self-Employed: 0.1%
- Part-Time: 1.0%

Plan, direct, or coordinate activities in such fields as architecture and engineering or research and development in these fields. Confer with management, production, and marketing staff to discuss project specifications and procedures. Coordinate and direct projects, making detailed plans to accomplish goals and directing the integration of technical activities. Analyze technology, resource needs, and market demand, to plan and assess the feasibility of projects. Plan and direct the installation, testing, operation, maintenance, and repair of facilities and equipment. Direct, review, and approve product design and changes. Recruit employees); assign, direct, and evaluate their work); and oversee the development and maintenance of staff competence. Prepare budgets, bids, and contracts, and direct the negotiation of research contracts. Develop and implement policies, standards and procedures for the engineering and technical work performed in the department, service, laboratory or firm. Perform administrative functions such as reviewing and writing reports, approving expenditures, enforcing rules, and making decisions about the purchase of materials or services. Review and recommend or approve contracts and cost estimates. Present and explain proposals, reports, and findings to clients. Consult or negotiate with clients to prepare project specifications. Set scientific and technical goals within broad outlines provided by top management. Administer highway planning, construction, and maintenance. Direct the engineering of water control, treatment, and distribution projects. Plan, direct, and coordinate survey work with other staff activities, certifying survey work, and writing land legal descriptions. Confer with and report to officials and the public to provide information and solicit support for projects. **SKILLS—Technology Design:** Generating or adapting equipment and technology to serve user needs. **Operations Analysis:** Analyzing needs and product requirements to create a design. **Science:** Using scientific rules and methods to solve problems. **Management of Financial Resources:** Determining how money will be spent to get the work done and accounting for these expenditures. **Installation:** Installing equipment, machines, wiring, or programs to meet specifications. **Negotiation:** Bringing others together and trying to reconcile differences. **Persuasion:** Persuading others to change their minds or behavior. **Time Management:** Managing one's own time and the time of others.

GOE—Interest Area: 15. Scientific Research, Engineering, and Mathematics. **Work Group:** 15.01. Managerial Work in Scientific Research, Engineering, and Mathematics. **Other Jobs in This Work Group:** Natural Sciences Managers. **PERSONALITY TYPE:** Enterprising. Enterprising occupations frequently involve starting up and carrying out projects. These occupations can involve leading people and making many decisions. They sometimes require risk taking and often deal with business.

EDUCATION/TRAINING PROGRAM(S)— Aerospace, Aeronautical and Astronautical Engineering; Agricultural/Biological Engineering and Bioengineering; Architectural Engineering; Architecture (BArch, BA/BS, MArch, MA/MS, PhD); Biomedical/Medical Engineering; Ceramic Sciences and Engineering; Chemical Engineering; City/Urban, Community and Regional Planning; Civil Engineering, General; Civil Engineering, Other; Computer Engineering, General; Computer Engineering, Other; Computer Hardware Engineering; Computer Software Engineering; Construction Engineering; Electrical, Electronics and Communications Engineering; Engineering Mechanics; Engineering Physics; Engineering Science; Engineering, General; Engineering, Other; Environmental Design/Architecture; Environmental/Environmental Health Engineering; Forest Engineering; Geological/Geophysical Engineering; Geotechnical Engineering; Industrial Engineering; Interior Architecture; Landscape Architecture (BS, BSLA, BLA, MSLA, MLA, PhD); Manufacturing Engineering; Materials Engineering; Materials Science; Mechanical Engineering; Metallurgical Engineering; Mining and Mineral Engineering; Naval Architecture and Marine Engineering; Nuclear Engineering; Ocean Engineering; Petroleum Engineering; Polymer/Plastics Engineering; Structural Engineering; Surveying Engineering; Systems Engineering; Textile Sciences and Engineering; Transportation and Highway Engineering; Water Resources Engineering. **RELATED KNOWLEDGE/COURSES—Engineering and Technology:** Knowledge of the practical application of engineering science and technology. This includes applying principles, techniques, procedures, and equipment to the design and production of various goods and services. **Design:** Knowledge of design techniques, tools, and principles involved in production of precision technical plans, blueprints, drawings, and models. **Physics:** Knowledge and prediction of physical principles and laws and their interrelationships and applications to understanding fluid, material, and atmospheric dynamics and mechanical, electrical, atomic, and subatomic structures and processes. **Mathematics:** Knowledge of arithmetic, algebra, geometry, calculus, and statistics and their applications. **Personnel and Human Resources:** Knowledge of principles and procedures for personnel recruitment, selection, training, compensation and benefits, labor relations and negotiation, and personnel information systems. **Administration and Management:** Knowledge of business and management principles involved in strategic planning, resource allocation, human resources modeling, leadership technique, production methods, and coordination of people and resources. **Building and Construction:** Knowledge of the materials, methods, and tools involved in the construction or repair of houses, buildings, or other structures such as highways and roads.

Engineering Teachers, Postsecondary

- Education/Training Required: Master's degree
- Annual Earnings: $71,070
- Growth: 38.1% for all Postsecondary Teachers
- Annual Job Openings: 216,000 for all Postsecondary Teachers
- Self-Employed: 0.3% for all Postsecondary Teachers
- Part-Time: 27.7% for all Postsecondary Teachers

Teach courses pertaining to the application of physical laws and principles of engineering for the development of machines, materials, instruments, processes, and services. Includes teachers of subjects, such as chemical, civil, electrical, industrial, mechanical, mineral, and petroleum engineering. Includes both teachers primarily engaged in teaching and those who do a combination of both teaching and research. Maintain regularly scheduled office hours in order to advise and assist students. Maintain student attendance records, grades, and other required records. Plan, evaluate, and revise curricula, course content, and course materials and methods of instruction. Prepare course materials such as syllabi, homework assignments, and handouts. Select and obtain materials and supplies such as textbooks and laboratory equipment. Supervise students' laboratory work. Supervise undergraduate and/or graduate teaching, internship, and research work. Act as advisers to student organizations. Collaborate with colleagues to address teaching and research issues. Conduct research in a particular field of knowledge, and publish findings in professional journals, books, and/or electronic media. Participate in campus and community events. Participate in student recruitment, registration, and placement activities. Perform administrative duties such as serving as department head. Provide professional consulting services to government and/or industry. Serve on academic or administrative committees that deal with institutional policies, departmental matters, and academic issues. Write grant proposals to procure external research funding. Evaluate and grade students' class work, laboratory work, assignments, and papers. Prepare and deliver lectures to undergraduate and/or graduate students on topics such as mechanics, hydraulics, and robotics. Advise students on academic and vocational curricula, and on career issues. Compile, administer, and grade examinations, or assign this work to others. Compile bibliographies of specialized materials for outside reading assignments. Initiate, facilitate, and moderate class discussions. Keep abreast of developments in their field by reading current literature, talking with colleagues, and participating in professional conferences. **SKILLS—Science:** Using scientific rules and methods to solve problems. **Mathematics:** Using mathematics to solve problems. **Instructing:** Teaching others how to do something. **Technology Design:** Generating or adapting equipment and technology to serve user needs. **Active Learning:** Understanding the implications of new information for both current and future problem-solving and decision-making. **Critical Thinking:** Using logic and reasoning to identify the strengths and weaknesses of alternative solutions, conclusions, or approaches to problems. **Learning Strategies:** Selecting and using training/instructional methods and procedures appropriate for the situation when learning or teaching new things. **Reading Comprehension:** Understanding written sentences and paragraphs in work-related documents. **Operations Analysis:** Analyzing needs and product requirements to create a design.

GOE—Interest Area: 05. Education and Training. **Work Group:** 05.03. Postsecondary and Adult Teaching and Instructing. **Other Jobs in This Work Group:** Adult Literacy, Remedial Education, and GED Teachers and Instructors; Agricultural Sciences Teachers, Postsecondary; Anthropology and Archeology Teachers, Postsecondary; Architecture Teachers, Postsecondary; Area, Ethnic, and Cultural Studies Teachers, Postsecondary; Art, Drama, and Music Teachers, Postsecondary; Atmospheric, Earth, Marine, and Space Sciences Teachers, Postsecondary; Biological Science Teachers, Postsecondary; Business Teachers, Postsecondary; Chemistry Teachers, Postsecondary; Communications Teachers, Postsecondary; Computer Science Teachers, Postsecondary; Criminal Justice and Law Enforcement Teachers, Postsecondary; Economics Teachers, Postsecondary; Education Teachers, Postsecondary; English Language and Literature Teachers, Postsecondary; Environmental Science Teachers, Postsecondary; Farm and Home Management Advisors; Foreign Language and Literature Teachers, Postsecondary; Forestry and Conservation

Science Teachers, Postsecondary; Geography Teachers, Postsecondary; Graduate Teaching Assistants; Health Specialties Teachers, Postsecondary; History Teachers, Postsecondary; Home Economics Teachers, Postsecondary; Law Teachers, Postsecondary; Library Science Teachers, Postsecondary; Mathematical Science Teachers, Postsecondary; Nursing Instructors and Teachers, Postsecondary; Philosophy and Religion Teachers, Postsecondary; Physics Teachers, Postsecondary; Political Science Teachers, Postsecondary; Psychology Teachers, Postsecondary; Recreation and Fitness Studies Teachers, Postsecondary; Self-Enrichment Education Teachers; Social Work Teachers, Postsecondary; Sociology Teachers, Postsecondary; Vocational Education Teachers, Postsecondary. **PERSONALITY TYPE:** Investigative. Investigative occupations frequently involve working with ideas and require an extensive amount of thinking. These occupations can involve searching for facts and figuring out problems mentally.

EDUCATION/TRAINING PROGRAM(S)— Aerospace, Aeronautical and Astronautical Engineering; Agricultural/Biological Engineering and Bioengineering; Architectural Engineering; Biomedical/Medical Engineering; Ceramic Sciences and Engineering; Chemical Engineering; Civil Engineering, General; Civil Engineering, Other; Computer Engineering, General; Computer Engineering, Other; Computer Hardware Engineering; Computer Software Engineering; Construction Engineering; Electrical, Electronics and Communications Engineering; Engineering Mechanics; Engineering Physics; Engineering Science; Engineering, General; Engineering, Other; Environmental/Environmental Health Engineering; Forest Engineering; Geological/Geophysical Engineering; Geotechnical Engineering; Industrial Engineering; Manufacturing Engineering; Materials Engineering; Materials Science; Mechanical Engineering; Metallurgical Engineering; Mining and Mineral Engineering; Naval Architecture and Marine Engineering; Nuclear Engineering; Ocean Engineering; Petroleum Engineering; Polymer/Plastics Engineering; Structural Engineering; Surveying Engineering; Systems Engineering; Teacher Education and Professional Development, Specific Subject Areas, Other; Textile Sciences and Engineering; Transportation and Highway Engineering; Water Resources Engineering. **RELATED KNOWLEDGE/COURSES—Engineering and Technology:** Knowledge of the practical application of engineering science and technology. This includes applying principles, techniques, procedures, and equipment to the design and production of various goods and services. **Education and Training:** Knowledge of principles and methods for curriculum and training design, teaching and instruction for individuals and groups, and the measurement of training effects. **Physics:** Knowledge and prediction of physical principles and laws and their interrelationships and applications to understanding fluid, material, and atmospheric dynamics and mechanical, electrical, atomic, and subatomic structures and processes. **Chemistry:** Knowledge of the chemical composition, structure, and properties of substances and of the chemical processes and transformations that they undergo. This includes uses of chemicals and their danger signs, production techniques, and disposal methods. **Design:** Knowledge of design techniques, tools, and principles involved in production of precision technical plans, blueprints, drawings, and models. **Mathematics:** Knowledge of arithmetic, algebra, geometry, calculus, and statistics and their applications.

English Language and Literature Teachers, Postsecondary

- Education/Training Required: Master's degree
- Annual Earnings: $47,560
- Growth: 38.1% for all Postsecondary Teachers
- Annual Job Openings: 216,000 for all Postsecondary Teachers
- Self-Employed: 0.3% for all Postsecondary Teachers
- Part-Time: 27.7% for all Postsecondary Teachers

Teach courses in English language and literature, including linguistics and comparative literature. Provide professional consulting services to government and/or industry. Recruit, train, and supervise student writing instructors. Serve on academic or administrative committees that deal with institutional policies, departmental matters, and academic issues. Write grant proposals to procure external research funding. Evaluate and grade students' class work, assignments, and papers. Prepare and deliver lectures to undergraduate and/or graduate students on topics such as poetry, novel structure, and translation and adaptation. Advise students on academic and vocational curricula, and on career issues. Compile, administer, and grade examinations, or assign this work to others. Compile bibliographies of specialized materials for outside reading assignments. Initiate, facilitate, and moderate classroom discussions. Keep abreast of developments in their field by reading current literature, talking with colleagues, and participating in professional conferences. Maintain regularly scheduled office hours in order to advise and assist students. Maintain student attendance records, grades, and other required records. Plan, evaluate, and revise curricula, course content,

E

and course materials and methods of instruction. Prepare course materials such as syllabi, homework assignments, and handouts. Select and obtain materials and supplies such as textbooks. Supervise undergraduate and/or graduate teaching, internship, and research work. Provide assistance to students in college writing centers. Act as advisers to student organizations. Collaborate with colleagues to address teaching and research issues. Conduct research in a particular field of knowledge, and publish findings in professional journals, books, and/or electronic media. Participate in campus and community events. Participate in student recruitment, registration, and placement activities. Perform administrative duties such as serving as department head. **SKILLS—Instructing:** Teaching others how to do something. **Learning Strategies:** Selecting and using training/instructional methods and procedures appropriate for the situation when learning or teaching new things. **Speaking:** Talking to others to convey information effectively. **Reading Comprehension:** Understanding written sentences and paragraphs in work-related documents. **Writing:** Communicating effectively in writing as appropriate for the needs of the audience. **Critical Thinking:** Using logic and reasoning to identify the strengths and weaknesses of alternative solutions, conclusions, or approaches to problems. **Active Learning:** Understanding the implications of new information for both current and future problem-solving and decision-making. **Active Listening:** Giving full attention to what other people are saying, taking time to understand the points being made, asking questions as appropriate, and not interrupting at inappropriate times.

GOE—Interest Area: 05. Education and Training. **Work Group:** 05.03. Postsecondary and Adult Teaching and Instructing. **Other Jobs in This Work Group:** Adult Literacy, Remedial Education, and GED Teachers and Instructors; Agricultural Sciences Teachers, Postsecondary; Anthropology and Archeology Teachers, Postsecondary; Architecture Teachers, Postsecondary; Area, Ethnic, and Cultural Studies Teachers, Postsecondary; Art, Drama, and Music Teachers, Postsecondary; Atmospheric, Earth, Marine, and Space Sciences Teachers, Postsecondary; Biological Science Teachers, Postsecondary; Business Teachers, Postsecondary; Chemistry Teachers, Postsecondary; Communications Teachers, Postsecondary; Computer Science Teachers, Postsecondary; Criminal Justice and Law Enforcement Teachers, Postsecondary; Economics Teachers, Postsecondary; Education Teachers, Postsecondary; Engineering Teachers, Postsecondary; Environmental Science Teachers, Postsecondary; Farm and Home Management Advisors; Foreign Language and Literature Teachers, Postsecondary; Forestry and Conservation Science Teachers, Postsecondary; Geography Teachers, Postsecondary; Graduate Teaching Assistants; Health Specialties Teachers, Postsecondary; History Teachers, Postsecondary; Home Economics Teachers, Postsecondary; Law Teachers, Postsecondary; Library Science Teachers, Postsecondary; Mathematical Science Teachers, Postsecondary; Nursing Instructors and Teachers, Postsecondary; Philosophy and Religion Teachers, Postsecondary; Physics Teachers, Postsecondary; Political Science Teachers, Postsecondary; Psychology Teachers, Postsecondary; Recreation and Fitness Studies Teachers, Postsecondary; Self-Enrichment Education Teachers; Social Work Teachers, Postsecondary; Sociology Teachers, Postsecondary; Vocational Education Teachers, Postsecondary. **PERSONALITY TYPE:** Artistic. Artistic occupations frequently involve working with forms, designs, and patterns. They often require self-expression, and the work can be done without following a clear set of rules.

EDUCATION/TRAINING PROGRAM(S)— American Literature (Canadian); American Literature (United States); Comparative Literature; Creative Writing; English Composition; English Language and Literature, General; English Language and Literature/Letters, Other; English Literature (British and Commonwealth); Technical and Business Writing. **RELATED KNOWLEDGE/ COURSES—Foreign Language:** Knowledge of the structure and content of a foreign (non-English) language, including the meaning and spelling of words, rules of composition and grammar, and pronunciation. **Education and Training:** Knowledge of principles and methods for curriculum and training design, teaching and instruction for individuals and groups, and the measurement of training effects. **English Language:** Knowledge of the structure and content of the English language, including the meaning and spelling of words, rules of composition, and grammar. **Communications and Media:** Knowledge of media production, communication, and dissemination techniques and methods. This includes alternative ways to inform and entertain via written, oral, and visual media. **Therapy and Counseling:** Knowledge of principles, methods, and procedures for diagnosis, treatment, and rehabilitation of physical and mental dysfunctions and for career counseling and guidance. **Clerical Practices:** Knowledge of administrative and clerical procedures and systems such as word processing, managing files and records, stenography and transcription, designing forms, and other office procedures and terminology.

Environmental Engineering Technicians

- ◎ Education/Training Required: Associate's degree
- ◎ Annual Earnings: $38,180
- ◎ Growth: 28.4%
- ◎ Annual Job Openings: 3,000
- ◎ Self-Employed: 0.4%
- ◎ Part-Time: 5.0%

Apply theory and principles of environmental engineering to modify, test, and operate equipment and devices used in the prevention, control, and remediation of environmental pollution, including waste treatment and site remediation.

May assist in the development of environmental pollution remediation devices under direction of engineer. Receive, set up, test, and decontaminate equipment. Maintain project logbook records and computer program files. Conduct pollution surveys, collecting and analyzing samples such as air and ground water. Perform environmental quality work in field and office settings. Review technical documents to ensure completeness and conformance to requirements. Perform laboratory work such as logging numerical and visual observations, preparing and packaging samples, recording test results, and performing photo documentation. Review work plans to schedule activities. Obtain product information, identify vendors and suppliers, and order materials and equipment to maintain inventory. Arrange for the disposal of lead, asbestos and other hazardous materials. Inspect facilities to monitor compliance with regulations governing substances such as asbestos, lead, and wastewater. Provide technical engineering support in the planning of projects, such as wastewater treatment plants, to ensure compliance with environmental regulations and policies. Improve chemical processes to reduce toxic emissions. Oversee support staff. Assist in the cleanup of hazardous material spills. Produce environmental assessment reports, tabulating data and preparing charts, graphs and sketches. Maintain process parameters and evaluate process anomalies. Work with customers to assess the environmental impact of proposed construction and to develop pollution prevention programs. Perform statistical analysis and correction of air and/or water pollution data submitted by industry and other agencies. Develop work plans, including writing specifications and establishing material, manpower and facilities needs. **SKILLS—Troubleshooting:** Determining causes of operating errors and deciding what to do about them. **Science:** Using scientific rules and methods to solve problems. **Coordination:** Adjusting actions in relation to others' actions. **Repairing:** Repairing machines or systems, using the needed tools. **Equipment Maintenance:** Performing routine maintenance on equipment and determining when and what kind of maintenance is needed. **Time Management:** Managing one's own time and the time of others. **Management of Financial Resources:** Determining how money will be spent to get the work done and accounting for these expenditures. **Service Orientation:** Actively looking for ways to help people.

GOE—Interest Area: 15. Scientific Research, Engineering, and Mathematics. **Work Group:** 15.09. Engineering Technology. **Other Jobs in This Work Group:** Aerospace Engineering and Operations Technicians; Calibration and Instrumentation Technicians; Cartographers and Photogrammetrists; Civil Engineering Technicians; Electrical Engineering Technicians; Electro-Mechanical Technicians; Electronic Drafters; Electronics Engineering Technicians; Mapping Technicians; Mechanical Drafters; Mechanical Engineering Technicians; Surveying Technicians. **PERSONALITY TYPE:** No data available.

EDUCATION/TRAINING PROGRAM(S)— Environmental Engineering Technology/Environmental Technology; Hazardous Materials Information Systems Technology/Technician. **RELATED KNOWLEDGE/COURSES—Engineering and Technology:** Knowledge of the practical application of engineering science and technology. This includes applying principles, techniques, procedures, and equipment to the design and production of various goods and services. **Design:** Knowledge of design techniques, tools, and principles involved in production of precision technical plans, blueprints, drawings, and models. **Building and Construction:** Knowledge of the materials, methods, and tools involved in the construction or repair of houses, buildings, or other structures such as highways and roads. **Physics:** Knowledge and prediction of physical principles and laws and their interrelationships and applications to understanding fluid, material, and atmospheric dynamics and mechanical, electrical, atomic, and subatomic structures and processes. **Customer and Personal Service:** Knowledge of principles and processes for providing customer and personal services. This includes customer needs assessment,

meeting quality standards for services, and evaluation of customer satisfaction. **Law and Government:** Knowledge of laws, legal codes, court procedures, precedents, government regulations, executive orders, agency rules, and the democratic political process.

Environmental Engineers

◎ Education/Training Required: Bachelor's degree
◎ Annual Earnings: $64,040
◎ Growth: 38.2%
◎ Annual Job Openings: 6,000
◎ Self-Employed: 0.4%
◎ Part-Time: 4.6%

Design, plan, or perform engineering duties in the prevention, control, and remediation of environmental health hazards utilizing various engineering disciplines. Work may include waste treatment, site remediation, or pollution control technology. Prepare, review, and update environmental investigation and recommendation reports. Collaborate with environmental scientists, planners, hazardous waste technicians, engineers, and other specialists, and experts in law and business to address environmental problems. Obtain, update, and maintain plans, permits, and standard operating procedures. Provide technical-level support for environmental remediation and litigation projects, including remediation system design and determination of regulatory applicability. Monitor progress of environmental improvement programs. Inspect industrial and municipal facilities and programs in order to evaluate operational effectiveness and ensure compliance with environmental regulations. Provide administrative support for projects by collecting data, providing project documentation, training staff, and performing other general administrative duties. Develop proposed project objectives and targets, and report to management on progress in attaining them. Advise corporations and government agencies of procedures to follow in cleaning up contaminated sites in order to protect people and the environment. Advise industries and government agencies about environmental policies and standards. Inform company employees and other interested parties of environmental issues. Assess the existing or potential environmental impact of land use projects on air, water, and land. Assist in budget implementation, forecasts, and administration. Develop site-specific health and safety protocols, such as spill contingency plans and methods for loading and transporting waste. Coordinate and manage environmental protection programs and projects, assigning and evaluating work. Serve as liaison with federal, state, and local agencies and officials on issues pertaining to solid and hazardous waste program requirements. Design systems, processes, and equipment for control, management, and remediation of water, air, and soil quality. Prepare hazardous waste manifests and land disposal restriction notifications. Serve on teams conducting multimedia inspections at complex facilities, providing assistance with planning, quality assurance, safety inspection protocols, and sampling. **SKILLS—Science:** Using scientific rules and methods to solve problems. **Management of Financial Resources:** Determining how money will be spent to get the work done and accounting for these expenditures. **Coordination:** Adjusting actions in relation to others' actions. **Writing:** Communicating effectively in writing as appropriate for the needs of the audience. **Persuasion:** Persuading others to change their minds or behavior. **Negotiation:** Bringing others together and trying to reconcile differences. **Mathematics:** Using mathematics to solve problems. **Technology Design:** Generating or adapting equipment and technology to serve user needs.

GOE—Interest Area: 01. Agriculture and Natural Resources. **Work Group:** 01.02. Resource Science/Engineering for Plants, Animals, and the Environment. **Other Jobs in This Work Group:** Agricultural Engineers; Animal Scientists; Foresters; Mining and Geological Engineers, Including Mining Safety Engineers; Petroleum Engineers; Plant Scientists; Range Managers; Soil Conservationists; Soil Scientists; Zoologists and Wildlife Biologists. **PERSONALITY TYPE:** No data available.

EDUCATION/TRAINING PROGRAM(S)—Environmental/Environmental Health Engineering. **RELATED KNOWLEDGE/COURSES—Education and Training:** Knowledge of principles and methods for curriculum and training design, teaching and instruction for individuals and groups, and the measurement of training effects. **Law and Government:** Knowledge of laws, legal codes, court procedures, precedents, government regulations, executive orders, agency rules, and the democratic political process. **Chemistry:** Knowledge of the chemical composition, structure, and properties of substances and of the chemical processes and transformations that they undergo. This includes uses of chemicals and their danger signs, production techniques, and disposal methods. **Public Safety and Security:** Knowledge of relevant equipment, policies, procedures, and strategies to promote effective local, state, or national security operations for the protection of people, data, property, and institutions. **Engineering and Technology:** Knowledge of the practical application of engineering science and technology. This includes applying principles, techniques, procedures, and equipment to the design and production of various goods and services. **Design:** Knowledge of design techniques, tools, and principles involved in production of precision technical plans, blueprints, drawings, and models.

Environmental Science and Protection Technicians, Including Health

◎ Education/Training Required: Associate's degree

◎ Annual Earnings: $35,790

◎ Growth: 36.8%

◎ Annual Job Openings: 4,000

◎ Self-Employed: 1.1%

◎ Part-Time: 20.2%

Performs laboratory and field tests to monitor the environment and investigate sources of pollution, including those that affect health. Under direction of an environmental scientist or specialist, may collect samples of gases, soil, water, and other materials for testing and take corrective actions as assigned. Record test data and prepare reports, summaries, and charts that interpret test results. Collect samples of gases, soils, water, industrial wastewater, and asbestos products to conduct tests on pollutant levels and identify sources of pollution. Respond to and investigate hazardous conditions or spills, or outbreaks of disease or food poisoning, collecting samples for analysis. Provide information and technical and program assistance to government representatives, employers and the general public on the issues of public health, environmental protection or workplace safety. Calibrate microscopes and test instruments. Make recommendations to control or eliminate unsafe conditions at workplaces or public facilities. Inspect sanitary conditions at public facilities. Prepare samples or photomicrographs for testing and analysis. Calculate amount of pollutant in samples or compute air pollution or gas flow in industrial processes, using chemical and mathematical formulas. Initiate procedures to close down or fine establishments violating environmental and/or health regulations. Determine amounts and kinds of chemicals to use in destroying harmful organisms and removing impurities from purification systems. Discuss test results and analyses with customers. Maintain files such as hazardous waste databases, chemical usage data, personnel exposure information and diagrams showing equipment locations. Perform statistical analysis of environmental data. Set up equipment or stations to monitor and collect pollutants from sites, such as smoke stacks, manufacturing plants, or mechanical equipment. Distribute permits, closure plans and cleanup plans. Inspect workplaces to ensure the absence of health and safety hazards such as high noise levels, radiation or potential lighting hazards. Weigh, analyze, and measure collected sample particles, such as lead, coal dust, or rock, to determine concentration of pollutants. Examine and analyze material for presence and concentration of contaminants such as asbestos, using variety of microscopes. Develop testing procedures, and direct activities of workers in laboratory. **SKILLS—Science:** Using scientific rules and methods to solve problems. **Persuasion:** Persuading others to change their minds or behavior. **Active Learning:** Understanding the implications of new information for both current and future problem-solving and decision-making. **Instructing:** Teaching others how to do something. **Critical Thinking:** Using logic and reasoning to identify the strengths and weaknesses of alternative solutions, conclusions, or approaches to problems. **Reading Comprehension:** Understanding written sentences and paragraphs in work-related documents. **Social Perceptiveness:** Being aware of others' reactions and understanding why they react as they do. **Troubleshooting:** Determining causes of operating errors and deciding what to do about them.

GOE—Interest Area: 01. Agriculture and Natural Resources. **Work Group:** 01.03. Resource Technologies for Plants, Animals, and the Environment. **Other Jobs in This Work Group:** Agricultural Technicians; Food Science Technicians; Food Scientists and Technologists; Geological Data Technicians; Geological Sample Test Technicians.

PERSONALITY TYPE: Investigative. Investigative occupations frequently involve working with ideas and require an extensive amount of thinking. These occupations can involve searching for facts and figuring out problems mentally.

EDUCATION/TRAINING PROGRAM(S)— Environmental Science; Environmental Studies; Physical Science Technologies/Technicians, Other; Science Technologies/Technicians, Other. **RELATED KNOWLEDGE/COURSES—Biology:** Knowledge of plant and animal organisms and their tissues, cells, functions, interdependencies, and interactions with each other and the environment. **Engineering and Technology:** Knowledge of the practical application of engineering science and technology. This includes applying principles, techniques, procedures, and equipment to the design and production of various goods and services. **Chemistry:** Knowledge of the chemical composition, structure, and properties of substances and of the chemical processes and transformations that they undergo. This includes uses of chemicals and their danger signs, production techniques, and disposal methods. **Customer and Personal Service:** Knowledge of principles and processes for providing customer and personal services. This includes customer needs assessment, meeting quality standards for services, and evaluation of customer satisfaction. **Education and Training:** Knowledge of principles and methods for curriculum and training design, teaching and instruction for individuals and groups, and the measurement of training effects. **Physics:** Knowledge and prediction of physical principles and laws and their interrelationships and applications to understanding fluid, material, and atmospheric dynamics and mechanical, electrical, atomic, and subatomic structures and processes.

Environmental Science Teachers, Postsecondary

- Education/Training Required: Master's degree
- Annual Earnings: $60,660
- Growth: 38.1% for all Postsecondary Teachers
- Annual Job Openings: 216,000 for all Postsecondary Teachers
- Self-Employed: 0.3% for all Postsecondary Teachers
- Part-Time: 27.7% for all Postsecondary Teachers

Teach courses in environmental science. Collaborate with colleagues to address teaching and research issues. Conduct research in a particular field of knowledge, and publish findings in professional journals, books, and/or electronic media. Participate in campus and community events. Participate in student recruitment, registration, and placement activities. Perform administrative duties such as serving as department head. Provide professional consulting services to government and/or industry. Serve on academic or administrative committees that deal with institutional policies, departmental matters, and academic issues. Write grant proposals to procure external research funding. Evaluate and grade students' class work, laboratory work, assignments, and papers. Prepare and deliver lectures to undergraduate and/or graduate students on topics such as hazardous waste management, industrial safety, and environmental toxicology. Advise students on academic and vocational curricula, and on career issues. Compile, administer, and grade examinations, or assign this work to others. Compile bibliographies of specialized materials for outside reading assignments. Initiate, facilitate, and moderate classroom discussions. Keep abreast of develop-

E

ments in their field by reading current literature, talking with colleagues, and participating in professional conferences. Maintain regularly scheduled office hours in order to advise and assist students. Maintain student attendance records, grades, and other required records. Plan, evaluate, and revise curricula, course content, and course materials and methods of instruction. Prepare course materials such as syllabi, homework assignments, and handouts. Select and obtain materials and supplies such as textbooks and laboratory equipment. Supervise students' laboratory and field work. Supervise undergraduate and/or graduate teaching, internship, and research work. Act as advisers to student organizations. **SKILLS**—No data available.

GOE—**Interest Area:** 05. Education and Training. **Work Group:** 05.03. Postsecondary and Adult Teaching and Instructing. **Other Jobs in This Work Group:** Adult Literacy, Remedial Education, and GED Teachers and Instructors; Agricultural Sciences Teachers, Postsecondary; Anthropology and Archeology Teachers, Postsecondary; Architecture Teachers, Postsecondary; Area, Ethnic, and Cultural Studies Teachers, Postsecondary; Art, Drama, and Music Teachers, Postsecondary; Atmospheric, Earth, Marine, and Space Sciences Teachers, Postsecondary; Biological Science Teachers, Postsecondary; Business Teachers, Postsecondary; Chemistry Teachers, Postsecondary; Communications Teachers, Postsecondary; Computer Science Teachers, Postsecondary; Criminal Justice and Law Enforcement Teachers, Postsecondary; Economics Teachers, Postsecondary; Education Teachers, Postsecondary; Engineering Teachers, Postsecondary; English Language and Literature Teachers, Postsecondary; Farm and Home Management Advisors; Foreign Language and Literature Teachers, Postsecondary; Forestry and Conservation Science Teachers, Postsecondary; Geography Teachers, Postsecondary; Graduate Teaching Assistants; Health Specialties Teachers, Postsecondary; History Teachers, Postsecondary; Home Economics Teachers, Postsecondary; Law Teachers, Postsecondary; Library Science Teachers, Postsecondary; Mathe-

matical Science Teachers, Postsecondary; Nursing Instructors and Teachers, Postsecondary; Philosophy and Religion Teachers, Postsecondary; Physics Teachers, Postsecondary; Political Science Teachers, Postsecondary; Psychology Teachers, Postsecondary; Recreation and Fitness Studies Teachers, Postsecondary; Self-Enrichment Education Teachers; Social Work Teachers, Postsecondary; Sociology Teachers, Postsecondary; Vocational Education Teachers, Postsecondary. **PERSONALITY TYPE:** No data available.

EDUCATION/TRAINING PROGRAM(S)—Environmental Science; Environmental Studies; Science Teacher Education/General Science Teacher Education. **RELATED KNOWLEDGE/COURSES**—No data available.

Environmental Scientists and Specialists, Including Health

◎ Education/Training Required: Bachelor's degree
◎ Annual Earnings: $50,070
◎ Growth: 23.7%
◎ Annual Job Openings: 6,000
◎ Self-Employed: 2.9%
◎ Part-Time: 7.7%

Conduct research or perform investigation for the purpose of identifying, abating, or eliminating sources of pollutants or hazards that affect either the environment or the health of the population. Utilizing knowledge of various scientific disciplines may collect, synthesize, study, report, and take action based on data derived from measurements or observations of air, food, soil, water, and

other sources. Conduct environmental audits and inspections, and investigations of violations. Evaluate violations or problems discovered during inspections in order to determine appropriate regulatory actions or to provide advice on the development and prosecution of regulatory cases. Communicate scientific and technical information through oral briefings, written documents, workshops, conferences, and public hearings. Review and implement environmental technical standards, guidelines, policies, and formal regulations that meet all appropriate requirements. Provide technical guidance, support, and oversight to environmental programs, industry, and the public. Provide advice on proper standards and regulations and the development of policies, strategies, and codes of practice for environmental management. Analyze data to determine validity, quality, and scientific significance, and to interpret correlations between human activities and environmental effects. Collect, synthesize, and analyze data derived from pollution emission measurements, atmospheric monitoring, meteorological and mineralogical information, and soil or water samples. Determine data collection methods to be employed in research projects and surveys. Prepare charts or graphs from data samples, and provide summary information on the environmental relevance of the data. Develop the technical portions of legal documents, administrative orders, or consent decrees. Investigate and report on accidents affecting the environment. Monitor environmental impacts of development activities. Supervise environmental technologists and technicians. Develop programs designed to obtain the most productive, non-damaging use of land. Research sources of pollution to determine their effects on the environment and to develop theories or methods of pollution abatement or control. Monitor effects of pollution and land degradation, and recommend means of prevention or control. Design and direct studies to obtain technical environmental information about planned projects. Conduct applied research on topics such as waste control and treatment and pollution control methods. **SKILLS—Service Orientation:** Actively looking for ways to help people. **Science:** Using scientific rules and methods to solve problems. **Coordination:** Adjusting actions in relation to others' actions. **Negotiation:** Bringing others together and trying to reconcile differences. **Persuasion:** Persuading others to change their minds or behavior. **Reading Comprehension:** Understanding written sentences and paragraphs in work-related documents. **Active Learning:** Understanding the implications of new information for both current and future problem-solving and decision-making. **Time Management:** Managing one's own time and the time of others.

GOE—Interest Area: 15. Scientific Research, Engineering, and Mathematics. **Work Group:** 15.03. Life Sciences. **Other Jobs in This Work Group:** Biochemists; Biologists; Biophysicists; Epidemiologists; Medical Scientists, Except Epidemiologists; Microbiologists. **PERSONALITY TYPE:** Investigative. Investigative occupations frequently involve working with ideas and require an extensive amount of thinking. These occupations can involve searching for facts and figuring out problems mentally.

EDUCATION/TRAINING PROGRAM(S)— Environmental Science; Environmental Studies. **RELATED KNOWLEDGE/COURSES—Biology:** Knowledge of plant and animal organisms and their tissues, cells, functions, interdependencies, and interactions with each other and the environment. **Geography:** Knowledge of principles and methods for describing the features of land, sea, and air masses, including their physical characteristics; locations; interrelationships; and distribution of plant, animal, and human life. **Law and Government:** Knowledge of laws, legal codes, court procedures, precedents, government regulations, executive orders, agency rules, and the democratic political process. **Chemistry:** Knowledge of the chemical composition, structure, and properties of substances and of the chemical processes and transformations that they undergo. This includes uses of chemicals and their danger signs, production techniques, and disposal methods. **Customer and Personal Service:** Knowledge of principles and processes for providing customer and personal services. This includes customer needs assessment, meeting quality standards for services, and evaluation of customer satisfaction. **Education and Training:** Knowledge of principles and methods for curriculum and training design, teaching and instruction for individuals and groups, and the measurement of training effects.

Epidemiologists

- ◎ Education/Training Required: Doctoral degree
- ◎ Annual Earnings: $53,660
- ◎ Growth: 32.5%
- ◎ Annual Job Openings: Fewer than 500
- ◎ Self-Employed: 2.1%
- ◎ Part-Time: 8.8%

Investigate and describe the determinants and distribution of disease, disability, and other health outcomes and develop the means for prevention and control. Identify and analyze public health issues related to foodborne parasitic diseases and their impact on public policies or scientific studies or surveys. Investigate diseases or parasites to determine cause and risk factors, progress, life cycle, or mode of transmission. Plan and direct studies to investigate human or animal disease, preventive methods, and treatments for disease. Prepare and analyze samples to study effects of drugs, gases, pesticides, or microorganisms on cell structure and tissue. Standardize drug dosages, methods of immunization, and procedures for manufacture of drugs and medicinal compounds. Conduct research to develop methodologies, instrumentation and procedures for medical application, analyzing data and presenting findings. Consult with and advise physicians, educators, researchers, government health officials and others regarding medical applications of sciences, such as physics, biology, and chemistry. Oversee public health programs, including statistical analysis, health care planning, surveil-lance systems, and public health improvement. Plan, administer and evaluate health safety standards and programs to improve public health, conferring with health department, industry personnel, physicians and others. Provide expertise in the design, management and evaluation of study protocols and health status questionnaires, sample selection and analysis. Supervise professional, technical and clerical personnel. Teach principles of medicine and medical and laboratory procedures to physicians, residents, students, and technicians. **SKILLS—Instructing:** Teaching others how to do something. **Science:** Using scientific rules and methods to solve problems. **Active Learning:** Understanding the implications of new information for both current and future problem-solving and decision-making. **Systems Evaluation:** Identifying measures or indicators of system performance and the actions needed to improve or correct performance relative to the goals of the system. **Writing:** Communicating effectively in writing as appropriate for the needs of the audience. **Systems Analysis:** Determining how a system should work and how changes in conditions, operations, and the environment will affect outcomes. **Reading Comprehension:** Understanding written sentences and paragraphs in work-related documents. **Service Orientation:** Actively looking for ways to help people.

GOE—Interest Area: 15. Scientific Research, Engineering, and Mathematics. **Work Group:** 15.03. Life Sciences. **Other Jobs in This Work Group:** Biochemists; Biologists; Biophysicists; Environmental Scientists and Specialists, Including Health; Medical Scientists, Except Epidemiologists; Microbiologists. **PERSONALITY TYPE:** Investigative. Investigative occupations frequently involve working with ideas and require an extensive amount of thinking. These occupations can involve searching for facts and figuring out problems mentally.

EDUCATION/TRAINING PROGRAM(S)— Cell/Cellular Biology and Histology; Epidemiology; Medical Scientist (MS, PhD). **RELATED KNOWLEDGE/COURSES—Biology:** Knowledge of plant and animal organisms and their tissues, cells, functions, interdependencies, and interactions with each other and the environment. **Medicine and Dentistry:** Knowledge of the information and techniques needed to diagnose and treat human injuries, diseases, and deformities. This includes symptoms, treatment alternatives, drug properties and interactions, and preventive health-care measures. **Chemistry:** Knowledge of the chemical composition, structure, and properties of substances and of the chemical processes and transformations that they undergo. This includes uses of chemicals and their danger signs, production techniques, and disposal methods. **Mathematics:** Knowledge of arithmetic, algebra, geometry, calculus, and statistics and their applications. **Education and Training:** Knowledge of principles and methods for curriculum and training design, teaching and instruction for individuals and groups, and the measurement of training effects. **Communications and Media:** Knowledge of media production, communication, and dissemination techniques and methods. This includes alternative ways to inform and entertain via written, oral, and visual media.

Family and General Practitioners

- ◎ Education/Training Required: First professional degree
- ◎ Annual Earnings: $137,670
- ◎ Growth: 19.5%
- ◎ Annual Job Openings: 38,000
- ◎ Self-Employed: 16.9%
- ◎ Part-Time: 8.1%

Diagnose, treat, and help prevent diseases and injuries that commonly occur in the general population. Advise patients and community members concerning diet, activity, hygiene, and disease prevention. Collect, record, and maintain patient information, such as medical history, reports, and examination results. Explain procedures and discuss test results or prescribed treatments with patients. Monitor the patients' conditions and progress and re-evaluate treatments as necessary. Order, perform and interpret tests, and analyze records, reports and examination information to diagnose patients' condition. Prescribe or administer treatment, therapy, medication, vaccination, and other specialized medical care to treat or prevent illness, disease, or injury. Refer patients to medical specialists or other practitioners when necessary. Conduct research to study anatomy and develop or test medications, treatments, or procedures to prevent or control disease or injury. Coordinate work with nurses, social workers, rehabilitation therapists, pharmacists, psychologists and other health-care providers. Deliver babies. Direct and coordinate activities of nurses, students, assistants, specialists, therapists, and other medical staff. Operate on patients to remove, repair, or improve functioning of diseased or injured body parts and systems. Plan, implement, or administer health programs or standards in hospital, business, or community for information, prevention, or treatment of injury or illness. Prepare reports for government or management of birth, death, and disease statistics, workforce evaluations, or medical status of individuals. SKILLS—**Science:** Using scientific rules and methods to solve problems. **Reading Comprehension:** Understanding written sentences and paragraphs in work-related documents. **Systems Evaluation:** Identifying measures or indicators of system performance and the actions needed to improve or correct performance relative to the goals of the system. **Active Learning:** Understanding the implications of new information for both current and future problem-solving and decision-making. **Judgment and Decision Making:** Considering the relative costs and benefits of potential actions to choose the most appropriate one. **Management of Personnel Resources:** Motivating, developing, and directing people as they work, identifying the best people for the job. **Social Perceptiveness:** Being aware of others' reactions and understanding why they react as they do. **Systems Analysis:** Determining how a system should work and how changes in conditions, operations, and the environment will affect outcomes.

GOE—Interest Area: 08. Health Science. **Work Group:** 08.02. Medicine and Surgery. **Other Jobs in This Work Group:** Anesthesiologists; Internists, General; Medical Assistants; Medical Transcriptionists; Obstetricians and Gynecologists; Pediatricians, General; Pharmacists; Pharmacy Aides; Pharmacy Technicians; Physician Assistants; Psychiatrists; Registered Nurses; Surgeons; Surgical Technologists. **PERSONALITY TYPE:** Investigative. Investigative occupations frequently involve working with ideas and require an extensive amount of thinking. These occupations can involve searching for facts and figuring out problems mentally.

EDUCATION/TRAINING PROGRAM(S)— Family Medicine; Medicine (MD); Osteopathic Medicine/Osteopathy (DO). **RELATED KNOWLEDGE/COURSES—Medicine and Dentistry:** Knowledge of the information and techniques needed to diagnose and treat human injuries, diseases, and deformities. This includes symptoms, treatment alternatives, drug properties and interactions, and preventive health-care measures. **Biology:** Knowledge of plant and animal organisms and their tissues, cells, functions, interdependencies, and interactions with each other and the environment. **Therapy and Counseling:** Knowledge of principles, methods, and procedures for diagnosis, treatment, and rehabilitation of physical and mental dysfunctions and for career counseling and guidance. **Chemistry:** Knowledge of the chemical composition, structure, and properties of substances and of the chemical processes and transformations that they undergo. This includes uses of chemicals and their danger signs, production techniques, and disposal methods. **Administration and Management:** Knowledge of business and management principles involved in strategic planning, resource allocation, human resources modeling, leadership technique, production methods, and coordination of people and resources. **Personnel and Human Resources:** Knowledge of principles and procedures for personnel recruitment, selection, training, compensation

and benefits, labor relations and negotiation, and personnel information systems. **Physics:** Knowledge and prediction of physical principles and laws and their interrelationships and applications to understanding fluid, material, and atmospheric dynamics and mechanical, electrical, atomic, and subatomic structures and processes.

Fashion Designers

- Education/Training Required: Bachelor's degree
- Annual Earnings: $54,530
- Growth: 10.6%
- Annual Job Openings: 2,000
- Self-Employed: 29.3%
- Part-Time: 16.5%

Design clothing and accessories. Create original garments or design garments that follow well-established fashion trends. May develop the line of color and kinds of materials. Test fabrics or oversee testing so that garment care labels can be created. Attend fashion shows and review garment magazines and manuals in order to gather information about fashion trends and consumer preferences. Design custom clothing and accessories for individuals, retailers, or theatrical, television, or film productions. Draw patterns for articles designed; then cut patterns, and cut material according to patterns, using measuring instruments and scissors. Examine sample garments on and off models; then modify designs to achieve desired effects. Select materials and production techniques to be used for products. Sketch rough and detailed drawings of apparel or accessories, and write specifications such as color schemes, construction, material types, and accessory requirements. Adapt other designers' ideas for the mass market. Collaborate with other designers to coordinate special products and designs. Confer with sales and management executives or with clients in order to discuss design ideas. Determine prices for styles. Develop a group of products and/or accessories, and market them through venues such as boutiques or mail-order catalogs. Direct and coordinate workers involved in drawing and cutting patterns and constructing samples or finished garments. Identify target markets for designs, looking at factors such as age, gender, and socioeconomic status. Provide sample garments to agents and sales representatives, and arrange for showings of sample garments at sales meetings or fashion shows. Purchase new or used clothing and accessory items as needed to complete designs. Read scripts and consult directors and other production staff in order to develop design concepts and plan productions. Research the styles and periods of clothing needed for film or theatrical productions. Sew together sections of material to form mockups or samples of garments or articles, using sewing equipment. Visit textile showrooms to keep up-to-date on the latest fabrics. **SKILLS—Persuasion:** Persuading others to change their minds or behavior. **Management of Financial Resources:** Determining how money will be spent to get the work done and accounting for these expenditures. **Operations Analysis:** Analyzing needs and product requirements to create a design. **Systems Analysis:** Determining how a system should work and how changes in conditions, operations, and the environment will affect outcomes. **Negotiation:** Bringing others together and trying to reconcile differences. **Management of Material Resources:** Obtaining and seeing to the appropriate use of equipment, facilities, and materials needed to do certain work. **Systems Evaluation:** Identifying measures or indicators of system performance and the actions needed to improve or correct performance relative to the goals of the system. **Coordination:** Adjusting actions in relation to others' actions.

GOE—Interest Area: 03. Arts and Communication. **Work Group:** 03.05. Design. **Other Jobs in This Work Group:** Commercial and Industrial Designers; Exhibit Designers; Floral Designers; Graphic Designers; Interior Designers; Merchandise Displayers and Window Trimmers; Set Designers.

PERSONALITY TYPE: Artistic. Artistic occupations frequently involve working with forms, designs, and patterns. They often require self-expression, and the work can be done without following a clear set of rules.

EDUCATION/TRAINING PROGRAM(S)— Apparel and Textile Manufacture; Fashion and Fabric Consultant; Fashion/Apparel Design; Textile Science. **RELATED KNOWLEDGE/COURSES—Design:** Knowledge of design techniques, tools, and principles involved in production of precision technical plans, blueprints, drawings, and models. **Fine Arts:** Knowledge of the theory and techniques required to compose, produce, and perform works of music, dance, visual arts, drama, and sculpture. **Production and Processing:** Knowledge of raw materials, production processes, quality control, costs, and other techniques for maximizing the effective manufacture and distribution of goods. **Sales and Marketing:** Knowledge of principles and methods for showing, promoting, and selling products or services. This includes marketing strategy and tactics, product demonstration, sales techniques, and sales control systems. **Education and Training:** Knowledge of principles and methods for curriculum and training design, teaching and instruction for individuals and groups, and the measurement of training effects. **Customer and Personal Service:** Knowledge of principles and processes for providing customer and personal services. This includes customer needs assessment, meeting quality standards for services, and evaluation of customer satisfaction.

Film and Video Editors

◎ Education/Training Required: Bachelor's degree

◎ Annual Earnings: $41,820

◎ Growth: 26.4%

◎ Annual Job Openings: 3,000

◎ Self-Employed: 21.9%

◎ Part-Time: 20.4%

Edit motion picture soundtracks, film, and video. Cut shot sequences to different angles at specific points in scenes, making each individual cut as fluid and seamless as possible. Study scripts to become familiar with production concepts and requirements. Edit films and videotapes to insert music, dialogue, and sound effects, to arrange films into sequences, and to correct errors, using editing equipment. Select and combine the most effective shots of each scene in order to form a logical and smoothly running story. Mark frames where a particular shot or piece of sound is to begin or end. Determine the specific audio and visual effects and music necessary to complete films. Verify key numbers and time codes on materials. Organize and string together raw footage into a continuous whole according to scripts and/or the instructions of directors and producers. Review assembled films or edited videotapes on screens or monitors in order to determine if corrections are necessary. Program computerized graphic effects. Review footage sequence by sequence in order to become familiar with it before assembling it into a final product. Set up and operate computer editing systems, electronic titling systems, video switching equipment, and digital video effects units in order to produce a final product. Record needed sounds, or obtain them from sound effects libraries. Confer with producers and directors concerning layout or editing approaches needed to increase dramatic or entertainment value of productions. Manipulate plot, score, sound, and graphics to make the parts into a continuous whole, working closely with people in audio, visual, music, optical and/or special effects departments. Supervise and coordinate activities of workers engaged in film editing, assembling, and recording activities. Trim film segments to specified lengths, and reassemble segments in sequences that present stories with maximum effect. Develop post-production models for films. Piece sounds together to develop film soundtracks. Conduct film screenings for directors and members of production staffs. Collaborate with music editors to select appropriate passages of music and develop production scores. **SKILLS—Equipment Selection:** Determining the kind of tools and equipment needed to do a job. **Coordination:** Adjusting actions in relation to others' actions. **Time Management:** Managing one's own time and the time of others. **Active Learning:** Understanding the implications of new information for both current and future problem-solving and decision-making. **Operations Analysis:** Analyzing needs and product requirements to create a design. **Equipment Maintenance:** Performing routine maintenance on equipment and determining when and what kind of maintenance is needed. **Troubleshooting:** Determining causes of operating errors and deciding what to do about them. **Critical Thinking:** Using logic and reasoning to identify the strengths and weaknesses of alternative solutions, conclusions, or approaches to problems.

GOE—Interest Area: 03. Arts and Communication. **Work Group:** 03.09. Media Technology. **Other Jobs in This Work Group:** Audio and Video Equipment Technicians; Broadcast Technicians; Camera Operators, Television, Video, and Motion Picture; Multi-Media Artists and Animators; Photographic Hand Developers; Photographic Reproduction Technicians; Photographic Retouchers and Restorers; Professional Photographers; Radio Operators; Sound Engineering Technicians. **PERSONALITY TYPE:** Artistic. Artistic occupations frequently involve working with forms, designs, and patterns. They often require self-expression, and the work can be done without following a clear set of rules.

EDUCATION/TRAINING PROGRAM(S)—Audiovisual Communications Technologies/Technicians, Other; Cinematography and Film/Video Production; Communications Technology/Technician; Photojournalism; Radio and Television; Radio and Television Broadcasting Technology/Technician. **RELATED KNOWLEDGE/COURSES—Communications and Media:** Knowledge of media production, communication, and dissemination techniques and methods. This includes alternative ways to inform and entertain via written, oral, and visual media. **Fine Arts:** Knowledge of the theory and techniques required to compose, produce, and perform works of music, dance, visual arts, drama, and sculpture. **Computers and Electronics:** Knowledge of circuit boards, processors, chips, electronic equipment, and computer hardware and software, including applications and programming. **Design:** Knowledge of design techniques, tools, and principles involved in production of precision technical plans, blueprints, drawings, and models. **Education and Training:** Knowledge of principles and methods for curriculum and training design, teaching and instruction for individuals and groups, and the measurement of training effects. **English Language:** Knowledge of the structure and content of the English language, including the meaning and spelling of words, rules of composition, and grammar.

Financial Analysts

- ◎ Education/Training Required: Bachelor's degree
- ◎ Annual Earnings: $61,130
- ◎ Growth: 18.7%
- ◎ Annual Job Openings: 22,000
- ◎ Self-Employed: 4.8%
- ◎ Part-Time: 10.2%

Conduct quantitative analyses of information affecting investment programs of public or private **institutions.** Analyze financial information to produce forecasts of business, industry, and economic conditions for use in making investment decisions. Assemble spreadsheets and draw charts and graphs used to illustrate technical reports, using computer. Evaluate and compare the relative quality of various securities in a given industry. Interpret data affecting investment programs, such as price, yield, stability, future trends in investment risks, and economic influences. Maintain knowledge and stay abreast of developments in the fields of industrial technology, business, finance, and economic theory. Monitor fundamental economic, industrial, and corporate developments through the analysis of information obtained from financial publications and services, investment banking firms, government agencies, trade publications, company sources, and personal interviews. Prepare plans of action for investment based on financial analyses. Present oral and written reports on general economic trends, individual corporations, and entire industries. Recommend investments and investment timing to companies, investment firm staff, or the investing public. Collaborate with investment bankers to attract new corporate clients to securities firms. Contact brokers and purchase investments for companies, according to company policy. Determine the prices at which securities should be syndicated and offered to the public. **SKILLS—Judgment and Decision Making:** Considering the relative costs and benefits of potential actions to choose the most appropriate one. **Systems Analysis:** Determining how a system should work and how changes in conditions, operations, and the environment will affect outcomes. **Critical Thinking:** Using logic and reasoning to identify the strengths and weaknesses of alternative solutions, conclusions, or approaches to problems. **Active Learning:** Understanding the implications of new information for both current and future problem-solving and decision-making. **Systems Evaluation:** Identifying measures or indicators of system performance and the actions needed to improve or correct performance relative to the goals of the system. **Reading Comprehension:** Understanding written sentences and paragraphs in work-related documents. **Mathematics:** Using mathematics to solve problems. **Management of Financial Resources:** Determining how money will be spent to get the work done and accounting for these expenditures.

GOE—Interest Area: 06. Finance and Insurance. **Work Group:** 06.02. Finance/Insurance Investigation and Analysis. **Other Jobs in This Work Group:** Appraisers, Real Estate; Assessors; Claims Examiners, Property and Casualty Insurance; Cost Estimators; Credit Analysts; Insurance Adjusters, Examiners, and Investigators; Insurance Appraisers, Auto Damage; Insurance Underwriters; Loan Counselors; Loan Officers; Market Research Analysts; Survey Researchers. **PERSONALITY TYPE:** Investigative. Investigative occupations frequently involve working with ideas and require an extensive amount of thinking. These occupations can involve searching for facts and figuring out problems mentally.

EDUCATION/TRAINING PROGRAM(S)— Accounting and Business/Management; Accounting and Finance; Finance, General. **RELATED KNOWLEDGE/COURSES—Economics and Accounting:** Knowledge of economic and accounting principles and practices, the financial markets, banking, and the analysis and reporting of financial data. **Mathematics:** Knowledge of arithmetic, algebra, geometry, calculus, and statistics and their applications. **Law and Government:** Knowledge of laws, legal codes, court procedures, precedents, government regulations, executive orders, agency rules, and the democratic political process. **Computers and Electronics:** Knowledge of circuit boards, processors, chips, electronic equipment, and computer hardware and software, including applications and programming. **Sales and Marketing:** Knowledge of principles and methods for showing, promoting, and selling products or services. This includes marketing strategy and tactics, product demonstration, sales techniques, and sales control systems. **English Language:** Knowledge of the structure and content of the English language, including the meaning and spelling of words, rules of composition, and grammar.

Financial Examiners

◎ Education/Training Required: Bachelor's degree
◎ Annual Earnings: $59,050
◎ Growth: 8.9%
◎ Annual Job Openings: 3,000
◎ Self-Employed: 0%
◎ Part-Time: 10.2%

Enforce or ensure compliance with laws and regulations governing financial and securities institutions and financial and real estate transactions. May examine, verify correctness of, or establish authenticity of records. Direct and participate in formal and informal meetings with bank directors, trustees, senior management, counsels, outside accountants and consultants in order to gather information and discuss findings. Investigate activities of institutions in order to enforce laws and regulations and to ensure legality of transactions and operations or financial solvency. Prepare reports, exhibits and other supporting schedules that detail an institution's safety and soundness, compliance with laws and regulations, and recommended solutions to questionable financial conditions. Recommend actions to ensure compliance with laws and regulations, or to protect solvency of institutions. Resolve problems concerning the overall financial integrity of banking institutions including loan investment portfolios, capital, earnings, and specific or large troubled accounts. Review audit reports of internal and external auditors in order to monitor adequacy of scope of reports or to discover specific weaknesses in internal routines. Review balance sheets, operating income and expense accounts, and loan documentation in order to confirm institution assets and liabilities. Verify and inspect cash reserves, assigned collateral, and bank-owned securities in order to check internal control procedures. Confer with officials of real estate, securities, or financial institution industries in order to exchange views and discuss issues or pending cases. Establish guidelines for procedures and policies that comply with new and revised regulations, and direct their implementation. Evaluate data processing applications for institutions under examination in order to develop recommendations for coordinating existing systems with examination procedures. Examine the minutes of meetings of directors, stockholders and committees in order to investigate the specific authority extended at various levels of management. Plan, supervise, and review work of assigned subordinates. Review and analyze new, proposed, or revised laws, regulations, policies, and procedures in order to interpret their meaning and determine their impact. **SKILLS—Reading Comprehension:** Understanding written sentences and paragraphs in work-related documents. **Negotiation:** Bringing others together and trying to reconcile differences. **Judgment and Decision Making:** Considering the relative costs and benefits of potential actions to choose the most appropriate one. **Writing:** Communicating effectively in writing as appropriate for the needs of the audience. **Management of Financial Resources:** Determining how money will be spent to get the work done and accounting for these expenditures. **Mathematics:** Using mathematics to solve problems. **Speaking:** Talking to others to convey information effectively. **Active Listening:** Giving full attention to what other people are saying, taking time to understand the points being made, asking questions as appropriate, and not interrupting at inappropriate times. **Persuasion:** Persuading others to change their minds or behavior. **Systems Analysis:** Determining how a system should work and how changes in conditions, operations, and the environment will affect outcomes.

GOE—Interest Area: 07. Government and Public Administration. **Work Group:** 07.03. Regulations Enforcement. **Other Jobs in This Work Group:** Agricultural Inspectors; Aviation Inspectors; Child Support, Missing Persons, and Unemployment Insurance Fraud Investigators; Environmental Compliance Inspectors; Equal Opportunity Representatives and Officers; Fire Inspectors; Fish and Game Wardens; Forest Fire Inspectors and Prevention Specialists; Government Property Inspectors and Investigators; Immigration and Customs Inspectors; Licensing Examiners and Inspectors; Marine Cargo Inspectors; Mechanical Inspectors; Motor Vehicle Inspectors; Nuclear Monitoring Technicians; Occupational Health and Safety Specialists; Pressure Vessel Inspectors; Railroad Inspectors; Tax Examiners, Collectors, and Revenue Agents. **PERSONALITY TYPE:** Enterprising. Enterprising occupations frequently involve starting up and carrying out projects. These occupations can involve leading people and making many decisions. They sometimes require risk taking and often deal with business.

EDUCATION/TRAINING PROGRAM(S)—Accounting; Taxation. **RELATED KNOWLEDGE/COURSES—Economics and Accounting:** Knowledge of economic and accounting principles and practices, the financial markets, banking, and the analysis and reporting of financial data. **Education and Training:** Knowledge of principles and methods for curriculum and training design, teaching and instruction for individuals and groups, and the measurement of training effects. **Mathematics:** Knowledge of arithmetic, algebra, geometry, calculus, and statistics and their applications. **Law and Government:** Knowledge of laws, legal codes, court procedures, precedents, government regulations, executive orders, agency rules, and the democratic political process. **Administration and Management:** Knowledge of business and management principles involved in strategic planning, resource allocation, human resources modeling, leadership technique, production methods, and coordination of people and resources. **English Language:** Knowledge of the structure and content of the English language, including the meaning and spelling of words, rules of composition, and grammar.

Financial Managers, Branch or Department

- Education/Training Required: Work experience plus degree
- Annual Earnings: $79,090
- Growth: 18.3%
- Annual Job Openings: 71,000
- Self-Employed: 3.1%
- Part-Time: 4.8%

Direct and coordinate financial activities of workers in a branch, office, or department of an establishment, such as branch bank, brokerage firm, risk and insurance department, or credit department. Examine, evaluate, and process loan applications. Monitor order flow and transactions that brokerage firm executes on the floor of exchange. Recruit staff members, and oversee training programs. Review collection reports to determine the status of collections and the amounts of outstanding balances. Review reports of securities transactions and price lists in order to analyze market conditions. Submit delinquent accounts to attorneys or outside agencies for collection. Analyze and classify risks and investments to determine their potential impacts on companies. Approve or reject, or coordinate the approval and rejection of, lines of credit and commercial, real estate, and personal loans. Develop and analyze information to assess the current and future financial status of firms. Establish procedures for custody and control of assets, records, loan collateral, and securities, in order to ensure safekeeping. Evaluate data pertaining to costs in order to plan budgets. Evaluate financial reporting systems, accounting and collection procedures, and investment activities, and make recommendations for changes to procedures, operating systems, budgets, and other financial control functions. Network within communities to find and attract new business. Oversee the flow of cash and financial instruments. Plan, direct, and coordinate risk and insurance programs of establishments to control risks and losses. Plan, direct, and coordinate the activities of workers in branches, offices, or departments of such establishments as branch banks, brokerage firms, risk and insurance departments, or credit departments. Prepare financial and regulatory reports required by laws, regulations, and boards of directors. Prepare operational and risk reports for management analysis. Communicate with stockholders and other investors to provide information, and to raise capital. Direct floor operations of brokerage firm engaged in buying and selling securities at exchange. Direct insurance negotiations, select insurance brokers and carriers, and place insurance. Establish and maintain relationships with individual and business customers, and provide assistance with problems these customers may encounter. **SKILLS—Management of Financial Resources:** Determining how money will be spent to get the work done and accounting for these expenditures. **Management of Personnel Resources:** Motivating, developing, and directing people as they work, identifying the best people for the job. **Systems Analysis:** Determining how a system should work and how changes in conditions, operations, and the environment will affect outcomes. **Systems Evaluation:** Identifying measures or indicators of system performance and the actions needed to improve or correct performance relative to the goals of the system. **Judgment and Decision Making:** Considering the relative costs and benefits of potential actions to choose the most appropriate one. **Monitoring:** Monitoring or assessing your performance or that of other individuals or organizations to make improvements or take corrective action. **Writing:** Communicating effectively in writing as appropriate for the needs of the audience. **Negotiation:** Bringing others together and trying to reconcile differences.

GOE—Interest Area: 06. Finance and Insurance. **Work Group:** 06.01. Managerial Work in Finance and Insurance. **Other Jobs in This Work Group:** Treasurers, Controllers, and Chief Financial Officers. **PERSONALITY TYPE:** Enterprising. Enterprising occupations frequently involve starting up and carrying out projects. These occupations can involve leading people and making many decisions. They sometimes require risk taking and often deal with business.

EDUCATION/TRAINING PROGRAM(S)— Accounting and Business/Management; Accounting and Finance; Credit Management; Finance and Financial Management Services, Other; Finance, General; International Finance; Public Finance. **RELATED KNOWLEDGE/COURSES—Economics and Accounting:** Knowledge of economic and accounting principles and practices, the financial markets, banking, and the analysis and reporting of financial data. **Administration and Management:** Knowledge of business and management principles involved in strategic planning, resource allocation, human resources modeling, leadership technique, production methods, and coordination of people and resources. **Law and Government:** Knowledge of laws, legal codes, court procedures, precedents, government regulations, executive orders, agency rules, and the democratic political process. **Mathematics:** Knowledge of arithmetic, algebra, geometry, calculus, and statistics and their applications. **Personnel and Human Resources:** Knowledge of principles and procedures for personnel recruitment, selection, training, compensation and benefits, labor relations and negotiation, and personnel information systems. **Psychology:** Knowledge of human behavior and performance; individual differences in ability, personality, and interests; learning and motivation; psychological research methods; and the assessment and treatment of behavioral and affective disorders.

Fire-Prevention and Protection Engineers

- Education/Training Required: Bachelor's degree
- Annual Earnings: $61,430
- Growth: 7.9%
- Annual Job Openings: 4,000
- Self-Employed: 1.6%
- Part-Time: 1.5%

Research causes of fires, determine fire protection methods, and design or recommend materials or equipment such as structural components or fire-detection equipment to assist organizations in safeguarding life and property against fire, explosion, and related hazards. Determines fire causes and methods of fire prevention. Conducts research on fire retardants and fire safety of materials and devices to determine cause and methods of fire prevention. Studies buildings to evaluate fire prevention factors, resistance of construction, contents, water supply and delivery, and exits. Recommends and advises on use of fire detection equipment, extinguishing devices, or methods to alleviate conditions conducive to fire. Advises and plans for prevention of destruction by fire, wind, water, or other causes of damage. Organizes and trains personnel to carry out fire protection programs. Designs fire detection equipment, alarm systems, fire extinguishing devices and systems, or structural components protection. Evaluates fire departments and laws and regulations affecting fire prevention or fire safety. **SKILLS—Technology Design:** Generating or adapting equipment and technology to serve user needs. **Instructing:** Teaching others how to do something. **Operations Analysis:** Analyzing needs and product requirements to create a design. **Science:** Using scientific rules and methods to solve problems. **Systems Evaluation:** Identifying measures or indicators of system performance and the actions needed to improve or correct performance relative to the goals of the system. **Active Learning:** Understanding the implications of new information for both current and future problem-solving and decision-making. **Speaking:** Talking to others to convey information effectively. **Quality Control Analysis:** Conducting tests and inspections of products, services, or processes to evaluate quality or performance.

GOE—Interest Area: 15. Scientific Research, Engineering, and Mathematics. **Work Group:** 15.08. Industrial and Safety Engineering. **Other Jobs in This Work Group:** Industrial Engineers; Industrial Safety and Health Engineers; Product Safety Engineers. **PERSONALITY TYPE:** Investigative. Investigative occupations frequently involve working with ideas and require an extensive amount of thinking. These occupations can involve searching for facts and figuring out problems mentally.

EDUCATION/TRAINING PROGRAM(S)— Environmental/Environmental Health Engineering. **RELATED KNOWLEDGE/COURSES—Public Safety and Security:** Knowledge of relevant equipment, policies, procedures, and strategies to promote effective local, state, or national security operations for the protection of people, data, property, and institutions. **Engineering and Technology:** Knowledge of the practical application of engineering science and technology. This includes applying principles, techniques, procedures, and equipment to the design and production of various goods and services. **Education and Training:** Knowledge of principles and methods for curriculum and training design, teaching and instruction for individuals and groups, and the measurement of training effects. **Design:** Knowledge of design techniques, tools, and principles involved in production of precision technical plans, blueprints, drawings, and models. **Chemistry:** Knowledge of the chemical composition, structure, and properties of substances and of the chemical processes and transformations that they undergo. This includes uses of chemicals and their danger signs, production techniques, and disposal methods. **Law and Government:** Knowledge of laws, legal codes, court procedures, precedents, government regulations, executive orders, agency rules, and the democratic political process.

Foreign Language and Literature Teachers, Postsecondary

- ◎ Education/Training Required: Master's degree
- ◎ Annual Earnings: $47,060
- ◎ Growth: 38.1% for all Postsecondary Teachers
- ◎ Annual Job Openings: 216,000 for all Postsecondary Teachers
- ◎ Self-Employed: 0.3% for all Postsecondary Teachers
- ◎ Part-Time: 27.7% for all Postsecondary Teachers

Teach courses in foreign (i.e., other than English) languages and literature. Evaluate and grade students' class work, assignments, and papers. Prepare and deliver lectures to undergraduate and/or graduate students on topics such as how to speak and write a foreign language, and the cultural aspects of areas where a particular language is used. Advise students on academic and vocational curricula, and on career issues. Compile, administer, and grade examinations, or assign this work to others. Compile bibliographies of specialized materials for outside reading assignments. Initiate, facilitate, and moderate classroom discussions. Keep abreast of developments in their field by reading current literature, talking with colleagues, and participating in professional organizations and activities. Maintain regularly scheduled office hours in order to advise and assist students. Maintain student attendance records, grades, and other required records. Plan, evaluate, and revise curricula, course content, and course materials and methods of instruction. Prepare course materials such as syllabi, homework assignments, and handouts. Select and obtain materials and supplies such as textbooks. Supervise undergraduate and/or graduate teaching, internship, and research work. Act as advisers to student organizations. Collaborate with colleagues to address teaching and research issues. Conduct research in a particular field of knowledge, and publish findings in scholarly journals, books, and/or electronic media. Participate in campus and community events. Participate in student recruitment, registration, and placement activities. Perform administrative duties such as serving as department head. Provide professional consulting services to government and/or industry. Serve on academic or administrative committees that deal with institutional policies, departmental matters, and academic issues. Write grant proposals to procure external research funding. **SKILLS—Instructing:** Teaching others how to do something. **Learning Strategies:** Selecting and using training/instructional methods and procedures appropriate for the situation when learning or teaching new things. **Speaking:** Talking to others to convey information effectively. **Reading Comprehension:** Understanding written sentences and paragraphs in work-related documents. **Writing:** Communicating effectively in writing as appropriate for the needs of the audience. **Critical Thinking:** Using logic and reasoning to identify the strengths and weaknesses of alternative solutions, conclusions, or approaches to problems. **Active Learning:** Understanding the implications of new information for both current and future problem-solving and decision-making. **Active Listening:** Giving full attention to what other people are saying, taking time to understand the points being made, asking questions as appropriate, and not interrupting at inappropriate times.

GOE—Interest Area: 05. Education and Training. **Work Group:** 05.03. Postsecondary and Adult Teaching and Instructing. **Other Jobs in This Work Group:** Adult Literacy, Remedial Education, and

GED Teachers and Instructors; Agricultural Sciences Teachers, Postsecondary; Anthropology and Archeology Teachers, Postsecondary; Architecture Teachers, Postsecondary; Area, Ethnic, and Cultural Studies Teachers, Postsecondary; Art, Drama, and Music Teachers, Postsecondary; Atmospheric, Earth, Marine, and Space Sciences Teachers, Postsecondary; Biological Science Teachers, Postsecondary; Business Teachers, Postsecondary; Chemistry Teachers, Postsecondary; Communications Teachers, Postsecondary; Computer Science Teachers, Postsecondary; Criminal Justice and Law Enforcement Teachers, Postsecondary; Economics Teachers, Postsecondary; Education Teachers, Postsecondary; Engineering Teachers, Postsecondary; English Language and Literature Teachers, Postsecondary; Environmental Science Teachers, Postsecondary; Farm and Home Management Advisors; Forestry and Conservation Science Teachers, Postsecondary; Geography Teachers, Postsecondary; Graduate Teaching Assistants; Health Specialties Teachers, Postsecondary; History Teachers, Postsecondary; Home Economics Teachers, Postsecondary; Law Teachers, Postsecondary; Library Science Teachers, Postsecondary; Mathematical Science Teachers, Postsecondary; Nursing Instructors and Teachers, Postsecondary; Philosophy and Religion Teachers, Postsecondary; Physics Teachers, Postsecondary; Political Science Teachers, Postsecondary; Psychology Teachers, Postsecondary; Recreation and Fitness Studies Teachers, Postsecondary; Self-Enrichment Education Teachers; Social Work Teachers, Postsecondary; Sociology Teachers, Postsecondary; Vocational Education Teachers, Postsecondary. **PERSONALITY TYPE:** Artistic. Artistic occupations frequently involve working with forms, designs, and patterns. They often require self-expression, and the work can be done without following a clear set of rules.

EDUCATION/TRAINING PROGRAM(S)— African Languages, Literatures, and Linguistics; Albanian Language and Literature; American Indian/Native American Languages, Literatures, and Linguistics; Ancient Near Eastern and Biblical Languages, Literatures, and Linguistics; Ancient/Classical Greek Language and Literature; Arabic Language and Literature; Australian/Oceanic/Pacific Languages, Literatures, and Linguistics; Bahasa Indonesian/Bahasa Malay Languages and Literatures; Baltic Languages, Literatures, and Linguistics; Bengali Language and Literature; Bulgarian Language and Literature; Burmese Language and Literature; Catalan Language and Literature; Celtic Languages, Literatures, and Linguistics; Chinese Language and Literature; Classics and Classical Languages, Literatures, and Linguistics, General; Classics and Classical Languages, Literatures, and Linguistics, Other; Czech Language and Literature; Danish Language and Literature; Dutch/Flemish Language and Literature; East Asian Languages, Literatures, and Linguistics, General; East Asian Languages, Literatures, and Linguistics, Other; Filipino/Tagalog Language and Literature; Finnish and Related Languages, Literatures, and Linguistics; Foreign Languages and Literatures, General; Foreign Languages, Literatures, and Linguistics, Other; French Language and Literature; German Language and Literature; Germanic Languages, Literatures, and Linguistics, General; Germanic Languages, Literatures, and Linguistics, Other; Hebrew Language and Literature; Hindi Language and Literature; Hungarian/Magyar Language and Literature; Iranian/Persian Languages, Literatures, and Linguistics; Italian Language and Literature; Japanese Language and Literature; Khmer/Cambodian Language and Literature; Korean Language and Literature; Language Interpretation and Translation; Lao/Laotian Language and Literature; Latin Language and Literature; Latin Teacher Education; Linguistics; Middle/Near Eastern and Semitic Languages, Literatures, and Linguistics, Other; others. **RELATED KNOWLEDGE/COURSES—Foreign Language:** Knowledge of the structure and content of a foreign (non-English) language, including the meaning and spelling of words, rules of composition and grammar, and pronunciation. **Education and Training:** Knowledge of principles and methods for curriculum and training design, teaching and instruction for individuals and groups, and the

measurement of training effects. **English Language:** Knowledge of the structure and content of the English language, including the meaning and spelling of words, rules of composition, and grammar. **Communications and Media:** Knowledge of media production, communication, and dissemination techniques and methods. This includes alternative ways to inform and entertain via written, oral, and visual media. **Therapy and Counseling:** Knowledge of principles, methods, and procedures for diagnosis, treatment, and rehabilitation of physical and mental dysfunctions and for career counseling and guidance. **Clerical Practices:** Knowledge of administrative and clerical procedures and systems such as word processing, managing files and records, stenography and transcription, designing forms, and other office procedures and terminology.

Forestry and Conservation Science Teachers, Postsecondary

- ◉ Education/Training Required: Master's degree
- ◉ Annual Earnings: $64,350
- ◉ Growth: 38.1% for all Postsecondary Teachers
- ◉ Annual Job Openings: 216,000 for all Postsecondary Teachers
- ◉ Self-Employed: 0.3% for all Postsecondary Teachers
- ◉ Part-Time: 27.7% for all Postsecondary Teachers

Teach courses in environmental and conservation science. Evaluate and grade students' class work, assignments, and papers. Prepare and deliver lectures to undergraduate and/or graduate students on topics such as forest resource policy, forest pathology, and mapping. Advise students on academic and vocational curricula, and on career issues. Compile, administer, and grade examinations, or assign this work to others. Compile bibliographies of specialized materials for outside reading assignments. Initiate, facilitate, and moderate classroom discussions. Keep abreast of developments in their field by reading current literature, talking with colleagues, and participating in professional conferences. Maintain regularly scheduled office hours in order to advise and assist students. Maintain student attendance records, grades, and other required records. Plan, evaluate, and revise curricula, course content, and course materials and methods of instruction. Prepare course materials such as syllabi, homework assignments, and handouts. Select and obtain materials and supplies such as textbooks and laboratory equipment. Supervise students' laboratory and/or field work. Supervise undergraduate and/or graduate teaching, internship, and research work. Act as advisers to student organizations. Collaborate with colleagues to address teaching and research issues. Conduct research in a particular field of knowledge, and publish findings in books, professional journals, and/or electronic media. Participate in campus and community events. Participate in student recruitment, registration, and placement activities. Perform administrative duties such as serving as department head. Provide professional consulting services to government and/or industry. Serve on academic or administrative committees that deal with institutional policies, departmental matters, and academic issues. Write grant proposals to procure external research funding. **SKILLS—Science:** Using scientific rules and methods to solve problems. **Instructing:** Teaching others how to do something. **Learning Strategies:** Selecting and using training/instructional methods and procedures appropriate for the situation when learning or teaching new things. **Reading Comprehension:** Understanding written sentences and paragraphs in work-related documents. **Active Learning:** Understanding the implications of new information for both current and future problem-solving and deci-

sion-making. **Writing:** Communicating effectively in writing as appropriate for the needs of the audience. **Critical Thinking:** Using logic and reasoning to identify the strengths and weaknesses of alternative solutions, conclusions, or approaches to problems. **Mathematics:** Using mathematics to solve problems.

GOE—Interest Area: 05. Education and Training. **Work Group:** 05.03. Postsecondary and Adult Teaching and Instructing. **Other Jobs in This Work Group:** Adult Literacy, Remedial Education, and GED Teachers and Instructors; Agricultural Sciences Teachers, Postsecondary; Anthropology and Archeology Teachers, Postsecondary; Architecture Teachers, Postsecondary; Area, Ethnic, and Cultural Studies Teachers, Postsecondary; Art, Drama, and Music Teachers, Postsecondary; Atmospheric, Earth, Marine, and Space Sciences Teachers, Postsecondary; Biological Science Teachers, Postsecondary; Business Teachers, Postsecondary; Chemistry Teachers, Postsecondary; Communications Teachers, Postsecondary; Computer Science Teachers, Postsecondary; Criminal Justice and Law Enforcement Teachers, Postsecondary; Economics Teachers, Postsecondary; Education Teachers, Postsecondary; Engineering Teachers, Postsecondary; English Language and Literature Teachers, Postsecondary; Environmental Science Teachers, Postsecondary; Farm and Home Management Advisors; Foreign Language and Literature Teachers, Postsecondary; Geography Teachers, Postsecondary; Graduate Teaching Assistants; Health Specialties Teachers, Postsecondary; History Teachers, Postsecondary; Home Economics Teachers, Postsecondary; Law Teachers, Postsecondary; Library Science Teachers, Postsecondary; Mathematical Science Teachers, Postsecondary; Nursing Instructors and Teachers, Postsecondary; Philosophy and Religion Teachers, Postsecondary; Physics Teachers, Postsecondary; Political Science Teachers, Postsecondary; Psychology Teachers, Postsecondary; Recreation and Fitness Studies Teachers, Postsecondary; Self-Enrichment Education Teachers; Social Work Teachers, Postsecondary; Sociology Teachers,

Postsecondary; Vocational Education Teachers, Postsecondary. **PERSONALITY TYPE:** Investigative. Investigative occupations frequently involve working with ideas and require an extensive amount of thinking. These occupations can involve searching for facts and figuring out problems mentally.

EDUCATION/TRAINING PROGRAM(S)— Science Teacher Education/General Science Teacher Education. **RELATED KNOWLEDGE/COURSES—Biology:** Knowledge of plant and animal organisms and their tissues, cells, functions, interdependencies, and interactions with each other and the environment. **Education and Training:** Knowledge of principles and methods for curriculum and training design, teaching and instruction for individuals and groups, and the measurement of training effects. **Medicine and Dentistry:** Knowledge of the information and techniques needed to diagnose and treat human injuries, diseases, and deformities. This includes symptoms, treatment alternatives, drug properties and interactions, and preventive health-care measures. **Chemistry:** Knowledge of the chemical composition, structure, and properties of substances and of the chemical processes and transformations that they undergo. This includes uses of chemicals and their danger signs, production techniques, and disposal methods. **Therapy and Counseling:** Knowledge of principles, methods, and procedures for diagnosis, treatment, and rehabilitation of physical and mental dysfunctions and for career counseling and guidance. **Psychology:** Knowledge of human behavior and performance; individual differences in ability, personality, and interests; learning and motivation; psychological research methods; and the assessment and treatment of behavioral and affective disorders.

Gaming Managers

- ◎ Education/Training Required: Work experience plus degree
- ◎ Annual Earnings: $57,930
- ◎ Growth: 12.4%
- ◎ Annual Job Openings: 1,000
- ◎ Self-Employed: 38.6%
- ◎ Part-Time: 6.9%

Plan, organize, direct, control, or coordinate gaming operations in a casino. Formulate gaming policies for their area of responsibility. Circulate among gaming tables to ensure that operations are conducted properly, that dealers follow house rules, and that players are not cheating. Direct the distribution of complimentary hotel rooms, meals, and other discounts or free items given to players based on their length of play and betting totals. Direct workers compiling summary sheets that show wager amounts and payoffs for races and events. Establish policies on issues such as the type of gambling offered and the odds, the extension of credit, and the serving of food and beverages. Maintain familiarity with all games used at a facility, as well as strategies and tricks employed in those games. Monitor credit extended to players. Monitor staffing levels to ensure that games and tables are adequately staffed for each shift, arranging for staff rotations and breaks, and locating substitute employees as necessary. Prepare work schedules and station assignments, and keep attendance records. Resolve customer complaints regarding problems such as payout errors. Review operational expenses, budget estimates, betting accounts, and collection reports for accuracy. Set and maintain a bank and table limit for each game. Track supplies of money to tables, and perform any required paperwork. Explain and interpret house rules, such as game rules and betting limits. Interview and hire workers. Notify board attendants of table vacancies so that waiting patrons can play. Record, collect, and pay off bets, issuing receipts as necessary. Remove suspected cheaters, such as card counters and other players who may have systems that shift the odds of winning to their favor. Train new workers and evaluate their performance. **SKILLS—Management of Financial Resources:** Determining how money will be spent to get the work done and accounting for these expenditures. **Management of Personnel Resources:** Motivating, developing, and directing people as they work, identifying the best people for the job. **Negotiation:** Bringing others together and trying to reconcile differences. **Management of Material Resources:** Obtaining and seeing to the appropriate use of equipment, facilities, and materials needed to do certain work. **Time Management:** Managing one's own time and the time of others. **Speaking:** Talking to others to convey information effectively. **Critical Thinking:** Using logic and reasoning to identify the strengths and weaknesses of alternative solutions, conclusions, or approaches to problems. **Social Perceptiveness:** Being aware of others' reactions and understanding why they react as they do.

GOE—Interest Area: 09. Hospitality, Tourism, and Recreation. **Work Group:** 09.01. Managerial Work in Hospitality and Tourism . **Other Jobs in This Work Group:** First-Line Supervisors/Managers of Food Preparation and Serving Workers; First-Line Supervisors/Managers of Personal Service Workers; Food Service Managers; Gaming Supervisors; Lodging Managers. **PERSONALITY TYPE:** Enterprising. Enterprising occupations frequently involve starting up and carrying out projects. These occupations can involve leading people and making many decisions. They sometimes require risk taking and often deal with business.

EDUCATION/TRAINING PROGRAM(S)— Personal and Culinary Services, Other. **RELATED KNOWLEDGE/COURSES—Economics and Accounting:** Knowledge of economic and accounting principles and practices, the financial markets, banking, and the analysis and reporting of financial data. **Administration and Management:** Knowledge of business and management principles involved in strategic planning, resource allocation,

human resources modeling, leadership technique, production methods, and coordination of people and resources. **Personnel and Human Resources:** Knowledge of principles and procedures for personnel recruitment, selection, training, compensation and benefits, labor relations and negotiation, and personnel information systems. **Customer and Personal Service:** Knowledge of principles and processes for providing customer and personal services. This includes customer needs assessment, meeting quality standards for services, and evaluation of customer satisfaction. **Mathematics:** Knowledge of arithmetic, algebra, geometry, calculus, and statistics and their applications. **Education and Training:** Knowledge of principles and methods for curriculum and training design, teaching and instruction for individuals and groups, and the measurement of training effects.

General and Operations Managers

- Education/Training Required: Work experience plus degree
- Annual Earnings: $74,600
- Growth: 18.4%
- Annual Job Openings: 260,000
- Self-Employed: 0.7%
- Part-Time: 2.6%

Plan, direct, or coordinate the operations of companies or public and private sector organizations. Duties and responsibilities include formulating policies, managing daily operations, and planning the use of materials and human resources, but are too diverse and general in nature to be classified in any one functional area of management or administration, such as personnel, purchasing, or administrative services. Includes owners and managers who head small business establishments whose duties are primarily managerial. Direct and coordinate activities of businesses or departments concerned with the production, pricing, sales, and/or distribution of products. Manage staff, preparing work schedules and assigning specific duties. Review financial statements, sales and activity reports, and other performance data to measure productivity and goal achievement and to determine areas needing cost reduction and program improvement. Establish and implement departmental policies, goals, objectives, and procedures, conferring with board members, organization officials, and staff members as necessary. Determine staffing requirements, and interview, hire and train new employees, or oversee those personnel processes. Monitor businesses and agencies to ensure that they efficiently and effectively provide needed services while staying within budgetary limits. Oversee activities directly related to making products or providing services. Direct and coordinate organization's financial and budget activities to fund operations, maximize investments, and increase efficiency. Determine goods and services to be sold, and set prices and credit terms, based on forecasts of customer demand. Manage the movement of goods into and out of production facilities. Locate, select, and procure merchandise for resale, representing management in purchase negotiations. Perform sales floor work such as greeting and assisting customers, stocking shelves, and taking inventory. Develop and implement product marketing strategies including advertising campaigns and sales promotions. Plan and direct activities such as sales promotions, coordinating with other department heads as required. Direct non-merchandising departments of businesses, such as advertising and purchasing. **SKILLS—Management of Financial Resources:** Determining how money will be spent to get the work done and accounting for these expenditures. **Management of Personnel Resources:** Motivating, developing, and directing people as they work, identifying the best people for the job. **Management of Material Resources:** Obtaining and seeing to the appropriate use of equipment, facilities, and materials needed to do certain work. **Negotiation:** Bringing others together and trying to reconcile differences. **Moni-**

toring: Monitoring or assessing your performance or that of other individuals or organizations to make improvements or take corrective action. **Persuasion:** Persuading others to change their minds or behavior. **Coordination:** Adjusting actions in relation to others' actions. **Social Perceptiveness:** Being aware of others' reactions and understanding why they react as they do.

GOE—Interest Area: 04. Business and Administration. **Work Group:** 04.01. Managerial Work in General Business. **Other Jobs in This Work Group:** Chief Executives; Compensation and Benefits Managers; Human Resources Managers; Private Sector Executives; Training and Development Managers. **PERSONALITY TYPE:** No data available.

EDUCATION/TRAINING PROGRAM(S)— Business Administration and Management, General; Business/Commerce, General; Entrepreneurship/Entrepreneurial Studies; International Business/Trade/Commerce; Public Administration. **RELATED KNOWLEDGE/COURSES—Sales and Marketing:** Knowledge of principles and methods for showing, promoting, and selling products or services. This includes marketing strategy and tactics, product demonstration, sales techniques, and sales control systems. **Customer and Personal Service:** Knowledge of principles and processes for providing customer and personal services. This includes customer needs assessment, meeting quality standards for services, and evaluation of customer satisfaction. **Administration and Management:** Knowledge of business and management principles involved in strategic planning, resource allocation, human resources modeling, leadership technique, production methods, and coordination of people and resources. **Personnel and Human Resources:** Knowledge of principles and procedures for personnel recruitment, selection, training, compensation and benefits, labor relations and negotiation, and personnel information systems. **Economics and Accounting:** Knowledge of economic and accounting principles and practices, the financial markets, banking, and the analysis and reporting of financial data. **Law and Government:** Knowledge of laws, legal codes, court procedures, precedents, government regulations, executive orders, agency rules, and the democratic political process.

Geographers

- ◎ Education/Training Required: Bachelor's degree
- ◎ Annual Earnings: $56,290
- ◎ Growth: 19.5%
- ◎ Annual Job Openings: Fewer than 500
- ◎ Self-Employed: 3.7%
- ◎ Part-Time: 16.8%

Study nature and use of areas of earth's surface, relating and interpreting interactions of physical and cultural phenomena. Conduct research on physical aspects of a region, including land forms, climates, soils, plants and animals, and conduct research on the spatial implications of human activities within a given area, including social characteristics, economic activities, and political organization, as well as researching interdependence between regions at scales ranging from local to global. Analyze geographic distributions of physical and cultural phenomena on local, regional, continental, and global scales. Collect data on physical characteristics of specified areas, such as geological formations, climates, and vegetation, using surveying or meteorological equipment. Create and modify maps, graphs, and diagrams, using geographical information software and related equipment, and principles of cartography such as coordinate systems, longitude, latitude, elevation, topography, and map scales. Gather and compile geographic data from sources including censuses, field observations, satellite imagery, aerial photographs, and existing maps. Locate and obtain existing geographic information databases. Write and present reports of research findings. Conduct fieldwork at outdoor sites. Develop, operate, and maintain geographical

information (GIS) computer systems, including hardware, software, plotters, digitizers, printers, and video cameras. Provide consulting services in fields including resource development and management, business location and market area analysis, environmental hazards, regional cultural history, and urban social planning. Provide geographical information systems support to the private and public sectors. Study the economic, political, and cultural characteristics of a specific region's population. Teach geography. **SKILLS—Writing:** Communicating effectively in writing as appropriate for the needs of the audience. **Reading Comprehension:** Understanding written sentences and paragraphs in work-related documents. **Mathematics:** Using mathematics to solve problems. **Science:** Using scientific rules and methods to solve problems. **Critical Thinking:** Using logic and reasoning to identify the strengths and weaknesses of alternative solutions, conclusions, or approaches to problems. **Active Learning:** Understanding the implications of new information for both current and future problem-solving and decision-making. **Speaking:** Talking to others to convey information effectively. **Systems Evaluation:** Identifying measures or indicators of system performance and the actions needed to improve or correct performance relative to the goals of the system.

GOE—Interest Area: 15. Scientific Research, Engineering, and Mathematics. **Work Group:** 15.02. Physical Sciences. **Other Jobs in This Work Group:** Astronomers; Atmospheric and Space Scientists; Chemists; Geologists; Hydrologists; Materials Scientists; Physicists. **PERSONALITY TYPE:** Investigative. Investigative occupations frequently involve working with ideas and require an extensive amount of thinking. These occupations can involve searching for facts and figuring out problems mentally.

EDUCATION/TRAINING PROGRAM(S)— Geography. **RELATED KNOWLEDGE/COURSES—Geography:** Knowledge of principles and methods for describing the features of land, sea, and air masses, including their physical characteristics; locations; interrelationships; and distribution of plant, animal, and human life. **Sociology and Anthropology:** Knowledge of group behavior and dynamics, societal trends and influences, human migrations, ethnicity, and cultures and their history and origins. **Biology:** Knowledge of plant and animal organisms and their tissues, cells, functions, interdependencies, and interactions with each other and the environment. **Physics:** Knowledge and prediction of physical principles and laws and their interrelationships and applications to understanding fluid, material, and atmospheric dynamics and mechanical, electrical, atomic, and subatomic structures and processes. **History and Archeology:** Knowledge of historical events and their causes, indicators, and effects on civilizations and cultures. **Design:** Knowledge of design techniques, tools, and principles involved in production of precision technical plans, blueprints, drawings, and models.

Geography Teachers, Postsecondary

◎ Education/Training Required: Master's degree

◎ Annual Earnings: $56,810

◎ Growth: 38.1% for all Postsecondary Teachers

◎ Annual Job Openings: 216,000 for all Postsecondary Teachers

◎ Self-Employed: 0.3% for all Postsecondary Teachers

◎ Part-Time: 27.7% for all Postsecondary Teachers

Teach courses in geography. Evaluate and grade students' class work, assignments, and papers. Prepare and deliver lectures to undergraduate and/or graduate students on topics such as urbanization, environmental systems, and cultural geography. Advise students on academic and vocational curricula, and

on career issues. Compile, administer, and grade examinations, or assign this work to others. Compile bibliographies of specialized materials for outside reading assignments. Initiate, facilitate, and moderate classroom discussions. Keep abreast of developments in their field by reading current literature, talking with colleagues, and participating in professional conferences. Maintain regularly scheduled office hours in order to advise and assist students. Maintain student attendance records, grades, and other required records. Plan, evaluate, and revise curricula, course content, and course materials and methods of instruction. Prepare course materials such as syllabi, homework assignments, and handouts. Select and obtain materials and supplies such as textbooks. Supervise students' laboratory and field work. Supervise undergraduate and/or graduate teaching, internship, and research work. Act as advisers to student organizations. Collaborate with colleagues to address teaching and research issues. Conduct research in a particular field of knowledge, and publish findings in professional journals, books, and/or electronic media. Maintain geographic information systems laboratories, performing duties such as updating software. Participate in campus and community events. Participate in student recruitment, registration, and placement activities. Perform administrative duties such as serving as department head. Perform spatial analysis and modeling, using geographic information system techniques. Provide professional consulting services to government and/or industry. Serve on academic or administrative committees that deal with institutional policies, departmental matters, and academic issues. Write grant proposals to procure external research funding. **SKILLS**—No data available.

GOE—Interest Area: 05. Education and Training. **Work Group:** 05.03. Postsecondary and Adult Teaching and Instructing. **Other Jobs in This Work Group:** Adult Literacy, Remedial Education, and GED Teachers and Instructors; Agricultural Sciences Teachers, Postsecondary; Anthropology and Archeology Teachers, Postsecondary; Architecture

Teachers, Postsecondary; Area, Ethnic, and Cultural Studies Teachers, Postsecondary; Art, Drama, and Music Teachers, Postsecondary; Atmospheric, Earth, Marine, and Space Sciences Teachers, Postsecondary; Biological Science Teachers, Postsecondary; Business Teachers, Postsecondary; Chemistry Teachers, Postsecondary; Communications Teachers, Postsecondary; Computer Science Teachers, Postsecondary; Criminal Justice and Law Enforcement Teachers, Postsecondary; Economics Teachers, Postsecondary; Education Teachers, Postsecondary; Engineering Teachers, Postsecondary; English Language and Literature Teachers, Postsecondary; Environmental Science Teachers, Postsecondary; Farm and Home Management Advisors; Foreign Language and Literature Teachers, Postsecondary; Forestry and Conservation Science Teachers, Postsecondary; Graduate Teaching Assistants; Health Specialties Teachers, Postsecondary; History Teachers, Postsecondary; Home Economics Teachers, Postsecondary; Law Teachers, Postsecondary; Library Science Teachers, Postsecondary; Mathematical Science Teachers, Postsecondary; Nursing Instructors and Teachers, Postsecondary; Philosophy and Religion Teachers, Postsecondary; Physics Teachers, Postsecondary; Political Science Teachers, Postsecondary; Psychology Teachers, Postsecondary; Recreation and Fitness Studies Teachers, Postsecondary; Self-Enrichment Education Teachers; Social Work Teachers, Postsecondary; Sociology Teachers, Postsecondary; Vocational Education Teachers, Postsecondary. **PERSONALITY TYPE:** No data available.

EDUCATION/TRAINING PROGRAM(S)— Geography; Geography Teacher Education. **RELATED KNOWLEDGE/COURSES—**No data available.

Geologists

- Education/Training Required: Bachelor's degree
- Annual Earnings: $68,570
- Growth: 11.5%
- Annual Job Openings: 2,000
- Self-Employed: 2.7%
- Part-Time: 7.7%

Study composition, structure, and history of the earth's crust; examine rocks, minerals, and fossil remains to identify and determine the sequence of processes affecting the development of the earth; apply knowledge of chemistry, physics, biology, and mathematics to explain these phenomena and to help locate mineral and petroleum deposits and underground water resources; prepare geologic reports and maps; and interpret research data to recommend further action for study. Analyze and interpret geological, geochemical, and geophysical information from sources such as survey data, well logs, boreholes, and aerial photos. Plan and conduct geological, geochemical, and geophysical field studies and surveys; sample collection; and drilling and testing programs used to collect data for research and/or application. Investigate the composition, structure, and history of the Earth's crust through the collection, examination, measurement, and classification of soils, minerals, rocks, and fossil remains. Prepare geological maps, cross-sectional diagrams, charts, and reports concerning mineral extraction, land use, and resource management, using results of field work and laboratory research. Locate and estimate probable natural gas, oil, and mineral ore deposits and underground water resources, using aerial photographs, charts, and research and survey results. Assess ground and surface water movement in order to provide advice regarding issues such as waste management, route and site selection, and the restoration of contaminated sites. Identify risks for natural disasters such as mud slides, earthquakes, and volcanic eruptions, and provide advice on ways in which potential damage can be mitigated. Conduct geological and geophysical studies to provide information for use in regional development, site selection, and the development of public works projects. Inspect construction projects in order to analyze engineering problems, applying geological knowledge and using test equipment and drilling machinery. Advise construction firms and government agencies on dam and road construction, foundation design, and land use and resource management. **SKILLS—Science:** Using scientific rules and methods to solve problems. **Management of Financial Resources:** Determining how money will be spent to get the work done and accounting for these expenditures. **Time Management:** Managing one's own time and the time of others. **Active Learning:** Understanding the implications of new information for both current and future problem-solving and decision-making. **Coordination:** Adjusting actions in relation to others' actions. **Critical Thinking:** Using logic and reasoning to identify the strengths and weaknesses of alternative solutions, conclusions, or approaches to problems. **Persuasion:** Persuading others to change their minds or behavior. **Negotiation:** Bringing others together and trying to reconcile differences.

GOE—Interest Area: 15. Scientific Research, Engineering, and Mathematics. **Work Group:** 15.02. Physical Sciences. **Other Jobs in This Work Group:** Astronomers; Atmospheric and Space Scientists; Chemists; Geographers; Hydrologists; Materials Scientists; Physicists. **PERSONALITY TYPE:** Investigative. Investigative occupations frequently involve working with ideas and require an extensive amount of thinking. These occupations can involve searching for facts and figuring out problems mentally.

EDUCATION/TRAINING PROGRAM(S)— Geochemistry; Geochemistry and Petrology; Geological and Earth Sciences/Geosciences, Other; Geology/Earth Science, General; Geophysics and Seismology; Oceanography, Chemical and Physical; Paleontology. **RELATED KNOWLEDGE/COURSES—Geography:** Knowledge of principles

and methods for describing the features of land, sea, and air masses, including their physical characteristics; locations; interrelationships; and distribution of plant, animal, and human life. **Physics:** Knowledge and prediction of physical principles and laws and their interrelationships and applications to understanding fluid, material, and atmospheric dynamics and mechanical, electrical, atomic, and subatomic structures and processes. **Chemistry:** Knowledge of the chemical composition, structure, and properties of substances and of the chemical processes and transformations that they undergo. This includes uses of chemicals and their danger signs, production techniques, and disposal methods. **Engineering and Technology:** Knowledge of the practical application of engineering science and technology. This includes applying principles, techniques, procedures, and equipment to the design and production of various goods and services. **Mathematics:** Knowledge of arithmetic, algebra, geometry, calculus, and statistics and their applications. **Biology:** Knowledge of plant and animal organisms and their tissues, cells, functions, interdependencies, and interactions with each other and the environment.

Government Service Executives

- Education/Training Required: Work experience plus degree
- Annual Earnings: $136,400
- Growth: 16.7%
- Annual Job Openings: 63,000
- Self-Employed: 14.6%
- Part-Time: 5.3%

Determine and formulate policies and provide overall direction of federal, state, local, or international government activities. Plan, direct, and coordinate operational activities at the highest level of management with the help of subordinate

managers. Directs organization charged with administering and monitoring regulated activities to interpret and clarify laws and ensure compliance with laws. Administers, interprets, and explains policies, rules, regulations, and laws to organizations and individuals under authority of commission or applicable legislation. Develops, plans, organizes, and administers policies and procedures for organization to ensure administrative and operational objectives are met. Directs and coordinates activities of workers in public organization to ensure continuing operations, maximize returns on investments, and increase productivity. Negotiates contracts and agreements with federal and state agencies and other organizations and prepares budget for funding and implementation of programs. Implements corrective action plan to solve problems. Reviews and analyzes legislation, laws, and public policy and recommends changes to promote and support interests of general population, as well as special groups. Develops, directs, and coordinates testing, hiring, training, and evaluation of staff personnel. Establishes and maintains comprehensive and current record keeping system of activities and operational procedures in business office. Testifies in court, before control or review board, or at legislature. Participates in activities to promote business and expand services, and provides technical assistance in conducting of conferences, seminars, and workshops. Delivers speeches, writes articles, and presents information for organization at meetings or conventions to promote services, exchange ideas, and accomplish objectives. Plans, promotes, organizes, and coordinates public community service program and maintains cooperative working relationships among public and agency participants. Conducts or directs investigations or hearings to resolve complaints and violations of laws. Prepares, reviews, and submits reports concerning activities, expenses, budget, government statutes and rulings, and other items affecting business or program services. Directs, coordinates, and conducts activities between United States government and foreign entities to provide information to promote international interest and harmony. **SKILLS—Management of**

Financial Resources: Determining how money will be spent to get the work done and accounting for these expenditures. **Systems Evaluation:** Identifying measures or indicators of system performance and the actions needed to improve or correct performance relative to the goals of the system. **Coordination:** Adjusting actions in relation to others' actions. **Systems Analysis:** Determining how a system should work and how changes in conditions, operations, and the environment will affect outcomes. **Management of Personnel Resources:** Motivating, developing, and directing people as they work, identifying the best people for the job. **Judgment and Decision Making:** Considering the relative costs and benefits of potential actions to choose the most appropriate one. **Negotiation:** Bringing others together and trying to reconcile differences. **Persuasion:** Persuading others to change their minds or behavior.

GOE—Interest Area: 07. Government and Public Administration. **Work Group:** 07.01. Managerial Work in Government and Public Administration. **Other Jobs in This Work Group:** Social and Community Service Managers. **PERSONALITY TYPE:** Enterprising. Enterprising occupations frequently involve starting up and carrying out projects. These occupations can involve leading people and making many decisions. They sometimes require risk taking and often deal with business.

EDUCATION/TRAINING PROGRAM(S)— Business Administration and Management, General; Business/Commerce, General; Entrepreneurship/Entrepreneurial Studies; International Business/Trade/Commerce; Public Administration; Public Administration and Social Service Professions, Other; Public Policy Analysis. **RELATED KNOWLEDGE/COURSES—Administration and Management:** Knowledge of business and management principles involved in strategic planning, resource allocation, human resources modeling, leadership technique, production methods, and coordination of people and resources. **Law and Government:** Knowledge of laws, legal codes, court procedures, precedents, government regulations, executive orders, agency rules, and the democratic political process. **Personnel and Human Resources:** Knowledge of principles and procedures for personnel recruitment, selection, training, compensation and benefits, labor relations and negotiation, and personnel information systems. **Economics and Accounting:** Knowledge of economic and accounting principles and practices, the financial markets, banking, and the analysis and reporting of financial data. **Education and Training:** Knowledge of principles and methods for curriculum and training design, teaching and instruction for individuals and groups, and the measurement of training effects. **Psychology:** Knowledge of human behavior and performance; individual differences in ability, personality, and interests; learning and motivation; psychological research methods; and the assessment and treatment of behavioral and affective disorders.

Graduate Teaching Assistants

- Education/Training Required: Master's degree
- Annual Earnings: $25,550
- Growth: 38.1%
- Annual Job Openings: 216,000
- Self-Employed: 0.3%
- Part-Time: 27.7%

Assist department chairperson, faculty members, or other professional staff members in college or university by performing teaching or teaching-related duties, such as teaching lower level courses, developing teaching materials, preparing and giving examinations, and grading examinations or papers. Graduate assistants must be enrolled in a graduate school program. Graduate assistants who primarily perform non-teaching duties, such as laboratory research, should be reported in the occupational category related to the work performed. Provide instructors with assistance in the use of audiovisual equipment. Provide assistance to library staff in maintaining library collections. Evaluate and grade examinations, assignments, and papers, and record grades. Lead discussion sections, tutorials, and laboratory sections. Teach undergraduate level courses. Develop teaching materials such as syllabi, visual aids, answer keys, supplementary notes, and course websites. Attend lectures given by the instructor whom they are assisting. Complete laboratory projects prior to assigning them to students so that any needed modifications can be made. Copy and distribute classroom materials. Demonstrate use of laboratory equipment, and enforce laboratory rules. Inform students of the procedures for completing and submitting class work such as lab reports. Meet with supervisors to discuss students' grades, and to complete required grade-related paperwork. Notify instructors of errors or problems with assignments. Order or obtain materials needed for classes. Prepare and proctor examinations. Return assignments to students in accordance with established deadlines. Schedule and maintain regular office hours to meet with students. Arrange for supervisors to conduct teaching observations; meet with supervisors to receive feedback about teaching performance. Assist faculty members or staff with student conferences. Provide assistance to faculty members or staff with laboratory or field research. **SKILLS—Instructing:** Teaching others how to do something. **Learning Strategies:** Selecting and using training/instructional methods and procedures appropriate for the situation when learning or teaching new things. **Speaking:** Talking to others to convey information effectively. **Reading Comprehension:** Understanding written sentences and paragraphs in work-related documents. **Science:** Using scientific rules and methods to solve problems. **Writing:** Communicating effectively in writing as appropriate for the needs of the audience. **Critical Thinking:** Using logic and reasoning to identify the strengths and weaknesses of alternative solutions, conclusions, or approaches to problems.

Mathematics: Using mathematics to solve problems. **Active Learning:** Understanding the implications of new information for both current and future problem-solving and decision-making.

GOE—Interest Area: 05. Education and Training. **Work Group:** 05.03. Postsecondary and Adult Teaching and Instructing. **Other Jobs in This Work Group:** Adult Literacy, Remedial Education, and GED Teachers and Instructors; Agricultural Sciences Teachers, Postsecondary; Anthropology and Archeology Teachers, Postsecondary; Architecture Teachers, Postsecondary; Area, Ethnic, and Cultural Studies Teachers, Postsecondary; Art, Drama, and Music Teachers, Postsecondary; Atmospheric, Earth, Marine, and Space Sciences Teachers, Postsecondary; Biological Science Teachers, Postsecondary; Business Teachers, Postsecondary; Chemistry Teachers, Postsecondary; Communications Teachers, Postsecondary; Computer Science Teachers, Postsecondary; Criminal Justice and Law Enforcement Teachers, Postsecondary; Economics Teachers, Postsecondary; Education Teachers, Postsecondary; Engineering Teachers, Postsecondary; English Language and Literature Teachers, Postsecondary; Environmental Science Teachers, Postsecondary; Farm and Home Management Advisors; Foreign Language and Literature Teachers, Postsecondary; Forestry and Conservation Science Teachers, Postsecondary; Geography Teachers, Postsecondary; Health Specialties Teachers, Postsecondary; History Teachers, Postsecondary; Home Economics Teachers, Postsecondary; Law Teachers, Postsecondary; Library Science Teachers, Postsecondary; Mathematical Science Teachers, Postsecondary; Nursing Instructors and Teachers, Postsecondary; Philosophy and Religion Teachers, Postsecondary; Physics Teachers, Postsecondary; Political Science Teachers, Postsecondary; Psychology Teachers, Postsecondary; Recreation and Fitness Studies Teachers, Postsecondary; Self-Enrichment Education Teachers; Social Work Teachers, Postsecondary; Sociology Teachers, Postsecondary; Vocational Education Teachers, Postsecondary. **PERSONALITY TYPE:** Social. Social occupations frequently involve working with, communicating with, and teaching people. These occupations often involve helping or providing service to others.

EDUCATION/TRAINING PROGRAM(S)— No data available. **RELATED KNOWLEDGE/ COURSES—Education and Training:** Knowledge of principles and methods for curriculum and training design, teaching and instruction for individuals and groups, and the measurement of training effects. **English Language:** Knowledge of the structure and content of the English language, including the meaning and spelling of words, rules of composition, and grammar. **Clerical Practices:** Knowledge of administrative and clerical procedures and systems such as word processing, managing files and records, stenography and transcription, designing forms, and other office procedures and terminology. **Mathematics:** Knowledge of arithmetic, algebra, geometry, calculus, and statistics and their applications. **Administration and Management:** Knowledge of business and management principles involved in strategic planning, resource allocation, human resources modeling, leadership technique, production methods, and coordination of people and resources. **Computers and Electronics:** Knowledge of circuit boards, processors, chips, electronic equipment, and computer hardware and software, including applications and programming.

Graphic Designers

- Education/Training Required: Bachelor's degree
- Annual Earnings: $36,930
- Growth: 21.9%
- Annual Job Openings: 29,000
- Self-Employed: 31.8%
- Part-Time: 16.5%

Design or create graphics to meet specific commercial or promotional needs, such as packaging,

displays, or logos. May use a variety of mediums to achieve artistic or decorative effects. Create designs, concepts, and sample layouts based on knowledge of layout principles and esthetic design concepts. Determine size and arrangement of illustrative material and copy, and select style and size of type. Use computer software to generate new images. Mark up, paste, and assemble final layouts to prepare layouts for printer. Draw and print charts, graphs, illustrations, and other artwork, using computer. Review final layouts and suggest improvements as needed. Confer with clients to discuss and determine layout design. Develop graphics and layouts for product illustrations, company logos, and Internet websites. Key information into computer equipment to create layouts for client or supervisor. Prepare illustrations or rough sketches of material, discussing them with clients and/or supervisors and making necessary changes. Study illustrations and photographs to plan presentation of materials, products, or services. Prepare notes and instructions for workers who assemble and prepare final layouts for printing. Develop negatives and prints to produce layout photographs, using negative and print developing equipment and tools. Photograph layouts, using camera, to make layout prints for supervisors or clients. Produce still and animated graphics for on-air and taped portions of television news broadcasts, using electronic video equipment. **SKILLS— Persuasion:** Persuading others to change their minds or behavior. **Time Management:** Managing one's own time and the time of others. **Troubleshooting:** Determining causes of operating errors and deciding what to do about them. **Instructing:** Teaching others how to do something. **Coordination:** Adjusting actions in relation to others' actions. **Social Perceptiveness:** Being aware of others' reactions and understanding why they react as they do. **Operations Analysis:** Analyzing needs and product requirements to create a design. **Complex Problem Solving:** Identifying complex problems and reviewing related information to develop and evaluate options and implement solutions.

GOE—Interest Area: 03. Arts and Communication. **Work Group:** 03.05. Design. **Other Jobs in This Work Group:** Commercial and Industrial Designers; Exhibit Designers; Fashion Designers; Floral Designers; Interior Designers; Merchandise Displayers and Window Trimmers; Set Designers. **PERSONALITY TYPE:** Artistic. Artistic occupations frequently involve working with forms, designs, and patterns. They often require self-expression, and the work can be done without following a clear set of rules.

EDUCATION/TRAINING PROGRAM(S)— Agricultural Communication/Journalism; Commercial and Advertising Art; Computer Graphics; Design and Visual Communications, General; Graphic Design; Industrial Design; Web Page, Digital/Multimedia and Information Resources Design. **RELATED KNOWLEDGE/COURSES—Fine Arts:** Knowledge of the theory and techniques required to compose, produce, and perform works of music, dance, visual arts, drama, and sculpture. **Design:** Knowledge of design techniques, tools, and principles involved in production of precision technical plans, blueprints, drawings, and models. **Computers and Electronics:** Knowledge of circuit boards, processors, chips, electronic equipment, and computer hardware and software, including applications and programming. **Communications and Media:** Knowledge of media production, communication, and dissemination techniques and methods. This includes alternative ways to inform and entertain via written, oral, and visual media. **Sales and Marketing:** Knowledge of principles and methods for showing, promoting, and selling products or services. This includes marketing strategy and tactics, product demonstration, sales techniques, and sales control systems. **Clerical Practices:** Knowledge of administrative and clerical procedures and systems such as word processing, managing files and records, stenography and transcription, designing forms, and other office procedures and terminology.

Health Educators

- ⊚ Education/Training Required: Master's degree
- ⊚ Annual Earnings: $38,100
- ⊚ Growth: 21.9%
- ⊚ Annual Job Openings: 8,000
- ⊚ Self-Employed: 0.2%
- ⊚ Part-Time: 10.6%

Promote, maintain, and improve individual and community health by assisting individuals and communities to adopt healthy behaviors. Collect and analyze data to identify community needs prior to planning, implementing, monitoring, and evaluating programs designed to encourage healthy lifestyles, policies, and environments. May also serve as a resource to assist individuals, other professionals, or the community and may administer fiscal resources for health education programs. Collaborate with health specialists and civic groups to determine community health needs and the availability of services, and to develop goals for meeting needs. Design and conduct evaluations and diagnostic studies to assess the quality and performance of health education programs. Develop and present health education and promotion programs such as training workshops, conferences, and school or community presentations. Develop operational plans and policies necessary to achieve health education objectives and services. Develop, conduct, or coordinate health needs assessments and other public health surveys. Prepare and distribute health education materials, including reports, bulletins, and visual aids such as films, videotapes, photographs, and posters. Provide guidance to agencies and organizations in the assessment of health education needs, and in the development and delivery of health education programs. Provide program information to the public by preparing and presenting press releases, conducting media campaigns, and/or maintaining program-related web sites. Develop and maintain cooperative working relationships with agencies and organizations interested in public health care. Develop and maintain health education libraries to provide resources for staff and community agencies. Develop, prepare, and coordinate grant applications and grant-related activities to obtain funding for health education programs and related work. Document activities, recording information such as the numbers of applications completed, presentations conducted, and persons assisted. Maintain databases, mailing lists, telephone networks, and other information to facilitate the functioning of health education programs. Supervise professional and technical staff in implementing health programs, objectives, and goals. **SKILLS— Speaking:** Talking to others to convey information effectively. **Coordination:** Adjusting actions in relation to others' actions. **Writing:** Communicating effectively in writing as appropriate for the needs of the audience. **Persuasion:** Persuading others to change their minds or behavior. **Systems Analysis:** Determining how a system should work and how changes in conditions, operations, and the environment will affect outcomes. **Active Learning:** Understanding the implications of new information for both current and future problem-solving and decision-making. **Systems Evaluation:** Identifying measures or indicators of system performance and the actions needed to improve or correct performance relative to the goals of the system. **Service Orientation:** Actively looking for ways to help people. **Complex Problem Solving:** Identifying complex problems and reviewing related information to develop and evaluate options and implement solutions.

GOE—Interest Area: 05. Education and Training. **Work Group:** 05.06. Counseling, Health, and Fitness Education. **Other Jobs in This Work Group:** Educational, Vocational, and School Counselors; Fitness Trainers and Aerobics Instructors. **PERSONALITY TYPE:** Social. Social occupations frequently involve working with, communicating with, and teaching people. These occupations often involve helping or providing service to others.

H

EDUCATION/TRAINING PROGRAM(S)—
Community Health Services/Liaison/Counseling;
Health Communication; International Public
Health/International Health; Maternal and Child
Health; Public Health Education and Promotion.
RELATED KNOWLEDGE/COURSES—Education and Training: Knowledge of principles and
methods for curriculum and training design, teaching and instruction for individuals and groups, and
the measurement of training effects. **Communications and Media:** Knowledge of media production,
communication, and dissemination techniques and
methods. This includes alternative ways to inform
and entertain via written, oral, and visual media.
Sales and Marketing: Knowledge of principles and
methods for showing, promoting, and selling products or services. This includes marketing strategy
and tactics, product demonstration, sales techniques, and sales control systems. **Therapy and
Counseling:** Knowledge of principles, methods, and
procedures for diagnosis, treatment, and rehabilitation of physical and mental dysfunctions and for
career counseling and guidance. **Medicine and
Dentistry:** Knowledge of the information and techniques needed to diagnose and treat human injuries,
diseases, and deformities. This includes symptoms,
treatment alternatives, drug properties and interactions, and preventive health-care measures. **English
Language:** Knowledge of the structure and content
of the English language, including the meaning
and spelling of words, rules of composition, and
grammar.

Health Specialties Teachers, Postsecondary

- ◎ Education/Training Required: Master's degree
- ◎ Annual Earnings: $63,250
- ◎ Growth: 38.1% for all Postsecondary Teachers
- ◎ Annual Job Openings: 216,000 for all Postsecondary Teachers
- ◎ Self-Employed: 0.3% for all Postsecondary Teachers
- ◎ Part-Time: 27.7% for all Postsecondary Teachers

Teach courses in health specialties, such as veterinary medicine, dentistry, pharmacy, therapy, laboratory technology, and public health. Evaluate and
grade students' class work, assignments, and papers.
Prepare and deliver lectures to undergraduate
and/or graduate students on topics such as public
health, stress management, and worksite health promotion. Advise students on academic and vocational curricula, and on career issues. Compile,
administer, and grade examinations, or assign this
work to others. Compile bibliographies of specialized materials for outside reading assignments. Initiate, facilitate, and moderate classroom discussions.
Keep abreast of developments in their field by reading current literature, talking with colleagues, and
participating in professional conferences. Maintain
regularly scheduled office hours in order to advise
and assist students. Maintain student attendance
records, grades, and other required records. Plan,
evaluate, and revise curricula, course content, and
course materials and methods of instruction. Prepare course materials such as syllabi, homework
assignments, and handouts. Select and obtain materials and supplies such as textbooks and laboratory

equipment. Supervise laboratory sessions. Supervise undergraduate and/or graduate teaching, internship, and research work. Act as advisers to student organizations. Collaborate with colleagues to address teaching and research issues. Conduct research in a particular field of knowledge, and publish findings in professional journals, books, and/or electronic media. Participate in campus and community events. Participate in student recruitment, registration, and placement activities. Perform administrative duties such as serving as department head. Provide professional consulting services to government and/or industry. Serve on academic or administrative committees that deal with institutional policies, departmental matters, and academic issues. Write grant proposals to procure external research funding. **SKILLS—Science:** Using scientific rules and methods to solve problems. **Instructing:** Teaching others how to do something. **Writing:** Communicating effectively in writing as appropriate for the needs of the audience. **Reading Comprehension:** Understanding written sentences and paragraphs in work-related documents. **Active Learning:** Understanding the implications of new information for both current and future problem-solving and decision-making. **Critical Thinking:** Using logic and reasoning to identify the strengths and weaknesses of alternative solutions, conclusions, or approaches to problems. **Learning Strategies:** Selecting and using training/instructional methods and procedures appropriate for the situation when learning or teaching new things. **Speaking:** Talking to others to convey information effectively.

GOE—Interest Area: 05. Education and Training. **Work Group:** 05.03. Postsecondary and Adult Teaching and Instructing. **Other Jobs in This Work Group:** Adult Literacy, Remedial Education, and GED Teachers and Instructors; Agricultural Sciences Teachers, Postsecondary; Anthropology and Archeology Teachers, Postsecondary; Architecture Teachers, Postsecondary; Area, Ethnic, and Cultural Studies Teachers, Postsecondary; Art, Drama, and Music Teachers, Postsecondary; Atmospheric, Earth, Marine, and Space Sciences Teachers, Post-secondary; Biological Science Teachers, Postsecondary; Business Teachers, Postsecondary; Chemistry Teachers, Postsecondary; Communications Teachers, Postsecondary; Computer Science Teachers, Postsecondary; Criminal Justice and Law Enforcement Teachers, Postsecondary; Economics Teachers, Postsecondary; Education Teachers, Postsecondary; Engineering Teachers, Postsecondary; English Language and Literature Teachers, Postsecondary; Environmental Science Teachers, Postsecondary; Farm and Home Management Advisors; Foreign Language and Literature Teachers, Postsecondary; Forestry and Conservation Science Teachers, Postsecondary; Geography Teachers, Postsecondary; Graduate Teaching Assistants; History Teachers, Postsecondary; Home Economics Teachers, Postsecondary; Law Teachers, Postsecondary; Library Science Teachers, Postsecondary; Mathematical Science Teachers, Postsecondary; Nursing Instructors and Teachers, Postsecondary; Philosophy and Religion Teachers, Postsecondary; Physics Teachers, Postsecondary; Political Science Teachers, Postsecondary; Psychology Teachers, Postsecondary; Recreation and Fitness Studies Teachers, Postsecondary; Self-Enrichment Education Teachers; Social Work Teachers, Postsecondary; Sociology Teachers, Postsecondary; Vocational Education Teachers, Postsecondary. **PERSONALITY TYPE:** Investigative. Investigative occupations frequently involve working with ideas and require an extensive amount of thinking. These occupations can involve searching for facts and figuring out problems mentally.

EDUCATION/TRAINING PROGRAM(S)— Allied Health and Medical Assisting Services, Other; Allied Health Diagnostic, Intervention, and Treatment Professions, Other; Art Therapy/Therapist; Asian Bodywork Therapy; Audiology/Audiologist and Hearing Sciences; Audiology/Audiologist and Speech-Language Pathology/Pathologist; Biostatistics; Blood Bank Technology Specialist; Cardiovascular Technology/Technologist; Chiropractic (DC); Clinical Laboratory Science/Medical Technology/Technologist; Clinical/Medical Laboratory Assistant; Clinical/Medical Laboratory Technician;

Communication Disorders, General; Cytotechnology/Cytotechnologist; Dance Therapy/Therapist; Dental Assisting/Assistant; Dental Clinical Sciences, General (MS, PhD); Dental Hygiene/Hygienist; Dental Laboratory Technology/Technician; Dental Services and Allied Professions, Other; Dentistry (DDS, DMD); Diagnostic Medical Sonography/Sonographer and Ultrasound Technician; Electrocardiograph Technology/Technician; Electroneurodiagnostic/Electroencephalographic Technology/Technologist; Emergency Medical Technology/Technician (EMT Paramedic); Environmental Health; Epidemiology; Health Occupations Teacher Education; Health/Medical Physics; Health/Medical Preparatory Programs, Other; Hematology Technology/Technician; Hypnotherapy/Hypnotherapist; Massage Therapy/Therapeutic Massage; Medical Radiologic Technology/Science—Radiation Therapist; Music Therapy/Therapist; Nuclear Medical Technology/Technologist; Occupational Health and Industrial Hygiene; Occupational Therapist Assistant; Occupational Therapy/Therapist; Orthotist/Prosthetist; Perfusion Technology/Perfusionist; Pharmacy (PharmD [USA]; PharmD, BS/BPharm [Canada]); Pharmacy Administration and Pharmacy Policy and Regulatory Affairs (MS, PhD); Pharmacy Technician/Assistant; Pharmacy, Pharmaceutical Sciences, and Administration, Other; Physical Therapist Assistant; Physical Therapy/Therapist; Physician Assistant; Pre-Dentistry Studies; Pre-Medicine/Pre-Medical Studies; Pre-Nursing Studies; others. **RELATED KNOWLEDGE/COURSES—Biology:** Knowledge of plant and animal organisms and their tissues, cells, functions, interdependencies, and interactions with each other and the environment. **Education and Training:** Knowledge of principles and methods for curriculum and training design, teaching and instruction for individuals and groups, and the measurement of training effects. **Medicine and Dentistry:** Knowledge of the information and techniques needed to diagnose and treat human injuries, diseases, and deformities. This includes symptoms, treatment alternatives, drug properties and interactions, and preventive health-care measures. **Therapy and Counseling:** Knowledge of principles, methods, and procedures for diagnosis, treatment, and rehabilitation of physical and mental dysfunctions and for career counseling and guidance. **English Language:** Knowledge of the structure and content of the English language, including the meaning and spelling of words, rules of composition, and grammar. **Chemistry:** Knowledge of the chemical composition, structure, and properties of substances and of the chemical processes and transformations that they undergo. This includes uses of chemicals and their danger signs, production techniques, and disposal methods.

History Teachers, Postsecondary

- ◉ Education/Training Required: Master's degree
- ◉ Annual Earnings: $53,130
- ◉ Growth: 38.1% for all Postsecondary Teachers
- ◉ Annual Job Openings: 216,000 for all Postsecondary Teachers
- ◉ Self-Employed: 0.3% for all Postsecondary Teachers
- ◉ Part-Time: 27.7% for all Postsecondary Teachers

Teach courses in human history and historiography. Perform administrative duties such as serving as department head. Provide professional consulting services to government, educational institutions, and/or industry. Serve on academic or administrative committees that deal with institutional policies, departmental matters, and academic issues. Write grant proposals to procure external research funding. Evaluate and grade students' class work, assignments, and papers. Prepare and deliver lectures to undergraduate and/or graduate students on topics such as ancient history, postwar civilizations, and the history of third-world countries. Advise students on academic and vocational curricula, and on career issues. Compile, administer, and grade examinations, or assign this work to others. Compile bibliographies of specialized materials for outside reading assignments. Initiate, facilitate, and moderate classroom discussions. Keep abreast of developments in their field by reading current literature, talking with colleagues, and participating in professional conferences. Maintain regularly scheduled office hours in order to advise and assist students. Maintain student attendance records, grades, and other required records. Plan, evaluate, and revise curricula, course content, and course materials and methods of instruction. Prepare course materials such as syllabi, homework assignments, and handouts. Select and obtain materials and supplies such as textbooks. Supervise undergraduate and/or graduate teaching, internship, and research work. Act as advisers to student organizations. Collaborate with colleagues to address teaching and research issues. Conduct research in a particular field of knowledge, and publish findings in professional journals, books, and/or electronic media. Participate in campus and community events. Participate in student recruitment, registration, and placement activities. **SKILLS— Instructing:** Teaching others how to do something. **Learning Strategies:** Selecting and using training/instructional methods and procedures appropriate for the situation when learning or teaching new things. **Reading Comprehension:** Understanding written sentences and paragraphs in work-related documents. **Active Learning:** Understanding the implications of new information for both current and future problem-solving and decision-making. **Speaking:** Talking to others to convey information effectively. **Writing:** Communicating effectively in writing as appropriate for the needs of the audience. **Science:** Using scientific rules and methods to solve problems. **Active Listening:** Giving full attention to what other people are saying,

taking time to understand the points being made, asking questions as appropriate, and not interrupting at inappropriate times. **Critical Thinking:** Using logic and reasoning to identify the strengths and weaknesses of alternative solutions, conclusions, or approaches to problems.

GOE—Interest Area: 05. Education and Training. **Work Group:** 05.03. Postsecondary and Adult Teaching and Instructing. **Other Jobs in This Work Group:** Adult Literacy, Remedial Education, and GED Teachers and Instructors; Agricultural Sciences Teachers, Postsecondary; Anthropology and Archeology Teachers, Postsecondary; Architecture Teachers, Postsecondary; Area, Ethnic, and Cultural Studies Teachers, Postsecondary; Art, Drama, and Music Teachers, Postsecondary; Atmospheric, Earth, Marine, and Space Sciences Teachers, Postsecondary; Biological Science Teachers, Postsecondary; Business Teachers, Postsecondary; Chemistry Teachers, Postsecondary; Communications Teachers, Postsecondary; Computer Science Teachers, Postsecondary; Criminal Justice and Law Enforcement Teachers, Postsecondary; Economics Teachers, Postsecondary; Education Teachers, Postsecondary; Engineering Teachers, Postsecondary; English Language and Literature Teachers, Postsecondary; Environmental Science Teachers, Postsecondary; Farm and Home Management Advisors; Foreign Language and Literature Teachers, Postsecondary; Forestry and Conservation Science Teachers, Postsecondary; Geography Teachers, Postsecondary; Graduate Teaching Assistants; Health Specialties Teachers, Postsecondary; Home Economics Teachers, Postsecondary; Law Teachers, Postsecondary; Library Science Teachers, Postsecondary; Mathematical Science Teachers, Postsecondary; Nursing Instructors and Teachers, Postsecondary; Philosophy and Religion Teachers, Postsecondary; Physics Teachers, Postsecondary; Political Science Teachers, Postsecondary; Psychology Teachers, Postsecondary; Recreation and Fitness Studies Teachers, Postsecondary; Self-Enrichment Education Teachers; Social Work Teachers, Postsecondary; Sociology Teachers, Postsecondary; Vocational Education Teachers, Postsecondary. **PER-SONALITY TYPE:** Social. Social occupations frequently involve working with, communicating with, and teaching people. These occupations often involve helping or providing service to others.

EDUCATION/TRAINING PROGRAM(S)— American History (United States); Asian History; Canadian History; European History; History and Philosophy of Science and Technology; History, General; History, Other; Public/Applied History and Archival Administration. **RELATED KNOWLEDGE/COURSES—Sociology and Anthropology:** Knowledge of group behavior and dynamics, societal trends and influences, human migrations, ethnicity, and cultures and their history and origins. **History and Archeology:** Knowledge of historical events and their causes, indicators, and effects on civilizations and cultures. **Education and Training:** Knowledge of principles and methods for curriculum and training design, teaching and instruction for individuals and groups, and the measurement of training effects. **Psychology:** Knowledge of human behavior and performance; individual differences in ability, personality, and interests; learning and motivation; psychological research methods; and the assessment and treatment of behavioral and affective disorders. **Economics and Accounting:** Knowledge of economic and accounting principles and practices, the financial markets, banking, and the analysis and reporting of financial data. **English Language:** Knowledge of the structure and content of the English language, including the meaning and spelling of words, rules of composition, and grammar.

Home Economics Teachers, Postsecondary

- ◉ Education/Training Required: Master's degree
- ◉ Annual Earnings: $46,780
- ◉ Growth: 38.1% for all Postsecondary Teachers
- ◉ Annual Job Openings: 216,000 for all Postsecondary Teachers
- ◉ Self-Employed: 0.3% for all Postsecondary Teachers
- ◉ Part-Time: 27.7% for all Postsecondary Teachers

Teach courses in child care, family relations, finance, nutrition, and related subjects as pertaining to home management. Evaluate and grade students' class work, laboratory work, projects, assignments, and papers. Prepare and deliver lectures to undergraduate and/or graduate students on topics such as food science, nutrition, and child care. Advise students on academic and vocational curricula, and on career issues. Compile, administer, and grade examinations, or assign this work to others. Compile bibliographies of specialized materials for outside reading assignments. Initiate, facilitate, and moderate classroom discussions. Keep abreast of developments in their field by reading current literature, talking with colleagues, and participating in professional conferences. Maintain regularly scheduled office hours in order to advise and assist students. Maintain student attendance records, grades, and other required records. Plan, evaluate, and revise curricula, course content, and course materials and methods of instruction. Prepare course materials such as syllabi, homework assignments, and handouts. Select and obtain materials and supplies such as textbooks. Supervise undergraduate and/or graduate teaching, internship, and research work. Act as advisers to student organizations. Collaborate with colleagues to address teaching and research issues. Conduct research in a particular field of knowledge, and publish findings in professional journals, books, and/or electronic media. Participate in campus and community events. Participate in student recruitment, registration, and placement activities. Perform administrative duties such as serving as department head. Provide professional consulting services to government and/or industry. Serve on academic or administrative committees that deal with institutional policies, departmental matters, and academic issues. Write grant proposals to procure external research funding. **SKILLS**—No data available.

GOE—Interest Area: 05. Education and Training. **Work Group:** 05.03. Postsecondary and Adult Teaching and Instructing. **Other Jobs in This Work Group:** Adult Literacy, Remedial Education, and GED Teachers and Instructors; Agricultural Sciences Teachers, Postsecondary; Anthropology and Archeology Teachers, Postsecondary; Architecture Teachers, Postsecondary; Area, Ethnic, and Cultural Studies Teachers, Postsecondary; Art, Drama, and Music Teachers, Postsecondary; Atmospheric, Earth, Marine, and Space Sciences Teachers, Postsecondary; Biological Science Teachers, Postsecondary; Business Teachers, Postsecondary; Chemistry Teachers, Postsecondary; Communications Teachers, Postsecondary; Computer Science Teachers, Postsecondary; Criminal Justice and Law Enforcement Teachers, Postsecondary; Economics Teachers, Postsecondary; Education Teachers, Postsecondary; Engineering Teachers, Postsecondary; English Language and Literature Teachers, Postsecondary; Environmental Science Teachers, Postsecondary; Farm and Home Management Advisors; Foreign Language and Literature Teachers, Postsecondary; Forestry and Conservation Science Teachers, Postsecondary; Geography Teachers, Postsecondary; Graduate Teaching Assistants; Health Specialties Teachers, Postsecondary; History Teachers, Postsecondary; Law Teachers, Postsecondary; Library Science Teachers, Postsecondary; Mathe-matical Science Teachers, Postsecondary; Nursing Instructors and Teachers, Postsecondary; Philosophy and Religion Teachers, Postsecondary; Physics Teachers, Postsecondary; Political Science Teachers, Postsecondary; Psychology Teachers, Postsecondary; Recreation and Fitness Studies Teachers, Postsecondary; Self-Enrichment Education Teachers; Social Work Teachers, Postsecondary; Sociology Teachers, Postsecondary; Vocational Education Teachers, Postsecondary. **PERSONALITY TYPE:** No data available.

EDUCATION/TRAINING PROGRAM(S)— Business Family and Consumer Sciences/Human Sciences; Child Care and Support Services Management; Family and Consumer Sciences/Human Sciences, General; Foodservice Systems Administration/Management; Human Development and Family Studies, General. **RELATED KNOWLEDGE/ COURSES**—No data available.

Human Resources Managers

- ◎ Education/Training Required: Work experience plus degree
- ◎ Annual Earnings: $70,350
- ◎ Growth: 19.4%
- ◎ Annual Job Openings: 21,000
- ◎ Self-Employed: 0%
- ◎ Part-Time: 3.7%

Plan, direct, and coordinate human resource management activities of an organization to maximize the strategic use of human resources and maintain functions such as employee compensation, recruitment, personnel policies, and regulatory compliance. Administer compensation, benefits and performance management systems, and safety and recreation programs. Identify staff vacancies and recruit, interview and select applicants. Allocate human resources, ensuring appropriate matches between personnel. Provide current and prospective employees with information about policies, job duties, working conditions, wages, opportunities for promotion and employee benefits. Perform difficult staffing duties, including dealing with under-staffing, refereeing disputes, firing employees, and administering disciplinary procedures. Advise managers on organizational policy matters such as equal employment opportunity and sexual harassment, and recommend needed changes. Analyze and modify compensation and benefits policies to establish competitive programs and ensure compliance with legal requirements. Plan and conduct new employee orientation to foster positive attitude toward organizational objectives. Serve as a link between management and employees by handling questions, interpreting and administering contracts and helping resolve work-related problems. Plan, direct, supervise, and coordinate work activities of subordinates and staff relating to employment, compensation, labor relations, and employee relations. Analyze training needs to design employee development, language training and health and safety programs. Maintain records and compile statistical reports concerning personnel-related data such as hires, transfers, performance appraisals, and absenteeism rates. Analyze statistical data and reports to identify and determine causes of personnel problems and develop recommendations for improvement of organization's personnel policies and practices. Plan, organize, direct, control or coordinate the personnel, training, or labor relations activities of an organization. Conduct exit interviews to identify reasons for employee termination. Investigate and report on industrial accidents for insurance carriers. Represent organization at personnel-related hearings and investigations. Negotiate bargaining agreements and help interpret labor contracts. **SKILLS—Management of Personnel Resources:** Motivating, developing, and directing people as they work, identifying the best people for the job. **Negotiation:** Bringing others together and trying to reconcile differences. **Persuasion:** Persuading others to change their minds or behavior. **Time Manage-**

ment: Managing one's own time and the time of others. **Social Perceptiveness:** Being aware of others' reactions and understanding why they react as they do. **Learning Strategies:** Selecting and using training/instructional methods and procedures appropriate for the situation when learning or teaching new things. **Active Listening:** Giving full attention to what other people are saying, taking time to understand the points being made, asking questions as appropriate, and not interrupting at inappropriate times. **Management of Financial Resources:** Determining how money will be spent to get the work done and accounting for these expenditures.

GOE—Interest Area: 04. Business and Administration. **Work Group:** 04.01. Managerial Work in General Business. **Other Jobs in This Work Group:** Chief Executives; Compensation and Benefits Managers; General and Operations Managers; Private Sector Executives; Training and Development Managers. **PERSONALITY TYPE:** Enterprising. Enterprising occupations frequently involve starting up and carrying out projects. These occupations can involve leading people and making many decisions. They sometimes require risk taking and often deal with business.

EDUCATION/TRAINING PROGRAM(S)— Human Resources Development; Human Resources Management/Personnel Administration, General; Labor and Industrial Relations; Labor Studies. **RELATED KNOWLEDGE/COURSES—Personnel and Human Resources:** Knowledge of principles and procedures for personnel recruitment, selection, training, compensation and benefits, labor relations and negotiation, and personnel information systems. **Clerical Practices:** Knowledge of administrative and clerical procedures and systems such as word processing, managing files and records, stenography and transcription, designing forms, and other office procedures and terminology. **Education and Training:** Knowledge of principles and methods for curriculum and training design, teaching and instruction for individuals and groups, and the measurement of training effects. **Law and Government:** Knowledge of laws, legal codes, court procedures, precedents, government regulations, executive orders, agency rules, and the democratic political process. **Customer and Personal Service:** Knowledge of principles and processes for providing customer and personal services. This includes customer needs assessment, meeting quality standards for services, and evaluation of customer satisfaction. **Economics and Accounting:** Knowledge of economic and accounting principles and practices, the financial markets, banking, and the analysis and reporting of financial data.

Hydrologists

- ◎ Education/Training Required: Bachelor's degree
- ◎ Annual Earnings: $59,010
- ◎ Growth: 21.0%
- ◎ Annual Job Openings: 1,000
- ◎ Self-Employed: 3.0%
- ◎ Part-Time: 7.7%

Research the distribution, circulation, and physical properties of underground and surface waters; study the form and intensity of precipitation, its rate of infiltration into the soil, movement through the earth, and its return to the ocean and atmosphere. Studies and analyzes physical aspects of earth, including atmosphere and hydrosphere, and interior structure. Studies waters of land areas to determine modes of return to ocean and atmosphere. Compiles and evaluates data to prepare navigational charts and maps, predict atmospheric conditions, and prepare environmental reports. Prepares and issues maps and reports indicating areas of seismic risk to existing or proposed construction or development. Evaluates data in reference to project planning, such as flood and drought control, water power and supply, drainage, irrigation, and inland navigation. Investigates origin and activity of glaciers, volcanoes, and earthquakes. Studies, maps, and charts distribution, disposition, and development of waters of land areas, including form and intensity of precipitation. Studies, measures, and interprets seismic, gravitational, electrical, thermal, and magnetic forces and data affecting the earth. **SKILLS—Science:** Using scientific rules and methods to solve problems. **Mathematics:** Using mathematics to solve problems. **Active Learning:** Understanding the implications of new information for both current and future problem-solving and decision-making. **Writing:** Communicating effectively in writing as appropriate for the needs of the audience. **Critical Thinking:** Using logic and reasoning to identify the strengths and weaknesses of alternative solutions, conclusions, or approaches to problems. **Systems Analysis:** Determining how a system should work and how changes in conditions, operations, and the environment will affect outcomes. **Complex Problem Solving:** Identifying complex problems and reviewing related information to develop and evaluate options and implement solutions. **Judgment and Decision Making:** Considering the relative costs and benefits of potential actions to choose the most appropriate one.

GOE—Interest Area: 15. Scientific Research, Engineering, and Mathematics. **Work Group:** 15.02. Physical Sciences. **Other Jobs in This Work Group:** Astronomers; Atmospheric and Space Scientists; Chemists; Geographers; Geologists; Materials Scientists; Physicists. **PERSONALITY TYPE:** Investigative. Investigative occupations frequently involve working with ideas and require an extensive amount of thinking. These occupations can involve searching for facts and figuring out problems mentally.

EDUCATION/TRAINING PROGRAM(S)— Geology/Earth Science, General; Hydrology and Water Resources Science; Oceanography, Chemical and Physical. **RELATED KNOWLEDGE/ COURSES—Physics:** Knowledge and prediction of physical principles and laws and their interrelationships and applications to understanding fluid, material, and atmospheric dynamics and mechanical, electrical, atomic, and subatomic structures and processes. **Geography:** Knowledge of principles and methods for describing the features of land, sea, and air masses, including their physical characteristics; locations; interrelationships; and distribution of plant, animal, and human life. **Mathematics:** Knowledge of arithmetic, algebra, geometry, calculus, and statistics and their applications. **Chemistry:** Knowledge of the chemical composition, structure, and properties of substances and of the chemical processes and transformations that they undergo. This includes uses of chemicals and their danger signs, production techniques, and disposal methods. **History and Archeology:** Knowledge of historical events and their causes, indicators, and effects on civilizations and cultures. **Communications and Media:** Knowledge of media production, communication, and dissemination techniques and methods. This includes alternative ways to inform and entertain via written, oral, and visual media.

Industrial Engineers

- ◎ Education/Training Required: Bachelor's degree
- ◎ Annual Earnings: $64,050
- ◎ Growth: 10.6%
- ◎ Annual Job Openings: 16,000
- ◎ Self-Employed: 1.5%
- ◎ Part-Time: 1.5%

Design, develop, test, and evaluate integrated systems for managing industrial production processes including human work factors, quality control, inventory control, logistics and material flow, cost analysis, and production coordination. Analyze statistical data and product specifications to determine standards and establish quality and reliability objectives of finished product. Develop manufacturing methods, labor utilization standards, and cost analysis systems to promote efficient staff and facility utilization. Recommend methods for improving utilization of personnel, material, and utilities. Plan and establish sequence of operations to fabricate and assemble parts or products and to promote efficient utilization. Apply statistical methods and perform mathematical calculations to determine manufacturing processes, staff requirements, and production standards. Coordinate quality control objectives and activities to resolve production problems, maximize product reliability, and minimize cost. Confer with vendors, staff, and management personnel regarding purchases, procedures, product specifications, manufacturing capabilities, and project status. Draft and design layout of equipment, materials, and workspace to illustrate maximum efficiency, using drafting tools and computer. Review production schedules, engineering specifications, orders, and related information to obtain knowledge of manufacturing methods, procedures, and activities. Communicate with management and user personnel to develop production and design standards. Estimate production cost and effect of product design changes for management review, action, and control. Formulate sampling procedures and designs and develop forms and instructions for recording, evaluating, and reporting quality and reliability data. Record or oversee recording of information to ensure currency of engineering drawings and documentation of production problems. Study operations sequence, material flow, functional statements, organization charts, and project information to determine worker functions and responsibilities. Direct workers engaged in product measurement, inspection, and testing activities to ensure quality control and reliability. Implement methods and procedures for disposition of discrepant material and defective or damaged parts, and assess cost and responsibility. SKILLS—**Equipment Selection:** Determining the kind of tools and equipment needed to do a job. **Negotiation:** Bringing others together and trying to reconcile differences. **Technology Design:** Generating or adapting equipment and technology to serve user needs. **Troubleshooting:** Determining causes of operating errors and deciding what to do about them. **Active Learning:** Understanding the implications of new information for both current and future problem-solving and decision-making. **Persuasion:** Persuading others to change their minds or behavior. **Judgment and Decision Making:** Considering the relative costs and benefits of potential actions to choose the most appropriate one. **Complex Problem Solving:** Identifying complex problems and reviewing related information to develop and evaluate options and implement solutions.

GOE—Interest Area: 15. Scientific Research, Engineering, and Mathematics. **Work Group:** 15.08. Industrial and Safety Engineering. **Other Jobs in This Work Group:** Fire-Prevention and Protection Engineers; Industrial Safety and Health Engineers; Product Safety Engineers. **PERSONALITY TYPE:** Enterprising. Enterprising occupations frequently involve starting up and carrying out projects. These occupations can involve leading people and making many decisions. They sometimes require risk taking and often deal with business.

EDUCATION/TRAINING PROGRAM(S)— Industrial Engineering. **RELATED KNOWLEDGE/COURSES—Engineering and Technology:** Knowledge of the practical application of engineering science and technology. This includes applying principles, techniques, procedures, and equipment to the design and production of various goods and services. **Design:** Knowledge of design techniques, tools, and principles involved in production of precision technical plans, blueprints, drawings, and models. **Production and Processing:** Knowledge of raw materials, production processes, quality control, costs, and other techniques for maximizing the effective manufacture and distribution of goods. **Mathematics:** Knowledge of arithmetic, algebra, geometry, calculus, and statistics and their applications. **Education and Training:** Knowledge of principles and methods for curriculum and training design, teaching and instruction for individuals and groups, and the measurement of training effects. **Mechanical Devices:** Knowledge of machines and tools, including their designs, uses, repair, and maintenance.

Industrial Production Managers

- Education/Training Required: Bachelor's degree
- Annual Earnings: $71,650
- Growth: 7.9%
- Annual Job Openings: 18,000
- Self-Employed: 1.5%
- Part-Time: 1.8%

Plan, direct, or coordinate the work activities and resources necessary for manufacturing products in accordance with cost, quality, and quantity specifications. Direct and coordinate production, processing, distribution, and marketing activities of industrial organization. Develop budgets and approve expenditures for supplies, materials, and human resources, ensuring that materials, labor and equipment are used efficiently to meet production targets. Review processing schedules and production orders to make decisions concerning inventory requirements, staffing requirements, work procedures, and duty assignments, considering budgetary limitations and time constraints. Review operations and confer with technical or administrative staff to resolve production or processing problems. Hire, train, evaluate, and discharge staff, and resolve personnel grievances. Initiate and coordinate inventory and cost control programs. Prepare and maintain production reports and personnel records. Set and monitor product standards, examining samples of raw products or directing testing during processing, to ensure finished products are of prescribed quality. Develop and implement production tracking and quality control systems, analyzing production, quality control, maintenance, and other operational reports, to detect production problems. Review plans and confer with research and support staff to develop new products and processes. Institute employee suggestion or involvement programs. Coordinate and recommend procedures for facility and equipment maintenance or modification, including the replacement of machines. Maintain current knowledge of the quality control field, relying on current literature pertaining to materials use, technological advances, and statistical studies. Negotiate materials prices with suppliers. SKILLS—**Management of Material Resources:** Obtaining and seeing to the appropriate use of equipment, facilities, and materials needed to do certain work. **Persuasion:** Persuading others to change their minds or behavior. **Management of Personnel Resources:** Motivating, developing, and directing people as they work, identifying the best people for the job. **Coordination:** Adjusting actions in relation to others' actions. **Monitoring:** Monitoring or assessing your performance or that of other individuals or organizations to make improvements or take corrective action. **Systems Evaluation:** Identifying measures or indicators of system performance and the actions needed to improve or correct performance relative to the goals of the system. **Time Management:** Managing one's own time and the time of others. **Negotiation:** Bringing others together and trying to reconcile differences.

GOE—**Interest Area:** 13. Manufacturing. **Work Group:** 13.01. Managerial Work in Manufacturing. **Other Jobs in This Work Group:** First-Line Supervisors/Managers of Helpers, Laborers, and Material Movers, Hand; First-Line Supervisors/Managers of Mechanics, Installers, and Repairers; First-Line Supervisors/Managers of Production and Operating Workers. **PERSONALITY TYPE:** Enterprising. Enterprising occupations frequently involve starting up and carrying out projects. These occupations can involve leading people and making many decisions. They sometimes require risk taking and often deal with business.

EDUCATION/TRAINING PROGRAM(S)— Business Administration and Management, General; Business/Commerce, General; Operations Management and Supervision. RELATED KNOWLEDGE/COURSES—**Production and Processing:** Knowledge of raw materials, production processes, quality control, costs, and other techniques for maximizing the effective manufacture

and distribution of goods. **Personnel and Human Resources:** Knowledge of principles and procedures for personnel recruitment, selection, training, compensation and benefits, labor relations and negotiation, and personnel information systems. **Education and Training:** Knowledge of principles and methods for curriculum and training design, teaching and instruction for individuals and groups, and the measurement of training effects. **Administration and Management:** Knowledge of business and management principles involved in strategic planning, resource allocation, human resources modeling, leadership technique, production methods, and coordination of people and resources. **Mechanical Devices:** Knowledge of machines and tools, including their designs, uses, repair, and maintenance. **Engineering and Technology:** Knowledge of the practical application of engineering science and technology. This includes applying principles, techniques, procedures, and equipment to the design and production of various goods and services.

Industrial Safety and Health Engineers

- ◉ Education/Training Required: Bachelor's degree
- ◉ Annual Earnings: $61,430
- ◉ Growth: 7.9%
- ◉ Annual Job Openings: 4,000
- ◉ Self-Employed: 1.6%
- ◉ Part-Time: 1.5%

Plan, implement, and coordinate safety programs, requiring application of engineering principles and technology, to prevent or correct unsafe environmental working conditions. Devises and implements safety or industrial health program to prevent, correct, or control unsafe environmental conditions. Installs or directs installation of safety devices on machinery. Maintains liaison with outside organizations, such as fire departments, mutual aid societies, and rescue teams. Prepares reports of findings from investigation of accidents, inspection of facilities, or testing of environment. Designs and builds safety devices for machinery or safety clothing. Checks floors of plant to ensure they are strong enough to support heavy machinery. Conducts plant or area surveys to determine safety levels for exposure to materials and conditions. Investigates causes of industrial accidents or injuries to develop solutions to minimize or prevent recurrence. Compiles, analyzes, and interprets statistical data related to exposure factors concerning occupational illnesses and accidents. Examines plans and specifications for new machinery or equipment to determine if all safety requirements have been included. Inspects facilities, machinery, and safety equipment to identify and correct potential hazards, and ensure compliance with safety regulations. Conducts or directs testing of air quality, noise, temperature, or radiation to verify compliance with health and safety regulations. Provides technical guidance to organizations regarding how to handle health-related problems, such as water and air pollution. Conducts or coordinates training of workers concerning safety laws and regulations, use of safety equipment, devices, and clothing, and first aid. **SKILLS—Operations Analysis:** Analyzing needs and product requirements to create a design. **Technology Design:** Generating or adapting equipment and technology to serve user needs. **Mathematics:** Using mathematics to solve problems. **Science:** Using scientific rules and methods to solve problems. **Instructing:** Teaching others how to do something. **Systems Evaluation:** Identifying measures or indicators of system performance and the actions needed to improve or correct performance relative to the goals of the system. **Systems Analysis:** Determining how a system should work and how changes in conditions, operations, and the environment will affect outcomes. **Quality Control Analysis:** Conducting tests and inspections of products, services, or processes to evaluate quality or performance.

GOE—Interest Area: 15. Scientific Research, Engineering, and Mathematics. **Work Group:** 15.08. Industrial and Safety Engineering. **Other Jobs in This Work Group:** Fire-Prevention and Protection Engineers; Industrial Engineers; Product Safety Engineers. **PERSONALITY TYPE:** Investigative. Investigative occupations frequently involve working with ideas and require an extensive amount of thinking. These occupations can involve searching for facts and figuring out problems mentally.

EDUCATION/TRAINING PROGRAM(S)— Environmental/Environmental Health Engineering. **RELATED KNOWLEDGE/COURSES—Engineering and Technology:** Knowledge of the practical application of engineering science and technology. This includes applying principles, techniques, procedures, and equipment to the design and production of various goods and services. **Design:** Knowledge of design techniques, tools, and principles involved in production of precision technical plans, blueprints, drawings, and models. **Public Safety and Security:** Knowledge of relevant equipment, policies, procedures, and strategies to promote effective local, state, or national security operations for the protection of people, data, property, and institutions. **Physics:** Knowledge and prediction of physical principles and laws and their interrelationships and applications to understanding fluid, material, and atmospheric dynamics and mechanical, electrical, atomic, and subatomic structures and processes. **Administration and Management:** Knowledge of business and management principles involved in strategic planning, resource allocation, human resources modeling, leadership technique, production methods, and coordination of people and resources. **Chemistry:** Knowledge of the chemical composition, structure, and properties of substances and of the chemical processes and transformations that they undergo. This includes uses of chemicals and their danger signs, production techniques, and disposal methods.

Industrial-Organizational Psychologists

◎ Education/Training Required: Master's degree

◎ Annual Earnings: $67,740

◎ Growth: 16.0%

◎ Annual Job Openings: Fewer than 500

◎ Self-Employed: 26.8%

◎ Part-Time: 27.2%

Apply principles of psychology to personnel, administration, management, sales, and marketing problems. Activities may include policy planning; employee screening, training and development; and organizational development and analysis. May work with management to reorganize the work setting to improve worker productivity. Analyze data, using statistical methods and applications, in order to evaluate the outcomes and effectiveness of workplace programs. Analyze job requirements and content in order to establish criteria for classification, selection, training, and other related personnel functions. Conduct research studies of physical work environments, organizational structures, communication systems, group interactions, morale, and motivation in order to assess organizational functioning. Develop and implement employee selection and placement programs. Develop interview techniques, rating scales, and psychological tests used to assess skills, abilities, and interests for the purpose of employee selection, placement, and promotion. Facilitate organizational development and change. Formulate and implement training programs, applying principles of learning and individual differences. Identify training and development needs. Observe and interview workers in order to obtain information about the physical, mental, and educational requirements of jobs as well as information about aspects such as job satisfaction. Study

organizational effectiveness, productivity, and efficiency, including the nature of workplace supervision and leadership. Advise management concerning personnel, managerial, and marketing policies and practices and their potential effects on organizational effectiveness and efficiency. Assess employee performance. Counsel workers about job and career-related issues. Participate in mediation and dispute resolution. Study consumers' reactions to new products and package designs, and to advertising efforts, using surveys and tests. Write reports on research findings and implications in order to contribute to general knowledge and to suggest potential changes in organizational functioning. **SKILLS—Systems Evaluation:** Identifying measures or indicators of system performance and the actions needed to improve or correct performance relative to the goals of the system. **Management of Personnel Resources:** Motivating, developing, and directing people as they work, identifying the best people for the job. **Science:** Using scientific rules and methods to solve problems. **Systems Analysis:** Determining how a system should work and how changes in conditions, operations, and the environment will affect outcomes. **Complex Problem Solving:** Identifying complex problems and reviewing related information to develop and evaluate options and implement solutions. **Mathematics:** Using mathematics to solve problems. **Active Learning:** Understanding the implications of new information for both current and future problem-solving and decision-making. **Social Perceptiveness:** Being aware of others' reactions and understanding why they react as they do.

GOE—Interest Area: 15. Scientific Research, Engineering, and Mathematics. **Work Group:** 15.04. Social Sciences. **Other Jobs in This Work Group:** Anthropologists; Archeologists; Economists; Educational Psychologists; Historians; Political Scientists; Sociologists. **PERSONALITY TYPE:** Investigative. Investigative occupations frequently involve working with ideas and require an extensive amount of thinking. These occupations can involve searching for facts and figuring out problems mentally.

EDUCATION/TRAINING PROGRAM(S)—Industrial and Organizational Psychology; Psychology, General. **RELATED KNOWLEDGE/COURSES—Personnel and Human Resources:** Knowledge of principles and procedures for personnel recruitment, selection, training, compensation and benefits, labor relations and negotiation, and personnel information systems. **Psychology:** Knowledge of human behavior and performance; individual differences in ability, personality, and interests; learning and motivation; psychological research methods; and the assessment and treatment of behavioral and affective disorders. **Education and Training:** Knowledge of principles and methods for curriculum and training design, teaching and instruction for individuals and groups, and the measurement of training effects. **Administration and Management:** Knowledge of business and management principles involved in strategic planning, resource allocation, human resources modeling, leadership technique, production methods, and coordination of people and resources. **Mathematics:** Knowledge of arithmetic, algebra, geometry, calculus, and statistics and their applications. **Sales and Marketing:** Knowledge of principles and methods for showing, promoting, and selling products or services. This includes marketing strategy and tactics, product demonstration, sales techniques, and sales control systems. **Therapy and Counseling:** Knowledge of principles, methods, and procedures for diagnosis, treatment, and rehabilitation of physical and mental dysfunctions and for career counseling and guidance.

Instructional Coordinators

- Education/Training Required: Master's degree
- Annual Earnings: $47,550
- Growth: 25.4%
- Annual Job Openings: 18,000
- Self-Employed: 2.7%
- Part-Time: 16.5%

Develop instructional material, coordinate educational content, and incorporate current technology in specialized fields that provide guidelines to educators and instructors for developing curricula and conducting courses. Advise teaching and administrative staff in curriculum development, use of materials and equipment, and implementation of state and federal programs and procedures. Research, evaluate, and prepare recommendations on curricula, instructional methods, and materials for school systems. Update the content of educational programs to ensure that students are being trained with equipment and processes that are technologically current. Confer with members of educational committees and advisory groups to obtain knowledge of subject areas, and to relate curriculum materials to specific subjects, individual student needs, and occupational areas. Coordinate activities of workers engaged in cataloging, distributing, and maintaining educational materials and equipment in curriculum libraries and laboratories. Develop classroom-based and distance learning training courses, using needs assessments and skill level analyses. Develop instructional materials to be used by educators and instructors. Develop tests, questionnaires, and procedures that measure the effectiveness of curricula, and use these tools to determine whether program objectives are being met. Organize production and design of curriculum materials. Prepare or approve manuals, guidelines, and reports on state educational policies and practices for distribution to school districts. Recommend, order, or authorize purchase of instructional materials, supplies, equipment, and visual aids designed to meet student educational needs and district standards. Advise and teach students. Conduct or participate in workshops, committees, and conferences designed to promote the intellectual, social, and physical welfare of students. Inspect instructional equipment to determine if repairs are needed; authorize necessary repairs. Observe work of teaching staff in order to evaluate performance, and to recommend changes that could strengthen teaching skills. Plan and conduct teacher training programs and conferences dealing with new classroom procedures, instructional materials and equipment, and teaching aids. Prepare grant proposals, budgets, and program policies and goals, or assist in their preparation. **SKILLS—Learning Strategies:** Selecting and using training/instructional methods and procedures appropriate for the situation when learning or teaching new things. **Instructing:** Teaching others how to do something. **Management of Personnel Resources:** Motivating, developing, and directing people as they work, identifying the best people for the job. **Speaking:** Talking to others to convey information effectively. **Systems Analysis:** Determining how a system should work and how changes in conditions, operations, and the environment will affect outcomes. **Writing:** Communicating effectively in writing as appropriate for the needs of the audience. **Management of Financial Resources:** Determining how money will be spent to get the work done and accounting for these expenditures. **Systems Evaluation:** Identifying measures or indicators of system performance and the actions needed to improve or correct performance relative to the goals of the system.

GOE—Interest Area: 05. Education and Training. **Work Group:** 05.01. Managerial Work in Education. **Other Jobs in This Work Group:** Education Administrators, Elementary and Secondary School; Education Administrators, Postsecondary; Education Administrators, Preschool and Child Care Center/Program. **PERSONALITY TYPE:** Social.

Social occupations frequently involve working with, communicating with, and teaching people. These occupations often involve helping or providing service to others.

EDUCATION/TRAINING PROGRAM(S)— Curriculum and Instruction; Educational/Instructional Media Design. **RELATED KNOWLEDGE/ COURSES—Education and Training:** Knowledge of principles and methods for curriculum and training design, teaching and instruction for individuals and groups, and the measurement of training effects. **Personnel and Human Resources:** Knowledge of principles and procedures for personnel recruitment, selection, training, compensation and benefits, labor relations and negotiation, and personnel information systems. **Psychology:** Knowledge of human behavior and performance; individual differences in ability, personality, and interests; learning and motivation; psychological research methods; and the assessment and treatment of behavioral and affective disorders. **Administration and Management:** Knowledge of business and management principles involved in strategic planning, resource allocation, human resources modeling, leadership technique, production methods, and coordination of people and resources. **English Language:** Knowledge of the structure and content of the English language, including the meaning and spelling of words, rules of composition, and grammar. **Economics and Accounting:** Knowledge of economic and accounting principles and practices, the financial markets, banking, and the analysis and reporting of financial data.

Insurance Sales Agents

◉ Education/Training Required: Bachelor's degree

◉ Annual Earnings: $40,370

◉ Growth: 8.4%

◉ Annual Job Openings: 52,000

◉ Self-Employed: 26.2%

◉ Part-Time: 9.2%

Sell life, property, casualty, health, automotive, or other types of insurance. May refer clients to independent brokers, work as independent broker, or be employed by an insurance company. Call on policyholders to deliver and explain policy, to analyze insurance program and suggest additions or changes, or to change beneficiaries. Calculate premiums and establish payment method. Customize insurance programs to suit individual customers, often covering a variety of risks. Sell various types of insurance policies to businesses and individuals on behalf of insurance companies, including automobile, fire, life, property, medical and dental insurance or specialized policies such as marine, farm/crop, and medical malpractice. Interview prospective clients to obtain data about their financial resources and needs, the physical condition of the person or property to be insured, and to discuss any existing coverage. Seek out new clients and develop clientele by networking to find new customers and generate lists of prospective clients. Explain features, advantages and disadvantages of various policies to promote sale of insurance plans. Contact underwriter and submit forms to obtain binder coverage. Ensure that policy requirements are fulfilled, including any necessary medical examinations and the completion of appropriate forms. Confer with clients to obtain and provide information when claims are made on a policy. Perform administrative tasks, such as maintaining records and handling policy renewals. Select company that offers type of coverage requested by client to underwrite policy. Monitor insurance claims to ensure they are settled equitably for both the client and the insurer. Develop marketing strategies to compete with other individuals or companies who sell insurance. Attend meetings, seminars and programs to learn about new products and services, learn new skills, and receive technical assistance in developing new accounts. Inspect property, examining its general condition, type of construction, age, and other characteristics, to decide if it is a good insurance risk. Install bookkeeping systems and resolve system problems. Plan and oversee incorporation of insurance program into bookkeeping system of company. Explain necessary bookkeeping requirements for customer to implement and provide group insurance program. **SKILLS—Persuasion:** Persuading others to change their minds or behavior. **Time Management:** Managing one's own time and the time of others. **Negotiation:** Bringing others together and trying to reconcile differences. **Service Orientation:** Actively looking for ways to help people. **Social Perceptiveness:** Being aware of others' reactions and understanding why they react as they do. **Judgment and Decision Making:** Considering the relative costs and benefits of potential actions to choose the most appropriate one. **Active Listening:** Giving full attention to what other people are saying, taking time to understand the points being made, asking questions as appropriate, and not interrupting at inappropriate times. **Speaking:** Talking to others to convey information effectively.

GOE—Interest Area: 06. Finance and Insurance. **Work Group:** 06.05. Finance/Insurance Sales and Support. **Other Jobs in This Work Group:** Advertising Sales Agents; Personal Financial Advisors; Sales Agents, Financial Services; Sales Agents, Securities and Commodities. **PERSONALITY TYPE:** Enterprising. Enterprising occupations frequently involve starting up and carrying out projects. These occupations can involve leading people and making many decisions. They sometimes require risk taking and often deal with business.

EDUCATION/TRAINING PROGRAM(S)— Insurance. **RELATED KNOWLEDGE/COURSES—Sales and Marketing:** Knowledge of principles and methods for showing, promoting, and selling products or services. This includes marketing strategy and tactics, product demonstration, sales techniques, and sales control systems. **Customer and Personal Service:** Knowledge of principles and processes for providing customer and personal services. This includes customer needs assessment, meeting quality standards for services, and evaluation of customer satisfaction. **Economics and Accounting:** Knowledge of economic and accounting principles and practices, the financial markets, banking, and the analysis and reporting of financial data. **Computers and Electronics:** Knowledge of circuit boards, processors, chips, electronic equipment, and computer hardware and software, including applications and programming. **Clerical Practices:** Knowledge of administrative and clerical procedures and systems such as word processing, managing files and records, stenography and transcription, designing forms, and other office procedures and terminology. **Mathematics:** Knowledge of arithmetic, algebra, geometry, calculus, and statistics and their applications. **Law and Government:** Knowledge of laws, legal codes, court procedures, precedents, government regulations, executive orders, agency rules, and the democratic political process.

Insurance Underwriters

- ◎ Education/Training Required: Bachelor's degree
- ◎ Annual Earnings: $48,370
- ◎ Growth: 10.0%
- ◎ Annual Job Openings: 12,000
- ◎ Self-Employed: 1.0%
- ◎ Part-Time: 4.5%

Review individual applications for insurance to evaluate degree of risk involved and determine acceptance of applications. Examine documents to determine degree of risk from such factors as applicant financial standing and value and condition of property. Decline excessive risks. Write to field representatives, medical personnel, and others to obtain further information, quote rates, or explain company underwriting policies. Evaluate possibility of losses due to catastrophe or excessive insurance. Decrease value of policy when risk is substandard and specify applicable endorsements or apply rating to ensure safe profitable distribution of risks, using reference materials. Review company records to determine amount of insurance in force on single risk or group of closely related risks. Authorize reinsurance of policy when risk is high. **SKILLS—Service Orientation:** Actively looking for ways to help people. **Writing:** Communicating effectively in writing as appropriate for the needs of the audience. **Active Learning:** Understanding the implications of new information for both current and future problem-solving and decision-making. **Learning Strategies:** Selecting and using training/instructional methods and procedures appropriate for the situation when learning or teaching new things. **Persuasion:** Persuading others to change their minds or behavior. **Active Listening:** Giving full attention to what other people are saying, taking time to understand the points being made, asking questions as appropriate, and not interrupting at inappropriate times. **Monitoring:** Monitoring or assessing your performance or that of other individuals or organizations to make improvements or take corrective action. **Negotiation:** Bringing others together and trying to reconcile differences.

GOE—Interest Area: 06. Finance and Insurance. **Work Group:** 06.02. Finance/Insurance Investigation and Analysis. **Other Jobs in This Work Group:** Appraisers, Real Estate; Assessors; Claims Examiners, Property and Casualty Insurance; Cost Estimators; Credit Analysts; Financial Analysts; Insurance Adjusters, Examiners, and Investigators; Insurance Appraisers, Auto Damage; Loan Counselors; Loan Officers; Market Research Analysts; Survey Researchers. **PERSONALITY TYPE:** Conventional. Conventional occupations frequently involve following set procedures and routines. These occupations can include working with data and details more than with ideas. Usually there is a clear line of authority to follow.

EDUCATION/TRAINING PROGRAM(S)— Insurance. RELATED KNOWLEDGE/COURSES—Customer and Personal Service: Knowledge of principles and processes for providing customer and personal services. This includes customer needs assessment, meeting quality standards for services, and evaluation of customer satisfaction. Clerical Practices: Knowledge of administrative and clerical procedures and systems such as word processing, managing files and records, stenography and transcription, designing forms, and other office procedures and terminology. Sales and Marketing: Knowledge of principles and methods for showing, promoting, and selling products or services. This includes marketing strategy and tactics, product demonstration, sales techniques, and sales control systems. Economics and Accounting: Knowledge of economic and accounting principles and practices, the financial markets, banking, and the analysis and reporting of financial data. Computers and Electronics: Knowledge of circuit boards, processors, chips, electronic equipment, and computer hardware and software, including applications and programming. Law and Government: Knowledge of laws, legal codes, court procedures, precedents, government regulations, executive orders, agency rules, and the democratic political process.

Interior Designers

- ⊚ Education/Training Required: Bachelor's degree
- ⊚ Annual Earnings: $40,420
- ⊚ Growth: 21.7%
- ⊚ Annual Job Openings: 8,000
- ⊚ Self-Employed: 32.2%
- ⊚ Part-Time: 16.5%

Plan, design, and furnish interiors of residential, commercial, or industrial buildings. Formulate design which is practical, aesthetic, and conducive to intended purposes, such as raising productivity, selling merchandise, or improving life style. May specialize in a particular field, style, or phase of interior design. Estimate material requirements and costs, and present design to client for approval. Confer with client to determine factors affecting planning interior environments, such as budget, architectural preferences, and purpose and function. Advise client on interior design factors, such as space planning, layout and utilization of furnishings and equipment, and color coordination. Select or design, and purchase furnishings, art works, and accessories. Formulate environmental plan to be practical, esthetic, and conducive to intended purposes, such as raising productivity or selling merchandise. Subcontract fabrication, installation, and arrangement of carpeting, fixtures, accessories, draperies, paint and wall coverings, art work, furniture, and related items. Render design ideas in form of paste-ups or drawings. SKILLS—Installation: Installing equipment, machines, wiring, or programs to meet specifications. Persuasion: Persuading others to change their minds or behavior. Management of Financial Resources: Determining how money will be spent to get the work done and accounting for these expenditures. Active Learning: Understanding the implications of new information for both current and future problem-solving and decision-making. Negotiation: Bringing others together and trying to reconcile differences. Speaking: Talking to others to convey information effectively. Troubleshooting: Determining causes of operating errors and deciding what to do about them. Critical Thinking: Using logic and reasoning to identify the strengths and weaknesses of alternative solutions, conclusions, or approaches to problems.

GOE—Interest Area: 03. Arts and Communication. Work Group: 03.05. Design. Other Jobs in This Work Group: Commercial and Industrial Designers; Exhibit Designers; Fashion Designers; Floral Designers; Graphic Designers; Merchandise

Displayers and Window Trimmers; Set Designers. **PERSONALITY TYPE:** Artistic. Artistic occupations frequently involve working with forms, designs, and patterns. They often require self-expression, and the work can be done without following a clear set of rules.

EDUCATION/TRAINING PROGRAM(S)— Facilities Planning and Management; Interior Architecture; Interior Design; Textile Science. **RELATED KNOWLEDGE/COURSES— Design:** Knowledge of design techniques, tools, and principles involved in production of precision technical plans, blueprints, drawings, and models. **Sales and Marketing:** Knowledge of principles and methods for showing, promoting, and selling products or services. This includes marketing strategy and tactics, product demonstration, sales techniques, and sales control systems. **Customer and Personal Service:** Knowledge of principles and processes for providing customer and personal services. This includes customer needs assessment, meeting quality standards for services, and evaluation of customer satisfaction. **Administration and Management:** Knowledge of business and management principles involved in strategic planning, resource allocation, human resources modeling, leadership technique, production methods, and coordination of people and resources. **Clerical Practices:** Knowledge of administrative and clerical procedures and systems such as word processing, managing files and records, stenography and transcription, designing forms, and other office procedures and terminology. **Building and Construction:** Knowledge of the materials, methods, and tools involved in the construction or repair of houses, buildings, or other structures such as highways and roads.

Internists, General

- Education/Training Required: First professional degree
- Annual Earnings: More than $145,000
- Growth: 19.5%
- Annual Job Openings: 38,000
- Self-Employed: 16.9%
- Part-Time: 8.1%

Diagnose and provide non-surgical treatment of diseases and injuries of internal organ systems. Provide care mainly for adults who have a wide range of problems associated with the internal organs. Provide consulting services to other doctors caring for patients with special or difficult problems. Plan, implement, or administer health programs in hospitals, businesses, or communities for prevention and treatment of injuries or illnesses. Prepare government or organizational reports on birth, death, and disease statistics, workforce evaluations, or the medical status of individuals. Advise patients and community members concerning diet, activity, hygiene, and disease prevention. Analyze records, reports, test results, or examination information to diagnose medical condition of patient. Collect, record, and maintain patient information, such as medical history, reports, and examination results. Make diagnoses when different illnesses occur together or in situations where the diagnosis may be obscure. Explain procedures and discuss test results or prescribed treatments with patients. Immunize patients to protect them from preventable diseases. Manage and treat common health problems, such as infections, influenza and pneumonia, as well as serious, chronic, and complex illnesses, in adolescents, adults, and the elderly. Monitor patients' conditions and progress and re-evaluate treatments as necessary. Prescribe or administer medication, therapy, and other specialized medical care to treat or prevent illness, disease, or injury. Provide and manage long-term, comprehensive medical care, including diagnosis and non-surgical treatment of diseases, for adult patients in an office or hospital. Refer patient to medical specialist or other practitioner when necessary. Treat internal disorders, such as hypertension, heart disease, diabetes, and problems of the lung, brain, kidney, and gastrointestinal tract. Advise surgeon of a patient's risk status and recommend appropriate intervention to minimize risk. Conduct research to develop or test medications, treatments, or procedures to prevent or control disease or injury. Direct and coordinate activities of nurses, students, assistants, specialists, therapists, and other medical staff. Operate on patients to remove, repair, or improve functioning of diseased or injured body parts and systems. **SKILLS—Science:** Using scientific rules and methods to solve problems. **Reading Comprehension:** Understanding written sentences and paragraphs in work-related documents. **Systems Evaluation:** Identifying measures or indicators of system performance and the actions needed to improve or correct performance relative to the goals of the system. **Active Learning:** Understanding the implications of new information for both current and future problem-solving and decision-making. **Judgment and Decision Making:** Considering the relative costs and benefits of potential actions to choose the most appropriate one. **Management of Personnel Resources:** Motivating, developing, and directing people as they work, identifying the best people for the job. **Social Perceptiveness:** Being aware of others' reactions and understanding why they react as they do. **Systems Analysis:** Determining how a system should work and how changes in conditions, operations, and the environment will affect outcomes.

GOE—Interest Area: 08. Health Science. **Work Group:** 08.02. Medicine and Surgery. **Other Jobs in This Work Group:** Anesthesiologists; Family and General Practitioners; Medical Assistants; Medical Transcriptionists; Obstetricians and Gynecologists; Pediatricians, General; Pharmacists; Pharmacy Aides; Pharmacy Technicians; Physician Assistants; Psychiatrists; Registered Nurses; Surgeons; Surgical Technologists. **PERSONALITY TYPE:** Investiga-tive. Investigative occupations frequently involve working with ideas and require an extensive amount of thinking. These occupations can involve searching for facts and figuring out problems mentally.

EDUCATION/TRAINING PROGRAM(S)— Cardiology; Critical Care Medicine; Endocrinology and Metabolism; Gastroenterology; Geriatric Medicine; Hematology; Infectious Disease; Internal Medicine; Nephrology; Neurology; Nuclear Medicine; Oncology; Pulmonary Disease; Rheumatology. **RELATED KNOWLEDGE/COURSES— Medicine and Dentistry:** Knowledge of the information and techniques needed to diagnose and treat human injuries, diseases, and deformities. This includes symptoms, treatment alternatives, drug properties and interactions, and preventive health-care measures. **Biology:** Knowledge of plant and animal organisms and their tissues, cells, functions, interdependencies, and interactions with each other and the environment. **Therapy and Counseling:** Knowledge of principles, methods, and procedures for diagnosis, treatment, and rehabilitation of physical and mental dysfunctions and for career counseling and guidance. **Chemistry:** Knowledge of the chemical composition, structure, and properties of substances and of the chemical processes and transformations that they undergo. This includes uses of chemicals and their danger signs, production techniques, and disposal methods. **Administration and Management:** Knowledge of business and management principles involved in strategic planning, resource allocation, human resources modeling, leadership technique, production methods, and coordination of people and resources. **Personnel and Human Resources:** Knowledge of principles and procedures for personnel recruitment, selection, training, compensation and benefits, labor relations and negotiation, and personnel information systems. **Physics:** Knowledge and prediction of physical principles and laws and their interrelationships and applications to understanding fluid, material, and atmospheric dynamics and mechanical, electrical, atomic, and subatomic structures and processes.

Judges, Magistrate Judges, and Magistrates

- Education/Training Required: Work experience plus degree
- Annual Earnings: $91,230
- Growth: 8.7%
- Annual Job Openings: 2,000
- Self-Employed: 0%
- Part-Time: 6.2%

Arbitrate, advise, adjudicate, or administer justice in a court of law. May sentence defendant in criminal cases according to government statutes. May determine liability of defendant in civil cases. May issue marriage licenses and perform wedding ceremonies. Advise attorneys, juries, litigants, and court personnel regarding conduct, issues, and proceedings. Award compensation for damages to litigants in civil cases in relation to findings by juries or by the court. Conduct preliminary hearings to decide issues such as whether there is reasonable and probable cause to hold defendants in felony cases. Grant divorces and divide assets between spouses. Impose restrictions upon parties in civil cases until trials can be held. Instruct juries on applicable laws, direct juries to deduce the facts from the evidence presented, and hear their verdicts. Interpret and enforce rules of procedure or establish new rules in situations where there are no procedures already established by law. Monitor proceedings to ensure that all applicable rules and procedures are followed. Preside over hearings and listen to allegations made by plaintiffs to determine whether the evidence supports the charges. Read documents on pleadings and motions to ascertain facts and issues. Research legal issues and write opinions on the issues. Rule on admissibility of evidence and methods of conducting testimony. Rule on custody and access disputes, and enforce court orders regarding custody and support of children. Sentence defendants in criminal cases, on conviction by jury, according to applicable government statutes. Settle disputes between opposing attorneys. Write decisions on cases. Participate in judicial tribunals to help resolve disputes. Perform wedding ceremonies. Supervise other judges, court officers, and the court's administrative staff. **SKILLS—Judgment and Decision Making:** Considering the relative costs and benefits of potential actions to choose the most appropriate one. **Active Listening:** Giving full attention to what other people are saying, taking time to understand the points being made, asking questions as appropriate, and not interrupting at inappropriate times. **Critical Thinking:** Using logic and reasoning to identify the strengths and weaknesses of alternative solutions, conclusions, or approaches to problems. **Reading Comprehension:** Understanding written sentences and paragraphs in work-related documents. **Active Learning:** Understanding the implications of new information for both current and future problem-solving and decision-making. **Systems Analysis:** Determining how a system should work and how changes in conditions, operations, and the environment will affect outcomes. **Writing:** Communicating effectively in writing as appropriate for the needs of the audience. **Speaking:** Talking to others to convey information effectively. **Negotiation:** Bringing others together and trying to reconcile differences.

GOE—Interest Area: 12. Law and Public Safety. **Work Group:** 12.02. Legal Practice and Justice Administration. **Other Jobs in This Work Group:** Administrative Law Judges, Adjudicators, and Hearing Officers; Arbitrators, Mediators, and Conciliators; Lawyers. **PERSONALITY TYPE:** Enterprising. Enterprising occupations frequently involve starting up and carrying out projects. These occupations can involve leading people and making many decisions. They sometimes require risk taking and often deal with business.

EDUCATION/TRAINING PROGRAM(S)— Law (LL.B., J.D.); Legal Professions and Studies, Other. **RELATED KNOWLEDGE/COURSES— Law and Government:** Knowledge of laws, legal codes, court procedures, precedents, government regulations, executive orders, agency rules, and the democratic political process. **Sociology and Anthropology:** Knowledge of group behavior and dynamics, societal trends and influences, human migrations, ethnicity, and cultures and their history and origins. **Philosophy and Theology:** Knowledge of different philosophical systems and religions. This includes their basic principles, values, ethics, ways of thinking, customs, and practices and their impact on human culture. **Public Safety and Security:** Knowledge of relevant equipment, policies, procedures, and strategies to promote effective local, state, or national security operations for the protection of people, data, property, and institutions. **English Language:** Knowledge of the structure and content of the English language, including the meaning and spelling of words, rules of composition, and grammar. **History and Archeology:** Knowledge of historical events and their causes, indicators, and effects on civilizations and cultures.

Kindergarten Teachers, Except Special Education

- ☺ Education/Training Required: Bachelor's degree
- ☺ Annual Earnings: $40,980
- ☺ Growth: 27.2%
- ☺ Annual Job Openings: 34,000
- ☺ Self-Employed: 2.2%
- ☺ Part-Time: 24.9%

Teach elemental natural and social science, personal hygiene, music, art, and literature to children from 4 to 6 years old. Promote physical, mental, and social development. May be required to hold State certification. Identify children showing signs of emotional, developmental, or health-related problems, and discuss them with supervisors, parents or guardians, and child development specialists. Instruct and monitor students in the use and care of equipment and materials, in order to prevent injuries and damage. Maintain accurate and complete student records, and prepare reports on children and activities, as required by laws, district policies, and administrative regulations. Meet with other professionals to discuss individual students' needs and progress. Meet with parents and guardians to discuss their children's progress, and to determine their priorities for their children and their resource needs. Organize and label materials and display children's work in a manner appropriate for their sizes and perceptual skills. Organize and lead activities designed to promote physical, mental, and social development such as games, arts and crafts, music, and storytelling. Plan and conduct activities for a balanced program of instruction, demonstration, and work time that provides students with opportunities to observe, question, and investigate. Plan and supervise class projects, field trips, visits by guests, or other experiential activities, and guide students in learning from those activities. Prepare and implement remedial programs for students requiring extra help. Prepare children for later grades by encouraging them to explore learning opportunities and to persevere with challenging tasks. Instruct students individually and in groups, adapting teaching methods to meet students' varying needs and interests. Observe and evaluate children's performance, behavior, social development, and physical health. Teach basic skills such as color, shape, number and letter recognition, personal hygiene, and social skills. Demonstrate activities to children. Assimilate arriving children to the school environment by greeting them, helping them remove outerwear, and selecting activities of interest to them. Confer with other staff members to plan and schedule lessons promoting learning, following approved curricula. **SKILLS—Learning Strategies:** Selecting and using training/instructional methods and procedures appropriate for the situation when learning or teaching new things. **Service Orientation:** Actively

K

looking for ways to help people. **Social Perceptiveness:** Being aware of others' reactions and understanding why they react as they do. **Monitoring:** Monitoring or assessing your performance or that of other individuals or organizations to make improvements or take corrective action. **Instructing:** Teaching others how to do something. **Speaking:** Talking to others to convey information effectively. **Management of Personnel Resources:** Motivating, developing, and directing people as they work, identifying the best people for the job. **Active Listening:** Giving full attention to what other people are saying, taking time to understand the points being made, asking questions as appropriate, and not interrupting at inappropriate times.

GOE—Interest Area: 05. Education and Training. **Work Group:** 05.02. Pre-school, Elementary, and Secondary Teaching and Instructing. **Other Jobs in This Work Group:** Elementary School Teachers, Except Special Education; Middle School Teachers, Except Special and Vocational Education; Preschool Teachers, Except Special Education; Secondary School Teachers, Except Special and Vocational Education; Special Education Teachers, Middle School; Special Education Teachers, Preschool, Kindergarten, and Elementary School; Special Education Teachers, Secondary School; Teacher Assistants; Vocational Education Teachers, Middle School; Vocational Education Teachers, Secondary School. **PERSONALITY TYPE:** Social. Social occupations frequently involve working with, communicating with, and teaching people. These occupations often involve helping or providing service to others.

EDUCATION/TRAINING PROGRAM(S)— Early Childhood Education and Teaching; Kindergarten/Preschool Education and Teaching. **RELATED KNOWLEDGE/COURSES—Education and Training:** Knowledge of principles and methods for curriculum and training design, teaching and instruction for individuals and groups, and the measurement of training effects. **Sociology and Anthropology:** Knowledge of group behavior and dynamics, societal trends and influences, human migrations, ethnicity, and cultures and their history and origins. **Psychology:** Knowledge of human behavior and performance; individual differences in ability, personality, and interests; learning and motivation; psychological research methods; and the assessment and treatment of behavioral and affective disorders. **Customer and Personal Service:** Knowledge of principles and processes for providing customer and personal services. This includes customer needs assessment, meeting quality standards for services, and evaluation of customer satisfaction. **Therapy and Counseling:** Knowledge of principles, methods, and procedures for diagnosis, treatment, and rehabilitation of physical and mental dysfunctions and for career counseling and guidance. **History and Archeology:** Knowledge of historical events and their causes, indicators, and effects on civilizations and cultures.

Landscape Architects

- Education/Training Required: Bachelor's degree
- Annual Earnings: $50,780
- Growth: 22.2%
- Annual Job Openings: 2,000
- Self-Employed: 23.4%
- Part-Time: 5.5%

Plan and design land areas for such projects as parks and other recreational facilities, airports, highways, hospitals, schools, land subdivisions, and commercial, industrial, and residential sites. Prepare site plans, specifications, and cost estimates for land development, coordinating arrangement of existing and proposed land features and structures. Confer with clients, engineering personnel, and architects on overall program. Compile and analyze data on conditions, such as location, drainage, and location of structures for environmental reports and landscaping plans. Inspect landscape work to ensure compliance with specifications, approve quality of materials and work, and advise client and construction personnel. **SKILLS—Coordination:** Adjusting actions in relation to others' actions. **Operations Analysis:** Analyzing needs and product requirements to create a design. **Management of Financial Resources:** Determining how money will be spent to get the work done and accounting for these expenditures. **Persuasion:** Persuading others to change their minds or behavior. **Social Perceptiveness:** Being aware of others' reactions and understanding why they react as they do. **Time Management:** Managing one's own time and the time of others. **Instructing:** Teaching others how to do something. **Complex Problem Solving:** Identifying complex problems and reviewing related information to develop and evaluate options and implement solutions.

GOE—Interest Area: 02. Architecture and Construction. **Work Group:** 02.02. Architectural Design. **Other Jobs in This Work Group:** Architects, Except Landscape and Naval. **PERSONALITY TYPE:** Artistic. Artistic occupations frequently involve working with forms, designs, and patterns. They often require self-expression, and the work can be done without following a clear set of rules.

EDUCATION/TRAINING PROGRAM(S)— Environmental Design/Architecture; Landscape Architecture (BS, BSLA, BLA, MSLA, MLA, PhD). **RELATED KNOWLEDGE/COURSES—Design:** Knowledge of design techniques, tools, and principles involved in production of precision technical plans, blueprints, drawings, and models. **Building and Construction:** Knowledge of the materials, methods, and tools involved in the construction or repair of houses, buildings, or other structures such as highways and roads. **Geography:** Knowledge of principles and methods for describing the features of land, sea, and air masses, including their physical characteristics; locations; interrelationships; and distribution of plant, animal, and human life. **Engineering and Technology:** Knowledge of the practical application of engineering science and technology. This includes applying

principles, techniques, procedures, and equipment to the design and production of various goods and services. **Biology:** Knowledge of plant and animal organisms and their tissues, cells, functions, interdependencies, and interactions with each other and the environment. **Sales and Marketing:** Knowledge of principles and methods for showing, promoting, and selling products or services. This includes marketing strategy and tactics, product demonstration, sales techniques, and sales control systems.

Law Teachers, Postsecondary

- Education/Training Required: First professional degree
- Annual Earnings: $86,360
- Growth: 38.1% for all Postsecondary Teachers
- Annual Job Openings: 216,000 for all Postsecondary Teachers
- Self-Employed: 0.3% for all Postsecondary Teachers
- Part-Time: 27.7% for all Postsecondary Teachers

Teach courses in law. Evaluate and grade students' class work, assignments, papers, and oral presentations. Prepare and deliver lectures to undergraduate and/or graduate students on topics such as civil procedure, contracts, and torts. Advise students on academic and vocational curricula, and on career issues. Assign cases for students to hear and try. Compile, administer, and grade examinations, or assign this work to others. Compile bibliographies of specialized materials for outside reading assignments. Initiate, facilitate, and moderate classroom discussions. Keep abreast of developments in their field by reading current literature, talking with colleagues, and participating in professional conferences. Maintain regularly scheduled office hours in order to advise and assist students. Maintain student attendance records, grades, and other required records. Plan, evaluate, and revise curricula, course content, and course materials and methods of instruction. Prepare course materials such as syllabi, homework assignments, and handouts. Conduct research in a particular field of knowledge, and publish findings in professional journals, books, and/or electronic media. Participate in campus and community events. Participate in student recruitment, registration, and placement activities. Perform administrative duties such as serving as department head. Provide professional consulting services to government and/or industry. Serve on academic or administrative committees that deal with institutional policies, departmental matters, and academic issues. Write grant proposals to procure external research funding. Select and obtain materials and supplies such as textbooks. Supervise undergraduate and/or graduate teaching, internship, and research work. Act as advisers to student organizations. Collaborate with colleagues to address teaching and research issues. **SKILLS**—No data available.

GOE—Interest Area: 05. Education and Training. **Work Group:** 05.03. Postsecondary and Adult Teaching and Instructing. **Other Jobs in This Work Group:** Adult Literacy, Remedial Education, and GED Teachers and Instructors; Agricultural Sciences Teachers, Postsecondary; Anthropology and Archeology Teachers, Postsecondary; Architecture Teachers, Postsecondary; Area, Ethnic, and Cultural Studies Teachers, Postsecondary; Art, Drama, and Music Teachers, Postsecondary; Atmospheric, Earth, Marine, and Space Sciences Teachers, Postsecondary; Biological Science Teachers, Postsecondary; Business Teachers, Postsecondary; Chemistry Teachers, Postsecondary; Communications Teachers, Postsecondary; Computer Science Teachers, Postsecondary; Criminal Justice and Law Enforcement Teachers, Postsecondary; Economics Teachers, Postsecondary; Education Teachers, Postsecondary; Engineering Teachers, Postsecondary; English Language and Literature Teachers, Postsec-

ondary; Environmental Science Teachers, Postsecondary; Farm and Home Management Advisors; Foreign Language and Literature Teachers, Postsecondary; Forestry and Conservation Science Teachers, Postsecondary; Geography Teachers, Postsecondary; Graduate Teaching Assistants; Health Specialties Teachers, Postsecondary; History Teachers, Postsecondary; Home Economics Teachers, Postsecondary; Library Science Teachers, Postsecondary; Mathematical Science Teachers, Postsecondary; Nursing Instructors and Teachers, Postsecondary; Philosophy and Religion Teachers, Postsecondary; Physics Teachers, Postsecondary; Political Science Teachers, Postsecondary; Psychology Teachers, Postsecondary; Recreation and Fitness Studies Teachers, Postsecondary; Self-Enrichment Education Teachers; Social Work Teachers, Postsecondary; Sociology Teachers, Postsecondary; Vocational Education Teachers, Postsecondary. **PERSONALITY TYPE:** No data available.

EDUCATION/TRAINING PROGRAM(S)— Law (LL.B., J.D.); Legal Studies, General. **RELATED KNOWLEDGE/COURSES—**No data available.

Lawyers

- Education/Training Required: First professional degree
- Annual Earnings: $92,730
- Growth: 17.0%
- Annual Job Openings: 53,000
- Self-Employed: 26.8%
- Part-Time: 6.2%

Represent clients in criminal and civil litigation and other legal proceedings, draw up legal documents, and manage or advise clients on legal transactions. May specialize in a single area or may practice broadly in many areas of law. Advise clients concerning business transactions, claim liability, advisability of prosecuting or defending lawsuits, or legal rights and obligations. Interpret laws, rulings and regulations for individuals and businesses. Analyze the probable outcomes of cases, using knowledge of legal precedents. Present and summarize cases to judges and juries. Evaluate findings and develop strategies and arguments in preparation for presentation of cases. Gather evidence to formulate defense or to initiate legal actions, by such means as interviewing clients and witnesses to ascertain the facts of a case. Represent clients in court or before government agencies. Examine legal data to determine advisability of defending or prosecuting lawsuit. Select jurors, argue motions, meet with judges and question witnesses during the course of a trial. Present evidence to defend clients or prosecute defendants in criminal or civil litigation. Study Constitution, statutes, decisions, regulations, and ordinances of quasi-judicial bodies to determine ramifications for cases. Prepare and draft legal documents, such as wills, deeds, patent applications, mortgages, leases, and contracts. Prepare legal briefs and opinions, and file appeals in state and federal courts of appeal. Negotiate settlements of civil disputes. Confer with colleagues with specialties in appropriate areas of legal issue to establish and verify bases for legal proceedings. Search for and examine public and other legal records to write opinions or establish ownership. Supervise legal assistants. Perform administrative and management functions related to the practice of law. Act as agent, trustee, guardian, or executor for businesses or individuals. Probate wills and represent and advise executors and administrators of estates. Help develop federal and state programs, draft and interpret laws and legislation, and establish enforcement procedures. Work in environmental law, representing public interest groups, waste disposal companies, or construction firms in their dealings with state and federal agencies. **SKILLS—Persuasion:** Persuading others to change their minds or behavior. **Negotiation:** Bringing others together and trying to reconcile differences. **Critical Thinking:** Using logic and reasoning to identify the strengths and weaknesses of alterna-

tive solutions, conclusions, or approaches to problems. **Active Learning:** Understanding the implications of new information for both current and future problem-solving and decision-making. **Social Perceptiveness:** Being aware of others' reactions and understanding why they react as they do. **Writing:** Communicating effectively in writing as appropriate for the needs of the audience. **Judgment and Decision Making:** Considering the relative costs and benefits of potential actions to choose the most appropriate one. **Time Management:** Managing one's own time and the time of others.

GOE—Interest Area: 12. Law and Public Safety. **Work Group:** 12.02. Legal Practice and Justice Administration. **Other Jobs in This Work Group:** Administrative Law Judges, Adjudicators, and Hearing Officers; Arbitrators, Mediators, and Conciliators; Judges, Magistrate Judges, and Magistrates. **PERSONALITY TYPE:** Enterprising. Enterprising occupations frequently involve starting up and carrying out projects. These occupations can involve leading people and making many decisions. They sometimes require risk taking and often deal with business.

EDUCATION/TRAINING PROGRAM(S)— Advanced Legal Research/Studies, General (LL.M., M.C.L., M.L.I., M.S.L., J.S.D./S.J.D.); American/U.S. Law/Legal Studies/Jurisprudence (LL.M., M.C.J., J.S.D./S.J.D.); Banking, Corporate, Finance, and Securities Law (LL.M., J.S.D./ S.J.D.); Canadian Law/Legal Studies/Jurisprudence (LL.M., M.C.J., J.S.D./S.J.D.); Comparative Law (LL.M., M.C.L., J.S.D./S.J.D.); Energy, Environment, and Natural Resources Law (LL.M., M.S., J.S.D./S.J.D.); Health Law (LL.M., M.J., J.S.D./S.J.D.); International Business, Trade, and Tax Law (LL.M., J.S.D./S.J.D.); International Law and Legal Studies (LL.M., J.S.D./S.J.D.); Law (LL.B., J.D.); Legal Professions and Studies, Other; Legal Research and Advanced Professional Studies, Other; Programs for Foreign Lawyers (LL.M., M.C.L.); Tax Law/Taxation (LL.M, J.S.D./S.J.D.). **RELATED KNOWLEDGE/COURSES—Law**

and Government: Knowledge of laws, legal codes, court procedures, precedents, government regulations, executive orders, agency rules, and the democratic political process. **English Language:** Knowledge of the structure and content of the English language, including the meaning and spelling of words, rules of composition, and grammar. **Customer and Personal Service:** Knowledge of principles and processes for providing customer and personal services. This includes customer needs assessment, meeting quality standards for services, and evaluation of customer satisfaction. **Personnel and Human Resources:** Knowledge of principles and procedures for personnel recruitment, selection, training, compensation and benefits, labor relations and negotiation, and personnel information systems. **Administration and Management:** Knowledge of business and management principles involved in strategic planning, resource allocation, human resources modeling, leadership technique, production methods, and coordination of people and resources. **Psychology:** Knowledge of human behavior and performance; individual differences in ability, personality, and interests; learning and motivation; psychological research methods; and the assessment and treatment of behavioral and affective disorders.

Librarians

- Education/Training Required: Master's degree
- Annual Earnings: $44,730
- Growth: 10.1%
- Annual Job Openings: 15,000
- Self-Employed: 0.1%
- Part-Time: 23.1%

Administer libraries and perform related library services. Work in a variety of settings, including public libraries, schools, colleges and universities,

museums, corporations, government agencies, law firms, non-profit organizations, and health-care providers. Tasks may include selecting, acquiring, cataloguing, classifying, circulating, and maintaining library materials; and furnishing reference, bibliographical, and readers' advisory services. May perform in-depth, strategic research, and synthesize, analyze, edit, and filter information. May set up or work with databases and information systems to catalogue and access information. Search standard reference materials, including on-line sources and the Internet, in order to answer patrons' reference questions. Analyze patrons' requests to determine needed information, and assist in furnishing or locating that information. Teach library patrons to search for information using databases. Keep records of circulation and materials. Supervise budgeting, planning, and personnel activities. Check books in and out of the library. Explain use of library facilities, resources, equipment, and services, and provide information about library policies. Review and evaluate resource material, such as book reviews and catalogs, in order to select and order print, audiovisual, and electronic resources. Code, classify, and catalog books, publications, films, audiovisual aids, and other library materials based on subject matter or standard library classification systems. Locate unusual or unique information in response to specific requests. Direct and train library staff in duties such as receiving, shelving, researching, cataloging, and equipment use. Respond to customer complaints, taking action as necessary. Organize collections of books, publications, documents, audiovisual aids, and other reference materials for convenient access. Develop library policies and procedures. Evaluate materials to determine outdated or unused items to be discarded. Develop information access aids such as indexes and annotated bibliographies, web pages, electronic pathfinders, and on-line tutorials. Plan and deliver client-centered programs and services such as special services for corporate clients, storytelling for children, newsletters, or programs for special groups. Compile lists of books, periodicals, articles, and audiovisual materials on particular subjects. Arrange for interlibrary loans of materials not available in a particular library. Assemble and arrange display materials. Confer with teachers, parents, and community organizations to develop, plan, and conduct programs in reading, viewing, and communication skills. Compile lists of overdue materials, and notify borrowers that their materials are overdue. **SKILLS—Management of Financial Resources:** Determining how money will be spent to get the work done and accounting for these expenditures. **Learning Strategies:** Selecting and using training/instructional methods and procedures appropriate for the situation when learning or teaching new things. **Service Orientation:** Actively looking for ways to help people. **Instructing:** Teaching others how to do something. **Persuasion:** Persuading others to change their minds or behavior. **Management of Material Resources:** Obtaining and seeing to the appropriate use of equipment, facilities, and materials needed to do certain work. **Monitoring:** Monitoring or assessing your performance or that of other individuals or organizations to make improvements or take corrective action. **Social Perceptiveness:** Being aware of others' reactions and understanding why they react as they do.

GOE—**Interest Area:** 05. Education and Training. **Work Group:** 05.04. Library Services. **Other Jobs in This Work Group:** Library Assistants, Clerical; Library Technicians. **PERSONALITY TYPE:** Artistic. Artistic occupations frequently involve working with forms, designs, and patterns. They often require self-expression, and the work can be done without following a clear set of rules.

EDUCATION/TRAINING PROGRAM(S)— Library Science, Other; Library Science/Librarianship; School Librarian/School Library Media Specialist. **RELATED KNOWLEDGE/COURSES—Customer and Personal Service:** Knowledge of principles and processes for providing customer and personal services. This includes customer needs assessment, meeting quality standards for services, and evaluation of customer satisfaction. **Clerical Practices:** Knowledge of administrative and clerical procedures and systems such as word processing,

managing files and records, stenography and transcription, designing forms, and other office procedures and terminology. **English Language:** Knowledge of the structure and content of the English language, including the meaning and spelling of words, rules of composition, and grammar. **Personnel and Human Resources:** Knowledge of principles and procedures for personnel recruitment, selection, training, compensation and benefits, labor relations and negotiation, and personnel information systems. **Communications and Media:** Knowledge of media production, communication, and dissemination techniques and methods. This includes alternative ways to inform and entertain via written, oral, and visual media. **Geography:** Knowledge of principles and methods for describing the features of land, sea, and air masses, including their physical characteristics; locations; interrelationships; and distribution of plant, animal, and human life.

Library Science Teachers, Postsecondary

- Education/Training Required: Master's degree
- Annual Earnings: $51,340
- Growth: 38.1% for all Postsecondary Teachers
- Annual Job Openings: 216,000 for all Postsecondary Teachers
- Self-Employed: 0.3% for all Postsecondary Teachers
- Part-Time: 27.7% for all Postsecondary Teachers

Teach courses in library science. Evaluate and grade students' class work, assignments, and papers. Prepare and deliver lectures to undergraduate and/or graduate students on topics such as collection development, archival methods, and indexing and abstracting. Advise students on academic and vocational curricula, and on career issues. Compile, administer, and grade examinations, or assign this work to others. Compile bibliographies of specialized materials for outside reading assignments. Initiate, facilitate, and moderate classroom discussions. Keep abreast of developments in their field by reading current literature, talking with colleagues, and participating in professional conferences. Maintain regularly scheduled office hours in order to advise and assist students. Maintain student attendance records, grades, and other required records. Plan, evaluate, and revise curricula, course content, and course materials and methods of instruction. Prepare course materials such as syllabi, homework assignments, and handouts. Select and obtain materials and supplies such as textbooks. Supervise undergraduate and/or graduate teaching, internship, and research work. Act as advisers to student organizations. Collaborate with colleagues to address teaching and research issues. Conduct research in a particular field of knowledge, and publish findings in professional journals, books, and/or electronic media. Participate in campus and community events. Participate in student recruitment, registration, and placement activities. Perform administrative duties such as serving as department head. Provide professional consulting services to government and/or industry. Serve on academic or administrative committees that deal with institutional policies, departmental matters, and academic issues. Write grant proposals to procure external research funding. **SKILLS**—No data available.

GOE—Interest Area: 05. Education and Training. **Work Group:** 05.03. Postsecondary and Adult Teaching and Instructing. **Other Jobs in This Work Group:** Adult Literacy, Remedial Education, and GED Teachers and Instructors; Agricultural Sciences Teachers, Postsecondary; Anthropology and Archeology Teachers, Postsecondary; Architecture Teachers, Postsecondary; Area, Ethnic, and Cultural Studies Teachers, Postsecondary; Art, Drama, and Music Teachers, Postsecondary; Atmospheric, Earth, Marine, and Space Sciences Teachers, Postsecondary; Biological Science Teachers, Postsecondary; Business Teachers, Postsecondary; Chemistry Teachers, Postsecondary; Communications Teachers, Postsecondary; Computer Science Teachers, Postsecondary; Criminal Justice and Law Enforcement Teachers, Postsecondary; Economics Teachers, Postsecondary; Education Teachers, Postsecondary; Engineering Teachers, Postsecondary; English Language and Literature Teachers, Postsecondary; Environmental Science Teachers, Postsecondary; Farm and Home Management Advisors; Foreign Language and Literature Teachers, Postsecondary; Forestry and Conservation Science Teachers, Postsecondary; Geography Teachers, Postsecondary; Graduate Teaching Assistants; Health Specialties Teachers, Postsecondary; History Teachers, Postsecondary; Home Economics Teachers, Postsecondary; Law Teachers, Postsecondary; Mathematical Science Teachers, Postsecondary; Nursing Instructors and Teachers, Postsecondary; Philosophy and Religion Teachers, Postsecondary; Physics Teachers, Postsecondary; Political Science Teachers, Postsecondary; Psychology Teachers, Postsecondary; Recreation and Fitness Studies Teachers, Postsecondary; Self-Enrichment Education Teachers; Social Work Teachers, Postsecondary; Sociology Teachers, Postsecondary; Vocational Education Teachers, Postsecondary. **PERSONALITY TYPE:** No data available.

EDUCATION/TRAINING PROGRAM(S)—Library Science/Librarianship; Teacher Education and Professional Development, Specific Subject Areas, Other. **RELATED KNOWLEDGE/COURSES**—No data available.

Loan Officers

- ◎ Education/Training Required: Bachelor's degree
- ◎ Annual Earnings: $47,530
- ◎ Growth: 18.8%
- ◎ Annual Job Openings: 30,000
- ◎ Self-Employed: 2.3%
- ◎ Part-Time: 5.0%

Evaluate, authorize, or recommend approval of commercial, real estate, or credit loans. Advise borrowers on financial status and methods of payments. Includes mortgage loan officers and agents, collection analysts, loan servicing officers, and loan underwriters. Approve loans within specified limits, and refer loan applications outside those limits to management for approval. Meet with applicants to obtain information for loan applications and to answer questions about the process. Analyze applicants' financial status, credit, and property evaluations to determine feasibility of granting loans. Explain to customers the different types of loans and credit options that are available, as well as the terms of those services. Obtain and compile copies of loan applicants' credit histories, corporate financial statements, and other financial information. Review and update credit and loan files. Review loan agreements to ensure that they are complete and accurate according to policy. Compute payment schedules. Stay abreast of new types of loans and other financial services and products in order to better meet customers' needs. Submit applications to credit analysts for verification and recommendation. Handle customer complaints and take appropriate action to resolve them. Work with clients to identify their financial goals and to find ways of reaching those goals. Confer with underwriters to aid in resolving mortgage application problems. Negotiate payment arrangements with customers who have delinquent loans. Market bank products to individuals and firms, promoting bank services that may meet customers' needs. Supervise loan personnel. Set credit policies, credit lines, procedures and standards in conjunction with senior managers. Provide special services such as investment banking for clients with more specialized needs. Analyze potential loan markets and develop referral networks in order to locate prospects for loans. Prepare reports to send to customers whose accounts are delinquent and forward irreconcilable accounts for collector action. Arrange for maintenance and liquidation of delinquent properties. Interview, hire, and train new employees. Petition courts to transfer titles and deeds of collateral to banks. **SKILLS—Persuasion:** Persuading others to change their minds or behavior. **Social Perceptiveness:** Being aware of others' reactions and understanding why they react as they do. **Service Orientation:** Actively looking for ways to help people. **Instructing:** Teaching others how to do something. **Negotiation:** Bringing others together and trying to reconcile differences. **Learning Strategies:** Selecting and using training/instructional methods and procedures appropriate for the situation when learning or teaching new things. **Complex Problem Solving:** Identifying complex problems and reviewing related information to develop and evaluate options and implement solutions. **Coordination:** Adjusting actions in relation to others' actions.

GOE—Interest Area: 06. Finance and Insurance. **Work Group:** 06.02. Finance/Insurance Investigation and Analysis. **Other Jobs in This Work Group:** Appraisers, Real Estate; Assessors; Claims Examiners, Property and Casualty Insurance; Cost Estimators; Credit Analysts; Financial Analysts; Insurance Adjusters, Examiners, and Investigators; Insurance Appraisers, Auto Damage; Insurance Underwriters; Loan Counselors; Market Research Analysts; Survey Researchers. **PERSONALITY TYPE:** Enterprising. Enterprising occupations frequently involve starting up and carrying out projects. These occupations can involve leading people and making many decisions. They sometimes require risk taking and often deal with business.

EDUCATION/TRAINING PROGRAM(S)— Credit Management; Finance, General. **RELATED KNOWLEDGE/COURSES—Economics and**

Accounting: Knowledge of economic and accounting principles and practices, the financial markets, banking, and the analysis and reporting of financial data. **Sales and Marketing:** Knowledge of principles and methods for showing, promoting, and selling products or services. This includes marketing strategy and tactics, product demonstration, sales techniques, and sales control systems. **Customer and Personal Service:** Knowledge of principles and processes for providing customer and personal services. This includes customer needs assessment, meeting quality standards for services, and evaluation of customer satisfaction. **Law and Government:** Knowledge of laws, legal codes, court procedures, precedents, government regulations, executive orders, agency rules, and the democratic political process. **English Language:** Knowledge of the structure and content of the English language, including the meaning and spelling of words, rules of composition, and grammar. **Mathematics:** Knowledge of arithmetic, algebra, geometry, calculus, and statistics and their applications.

Logisticians

- ◎ Education/Training Required: Bachelor's degree
- ◎ Annual Earnings: $49,740
- ◎ Growth: 27.5%
- ◎ Annual Job Openings: 162,000
- ◎ Self-Employed: No data available
- ◎ Part-Time: 7.4%

Analyze and coordinate the logistical functions of a firm or organization. Responsible for the entire life cycle of a product, including acquisition, distribution, internal allocation, delivery, and final disposal of resources. Develop and implement technical project management tools such as plans, schedules, and responsibility and compliance matrices. Develop proposals that include documentation for esti-

mates. Direct and support the compilation and analysis of technical source data necessary for product development. Direct availability and allocation of materials, supplies, and finished products. Direct team activities, establishing task priorities, scheduling and tracking work assignments, providing guidance, and ensuring the availability of resources. Manage the logistical aspects of product life cycles, including coordination or provisioning of samples, and the minimization of obsolescence. Participate in the assessment and review of design alternatives and design change proposal impacts. Perform system life-cycle cost analysis, and develop component studies. Plan, organize, and execute logistics support activities such as maintenance planning, repair analysis, and test equipment recommendations. Provide project management services, including the provision and analysis of technical data. Redesign the movement of goods in order to maximize value and minimize costs. Report project plans, progress, and results. Stay informed of logistics technology advances, and apply appropriate technology in order to improve logistics processes. Collaborate with other departments as necessary to meet customer requirements, to take advantage of sales opportunities or, in the case of shortages, to minimize negative impacts on a business. Develop an understanding of customers' needs, and take actions to ensure that such needs are met. Explain proposed solutions to customers, management, or other interested parties through written proposals and oral presentations. Maintain and develop positive business relationships with a customer's key personnel involved in or directly relevant to a logistics activity. Manage subcontractor activities, reviewing proposals, developing performance specifications, and serving as liaisons between subcontractors and organizations. Protect and control proprietary materials. Review logistics performance with customers against targets, benchmarks and service agreements. **SKILLS**—No data available.

GOE—Interest Area: 04. Business and Administration. **Work Group:** 04.05. Accounting, Auditing, and Analytical Support. **Other Jobs in This Work**

Group: Accountants; Auditors; Budget Analysts; Industrial Engineering Technicians; Management Analysts; Operations Research Analysts. **PERSONALITY TYPE:** No data available.

EDUCATION/TRAINING PROGRAM(S)— Logistics and Materials Management; Operations Management and Supervision. **RELATED KNOWLEDGE/COURSES—**No data available.

Management Analysts

- ◎ Education/Training Required: Work experience plus degree
- ◎ Annual Earnings: $63,090
- ◎ Growth: 30.4%
- ◎ Annual Job Openings: 78,000
- ◎ Self-Employed: 29.8%
- ◎ Part-Time: 14.0%

Conduct organizational studies and evaluations, design systems and procedures, conduct work simplifications and measurement studies, and prepare operations and procedures manuals to assist management in operating more efficiently and effectively. Includes program analysts and management consultants. Review forms and reports, and confer with management and users about format, distribution, and purpose, and to identify problems and improvements. Develop and implement records management program for filing, protection, and retrieval of records, and assure compliance with program. Interview personnel and conduct on-site observation to ascertain unit functions, work performed, and methods, equipment, and personnel used. Prepare manuals and train workers in use of new forms, reports, procedures or equipment, according to organizational policy. Design, evaluate, recommend, and approve changes of forms and reports. Recommend purchase of storage equipment, and design area layout to locate equipment in space available. Plan study of work problems and procedures, such as organizational change, communications, information flow, integrated production methods, inventory control, or cost analysis. Gather and organize information on problems or procedures. Analyze data gathered and develop solutions or alternative methods of proceeding. Document findings of study and prepare recommendations for implementation of new systems, procedures, or organizational changes. Confer with personnel concerned to ensure successful functioning of newly implemented systems or procedures. **SKILLS—Systems Evaluation:** Identifying measures or indicators of system performance and the actions needed to improve or correct performance relative to the goals of the system. **Management of Personnel Resources:** Motivating, developing, and directing people as they work, identifying the best people for the job. **Systems Analysis:** Determining how a system should work and how changes in conditions, operations, and the environment will affect outcomes. **Management of Material Resources:** Obtaining and seeing to the appropriate use of equipment, facilities, and materials needed to do certain work. **Operations Analysis:** Analyzing needs and product requirements to create a design. **Judgment and Decision Making:** Considering the relative costs and benefits of potential actions to choose the most appropriate one. **Monitoring:** Monitoring or assessing your performance or that of other individuals or organizations to make improvements or take corrective action. **Complex Problem Solving:** Identifying complex problems and reviewing related information to develop and evaluate options and implement solutions.

GOE—Interest Area: 04. Business and Administration. **Work Group:** 04.05. Accounting, Auditing, and Analytical Support. **Other Jobs in This Work Group:** Accountants; Auditors; Budget Analysts; Industrial Engineering Technicians; Logisticians; Operations Research Analysts. **PERSONALITY TYPE:** Enterprising. Enterprising occupations frequently involve starting up and carrying out projects. These occupations can involve leading people and making many decisions. They sometimes require risk taking and often deal with business.

EDUCATION/TRAINING PROGRAM(S)—Business Administration and Management, General; Business/Commerce, General. **RELATED KNOWLEDGE/COURSES—Administration and Management:** Knowledge of business and management principles involved in strategic planning, resource allocation, human resources modeling, leadership technique, production methods, and coordination of people and resources. **Personnel and Human Resources:** Knowledge of principles and procedures for personnel recruitment, selection, training, compensation and benefits, labor relations and negotiation, and personnel information systems. **Education and Training:** Knowledge of principles and methods for curriculum and training design, teaching and instruction for individuals and groups, and the measurement of training effects. **Economics and Accounting:** Knowledge of economic and accounting principles and practices, the financial markets, banking, and the analysis and reporting of financial data. **Clerical Practices:** Knowledge of administrative and clerical procedures and systems such as word processing, managing files and records, stenography and transcription, designing forms, and other office procedures and terminology. **English Language:** Knowledge of the structure and content of the English language, including the meaning and spelling of words, rules of composition, and grammar.

Market Research Analysts

- ◎ Education/Training Required: Bachelor's degree
- ◎ Annual Earnings: $54,830
- ◎ Growth: 23.4%
- ◎ Annual Job Openings: 18,000
- ◎ Self-Employed: 7.3%
- ◎ Part-Time: 11.7%

Research market conditions in local, regional, or national areas to determine potential sales of a product or service. May gather information on competitors, prices, sales, and methods of marketing and distribution. May use survey results to create a marketing campaign based on regional preferences and buying habits. Collect and analyze data on customer demographics, preferences, needs, and buying habits to identify potential markets and factors affecting product demand. Conduct research on consumer opinions and marketing strategies, collaborating with marketing professionals, statisticians, pollsters, and other professionals. Develop and implement procedures for identifying advertising needs. Devise and evaluate methods and procedures for collecting data (such as surveys, opinion polls, or questionnaires), or arrange to obtain existing data. Forecast and track marketing and sales trends, analyzing collected data. Gather data on competitors and analyze their prices, sales, and method of marketing and distribution. Measure and assess customer and employee satisfaction. Measure the effectiveness of marketing, advertising, and communications programs and strategies. Monitor industry statistics and follow trends in trade literature. Prepare reports of findings, illustrating data graphically and translating complex findings into written text. Attend staff conferences to provide management with information and proposals concerning the promotion, distribution, design, and pricing of company products or services. Direct trained survey interviewers. Seek and provide information to help companies determine their position in the marketplace. **SKILLS—Programming:** Writing computer programs for various purposes. **Writing:** Communicating effectively in writing as appropriate for the needs of the audience. **Systems Analysis:** Determining how a system should work and how changes in conditions, operations, and the environment will affect outcomes. **Mathematics:** Using mathematics to solve problems. **Operations Analysis:** Analyzing needs and product requirements to create a design. **Systems Evaluation:** Identifying measures or indicators of system performance and the actions needed to improve or correct performance relative to the goals of the system. **Monitoring:** Monitoring or assessing your performance or that of other individuals or organizations to make improvements or take corrective action. **Active Learning:** Understanding the implications of new information for both current and future problem-solving and decision-making. **Complex Problem Solving:** Identifying complex problems and reviewing related information to develop and evaluate options and implement solutions.

GOE—Interest Area: 06. Finance and Insurance. **Work Group:** 06.02. Finance/Insurance Investigation and Analysis. **Other Jobs in This Work Group:** Appraisers, Real Estate; Assessors; Claims Examiners, Property and Casualty Insurance; Cost Estimators; Credit Analysts; Financial Analysts; Insurance Adjusters, Examiners, and Investigators; Insurance Appraisers, Auto Damage; Insurance Underwriters; Loan Counselors; Loan Officers; Survey Researchers. **PERSONALITY TYPE:** Investigative. Investigative occupations frequently involve working with ideas and require an extensive amount of thinking. These occupations can involve searching for facts and figuring out problems mentally.

EDUCATION/TRAINING PROGRAM(S)— Applied Economics; Business/Managerial Economics; Econometrics and Quantitative Economics; Economics, General; International Economics; Marketing Research. **RELATED KNOWLEDGE/COURSES—Sales and Marketing:** Knowledge of principles and methods for showing, promoting, and selling products or services. This includes marketing strategy and tactics, product demonstration, sales techniques, and sales control systems. **Psychology:** Knowledge of human behavior and performance; individual differences in ability, personality, and interests; learning and motivation; psychological research methods; and the assessment and treatment of behavioral and affective disorders. **Mathematics:** Knowledge of arithmetic, algebra, geometry, calculus, and statistics and their applications. **Economics and Accounting:** Knowledge of economic and accounting principles and practices, the financial markets, banking, and the analysis and reporting of financial data. **Computers and Electronics:** Knowledge of circuit boards, processors, chips, electronic equipment, and computer hardware and software, including applications and programming. **Food Production:** Knowledge of techniques and equipment for planting, growing, and harvesting food products (both plant and animal) for consumption, including storage/handling techniques.

Marketing Managers

- Education/Training Required: Work experience plus degree
- Annual Earnings: $85,220
- Growth: 21.3%
- Annual Job Openings: 30,000
- Self-Employed: 3.1%
- Part-Time: 4.7%

Determine the demand for products and services offered by a firm and its competitors and identify potential customers. Develop pricing strategies with the goal of maximizing the firm's profits or share of the market while ensuring the firm's customers are satisfied. Oversee product development or monitor trends that indicate the need for new products and services. Develop pricing strategies, balancing firm objectives and customer satisfaction. Identify, develop, and evaluate marketing strategy, based on knowledge of establishment objectives, market characteristics, and cost and markup factors. Evaluate the financial aspects of product development, such as budgets, expenditures, research and development appropriations, and return-on-investment and profit-loss projections. Formulate, direct and coordinate marketing activities and policies to promote products and services, working with advertising and promotion managers. Direct the hiring, training, and performance evaluations of marketing and sales staff and oversee their daily activities. Negotiate contracts with vendors and distributors to manage product distribution, establishing distribution networks and developing distribution strategies. Consult with product development personnel on product specifications such as design, color, and packaging. Compile lists describing product or service offerings. Use sales forecasting and strategic planning to ensure the sale and profitability of products, lines, or services, analyzing business developments and monitoring market trends. Select products and accessories to be displayed at trade or special production shows. Confer with legal staff to resolve problems, such as copyright infringement and royalty sharing with outside producers and distributors. Coordinate and participate in promotional activities and trade shows, working with developers, advertisers, and production managers, to market products and services. Advise business and other groups on local, national, and international factors affecting the buying and selling of products and services. Initiate market research studies and analyze their findings. Consult with buying personnel to gain advice regarding the types of products or services expected to be in demand. Conduct economic and commercial surveys to identify potential markets for products and services. **SKILLS—Management of Financial Resources:** Determining how money will be spent to get the work done and accounting for these expenditures. **Management of Personnel Resources:** Motivating, developing, and directing people as they work, identifying the best people for the job. **Negotiation:** Bringing others together and trying to reconcile differences. **Operations Analysis:** Analyzing needs and product requirements to create a design. **Persuasion:** Persuading others to change their minds or behavior. **Coordination:** Adjusting actions in relation to others' actions. **Instructing:** Teaching others how to do something. **Time Management:** Managing one's own time and the time of others.

GOE—Interest Area: 14. Retail and Wholesale Sales and Service. **Work Group:** 14.01. Managerial

Work in Retail/Wholesale Sales and Service. **Other Jobs in This Work Group:** Advertising and Promotions Managers; First-Line Supervisors/Managers of Non-Retail Sales Workers; First-Line Supervisors/Managers of Retail Sales Workers; Funeral Directors; Property, Real Estate, and Community Association Managers; Purchasing Managers; Sales Managers. **PERSONALITY TYPE:** Enterprising. Enterprising occupations frequently involve starting up and carrying out projects. These occupations can involve leading people and making many decisions. They sometimes require risk taking and often deal with business.

EDUCATION/TRAINING PROGRAM(S)— Apparel and Textile Marketing Management; Consumer Merchandising/Retailing Management; International Marketing; Marketing Research; Marketing, Other; Marketing/Marketing Management, General. **RELATED KNOWLEDGE/COURSES—Sales and Marketing:** Knowledge of principles and methods for showing, promoting, and selling products or services. This includes marketing strategy and tactics, product demonstration, sales techniques, and sales control systems. **Customer and Personal Service:** Knowledge of principles and processes for providing customer and personal services. This includes customer needs assessment, meeting quality standards for services, and evaluation of customer satisfaction. **Administration and Management:** Knowledge of business and management principles involved in strategic planning, resource allocation, human resources modeling, leadership technique, production methods, and coordination of people and resources. **Personnel and Human Resources:** Knowledge of principles and procedures for personnel recruitment, selection, training, compensation and benefits, labor relations and negotiation, and personnel information systems. **Education and Training:** Knowledge of principles and methods for curriculum and training design, teaching and instruction for individuals and groups, and the measurement of training effects. **English Language:** Knowledge of the structure and content of the English language, including the meaning and spelling of words, rules of composition, and grammar.

Marriage and Family Therapists

- Education/Training Required: Master's degree
- Annual Earnings: $38,210
- Growth: 22.4%
- Annual Job Openings: 3,000
- Self-Employed: 4.2%
- Part-Time: 14.6%

Diagnose and treat mental and emotional disorders, whether cognitive, affective, or behavioral, within the context of marriage and family systems. Apply psychotherapeutic and family systems theories and techniques in the delivery of professional services to individuals, couples, and families for the purpose of treating such diagnosed nervous and mental disorders. Ask questions that will help clients identify their feelings and behaviors. Collect information about clients, using techniques such as testing, interviewing, discussion, and observation. Confer with clients in order to develop plans for post-treatment activities. Counsel clients on concerns such as unsatisfactory relationships, divorce and separation, child rearing, home management, and financial difficulties. Determine whether clients should be counseled or referred to other specialists in such fields as medicine, psychiatry and legal aid. Develop and implement individualized treatment plans addressing family relationship problems. Encourage individuals and family members to develop and use skills and strategies for confronting their problems in a constructive manner. Maintain case files that include activities, progress notes, evaluations, and recommendations. Confer with other counselors in order to analyze individual cases and to coordinate counseling services. Contact doctors, schools, social workers, juvenile counselors, law enforcement personnel and others to gather information in order to make recommendations to courts for the resolution of child custody or visitation disputes. Follow up on results of counseling programs and clients' adjustments in order to determine effectiveness of programs. Provide family counseling and treatment services to inmates participating in substance abuse programs. Provide instructions to clients on how to obtain help with legal, financial, and other personal issues. Supervise other counselors, social service staff and assistants. Write evaluations of parents and children for use by courts deciding divorce and custody cases, testifying in court if necessary. Provide public education and consultation to other professionals or groups regarding counseling services, issues and methods. **SKILLS**—No data available.

GOE—Interest Area: 10. Human Service. **Work Group:** 10.01. Counseling and Social Work. **Other Jobs in This Work Group:** Child, Family, and School Social Workers; Clinical Psychologists; Counseling Psychologists; Medical and Public Health Social Workers; Mental Health and Substance Abuse Social Workers; Mental Health Counselors; Probation Officers and Correctional Treatment Specialists; Rehabilitation Counselors; Residential Advisors; Social and Human Service Assistants; Substance Abuse and Behavioral Disorder Counselors. **PERSONALITY TYPE:** No data available.

EDUCATION/TRAINING PROGRAM(S)— Clinical Pastoral Counseling/Patient Counseling; Marriage and Family Therapy/Counseling; Social Work. **RELATED KNOWLEDGE/COURSES**— No data available.

M

Materials Engineers

- Education/Training Required: Bachelor's degree
- Annual Earnings: $65,010
- Growth: 4.1%
- Annual Job Openings: 2,000
- Self-Employed: 3.6%
- Part-Time: 1.0%

Evaluate materials and develop machinery and processes to manufacture materials for use in products that must meet specialized design and performance specifications. Develop new uses for known materials. Includes those working with composite materials or specializing in one type of material, such as graphite, metal and metal alloys, ceramics and glass, plastics and polymers, and naturally occurring materials. Design processing plants and equipment. Guide technical staff engaged in developing materials for specific uses in projected products or devices. Modify properties of metal alloys, using thermal and mechanical treatments. Perform managerial functions such as preparing proposals and budgets, analyzing labor costs, and writing reports. Plan and evaluate new projects, consulting with other engineers and corporate executives as necessary. Remove metals from ores, and refine and alloy them to obtain useful metal. Replicate the characteristics of materials and their components with computers. Supervise the work of technologists, technicians and other engineers and scientists. Sell and service metal products. Teach in colleges and universities. Write for technical magazines, journals, and trade association publications. Analyze product failure data and laboratory test results in order to determine causes of problems and develop solutions. Conduct or supervise tests on raw materials or finished products in order to ensure their quality. Design and direct the testing and/or control of processing procedures. Determine appropriate methods for fabricating and joining materials. Evaluate technical specifications and economic factors relating to process or product design objectives. Monitor material performance and evaluate material deterioration. Plan and implement laboratory operations for the purpose of developing material and fabrication procedures that meet cost, product specification, and performance standards. Review new product plans and make recommendations for material selection based on design objectives, such as strength, weight, heat resistance, electrical conductivity, and cost. Solve problems in a number of engineering fields, such as mechanical, chemical, electrical, civil, nuclear and aerospace. Supervise production and testing processes in industrial settings such as metal refining facilities, smelting or foundry operations, or non-metallic materials production operations. Conduct training sessions on new material products, applications, or manufacturing methods for customers and their employees. SKILLS—Science: Using scientific rules and methods to solve problems. Operations Analysis: Analyzing needs and product requirements to create a design. Technology Design: Generating or adapting equipment and technology to serve user needs. Mathematics: Using mathematics to solve problems. Judgment and Decision Making: Considering the relative costs and benefits of potential actions to choose the most appropriate one. Systems Evaluation: Identifying measures or indicators of system performance and the actions needed to improve or correct performance relative to the goals of the system. Active Learning: Understanding the implications of new information for both current and future problem-solving and decision-making. Complex Problem Solving: Identifying complex problems and reviewing related information to develop and evaluate options and implement solutions.

GOE—Interest Area: 15. Scientific Research, Engineering, and Mathematics. Work Group: 15.07. Research and Design Engineering. Other Jobs in This Work Group: Aerospace Engineers; Biomedical Engineers; Chemical Engineers; Civil Engineers; Computer Hardware Engineers; Electrical Engineers; Electronics Engineers, Except Computer; Marine Architects; Marine Engineers; Mechanical Engineers; Nuclear Engineers. **PERSONALITY TYPE:** Investigative. Investigative occupations frequently involve working with ideas and require an extensive amount of thinking. These occupations can involve searching for facts and figuring out problems mentally.

EDUCATION/TRAINING PROGRAM(S)— Ceramic Sciences and Engineering; Materials Engineering; Metallurgical Engineering. **RELATED KNOWLEDGE/COURSES—Engineering and Technology:** Knowledge of the practical application of engineering science and technology. This includes applying principles, techniques, procedures, and equipment to the design and production of various goods and services. **Design:** Knowledge of design techniques, tools, and principles involved in production of precision technical plans, blueprints, drawings, and models. **Mathematics:** Knowledge of arithmetic, algebra, geometry, calculus, and statistics and their applications. **Production and Processing:** Knowledge of raw materials, production processes, quality control, costs, and other techniques for maximizing the effective manufacture and distribution of goods. **Physics:** Knowledge and prediction of physical principles and laws and their interrelationships and applications to understanding fluid, material, and atmospheric dynamics and mechanical, electrical, atomic, and subatomic structures and processes. **Economics and Accounting:** Knowledge of economic and accounting principles and practices, the financial markets, banking, and the analysis and reporting of financial data.

Materials Scientists

- ◉ Education/Training Required: Bachelor's degree
- ◉ Annual Earnings: $71,090
- ◉ Growth: 8.5%
- ◉ Annual Job Openings: 1,000
- ◉ Self-Employed: 0.2%
- ◉ Part-Time: 4.2%

M

Research and study the structures and chemical properties of various natural and manmade materials, including metals, alloys, rubber, ceramics, semiconductors, polymers, and glass. Determine ways to strengthen or combine materials or develop new materials with new or specific properties for use in a variety of products and applications. Conduct research into the structures and properties of materials, such as metals, alloys, polymers, and ceramics in order to obtain information that could be used to develop new products or enhance existing ones. Determine ways to strengthen or combine materials, or develop new materials with new or specific properties for use in a variety of products and applications. Devise testing methods to evaluate the effects of various conditions on particular materials. Plan laboratory experiments to confirm feasibility of processes and techniques used in the production of materials having special characteristics. Prepare reports of materials study findings for the use of other scientists and requestors. Recommend materials for reliable performance in various environments. Research methods of processing, forming, and firing materials in order to develop such products as ceramic fillings for teeth, unbreakable dinner plates, and telescope lenses. Study the nature, structure and physical properties of metals and their alloys, and their responses to applied forces. Test material samples for tolerance under tension, compression and shear, to determine the cause of metal failures. Confer with customers in order to determine how materials can be tailored to suit their needs. Monitor production processes in order to ensure that equipment is used efficiently and that projects are completed within appropriate time frames and budgets. Receive molten metal from smelters, and further alloy and refine it in oxygen, open-hearth or other kinds of furnaces. Teach in colleges and universities. Test individual parts and products in order to ensure that manufacturer and governmental quality and safety standards are met. Test metals in order to determine whether they meet specifications of mechanical strength, strength-weight ratio, ductility, magnetic and electrical properties, and resistance to abrasion, corrosion, heat and cold. Visit suppliers of materials or users of products in order to gather specific information. **SKILLS—Science:** Using scientific rules and methods to solve problems. **Active Learning:** Understanding the implications of new information for both current and future problem-solving and decision-making. **Writing:** Communicating effectively in writing as appropriate for the needs of the audience. **Mathematics:** Using mathematics to solve problems. **Reading Comprehension:** Understanding written sentences and paragraphs in work-related documents. **Operations Analysis:** Analyzing needs and product requirements to create a design. **Quality Control Analysis:** Conducting tests and inspections of products, services, or processes to evaluate quality or performance. **Speaking:** Talking to others to convey information effectively. **Critical Thinking:** Using logic and reasoning to identify the strengths and weaknesses of alternative solutions, conclusions, or approaches to problems. **Systems Evaluation:** Identifying measures or indicators of system performance and the actions needed to improve or correct performance relative to the goals of the system.

GOE—Interest Area: 15. Scientific Research, Engineering, and Mathematics. **Work Group:** 15.02. Physical Sciences. **Other Jobs in This Work Group:** Astronomers; Atmospheric and Space Scientists; Chemists; Geographers; Geologists; Hydrologists; Physicists. **PERSONALITY TYPE:** Investigative. Investigative occupations frequently involve working with ideas and require an extensive amount of thinking. These occupations can involve searching for facts and figuring out problems mentally.

EDUCATION/TRAINING PROGRAM(S)— Materials Science. **RELATED KNOWLEDGE/ COURSES—Chemistry:** Knowledge of the chemical composition, structure, and properties of substances and of the chemical processes and transformations that they undergo. This includes uses of chemicals and their danger signs, production techniques, and disposal methods. **Physics:** Knowledge and prediction of physical principles and laws and their interrelationships and applications to understanding fluid, material, and atmospheric dynamics and mechanical, electrical, atomic, and subatomic structures and processes. **Engineering and Technology:** Knowledge of the practical application of engineering science and technology. This includes applying principles, techniques, procedures, and equipment to the design and production of various goods and services. **Mathematics:** Knowledge of arithmetic, algebra, geometry, calculus, and statistics and their applications. **Administration and Management:** Knowledge of business and management principles involved in strategic planning, resource allocation, human resources modeling, leadership technique, production methods, and coordination of people and resources. **English Language:** Knowledge of the structure and content of the English language, including the meaning and spelling of words, rules of composition, and grammar.

Mathematical Science Teachers, Postsecondary

- Education/Training Required: Master's degree
- Annual Earnings: $51,820
- Growth: 38.1% for all Postsecondary Teachers
- Annual Job Openings: 216,000 for all Postsecondary Teachers
- Self-Employed: 0.3% for all Postsecondary Teachers
- Part-Time: 27.7% for all Postsecondary Teachers

Teach courses pertaining to mathematical concepts, statistics, and actuarial science and to the application of original and standardized mathematical techniques in solving specific problems and situations. Maintain regularly scheduled office hours in order to advise and assist students. Maintain student attendance records, grades, and other required records. Plan, evaluate, and revise curricula, course content, and course materials and methods of instruction. Prepare course materials such as syllabi, homework assignments, and handouts. Select and obtain materials and supplies such as textbooks. Supervise undergraduate and/or graduate teaching, internship, and research work. Act as advisers to student organizations. Collaborate with colleagues to address teaching and research issues. Conduct research in a particular field of knowledge, and publish findings in books, professional journals, and/or electronic media. Participate in campus and community events. Participate in student recruitment, registration, and placement activities. Perform administrative duties such as serving as department head. Provide professional consulting services to government and/or industry. Serve on academic or administrative committees that deal with institutional policies, departmental matters, and academic issues. Write grant proposals to procure external research funding. Evaluate and grade students' class work, assignments, and papers. Prepare and deliver lectures to undergraduate and/or graduate students on topics such as linear algebra, differential equations, and discrete mathematics. Advise students on academic and vocational curricula, and on career issues. Compile, administer, and grade examinations, or assign this work to others. Compile bibliographies of specialized materials for outside reading assignments. Initiate, facilitate, and moderate classroom discussions. Keep abreast of developments in their field by reading current literature, talking with colleagues, and participating in professional conferences. **SKILLS—Mathematics:** Using mathematics to solve problems. **Instructing:** Teaching others how to do something. **Learning Strategies:** Selecting and using training/instructional methods and procedures appropriate for the situation when learning or teaching new things. **Active Learning:** Understanding the implications of new information for both current and future problem-solving and decision-making. **Reading Comprehension:** Understanding written sentences and paragraphs in work-related documents. **Writing:** Communicating effectively in writing as appropriate for the needs of the audience. **Critical Thinking:** Using logic and reasoning to identify the strengths and weaknesses of alternative solutions, conclusions, or approaches to problems. **Speaking:** Talking to others to convey information effectively.

GOE—Interest Area: 05. Education and Training. **Work Group:** 05.03. Postsecondary and Adult Teaching and Instructing. **Other Jobs in This Work Group:** Adult Literacy, Remedial Education, and GED Teachers and Instructors; Agricultural Sciences Teachers, Postsecondary; Anthropology and Archeology Teachers, Postsecondary; Architecture Teachers, Postsecondary; Area, Ethnic, and Cultural Studies Teachers, Postsecondary; Art, Drama, and Music Teachers, Postsecondary; Atmospheric, Earth, Marine, and Space Sciences Teachers, Postsecondary; Biological Science Teachers, Postsecondary; Business Teachers, Postsecondary; Chemistry Teachers, Postsecondary; Communications Teachers, Postsecondary; Computer Science Teachers, Postsecondary; Criminal Justice and Law Enforcement Teachers, Postsecondary; Economics Teachers, Postsecondary; Education Teachers, Postsecondary; Engineering Teachers, Postsecondary; English Language and Literature Teachers, Postsecondary; Environmental Science Teachers, Postsecondary; Farm and Home Management Advisors; Foreign Language and Literature Teachers, Postsecondary; Forestry and Conservation Science Teachers, Postsecondary; Geography Teachers, Postsecondary; Graduate Teaching Assistants; Health Specialties Teachers, Postsecondary; History Teachers, Postsecondary; Home Economics Teachers, Postsecondary; Law Teachers, Postsecondary; Library Science Teachers, Postsecondary; Nursing Instructors and Teachers, Postsecondary; Philosophy and Religion Teachers, Postsecondary; Physics Teachers, Postsecondary; Political Science Teachers, Postsecondary; Psychology Teachers, Postsecondary; Recreation and Fitness Studies Teachers, Postsecondary; Self-Enrichment Education Teachers; Social Work Teachers, Postsecondary; Sociology Teachers, Postsecondary; Vocational Education Teachers, Postsecondary. **PERSONALITY TYPE:** Investigative. Investigative occupations frequently involve working with ideas and require an extensive amount of thinking. These occupations can involve searching for facts and figuring out problems mentally.

EDUCATION/TRAINING PROGRAM(S)— Algebra and Number Theory; Analysis and Functional Analysis; Applied Mathematics; Business Statistics; Geometry/Geometric Analysis; Logic; Mathematical Statistics and Probability; Mathematics and Statistics, Other; Mathematics, General; Mathematics, Other; Statistics, General; Topology and Foundations. **RELATED KNOWLEDGE/ COURSES—Mathematics:** Knowledge of arithmetic, algebra, geometry, calculus, and statistics and their applications. **Education and Training:** Knowledge of principles and methods for curriculum and training design, teaching and instruction for indi-

viduals and groups, and the measurement of training effects. **English Language:** Knowledge of the structure and content of the English language, including the meaning and spelling of words, rules of composition, and grammar. **Clerical Practices:** Knowledge of administrative and clerical procedures and systems such as word processing, managing files and records, stenography and transcription, designing forms, and other office procedures and terminology. **Communications and Media:** Knowledge of media production, communication, and dissemination techniques and methods. This includes alternative ways to inform and entertain via written, oral, and visual media. **Administration and Management:** Knowledge of business and management principles involved in strategic planning, resource allocation, human resources modeling, leadership technique, production methods, and coordination of people and resources.

Mechanical Engineers

- Education/Training Required: Bachelor's degree
- Annual Earnings: $65,210
- Growth: 4.8%
- Annual Job Openings: 14,000
- Self-Employed: 3.0%
- Part-Time: 2.4%

Perform engineering duties in planning and designing tools, engines, machines, and other mechanically functioning equipment. Oversee installation, operation, maintenance, and repair of such equipment as centralized heat, gas, water, and steam systems. Read and interpret blueprints, technical drawings, schematics, and computer-generated reports. Confer with engineers and other personnel to implement operating procedures, resolve system malfunctions, and provide technical information. Research and analyze customer design proposals, specifications, manuals, and other data to evaluate the feasibility, cost, and maintenance requirements of designs or applications. Specify system components or direct modification of products to ensure conformance with engineering design and performance specifications. Research, design, evaluate, install, operate, and maintain mechanical products, equipment, systems and processes to meet requirements, applying knowledge of engineering principles. Investigate equipment failures and difficulties to diagnose faulty operation, and to make recommendations to maintenance crew. Assist drafters in developing the structural design of products, using drafting tools or computer-assisted design/drafting equipment and software. Provide feedback to design engineers on customer problems and needs. Oversee installation, operation, maintenance, and repair to ensure that machines and equipment are installed and functioning according to specifications. Conduct research that tests and analyzes the feasibility, design, operation and performance of equipment, components and systems. Recommend design modifications to eliminate machine or system malfunctions. Develop and test models of alternate designs and processing methods to assess feasibility, operating condition effects, possible new applications and necessity of modification. Develop, coordinate, and monitor all aspects of production, including selection of manufacturing methods, fabrication, and operation of product designs. Estimate costs and submit bids for engineering, construction, or extraction projects, and prepare contract documents. Perform personnel functions, such as supervision of production workers, technicians, technologists and other engineers, and design of evaluation programs. Solicit new business and provide technical customer service. Establish and coordinate the maintenance and safety procedures, service schedule, and supply of materials required to maintain machines and equipment in the prescribed condition. **SKILLS— Science:** Using scientific rules and methods to solve problems. **Operations Analysis:** Analyzing needs and product requirements to create a design. **Complex Problem Solving:** Identifying complex problems and reviewing related information to develop

and evaluate options and implement solutions. **Installation:** Installing equipment, machines, wiring, or programs to meet specifications. **Coordination:** Adjusting actions in relation to others' actions. **Mathematics:** Using mathematics to solve problems. **Negotiation:** Bringing others together and trying to reconcile differences. **Judgment and Decision Making:** Considering the relative costs and benefits of potential actions to choose the most appropriate one.

GOE—Interest Area: 15. Scientific Research, Engineering, and Mathematics. **Work Group:** 15.07. Research and Design Engineering. **Other Jobs in This Work Group:** Aerospace Engineers; Biomedical Engineers; Chemical Engineers; Civil Engineers; Computer Hardware Engineers; Electrical Engineers; Electronics Engineers, Except Computer; Marine Architects; Marine Engineers; Materials Engineers; Nuclear Engineers. **PERSONALITY TYPE:** Realistic. Realistic occupations frequently involve work activities that include practical, hands-on problems and solutions. They often deal with plants, animals, and real-world materials like wood, tools, and machinery. Many of the occupations require working outside and do not involve a lot of paperwork or working closely with others.

EDUCATION/TRAINING PROGRAM(S)— Mechanical Engineering. **RELATED KNOWLEDGE/COURSES—Design:** Knowledge of design techniques, tools, and principles involved in production of precision technical plans, blueprints, drawings, and models. **Engineering and Technology:** Knowledge of the practical application of engineering science and technology. This includes applying principles, techniques, procedures, and equipment to the design and production of various goods and services. **Mechanical Devices:** Knowledge of machines and tools, including their designs, uses, repair, and maintenance. **Production and Processing:** Knowledge of raw materials, production processes, quality control, costs, and other techniques for maximizing the effective manufacture and distribution of goods. **Administration and Management:** Knowledge of business and management principles involved in strategic planning, resource allocation, human resources modeling, leadership technique, production methods, and coordination of people and resources. **Physics:** Knowledge and prediction of physical principles and laws and their interrelationships and applications to understanding fluid, material, and atmospheric dynamics and mechanical, electrical, atomic, and subatomic structures and processes.

Medical and Clinical Laboratory Technicians

◉ Education/Training Required: Associate's degree

◉ Annual Earnings: $30,140

◉ Growth: 19.4%

◉ Annual Job Openings: 21,000

◉ Self-Employed: 1.6%

◉ Part-Time: 16.0%

Perform routine medical laboratory tests for the diagnosis, treatment, and prevention of disease. May work under the supervision of a medical technologist. Conduct chemical analyses of body fluids, such as blood and urine, using microscope or automatic analyzer to detect abnormalities or diseases, and enter findings into computer. Set up, adjust, maintain and clean medical laboratory equipment. Analyze the results of tests and experiments to ensure conformity to specifications, using special mechanical and electrical devices. Analyze and record test data to issue reports that use charts, graphs and narratives. Perform medical research to further control and cure disease. Conduct blood tests for transfusion purposes and perform blood counts. Obtain specimens, cultivating, isolating and identifying microorganisms for analysis. Examine cells stained with dye to locate abnormalities. Collect blood or tissue samples from patients, observing

principles of asepsis to obtain blood sample. Consult with a pathologist to determine a final diagnosis when abnormal cells are found. Inoculate fertilized eggs, broths, or other bacteriological media with organisms. Cut, stain and mount tissue samples for examination by pathologists. Supervise and instruct other technicians and laboratory assistants. Prepare standard volumetric solutions and reagents to be combined with samples, following standardized formulas or experimental procedures. Prepare vaccines and serums by standard laboratory methods, testing for virus inactivity and sterility. Test raw materials, processes and finished products to determine quality and quantity of materials or characteristics of a substance. **SKILLS—Equipment Maintenance:** Performing routine maintenance on equipment and determining when and what kind of maintenance is needed. **Science:** Using scientific rules and methods to solve problems. **Troubleshooting:** Determining causes of operating errors and deciding what to do about them. **Instructing:** Teaching others how to do something. **Monitoring:** Monitoring or assessing your performance or that of other individuals or organizations to make improvements or take corrective action. **Time Management:** Managing one's own time and the time of others. **Service Orientation:** Actively looking for ways to help people. **Active Learning:** Understanding the implications of new information for both current and future problem-solving and decision-making.

GOE—Interest Area: 08. Health Science. **Work Group:** 08.06. Medical Technology. **Other Jobs in This Work Group:** Biological Technicians; Cardiovascular Technologists and Technicians; Diagnostic Medical Sonographers; Medical and Clinical Laboratory Technologists; Medical Equipment Preparers; Medical Records and Health Information Technicians; Nuclear Medicine Technologists; Opticians, Dispensing; Orthotists and Prosthetists; Radiologic Technicians; Radiologic Technologists. **PERSONALITY TYPE:** Realistic. Realistic occupations frequently involve work activities that include practical, hands-on problems and solutions. They often deal with plants, animals, and real-world materials like wood, tools, and machinery. Many of the occupations require working outside and do not involve a lot of paperwork or working closely with others.

EDUCATION/TRAINING PROGRAM(S)— Blood Bank Technology Specialist; Clinical/Medical Laboratory Assistant; Clinical/Medical Laboratory Technician; Hematology Technology/Technician; Histologic Technician. **RELATED KNOWLEDGE/COURSES—Medicine and Dentistry:** Knowledge of the information and techniques needed to diagnose and treat human injuries, diseases, and deformities. This includes symptoms, treatment alternatives, drug properties and interactions, and preventive health-care measures. **Clerical Practices:** Knowledge of administrative and clerical procedures and systems such as word processing, managing files and records, stenography and transcription, designing forms, and other office procedures and terminology. **Therapy and Counseling:** Knowledge of principles, methods, and procedures for diagnosis, treatment, and rehabilitation of physical and mental dysfunctions and for career counseling and guidance. **Biology:** Knowledge of plant and animal organisms and their tissues, cells, functions, interdependencies, and interactions with each other and the environment. **Chemistry:** Knowledge of the chemical composition, structure, and properties of substances and of the chemical processes and transformations that they undergo. This includes uses of chemicals and their danger signs, production techniques, and disposal methods. **Customer and Personal Service:** Knowledge of principles and processes for providing customer and personal services. This includes customer needs assessment, meeting quality standards for services, and evaluation of customer satisfaction.

Medical and Clinical Laboratory Technologists

- ◉ Education/Training Required: Bachelor's degree
- ◉ Annual Earnings: $44,460
- ◉ Growth: 19.3%
- ◉ Annual Job Openings: 21,000
- ◉ Self-Employed: 1.6%
- ◉ Part-Time: 16.0%

Perform complex medical laboratory tests for diagnosis, treatment, and prevention of disease. May train or supervise staff. Analyze laboratory findings to check the accuracy of the results. Conduct chemical analysis of body fluids, including blood, urine, and spinal fluid, to determine presence of normal and abnormal components. Operate, calibrate and maintain equipment used in quantitative and qualitative analysis, such as spectrophotometers, calorimeters, flame photometers, and computer-controlled analyzers. Enter data from analysis of medical tests and clinical results into computer for storage. Analyze samples of biological material for chemical content or reaction. Establish and monitor programs to ensure the accuracy of laboratory results. Set up, clean, and maintain laboratory equipment. Provide technical information about test results to physicians, family members and researchers. Supervise, train, and direct lab assistants, medical and clinical laboratory technicians and technologists, and other medical laboratory workers engaged in laboratory testing. Develop, standardize, evaluate, and modify procedures, techniques and tests used in the analysis of specimens and in medical laboratory experiments. Cultivate, isolate, and assist in identifying microbial organisms, and perform various tests on these microorganisms. Study blood samples to determine the number of cells and their morphology, as well as the blood group, type and compatibility for transfusion purposes, using microscopic technique. Obtain, cut, stain, and mount biological material on slides for microscopic study and diagnosis, following standard laboratory procedures. Select and prepare specimen and media for cell culture, using aseptic technique and knowledge of medium components and cell requirements. Conduct medical research under direction of microbiologist or biochemist. Harvest cell cultures at optimum time based on knowledge of cell cycle differences and culture conditions. **SKILLS—Equipment Maintenance:** Performing routine maintenance on equipment and determining when and what kind of maintenance is needed. **Operation Monitoring:** Watching gauges, dials, or other indicators to make sure a machine is working properly. **Quality Control Analysis:** Conducting tests and inspections of products, services, or processes to evaluate quality or performance. **Science:** Using scientific rules and methods to solve problems. **Troubleshooting:** Determining causes of operating errors and deciding what to do about them. **Instructing:** Teaching others how to do something. **Repairing:** Repairing machines or systems, using the needed tools. **Operation and Control:** Controlling operations of equipment or systems.

GOE—Interest Area: 08. Health Science. **Work Group:** 08.06. Medical Technology. **Other Jobs in This Work Group:** Biological Technicians; Cardiovascular Technologists and Technicians; Diagnostic Medical Sonographers; Medical and Clinical Laboratory Technicians; Medical Equipment Preparers; Medical Records and Health Information Technicians; Nuclear Medicine Technologists; Opticians, Dispensing; Orthotists and Prosthetists; Radiologic Technicians; Radiologic Technologists. **PERSONALITY TYPE:** Investigative. Investigative occupations frequently involve working with ideas and require an extensive amount of thinking. These occupations can involve searching for facts and figuring out problems mentally.

EDUCATION/TRAINING PROGRAM(S)— Clinical Laboratory Science/Medical Technology/Technologist; Clinical/Medical Laboratory Science and Allied Professions, Other; Cytogenetics/Genetics/Clinical Genetics Technology/Technologist; Cytotechnology/Cytotechnologist; Histologic Technology/Histotechnologist; Renal/Dialysis Technologist/Technician. **RELATED KNOWLEDGE/COURSES—Biology:** Knowledge of plant and animal organisms and their tissues, cells, functions, interdependencies, and interactions with each other and the environment. **Chemistry:** Knowledge of the chemical composition, structure, and properties of substances and of the chemical processes and transformations that they undergo. This includes uses of chemicals and their danger signs, production techniques, and disposal methods. **Computers and Electronics:** Knowledge of circuit boards, processors, chips, electronic equipment, and computer hardware and software, including applications and programming. **Public Safety and Security:** Knowledge of relevant equipment, policies, procedures, and strategies to promote effective local, state, or national security operations for the protection of people, data, property, and institutions. **Customer and Personal Service:** Knowledge of principles and processes for providing customer and personal services. This includes customer needs assessment, meeting quality standards for services, and evaluation of customer satisfaction. **Mathematics:** Knowledge of arithmetic, algebra, geometry, calculus, and statistics and their applications.

Medical and Health Services Managers

- Education/Training Required: Work experience plus degree
- Annual Earnings: $66,360
- Growth: 29.3%
- Annual Job Openings: 33,000
- Self-Employed: 5.3%
- Part-Time: 5.4%

Plan, direct, or coordinate medicine and health services in hospitals, clinics, managed care organizations, public health agencies, or similar organizations. Direct, supervise and evaluate work activities of medical, nursing, technical, clerical, service, maintenance, and other personnel. Establish objectives and evaluative or operational criteria for units they manage. Direct or conduct recruitment, hiring and training of personnel. Develop and maintain computerized record management systems to store and process data, such as personnel activities and information, and to produce reports. Develop and implement organizational policies and procedures for the facility or medical unit. Conduct and administer fiscal operations, including accounting, planning budgets, authorizing expenditures, establishing rates for services, and coordinating financial reporting. Establish work schedules and assignments for staff, according to workload, space and equipment availability. Maintain communication between governing boards, medical staff, and department heads by attending board meetings and coordinating interdepartmental functioning. Monitor the use of diagnostic services, inpatient beds, facilities, and staff to ensure effective use of resources and assess the need for additional staff, equipment, and services. Maintain awareness of advances in medicine, computerized diagnostic and treatment equipment, data processing technology, government regulations, health insurance changes, and financing options. Manage change in integrated health-care delivery systems, such as work restructuring, technological innovations, and shifts in the focus of care. Prepare activity reports to inform management of the status and implementation plans of programs, services, and quality initiatives. Plan, implement and administer programs and services in a health-care or medical facility, including personnel administration, training, and coordination of medical, nursing and physical plant staff. Consult with medical, business, and community groups to discuss service problems, respond to community needs, enhance public relations, coordinate activities and plans, and promote health pro-

grams. Inspect facilities and recommend building or equipment modifications to ensure emergency readiness and compliance to access, safety, and sanitation regulations. **SKILLS—Persuasion:** Persuading others to change their minds or behavior. **Management of Personnel Resources:** Motivating, developing, and directing people as they work, identifying the best people for the job. **Service Orientation:** Actively looking for ways to help people. **Management of Material Resources:** Obtaining and seeing to the appropriate use of equipment, facilities, and materials needed to do certain work. **Monitoring:** Monitoring or assessing your performance or that of other individuals or organizations to make improvements or take corrective action. **Social Perceptiveness:** Being aware of others' reactions and understanding why they react as they do. **Management of Financial Resources:** Determining how money will be spent to get the work done and accounting for these expenditures. **Critical Thinking:** Using logic and reasoning to identify the strengths and weaknesses of alternative solutions, conclusions, or approaches to problems. **Learning Strategies:** Selecting and using training/instructional methods and procedures appropriate for the situation when learning or teaching new things.

GOE—Interest Area: 08. Health Science. **Work Group:** 08.01. Managerial Work in Medical and Health Services. **Other Jobs in This Work Group:** Coroners; First-Line Supervisors and Manager/Supervisors—Animal Care Workers, Except Livestock. **PERSONALITY TYPE:** Enterprising. Enterprising occupations frequently involve starting up and carrying out projects. These occupations can involve leading people and making many decisions. They sometimes require risk taking and often deal with business.

EDUCATION/TRAINING PROGRAM(S)— Community Health and Preventive Medicine; Health and Medical Administrative Services, Other; Health Information/Medical Records Administration/Administrator; Health Services Administration; Health Unit Manager/Ward Supervisor;

Health/Health Care Administration/Management; Hospital and Health Care Facilities Administration/Management; Medical Staff Services Technology/Technician; Nursing Administration (MSN, MS, PhD); Public Health, General (MPH, DPH). **RELATED KNOWLEDGE/COURSES—Therapy and Counseling:** Knowledge of principles, methods, and procedures for diagnosis, treatment, and rehabilitation of physical and mental dysfunctions and for career counseling and guidance. **Customer and Personal Service:** Knowledge of principles and processes for providing customer and personal services. This includes customer needs assessment, meeting quality standards for services, and evaluation of customer satisfaction. **Personnel and Human Resources:** Knowledge of principles and procedures for personnel recruitment, selection, training, compensation and benefits, labor relations and negotiation, and personnel information systems. **Medicine and Dentistry:** Knowledge of the information and techniques needed to diagnose and treat human injuries, diseases, and deformities. This includes symptoms, treatment alternatives, drug properties and interactions, and preventive health-care measures. **Psychology:** Knowledge of human behavior and performance; individual differences in ability, personality, and interests; learning and motivation; psychological research methods; and the assessment and treatment of behavioral and affective disorders. **Sociology and Anthropology:** Knowledge of group behavior and dynamics, societal trends and influences, human migrations, ethnicity, and cultures and their history and origins. **Education and Training:** Knowledge of principles and methods for curriculum and training design, teaching and instruction for individuals and groups, and the measurement of training effects. **Philosophy and Theology:** Knowledge of different philosophical systems and religions. This includes their basic principles, values, ethics, ways of thinking, customs, and practices and their impact on human culture.

Medical and Public Health Social Workers

◎ Education/Training Required: Bachelor's degree
◎ Annual Earnings: $39,160
◎ Growth: 28.6%
◎ Annual Job Openings: 18,000
◎ Self-Employed: 1.7%
◎ Part-Time: 8.7%

Provide persons, families, or vulnerable populations with the psychosocial support needed to cope with chronic, acute, or terminal illnesses, such as Alzheimer's, cancer, or AIDS. Services include advising family care givers, providing patient education and counseling, and making necessary referrals for other social services. Collaborate with other professionals to evaluate patients' medical or physical condition and to assess client needs. Investigate child abuse or neglect cases and take authorized protective action when necessary. Refer patient, client, or family to community resources to assist in recovery from mental or physical illness and to provide access to services such as financial assistance, legal aid, housing, job placement or education. Counsel clients and patients in individual and group sessions to help them overcome dependencies, recover from illness, and adjust to life. Organize support groups or counsel family members to assist them in understanding, dealing with, and supporting the client or patient. Advocate for clients or patients to resolve crises. Identify environmental impediments to client or patient progress through interviews and review of patient records. Utilize consultation data and social work experience to plan and coordinate client or patient care and rehabilitation, following through to ensure service efficacy. Modify treatment plans to comply with changes in clients' status. Monitor, evaluate, and record client progress according to measurable goals described in treatment and care plan. Supervise and direct other workers providing services to clients or patients. Develop or advise on social policy and assist in community development. Oversee Medicaid- and Medicare-related paperwork and record-keeping in hospitals. Conduct social research to advance knowledge in the social work field. Plan and conduct programs to combat social problems, prevent substance abuse, or improve community health and counseling services. **SKILLS—Social Perceptiveness:** Being aware of others' reactions and understanding why they react as they do. **Service Orientation:** Actively looking for ways to help people. **Negotiation:** Bringing others together and trying to reconcile differences. **Coordination:** Adjusting actions in relation to others' actions. **Active Listening:** Giving full attention to what other people are saying, taking time to understand the points being made, asking questions as appropriate, and not interrupting at inappropriate times. **Critical Thinking:** Using logic and reasoning to identify the strengths and weaknesses of alternative solutions, conclusions, or approaches to problems. **Learning Strategies:** Selecting and using training/instructional methods and procedures appropriate for the situation when learning or teaching new things. **Instructing:** Teaching others how to do something.

GOE—Interest Area: 10. Human Service. **Work Group:** 10.01. Counseling and Social Work. **Other Jobs in This Work Group:** Child, Family, and School Social Workers; Clinical Psychologists; Counseling Psychologists; Marriage and Family Therapists; Mental Health and Substance Abuse Social Workers; Mental Health Counselors; Probation Officers and Correctional Treatment Specialists; Rehabilitation Counselors; Residential Advisors; Social and Human Service Assistants; Substance Abuse and Behavioral Disorder Counselors. **PERSONALITY TYPE:** Social. Social occupations frequently involve working with, communicating with, and teaching people. These occupations often involve helping or providing service to others.

EDUCATION/TRAINING PROGRAM(S)— Clinical/Medical Social Work. **RELATED KNOWLEDGE/COURSES—Psychology:** Knowledge of human behavior and performance; individual differences in ability, personality, and interests; learning and motivation; psychological research methods; and the assessment and treatment of behavioral and affective disorders. **Therapy and Counseling:** Knowledge of principles, methods, and procedures for diagnosis, treatment, and rehabilitation of physical and mental dysfunctions and for career counseling and guidance. **Customer and Personal Service:** Knowledge of principles and processes for providing customer and personal services. This includes customer needs assessment, meeting quality standards for services, and evaluation of customer satisfaction. **Sociology and Anthropology:** Knowledge of group behavior and dynamics, societal trends and influences, human migrations, ethnicity, and cultures and their history and origins. **Philosophy and Theology:** Knowledge of different philosophical systems and religions. This includes their basic principles, values, ethics, ways of thinking, customs, and practices and their impact on human culture. **Medicine and Dentistry:** Knowledge of the information and techniques needed to diagnose and treat human injuries, diseases, and deformities. This includes symptoms, treatment alternatives, drug properties and interactions, and preventive health-care measures.

Medical Records and Health Information Technicians

- Education/Training Required: Associate's degree
- Annual Earnings: $24,920
- Growth: 46.8%
- Annual Job Openings: 24,000
- Self-Employed: 1.1%
- Part-Time: 17.6%

Compile, process, and maintain medical records of hospital and clinic patients in a manner consistent with medical, administrative, ethical, legal, and regulatory requirements of the health-care system. Process, maintain, compile, and report patient information for health requirements and standards. Protect the security of medical records to ensure that confidentiality is maintained. Process patient admission and discharge documents. Review records for completeness, accuracy and compliance with regulations. Compile and maintain patients' medical records to document condition and treatment and to provide data for research or cost control and care improvement efforts. Enter data, such as demographic characteristics, history and extent of disease, diagnostic procedures and treatment into computer. Release information to persons and agencies according to regulations. Plan, develop, maintain and operate a variety of health record indexes and storage and retrieval systems to collect, classify, store and analyze information. Manage the department and supervise clerical workers, directing and controlling activities of personnel in the medical records department. Transcribe medical reports. Identify, compile, abstract and code patient data, using standard classification systems. Resolve/clarify codes and diagnoses with conflicting, missing, or unclear information by consulting with doctors or others to get additional information and by participating in the coding team's regular meetings. Train medical records staff. Assign the patient to one of several hundred "diagnosis-related groups", or DRGs, using appropriate computer software. Post medical insurance billings. Process and prepare business and government forms. Contact discharged patients, their families, and physicians to maintain registry with follow-up information, such as quality of life and length of survival of cancer patients. Prepare statistical reports, narrative reports and graphic presentations of information such as tumor registry data for use by hospital staff, researchers, and other users. Consult classification manuals to locate information about disease processes. Compile medical care and census data for statistical reports on diseases treated, surgery performed, and use of hospital beds. Develop in-service educational materials. **SKILLS—Instructing:** Teaching others how to do something. **Systems Evaluation:** Identifying measures or indicators of system performance and the actions needed to improve or correct performance relative to the goals of the system. **Time Management:** Managing one's own time and the time of others. **Active Listening:** Giving full attention to what other people are saying, taking time to understand the points being made, asking questions as appropriate, and not interrupting at inappropriate times. **Critical Thinking:** Using logic and reasoning to identify the strengths and weaknesses of alternative solutions, conclusions, or approaches to problems. **Learning Strategies:** Selecting and using training/instructional methods and procedures appropriate for the situation when learning or teaching new things. **Service Orientation:** Actively looking for ways to help people. **Reading Comprehension:** Understanding written sentences and paragraphs in work-related documents. **Active Learning:** Understanding the implications of new information for both current and future problem-solving and decision-making. **Social Perceptiveness:** Being aware of others' reactions and understanding why they react as they do.

GOE—Interest Area: 08. Health Science. **Work Group:** 08.06. Medical Technology. **Other Jobs in This Work Group:** Biological Technicians; Cardiovascular Technologists and Technicians; Diagnostic Medical Sonographers; Medical and Clinical Laboratory Technicians; Medical and Clinical Laboratory Technologists; Medical Equipment Preparers; Nuclear Medicine Technologists; Opticians, Dispensing; Orthotists and Prosthetists; Radiologic Technicians; Radiologic Technologists. **PERSONALITY TYPE:** Conventional. Conventional occupations frequently involve following set procedures and routines. These occupations can include working with data and details more than with ideas. Usually there is a clear line of authority to follow.

EDUCATION/TRAINING PROGRAM(S)— Health Information/Medical Records Technology/Technician; Medical Insurance Coding

Specialist/Coder. **RELATED KNOWLEDGE/ COURSES—Clerical Practices:** Knowledge of administrative and clerical procedures and systems such as word processing, managing files and records, stenography and transcription, designing forms, and other office procedures and terminology. **Customer and Personal Service:** Knowledge of principles and processes for providing customer and personal services. This includes customer needs assessment, meeting quality standards for services, and evaluation of customer satisfaction. **Personnel and Human Resources:** Knowledge of principles and procedures for personnel recruitment, selection, training, compensation and benefits, labor relations and negotiation, and personnel information systems. **Medicine and Dentistry:** Knowledge of the information and techniques needed to diagnose and treat human injuries, diseases, and deformities. This includes symptoms, treatment alternatives, drug properties and interactions, and preventive health-care measures. **Administration and Management:** Knowledge of business and management principles involved in strategic planning, resource allocation, human resources modeling, leadership technique, production methods, and coordination of people and resources. **Computers and Electronics:** Knowledge of circuit boards, processors, chips, electronic equipment, and computer hardware and software, including applications and programming.

Medical Scientists, Except Epidemiologists

- ◉ Education/Training Required: Doctoral degree
- ◉ Annual Earnings: $60,200
- ◉ Growth: 26.9%
- ◉ Annual Job Openings: 6,000
- ◉ Self-Employed: 1.7%
- ◉ Part-Time: 8.8%

Conduct research dealing with the understanding of human diseases and the improvement of human health. Engage in clinical investigation or other research, production, technical writing, or related activities. Prepare and analyze organ, tissue and cell samples to identify toxicity, bacteria, or microorganisms, or to study cell structure. Standardize drug dosages, methods of immunization, and procedures for manufacture of drugs and medicinal compounds. Confer with health department, industry personnel, physicians, and others to develop health safety standards and public health improvement programs. Study animal and human health and physiological processes. Consult with and advise physicians, educators, researchers, and others regarding medical applications of physics, biology, and chemistry. Teach principles of medicine and medical and laboratory procedures to physicians, residents, students, and technicians. Use equipment such as atomic absorption spectrometers, electron microscopes, flow cytometers and chromatography systems. Conduct research to develop methodologies, instrumentation and procedures for medical application, analyzing data and presenting findings. Evaluate effects of drugs, gases, pesticides, parasites, and microorganisms at various levels. Follow strict safety procedures when handling toxic materials to avoid contamination. Investigate cause, progress, life cycle, or mode of transmission of diseases or parasites. Plan and direct studies to investigate human or animal disease, preventive methods, and treatments for disease. **SKILLS—Instructing:** Teaching others how to do something. **Science:** Using scientific rules and methods to solve problems. **Active Learning:** Understanding the implications of new information for both current and future problem-solving and decision-making. **Systems Evaluation:** Identifying measures or indicators of system performance and the actions needed to improve or correct performance relative to the goals of the system. **Writing:** Communicating effectively in writing as appropriate for the needs of the audience. **Systems Analysis:** Determining how a system should work and how changes in conditions, operations, and the environment will affect outcomes. **Reading Com-**

M

prehension: Understanding written sentences and paragraphs in work-related documents. **Service Orientation:** Actively looking for ways to help people.

GOE—Interest Area: 15. Scientific Research, Engineering, and Mathematics. **Work Group:** 15.03. Life Sciences. **Other Jobs in This Work Group:** Biochemists; Biologists; Biophysicists; Environmental Scientists and Specialists, Including Health; Epidemiologists; Microbiologists. **PERSONALITY TYPE:** Investigative. Investigative occupations frequently involve working with ideas and require an extensive amount of thinking. These occupations can involve searching for facts and figuring out problems mentally.

EDUCATION/TRAINING PROGRAM(S)— Anatomy; Biochemistry; Biomedical Sciences, General; Biophysics; Biostatistics; Cardiovascular Science; Cell Physiology; Cell/Cellular Biology and Histology; Endocrinology; Environmental Toxicology; Epidemiology; Exercise Physiology; Human/Medical Genetics; Immunology; Medical Microbiology and Bacteriology; Medical Scientist (MS, PhD); Molecular Biology; Molecular Pharmacology; Molecular Physiology; Molecular Toxicology; Neurobiology and Neurophysiology; Neuropharmacology; Oncology and Cancer Biology; Pathology/Experimental Pathology; Pharmacology; Pharmacology and Toxicology; Pharmacology and Toxicology, Other; Physiology, General; Physiology, Pathology, and Related Sciences, Other; Reproductive Biology; Toxicology; Vision Science/Physiological Optics. **RELATED KNOWLEDGE/COURSES—Biology:** Knowledge of plant and animal organisms and their tissues, cells, functions, interdependencies, and interactions with each other and the environment. **Medicine and Dentistry:** Knowledge of the information and techniques needed to diagnose and treat human injuries, diseases, and deformities. This includes symptoms, treatment alternatives, drug properties and interactions, and preventive health-care measures. **Chemistry:** Knowledge of the chemical composition, structure, and properties of substances and of the chemical processes and transformations that they

undergo. This includes uses of chemicals and their danger signs, production techniques, and disposal methods. **Mathematics:** Knowledge of arithmetic, algebra, geometry, calculus, and statistics and their applications. **Education and Training:** Knowledge of principles and methods for curriculum and training design, teaching and instruction for individuals and groups, and the measurement of training effects. **Communications and Media:** Knowledge of media production, communication, and dissemination techniques and methods. This includes alternative ways to inform and entertain via written, oral, and visual media.

Medical Transcriptionists

◎ Education/Training Required: Associate's degree

◎ Annual Earnings: $27,790

◎ Growth: 22.6%

◎ Annual Job Openings: 18,000

◎ Self-Employed: 2.3%

◎ Part-Time: 25.3%

Use transcribing machines with headset and foot pedal to listen to recordings by physicians and other health-care professionals dictating a variety of medical reports, such as emergency room visits, diagnostic imaging studies, operations, chart reviews, and final summaries. Transcribe dictated reports and translate medical jargon and abbreviations into their expanded forms. Edit as necessary and return reports in either printed or electronic form to the dictator for review and signature, or correction. Decide which information should be included or excluded in reports. Distinguish between homonyms, and recognize inconsistencies and mistakes in medical terms, referring to dictionaries, drug references, and other sources on anatomy, physiology, and medicine. Identify mistakes in reports, and check with doctors to obtain the correct information. Perform data entry and data retrieval services, providing data for inclusion in medical records and for transmission to physicians. Produce medical reports, correspondence, records, patient-care information, statistics, medical research, and administrative material. Return dictated reports in printed or electronic form for physicians' review, signature, and corrections, and for inclusion in patients' medical records. Review and edit transcribed reports or dictated material for spelling, grammar, clarity, consistency, and proper medical terminology. Take dictation using either shorthand or a stenotype machine, or using headsets and transcribing machines; then convert dictated materials or rough notes to written form. Transcribe dictation for a variety of medical reports such as patient histories, physical examinations, emergency room visits, operations, chart reviews, consultation, and/or discharge summaries. Translate medical jargon and abbreviations into their expanded forms to ensure the accuracy of patient and health-care facility records. Answer inquiries concerning the progress of medical cases, within the limits of confidentiality laws. Perform a variety of clerical and office tasks, such as handling incoming and outgoing mail, completing and submitting insurance claims, typing, filing, and operating office machines. Receive patients, schedule appointments, and maintain patient records. Set up and maintain medical files and databases, including records such as x-ray, lab, and procedure reports, medical histories, diagnostic workups, admission and discharge summaries, and clinical resumes. Receive and screen telephone calls and visitors. **SKILLS**—No data available.

GOE—Interest Area: 08. Health Science. **Work Group:** 08.02. Medicine and Surgery. **Other Jobs in This Work Group:** Anesthesiologists; Family and General Practitioners; Internists, General; Medical Assistants; Obstetricians and Gynecologists; Pediatricians, General; Pharmacists; Pharmacy Aides; Pharmacy Technicians; Physician Assistants; Psychiatrists; Registered Nurses; Surgeons; Surgical Technologists. **PERSONALITY TYPE:** No data available.

EDUCATION/TRAINING PROGRAM(S)—Medical Transcription/Transcriptionist. **RELATED KNOWLEDGE/COURSES**—No data available.

Meeting and Convention Planners

- Education/Training Required: Bachelor's degree
- Annual Earnings: $39,070
- Growth: 21.3%
- Annual Job Openings: 7,000
- Self-Employed: 1.8%
- Part-Time: 14.4%

Coordinate activities of staff and convention personnel to make arrangements for group meetings and conventions. Consult with customers in order to determine objectives and requirements for events such as meetings, conferences, and conventions. Monitor event activities in order to ensure compliance with applicable regulations and laws, satisfaction of participants, and resolution of any problems that arise. Confer with staff at a chosen event site in order to coordinate details. Review event bills for accuracy, and approve payment. Plan and develop programs, agendas, budgets, and services according to customer requirements. Coordinate services for events, such as accommodation and transportation for participants, facilities, catering, signage, displays, special needs requirements, printing and event security. Arrange the availability of audio-visual equipment, transportation, displays, and other event needs. Inspect event facilities in order to ensure that they conform to customer requirements. Maintain records of event aspects, including financial details. Conduct post-event evaluations in order to determine how future events could be improved. Negotiate contracts with such service providers and suppliers as hotels, convention centers, and speakers. Meet with sponsors and organizing committees in order to plan scope and format of events, to establish and monitor budgets, and to review administrative procedures and event progress. Direct administrative details such as financial operations, dissemination of promotional materials, and responses to inquiries. Evaluate and select providers of services according to customer requirements. Read trade publications, attend seminars, and consult with other meeting professionals in order to keep abreast of meeting management standards and trends. Organize registration of event participants. Design and implement efforts to publicize events and promote sponsorships. Hire, train, and supervise volunteers and support staff required for events. Obtain permits from fire and health departments to erect displays and exhibits and serve food at events. Promote conference, convention and trades show services by performing tasks such as meeting with professional and trade associations, and producing brochures and other publications. **SKILLS—Service Orientation:** Actively looking for ways to help people. **Coordination:** Adjusting actions in relation to others' actions. **Negotiation:** Bringing others together and trying to reconcile differences. **Time Management:** Managing one's own time and the time of others. **Persuasion:** Persuading others to change their minds or behavior. **Social Perceptiveness:** Being aware of others' reactions and understanding why they react as they do. **Operations Analysis:** Analyzing needs and product requirements to create a design. **Management of Financial Resources:** Determining how money will be spent to get the work done and accounting for these expenditures.

GOE—Interest Area: 04. Business and Administration. **Work Group:** 04.02. Managerial Work in Business Detail. **Other Jobs in This Work Group:** Administrative Services Managers; First-Line Supervisors, Administrative Support; First-Line Supervisors, Customer Service; Housekeeping Supervisors; Janitorial Supervisors. **PERSONALITY TYPE:** Enterprising. Enterprising occupations frequently involve starting up and carrying out projects. These occupations can involve leading people and making many decisions. They sometimes require risk taking and often deal with business.

EDUCATION/TRAINING PROGRAM(S)— Selling Skills and Sales Operations. **RELATED KNOWLEDGE/COURSES—Sales and Marketing:** Knowledge of principles and methods for showing, promoting, and selling products or services. This includes marketing strategy and tactics, product demonstration, sales techniques, and sales control systems. **Customer and Personal Service:** Knowledge of principles and processes for providing customer and personal services. This includes customer needs assessment, meeting quality standards for services, and evaluation of customer satisfaction. **Personnel and Human Resources:** Knowledge of principles and procedures for personnel recruitment, selection, training, compensation and benefits, labor relations and negotiation, and personnel information systems. **Administration and Management:** Knowledge of business and management principles involved in strategic planning, resource allocation, human resources modeling, leadership technique, production methods, and coordination of people and resources. **Education and Training:** Knowledge of principles and methods for curriculum and training design, teaching and instruction for individuals and groups, and the measurement of training effects. **Clerical Practices:** Knowledge of administrative and clerical procedures and systems such as word processing, managing files and records, stenography and transcription, designing forms, and other office procedures and terminology.

Mental Health and Substance Abuse Social Workers

- Education/Training Required: Master's degree
- Annual Earnings: $33,650
- Growth: 34.5%
- Annual Job Openings: 17,000
- Self-Employed: 1.6%
- Part-Time: 8.7%

Assess and treat individuals with mental, emotional, or substance abuse problems, including abuse of alcohol, tobacco, and/or other drugs. Activities may include individual and group therapy, crisis intervention, case management, client advocacy, prevention, and education. Counsel clients in individual and group sessions to assist them in dealing with substance abuse, mental and physical illness, poverty, unemployment, or physical abuse. Interview clients, review records, and confer with other professionals to evaluate mental or physical condition of client or patient. Collaborate with counselors, physicians, and nurses to plan and coordinate treatment, drawing on social work experience and patient needs. Monitor, evaluate, and record client progress with respect to treatment goals. Refer patient, client, or family to community resources for housing or treatment to assist in recovery from mental or physical illness, following through to ensure service efficacy. Counsel and aid family members to assist them in understanding, dealing with, and supporting the client or patient. Modify treatment plans according to changes in client status. Plan and conduct programs to prevent substance abuse, to combat social problems, or to improve health and counseling services in community. Supervise and direct other workers who provide services to clients or patients. Develop or advise on social policy and assist in community development. **SKILLS—Social**

Perceptiveness: Being aware of others' reactions and understanding why they react as they do. **Service Orientation:** Actively looking for ways to help people. **Negotiation:** Bringing others together and trying to reconcile differences. **Persuasion:** Persuading others to change their minds or behavior. **Active Listening:** Giving full attention to what other people are saying, taking time to understand the points being made, asking questions as appropriate, and not interrupting at inappropriate times. **Critical Thinking:** Using logic and reasoning to identify the strengths and weaknesses of alternative solutions, conclusions, or approaches to problems. **Coordination:** Adjusting actions in relation to others' actions. **Judgment and Decision Making:** Considering the relative costs and benefits of potential actions to choose the most appropriate one.

GOE—Interest Area: 10. Human Service. **Work Group:** 10.01. Counseling and Social Work. **Other Jobs in This Work Group:** Child, Family, and School Social Workers; Clinical Psychologists; Counseling Psychologists; Marriage and Family Therapists; Medical and Public Health Social Workers; Mental Health Counselors; Probation Officers and Correctional Treatment Specialists; Rehabilitation Counselors; Residential Advisors; Social and Human Service Assistants; Substance Abuse and Behavioral Disorder Counselors. **PERSONALITY TYPE:** Social. Social occupations frequently involve working with, communicating with, and teaching people. These occupations often involve helping or providing service to others.

EDUCATION/TRAINING PROGRAM(S)— Clinical/Medical Social Work. **RELATED KNOWLEDGE/COURSES—Psychology:** Knowledge of human behavior and performance; individual differences in ability, personality, and interests; learning and motivation; psychological research methods; and the assessment and treatment of behavioral and affective disorders. **Therapy and Counseling:** Knowledge of principles, methods, and procedures for diagnosis, treatment, and rehabilitation of physical and mental dysfunctions and for career counseling and guidance. **Customer and Per-**

sonal Service: Knowledge of principles and processes for providing customer and personal services. This includes customer needs assessment, meeting quality standards for services, and evaluation of customer satisfaction. **Sociology and Anthropology:** Knowledge of group behavior and dynamics, societal trends and influences, human migrations, ethnicity, and cultures and their history and origins. **Medicine and Dentistry:** Knowledge of the information and techniques needed to diagnose and treat human injuries, diseases, and deformities. This includes symptoms, treatment alternatives, drug properties and interactions, and preventive healthcare measures. **Philosophy and Theology:** Knowledge of different philosophical systems and religions. This includes their basic principles, values, ethics, ways of thinking, customs, and practices and their impact on human culture.

Mental Health Counselors

- Education/Training Required: Master's degree
- Annual Earnings: $32,040
- Growth: 26.7%
- Annual Job Openings: 13,000
- Self-Employed: 4.1%
- Part-Time: 14.6%

Counsel with emphasis on prevention. Work with individuals and groups to promote optimum mental health. May help individuals deal with addictions and substance abuse; family, parenting, and marital problems; suicide; stress management; problems with self-esteem; and issues associated with aging and mental and emotional health. Maintain confidentiality of records relating to clients' treatment. Encourage clients to express their feelings and discuss what is happening in their lives,

and help them to develop insight into themselves and their relationships. Guide clients in the development of skills and strategies for dealing with their problems. Prepare and maintain all required treatment records and reports. Counsel clients and patients, individually and in group sessions, to assist in overcoming dependencies, adjusting to life, and making changes. Collect information about clients through interviews, observation, and tests. Act as client advocates in order to coordinate required services or to resolve emergency problems in crisis situations. Develop and implement treatment plans based on clinical experience and knowledge. Collaborate with other staff members to perform clinical assessments and develop treatment plans. Evaluate clients' physical or mental condition based on review of client information. Meet with families, probation officers, police, and other interested parties in order to exchange necessary information during the treatment process. Refer patients, clients, or family members to community resources or to specialists as necessary. Counsel family members to assist them in understanding, dealing with, and supporting clients or patients. Evaluate the effectiveness of counseling programs and clients' progress in resolving identified problems and moving towards defined objectives. Plan, organize and lead structured programs of counseling, work, study, recreation and social activities for clients. Modify treatment activities and approaches as needed in order to comply with changes in clients' status. Learn about new developments in their field by reading professional literature, attending courses and seminars, and establishing and maintaining contact with other social service agencies. Discuss with individual patients their plans for life after leaving therapy. Gather information about community mental health needs and resources that could be used in conjunction with therapy. Monitor clients' use of medications. SKILLS—**Social Perceptiveness:** Being aware of others' reactions and understanding why they react as they do. **Service Orientation:** Actively looking for ways to help people. **Negotiation:** Bringing others together and trying to reconcile differences. **Learning Strategies:**

Selecting and using training/instructional methods and procedures appropriate for the situation when learning or teaching new things. **Persuasion:** Persuading others to change their minds or behavior. **Active Listening:** Giving full attention to what other people are saying, taking time to understand the points being made, asking questions as appropriate, and not interrupting at inappropriate times. **Critical Thinking:** Using logic and reasoning to identify the strengths and weaknesses of alternative solutions, conclusions, or approaches to problems. **Active Learning:** Understanding the implications of new information for both current and future problem-solving and decision-making. **Instructing:** Teaching others how to do something.

GOE—Interest Area: 10. Human Service. **Work Group:** 10.01. Counseling and Social Work. **Other Jobs in This Work Group:** Child, Family, and School Social Workers; Clinical Psychologists; Counseling Psychologists; Marriage and Family Therapists; Medical and Public Health Social Workers; Mental Health and Substance Abuse Social Workers; Probation Officers and Correctional Treatment Specialists; Rehabilitation Counselors; Residential Advisors; Social and Human Service Assistants; Substance Abuse and Behavioral Disorder Counselors. **PERSONALITY TYPE:** Social. Social occupations frequently involve working with, communicating with, and teaching people. These occupations often involve helping or providing service to others.

EDUCATION/TRAINING PROGRAM(S)— Clinical/Medical Social Work; Mental and Social Health Services and Allied Professions, Other; Mental Health Counseling/Counselor; Substance Abuse/Addiction Counseling. **RELATED KNOWLEDGE/COURSES—Therapy and Counseling:** Knowledge of principles, methods, and procedures for diagnosis, treatment, and rehabilitation of physical and mental dysfunctions and for career counseling and guidance. **Psychology:** Knowledge of human behavior and performance; individual differences in ability, personality, and interests; learning and motivation; psychological

research methods; and the assessment and treatment of behavioral and affective disorders. **Sociology and Anthropology:** Knowledge of group behavior and dynamics, societal trends and influences, human migrations, ethnicity, and cultures and their history and origins. **Customer and Personal Service:** Knowledge of principles and processes for providing customer and personal services. This includes customer needs assessment, meeting quality standards for services, and evaluation of customer satisfaction. **Philosophy and Theology:** Knowledge of different philosophical systems and religions. This includes their basic principles, values, ethics, ways of thinking, customs, and practices and their impact on human culture. **Education and Training:** Knowledge of principles and methods for curriculum and training design, teaching and instruction for individuals and groups, and the measurement of training effects.

Microbiologists

- Education/Training Required: Doctoral degree
- Annual Earnings: $52,100
- Growth: 20.0%
- Annual Job Openings: 1,000
- Self-Employed: 2.6%
- Part-Time: 7.1%

Investigate the growth, structure, development, and other characteristics of microscopic organisms, such as bacteria, algae, or fungi. Includes medical microbiologists who study the relationship between organisms and disease or the effects of antibiotics on microorganisms. Isolate and make cultures of bacteria or other microorganisms in prescribed media, controlling moisture, aeration, temperature, and nutrition. Perform tests on water, food and the environment to detect harmful microorganisms and to obtain information about sources of

M

pollution and contamination. Examine physiological, morphological, and cultural characteristics, using microscope, to identify and classify microorganisms in human, water, and food specimens. Provide laboratory services for health departments, for community environmental health programs and for physicians needing information for diagnosis and treatment. Observe action of microorganisms upon living tissues of plants, higher animals, and other microorganisms, and on dead organic matter. Investigate the relationship between organisms and disease, including the control of epidemics and the effects of antibiotics on microorganisms. Supervise biological technologists and technicians and other scientists. Study growth, structure, development, and general characteristics of bacteria and other microorganisms to understand their relationship to human, plant, and animal health. Prepare technical reports and recommendations based upon research outcomes. Study the structure and function of human, animal and plant tissues, cells, pathogens and toxins. Use a variety of specialized equipment such as electron microscopes, gas chromatographs and high pressure liquid chromatographs, electrophoresis units, thermocyclers, fluorescence activated cell sorters and phosphoimagers. Conduct chemical analyses of substances, such as acids, alcohols, and enzymes. **SKILLS—Science:** Using scientific rules and methods to solve problems. **Operation Monitoring:** Watching gauges, dials, or other indicators to make sure a machine is working properly. **Instructing:** Teaching others how to do something. **Equipment Maintenance:** Performing routine maintenance on equipment and determining when and what kind of maintenance is needed. **Active Listening:** Giving full attention to what other people are saying, taking time to understand the points being made, asking questions as appropriate, and not interrupting at inappropriate times. **Troubleshooting:** Determining causes of operating errors and deciding what to do about them. **Time Management:** Managing one's own time and the time of others. **Technology Design:** Generating or adapting equipment and technology to serve user needs.

GOE—Interest Area: 15. Scientific Research, Engineering, and Mathematics. **Work Group:** 15.03. Life Sciences. **Other Jobs in This Work Group:** Biochemists; Biologists; Biophysicists; Environmental Scientists and Specialists, Including Health; Epidemiologists; Medical Scientists, Except Epidemiologists. **PERSONALITY TYPE:** Investigative. Investigative occupations frequently involve working with ideas and require an extensive amount of thinking. These occupations can involve searching for facts and figuring out problems mentally.

EDUCATION/TRAINING PROGRAM(S)—Biochemistry/Biophysics and Molecular Biology; Cell/Cellular Biology and Anatomical Sciences, Other; Microbiology, General; Neuroanatomy; Soil Microbiology; Structural Biology. **RELATED KNOWLEDGE/COURSES—Biology:** Knowledge of plant and animal organisms and their tissues, cells, functions, interdependencies, and interactions with each other and the environment. **Chemistry:** Knowledge of the chemical composition, structure, and properties of substances and of the chemical processes and transformations that they undergo. This includes uses of chemicals and their danger signs, production techniques, and disposal methods. **Clerical Practices:** Knowledge of administrative and clerical procedures and systems such as word processing, managing files and records, stenography and transcription, designing forms, and other office procedures and terminology. **English Language:** Knowledge of the structure and content of the English language, including the meaning and spelling of words, rules of composition, and grammar. **Computers and Electronics:** Knowledge of circuit boards, processors, chips, electronic equipment, and computer hardware and software, including applications and programming. **Administration and Management:** Knowledge of business and management principles involved in strategic planning, resource allocation, human resources modeling, leadership technique, production methods, and coordination of people and resources.

Middle School Teachers, Except Special and Vocational Education

- ⊚ Education/Training Required: Bachelor's degree
- ⊚ Annual Earnings: $42,960
- ⊚ Growth: 9.0%
- ⊚ Annual Job Openings: 69,000
- ⊚ Self-Employed: 0.1%
- ⊚ Part-Time: 9.2%

Teach students in public or private schools in one or more subjects at the middle, intermediate, or junior high level, which falls between elementary and senior high school as defined by applicable State laws and regulations. Meet with other professionals to discuss individual students' needs and progress. Meet with parents and guardians to discuss their children's progress, and to determine their priorities for their children and their resource needs. Observe and evaluate students' performance, behavior, social development, and physical health. Organize and label materials, and display students' work. Organize and supervise games and other recreational activities to promote physical, mental, and social development. Plan and conduct activities for a balanced program of instruction, demonstration, and work time that provides students with opportunities to observe, question, and investigate. Plan and supervise class projects, field trips, visits by guest speakers or other experiential activities, and guide students in learning from such activities. Prepare and implement remedial programs for students requiring extra help. Prepare for assigned classes, and show written evidence of preparation upon request of immediate supervisors. Prepare materials and classrooms for class activities. Prepare objectives and outlines for courses of study, following curriculum guidelines or requirements of states and schools. Use computers, audiovisual aids, and other equipment and materials to supplement presentations. Prepare reports on students and activities as required by administration. Prepare students for later grades by encouraging them to explore learning opportunities and to persevere with challenging tasks. Supervise, evaluate, and plan assignments for teacher assistants and volunteers. Administer standardized ability and achievement tests, and interpret results to determine student strengths and areas of need. Attend professional meetings, educational conferences, and teacher training workshops in order to maintain and improve professional competence. Attend staff meetings, and serve on staff committees as required. Collaborate with other teachers and administrators in the development, evaluation, and revision of middle school programs. Perform administrative duties such as assisting in school libraries, hall and cafeteria monitoring, and bus loading and unloading. **SKILLS—Learning Strategies:** Selecting and using training/instructional methods and procedures appropriate for the situation when learning or teaching new things. **Instructing:** Teaching others how to do something. **Speaking:** Talking to others to convey information effectively. **Social Perceptiveness:** Being aware of others' reactions and understanding why they react as they do. **Mathematics:** Using mathematics to solve problems. **Reading Comprehension:** Understanding written sentences and paragraphs in work-related documents. **Monitoring:** Monitoring or assessing your performance or that of other individuals or organizations to make improvements or take corrective action. **Active Learning:** Understanding the implications of new information for both current and future problem-solving and decision-making.

GOE—Interest Area: 05. Education and Training. **Work Group:** 05.02. Pre-school, Elementary, and Secondary Teaching and Instructing. **Other Jobs in This Work Group:** Elementary School Teachers, Except Special Education; Kindergarten Teachers, Except Special Education; Preschool Teachers, Except Special Education; Secondary School Teachers, Except Special and

Vocational Education; Special Education Teachers, Middle School; Special Education Teachers, Preschool, Kindergarten, and Elementary School; Special Education Teachers, Secondary School; Teacher Assistants; Vocational Education Teachers, Middle School; Vocational Education Teachers, Secondary School. **PERSONALITY TYPE:** Social. Social occupations frequently involve working with, communicating with, and teaching people. These occupations often involve helping or providing service to others.

EDUCATION/TRAINING PROGRAM(S)— Art Teacher Education; Computer Teacher Education; English/Language Arts Teacher Education; Family and Consumer Sciences/Home Economics Teacher Education; Foreign Language Teacher Education; Health Occupations Teacher Education; Health Teacher Education; History Teacher Education; Junior High/Intermediate/Middle School Education and Teaching; Mathematics Teacher Education; Music Teacher Education; Physical Education Teaching and Coaching; Reading Teacher Education; Science Teacher Education/General Science Teacher Education; Social Science Teacher Education; Social Studies Teacher Education; Teacher Education and Professional Development, Specific Subject Areas, Other; Technology Teacher Education/Industrial Arts Teacher Education. **RELATED KNOWLEDGE/COURSES—Education and Training:** Knowledge of principles and methods for curriculum and training design, teaching and instruction for individuals and groups, and the measurement of training effects. **Therapy and Counseling:** Knowledge of principles, methods, and procedures for diagnosis, treatment, and rehabilitation of physical and mental dysfunctions and for career counseling and guidance. **English Language:** Knowledge of the structure and content of the English language, including the meaning and spelling of words, rules of composition, and grammar. **History and Archeology:** Knowledge of historical events and their causes, indicators, and effects on civilizations and cultures. **Sociology and Anthropology:** Knowledge of group behavior and dynamics, societal trends and influences, human migrations, ethnicity,

and cultures and their history and origins. **Geography:** Knowledge of principles and methods for describing the features of land, sea, and air masses, including their physical characteristics; locations; interrelationships; and distribution of plant, animal, and human life.

Multi-Media Artists and Animators

- ◎ Education/Training Required: Bachelor's degree
- ◎ Annual Earnings: $46,770
- ◎ Growth: 15.8%
- ◎ Annual Job Openings: 12,000
- ◎ Self-Employed: 53.5%
- ◎ Part-Time: 20.0%

Create special effects, animation, or other visual images using film, video, computers, or other electronic tools and media for use in products or creations, such as computer games, movies, music videos, and commercials. Apply story development, directing, cinematography, and editing to animation to create storyboards that show the flow of the animation and map out key scenes and characters. Assemble, typeset, scan and produce digital camera-ready art or film negatives and printer's proofs. Convert real objects to animated objects through modeling, using techniques such as optical scanning. Create and install special effects as required by the script, mixing chemicals and fabricating needed parts from wood, metal, plaster, and clay. Create basic designs, drawings, and illustrations for product labels, cartons, direct mail, or television. Create pen-and-paper images to be scanned, edited, colored, textured or animated by computer. Create two-dimensional and three-dimensional images depicting objects in motion or illustrating a process, using computer animation or modeling programs. Design complex graphics and animation, using independent judgment, creativity, and computer equipment. Develop briefings, brochures, multimedia presentations, web pages, promotional products, technical illustrations, and computer artwork for use in products, technical manuals, literature, newsletters and slide shows. Implement and maintain configuration control systems. Make objects or characters appear lifelike by manipulating light, color, texture, shadow, and transparency, and/or manipulating static images to give the illusion of motion. Script, plan, and create animated narrative sequences under tight deadlines, using computer software and hand drawing techniques. Use models to simulate the behavior of animated objects in the finished sequence. Participate in design and production of multimedia campaigns, handling budgeting and scheduling, and assisting with such responsibilities as production coordination, background design and progress tracking. **SKILLS**—No data available.

GOE—Interest Area: 03. Arts and Communication. **Work Group:** 03.09. Media Technology. **Other Jobs in This Work Group:** Audio and Video Equipment Technicians; Broadcast Technicians; Camera Operators, Television, Video, and Motion Picture; Film and Video Editors; Photographic Hand Developers; Photographic Reproduction Technicians; Photographic Retouchers and Restorers; Professional Photographers; Radio Operators; Sound Engineering Technicians. **PERSONALITY TYPE:** No data available.

EDUCATION/TRAINING PROGRAM(S)— Animation, Interactive Technology, Video Graphics and Special Effects; Drawing; Graphic Design; Intermedia/Multimedia; Painting; Printmaking; Web Page, Digital/Multimedia and Information Resources Design. **RELATED KNOWLEDGE/ COURSES**—No data available.

Natural Sciences Managers

- ◉ Education/Training Required: Work experience plus degree
- ◉ Annual Earnings: $86,910
- ◉ Growth: 11.3%
- ◉ Annual Job Openings: 5,000
- ◉ Self-Employed: 1.2%
- ◉ Part-Time: 0.9%

Plan, direct, or coordinate activities in such fields as life sciences, physical sciences, mathematics, statistics, and research and development in these fields. Confer with scientists, engineers, regulators, and others, to plan and review projects, and to provide technical assistance. Design and coordinate successive phases of problem analysis, solution proposals, and testing. Determine scientific and technical goals within broad outlines provided by top management and make detailed plans to accomplish these goals. Develop and implement policies, standards and procedures for the architectural, scientific and technical work performed, to ensure regulatory compliance and operations enhancement. Plan and direct research, development, and production activities. Prepare project proposals. Advise and assist in obtaining patents or meeting other legal requirements. Conduct own research in field of expertise. Develop client relationships and communicate with clients to explain proposals, present research findings, establish specifications or discuss project status. Develop innovative technology and train staff for its implementation. Hire, supervise and evaluate engineers, technicians, researchers and other staff. Prepare and administer budget, approve and review expenditures, and prepare financial reports. Recruit personnel and oversee the development and maintenance of staff competence. Review project activities, and prepare and review research, testing, and operational reports. Make presentations at professional meetings to further knowledge in the field. Provide for stewardship of plant and animal resources and habitats, studying land use, monitoring animal populations and/or providing shelter, resources, and medical treatment for animals. **SKILLS—Management of Material Resources:** Obtaining and seeing to the appropriate use of equipment, facilities, and materials needed to do certain work. **Management of Financial Resources:** Determining how money will be spent to get the work done and accounting for these expenditures. **Science:** Using scientific rules and methods to solve problems. **Management of Personnel Resources:** Motivating, developing, and directing people as they work, identifying the best people for the job. **Coordination:** Adjusting actions in relation to others' actions. **Systems Analysis:** Determining how a system should work and how changes in conditions, operations, and the environment will affect outcomes. **Systems Evaluation:** Identifying measures or indicators of system performance and the actions needed to improve or correct performance relative to the goals of the system. **Time Management:** Managing one's own time and the time of others.

GOE—Interest Area: 15. Scientific Research, Engineering, and Mathematics. **Work Group:** 15.01. Managerial Work in Scientific Research, Engineering, and Mathematics. **Other Jobs in This Work Group:** Engineering Managers. **PERSONALITY TYPE:** Investigative. Investigative occupations frequently involve working with ideas and require an extensive amount of thinking. These occupations can involve searching for facts and figuring out problems mentally.

EDUCATION/TRAINING PROGRAM(S)— Acoustics; Algebra and Number Theory; Analysis and Functional Analysis; Analytical Chemistry; Anatomy; Animal Genetics; Animal Physiology; Applied Mathematics; Applied Mathematics, Other; Astronomy; Astrophysics; Atmospheric Chemistry and Climatology; Atmospheric Physics and Dynamics; Atmospheric Sciences and Meteorology, General; Atmospheric Sciences and Meteorology, Other; Atomic/Molecular Physics; Biochemistry; Biological and Biomedical Sciences,

Other; Biological and Physical Sciences; Biology/Biological Sciences, General; Biometry/Biometrics; Biophysics; Biopsychology; Biostatistics; Biotechnology; Botany/Plant Biology; Botany/Plant Biology, Other; Cell/Cellular Biology and Anatomical Sciences, Other; Cell/Cellular Biology and Histology; Chemical Physics; Chemistry, General; Chemistry, Other; Computational Mathematics; Ecology; Ecology, Evolution, Systematics and Population Biology, Other; Elementary Particle Physics; Entomology; Evolutionary Biology; Geochemistry; Geochemistry and Petrology; Geological and Earth Sciences/Geosciences, Other; Geology/Earth Science, General; Geometry/Geometric Analysis; Geophysics and Seismology; Hydrology and Water Resources Science; Immunology; Inorganic Chemistry; Logic; Marine Biology and Biological Oceanography; Mathematics and Computer Science; Mathematics and Statistics, Other; Mathematics, General; Medical Microbiology and Bacteriology; Meteorology; Microbiology, General; Molecular Biology; Natural Sciences; Neuroscience; Nuclear Physics; Nutrition Sciences; Oceanography, Chemical and Physical; Operations Research; Optics/Optical Sciences; Organic Chemistry; Paleontology; Parasitology; Pathology/Experimental Pathology; Pharmacology; Physical and Theoretical Chemistry; Physical Sciences; Physical Sciences, Other; Physics, General; Physics, Other; Planetary Astronomy and Science; Plant Genetics; Plant Pathology/Phytopathology; Plant Physiology; Plasma and High-Temperature Physics; Polymer Chemistry; others. **RELATED KNOWLEDGE/ COURSES—Chemistry:** Knowledge of the chemical composition, structure, and properties of substances and of the chemical processes and transformations that they undergo. This includes uses of chemicals and their danger signs, production techniques, and disposal methods. **Administration and Management:** Knowledge of business and management principles involved in strategic planning, resource allocation, human resources modeling, leadership technique, production methods, and coordination of people and resources. **Economics and Accounting:** Knowledge of economic and accounting principles and practices, the financial markets, banking, and the analysis and reporting of financial data. **Physics:** Knowledge and prediction of physical principles and laws and their interrelationships and applications to understanding fluid, material, and atmospheric dynamics and mechanical, electrical, atomic, and subatomic structures and processes. **Law and Government:** Knowledge of laws, legal codes, court procedures, precedents, government regulations, executive orders, agency rules, and the democratic political process. **Mathematics:** Knowledge of arithmetic, algebra, geometry, calculus, and statistics and their applications.

Network and Computer Systems Administrators

◉ Education/Training Required: Bachelor's degree

◉ Annual Earnings: $57,060

◉ Growth: 37.4%

◉ Annual Job Openings: 35,000

◉ Self-Employed: 0.5%

◉ Part-Time: 3.9%

Install, configure, and support an organization's local area network (LAN), wide area network (WAN), and Internet system or a segment of a network system. Maintain network hardware and software. Monitor network to ensure network availability to all system users and perform necessary maintenance to support network availability. May supervise other network support and client server specialists and plan, coordinate, and implement network security measures. Diagnose hardware and software problems, and replace defective components. Perform data backups and disaster recovery operations. Maintain and administer computer networks and related computing environments, including computer hardware, systems software, applications software, and all configurations. Plan, coordinate, and implement network security measures in order to protect data, software, and hardware. Operate master consoles in order to monitor the performance of computer systems and networks, and to coordinate computer network access and use. Perform routine network startup and shutdown procedures, and maintain control records. Design, configure, and test computer hardware, networking software and operating system software. Recommend changes to improve systems and network configurations, and determine hardware or software requirements related to such changes. Confer with network users about how to solve existing system problems. Monitor network performance in order to determine whether adjustments need to be made, and to determine where changes will need to be made in the future. Train people in computer system use. Load computer tapes and disks, and install software and printer paper or forms. Gather data pertaining to customer needs, and use the information to identify, predict, interpret, and evaluate system and network requirements. Analyze equipment performance records in order to determine the need for repair or replacement. Maintain logs related to network functions, as well as maintenance and repair records. Research new technology, and implement it or recommend its implementation. Maintain an inventory of parts for emergency repairs. Coordinate with vendors and with company personnel in order to facilitate purchases. **SKILLS—Troubleshooting:** Determining causes of operating errors and deciding what to do about them. **Installation:** Installing equipment, machines, wiring, or programs to meet specifications. **Repairing:** Repairing machines or systems, using the needed tools. **Service Orientation:** Actively looking for ways to help people. **Technology Design:** Generating or adapting equipment and technology to serve user needs. **Systems Evaluation:** Identifying measures or indicators of system performance and the actions needed to improve or correct performance relative to the goals of the system. **Programming:** Writing computer programs for various purposes. **Systems Analysis:** Determining how

N

a system should work and how changes in conditions, operations, and the environment will affect outcomes.

GOE—Interest Area: 11. Information Technology. **Work Group:** 11.01. Managerial Work in Information Technology . **Other Jobs in This Work Group:** Computer and Information Systems Managers. **PERSONALITY TYPE:** No data available.

EDUCATION/TRAINING PROGRAM(S)— Computer and Information Sciences and Support Services, Other; Computer and Information Sciences, General; Computer and Information Systems Security; Computer Systems Analysis/Analyst; Computer Systems Networking and Telecommunications; Information Science/Studies; System Administration/Administrator; System, Networking, and LAN/WAN Management/Manager. **RELATED KNOWLEDGE/COURSES—Computers and Electronics:** Knowledge of circuit boards, processors, chips, electronic equipment, and computer hardware and software, including applications and programming. **Telecommunications:** Knowledge of transmission, broadcasting, switching, control, and operation of telecommunications systems. **Customer and Personal Service:** Knowledge of principles and processes for providing customer and personal services. This includes customer needs assessment, meeting quality standards for services, and evaluation of customer satisfaction. **Education and Training:** Knowledge of principles and methods for curriculum and training design, teaching and instruction for individuals and groups, and the measurement of training effects. **Engineering and Technology:** Knowledge of the practical application of engineering science and technology. This includes applying principles, techniques, procedures, and equipment to the design and production of various goods and services. **Administration and Management:** Knowledge of business and management principles involved in strategic planning, resource allocation, human resources modeling, leadership technique, production methods, and coordination of people and resources.

Network Systems and Data Communications Analysts

- ◎ Education/Training Required: Bachelor's degree
- ◎ Annual Earnings: $59,300
- ◎ Growth: 57.0%
- ◎ Annual Job Openings: 29,000
- ◎ Self-Employed: 23.6%
- ◎ Part-Time: 7.9%

Analyze, design, test, and evaluate network systems, such as local area networks (LAN), wide area networks (WAN), Internet, intranet, and other data communications systems. Perform network modeling, analysis, and planning. Research and recommend network and data communications hardware and software. Includes telecommunications specialists who deal with the interfacing of computer and communications equipment. May supervise computer programmers. Maintain needed files by adding and deleting files on the network server and backing up files to guarantee their safety in the event of problems with the network. Monitor system performance and provide security measures, troubleshooting and maintenance as needed. Assist users to diagnose and solve data communication problems. Set up user accounts, regulating and monitoring file access to ensure confidentiality and proper use. Design and implement network configurations, network architecture (including hardware and software technology, site locations, and integration of technologies), and systems. Maintain the peripherals, such as printers, that are connected to the network. Identify areas of operation that need upgraded equipment such as modems, fiber optic cables, and telephone wires. Train users in use of equipment. Develop and write procedures for installation, use, and troubleshooting of communications hardware and software. Adapt and modify existing software to meet specific needs. Work with other engineers, systems analysts, programmers, technicians, scientists and top-level managers in the design, testing and evaluation of systems. Test and evaluate hardware and software to determine efficiency, reliability, and compatibility with existing system, and make purchase recommendations. Read technical manuals and brochures to determine which equipment meets establishment requirements. Consult customers, visit workplaces or conduct surveys to determine present and future user needs. Visit vendors, attend conferences or training and study technical journals to keep up with changes in technology. **SKILLS—Installation:** Installing equipment, machines, wiring, or programs to meet specifications. **Troubleshooting:** Determining causes of operating errors and deciding what to do about them. **Technology Design:** Generating or adapting equipment and technology to serve user needs. **Management of Material Resources:** Obtaining and seeing to the appropriate use of equipment, facilities, and materials needed to do certain work. **Systems Analysis:** Determining how a system should work and how changes in conditions, operations, and the environment will affect outcomes. **Systems Evaluation:** Identifying measures or indicators of system performance and the actions needed to improve or correct performance relative to the goals of the system. **Operations Analysis:** Analyzing needs and product requirements to create a design. **Equipment Maintenance:** Performing routine maintenance on equipment and determining when and what kind of maintenance is needed.

GOE—Interest Area: 11. Information Technology. **Work Group:** 11.02. Information Technology Specialties. **Other Jobs in This Work Group:** Computer Operators; Computer Programmers; Computer Security Specialists; Computer Software Engineers, Applications; Computer Software Engineers, Systems Software; Computer Support Specialists; Computer Systems Analysts; Database Administrators. **PERSONALITY TYPE:** Investigative. Investigative occupations frequently involve working with ideas and require an extensive amount of thinking. These occupations can involve searching for facts and figuring out problems mentally.

EDUCATION/TRAINING PROGRAM(S)— Computer and Information Sciences, General; Computer and Information Systems Security; Computer Systems Analysis/Analyst; Computer Systems Networking and Telecommunications; Information Technology. **RELATED KNOWLEDGE/COURSES—Customer and Personal Service:** Knowledge of principles and processes for providing customer and personal services. This includes customer needs assessment, meeting quality standards for services, and evaluation of customer satisfaction. **Computers and Electronics:** Knowledge of circuit boards, processors, chips, electronic equipment, and computer hardware and software, including applications and programming. **Telecommunications:** Knowledge of transmission, broadcasting, switching, control, and operation of telecommunications systems. **Education and Training:** Knowledge of principles and methods for curriculum and training design, teaching and instruction for individuals and groups, and the measurement of training effects. **Engineering and Technology:** Knowledge of the practical application of engineering science and technology. This includes applying principles, techniques, procedures, and equipment to the design and production of various goods and services. **Design:** Knowledge of design techniques, tools, and principles involved in production of precision technical plans, blueprints, drawings, and models.

N

Nuclear Engineers

◎ Education/Training Required: Bachelor's degree

◎ Annual Earnings: $83,260

◎ Growth: –0.1%

◎ Annual Job Openings: 1,000

◎ Self-Employed: 0%

◎ Part-Time: 1.8%

Conduct research on nuclear engineering problems or apply principles and theory of nuclear science to problems concerned with release, control, and utilization of nuclear energy and nuclear waste disposal. Analyze available data and consult with other scientists in order to determine parameters of experimentation and suitability of analytical models. Conduct tests of nuclear fuel behavior and cycles and performance of nuclear machinery and equipment, in order to optimize performance of existing plants. Design and develop nuclear equipment such as reactor cores, radiation shielding, and associated instrumentation and control mechanisms. Design and direct nuclear research projects in order to discover facts, to test or modify theoretical models, or to develop new theoretical models or new uses for current models. Examine accidents in order to obtain data that can be used to design preventive measures. Formulate equations that describe phenomena occurring during fission of nuclear fuels, and develop research models based on the equations. Keep abreast of developments and changes in the nuclear field by reading technical journals and by independent study and research. Monitor nuclear facility operations in order to identify any design, construction, or operation practices that violate safety regulations and laws or that could jeopardize the safety of operations. Perform experiments that will provide information about acceptable methods of nuclear material usage, nuclear fuel reclamation, and waste disposal. Recommend preventive measures to be taken in the handling of nuclear technology, based on data obtained from operations monitoring or from evaluation of test results. Synthesize analyses of test results, and use the results to prepare technical reports of findings and recommendations. Design and oversee construction and operation of nuclear reactors and power plants and nuclear fuels reprocessing and reclamation systems. Develop new medical scanning technologies. Direct operating and maintenance activities of operational nuclear power plants in order to ensure efficiency and conformity to safety standards. Initiate corrective actions and/or order plant shutdowns in emergency situations. Prepare construction project proposals that include cost estimates, and discuss proposals with interested parties such as vendors, contractors, and nuclear facility review boards. **SKILLS—Science:** Using scientific rules and methods to solve problems. **Technology Design:** Generating or adapting equipment and technology to serve user needs. **Operations Analysis:** Analyzing needs and product requirements to create a design. **Quality Control Analysis:** Conducting tests and inspections of products, services, or processes to evaluate quality or performance. **Systems Evaluation:** Identifying measures or indicators of system performance and the actions needed to improve or correct performance relative to the goals of the system. **Operation Monitoring:** Watching gauges, dials, or other indicators to make sure a machine is working properly. **Systems Analysis:** Determining how a system should work and how changes in conditions, operations, and the environment will affect outcomes. **Mathematics:** Using mathematics to solve problems.

GOE—Interest Area: 15. Scientific Research, Engineering, and Mathematics. **Work Group:** 15.07. Research and Design Engineering. **Other Jobs in This Work Group:** Aerospace Engineers; Biomedical Engineers; Chemical Engineers; Civil Engineers; Computer Hardware Engineers; Electrical Engineers; Electronics Engineers, Except Computer; Marine Architects; Marine Engineers; Materials Engineers; Mechanical Engineers. **PERSONALITY TYPE:** Investigative. Investigative occupations frequently involve working with ideas and require an extensive amount of thinking. These occupations can involve searching for facts and figuring out problems mentally.

EDUCATION/TRAINING PROGRAM(S)—Nuclear Engineering. **RELATED KNOWLEDGE/COURSES—Engineering and Technology:** Knowledge of the practical application of engineering science and technology. This includes applying principles, techniques, procedures, and equipment to the design and production of various goods and services. **Physics:** Knowledge and prediction of physical principles and laws and their interrelationships and applications to understanding fluid, material, and atmospheric dynamics and mechanical, electrical, atomic, and subatomic structures and processes. **Design:** Knowledge of design techniques, tools, and principles involved in production of precision technical plans, blueprints, drawings, and models. **Mathematics:** Knowledge of arithmetic, algebra, geometry, calculus, and statistics and their applications. **Chemistry:** Knowledge of the chemical composition, structure, and properties of substances and of the chemical processes and transformations that they undergo. This includes uses of chemicals and their danger signs, production techniques, and disposal methods. **Administration and Management:** Knowledge of business and management principles involved in strategic planning, resource allocation, human resources modeling, leadership technique, production methods, and coordination of people and resources.

Nuclear Medicine Technologists

- Education/Training Required: Associate's degree
- Annual Earnings: $53,680
- Growth: 23.6%
- Annual Job Openings: 2,000
- Self-Employed: 0.2%
- Part-Time: 17.5%

Prepare, administer, and measure radioactive isotopes in therapeutic, diagnostic, and tracer studies utilizing a variety of radioisotope equipment. Prepare stock solutions of radioactive materials and calculate doses to be administered by radiologists. Subject patients to radiation. Execute blood volume, red cell survival, and fat absorption studies following standard laboratory techniques. Calculate, measure and record radiation dosage or radiopharmaceuticals received, used and disposed, using computer and following physician's prescription. Detect and map radiopharmaceuticals in patients' bodies, using a camera to produce photographic or computer images. Explain test procedures and safety precautions to patients and provide them with assistance during test procedures. Administer radiopharmaceuticals or radiation to patients to detect or treat diseases, using radioisotope equipment, under direction of physician. Produce a computer-generated or film image for interpretation by a physician. Process cardiac function studies, using computer. Dispose of radioactive materials and store radiopharmaceuticals, following radiation safety procedures. Record and process results of procedures. Prepare stock radiopharmaceuticals, adhering to safety standards that minimize radiation exposure to workers and patients. Maintain and calibrate radioisotope and laboratory equipment. Gather information on patients' illnesses and medical history to guide the choice of diagnostic procedures for therapy. Measure glandular activity, blood volume, red cell survival, and radioactivity of patient, using scanners, Geiger counters, scintillometers, and other laboratory equipment. Train and supervise student or subordinate nuclear medicine technologists. Position radiation fields, radiation beams, and patient to allow for most effective treatment of patient's disease, using computer. Add radioactive substances to biological specimens, such as blood, urine and feces, to determine therapeutic drug or hormone levels. Develop treatment procedures for nuclear medicine treatment programs. **SKILLS—Science:** Using scientific rules and methods to solve problems. **Social Perceptiveness:** Being aware of others' reactions and understanding why they react as they do. **Operation Monitoring:** Watching gauges, dials, or other indicators to make sure a machine is working properly. **Service Orientation:** Actively looking for ways to help people. **Instructing:** Teaching others how to do something. **Active Learning:** Understanding the implications of new information for both current and future problem-solving and decision-making. **Coordination:** Adjusting actions in relation to others' actions. **Operation and Control:** Controlling operations of equipment or systems.

GOE—Interest Area: 08. Health Science. **Work Group:** 08.06. Medical Technology. **Other Jobs in This Work Group:** Biological Technicians; Cardiovascular Technologists and Technicians; Diagnostic Medical Sonographers; Medical and Clinical Laboratory Technicians; Medical and Clinical Laboratory Technologists; Medical Equipment Preparers; Medical Records and Health Information Technicians; Opticians, Dispensing; Orthotists and Prosthetists; Radiologic Technicians; Radiologic Technologists. **PERSONALITY TYPE:** Investigative. Investigative occupations frequently involve working with ideas and require an extensive amount of thinking. These occupations can involve searching for facts and figuring out problems mentally.

EDUCATION/TRAINING PROGRAM(S)— Nuclear Medical Technology/Technologist; Radiation Protection/Health Physics Technician. **RELATED KNOWLEDGE/COURSES—Medi-** cine and Dentistry: Knowledge of the information and techniques needed to diagnose and treat human injuries, diseases, and deformities. This includes symptoms, treatment alternatives, drug properties and interactions, and preventive health-care measures. **Customer and Personal Service:** Knowledge of principles and processes for providing customer and personal services. This includes customer needs assessment, meeting quality standards for services, and evaluation of customer satisfaction. **Biology:** Knowledge of plant and animal organisms and their tissues, cells, functions, interdependencies, and interactions with each other and the environment. **Physics:** Knowledge and prediction of physical principles and laws and their interrelationships and applications to understanding fluid, material, and atmospheric dynamics and mechanical, electrical, atomic, and subatomic structures and processes. **Chemistry:** Knowledge of the chemical composition, structure, and properties of substances and of the chemical processes and transformations that they undergo. This includes uses of chemicals and their danger signs, production techniques, and disposal methods. **Computers and Electronics:** Knowledge of circuit boards, processors, chips, electronic equipment, and computer hardware and software, including applications and programming.

Nursing Instructors and Teachers, Postsecondary

◉ Education/Training Required: Master's degree

◉ Annual Earnings: $51,310

◉ Growth: 38.1% for all Postsecondary Teachers

◉ Annual Job Openings: 216,000 for all Postsecondary Teachers

◉ Self-Employed: 0.3% for all Postsecondary Teachers

◉ Part-Time: 27.7% for all Postsecondary Teachers

Demonstrate and teach patient care in classroom and clinical units to nursing students. Includes both teachers primarily engaged in teaching and those who do a combination of both teaching and research. Plan, evaluate, and revise curricula, course content, and course materials and methods of instruction. Prepare course materials such as syllabi, homework assignments, and handouts. Select and obtain materials and supplies such as textbooks and laboratory equipment. Supervise students' laboratory and clinical work. Supervise undergraduate and/or graduate teaching, internship, and research work. Act as advisers to student organizations. Assess clinical education needs, and patient and client teaching needs, utilizing a variety of methods. Collaborate with colleagues to address teaching and research issues. Conduct research in a particular field of knowledge, and publish findings in professional journals, books, and/or electronic media. Coordinate training programs with area universities, clinics, hospitals, health agencies, and/or vocational schools. Participate in campus and community events. Evaluate and grade students' class work, laboratory and clinic work, assignments, and papers. Prepare and deliver lectures to undergraduate and/or graduate students on topics such as pharmacology, mental health nursing, and community health-care practices. Advise students on academic and vocational curricula, and on career issues. Compile, administer, and grade examinations, or assign this work to others. Compile bibliographies of specialized materials for outside reading assignments. Demonstrate patient care in clinical units of hospitals. Initiate, facilitate, and moderate classroom discussions. Keep abreast of developments in their field by reading current literature, talking with colleagues, and participating in professional conferences. Maintain regularly scheduled office hours in order to advise and assist students. Maintain student attendance records, grades, and other required records. Participate in student recruitment, registration, and placement activities. Perform administrative duties such as serving as department head. Provide professional consulting services to government and/or industry. Serve on academic or administrative committees that deal with institutional policies, departmental matters, and academic issues. **SKILLS—Learning Strategies:** Selecting and using training/instructional methods and procedures appropriate for the situation when learning or teaching new things. **Instructing:** Teaching others how to do something. **Management of Personnel Resources:** Motivating, developing, and directing people as they work, identifying the best people for the job. **Science:** Using scientific rules and methods to solve problems. **Reading Comprehension:** Understanding written sentences and paragraphs in work-related documents. **Service Orientation:** Actively looking for ways to help people. **Social Perceptiveness:** Being aware of others' reactions and understanding why they react as they do. **Speaking:** Talking to others to convey information effectively. **Time Management:** Managing one's own time and the time of others.

GOE—Interest Area: 05. Education and Training. **Work Group:** 05.03. Postsecondary and Adult Teaching and Instructing. **Other Jobs in This Work Group:** Adult Literacy, Remedial Education, and GED Teachers and Instructors; Agricultural

Sciences Teachers, Postsecondary; Anthropology and Archeology Teachers, Postsecondary; Architecture Teachers, Postsecondary; Area, Ethnic, and Cultural Studies Teachers, Postsecondary; Art, Drama, and Music Teachers, Postsecondary; Atmospheric, Earth, Marine, and Space Sciences Teachers, Postsecondary; Biological Science Teachers, Postsecondary; Business Teachers, Postsecondary; Chemistry Teachers, Postsecondary; Communications Teachers, Postsecondary; Computer Science Teachers, Postsecondary; Criminal Justice and Law Enforcement Teachers, Postsecondary; Economics Teachers, Postsecondary; Education Teachers, Postsecondary; Engineering Teachers, Postsecondary; English Language and Literature Teachers, Postsecondary; Environmental Science Teachers, Postsecondary; Farm and Home Management Advisors; Foreign Language and Literature Teachers, Postsecondary; Forestry and Conservation Science Teachers, Postsecondary; Geography Teachers, Postsecondary; Graduate Teaching Assistants; Health Specialties Teachers, Postsecondary; History Teachers, Postsecondary; Home Economics Teachers, Postsecondary; Law Teachers, Postsecondary; Library Science Teachers, Postsecondary; Mathematical Science Teachers, Postsecondary; Philosophy and Religion Teachers, Postsecondary; Physics Teachers, Postsecondary; Political Science Teachers, Postsecondary; Psychology Teachers, Postsecondary; Recreation and Fitness Studies Teachers, Postsecondary; Self-Enrichment Education Teachers; Social Work Teachers, Postsecondary; Sociology Teachers, Postsecondary; Vocational Education Teachers, Postsecondary. **PERSONALITY TYPE:** Social. Social occupations frequently involve working with, communicating with, and teaching people. These occupations often involve helping or providing service to others.

EDUCATION/TRAINING PROGRAM(S)— Adult Health Nurse/Nursing; Clinical Nurse Specialist; Family Practice Nurse/Nurse Practitioner; Maternal/Child Health and Neonatal Nurse/Nursing; Nurse Anesthetist; Nurse Midwife/Nursing

Midwifery; Nursing—Registered Nurse Training (RN, ASN, BSN, MSN); Nursing Science (MS, PhD); Nursing, Other; Pediatric Nurse/Nursing; Perioperative/Operating Room and Surgical Nurse/Nursing; Pre-Nursing Studies; Psychiatric/Mental Health Nurse/Nursing; Public Health/Community Nurse/Nursing. **RELATED KNOWLEDGE/COURSES—Education and Training:** Knowledge of principles and methods for curriculum and training design, teaching and instruction for individuals and groups, and the measurement of training effects. **Medicine and Dentistry:** Knowledge of the information and techniques needed to diagnose and treat human injuries, diseases, and deformities. This includes symptoms, treatment alternatives, drug properties and interactions, and preventive health-care measures. **Biology:** Knowledge of plant and animal organisms and their tissues, cells, functions, interdependencies, and interactions with each other and the environment. **Psychology:** Knowledge of human behavior and performance; individual differences in ability, personality, and interests; learning and motivation; psychological research methods; and the assessment and treatment of behavioral and affective disorders. **Chemistry:** Knowledge of the chemical composition, structure, and properties of substances and of the chemical processes and transformations that they undergo. This includes uses of chemicals and their danger signs, production techniques, and disposal methods. **Therapy and Counseling:** Knowledge of principles, methods, and procedures for diagnosis, treatment, and rehabilitation of physical and mental dysfunctions and for career counseling and guidance.

Obstetricians and Gynecologists

- Education/Training Required: First professional degree
- Annual Earnings: More than $145,000
- Growth: 19.5%
- Annual Job Openings: 38,000
- Self-Employed: 16.9%
- Part-Time: 8.1%

Diagnose, treat, and help prevent diseases of women, especially those affecting the reproductive system and the process of childbirth. Conduct research to develop or test medications, treatments, or procedures to prevent or control disease or injury. Consult with, or provide consulting services to, other physicians. Direct and coordinate activities of nurses, students, assistants, specialists, therapists, and other medical staff. Plan, implement, or administer health programs in hospitals, businesses, or communities for prevention and treatment of injuries or illnesses. Prepare government and organizational reports on birth, death, and disease statistics, workforce evaluations, or the medical status of individuals. Advise patients and community members concerning diet, activity, hygiene, and disease prevention. Analyze records, reports, test results, or examination information to diagnose medical condition of patient. Care for and treat women during prenatal, natal and post-natal periods. Collect, record, and maintain patient information, such as medical histories, reports, and examination results. Explain procedures and discuss test results or prescribed treatments with patients. Monitor patients' condition and progress and re-evaluate treatments as necessary. Perform cesarean sections or other surgical procedures as needed to preserve patients' health and deliver babies safely. Prescribe or administer therapy, medication, and other specialized medical care to treat or prevent illness, disease, or injury. Refer patient to medical specialist or other practitioner when necessary. Treat diseases of female organs. **SKILLS—Science:** Using scientific rules and methods to solve problems. **Reading Comprehension:** Understanding written sentences and paragraphs in work-related documents. **Systems Evaluation:** Identifying measures or indicators of system performance and the actions needed to improve or correct performance relative to the goals of the system. **Active Learning:** Understanding the implications of new information for both current and future problem-solving and decision-making. **Judgment and Decision Making:** Considering the relative costs and benefits of potential actions to choose the most appropriate one. **Management of Personnel Resources:** Motivating, developing, and directing people as they work, identifying the best people for the job. **Social Perceptiveness:** Being aware of others' reactions and understanding why they react as they do. **Systems Analysis:** Determining how a system should work and how changes in conditions, operations, and the environment will affect outcomes.

GOE—Interest Area: 08. Health Science. **Work Group:** 08.02. Medicine and Surgery. **Other Jobs in This Work Group:** Anesthesiologists; Family and General Practitioners; Internists, General; Medical Assistants; Medical Transcriptionists; Pediatricians, General; Pharmacists; Pharmacy Aides; Pharmacy Technicians; Physician Assistants; Psychiatrists; Registered Nurses; Surgeons; Surgical Technologists. **PERSONALITY TYPE:** Investigative. Investigative occupations frequently involve working with ideas and require an extensive amount of thinking. These occupations can involve searching for facts and figuring out problems mentally.

EDUCATION/TRAINING PROGRAM(S)— Neonatal-Perinatal Medicine; Obstetrics and Gynecology. **RELATED KNOWLEDGE/COURSES— Medicine and Dentistry:** Knowledge of the information and techniques needed to diagnose and treat human injuries, diseases, and deformities. This includes symptoms, treatment alternatives, drug properties and interactions, and preventive health-care measures. **Biology:** Knowledge of plant and animal organisms and their tissues, cells, functions, interdependencies, and interactions with each other and the environment. **Therapy and Counseling:** Knowledge of principles, methods, and procedures for diagnosis, treatment, and rehabilitation of physical and mental dysfunctions and for career counseling and guidance. **Chemistry:** Knowledge of the chemical composition, structure, and properties of substances and of the chemical processes and transformations that they undergo. This includes uses of chemicals and their danger signs, production techniques, and disposal methods. **Administration and Management:** Knowledge of business and management principles involved in strategic planning, resource allocation, human resources modeling, leadership technique, production methods, and coordination of people and resources. **Personnel and Human Resources:** Knowledge of principles and procedures for personnel recruitment, selection, training, compensation and benefits, labor relations and negotiation, and personnel information systems. **Physics:** Knowledge and prediction of physical principles and laws and their interrelationships and applications to understanding fluid, material, and atmospheric dynamics and mechanical, electrical, atomic, and subatomic structures and processes.

Occupational Health and Safety Specialists

- ◎ Education/Training Required: Master's degree
- ◎ Annual Earnings: $48,330
- ◎ Growth: 13.2%
- ◎ Annual Job Openings: 6,000
- ◎ Self-Employed: 2.4%
- ◎ Part-Time: 6.5%

Review, evaluate, and analyze work environments and design programs and procedures to control,

eliminate, and prevent disease or injury caused by chemical, physical, and biological agents or ergonomic factors. May conduct inspections and enforce adherence to laws and regulations governing the health and safety of individuals. May be employed in the public or private sector. Investigates adequacy of ventilation, exhaust equipment, lighting, and other conditions which may affect employee health, comfort, or efficiency. Conducts evaluations of exposure to ionizing and nonionizing radiation and to noise. Collects samples of dust, gases, vapors, and other potentially toxic materials for analysis. Recommends measures to ensure maximum employee protection. Collaborates with engineers and physicians to institute control and remedial measures for hazardous and potentially hazardous conditions of equipment. Participates in educational meetings to instruct employees in matters pertaining to occupational health and prevention of accidents. Prepares reports including observations, analysis of contaminants, and recommendation for control and correction of hazards. Reviews physicians' reports and conducts worker studies to determine if diseases or illnesses are job related. Prepares and calibrates equipment used to collect and analyze samples. Prepares documents to be used in legal proceedings and gives testimony in court proceedings. Uses cost-benefit analysis to justify money spent. **SKILLS—Science:** Using scientific rules and methods to solve problems. **Writing:** Communicating effectively in writing as appropriate for the needs of the audience. **Speaking:** Talking to others to convey information effectively. **Mathematics:** Using mathematics to solve problems. **Management of Financial Resources:** Determining how money will be spent to get the work done and accounting for these expenditures. **Reading Comprehension:** Understanding written sentences and paragraphs in work-related documents. **Operation Monitoring:** Watching gauges, dials, or other indicators to make sure a machine is working properly. **Systems Analysis:** Determining how a system should work and how changes in conditions, operations, and the environment will affect outcomes.

GOE—Interest Area: 07. Government and Public Administration. Work Group: 07.03. Regulations Enforcement. Other Jobs in This Work Group: Agricultural Inspectors; Aviation Inspectors; Child Support, Missing Persons, and Unemployment Insurance Fraud Investigators; Environmental Compliance Inspectors; Equal Opportunity Representatives and Officers; Financial Examiners; Fire Inspectors; Fish and Game Wardens; Forest Fire Inspectors and Prevention Specialists; Government Property Inspectors and Investigators; Immigration and Customs Inspectors; Licensing Examiners and Inspectors; Marine Cargo Inspectors; Mechanical Inspectors; Motor Vehicle Inspectors; Nuclear Monitoring Technicians; Pressure Vessel Inspectors; Railroad Inspectors; Tax Examiners, Collectors, and Revenue Agents. **PERSONALITY TYPE:** Social. Social occupations frequently involve working with, communicating with, and teaching people. These occupations often involve helping or providing service to others.

EDUCATION/TRAINING PROGRAM(S)— Environmental Health; Industrial Safety Technology/Technician; Occupational Health and Industrial Hygiene; Occupational Safety and Health Technology/Technician; Quality Control and Safety Technologies/Technicians, Other. **RELATED KNOWLEDGE/COURSES—Public Safety and Security:** Knowledge of relevant equipment, policies, procedures, and strategies to promote effective local, state, or national security operations for the protection of people, data, property, and institutions. **Medicine and Dentistry:** Knowledge of the information and techniques needed to diagnose and treat human injuries, diseases, and deformities. This includes symptoms, treatment alternatives, drug properties and interactions, and preventive health-care measures. **Chemistry:** Knowledge of the chemical composition, structure, and properties of substances and of the chemical processes and transformations that they undergo. This includes uses of chemicals and their danger signs, production techniques, and disposal methods. **Physics:** Knowledge and prediction of physical principles and laws and

their interrelationships and applications to understanding fluid, material, and atmospheric dynamics and mechanical, electrical, atomic, and subatomic structures and processes. **Law and Government:** Knowledge of laws, legal codes, court procedures, precedents, government regulations, executive orders, agency rules, and the democratic political process. **Economics and Accounting:** Knowledge of economic and accounting principles and practices, the financial markets, banking, and the analysis and reporting of financial data. **Biology:** Knowledge of plant and animal organisms and their tissues, cells, functions, interdependencies, and interactions with each other and the environment.

Occupational Therapist Assistants

- ◎ Education/Training Required: Associate's degree
- ◎ Annual Earnings: $38,120
- ◎ Growth: 39.2%
- ◎ Annual Job Openings: 3,000
- ◎ Self-Employed: 2.9%
- ◎ Part-Time: 25.5%

Assist occupational therapists in providing occupational therapy treatments and procedures. May, in accordance with State laws, assist in development of treatment plans, carry out routine functions, direct activity programs, and document the progress of treatments. Generally requires formal training. Observe and record patients' progress, attitudes, and behavior, and maintain this information in client records. Maintain and promote a positive attitude toward clients and their treatment programs. Monitor patients' performance in therapy activities, providing encouragement. Select therapy activities to fit patients' needs and capabilities. Instruct, or assist in instructing, patients and families in home programs, basic living skills, and the care and use of adaptive equipment. Evaluate the daily living skills and capacities of physically, developmentally or emotionally disabled clients. Aid patients in dressing and grooming themselves. Implement, or assist occupational therapists with implementing, treatment plans designed to help clients function independently. Report to supervisors, verbally or in writing, on patients' progress, attitudes and behavior. Alter treatment programs to obtain better results if treatment is not having the intended effect. Work under the direction of occupational therapists to plan, implement and administer educational, vocational, and recreational programs that restore and enhance performance in individuals with functional impairments. Design, fabricate, and repair assistive devices and make adaptive changes to equipment and environments. Assemble, clean, and maintain equipment and materials for patient use. Teach patients how to deal constructively with their emotions. Perform clerical duties such as scheduling appointments, collecting data, and documenting health insurance billings. Transport patients to and from the occupational therapy work area. Demonstrate therapy techniques, such as manual and creative arts, and games. Order any needed educational or treatment supplies. Assist educational specialists or clinical psychologists in administering situational or diagnostic tests to measure client's abilities or progress. **SKILLS—Social Perceptiveness:** Being aware of others' reactions and understanding why they react as they do. **Instructing:** Teaching others how to do something. **Service Orientation:** Actively looking for ways to help people. **Persuasion:** Persuading others to change their minds or behavior. **Time Management:** Managing one's own time and the time of others. **Learning Strategies:** Selecting and using training/instructional methods and procedures appropriate for the situation when learning or teaching new things. **Monitoring:** Monitoring or assessing your performance or that of other individuals or organizations to make improvements or take corrective action. **Active Listening:** Giving full attention to what other people are saying, taking time to understand the points being made, asking

questions as appropriate, and not interrupting at inappropriate times. **Writing:** Communicating effectively in writing as appropriate for the needs of the audience. **Critical Thinking:** Using logic and reasoning to identify the strengths and weaknesses of alternative solutions, conclusions, or approaches to problems.

GOE—Interest Area: 08. Health Science. **Work Group:** 08.07. Medical Therapy. **Other Jobs in This Work Group:** Audiologists; Massage Therapists; Occupational Therapist Aides; Occupational Therapists; Physical Therapist Aides; Physical Therapist Assistants; Physical Therapists; Radiation Therapists; Recreational Therapists; Respiratory Therapists; Respiratory Therapy Technicians; Speech-Language Pathologists. **PERSONALITY TYPE:** Social. Social occupations frequently involve working with, communicating with, and teaching people. These occupations often involve helping or providing service to others.

EDUCATION/TRAINING PROGRAM(S)— Occupational Therapist Assistant. **RELATED KNOWLEDGE/COURSES—Psychology:** Knowledge of human behavior and performance; individual differences in ability, personality, and interests; learning and motivation; psychological research methods; and the assessment and treatment of behavioral and affective disorders. **Therapy and Counseling:** Knowledge of principles, methods, and procedures for diagnosis, treatment, and rehabilitation of physical and mental dysfunctions and for career counseling and guidance. **Sociology and Anthropology:** Knowledge of group behavior and dynamics, societal trends and influences, human migrations, ethnicity, and cultures and their history and origins. **Philosophy and Theology:** Knowledge of different philosophical systems and religions. This includes their basic principles, values, ethics, ways of thinking, customs, and practices and their impact on human culture. **Customer and Personal Service:** Knowledge of principles and processes for providing customer and personal services. This includes customer needs assessment, meeting quality standards for services, and evaluation of customer satisfaction. **Medicine and Dentistry:** Knowledge of the information and techniques needed to diagnose and treat human injuries, diseases, and deformities. This includes symptoms, treatment alternatives, drug properties and interactions, and preventive health-care measures.

Occupational Therapists

- Education/Training Required: Bachelor's degree
- Annual Earnings: $53,320
- Growth: 35.2%
- Annual Job Openings: 10,000
- Self-Employed: 4.0%
- Part-Time: 31.1%

Assess, plan, organize, and participate in rehabilitative programs that help restore vocational, homemaking, and daily living skills, as well as general independence, to disabled persons. Complete and maintain necessary records. Evaluate patients' progress and prepare reports that detail progress. Test and evaluate patients' physical and mental abilities and analyze medical data to determine realistic rehabilitation goals for patients. Select activities that will help individuals learn work and life-management skills within limits of their mental and physical capabilities. Plan, organize, and conduct occupational therapy programs in hospital, institutional, or community settings to help rehabilitate those impaired because of illness, injury or psychological or developmental problems. Recommend changes in patients' work or living environments, consistent with their needs and capabilities. Consult with rehabilitation team to select activity programs and coordinate occupational therapy with other therapeutic activities. Help clients improve decision making, abstract reasoning, memory, sequencing, coordination and perceptual skills, using computer programs. Develop and participate in health pro-

motion programs, group activities, or discussions to promote client health, facilitate social adjustment, alleviate stress, and prevent physical or mental disability. Provide training and supervision in therapy techniques and objectives for students and nurses and other medical staff. Design and create, or requisition, special supplies and equipment, such as splints, braces and computer-aided adaptive equipment. Plan and implement programs and social activities to help patients learn work and school skills and adjust to handicaps. Lay out materials such as puzzles, scissors and eating utensils for use in therapy, and clean and repair these tools after therapy sessions. Advise on health risks in the workplace and on health-related transition to retirement. Conduct research in occupational therapy. **SKILLS—Social Perceptiveness:** Being aware of others' reactions and understanding why they react as they do. **Service Orientation:** Actively looking for ways to help people. **Instructing:** Teaching others how to do something. **Science:** Using scientific rules and methods to solve problems. **Coordination:** Adjusting actions in relation to others' actions. **Technology Design:** Generating or adapting equipment and technology to serve user needs. **Persuasion:** Persuading others to change their minds or behavior. **Reading Comprehension:** Understanding written sentences and paragraphs in work-related documents. **Active Learning:** Understanding the implications of new information for both current and future problem-solving and decision-making.

GOE—Interest Area: 08. Health Science. **Work Group:** 08.07. Medical Therapy. **Other Jobs in This Work Group:** Audiologists; Massage Therapists; Occupational Therapist Aides; Occupational Therapist Assistants; Physical Therapist Aides; Physical Therapist Assistants; Physical Therapists; Radiation Therapists; Recreational Therapists; Respiratory Therapists; Respiratory Therapy Technicians; Speech-Language Pathologists. **PERSONALITY TYPE:** Social. Social occupations frequently involve working with, communicating with, and teaching people. These occupations often involve helping or providing service to others.

EDUCATION/TRAINING PROGRAM(S)—Occupational Therapy/Therapist. **RELATED KNOWLEDGE/COURSES**—**Therapy and Counseling:** Knowledge of principles, methods, and procedures for diagnosis, treatment, and rehabilitation of physical and mental dysfunctions and for career counseling and guidance. **Psychology:** Knowledge of human behavior and performance; individual differences in ability, personality, and interests; learning and motivation; psychological research methods; and the assessment and treatment of behavioral and affective disorders. **Customer and Personal Service:** Knowledge of principles and processes for providing customer and personal services. This includes customer needs assessment, meeting quality standards for services, and evaluation of customer satisfaction. **Medicine and Dentistry:** Knowledge of the information and techniques needed to diagnose and treat human injuries, diseases, and deformities. This includes symptoms, treatment alternatives, drug properties and interactions, and preventive health-care measures. **Education and Training:** Knowledge of principles and methods for curriculum and training design, teaching and instruction for individuals and groups, and the measurement of training effects. **Sociology and Anthropology:** Knowledge of group behavior and dynamics, societal trends and influences, human migrations, ethnicity, and cultures and their history and origins.

Operations Research Analysts

- Education/Training Required: Master's degree
- Annual Earnings: $59,090
- Growth: 6.2%
- Annual Job Openings: 6,000
- Self-Employed: 5.8%
- Part-Time: 2.7%

Formulate and apply mathematical modeling and other optimizing methods using a computer to develop and interpret information that assists management with decision making, policy formulation, or other managerial functions. May develop related software, service, or products. Frequently concentrates on collecting and analyzing data and developing decision support software. May develop and supply optimal time, cost, or logistics networks for program evaluation, review, or implementation. Prepares for management reports defining problem, evaluation, and possible solution. Studies information and selects plan from competitive proposals that afford maximum probability of profit or effectiveness relating to cost or risk. Defines data requirements and gathers and validates information, applying judgment and statistical tests. Designs, conducts, and evaluates experimental operational models where insufficient data exists to formulate model. Performs validation and testing of model to ensure adequacy, or determines need for reformulation. Analyzes problem in terms of management information and conceptualizes and defines problem. Prepares model of problem in form of one or several equations that relates constants and variables, restrictions, alternatives, conflicting objectives and their numerical parameters. Specifies manipulative or computational methods to be applied to model. Evaluates implementation and effectiveness of research. Develops and applies time and cost networks to plan and control large projects. **SKILLS—Systems Evaluation:** Identifying measures or indicators of system performance and the actions needed to improve or correct performance relative to the goals of the system. **Systems Analysis:** Determining how a system should work and how changes in conditions, operations, and the environment will affect outcomes. **Mathematics:** Using mathematics to solve problems. **Judgment and Decision Making:** Considering the relative costs and benefits of potential actions to choose the most appropriate one. **Science:** Using scientific rules and methods to solve problems. **Monitoring:** Monitoring or assessing your performance or that of other individuals or organizations to make improvements or take corrective action. **Critical Thinking:** Using logic and reasoning to identify the strengths and weaknesses of alternative solutions, conclusions, or approaches to problems. **Complex Problem Solving:** Identifying complex problems and reviewing related information to develop and evaluate options and implement solutions.

GOE—**Interest Area:** 04. Business and Administration. **Work Group:** 04.05. Accounting, Auditing, and Analytical Support. **Other Jobs in This Work Group:** Accountants; Auditors; Budget Analysts; Industrial Engineering Technicians; Logisticians; Management Analysts. **PERSONALITY TYPE:** Investigative. Investigative occupations frequently involve working with ideas and require an extensive amount of thinking. These occupations can involve searching for facts and figuring out problems mentally.

EDUCATION/TRAINING PROGRAM(S)— Management Science, General; Management Sciences and Quantitative Methods, Other; Operations Research. **RELATED KNOWLEDGE/COURSES—Mathematics:** Knowledge of arithmetic, algebra, geometry, calculus, and statistics and their applications. **Economics and Accounting:** Knowledge of economic and accounting principles and practices, the financial markets, banking, and the analysis and reporting of financial data. **Administration and Management:** Knowledge of business and management principles involved in strategic planning, resource allocation, human resources modeling, leadership technique, production methods, and coordination of people and resources. **Production and Processing:** Knowledge of raw materials, production processes, quality control, costs, and other techniques for maximizing the effective manufacture and distribution of goods. **Computers and Electronics:** Knowledge of circuit boards, processors, chips, electronic equipment, and computer hardware and software, including applications and programming. **Personnel and Human Resources:** Knowledge of principles and procedures for personnel recruitment, selection, training, compensation and benefits, labor relations and negotiation, and personnel information systems.

Optometrists

- ◎ Education/Training Required: First professional degree
- ◎ Annual Earnings: $87,340
- ◎ Growth: 17.1%
- ◎ Annual Job Openings: 2,000
- ◎ Self-Employed: 29.2%
- ◎ Part-Time: 25.1%

Diagnose, manage, and treat conditions and diseases of the human eye and visual system. Examine eyes and visual system, diagnose problems or impairments, prescribe corrective lenses, and provide treatment. May prescribe therapeutic drugs to treat specific eye conditions. Examine eyes, using observation, instruments and pharmaceutical agents, to determine visual acuity and perception, focus and coordination and to diagnose diseases and other abnormalities such as glaucoma or color blindness. Analyze test results and develop a treatment plan. Prescribe, supply, fit and adjust eyeglasses, contact lenses and other vision aids. Prescribe medications to treat eye diseases if state laws permit. Educate and counsel patients on contact lens care, visual hygiene, lighting arrangements and safety factors. Consult with and refer patients to ophthalmologist or other health-care practitioner if additional medical treatment is determined necessary. Remove foreign bodies from the eye. Provide patients undergoing eye surgeries, such as cataract and laser vision correction, with pre- and post-operative care. Prescribe therapeutic procedures to correct or conserve vision. Provide vision therapy and low vision rehabilitation. **SKILLS—Science:** Using scientific rules and methods to solve problems. **Persuasion:** Persuading others to change their minds or behavior. **Judgment and Decision Making:** Considering the relative costs and benefits of potential actions to choose the most appropriate one. **Management of Personnel Resources:** Motivating, developing, and directing people as they work, identifying the best people for the job. **Service Orientation:** Actively looking for ways to help people. **Active Listening:** Giving full attention to what other people are saying, taking time to understand the points being made, asking questions as appropriate, and not interrupting at inappropriate times. **Reading Comprehension:** Understanding written sentences and paragraphs in work-related documents. **Active Learning:** Understanding the implications of new information for both current and future problem-solving and decision-making. **Instructing:** Teaching others how to do something.

GOE—Interest Area: 08. Health Science. **Work Group:** 08.04. Health Specialties. **Other Jobs in This Work Group:** Chiropractors; Podiatrists. **PERSONALITY TYPE:** Investigative. Investigative occupations frequently involve working with ideas and require an extensive amount of thinking. These occupations can involve searching for facts and figuring out problems mentally.

EDUCATION/TRAINING PROGRAM(S)— Optometry (OD). **RELATED KNOWLEDGE/ COURSES—Medicine and Dentistry:** Knowledge of the information and techniques needed to diagnose and treat human injuries, diseases, and deformities. This includes symptoms, treatment alternatives, drug properties and interactions, and preventive health-care measures. **Biology:** Knowledge of plant and animal organisms and their tissues, cells, functions, interdependencies, and interactions with each other and the environment. **Psychology:** Knowledge of human behavior and performance; individual differences in ability, personality, and interests; learning and motivation; psychological research methods; and the assessment and treatment of behavioral and affective disorders. **Customer and Personal Service:** Knowledge of principles and processes for providing customer and personal services. This includes customer needs assessment, meeting quality standards for

services, and evaluation of customer satisfaction. **Personnel and Human Resources:** Knowledge of principles and procedures for personnel recruitment, selection, training, compensation and benefits, labor relations and negotiation, and personnel information systems. **Sales and Marketing:** Knowledge of principles and methods for showing, promoting, and selling products or services. This includes marketing strategy and tactics, product demonstration, sales techniques, and sales control systems.

Oral and Maxillofacial Surgeons

- Education/Training Required: First professional degree
- Annual Earnings: $120,420
- Growth: 4.1%
- Annual Job Openings: 7,000
- Self-Employed: 39.9%
- Part-Time: 22.3%

Perform surgery on mouth, jaws, and related head and neck structure to execute difficult and multiple extractions of teeth, to remove tumors and other abnormal growths, to correct abnormal jaw relations by mandibular or maxillary revision, to prepare mouth for insertion of dental prosthesis, or to treat fractured jaws. Administer general and local anesthetics. Collaborate with other professionals such as restorative dentists and orthodontists in order to plan treatment. Perform surgery on the mouth and jaws in order to treat conditions such as cleft lip and palate and jaw growth problems. Perform surgery to prepare the mouth for dental implants, and to aid in the regeneration of deficient bone and gum tissues. Provide emergency treatment of facial injuries including facial lacerations, intra-oral lacerations, and fractured facial bones. Remove impacted, damaged, and non-restorable teeth.

Remove tumors and other abnormal growths of the oral and facial regions, using surgical instruments. Restore form and function by moving skin, bone, nerves, and other tissues from other parts of the body in order to reconstruct the jaws and face. Evaluate the position of the wisdom teeth in order to determine whether problems exist currently or might occur in the future. Perform minor cosmetic procedures such as chin and cheek-bone enhancements, and minor facial rejuvenation procedures including the use of Botox and laser technology. Treat infections of the oral cavity, salivary glands, jaws, and neck. Treat problems affecting the oral mucosa such as mouth ulcers and infections. Treat snoring problems, using laser surgery. **SKILLS— Science:** Using scientific rules and methods to solve problems. **Reading Comprehension:** Understanding written sentences and paragraphs in work-related documents. **Judgment and Decision Making:** Considering the relative costs and benefits of potential actions to choose the most appropriate one. **Critical Thinking:** Using logic and reasoning to identify the strengths and weaknesses of alternative solutions, conclusions, or approaches to problems. **Active Learning:** Understanding the implications of new information for both current and future problem-solving and decision-making. **Learning Strategies:** Selecting and using training/instructional methods and procedures appropriate for the situation when learning or teaching new things. **Service Orientation:** Actively looking for ways to help people. **Monitoring:** Monitoring or assessing your performance or that of other individuals or organizations to make improvements or take corrective action.

GOE—Interest Area: 08. Health Science. **Work Group:** 08.03. Dentistry. **Other Jobs in This Work Group:** Dental Assistants; Dental Hygienists; Dentists, General; Orthodontists; Prosthodontists. **PERSONALITY TYPE:** Investigative. Investigative occupations frequently involve working with ideas and require an extensive amount of thinking. These occupations can involve searching for facts and figuring out problems mentally.

EDUCATION/TRAINING PROGRAM(S)— Dental/Oral Surgery Specialty; Oral/Maxillofacial Surgery (Cert, MS, PhD). **RELATED KNOWLEDGE/COURSES—Medicine and Dentistry:** Knowledge of the information and techniques needed to diagnose and treat human injuries, diseases, and deformities. This includes symptoms, treatment alternatives, drug properties and interactions, and preventive health-care measures. **Chemistry:** Knowledge of the chemical composition, structure, and properties of substances and of the chemical processes and transformations that they undergo. This includes uses of chemicals and their danger signs, production techniques, and disposal methods. **Biology:** Knowledge of plant and animal organisms and their tissues, cells, functions, interdependencies, and interactions with each other and the environment. **Psychology:** Knowledge of human behavior and performance; individual differences in ability, personality, and interests; learning and motivation; psychological research methods; and the assessment and treatment of behavioral and affective disorders. **Therapy and Counseling:** Knowledge of principles, methods, and procedures for diagnosis, treatment, and rehabilitation of physical and mental dysfunctions and for career counseling and guidance. **English Language:** Knowledge of the structure and content of the English language, including the meaning and spelling of words, rules of composition, and grammar.

Orthodontists

- Education/Training Required: First professional degree
- Annual Earnings: $120,420
- Growth: 4.1%
- Annual Job Openings: 7,000
- Self-Employed: 39.9%
- Part-Time: 22.3%

Examine, diagnose, and treat dental malocclusions and oral cavity anomalies. Design and fabricate appliances to realign teeth and jaws to produce and maintain normal function and to improve appearance. Adjust dental appliances periodically in order to produce and maintain normal function. Coordinate orthodontic services with other dental and medical services. Design and fabricate appliances, such as space maintainers, retainers, and labial and lingual arch wires. Diagnose teeth and jaw or other dental-facial abnormalities. Examine patients in order to assess abnormalities of jaw development, tooth position, and other dental-facial structures. Fit dental appliances in patients' mouths in order to alter the position and relationship of teeth and jaws, and to realign teeth. Prepare diagnostic and treatment records. Provide patients with proposed treatment plans and cost estimates. Study diagnostic records such as medical/dental histories, plaster models of the teeth, photos of a patient's face and teeth, and X-rays in order to develop patient treatment plans. Instruct dental officers and technical assistants in orthodontic procedures and techniques. **SKILLS—Science:** Using scientific rules and methods to solve problems. **Technology Design:** Generating or adapting equipment and technology to serve user needs. **Reading Comprehension:** Understanding written sentences and paragraphs in work-related documents. **Active Learning:** Understanding the implications of new information for both current and future problem-solving and decision-making. **Service Orientation:** Actively looking for ways to help people. **Operations Analysis:** Analyzing needs and product requirements to create a design. **Critical Thinking:** Using logic and reasoning to identify the strengths and weaknesses of alternative solutions, conclusions, or approaches to problems. **Complex Problem Solving:** Identifying complex problems and reviewing related information to develop and evaluate options and implement solutions. **Equipment Selection:** Determining the kind of tools and equipment needed to do a job. **Judgment and Decision Making:** Considering the relative costs and benefits of potential actions to choose the most appropriate one.

GOE—Interest Area: 08. Health Science. **Work Group:** 08.03. Dentistry. **Other Jobs in This Work Group:** Dental Assistants; Dental Hygienists; Dentists, General; Oral and Maxillofacial Surgeons; Prosthodontists. **PERSONALITY TYPE:** Investigative. Investigative occupations frequently involve working with ideas and require an extensive amount of thinking. These occupations can involve searching for facts and figuring out problems mentally.

EDUCATION/TRAINING PROGRAM(S)— Orthodontics Specialty; Orthodontics/Orthodontology (Cert, MS, PhD). **RELATED KNOWLEDGE/COURSES—Medicine and Dentistry:** Knowledge of the information and techniques needed to diagnose and treat human injuries, diseases, and deformities. This includes symptoms, treatment alternatives, drug properties and interactions, and preventive health-care measures. **Biology:** Knowledge of plant and animal organisms and their tissues, cells, functions, interdependencies, and interactions with each other and the environment. **Therapy and Counseling:** Knowledge of principles, methods, and procedures for diagnosis, treatment, and rehabilitation of physical and mental dysfunctions and for career counseling and guidance. **Chemistry:** Knowledge of the chemical composition, structure, and properties of substances and of the chemical processes and transformations that they undergo. This includes uses of chemicals and their danger signs, production techniques, and disposal methods. **Administration and Management:** Knowledge of business and management principles involved in strategic planning, resource allocation, human resources modeling, leadership technique, production methods, and coordination of people and resources. **Design:** Knowledge of design techniques, tools, and principles involved in production of precision technical plans, blueprints, drawings, and models.

Orthotists and Prosthetists

⊚ Education/Training Required: Bachelor's degree

⊚ Annual Earnings: $49,860

⊚ Growth: 18.9%

⊚ Annual Job Openings: 1,000

⊚ Self-Employed: 2.1%

⊚ Part-Time: 14.6%

Assist patients with disabling conditions of limbs and spine or with partial or total absence of limb by fitting and preparing orthopedic braces or prostheses. Train and supervise orthopedic and prosthetic assistants and technicians, and other support staff. Update skills and knowledge by attending conferences and seminars. Confer with physicians in order to formulate specifications and prescriptions for orthopedic and/or prosthetic devices. Construct and fabricate appliances or supervise others who are constructing the appliances. Design orthopedic and prosthetic devices, based on physicians' prescriptions, and examination and measurement of patients. Examine, interview, and measure patients in order to determine their appliance needs, and to identify factors that could affect appliance fit. Fit, test, and evaluate devices on patients, and make adjustments for proper fit, function, and comfort. Instruct patients in the use and care of orthoses and prostheses. Make and modify plaster casts of areas that will be fitted with prostheses or orthoses, for use in the device construction process. Repair, rebuild, and modify prosthetic and orthopedic appliances. Select materials and components to be used, based on device design. Maintain patients' records. Publish research findings, and present them at conferences and seminars. Research new ways to construct and use orthopedic and prosthetic devices. Show and explain orthopedic and prosthetic appliances to health-care workers. **SKILLS—Technology Design:** Generating or adapting equipment and technology to serve user needs. **Social Perceptiveness:** Being aware of others' reactions and understanding why they react as they do. **Speaking:** Talking to others to convey information effectively. **Instructing:** Teaching others how to do something. **Science:** Using scientific rules and methods to solve problems. **Management of Personnel Resources:** Motivating, developing, and directing people as they work, identifying the best people for the job. **Active Listening:** Giving full attention to what other people are saying, taking time to understand the points being made, asking questions as appropriate, and not interrupting at inappropriate times. **Service Orientation:** Actively looking for ways to help people.

GOE—Interest Area: 08. Health Science. **Work Group:** 08.06. Medical Technology. **Other Jobs in This Work Group:** Biological Technicians; Cardiovascular Technologists and Technicians; Diagnostic Medical Sonographers; Medical and Clinical Laboratory Technicians; Medical and Clinical Laboratory Technologists; Medical Equipment Preparers; Medical Records and Health Information Technicians; Nuclear Medicine Technologists; Opticians, Dispensing; Radiologic Technicians; Radiologic Technologists. **PERSONALITY TYPE:** Social. Social occupations frequently involve working with, communicating with, and teaching people. These occupations often involve helping or providing service to others.

EDUCATION/TRAINING PROGRAM(S)— Assistive/Augmentative Technology and Rehabilitation Engineering; Orthotist/Prosthetist. **RELATED KNOWLEDGE/COURSES—Medicine and Dentistry:** Knowledge of the information and techniques needed to diagnose and treat human injuries, diseases, and deformities. This includes symptoms, treatment alternatives, drug properties and interactions, and preventive health-care measures. **Design:** Knowledge of design techniques, tools, and principles involved in production of precision technical plans, blueprints, drawings, and models. **Building and Construction:** Knowledge of the materials, methods, and tools involved in the construction or repair of houses, buildings, or other structures such as highways and roads. **Therapy and Counseling:** Knowledge of principles, methods, and procedures for diagnosis, treatment, and rehabilitation of physical and mental dysfunctions and for career counseling and guidance. **Engineering and Technology:** Knowledge of the practical application of engineering science and technology. This includes applying principles, techniques, procedures, and equipment to the design and production of various goods and services. **Customer and Personal Service:** Knowledge of principles and processes for providing customer and personal services. This includes customer needs assessment, meeting quality standards for services, and evaluation of customer satisfaction. **Physics:** Knowledge and prediction of physical principles and laws and their interrelationships and applications to understanding fluid, material, and atmospheric dynamics and mechanical, electrical, atomic, and subatomic structures and processes. **Education and Training:** Knowledge of principles and methods for curriculum and training design, teaching and instruction for individuals and groups, and the measurement of training effects.

Paralegals and Legal Assistants

- Education/Training Required: Associate's degree
- Annual Earnings: $38,440
- Growth: 28.7%
- Annual Job Openings: 29,000
- Self-Employed: 2.3%
- Part-Time: 10.8%

Assist lawyers by researching legal precedent, investigating facts, or preparing legal documents. Conduct research to support a legal proceeding, to formulate a defense, or to initiate legal action. Prepare legal documents, including briefs, pleadings, appeals, wills, contracts, and real estate closing statements. Prepare affidavits or other documents, maintain document file, and file pleadings with court clerk. Gather and analyze research data, such as statutes, decisions, and legal articles, codes, and documents. Investigate facts and law of cases to determine causes of action and to prepare cases. Call upon witnesses to testify at hearing. Direct and coordinate law office activity, including delivery of subpoenas. Arbitrate disputes between parties and assist in real estate closing process. Keep and monitor legal volumes to ensure that law library is up-to-date. Appraise and inventory real and personal property for estate planning. **SKILLS—Time Management:** Managing one's own time and the time of others. **Instructing:** Teaching others how to do something. **Active Listening:** Giving full attention to what other people are saying, taking time to understand the points being made, asking questions as appropriate, and not interrupting at inappropriate times. **Writing:** Communicating effectively in writing as appropriate for the needs of the audience. **Speaking:** Talking to others to convey information effectively. **Monitoring:** Monitoring or assessing your performance or that of other individuals or organizations to make improvements or take corrective action. **Social Perceptiveness:** Being aware of others' reactions and understanding why they react as they do. **Service Orientation:** Actively looking for ways to help people.

GOE—Interest Area: 12. Law and Public Safety. **Work Group:** 12.03. Legal Support. **Other Jobs in This Work Group:** Law Clerks; Title Examiners and Abstractors; Title Searchers. **PERSONALITY TYPE:** Enterprising. Enterprising occupations frequently involve starting up and carrying out projects. These occupations can involve leading people and making many decisions. They sometimes require risk taking and often deal with business.

EDUCATION/TRAINING PROGRAM(S)— Legal Assistant/Paralegal. **RELATED KNOWLEDGE/COURSES—Clerical Practices:** Knowledge of administrative and clerical procedures and systems such as word processing, managing files and records, stenography and transcription, designing forms, and other office procedures and terminology. **Law and Government:** Knowledge of laws, legal codes, court procedures, precedents, government regulations, executive orders, agency rules, and the democratic political process. **Customer and Personal Service:** Knowledge of principles and processes for providing customer and personal services. This includes customer needs assessment, meeting quality standards for services, and evaluation of customer satisfaction. **Computers and Electronics:** Knowledge of circuit boards, processors, chips, electronic equipment, and computer hardware and software, including applications and programming. **English Language:** Knowledge of the structure and content of the English language, including the meaning and spelling of words, rules of composition, and grammar. **Personnel and Human Resources:** Knowledge of principles and procedures for personnel recruitment, selection, training, compensation and benefits, labor relations and negotiation, and personnel information systems.

Pediatricians, General

- ◎ Education/Training Required: First professional degree
- ◎ Annual Earnings: $136,490
- ◎ Growth: 19.5%
- ◎ Annual Job Openings: 38,000
- ◎ Self-Employed: 16.9%
- ◎ Part-Time: 8.1%

Diagnose, treat, and help prevent children's diseases and injuries. Advise patients, parents or guardians and community members concerning diet, activity, hygiene, and disease prevention. Collect, record, and maintain patient information, such as medical history, reports, and examination results. Examine children regularly to assess their growth and development. Examine patients or order, per-

form and interpret diagnostic tests to obtain information on medical condition and determine diagnosis. Explain procedures and discuss test results or prescribed treatments with patients and parents or guardians. Monitor patients' condition and progress and re-evaluate treatments as necessary. Plan and execute medical care programs to aid in the mental and physical growth and development of children and adolescents. Prescribe or administer treatment, therapy, medication, vaccination, and other specialized medical care to treat or prevent illness, disease, or injury in infants and children. Refer patient to medical specialist or other practitioner when necessary. Treat children who have minor illnesses, acute and chronic health problems, and growth and development concerns. Conduct research to study anatomy and develop or test medications, treatments, or procedures to prevent, or control disease or injury. Direct and coordinate activities of nurses, students, assistants, specialists, therapists, and other medical staff. Operate on patients to remove, repair, or improve functioning of diseased or injured body parts and systems. Plan, implement, or administer health programs or standards in hospital, business, or community for information, prevention, or treatment of injury or illness. Provide consulting services to other physicians. Prepare reports for government or management of birth, death, and disease statistics, workforce evaluations, or medical status of individuals. **SKILLS—Science:** Using scientific rules and methods to solve problems. **Reading Comprehension:** Understanding written sentences and paragraphs in work-related documents. **Systems Evaluation:** Identifying measures or indicators of system performance and the actions needed to improve or correct performance relative to the goals of the system. **Active Learning:** Understanding the implications of new information for both current and future problem-solving and decision-making. **Judgment and Decision Making:** Considering the relative costs and benefits of potential actions to choose the most appropriate one. **Management of Personnel Resources:** Motivating, developing, and directing people as they work, identifying the best people for the job. **Social Percep-**

tiveness: Being aware of others' reactions and understanding why they react as they do. **Systems Analysis:** Determining how a system should work and how changes in conditions, operations, and the environment will affect outcomes.

GOE—Interest Area: 08. Health Science. **Work Group:** 08.02. Medicine and Surgery. **Other Jobs in This Work Group:** Anesthesiologists; Family and General Practitioners; Internists, General; Medical Assistants; Medical Transcriptionists; Obstetricians and Gynecologists; Pharmacists; Pharmacy Aides; Pharmacy Technicians; Physician Assistants; Psychiatrists; Registered Nurses; Surgeons; Surgical Technologists. **PERSONALITY TYPE:** Investigative. Investigative occupations frequently involve working with ideas and require an extensive amount of thinking. These occupations can involve searching for facts and figuring out problems mentally.

EDUCATION/TRAINING PROGRAM(S)— Child/Pediatric Neurology; Family Medicine; Neonatal-Perinatal Medicine; Pediatric Cardiology; Pediatric Endocrinology; Pediatric Hemato-Oncology; Pediatric Nephrology; Pediatric Orthopedics; Pediatric Surgery; Pediatrics. **RELATED KNOWLEDGE/COURSES—Medicine and Dentistry:** Knowledge of the information and techniques needed to diagnose and treat human injuries, diseases, and deformities. This includes symptoms, treatment alternatives, drug properties and interactions, and preventive health-care measures. **Biology:** Knowledge of plant and animal organisms and their tissues, cells, functions, interdependencies, and interactions with each other and the environment. **Therapy and Counseling:** Knowledge of principles, methods, and procedures for diagnosis, treatment, and rehabilitation of physical and mental dysfunctions and for career counseling and guidance. **Chemistry:** Knowledge of the chemical composition, structure, and properties of substances and of the chemical processes and transformations that they undergo. This includes uses of chemicals and their danger signs, production techniques, and disposal methods. **Administration and Management:**

Knowledge of business and management principles involved in strategic planning, resource allocation, human resources modeling, leadership technique, production methods, and coordination of people and resources. **Personnel and Human Resources:** Knowledge of principles and procedures for personnel recruitment, selection, training, compensation and benefits, labor relations and negotiation, and personnel information systems. **Physics:** Knowledge and prediction of physical principles and laws and their interrelationships and applications to understanding fluid, material, and atmospheric dynamics and mechanical, electrical, atomic, and subatomic structures and processes.

Personal Financial Advisors

◎ Education/Training Required: Bachelor's degree
◎ Annual Earnings: $60,230
◎ Growth: 34.6%
◎ Annual Job Openings: 18,000
◎ Self-Employed: 37.7%
◎ Part-Time: 7.0%

Advise clients on financial plans utilizing knowledge of tax and investment strategies, securities, insurance, pension plans, and real estate. Duties include assessing clients' assets, liabilities, cash flow, insurance coverage, tax status, and financial objectives to establish investment strategies. Analyze financial information obtained from clients to determine strategies for meeting clients' financial objectives. Answer clients' questions about the purposes and details of financial plans and strategies. Build and maintain client bases, keeping current client plans up-to-date and recruiting new clients on an ongoing basis. Contact clients periodically to determine if there have been changes in their financial status. Devise debt liquidation plans that include payoff priorities and timelines. Explain and document for clients the types of services that are to be provided, and the responsibilities to be taken by the personal financial advisor. Explain to individuals and groups the details of financial assistance available to college and university students, such as loans, grants, and scholarships. Guide clients in the gathering of information such as bank account records, income tax returns, life and disability insurance records, pension plan information, and wills. Implement financial planning recommendations, or refer clients to someone who can assist them with plan implementation. Interview clients to determine their current income, expenses, insurance coverage, tax status, financial objectives, risk tolerance, and other information needed to develop a financial plan. Monitor financial market trends to ensure that plans are effective, and to identify any necessary updates. Prepare and interpret for clients information such as investment performance reports, financial document summaries, and income projections. Recommend strategies clients can use to achieve their financial goals and objectives, including specific recommendations in such areas as cash management, insurance coverage, and investment planning. Research and investigate available investment opportunities to determine whether they fit into financial plans. Review clients' accounts and plans regularly to determine whether life changes, economic changes, or financial performance indicate a need for plan reassessment. Sell financial products such as stocks, bonds, mutual funds, and insurance if licensed to do so. **SKILLS—Service Orientation:** Actively looking for ways to help people. **Speaking:** Talking to others to convey information effectively. **Management of Financial Resources:** Determining how money will be spent to get the work done and accounting for these expenditures. **Active Listening:** Giving full attention to what other people are saying, taking time to understand the points being made, asking questions as appropriate, and not interrupting at inappropriate times. **Judgment and Decision Making:** Considering the relative costs

and benefits of potential actions to choose the most appropriate one. **Mathematics:** Using mathematics to solve problems. **Critical Thinking:** Using logic and reasoning to identify the strengths and weaknesses of alternative solutions, conclusions, or approaches to problems. **Reading Comprehension:** Understanding written sentences and paragraphs in work-related documents. **Writing:** Communicating effectively in writing as appropriate for the needs of the audience.

GOE—Interest Area: 06. Finance and Insurance. **Work Group:** 06.05. Finance/Insurance Sales and Support. **Other Jobs in This Work Group:** Advertising Sales Agents; Insurance Sales Agents; Sales Agents, Financial Services; Sales Agents, Securities and Commodities. **PERSONALITY TYPE:** Social. Social occupations frequently involve working with, communicating with, and teaching people. These occupations often involve helping or providing service to others.

EDUCATION/TRAINING PROGRAM(S)— Finance, General; Financial Planning and Services. **RELATED KNOWLEDGE/COURSES—Economics and Accounting:** Knowledge of economic and accounting principles and practices, the financial markets, banking, and the analysis and reporting of financial data. **Mathematics:** Knowledge of arithmetic, algebra, geometry, calculus, and statistics and their applications. **Administration and Management:** Knowledge of business and management principles involved in strategic planning, resource allocation, human resources modeling, leadership technique, production methods, and coordination of people and resources. **Law and Government:** Knowledge of laws, legal codes, court procedures, precedents, government regulations, executive orders, agency rules, and the democratic political process. **Customer and Personal Service:** Knowledge of principles and processes for providing customer and personal services. This includes customer needs assessment, meeting quality standards for services, and evaluation of customer satisfaction. **Therapy and Counseling:** Knowledge of principles, methods, and procedures for diagnosis, treatment, and rehabilitation of physical and mental dysfunctions and for career counseling and guidance.

Personnel Recruiters

- ◎ Education/Training Required: Bachelor's degree
- ◎ Annual Earnings: $40,970
- ◎ Growth: 27.3%
- ◎ Annual Job Openings: 29,000
- ◎ Self-Employed: 0.8%
- ◎ Part-Time: 7.7%

Seek out, interview, and screen applicants to fill existing and future job openings and promote career opportunities within an organization. Establish and maintain relationships with hiring managers to stay abreast of current and future hiring and business needs. Interview applicants to obtain information on work history, training, education, and job skills. Maintain current knowledge of Equal Employment Opportunity (EEO) and affirmative action guidelines and laws, such as the Americans with Disabilities Act. Perform searches for qualified candidates according to relevant job criteria, using computer databases, networking, Internet recruiting resources, cold calls, media, recruiting firms, and employee referrals. Prepare and maintain employment records. Contact applicants to inform them of employment possibilities, consideration, and selection. Inform potential applicants about facilities, operations, benefits, and job or career opportunities in organizations. Screen and refer applicants to hiring personnel in the organization, making hiring recommendations when appropriate. Arrange for interviews and provide travel arrangements as necessary. Advise managers and employees on staffing policies and procedures. Review and evaluate applicant qualifications or eligibility for specified licensing, according to established guidelines and designated licensing codes. Hire applicants and authorize paperwork assigning them to positions. Conduct reference and background checks on applicants. Evaluate recruitment and selection criteria to ensure conformance to professional, statistical, and testing standards, recommending revision as needed. Recruit applicants for open positions, arranging job fairs with college campus representatives. Advise management on organizing, preparing, and implementing recruiting and retention programs. Supervise personnel clerks performing filing, typing and record-keeping duties. Project yearly recruitment expenditures for budgetary consideration and control. **SKILLS—Management of Personnel Resources:** Motivating, developing, and directing people as they work, identifying the best people for the job. **Negotiation:** Bringing others together and trying to reconcile differences. **Persuasion:** Persuading others to change their minds or behavior. **Service Orientation:** Actively looking for ways to help people. **Time Management:** Managing one's own time and the time of others. **Management of Financial Resources:** Determining how money will be spent to get the work done and accounting for these expenditures. **Monitoring:** Monitoring or assessing your performance or that of other individuals or organizations to make improvements or take corrective action. **Social Perceptiveness:** Being aware of others' reactions and understanding why they react as they do.

GOE—Interest Area: 04. Business and Administration. **Work Group:** 04.03. Human Resources Support. **Other Jobs in This Work Group:** Compensation, Benefits, and Job Analysis Specialists; Employment Interviewers, Private or Public Employment Service; Training and Development Specialists. **PERSONALITY TYPE:** Enterprising. Enterprising occupations frequently involve starting up and carrying out projects. These occupations can involve leading people and making many decisions. They sometimes require risk taking and often deal with business.

EDUCATION/TRAINING PROGRAM(S)— Human Resources Management/Personnel Administration, General; Labor and Industrial Relations.

RELATED KNOWLEDGE/COURSES—Personnel and Human Resources: Knowledge of principles and procedures for personnel recruitment, selection, training, compensation and benefits, labor relations and negotiation, and personnel information systems. **Clerical Practices:** Knowledge of administrative and clerical procedures and systems such as word processing, managing files and records, stenography and transcription, designing forms, and other office procedures and terminology. **Education and Training:** Knowledge of principles and methods for curriculum and training design, teaching and instruction for individuals and groups, and the measurement of training effects. **Sales and Marketing:** Knowledge of principles and methods for showing, promoting, and selling products or services. This includes marketing strategy and tactics, product demonstration, sales techniques, and sales control systems. **Administration and Management:** Knowledge of business and management principles involved in strategic planning, resource allocation, human resources modeling, leadership technique, production methods, and coordination of people and resources. **Computers and Electronics:** Knowledge of circuit boards, processors, chips, electronic equipment, and computer hardware and software, including applications and programming.

Pharmacists

- Education/Training Required: First professional degree
- Annual Earnings: $82,520
- Growth: 30.1%
- Annual Job Openings: 23,000
- Self-Employed: 3.4%
- Part-Time: 17.3%

Compound and dispense medications following prescriptions issued by physicians, dentists, or other authorized medical practitioners. Review prescriptions to assure accuracy, to ascertain the needed ingredients, and to evaluate their suitability. Provide information and advice regarding drug interactions, side effects, dosage and proper medication storage. Analyze prescribing trends to monitor patient compliance and to prevent excessive usage or harmful interactions. Order and purchase pharmaceutical supplies, medical supplies, and drugs, maintaining stock and storing and handling it properly. Maintain records, such as pharmacy files, patient profiles, charge system files, inventories, control records for radioactive nuclei, and registries of poisons, narcotics, and controlled drugs. Provide specialized services to help patients manage conditions such as diabetes, asthma, smoking cessation, or high blood pressure. Advise customers on the selection of medication brands, medical equipment and health-care supplies. Collaborate with other health-care professionals to plan, monitor, review, and evaluate the quality and effectiveness of drugs and drug regimens, providing advice on drug applications and characteristics. Compound and dispense medications as prescribed by doctors and dentists, by calculating, weighing, measuring, and mixing ingredients, or oversee these activities. Offer health promotion and prevention activities, for example, training people to use devices such as blood pressure or diabetes monitors. Refer patients to other health professionals and agencies when appropriate. Prepare sterile solutions and infusions for use in surgical procedures, emergency rooms, or patients' homes. Plan, implement, and maintain procedures for mixing, packaging, and labeling pharmaceuticals, according to policy and legal requirements, to ensure quality, security, and proper disposal. Assay radiopharmaceuticals, verify rates of disintegration, and calculate the volume required to produce the desired results, to ensure proper dosages. Manage pharmacy operations, hiring and supervising staff, performing administrative duties, and buying and selling non-pharmaceutical merchandise. Work in hospitals, clinics, or for HMOs, dispensing prescriptions, serving as a medical team consultants, or specializing in specific drug therapy areas such as oncology or nuclear pharmacotherapy. SKILLS—

Instructing: Teaching others how to do something. **Social Perceptiveness:** Being aware of others' reactions and understanding why they react as they do. **Reading Comprehension:** Understanding written sentences and paragraphs in work-related documents. **Active Listening:** Giving full attention to what other people are saying, taking time to understand the points being made, asking questions as appropriate, and not interrupting at inappropriate times. **Critical Thinking:** Using logic and reasoning to identify the strengths and weaknesses of alternative solutions, conclusions, or approaches to problems. **Science:** Using scientific rules and methods to solve problems. **Speaking:** Talking to others to convey information effectively. **Active Learning:** Understanding the implications of new information for both current and future problem-solving and decision-making.

GOE—Interest Area: 08. Health Science. **Work Group:** 08.02. Medicine and Surgery. **Other Jobs in This Work Group:** Anesthesiologists; Family and General Practitioners; Internists, General; Medical Assistants; Medical Transcriptionists; Obstetricians and Gynecologists; Pediatricians, General; Pharmacy Aides; Pharmacy Technicians; Physician Assistants; Psychiatrists; Registered Nurses; Surgeons; Surgical Technologists. **PERSONALITY TYPE:** Investigative. Investigative occupations frequently involve working with ideas and require an extensive amount of thinking. These occupations can involve searching for facts and figuring out problems mentally.

EDUCATION/TRAINING PROGRAM(S)— Clinical and Industrial Drug Development (MS, PhD); Clinical, Hospital, and Managed Care Pharmacy (MS, PhD); Industrial and Physical Pharmacy and Cosmetic Sciences (MS, PhD); Medicinal and Pharmaceutical Chemistry (MS, PhD); Natural Products Chemistry and Pharmacognosy (MS, PhD); Pharmaceutics and Drug Design (MS, PhD); Pharmacoeconomics/Pharmaceutical Economics (MS, PhD); Pharmacy (PharmD [USA]; PharmD, BS/BPharm [Canada]); Pharmacy Administration and Pharmacy Policy and Regulatory Affairs (MS, PhD); Pharmacy, Pharmaceutical Sciences, and Administration, Other. **RELATED KNOWLEDGE/COURSES—Medicine and Dentistry:** Knowledge of the information and techniques needed to diagnose and treat human injuries, diseases, and deformities. This includes symptoms, treatment alternatives, drug properties and interactions, and preventive health-care measures. **Chemistry:** Knowledge of the chemical composition, structure, and properties of substances and of the chemical processes and transformations that they undergo. This includes uses of chemicals and their danger signs, production techniques, and disposal methods. **Customer and Personal Service:** Knowledge of principles and processes for providing customer and personal services. This includes customer needs assessment, meeting quality standards for services, and evaluation of customer satisfaction. **Psychology:** Knowledge of human behavior and performance; individual differences in ability, personality, and interests; learning and motivation; psychological research methods; and the assessment and treatment of behavioral and affective disorders. **Therapy and Counseling:** Knowledge of principles, methods, and procedures for diagnosis, treatment, and rehabilitation of physical and mental dysfunctions and for career counseling and guidance. **Mathematics:** Knowledge of arithmetic, algebra, geometry, calculus, and statistics and their applications.

Philosophy and Religion Teachers, Postsecondary

◉ Education/Training Required: Master's degree

◉ Annual Earnings: $50,110

◉ Growth: 38.1% for all Postsecondary Teachers

◉ Annual Job Openings: 216,000 for all Postsecondary Teachers

◉ Self-Employed: 0.3% for all Postsecondary Teachers

◉ Part-Time: 27.7% for all Postsecondary Teachers

Teach courses in philosophy, religion, and theology. Evaluate and grade students' class work, assignments, and papers. Prepare and deliver lectures to undergraduate and/or graduate students on topics such as ethics, logic, and contemporary religious thought. Advise students on academic and vocational curricula, and on career issues. Compile, administer, and grade examinations, or assign this work to others. Compile bibliographies of specialized materials for outside reading assignments. Initiate, facilitate, and moderate classroom discussions. Keep abreast of developments in their field by reading current literature, talking with colleagues, and participating in professional conferences. Maintain regularly scheduled office hours in order to advise and assist students. Maintain student attendance records, grades, and other required records. Plan, evaluate, and revise curricula, course content, and course materials and methods of instruction. Prepare course materials such as syllabi, homework assignments, and handouts. Select and obtain materials and supplies such as textbooks. Supervise undergraduate and/or graduate teaching, internship, and research work. Act as advisers to student organizations. Collaborate with colleagues to address teaching and research issues. Conduct research in a particular field of knowledge, and publish findings in professional journals, books, and/or electronic media. Participate in campus and community events. Participate in student recruitment, registration, and placement activities. Perform administrative duties such as serving as department head. Provide professional consulting services to government and/or industry. Serve on academic or administrative committees that deal with institutional policies, departmental matters, and academic issues. Write grant proposals to procure external research funding. **SKILLS**—No data available.

GOE—Interest Area: 05. Education and Training. **Work Group:** 05.03. Postsecondary and Adult Teaching and Instructing. **Other Jobs in This Work Group:** Adult Literacy, Remedial Education, and GED Teachers and Instructors; Agricultural Sciences Teachers, Postsecondary; Anthropology and Archeology Teachers, Postsecondary; Architecture Teachers, Postsecondary; Area, Ethnic, and Cultural Studies Teachers, Postsecondary; Art, Drama, and Music Teachers, Postsecondary; Atmospheric, Earth, Marine, and Space Sciences Teachers, Postsecondary; Biological Science Teachers, Postsecondary; Business Teachers, Postsecondary; Chemistry Teachers, Postsecondary; Communications Teachers, Postsecondary; Computer Science Teachers, Postsecondary; Criminal Justice and Law Enforcement Teachers, Postsecondary; Economics Teachers, Postsecondary; Education Teachers, Postsecondary; Engineering Teachers, Postsecondary; English Language and Literature Teachers, Postsecondary; Environmental Science Teachers, Postsecondary; Farm and Home Management Advisors; Foreign Language and Literature Teachers, Postsecondary; Forestry and Conservation Science Teachers, Postsecondary; Geography Teachers, Postsecondary; Graduate Teaching Assistants; Health Specialties Teachers, Postsecondary; History Teachers, Postsecondary; Home Economics Teachers, Postsecondary; Law Teachers, Postsecondary; Library Science Teachers, Postsecondary; Mathematical Science Teachers, Postsecondary; Nursing

P

Instructors and Teachers, Postsecondary; Physics Teachers, Postsecondary; Political Science Teachers, Postsecondary; Psychology Teachers, Postsecondary; Recreation and Fitness Studies Teachers, Postsecondary; Self-Enrichment Education Teachers; Social Work Teachers, Postsecondary; Sociology Teachers, Postsecondary; Vocational Education Teachers, Postsecondary. **PERSONALITY TYPE:** No data available.

EDUCATION/TRAINING PROGRAM(S)— Bible/Biblical Studies; Buddhist Studies; Christian Studies; Divinity/Ministry (BD, MDiv.); Ethics; Hindu Studies; Missions/Missionary Studies and Missiology; Pastoral Counseling and Specialized Ministries, Other; Pastoral Studies/Counseling; Philosophy; Philosophy and Religious Studies, Other; Philosophy, Other; Pre-Theology/Pre-Ministerial Studies; Rabbinical Studies; Religion/Religious Studies; Religious Education; Religious/Sacred Music; Talmudic Studies; Theological and Ministerial Studies, Other; Theology and Religious Vocations, Other; Theology/Theological Studies. **RELATED KNOWLEDGE/COURSES—**No data available.

Physical Therapist Aides

- ⊚ Education/Training Required: Associate's degree
- ⊚ Annual Earnings: $21,070
- ⊚ Growth: 46.4%
- ⊚ Annual Job Openings: 8,000
- ⊚ Self-Employed: 0.4%
- ⊚ Part-Time: 22.8%

Under close supervision of a physical therapist or physical therapy assistant, perform only delegated, selected, or routine tasks in specific situations. These duties include preparing the patient and the treatment area. Clean and organize work area and disinfect equipment after treatment. Observe patients during treatment to compile and evaluate data on patients' responses and progress, and report to physical therapist. Instruct, motivate, safeguard and assist patients practicing exercises and functional activities, under direction of medical staff. Secure patients into or onto therapy equipment. Transport patients to and from treatment areas, using wheelchairs or providing standing support. Confer with physical therapy staff and others to discuss and evaluate patient information for planning, modifying, and coordinating treatment. Record treatment given and equipment used. Perform clerical duties, such as taking inventory, ordering supplies, answering telephone, taking messages, and filling out forms. Maintain equipment and furniture to keep it in good working condition, including performing the assembly and disassembly of equipment and accessories. Administer active and passive manual therapeutic exercises, therapeutic massage, and heat, light, sound, water, and electrical modality treatments, such as ultrasound. Change linens, such as bed sheets and pillow cases. Arrange treatment supplies to keep them in order. Assist patients to dress, undress, and put on and remove supportive devices, such as braces, splints, and slings. Measure patient's range-of-joint motion, body parts, and vital signs to determine effects of treatments or for patient evaluations. Train patients to use orthopedic braces, prostheses and supportive devices. Fit patients for orthopedic braces, prostheses, and supportive devices, adjusting fit as needed. Participate in patient care tasks, such as assisting with passing food trays and feeding residents, and bathing residents on bed rest. Administer traction to relieve neck and back pain, using intermittent and static traction equipment. **SKILLS—Social Perceptiveness:** Being aware of others' reactions and understanding why they react as they do. **Service Orientation:** Actively looking for ways to help people. **Time Management:** Managing one's own time and the time of others. **Learning Strategies:** Selecting and using training/instructional methods and procedures appropriate for the situation when learning or teaching new things. **Negotiation:** Bringing others together and trying to reconcile differences. **Persuasion:** Persuading others to change their minds or behavior. **Operation Monitoring:** Watching gauges, dials, or other indicators to make sure a machine is working properly. **Equipment Maintenance:** Performing routine maintenance on equipment and determining when and what kind of maintenance is needed.

GOE—Interest Area: 08. Health Science. **Work Group:** 08.07. Medical Therapy. **Other Jobs in This Work Group:** Audiologists; Massage Therapists; Occupational Therapist Aides; Occupational Therapist Assistants; Occupational Therapists; Physical Therapist Assistants; Physical Therapists; Radiation Therapists; Recreational Therapists; Respiratory Therapists; Respiratory Therapy Technicians; Speech-Language Pathologists. **PERSONALITY TYPE:** Social. Social occupations frequently involve working with, communicating with, and teaching people. These occupations often involve helping or providing service to others.

EDUCATION/TRAINING PROGRAM(S)— Physical Therapist Assistant. **RELATED KNOWLEDGE/COURSES—Psychology:** Knowledge of human behavior and performance; individual differences in ability, personality, and interests; learning and motivation; psychological research methods; and the assessment and treatment of behavioral and affective disorders. **Customer and Personal Service:** Knowledge of principles and processes for providing customer and personal services. This includes customer needs assessment, meeting quality standards for services, and evaluation of customer satisfaction. **Medicine and Dentistry:** Knowledge of the information and techniques needed to diagnose and treat human injuries, diseases, and deformities. This includes symptoms, treatment alternatives, drug properties and interactions, and preventive health-care measures. **Therapy and Counseling:** Knowledge of principles, methods, and procedures for diagnosis, treatment, and rehabilitation of physical and mental

dysfunctions and for career counseling and guidance. **Philosophy and Theology:** Knowledge of different philosophical systems and religions. This includes their basic principles, values, ethics, ways of thinking, customs, and practices and their impact on human culture. **Clerical Practices:** Knowledge of administrative and clerical procedures and systems such as word processing, managing files and records, stenography and transcription, designing forms, and other office procedures and terminology.

Physical Therapist Assistants

- ◎ Education/Training Required: Associate's degree
- ◎ Annual Earnings: $37,280
- ◎ Growth: 44.6%
- ◎ Annual Job Openings: 10,000
- ◎ Self-Employed: 0.4%
- ◎ Part-Time: 22.8%

Assist physical therapists in providing physical therapy treatments and procedures. May, in accordance with state laws, assist in the development of treatment plans, carry out routine functions, document the progress of treatment, and modify specific treatments in accordance with patient status and within the scope of treatment plans established by a physical therapist. Generally requires formal training. Instruct, motivate, safeguard and assist patients as they practice exercises and functional activities. Confer with physical therapy staff and others to discuss and evaluate patient information for planning, modifying, and coordinating treatment. Administer active and passive manual therapeutic exercises, therapeutic massage, and heat, light, sound, water, and electrical modality treatments, such as ultrasound. Observe patients during treatments to compile and evaluate data on patients'

P

responses and progress, and report to physical therapist. Measure patients' range-of-joint motion, body parts, and vital signs to determine effects of treatments or for patient evaluations. Secure patients into or onto therapy equipment. Fit patients for orthopedic braces, prostheses, and supportive devices, such as crutches. Train patients in the use of orthopedic braces, prostheses, and supportive devices. Transport patients to and from treatment areas, lifting and transferring them according to positioning requirements. Monitor operation of equipment and record use of equipment and administration of treatment. Clean work area and check and store equipment after treatment. Assist patients to dress, undress, and put on and remove supportive devices, such as braces, splints, and slings. Administer traction to relieve neck and back pain, using intermittent and static traction equipment. Perform clerical duties, such as taking inventory, ordering supplies, answering telephone, taking messages, and filling out forms. Prepare treatment areas and electrotherapy equipment for use by physiotherapists. Perform postural drainage, percussions and vibrations, and teach deep breathing exercises to treat respiratory conditions. **SKILLS—Social Perceptiveness:** Being aware of others' reactions and understanding why they react as they do. **Service Orientation:** Actively looking for ways to help people. **Instructing:** Teaching others how to do something. **Time Management:** Managing one's own time and the time of others. **Active Learning:** Understanding the implications of new information for both current and future problem-solving and decision-making. **Critical Thinking:** Using logic and reasoning to identify the strengths and weaknesses of alternative solutions, conclusions, or approaches to problems. **Learning Strategies:** Selecting and using training/instructional methods and procedures appropriate for the situation when learning or teaching new things. **Writing:** Communicating effectively in writing as appropriate for the needs of the audience. **Speaking:** Talking to others to convey information effectively.

GOE—Interest Area: 08. Health Science. **Work Group:** 08.07. Medical Therapy. **Other Jobs in This Work Group:** Audiologists; Massage Therapists; Occupational Therapist Aides; Occupational Therapist Assistants; Occupational Therapists; Physical Therapist Aides; Physical Therapists; Radiation Therapists; Recreational Therapists; Respiratory Therapists; Respiratory Therapy Technicians; Speech-Language Pathologists. **PERSONALITY TYPE:** Social. Social occupations frequently involve working with, communicating with, and teaching people. These occupations often involve helping or providing service to others.

EDUCATION/TRAINING PROGRAM(S)— Physical Therapist Assistant. **RELATED KNOWLEDGE/COURSES—Psychology:** Knowledge of human behavior and performance; individual differences in ability, personality, and interests; learning and motivation; psychological research methods; and the assessment and treatment of behavioral and affective disorders. **Therapy and Counseling:** Knowledge of principles, methods, and procedures for diagnosis, treatment, and rehabilitation of physical and mental dysfunctions and for career counseling and guidance. **Medicine and Dentistry:** Knowledge of the information and techniques needed to diagnose and treat human injuries, diseases, and deformities. This includes symptoms, treatment alternatives, drug properties and interactions, and preventive health-care measures. **Education and Training:** Knowledge of principles and methods for curriculum and training design, teaching and instruction for individuals and groups, and the measurement of training effects. **Customer and Personal Service:** Knowledge of principles and processes for providing customer and personal services. This includes customer needs assessment, meeting quality standards for services, and evaluation of customer satisfaction. **Sociology and Anthropology:** Knowledge of group behavior and dynamics, societal trends and influences, human migrations, ethnicity, and cultures and their history and origins.

Physical Therapists

- Education/Training Required: Master's degree
- Annual Earnings: $58,700
- Growth: 35.3%
- Annual Job Openings: 16,000
- Self-Employed: 5.7%
- Part-Time: 23.8%

Assess, plan, organize, and participate in rehabilitative programs that improve mobility, relieve pain, increase strength, and decrease or prevent deformity of patients suffering from disease or injury. Plan, prepare, and carry out individually designed programs of physical treatment to maintain, improve, or restore physical functioning; alleviate pain; and prevent physical dysfunction in patients. Perform and document an initial exam, evaluating the data to identify problems and determine a diagnosis prior to intervention. Evaluate effects of treatment at various stages and adjust treatments to achieve maximum benefit. Administer manual exercises, massage and/or traction to help relieve pain, increase the patient's strength, and decrease or prevent deformity and crippling. Instruct patient and family in treatment procedures to be continued at home. Confer with the patient, medical practitioners and appropriate others to plan, implement and assess the intervention program. Review physician's referral and patient's medical records to help determine diagnosis and physical therapy treatment required. Record prognosis, treatment, response, and progress in patient's chart or enter information into computer. Obtain patients' informed consent to proposed interventions. Discharge patient from physical therapy when goals or projected outcomes have been attained and provide for appropriate followup care or referrals. Test and measure patient's strength, motor development and function, sensory perception, functional capacity, and respiratory and circulatory efficiency and record data. Identify and document goals, anticipated progress and plans for reevaluation. Provide information to the patient about the proposed intervention, its material risks and expected benefits and any reasonable alternatives. Inform the patient when diagnosis reveals findings outside their scope and refer to an appropriate practitioner. Direct and supervise supportive personnel, assessing their competence, delegating specific tasks to them and establishing channels of communication. Administer treatment involving application of physical agents, using equipment, moist packs, ultraviolet and infrared lamps, and ultrasound machines. Teach physical therapy students as well as those in other health professions. Evaluate, fit, and adjust prosthetic and orthotic devices and recommend modification to orthotist. **SKILLS—Instructing:** Teaching others how to do something. **Social Perceptiveness:** Being aware of others' reactions and understanding why they react as they do. **Reading Comprehension:** Understanding written sentences and paragraphs in work-related documents. **Learning Strategies:** Selecting and using training/instructional methods and procedures appropriate for the situation when learning or teaching new things. **Science:** Using scientific rules and methods to solve problems. **Service Orientation:** Actively looking for ways to help people. **Time Management:** Managing one's own time and the time of others. **Critical Thinking:** Using logic and reasoning to identify the strengths and weaknesses of alternative solutions, conclusions, or approaches to problems. **Coordination:** Adjusting actions in relation to others' actions.

GOE—Interest Area: 08. Health Science. **Work Group:** 08.07. Medical Therapy. **Other Jobs in This Work Group:** Audiologists; Massage Therapists; Occupational Therapist Aides; Occupational Therapist Assistants; Occupational Therapists; Physical Therapist Aides; Physical Therapist Assistants; Radiation Therapists; Recreational Therapists; Respiratory Therapists; Respiratory Therapy Technicians; Speech-Language Pathologists. **PERSONALITY TYPE:** Social. Social occupations frequently involve working with, communicating with, and teaching people. These occupations often involve helping or providing service to others.

EDUCATION/TRAINING PROGRAM(S)— Kinesiotherapy/Kinesiotherapist; Physical Therapy/Therapist. **RELATED KNOWLEDGE/ COURSES—Psychology:** Knowledge of human behavior and performance; individual differences in ability, personality, and interests; learning and motivation; psychological research methods; and the assessment and treatment of behavioral and affective disorders. **Therapy and Counseling:** Knowledge of principles, methods, and procedures for diagnosis, treatment, and rehabilitation of physical and mental dysfunctions and for career counseling and guidance. **Customer and Personal Service:** Knowledge of principles and processes for providing customer and personal services. This includes customer needs assessment, meeting quality standards for services, and evaluation of customer satisfaction. **Medicine and Dentistry:** Knowledge of the information and techniques needed to diagnose and treat human injuries, diseases, and deformities. This includes symptoms, treatment alternatives, drug properties and interactions, and preventive health-care measures. **Biology:** Knowledge of plant and animal organisms and their tissues, cells, functions, interdependencies, and interactions with each other and the environment. **Sociology and Anthropology:** Knowledge of group behavior and dynamics, societal trends and influences, human migrations, ethnicity, and cultures and their history and origins.

Physician Assistants

- Education/Training Required: Bachelor's degree
- Annual Earnings: $68,200
- Growth: 48.9%
- Annual Job Openings: 7,000
- Self-Employed: 0.8%
- Part-Time: 16.3%

Provide health-care services typically performed by a physician, under the supervision of a physician.

Conduct complete physicals, provide treatment, and counsel patients. May, in some cases, prescribe medication. Must graduate from an accredited educational program for physician assistants. Examine patients to obtain information about their physical condition. Interpret diagnostic test results for deviations from normal. Make tentative diagnoses and decisions about management and treatment of patients. Obtain, compile and record patient medical data, including health history, progress notes and results of physical examination. Administer or order diagnostic tests, such as x-ray, electrocardiogram, and laboratory tests. Prescribe therapy or medication with physician approval. Perform therapeutic procedures, such as injections, immunizations, suturing and wound care, and infection management. Instruct and counsel patients about prescribed therapeutic regimens, normal growth and development, family planning, emotional problems of daily living, and health maintenance. Provide physicians with assistance during surgery or complicated medical procedures. Supervise and coordinate activities of technicians and technical assistants. Visit and observe patients on hospital rounds or house calls, updating charts, ordering therapy, and reporting back to physician. **SKILLS—Social Perceptiveness:** Being aware of others' reactions and understanding why they react as they do. **Science:** Using scientific rules and methods to solve problems. **Instructing:** Teaching others how to do something. **Critical Thinking:** Using logic and reasoning to identify the strengths and weaknesses of alternative solutions, conclusions, or approaches to problems. **Reading Comprehension:** Understanding written sentences and paragraphs in work-related documents. **Time Management:** Managing one's own time and the time of others. **Active Listening:** Giving full attention to what other people are saying, taking time to understand the points being made, asking questions as appropriate, and not interrupting at inappropriate times. **Active Learning:** Understanding the implications of new information for both current and future problem-solving and decision-making.

GOE—**Interest Area:** 08. Health Science. **Work Group:** 08.02. Medicine and Surgery. **Other Jobs in This Work Group:** Anesthesiologists; Family and General Practitioners; Internists, General; Medical Assistants; Medical Transcriptionists; Obstetricians and Gynecologists; Pediatricians, General; Pharmacists; Pharmacy Aides; Pharmacy Technicians; Psychiatrists; Registered Nurses; Surgeons; Surgical Technologists. **PERSONALITY TYPE:** Investigative. Investigative occupations frequently involve working with ideas and require an extensive amount of thinking. These occupations can involve searching for facts and figuring out problems mentally.

EDUCATION/TRAINING PROGRAM(S)— Physician Assistant. **RELATED KNOWLEDGE/COURSES—Medicine and Dentistry:** Knowledge of the information and techniques needed to diagnose and treat human injuries, diseases, and deformities. This includes symptoms, treatment alternatives, drug properties and interactions, and preventive health-care measures. **Biology:** Knowledge of plant and animal organisms and their tissues, cells, functions, interdependencies, and interactions with each other and the environment. **Psychology:** Knowledge of human behavior and performance; individual differences in ability, personality, and interests; learning and motivation; psychological research methods; and the assessment and treatment of behavioral and affective disorders. **Therapy and Counseling:** Knowledge of principles, methods, and procedures for diagnosis, treatment, and rehabilitation of physical and mental dysfunctions and for career counseling and guidance. **Customer and Personal Service:** Knowledge of principles and processes for providing customer and personal services. This includes customer needs assessment, meeting quality standards for services, and evaluation of customer satisfaction. **Chemistry:** Knowledge of the chemical composition, structure, and properties of substances and of the chemical processes and transformations that they undergo. This includes uses of chemicals and their danger signs, production techniques, and disposal methods.

Physicists

- Education/Training Required: Doctoral degree
- Annual Earnings: $83,570
- Growth: 6.9%
- Annual Job Openings: 1,000
- Self-Employed: 9.9%
- Part-Time: 2.4%

Conduct research into the phases of physical phenomena, develop theories and laws on the basis of observation and experiments, and devise methods to apply laws and theories to industry and other fields. Analyze data from research conducted to detect and measure physical phenomena. Describe and express observations and conclusions in mathematical terms. Design computer simulations to model physical data so that it can be better understood. Develop theories and laws on the basis of observation and experiments, and apply these theories and laws to problems in areas such as nuclear energy, optics, and aerospace technology. Observe the structure and properties of matter, and the transformation and propagation of energy, using equipment such as masers, lasers, and telescopes, in order to explore and identify the basic principles governing these phenomena. Perform complex calculations as part of the analysis and evaluation of data, using computers. Report experimental results by writing papers for scientific journals or by presenting information at scientific conferences. Collaborate with other scientists in the design, development, and testing of experimental, industrial, or medical equipment, instrumentation, and procedures. Conduct application evaluations and analyze results in order to determine commercial, industrial, scientific, medical, military, or other uses for electro-optical devices. Develop manufacturing, assembly, and fabrication processes of lasers, masers, infrared, and other light-emitting and light-sensitive devices. Provide support services for activities such as radiation therapy, diagnostic imaging, or seismology. Teach

P

physics to students. Advise authorities of procedures to be followed in radiation incidents or hazards, and assist in civil defense planning. Conduct research pertaining to potential environmental impacts of atomic energy-related industrial development in order to determine licensing qualifications. Develop standards of permissible concentrations of radioisotopes in liquids and gases. Direct testing and monitoring of contamination of radioactive equipment, and recording of personnel and plant area radiation exposure data. **SKILLS—Science:** Using scientific rules and methods to solve problems. **Mathematics:** Using mathematics to solve problems. **Writing:** Communicating effectively in writing as appropriate for the needs of the audience. **Active Learning:** Understanding the implications of new information for both current and future problem-solving and decision-making. **Technology Design:** Generating or adapting equipment and technology to serve user needs. **Reading Comprehension:** Understanding written sentences and paragraphs in work-related documents. **Critical Thinking:** Using logic and reasoning to identify the strengths and weaknesses of alternative solutions, conclusions, or approaches to problems. **Operations Analysis:** Analyzing needs and product requirements to create a design.

GOE—Interest Area: 15. Scientific Research, Engineering, and Mathematics. **Work Group:** 15.02. Physical Sciences. **Other Jobs in This Work Group:** Astronomers; Atmospheric and Space Scientists; Chemists; Geographers; Geologists; Hydrologists; Materials Scientists. **PERSONALITY TYPE:** Investigative. Investigative occupations frequently involve working with ideas and require an extensive amount of thinking. These occupations can involve searching for facts and figuring out problems mentally.

EDUCATION/TRAINING PROGRAM(S)— Acoustics; Astrophysics; Atomic/Molecular Physics; Elementary Particle Physics; Health/Medical Physics; Nuclear Physics; Optics/Optical Sciences; Physics, General; Physics, Other; Plasma and High-Temperature Physics; Solid State and Low-Temperature Physics; Theoretical and Mathematical Physics. **RELATED KNOWLEDGE/**

COURSES—Physics: Knowledge and prediction of physical principles and laws and their interrelationships and applications to understanding fluid, material, and atmospheric dynamics and mechanical, electrical, atomic, and subatomic structures and processes. **Mathematics:** Knowledge of arithmetic, algebra, geometry, calculus, and statistics and their applications. **Education and Training:** Knowledge of principles and methods for curriculum and training design, teaching and instruction for individuals and groups, and the measurement of training effects. **Engineering and Technology:** Knowledge of the practical application of engineering science and technology. This includes applying principles, techniques, procedures, and equipment to the design and production of various goods and services. **Design:** Knowledge of design techniques, tools, and principles involved in production of precision technical plans, blueprints, drawings, and models. **English Language:** Knowledge of the structure and content of the English language, including the meaning and spelling of words, rules of composition, and grammar.

Physics Teachers, Postsecondary

- Education/Training Required: Master's degree
- Annual Earnings: $63,790
- Growth: 38.1% for all Postsecondary Teachers
- Annual Job Openings: 216,000 for all Postsecondary Teachers
- Self-Employed: 0.3% for all Postsecondary Teachers
- Part-Time: 27.7% for all Postsecondary Teachers

Teach courses pertaining to the laws of matter and energy. Includes both teachers primarily engaged in teaching and those who do a combination of both teaching and research. Evaluate and grade students' class work, laboratory work, assignments, and papers. Prepare and deliver lectures to undergraduate and/or graduate students on topics such as quantum mechanics, particle physics, and optics. Advise students on academic and vocational curricula, and on career issues. Compile, administer, and grade examinations, or assign this work to others. Compile bibliographies of specialized materials for outside reading assignments. Initiate, facilitate, and moderate classroom discussions. Keep abreast of developments in their field by reading current literature, talking with colleagues, and participating in professional conferences. Maintain regularly scheduled office hours in order to advise and assist students. Maintain student attendance records, grades, and other required records. Plan, evaluate, and revise curricula, course content, and course materials and methods of instruction. Prepare course materials such as syllabi, homework assignments, and handouts. Select and obtain materials and supplies such as textbooks and laboratory equipment. Supervise students' laboratory work. Supervise undergraduate and/or graduate teaching, internship, and research work. Act as advisers to student organizations. Collaborate with colleagues to address teaching and research issues. Conduct research in a particular field of knowledge, and publish findings in professional journals, books, and/or electronic media. Participate in campus and community events. Participate in student recruitment, registration, and placement activities. Perform administrative duties such as serving as department head. Provide professional consulting services to government and/or industry. Serve on academic or administrative committees that deal with institutional policies, departmental matters, and academic issues. Write grant proposals to procure external research funding. **SKILLS—Science:** Using scientific rules and methods to solve problems. **Instructing:** Teaching others how to do something. **Writing:** Communicating effectively in writing as appropriate for the needs of the audience. **Learning Strategies:** Selecting and using training/instructional

methods and procedures appropriate for the situation when learning or teaching new things. **Reading Comprehension:** Understanding written sentences and paragraphs in work-related documents. **Active Learning:** Understanding the implications of new information for both current and future problem-solving and decision-making. **Critical Thinking:** Using logic and reasoning to identify the strengths and weaknesses of alternative solutions, conclusions, or approaches to problems. **Complex Problem Solving:** Identifying complex problems and reviewing related information to develop and evaluate options and implement solutions. **Judgment and Decision Making:** Considering the relative costs and benefits of potential actions to choose the most appropriate one.

GOE—Interest Area: 05. Education and Training. **Work Group:** 05.03. Postsecondary and Adult Teaching and Instructing. **Other Jobs in This Work Group:** Adult Literacy, Remedial Education, and GED Teachers and Instructors; Agricultural Sciences Teachers, Postsecondary; Anthropology and Archeology Teachers, Postsecondary; Architecture Teachers, Postsecondary; Area, Ethnic, and Cultural Studies Teachers, Postsecondary; Art, Drama, and Music Teachers, Postsecondary; Atmospheric, Earth, Marine, and Space Sciences Teachers, Postsecondary; Biological Science Teachers, Postsecondary; Business Teachers, Postsecondary; Chemistry Teachers, Postsecondary; Communications Teachers, Postsecondary; Computer Science Teachers, Postsecondary; Criminal Justice and Law Enforcement Teachers, Postsecondary; Economics Teachers, Postsecondary; Education Teachers, Postsecondary; Engineering Teachers, Postsecondary; English Language and Literature Teachers, Postsecondary; Environmental Science Teachers, Postsecondary; Farm and Home Management Advisors; Foreign Language and Literature Teachers, Postsecondary; Forestry and Conservation Science Teachers, Postsecondary; Geography Teachers, Postsecondary; Graduate Teaching Assistants; Health Specialties Teachers, Postsecondary; History Teachers, Postsecondary; Home Economics Teachers, Postsecondary; Law Teachers, Postsecondary; Library Science Teachers, Postsecondary; Mathematical Science Teachers, Postsecondary; Nursing Instructors and Teachers, Postsecondary; Philosophy and Religion Teachers, Postsecondary; Political Science Teachers, Postsecondary; Psychology Teachers, Postsecondary; Recreation and Fitness Studies Teachers, Postsecondary; Self-Enrichment Education Teachers; Social Work Teachers, Postsecondary; Sociology Teachers, Postsecondary; Vocational Education Teachers, Postsecondary. **PERSONALITY TYPE:** Investigative. Investigative occupations frequently involve working with ideas and require an extensive amount of thinking. These occupations can involve searching for facts and figuring out problems mentally.

EDUCATION/TRAINING PROGRAM(S)— Acoustics; Atomic/Molecular Physics; Elementary Particle Physics; Nuclear Physics; Optics/Optical Sciences; Physics, General; Physics, Other; Plasma and High-Temperature Physics; Solid State and Low-Temperature Physics; Theoretical and Mathematical Physics. **RELATED KNOWLEDGE/ COURSES—Physics:** Knowledge and prediction of physical principles and laws and their interrelationships and applications to understanding fluid, material, and atmospheric dynamics and mechanical, electrical, atomic, and subatomic structures and processes. **Education and Training:** Knowledge of principles and methods for curriculum and training design, teaching and instruction for individuals and groups, and the measurement of training effects. **Mathematics:** Knowledge of arithmetic, algebra, geometry, calculus, and statistics and their applications. **English Language:** Knowledge of the structure and content of the English language, including the meaning and spelling of words, rules of composition, and grammar. **Administration and Management:** Knowledge of business and management principles involved in strategic planning, resource allocation, human resources modeling, leadership technique, production methods, and coordination of people and resources. **Chemistry:** Knowledge of the chemical composition, structure, and properties

of substances and of the chemical processes and transformations that they undergo. This includes uses of chemicals and their danger signs, production techniques, and disposal methods.

Podiatrists

- ◎ Education/Training Required: First professional degree
- ◎ Annual Earnings: $95,550
- ◎ Growth: 15.0%
- ◎ Annual Job Openings: 1,000
- ◎ Self-Employed: 44.4%
- ◎ Part-Time: 15.6%

Diagnose and treat diseases and deformities of the human foot. Advise patients about treatments and foot care techniques necessary for prevention of future problems. Correct deformities by means of plaster casts and strapping. Diagnose diseases and deformities of the foot using medical histories, physical examinations, x-rays, and laboratory test results. Make and fit prosthetic appliances. Prescribe medications, corrective devices, physical therapy, or surgery. Refer patients to physicians when symptoms indicative of systemic disorders, such as arthritis or diabetes, are observed in feet and legs. Treat bone, muscle, and joint disorders affecting the feet. Treat conditions such as corns, calluses, ingrown nails, tumors, shortened tendons, bunions, cysts, and abscesses by surgical methods. Treat deformities using mechanical methods, such as whirlpool or paraffin baths, and electrical methods, such as short wave and low voltage currents. Educate the public about the benefits of foot care through techniques such as speaking engagements, advertising, and other forums. Perform administrative duties such as hiring employees, ordering supplies, and keeping records. **SKILLS—Active Learning:** Understanding the implications of new information for both current and future problem-solving and decision-making. **Reading Comprehension:** Understanding written sentences and paragraphs in work-related documents. **Technology Design:** Generating or adapting equipment and technology to serve user needs. **Judgment and Decision Making:** Considering the relative costs and benefits of potential actions to choose the most appropriate one. **Service Orientation:** Actively looking for ways to help people. **Equipment Selection:** Determining the kind of tools and equipment needed to do a job. **Active Listening:** Giving full attention to what other people are saying, taking time to understand the points being made, asking questions as appropriate, and not interrupting at inappropriate times. **Critical Thinking:** Using logic and reasoning to identify the strengths and weaknesses of alternative solutions, conclusions, or approaches to problems. **Complex Problem Solving:** Identifying complex problems and reviewing related information to develop and evaluate options and implement solutions. **Systems Evaluation:** Identifying measures or indicators of system performance and the actions needed to improve or correct performance relative to the goals of the system.

GOE—Interest Area: 08. Health Science. **Work Group:** 08.04. Health Specialties. **Other Jobs in This Work Group:** Chiropractors; Optometrists. **PERSONALITY TYPE:** Social. Social occupations frequently involve working with, communicating with, and teaching people. These occupations often involve helping or providing service to others.

EDUCATION/TRAINING PROGRAM(S)— Podiatric Medicine/Podiatry (DPM). **RELATED KNOWLEDGE/COURSES—Medicine and Dentistry:** Knowledge of the information and techniques needed to diagnose and treat human injuries, diseases, and deformities. This includes symptoms, treatment alternatives, drug properties and interactions, and preventive health-care measures. **Biology:** Knowledge of plant and animal organisms and their tissues, cells, functions, interdependencies, and interactions with each other and the environment. **Chemistry:** Knowledge of the chemical composition, structure, and properties of substances and of the chemical processes and transformations that they undergo. This includes uses of chemicals and their danger signs, production techniques, and disposal methods. **Therapy and Counseling:** Knowledge of principles, methods, and procedures for diagnosis, treatment, and rehabilitation of physical and mental dysfunctions and for career counseling and guidance. **English Language:** Knowledge of the structure and content of the English language, including the meaning and spelling of words, rules of composition, and grammar. **Physics:** Knowledge and prediction of physical principles and laws and their interrelationships and applications to understanding fluid, material, and atmospheric dynamics and mechanical, electrical, atomic, and subatomic structures and processes.

Poets and Lyricists

- Education/Training Required: Bachelor's degree
- Annual Earnings: $43,340
- Growth: 16.1%
- Annual Job Openings: 23,000
- Self-Employed: 67.9%
- Part-Time: 24.2%

Write poetry or song lyrics for publication or performance. Writes words to fit musical compositions, including lyrics for operas, musical plays, and choral works. Chooses subject matter and suitable form to express personal feeling and experience or ideas or to narrate story or event. Adapts text to accommodate musical requirements of composer and singer. Writes narrative, dramatic, lyric, or other types of poetry for publication. **SKILLS—Writing:** Communicating effectively in writing as appropriate for the needs of the audience. **Reading Comprehension:** Understanding written sentences and paragraphs in work-related documents. **Learning**

P

Strategies: Selecting and using training/instructional methods and procedures appropriate for the situation when learning or teaching new things.

GOE—Interest Area: 03. Arts and Communication. **Work Group:** 03.02. Writing and Editing. **Other Jobs in This Work Group:** Copy Writers; Creative Writers; Editors; Technical Writers. **PERSONALITY TYPE:** Artistic. Artistic occupations frequently involve working with forms, designs, and patterns. They often require self-expression, and the work can be done without following a clear set of rules.

EDUCATION/TRAINING PROGRAM(S)— Broadcast Journalism; Business/Corporate Communications; Communication Studies/Speech Communication and Rhetoric; Communication, Journalism, and Related Programs, Other; Creative Writing; English Composition; Family and Consumer Sciences/Human Sciences Communication; Journalism; Mass Communication/Media Studies; Playwriting and Screenwriting; Technical and Business Writing. **RELATED KNOWLEDGE/ COURSES—Fine Arts:** Knowledge of the theory and techniques required to compose, produce, and perform works of music, dance, visual arts, drama, and sculpture. **Communications and Media:** Knowledge of media production, communication, and dissemination techniques and methods. This includes alternative ways to inform and entertain via written, oral, and visual media. **English Language:** Knowledge of the structure and content of the English language, including the meaning and spelling of words, rules of composition, and grammar.

Political Science Teachers, Postsecondary

- Education/Training Required: Master's degree
- Annual Earnings: $58,530
- Growth: 38.1% for all Postsecondary Teachers
- Annual Job Openings: 216,000 for all Postsecondary Teachers
- Self-Employed: 0.3% for all Postsecondary Teachers
- Part-Time: 27.7% for all Postsecondary Teachers

Teach courses in political science, international affairs, and international relations. Evaluate and grade students' class work, assignments, and papers. Prepare and deliver lectures to undergraduate and/or graduate students on topics such as classical political thought, international relations, and democracy and citizenship. Advise students on academic and vocational curricula, and on career issues. Compile, administer, and grade examinations, or assign this work to others. Compile bibliographies of specialized materials for outside reading assignments. Initiate, facilitate, and moderate classroom discussions. Keep abreast of developments in their field by reading current literature, talking with colleagues, and participating in professional conferences. Maintain regularly scheduled office hours in order to advise and assist students. Maintain student attendance records, grades, and other required records. Plan, evaluate, and revise curricula, course content, and course materials and methods of instruction. Prepare course materials such as syllabi, homework assignments, and handouts. Select and obtain materials and supplies such as textbooks. Supervise undergraduate and/or graduate teaching, internship, and research work. Act as advisers to student organizations. Collaborate with colleagues to address teaching and research issues. Conduct research in a particular field of knowledge, and publish findings in professional journals, books, and/or electronic media. Participate in campus and community events. Participate in student recruitment, registration, and placement activities. Perform administrative duties such as serving as department head. Provide professional consulting services to government and/or industry. Serve on academic or administrative committees that deal with institutional policies, departmental matters, and academic issues. Write grant proposals to procure external research funding. **SKILLS—Instructing:** Teaching others how to do something. **Learning Strategies:** Selecting and using training/instructional methods and procedures appropriate for the situation when learning or teaching new things. **Reading Comprehension:** Understanding written sentences and paragraphs in work-related documents. **Active Learning:** Understanding the implications of new information for both current and future problem-solving and decision-making. **Speaking:** Talking to others to convey information effectively. **Writing:** Communicating effectively in writing as appropriate for the needs of the audience. **Science:** Using scientific rules and methods to solve problems. **Active Listening:** Giving full attention to what other people are saying, taking time to understand the points being made, asking questions as appropriate, and not interrupting at inappropriate times. **Critical Thinking:** Using logic and reasoning to identify the strengths and weaknesses of alternative solutions, conclusions, or approaches to problems.

GOE—Interest Area: 05. Education and Training. **Work Group:** 05.03. Postsecondary and Adult Teaching and Instructing. **Other Jobs in This Work Group:** Adult Literacy, Remedial Education, and GED Teachers and Instructors; Agricultural Sciences Teachers, Postsecondary; Anthropology and Archeology Teachers, Postsecondary; Architecture Teachers, Postsecondary; Area, Ethnic, and Cultural Studies Teachers, Postsecondary; Art, Drama, and Music Teachers, Postsecondary; Atmospheric, Earth, Marine, and Space Sciences Teachers, Postsecondary; Biological Science Teachers, Postsecondary; Business Teachers, Postsecondary; Chemistry Teachers, Postsecondary; Communications Teachers, Postsecondary; Computer Science Teachers, Postsecondary; Criminal Justice and Law Enforcement Teachers, Postsecondary; Economics Teachers, Postsecondary; Education Teachers, Postsecondary; Engineering Teachers, Postsecondary; English Language and Literature Teachers, Postsecondary; Environmental Science Teachers, Postsecondary; Farm and Home Management Advisors; Foreign Language and Literature Teachers, Postsecondary; Forestry and Conservation Science Teachers, Postsecondary; Geography Teachers, Postsecondary; Graduate Teaching Assistants; Health Specialties Teachers, Postsecondary; History Teachers, Postsecondary; Home Economics Teachers, Postsecondary; Law Teachers, Postsecondary; Library Science Teachers, Postsecondary; Mathematical Science Teachers, Postsecondary; Nursing Instructors and Teachers, Postsecondary; Philosophy and Religion Teachers, Postsecondary; Physics Teachers, Postsecondary; Psychology Teachers, Postsecondary; Recreation and Fitness Studies Teachers, Postsecondary; Self-Enrichment Education Teachers; Social Work Teachers, Postsecondary; Sociology Teachers, Postsecondary; Vocational Education Teachers, Postsecondary. **PERSONALITY TYPE:** Social. Social occupations frequently involve working with, communicating with, and teaching people. These occupations often involve helping or providing service to others.

EDUCATION/TRAINING PROGRAM(S)— American Government and Politics (United States); Political Science and Government, General; Political Science and Government, Other; Social Science Teacher Education. **RELATED KNOWLEDGE/COURSES—Sociology and Anthropology:** Knowledge of group behavior and dynamics, societal trends and influences, human migrations, ethnicity, and cultures and their history and origins. **History and Archeology:** Knowledge of historical events and their causes, indicators, and effects on

P

civilizations and cultures. **Education and Training:** Knowledge of principles and methods for curriculum and training design, teaching and instruction for individuals and groups, and the measurement of training effects. **Psychology:** Knowledge of human behavior and performance; individual differences in ability, personality, and interests; learning and motivation; psychological research methods; and the assessment and treatment of behavioral and affective disorders. **Economics and Accounting:** Knowledge of economic and accounting principles and practices, the financial markets, banking, and the analysis and reporting of financial data. **English Language:** Knowledge of the structure and content of the English language, including the meaning and spelling of words, rules of composition, and grammar.

Political Scientists

- Education/Training Required: Master's degree
- Annual Earnings: $81,670
- Growth: 5.9%
- Annual Job Openings: 1,000
- Self-Employed: 2.9%
- Part-Time: 16.8%

Study the origin, development, and operation of political systems. Research a wide range of subjects, such as relations between the United States and foreign countries, the beliefs and institutions of foreign nations, or the politics of small towns or a major metropolis. May study topics, such as public opinion, political decision making, and ideology. May analyze the structure and operation of governments, as well as various political entities. May conduct public opinion surveys, analyze election results, or analyze public documents. Conducts research into political philosophy and theories of political systems, such as governmental institu-

tions, public laws, and international law. Analyzes and interprets results of studies, and prepares reports detailing findings, recommendations, or conclusions. Organizes and conducts public opinion surveys and interprets results. Recommends programs and policies to institutions and organizations. Prepares reports detailing findings and conclusions. Consults with government officials, civic bodies, research agencies, and political parties. **SKILLS— Systems Analysis:** Determining how a system should work and how changes in conditions, operations, and the environment will affect outcomes. **Writing:** Communicating effectively in writing as appropriate for the needs of the audience. **Mathematics:** Using mathematics to solve problems. **Active Learning:** Understanding the implications of new information for both current and future problem-solving and decision-making. **Social Perceptiveness:** Being aware of others' reactions and understanding why they react as they do. **Systems Evaluation:** Identifying measures or indicators of system performance and the actions needed to improve or correct performance relative to the goals of the system. **Reading Comprehension:** Understanding written sentences and paragraphs in work-related documents. **Speaking:** Talking to others to convey information effectively.

GOE—Interest Area: 15. Scientific Research, Engineering, and Mathematics. **Work Group:** 15.04. Social Sciences. **Other Jobs in This Work Group:** Anthropologists; Archeologists; Economists; Educational Psychologists; Historians; Industrial-Organizational Psychologists; Sociologists. **PERSONALITY TYPE:** Investigative. Investigative occupations frequently involve working with ideas and require an extensive amount of thinking. These occupations can involve searching for facts and figuring out problems mentally.

EDUCATION/TRAINING PROGRAM(S)— American Government and Politics (United States); Canadian Government and Politics; International/Global Studies; Political Science and Government, General; Political Science and Government, Other. **RELATED KNOWLEDGE/COURSES—**

Law and Government: Knowledge of laws, legal codes, court procedures, precedents, government regulations, executive orders, agency rules, and the democratic political process. Philosophy and Theology: Knowledge of different philosophical systems and religions. This includes their basic principles, values, ethics, ways of thinking, customs, and practices and their impact on human culture. History and Archeology: Knowledge of historical events and their causes, indicators, and effects on civilizations and cultures. Sociology and Anthropology: Knowledge of group behavior and dynamics, societal trends and influences, human migrations, ethnicity, and cultures and their history and origins. Communications and Media: Knowledge of media production, communication, and dissemination techniques and methods. This includes alternative ways to inform and entertain via written, oral, and visual media. Geography: Knowledge of principles and methods for describing the features of land, sea, and air masses, including their physical characteristics; locations; interrelationships; and distribution of plant, animal, and human life. English Language: Knowledge of the structure and content of the English language, including the meaning and spelling of words, rules of composition, and grammar.

Postsecondary Teachers

- ◎ Education/Training Required: Master's degree
- ◎ Annual Earnings: $51,815
- ◎ Growth: 38.1%
- ◎ Annual Job Openings: 216,000
- ◎ Self-Employed: 0.3%
- ◎ Part-Time: 27.7%

For detailed information, see

- ◎ Agricultural Sciences Teachers, Postsecondary
- ◎ Anthropology and Archeology Teachers, Postsecondary
- ◎ Architecture Teachers, Postsecondary
- ◎ Area, Ethnic, and Cultural Studies Teachers, Postsecondary
- ◎ Art, Drama, and Music Teachers, Postsecondary
- ◎ Atmospheric, Earth, Marine, and Space Sciences Teachers, Postsecondary
- ◎ Biological Science Teachers, Postsecondary
- ◎ Business Teachers, Postsecondary
- ◎ Chemistry Teachers, Postsecondary
- ◎ Communications Teachers, Postsecondary
- ◎ Computer Science Teachers, Postsecondary
- ◎ Criminal Justice and Law Enforcement Teachers, Postsecondary
- ◎ Economics Teachers, Postsecondary
- ◎ Education Teachers, Postsecondary
- ◎ Engineering Teachers, Postsecondary
- ◎ English Language and Literature Teachers, Postsecondary
- ◎ Environmental Science Teachers, Postsecondary
- ◎ Foreign Language and Literature Teachers, Postsecondary
- ◎ Forestry and Conservation Science Teachers, Postsecondary
- ◎ Geography Teachers, Postsecondary
- ◎ Graduate Teaching Assistants
- ◎ Health Specialties Teachers, Postsecondary
- ◎ History Teachers, Postsecondary
- ◎ Home Economics Teachers, Postsecondary
- ◎ Law Teachers, Postsecondary
- ◎ Library Science Teachers, Postsecondary
- ◎ Mathematical Science Teachers, Postsecondary
- ◎ Nursing Instructors and Teachers, Postsecondary
- ◎ Philosophy and Religion Teachers, Postsecondary
- ◎ Physics Teachers, Postsecondary
- ◎ Political Science Teachers, Postsecondary
- ◎ Psychology Teachers, Postsecondary
- ◎ Recreation and Fitness Studies Teachers, Postsecondary
- ◎ Social Work Teachers, Postsecondary
- ◎ Sociology Teachers, Postsecondary

P

Preschool Teachers, Except Special Education

- ◎ Education/Training Required: Bachelor's degree
- ◎ Annual Earnings: $20,450
- ◎ Growth: 36.2%
- ◎ Annual Job Openings: 88,000
- ◎ Self-Employed: 2.2%
- ◎ Part-Time: 24.9%

Instruct children (normally up to 5 years of age) in activities designed to promote social, physical, and intellectual growth needed for primary school in preschool, day care center, or other child development facility. May be required to hold state certification. Demonstrate activities to children. Enforce all administration policies and rules governing students. Establish and enforce rules for behavior, and procedures for maintaining order. Identify children showing signs of emotional, developmental, or health-related problems, and discuss them with supervisors, parents or guardians, and child development specialists. Maintain accurate and complete student records as required by laws, district policies, and administrative regulations. Meet with other professionals to discuss individual students' needs and progress. Meet with parents and guardians to discuss their children's progress and needs, determine their priorities for their children, and suggest ways that they can promote learning and development. Observe and evaluate children's performance, behavior, social development, and physical health. Organize and label materials, and display students' work in a manner appropriate for their ages and perceptual skills. Prepare and implement remedial programs for students requiring extra help. Prepare reports on students and activities as required by administration. Establish clear objectives for all lessons, units, and projects, and communicate those objectives to children. Organize and lead activities designed to promote physical, mental and social development, such as games, arts and crafts, music, storytelling, and field trips. Plan and conduct activities for a balanced program of instruction, demonstration, and work time that provides students with opportunities to observe, question, and investigate. Prepare materials and classrooms for class activities. Teach basic skills such as color, shape, number and letter recognition, personal hygiene, and social skills. Plan and supervise class projects, field trips, visits by guests, or other experiential activities, and guide students in learning from those activities. Adapt teaching methods and instructional materials to meet students' varying needs and interests. Arrange indoor and outdoor space to facilitate creative play, motor-skill activities, and safety. Assimilate arriving children to the school environment by greeting them, helping them remove outerwear, and selecting activities of interest to them. SKILLS— **Social Perceptiveness:** Being aware of others' reactions and understanding why they react as they do. **Learning Strategies:** Selecting and using training/instructional methods and procedures appropriate for the situation when learning or teaching new things. **Monitoring:** Monitoring or assessing your performance or that of other individuals or organizations to make improvements or take corrective action. **Instructing:** Teaching others how to do something. **Management of Personnel Resources:** Motivating, developing, and directing people as they work, identifying the best people for the job. **Speaking:** Talking to others to convey information effectively. **Coordination:** Adjusting actions in relation to others' actions. **Active Listening:** Giving full attention to what other people are saying, taking time to understand the points being made, asking questions as appropriate, and not interrupting at inappropriate times. **Service Orientation:** Actively looking for ways to help people. **Management of Material Resources:** Obtaining and seeing to the appropriate use of equipment, facilities, and materials needed to do certain work.

GOE—**Interest Area:** 05. Education and Training. **Work Group:** 05.02. Pre-school, Elementary, and Secondary Teaching and Instructing. **Other Jobs in This Work Group:** Elementary School Teachers, Except Special Education; Kindergarten Teachers, Except Special Education; Middle School Teachers, Except Special and Vocational Education; Secondary School Teachers, Except Special and Vocational Education; Special Education Teachers, Middle School; Special Education Teachers, Preschool, Kindergarten, and Elementary School; Special Education Teachers, Secondary School; Teacher Assistants; Vocational Education Teachers, Middle School; Vocational Education Teachers, Secondary School. **PERSONALITY TYPE:** Social. Social occupations frequently involve working with, communicating with, and teaching people. These occupations often involve helping or providing service to others.

EDUCATION/TRAINING PROGRAM(S)— Child Care and Support Services Management; Early Childhood Education and Teaching; Kindergarten/Preschool Education and Teaching. **RELATED KNOWLEDGE/COURSES—Customer and Personal Service:** Knowledge of principles and processes for providing customer and personal services. This includes customer needs assessment, meeting quality standards for services, and evaluation of customer satisfaction. **Education and Training:** Knowledge of principles and methods for curriculum and training design, teaching and instruction for individuals and groups, and the measurement of training effects. **Psychology:** Knowledge of human behavior and performance; individual differences in ability, personality, and interests; learning and motivation; psychological research methods; and the assessment and treatment of behavioral and affective disorders. **Therapy and Counseling:** Knowledge of principles, methods, and procedures for diagnosis, treatment, and rehabilitation of physical and mental dysfunctions and for career counseling and guidance. **Sociology and Anthropology:** Knowledge of group behavior and dynamics, societal trends and influences, human migrations, ethnicity, and cultures and their history and origins. **Fine Arts:** Knowledge of the theory and techniques required to compose, produce, and perform works of music, dance, visual arts, drama, and sculpture.

Private Sector Executives

- Education/Training Required: Work experience plus degree
- Annual Earnings: $136,400
- Growth: 16.7%
- Annual Job Openings: 63,000
- Self-Employed: 14.6%
- Part-Time: 5.3%

Determine and formulate policies and business strategies and provide overall direction of private sector organizations. Plan, direct, and coordinate operational activities at the highest level of management with the help of subordinate managers. Directs, plans, and implements policies and objectives of organization or business in accordance with charter and board of directors. Directs activities of organization to plan procedures, establish responsibilities, and coordinate functions among departments and sites. Analyzes operations to evaluate performance of company and staff and to determine areas of cost reduction and program improvement. Confers with board members, organization officials, and staff members to establish policies and formulate plans. Reviews financial statements and sales and activity reports to ensure that organization's objectives are achieved. Assigns or delegates responsibilities to subordinates. Directs and coordinates activities of business involved with buying and selling investment products and financial services. Establishes internal control procedures. Presides over or serves on board of directors, management

P

committees, or other governing boards. Directs inservice training of staff. Administers program for selection of sites, construction of buildings, and provision of equipment and supplies. Screens, selects, hires, transfers, and discharges employees. Promotes objectives of institution or business before associations, public, government agencies, or community groups. Negotiates or approves contracts with suppliers and distributors, and with maintenance, janitorial, and security providers. Prepares reports and budgets. Directs non-merchandising departments of business, such as advertising, purchasing, credit, and accounting. Directs and coordinates activities of business or department concerned with production, pricing, sales, and/or distribution of products. Directs and coordinates organization's financial and budget activities to fund operations, maximize investments, and increase efficiency. **SKILLS— Management of Financial Resources:** Determining how money will be spent to get the work done and accounting for these expenditures. **Systems Evaluation:** Identifying measures or indicators of system performance and the actions needed to improve or correct performance relative to the goals of the system. **Systems Analysis:** Determining how a system should work and how changes in conditions, operations, and the environment will affect outcomes. **Management of Personnel Resources:** Motivating, developing, and directing people as they work, identifying the best people for the job. **Coordination:** Adjusting actions in relation to others' actions. **Judgment and Decision Making:** Considering the relative costs and benefits of potential actions to choose the most appropriate one. **Management of Material Resources:** Obtaining and seeing to the appropriate use of equipment, facilities, and materials needed to do certain work. **Negotiation:** Bringing others together and trying to reconcile differences.

GOE—Interest Area: 04. Business and Administration. **Work Group:** 04.01. Managerial Work in General Business. **Other Jobs in This Work Group:** Chief Executives; Compensation and Benefits Man-

agers; General and Operations Managers; Human Resources Managers; Training and Development Managers. **PERSONALITY TYPE:** Enterprising. Enterprising occupations frequently involve starting up and carrying out projects. These occupations can involve leading people and making many decisions. They sometimes require risk taking and often deal with business.

EDUCATION/TRAINING PROGRAM(S)— Business Administration and Management, General; Business/Commerce, General; Entrepreneurship/Entrepreneurial Studies; International Business/Trade/Commerce; Public Administration; Public Administration and Social Service Professions, Other; Public Policy Analysis. **RELATED KNOWLEDGE/COURSES—Economics and Accounting:** Knowledge of economic and accounting principles and practices, the financial markets, banking, and the analysis and reporting of financial data. **Production and Processing:** Knowledge of raw materials, production processes, quality control, costs, and other techniques for maximizing the effective manufacture and distribution of goods. **Administration and Management:** Knowledge of business and management principles involved in strategic planning, resource allocation, human resources modeling, leadership technique, production methods, and coordination of people and resources. **Sales and Marketing:** Knowledge of principles and methods for showing, promoting, and selling products or services. This includes marketing strategy and tactics, product demonstration, sales techniques, and sales control systems. **Personnel and Human Resources:** Knowledge of principles and procedures for personnel recruitment, selection, training, compensation and benefits, labor relations and negotiation, and personnel information systems. **Psychology:** Knowledge of human behavior and performance; individual differences in ability, personality, and interests; learning and motivation; psychological research methods; and the assessment and treatment of behavioral and affective disorders.

Probation Officers and Correctional Treatment Specialists

- Education/Training Required: Bachelor's degree
- Annual Earnings: $39,200
- Growth: 14.7%
- Annual Job Openings: 15,000
- Self-Employed: 0.2%
- Part-Time: 10.6%

Provide social services to assist in rehabilitation of law offenders in custody or on probation or parole. Make recommendations for actions involving formulation of rehabilitation plan and treatment of offender, including conditional release and education and employment stipulations. Prepare and maintain case folder for each assigned inmate or offender. Write reports describing offenders' progress. Inform offenders or inmates of requirements of conditional release, such as office visits, restitution payments, or educational and employment stipulations. Discuss with offenders how such issues as drug and alcohol abuse, and anger management problems might have played roles in their criminal behavior. Gather information about offenders' backgrounds by talking to offenders, their families and friends, and other people who have relevant information. Develop rehabilitation programs for assigned offenders or inmates, establishing rules of conduct, goals, and objectives. Develop liaisons and networks with other parole officers, community agencies, staff in correctional institutions, psychiatric facilities and after-care agencies in order to make plans for helping offenders with life adjustments. Arrange for medical, mental health, or substance abuse treatment services according to individual needs and/or court orders. Provide offenders or inmates with assistance in matters concerning detainers, sentences in other jurisdictions, writs, and applications for social assistance. Arrange for post-release services such as employment, housing, counseling, education, and social activities. Recommend remedial action or initiate court action when terms of probation or parole are not complied with. Interview probationers and parolees regularly to evaluate their progress in accomplishing goals and maintaining the terms specified in their probation contracts and rehabilitation plans. Supervise people on community-based sentences, including people on electronically monitored home detention. Assess the suitability of penitentiary inmates for release under parole and statutory release programs, and submit recommendations to parole boards. Investigate alleged parole violations, using interviews, surveillance, and search and seizure. Conduct prehearing and presentencing investigations, and testify in court regarding offenders' backgrounds and recommended sentences and sentencing conditions. **SKILLS—Social Perceptiveness:** Being aware of others' reactions and understanding why they react as they do. **Persuasion:** Persuading others to change their minds or behavior. **Time Management:** Managing one's own time and the time of others. **Negotiation:** Bringing others together and trying to reconcile differences. **Learning Strategies:** Selecting and using training/instructional methods and procedures appropriate for the situation when learning or teaching new things. **Coordination:** Adjusting actions in relation to others' actions. **Management of Personnel Resources:** Motivating, developing, and directing people as they work, identifying the best people for the job. **Instructing:** Teaching others how to do something.

GOE—Interest Area: 10. Human Service. **Work Group:** 10.01. Counseling and Social Work. **Other Jobs in This Work Group:** Child, Family, and School Social Workers; Clinical Psychologists; Counseling Psychologists; Marriage and Family Therapists; Medical and Public Health Social Workers; Mental Health and Substance Abuse Social Workers; Mental Health Counselors; Rehabilitation Counselors; Residential Advisors; Social and Human Service Assistants; Substance Abuse and

Behavioral Disorder Counselors. **PERSONALITY TYPE:** Social. Social occupations frequently involve working with, communicating with, and teaching people. These occupations often involve helping or providing service to others.

EDUCATION/TRAINING PROGRAM(S)— Social Work. **RELATED KNOWLEDGE/ COURSES—Therapy and Counseling:** Knowledge of principles, methods, and procedures for diagnosis, treatment, and rehabilitation of physical and mental dysfunctions and for career counseling and guidance. **Psychology:** Knowledge of human behavior and performance; individual differences in ability, personality, and interests; learning and motivation; psychological research methods; and the assessment and treatment of behavioral and affective disorders. **Sociology and Anthropology:** Knowledge of group behavior and dynamics, societal trends and influences, human migrations, ethnicity, and cultures and their history and origins. **Public Safety and Security:** Knowledge of relevant equipment, policies, procedures, and strategies to promote effective local, state, or national security operations for the protection of people, data, property, and institutions. **Philosophy and Theology:** Knowledge of different philosophical systems and religions. This includes their basic principles, values, ethics, ways of thinking, customs, and practices and their impact on human culture. **Law and Government:** Knowledge of laws, legal codes, court procedures, precedents, government regulations, executive orders, agency rules, and the democratic political process.

Producers

- ◎ Education/Training Required: Work experience plus degree
- ◎ Annual Earnings: $51,870
- ◎ Growth: 18.3%
- ◎ Annual Job Openings: 10,000
- ◎ Self-Employed: 32.8%
- ◎ Part-Time: 9.1%

Plan and coordinate various aspects of radio, television, stage, or motion picture production, such as selecting script, coordinating writing, directing and editing, and arranging financing. Coordinate the activities of writers, directors, managers, and other personnel throughout the production process. Monitor post-production processes in order to ensure accurate completion of all details. Perform management activities such as budgeting, scheduling, planning, and marketing. Determine production size, content, and budget, establishing details such as production schedules and management policies. Compose and edit scripts, or provide screenwriters with story outlines from which scripts can be written. Conduct meetings with staff to discuss production progress and to ensure production objectives are attained. Resolve personnel problems that arise during the production process by acting as liaisons between dissenting parties when necessary. Produce shows for special occasions, such as holidays or testimonials. Edit and write news stories from information collected by reporters. Write and submit proposals to bid on contracts for projects. Hire directors, principal cast members, and key production staff members. Arrange financing for productions. Select plays, scripts, books, or ideas to be produced. Review film, recordings, or rehearsals to ensure conformance to production and broadcast standards. Perform administrative duties such as preparing operational reports, distributing rehearsal call sheets and script copies, and arranging for rehearsal quarters. Obtain and distribute costumes, props, music, and studio equipment needed to complete productions. Negotiate contracts with artistic personnel, often in accordance with collective bargaining agreements. Maintain knowledge of minimum wages and working conditions established by unions and/or associations of actors and technicians. Plan and coordinate the production of musical recordings, selecting music and directing performers. Negotiate with parties including independent producers, and the distributors and broadcasters who will be handling completed productions. Develop marketing plans for finished products, collaborating with sales associates to supervise product distribution. Determine and direct the content of radio programming. **SKILLS—Coordination:** Adjusting actions in relation to others' actions. **Negotiation:** Bringing others together and trying to reconcile differences. **Monitoring:** Monitoring or assessing your performance or that of other individuals or organizations to make improvements or take corrective action. **Management of Personnel Resources:** Motivating, developing, and directing people as they work, identifying the best people for the job. **Writing:** Communicating effectively in writing as appropriate for the needs of the audience. **Time Management:** Managing one's own time and the time of others. **Social Perceptiveness:** Being aware of others' reactions and understanding why they react as they do. **Management of Financial Resources:** Determining how money will be spent to get the work done and accounting for these expenditures.

GOE—Interest Area: 03. Arts and Communication. **Work Group:** 03.01. Managerial Work in Arts and Communication. **Other Jobs in This Work Group:** Agents and Business Managers of Artists, Performers, and Athletes; Art Directors; Program Directors; Public Relations Managers; Technical Directors/Managers. **PERSONALITY TYPE:** Artistic. Artistic occupations frequently involve working with forms, designs, and patterns. They often require self-expression, and the work can be done without following a clear set of rules.

EDUCATION/TRAINING PROGRAM(S)— Cinematography and Film/Video Production; Directing and Theatrical Production; Drama and Dramatics/Theatre Arts, General; Dramatic/Theatre Arts and Stagecraft, Other; Film/Cinema Studies; Radio and Television; Theatre/Theatre Arts Management. **RELATED KNOWLEDGE/COURSES— Communications and Media:** Knowledge of media production, communication, and dissemination techniques and methods. This includes alternative ways to inform and entertain via written, oral, and visual media. **Clerical Practices:** Knowledge of administrative and clerical procedures and systems such as word processing, managing files and records, stenography and transcription, designing forms, and other office procedures and terminology. **Administration and Management:** Knowledge of business and management principles involved in strategic planning, resource allocation, human resources modeling, leadership technique, production methods, and coordination of people and resources. **English Language:** Knowledge of the structure and content of the English language, including the meaning and spelling of words, rules of composition, and grammar. **Fine Arts:** Knowledge of the theory and techniques required to compose, produce, and perform works of music, dance, visual arts, drama, and sculpture. **Sales and Marketing:** Knowledge of principles and methods for showing, promoting, and selling products or services. This includes marketing strategy and tactics, product demonstration, sales techniques, and sales control systems.

Product Safety Engineers

- Education/Training Required: Bachelor's degree
- Annual Earnings: $61,430
- Growth: 7.9%
- Annual Job Openings: 4,000
- Self-Employed: 1.6%
- Part-Time: 1.5%

Develop and conduct tests to evaluate product safety levels and recommend measures to reduce or eliminate hazards. Participates in preparation of product usage and precautionary label instructions. Prepares reports of findings from investigation of accidents. Investigates causes of accidents, injuries, or illnesses from product usage to develop solutions to minimize or prevent recurrence. Evaluates potential health hazards or damage which could occur from misuse of product and engineers solutions to improve safety. Conducts research to evaluate safety levels for products. Advises and recommends procedures for detection, prevention, and elimination of physical, chemical, or other product hazards. **SKILLS—Quality Control Analysis:** Conducting tests and inspections of products, services, or processes to evaluate quality or performance. **Operations Analysis:** Analyzing needs and product requirements to create a design. **Science:** Using scientific rules and methods to solve problems. **Mathematics:** Using mathematics to solve problems. **Technology Design:** Generating or adapting equipment and technology to serve user needs. **Active Learning:** Understanding the implications of new information for both current and future problem-solving and decision-making. **Writing:** Communicating effectively in writing as appropriate for the needs of the audience. **Troubleshooting:** Determining causes of operating errors and deciding what to do about them.

GOE—Interest Area: 15. Scientific Research, Engineering, and Mathematics. **Work Group:** 15.08. Industrial and Safety Engineering. **Other Jobs in This Work Group:** Fire-Prevention and Protection Engineers; Industrial Engineers; Industrial Safety and Health Engineers. **PERSONALITY TYPE:** Investigative. Investigative occupations frequently involve working with ideas and require an extensive amount of thinking. These occupations can involve searching for facts and figuring out problems mentally.

EDUCATION/TRAINING PROGRAM(S)— Environmental/Environmental Health Engineering.

RELATED KNOWLEDGE/COURSES—Chemistry: Knowledge of the chemical composition, structure, and properties of substances and of the chemical processes and transformations that they undergo. This includes uses of chemicals and their danger signs, production techniques, and disposal methods. **Engineering and Technology:** Knowledge of the practical application of engineering science and technology. This includes applying principles, techniques, procedures, and equipment to the design and production of various goods and services. **Physics:** Knowledge and prediction of physical principles and laws and their interrelationships and applications to understanding fluid, material, and atmospheric dynamics and mechanical, electrical, atomic, and subatomic structures and processes. **Public Safety and Security:** Knowledge of relevant equipment, policies, procedures, and strategies to promote effective local, state, or national security operations for the protection of people, data, property, and institutions. **Production and Processing:** Knowledge of raw materials, production processes, quality control, costs, and other techniques for maximizing the effective manufacture and distribution of goods. **Biology:** Knowledge of plant and animal organisms and their tissues, cells, functions, interdependencies, and interactions with each other and the environment.

Program Directors

- Education/Training Required: Work experience plus degree
- Annual Earnings: $51,870
- Growth: 18.3%
- Annual Job Openings: 10,000
- Self-Employed: 32.8%
- Part-Time: 9.1%

Direct and coordinate activities of personnel engaged in preparation of radio or television sta-

tion program schedules and programs, such as sports or news. Check completed program logs for accuracy and conformance with FCC rules and regulations, and resolve program log inaccuracies. Confer with directors and production staff to discuss issues such as production and casting problems, budgets, policies, and news coverage. Coordinate activities between departments, such as news and programming. Cue announcers, actors, performers, and guests. Develop promotions for current programs and specials. Direct and coordinate activities of personnel engaged in broadcast news, sports, or programming. Establish work schedules and assign work to staff members. Evaluate new and existing programming for suitability and in order to assess the need for changes, using information such as audience surveys and feedback. Monitor and review programming in order to ensure that schedules are met, guidelines are adhered to, and performances are of adequate quality. Monitor network transmissions for advisories concerning daily program schedules, program content, special feeds, and/or program changes. Perform personnel duties such as hiring staff and evaluating work performance. Plan and schedule programming and event coverage based on broadcast length, time availability, and other factors such as community needs, ratings data, and viewer demographics. Act as a liaison between talent and directors, providing information that performers/guests need to prepare for appearances, and communicating relevant information from guests, performers, or staff to directors. Conduct interviews for broadcasts. Develop budgets for programming and broadcasting activities, and monitor expenditures to ensure that they remain within budgetary limits. Develop ideas for programs and features that a station could produce. Operate and maintain on-air and production audio equipment. Prepare copy and edit tape so that material is ready for broadcasting. Read news, read and/or record public service and promotional announcements, and otherwise participate as a member of an on-air shift as required. Review information about programs and schedules in order to ensure accuracy and provide such information to local media outlets as necessary.

SKILLS—Management of Personnel Resources: Motivating, developing, and directing people as they work, identifying the best people for the job. **Coordination:** Adjusting actions in relation to others' actions. **Management of Financial Resources:** Determining how money will be spent to get the work done and accounting for these expenditures. **Management of Material Resources:** Obtaining and seeing to the appropriate use of equipment, facilities, and materials needed to do certain work. **Writing:** Communicating effectively in writing as appropriate for the needs of the audience. **Time Management:** Managing one's own time and the time of others. **Active Learning:** Understanding the implications of new information for both current and future problem-solving and decision-making. **Reading Comprehension:** Understanding written sentences and paragraphs in work-related documents.

GOE—Interest Area: 03. Arts and Communication. **Work Group:** 03.01. Managerial Work in Arts and Communication. **Other Jobs in This Work Group:** Agents and Business Managers of Artists, Performers, and Athletes; Art Directors; Producers; Public Relations Managers; Technical Directors/Managers. **PERSONALITY TYPE:** Enterprising. Enterprising occupations frequently involve starting up and carrying out projects. These occupations can involve leading people and making many decisions. They sometimes require risk taking and often deal with business.

EDUCATION/TRAINING PROGRAM(S)— Cinematography and Film/Video Production; Directing and Theatrical Production; Drama and Dramatics/Theatre Arts, General; Dramatic/Theatre Arts and Stagecraft, Other; Film/Cinema Studies; Radio and Television; Theatre/Theatre Arts Management. **RELATED KNOWLEDGE/ COURSES—Communications and Media:** Knowledge of media production, communication, and dissemination techniques and methods. This includes alternative ways to inform and entertain via written, oral, and visual media. **Administration and Management:** Knowledge of business and management principles involved in strategic planning, resource allocation, human resources modeling, leadership technique, production methods, and coordination of people and resources. **Personnel and Human Resources:** Knowledge of principles and procedures for personnel recruitment, selection, training, compensation and benefits, labor relations and negotiation, and personnel information systems. **Economics and Accounting:** Knowledge of economic and accounting principles and practices, the financial markets, banking, and the analysis and reporting of financial data. **Telecommunications:** Knowledge of transmission, broadcasting, switching, control, and operation of telecommunications systems. **English Language:** Knowledge of the structure and content of the English language, including the meaning and spelling of words, rules of composition, and grammar.

Property, Real Estate, and Community Association Managers

- Education/Training Required: Bachelor's degree
- Annual Earnings: $38,750
- Growth: 12.8%
- Annual Job Openings: 35,000
- Self-Employed: 46.0%
- Part-Time: 15.3%

Plan, direct, or coordinate selling, buying, leasing, or governance activities of commercial, industrial, or residential real estate properties. Act as liaisons between on-site managers or tenants and owners. Confer regularly with community association members to ensure their needs are being met. Determine and certify the eligibility of prospective tenants, following government regulations. Direct and coordi-

nate the activities of staff and contract personnel, and evaluate their performance. Direct collection of monthly assessments, rental fees, and deposits and payment of insurance premiums, mortgage, taxes, and incurred operating expenses. Inspect grounds, facilities, and equipment routinely to determine necessity of repairs or maintenance. Investigate complaints, disturbances and violations, and resolve problems, following management rules and regulations. Maintain records of sales, rental or usage activity, special permits issued, maintenance and operating costs, or property availability. Manage and oversee operations, maintenance, administration, and improvement of commercial, industrial, or residential properties. Market vacant space to prospective tenants through leasing agents, advertising, or other methods. Meet with prospective tenants to show properties, explain terms of occupancy, and provide information about local areas. Negotiate the sale, lease, or development of property, and complete or review appropriate documents and forms. Plan, schedule, and coordinate general maintenance, major repairs, and remodeling or construction projects for commercial or residential properties. Prepare and administer contracts for provision of property services such as cleaning, maintenance, and security services. Prepare detailed budgets and financial reports for properties. Purchase building and maintenance supplies, equipment, or furniture. Analyze information on property values, taxes, zoning, population growth, and traffic volume and patterns in order to determine if properties should be acquired. Clean common areas, change light bulbs, and make minor property repairs. Confer with legal authorities to ensure that renting and advertising practices are not discriminatory and that properties comply with state and federal regulations. SKILLS—**Management of Financial Resources:** Determining how money will be spent to get the work done and accounting for these expenditures. **Management of Personnel Resources:** Motivating, developing, and directing people as they work, identifying the best people for the job. **Negotiation:** Bringing others together and trying to reconcile differences. **Management of Material Resources:** Obtaining and seeing to the appropriate use of equipment, facilities, and materials needed to do certain work. **Coordination:** Adjusting actions in relation to others' actions. **Systems Evaluation:** Identifying measures or indicators of system performance and the actions needed to improve or correct performance relative to the goals of the system. **Judgment and Decision Making:** Considering the relative costs and benefits of potential actions to choose the most appropriate one. **Time Management:** Managing one's own time and the time of others.

GOE—**Interest Area:** 14. Retail and Wholesale Sales and Service. **Work Group:** 14.01. Managerial Work in Retail/Wholesale Sales and Service. **Other Jobs in This Work Group:** Advertising and Promotions Managers; First-Line Supervisors/Managers of Non-Retail Sales Workers; First-Line Supervisors/Managers of Retail Sales Workers; Funeral Directors; Marketing Managers; Purchasing Managers; Sales Managers. **PERSONALITY TYPE:** Enterprising. Enterprising occupations frequently involve starting up and carrying out projects. These occupations can involve leading people and making many decisions. They sometimes require risk taking and often deal with business.

EDUCATION/TRAINING PROGRAM(S)— Real Estate. **RELATED KNOWLEDGE/ COURSES—Administration and Management:** Knowledge of business and management principles involved in strategic planning, resource allocation, human resources modeling, leadership technique, production methods, and coordination of people and resources. **Law and Government:** Knowledge of laws, legal codes, court procedures, precedents, government regulations, executive orders, agency rules, and the democratic political process. **Sales and Marketing:** Knowledge of principles and methods for showing, promoting, and selling products or services. This includes marketing strategy and tactics, product demonstration, sales techniques, and sales control systems. **Personnel and Human Resources:** Knowledge of principles and procedures

for personnel recruitment, selection, training, compensation and benefits, labor relations and negotiation, and personnel information systems. **Economics and Accounting:** Knowledge of economic and accounting principles and practices, the financial markets, banking, and the analysis and reporting of financial data. **Building and Construction:** Knowledge of the materials, methods, and tools involved in the construction or repair of houses, buildings, or other structures such as highways and roads.

Prosthodontists

- Education/Training Required: First professional degree
- Annual Earnings: $120,420
- Growth: 4.1%
- Annual Job Openings: 7,000
- Self-Employed: 39.9%
- Part-Time: 22.3%

Construct oral prostheses to replace missing teeth and other oral structures to correct natural and acquired deformation of mouth and jaws, to restore and maintain oral function, such as chewing and speaking, and to improve appearance. Repair, reline, and/or rebase dentures. Treat facial pain and jaw joint problems. Use bonding technology on the surface of the teeth in order to change tooth shape or to close gaps. Collaborate with general dentists, specialists, and other health professionals in order to develop solutions to dental and oral health concerns. Design and fabricate dental prostheses, or supervise dental technicians and laboratory bench workers who construct the devices. Fit prostheses to patients, making any necessary adjustments and modifications. Measure and take impressions of patients' jaws and teeth in order to determine the shape and size of dental prostheses, using face bows, dental articulators, recording devices, and other materials. Replace missing teeth and associated oral structures with permanent fixtures, such as crowns and bridges, or removable fixtures, such as dentures. Restore function and aesthetics to traumatic injury victims, or to individuals with diseases or birth defects. Bleach discolored teeth in order to brighten and whiten them. Place veneers onto teeth in order to conceal defects. **SKILLS—Science:** Using scientific rules and methods to solve problems. **Technology Design:** Generating or adapting equipment and technology to serve user needs. **Reading Comprehension:** Understanding written sentences and paragraphs in work-related documents. **Critical Thinking:** Using logic and reasoning to identify the strengths and weaknesses of alternative solutions, conclusions, or approaches to problems. **Judgment and Decision Making:** Considering the relative costs and benefits of potential actions to choose the most appropriate one. **Service Orientation:** Actively looking for ways to help people. **Equipment Selection:** Determining the kind of tools and equipment needed to do a job. **Mathematics:** Using mathematics to solve problems. **Active Learning:** Understanding the implications of new information for both current and future problem-solving and decision-making. **Operations Analysis:** Analyzing needs and product requirements to create a design.

GOE—Interest Area: 08. Health Science. **Work Group:** 08.03. Dentistry. **Other Jobs in This Work Group:** Dental Assistants; Dental Hygienists; Dentists, General; Oral and Maxillofacial Surgeons; Orthodontists. **PERSONALITY TYPE:** Investigative. Investigative occupations frequently involve working with ideas and require an extensive amount of thinking. These occupations can involve searching for facts and figuring out problems mentally.

EDUCATION/TRAINING PROGRAM(S)— Prosthodontics Specialty; Prosthodontics/Prosthodontology (Cert, MS, PhD). **RELATED KNOWLEDGE/COURSES—Medicine and Dentistry:** Knowledge of the information and techniques needed to diagnose and treat human injuries, diseases, and deformities. This includes symptoms, treatment alternatives, drug properties and interactions, and preventive health-care measures. **Chemistry:** Knowledge of the chemical composition, structure, and properties of substances and of the chemical processes and transformations that they undergo. This includes uses of chemicals and their danger signs, production techniques, and disposal methods. **Biology:** Knowledge of plant and animal organisms and their tissues, cells, functions, interdependencies, and interactions with each other and the environment. **English Language:** Knowledge of the structure and content of the English language, including the meaning and spelling of words, rules of composition, and grammar. **Design:** Knowledge of design techniques, tools, and principles involved in production of precision technical plans, blueprints, drawings, and models.

Psychiatrists

- Education/Training Required: First professional degree
- Annual Earnings: $135,440
- Growth: 19.5%
- Annual Job Openings: 38,000
- Self-Employed: 16.9%
- Part-Time: 8.1%

Diagnose, treat, and help prevent disorders of the mind. Analyze and evaluate patient data and test or examination findings to diagnose nature and extent of mental disorder. Prescribe, direct, and administer psychotherapeutic treatments or medications to treat mental, emotional, or behavioral disorders. Collaborate with physicians, psychologists, social workers, psychiatric nurses, or other professionals to discuss treatment plans and progress. Gather and maintain patient information and records, including social and medical history obtained from patients, relatives, and other professionals. Counsel outpatients and other patients during office visits.

Design individualized care plans, using a variety of treatments. Examine or conduct laboratory or diagnostic tests on patient to provide information on general physical condition and mental disorder. Advise and inform guardians, relatives, and significant others of patients' conditions and treatment. Review and evaluate treatment procedures and outcomes of other psychiatrists and medical professionals. Teach, conduct research, and publish findings to increase understanding of mental, emotional, and behavioral states and disorders. Prepare and submit case reports and summaries to government and mental health agencies. Serve on committees to promote and maintain community mental health services and delivery systems. **SKILLS—Social Perceptiveness:** Being aware of others' reactions and understanding why they react as they do. **Persuasion:** Persuading others to change their minds or behavior. **Active Learning:** Understanding the implications of new information for both current and future problem-solving and decision-making. **Science:** Using scientific rules and methods to solve problems. **Active Listening:** Giving full attention to what other people are saying, taking time to understand the points being made, asking questions as appropriate, and not interrupting at inappropriate times. **Negotiation:** Bringing others together and trying to reconcile differences. **Critical Thinking:** Using logic and reasoning to identify the strengths and weaknesses of alternative solutions, conclusions, or approaches to problems. **Learning Strategies:** Selecting and using training/instructional methods and procedures appropriate for the situation when learning or teaching new things. **Complex Problem Solving:** Identifying complex problems and reviewing related information to develop and evaluate options and implement solutions.

GOE—Interest Area: 08. Health Science. **Work Group:** 08.02. Medicine and Surgery. **Other Jobs in This Work Group:** Anesthesiologists; Family and General Practitioners; Internists, General; Medical Assistants; Medical Transcriptionists; Obstetricians and Gynecologists; Pediatricians, General; Pharmacists; Pharmacy Aides; Pharmacy Technicians;

Physician Assistants; Registered Nurses; Surgeons; Surgical Technologists. **PERSONALITY TYPE:** Investigative. Investigative occupations frequently involve working with ideas and require an extensive amount of thinking. These occupations can involve searching for facts and figuring out problems mentally.

EDUCATION/TRAINING PROGRAM(S)— Child Psychiatry; Physical Medical and Rehabilitation/Psychiatry; Psychiatry. **RELATED KNOWLEDGE/COURSES—Therapy and Counseling:** Knowledge of principles, methods, and procedures for diagnosis, treatment, and rehabilitation of physical and mental dysfunctions and for career counseling and guidance. **Medicine and Dentistry:** Knowledge of the information and techniques needed to diagnose and treat human injuries, diseases, and deformities. This includes symptoms, treatment alternatives, drug properties and interactions, and preventive health-care measures. **Psychology:** Knowledge of human behavior and performance; individual differences in ability, personality, and interests; learning and motivation; psychological research methods; and the assessment and treatment of behavioral and affective disorders. **Biology:** Knowledge of plant and animal organisms and their tissues, cells, functions, interdependencies, and interactions with each other and the environment. **Philosophy and Theology:** Knowledge of different philosophical systems and religions. This includes their basic principles, values, ethics, ways of thinking, customs, and practices and their impact on human culture. **Sociology and Anthropology:** Knowledge of group behavior and dynamics, societal trends and influences, human migrations, ethnicity, and cultures and their history and origins.

P

Psychology Teachers, Postsecondary

- Education/Training Required: Master's degree
- Annual Earnings: $54,530
- Growth: 38.1% for all Postsecondary Teachers
- Annual Job Openings: 216,000 for all Postsecondary Teachers
- Self-Employed: 0.3% for all Postsecondary Teachers
- Part-Time: 27.7% for all Postsecondary Teachers

Teach courses in psychology, such as child, clinical, and developmental psychology, and psychological counseling. Evaluate and grade students' class work, laboratory work, assignments, and papers. Prepare and deliver lectures to undergraduate and/or graduate students on topics such as abnormal psychology, cognitive processes, and work motivation. Advise students on academic and vocational curricula, and on career issues. Compile, administer, and grade examinations, or assign this work to others. Compile bibliographies of specialized materials for outside reading assignments. Initiate, facilitate, and moderate classroom discussions. Keep abreast of developments in their field by reading current literature, talking with colleagues, and participating in professional conferences. Maintain regularly scheduled office hours in order to advise and assist students. Maintain student attendance records, grades, and other required records. Plan, evaluate, and revise curricula, course content, and course materials and methods of instruction. Prepare course materials such as syllabi, homework assignments, and handouts. Select and obtain materials and supplies such as textbooks. Supervise students' laboratory work. Supervise undergraduate and/or graduate teaching, internship, and research work. Act as advisers to student organizations. Collaborate with colleagues to address teaching and research issues. Conduct research in a particular field of knowledge, and publish findings in professional journals, books, and/or electronic media. Participate in campus and community events. Participate in student recruitment, registration, and placement activities. Perform administrative duties such as serving as department head. Provide professional consulting services to government and/or industry. Serve on academic or administrative committees that deal with institutional policies, departmental matters, and academic issues. Write grant proposals to procure external research funding. **SKILLS—Instructing:** Teaching others how to do something. **Learning Strategies:** Selecting and using training/instructional methods and procedures appropriate for the situation when learning or teaching new things. **Reading Comprehension:** Understanding written sentences and paragraphs in work-related documents. **Active Learning:** Understanding the implications of new information for both current and future problem-solving and decision-making. **Speaking:** Talking to others to convey information effectively. **Writing:** Communicating effectively in writing as appropriate for the needs of the audience. **Science:** Using scientific rules and methods to solve problems. **Active Listening:** Giving full attention to what other people are saying, taking time to understand the points being made, asking questions as appropriate, and not interrupting at inappropriate times. **Critical Thinking:** Using logic and reasoning to identify the strengths and weaknesses of alternative solutions, conclusions, or approaches to problems.

GOE—Interest Area: 05. Education and Training. **Work Group:** 05.03. Postsecondary and Adult Teaching and Instructing. **Other Jobs in This Work Group:** Adult Literacy, Remedial Education, and GED Teachers and Instructors; Agricultural Sciences Teachers, Postsecondary; Anthropology and Archeology Teachers, Postsecondary; Architecture Teachers, Postsecondary; Area, Ethnic, and Cultural Studies Teachers, Postsecondary; Art, Drama, and Music Teachers, Postsecondary; Atmospheric,

Earth, Marine, and Space Sciences Teachers, Postsecondary; Biological Science Teachers, Postsecondary; Business Teachers, Postsecondary; Chemistry Teachers, Postsecondary; Communications Teachers, Postsecondary; Computer Science Teachers, Postsecondary; Criminal Justice and Law Enforcement Teachers, Postsecondary; Economics Teachers, Postsecondary; Education Teachers, Postsecondary; Engineering Teachers, Postsecondary; English Language and Literature Teachers, Postsecondary; Environmental Science Teachers, Postsecondary; Farm and Home Management Advisors; Foreign Language and Literature Teachers, Postsecondary; Forestry and Conservation Science Teachers, Postsecondary; Geography Teachers, Postsecondary; Graduate Teaching Assistants; Health Specialties Teachers, Postsecondary; History Teachers, Postsecondary; Home Economics Teachers, Postsecondary; Law Teachers, Postsecondary; Library Science Teachers, Postsecondary; Mathematical Science Teachers, Postsecondary; Nursing Instructors and Teachers, Postsecondary; Philosophy and Religion Teachers, Postsecondary; Physics Teachers, Postsecondary; Political Science Teachers, Postsecondary; Recreation and Fitness Studies Teachers, Postsecondary; Self-Enrichment Education Teachers; Social Work Teachers, Postsecondary; Sociology Teachers, Postsecondary; Vocational Education Teachers, Postsecondary. **PERSONALITY TYPE:** Social. Social occupations frequently involve working with, communicating with, and teaching people. These occupations often involve helping or providing service to others.

EDUCATION/TRAINING PROGRAM(S)— Clinical Psychology; Cognitive Psychology and Psycholinguistics; Community Psychology; Comparative Psychology; Counseling Psychology; Developmental and Child Psychology; Educational Psychology; Experimental Psychology; Industrial and Organizational Psychology; Marriage and Family Therapy/Counseling; Personality Psychology; Physiological Psychology/Psychobiology; Psychology Teacher Education; Psychology, General; Psychology, Other; Psychometrics and Quantitative

Psychology; School Psychology; Social Psychology; Social Science Teacher Education. **RELATED KNOWLEDGE/COURSES—Sociology and Anthropology:** Knowledge of group behavior and dynamics, societal trends and influences, human migrations, ethnicity, and cultures and their history and origins. **History and Archeology:** Knowledge of historical events and their causes, indicators, and effects on civilizations and cultures. **Education and Training:** Knowledge of principles and methods for curriculum and training design, teaching and instruction for individuals and groups, and the measurement of training effects. **Psychology:** Knowledge of human behavior and performance; individual differences in ability, personality, and interests; learning and motivation; psychological research methods; and the assessment and treatment of behavioral and affective disorders. **Economics and Accounting:** Knowledge of economic and accounting principles and practices, the financial markets, banking, and the analysis and reporting of financial data. **English Language:** Knowledge of the structure and content of the English language, including the meaning and spelling of words, rules of composition, and grammar.

Public Relations Managers

- Education/Training Required: Work experience plus degree
- Annual Earnings: $67,810
- Growth: 23.4%
- Annual Job Openings: 10,000
- Self-Employed: 0.9%
- Part-Time: 4.8%

Plan and direct public relations programs designed to create and maintain a favorable public image for employer or client; or if engaged in fundraising,

plan and direct activities to solicit and maintain funds for special projects and nonprofit organizations. Identify main client groups and audiences and determine the best way to communicate publicity information to them. Write interesting and effective press releases, prepare information for media kits and develop and maintain company internet or intranet web pages. Develop and maintain the company's corporate image and identity, which includes the use of logos and signage. Manage communications budgets. Manage special events such as sponsorship of races, parties introducing new products, or other activities the firm supports in order to gain public attention through the media without advertising directly. Draft speeches for company executives, and arrange interviews and other forms of contact for them. Assign, supervise and review the activities of public relations staff. Evaluate advertising and promotion programs for compatibility with public relations efforts. Establish and maintain effective working relationships with local and municipal government officials and media representatives. Confer with labor relations managers to develop internal communications that keep employees informed of company activities. Direct activities of external agencies, establishments and departments that develop and implement communication strategies and information programs. Formulate policies and procedures related to public information programs, working with public relations executives. Respond to requests for information about employers' activities or status. Establish goals for soliciting funds, develop policies for collection and safeguarding of contributions, and coordinate disbursement of funds. Facilitate consumer relations, or the relationship between parts of the company such as the managers and employees, or different branch offices. Maintain company archives. Manage in-house communication courses. Produce films and other video products, regulate their distribution, and operate film library. **SKILLS—Management of Financial Resources:** Determining how money will be spent to get the work done and accounting for these expenditures. **Social Perceptiveness:** Being aware of others' reactions and understanding why they react as they do. **Service Orientation:** Actively looking for ways to help people. **Monitoring:** Monitoring or assessing your performance or that of other individuals or organizations to make improvements or take corrective action. **Persuasion:** Persuading others to change their minds or behavior. **Coordination:** Adjusting actions in relation to others' actions. **Negotiation:** Bringing others together and trying to reconcile differences. **Time Management:** Managing one's own time and the time of others.

GOE—Interest Area: 03. Arts and Communication. **Work Group:** 03.01. Managerial Work in Arts and Communication. **Other Jobs in This Work Group:** Agents and Business Managers of Artists, Performers, and Athletes; Art Directors; Producers; Program Directors; Technical Directors/Managers. **PERSONALITY TYPE:** No data available.

EDUCATION/TRAINING PROGRAM(S)— Public Relations/Image Management. **RELATED KNOWLEDGE/COURSES—Sales and Marketing:** Knowledge of principles and methods for showing, promoting, and selling products or services. This includes marketing strategy and tactics, product demonstration, sales techniques, and sales control systems. **Economics and Accounting:** Knowledge of economic and accounting principles and practices, the financial markets, banking, and the analysis and reporting of financial data. **Education and Training:** Knowledge of principles and methods for curriculum and training design, teaching and instruction for individuals and groups, and the measurement of training effects. **Law and Government:** Knowledge of laws, legal codes, court procedures, precedents, government regulations, executive orders, agency rules, and the democratic political process. **Customer and Personal Service:** Knowledge of principles and processes for providing customer and personal services. This includes customer needs assessment, meeting quality standards for services, and evaluation of customer satisfaction. **English Language:** Knowledge of the structure and content of the English language, including the meaning and spelling of words, rules of composition, and grammar. **Foreign Language:** Knowledge of the structure and content of a foreign (non-English) language, including the meaning and spelling of words, rules of composition and grammar, and pronunciation.

Public Relations Specialists

- Education/Training Required: Bachelor's degree
- Annual Earnings: $43,050
- Growth: 32.9%
- Annual Job Openings: 28,000
- Self-Employed: 6.1%
- Part-Time: 12.5%

Engage in promoting or creating good will for individuals, groups, or organizations by writing or selecting favorable publicity material and releasing it through various communications media. May prepare and arrange displays, and make speeches. Prepare or edit organizational publications for internal and external audiences, including employee newsletters and stockholders' reports. Respond to requests for information from the media or designate another appropriate spokesperson or information source. Establish and maintain cooperative relationships with representatives of community, consumer, employee, and public interest groups. Plan and direct development and communication of informational programs to maintain favorable public and stockholder perceptions of an organization's accomplishments and agenda. Confer with production and support personnel to produce or coordinate production of advertisements and promotions. Arrange public appearances, lectures, contests, or exhibits for clients to increase product and service awareness and to promote goodwill. Study the objectives, promotional policies and needs of organizations to develop public relations strategies that will influence public opinion or promote ideas, products and services. Confer with other managers to identify trends and key group interests and concerns or to provide advice on business decisions. Consult with advertising agencies or staff to arrange promotional campaigns in all types of media for products, organizations, or individuals. Coach client representatives in effective communication with the public and with employees. Prepare and deliver speeches to further public relations objectives. Purchase advertising space and time as required to promote client's product or agenda. Plan and conduct market and public opinion research to test products or determine potential for product success, communicating results to client or management. **SKILLS—Persuasion:** Persuading others to change their minds or behavior. **Service Orientation:** Actively looking for ways to help people. **Negotiation:** Bringing others together and trying to reconcile differences. **Social Perceptiveness:** Being aware of others' reactions and understanding why they react as they do. **Coordination:** Adjusting actions in relation to others' actions. **Management of Financial Resources:** Determining how money will be spent to get the work done and accounting for these expenditures. **Monitoring:** Monitoring or assessing your performance or that of other individuals or organizations to make improvements or take corrective action. **Writing:** Communicating effectively in writing as appropriate for the needs of the audience. **Time Management:** Managing one's own time and the time of others.

GOE—Interest Area: 03. Arts and Communication. **Work Group:** 03.03. News, Broadcasting, and Public Relations. **Other Jobs in This Work Group:** Broadcast News Analysts; Caption Writers; Interpreters and Translators; Reporters and Correspondents. **PERSONALITY TYPE:** Enterprising. Enterprising occupations frequently involve starting up and carrying out projects. These occupations can involve leading people and making many decisions. They sometimes require risk taking and often deal with business.

P

EDUCATION/TRAINING PROGRAM(S)—Communication Studies/Speech Communication and Rhetoric; Family and Consumer Sciences/Human Sciences Communication; Health Communication; Political Communication; Public Relations/Image Management. **RELATED KNOWLEDGE/COURSES**—**Sales and Marketing:** Knowledge of principles and methods for showing, promoting, and selling products or services. This includes marketing strategy and tactics, product demonstration, sales techniques, and sales control systems. **Customer and Personal Service:** Knowledge of principles and processes for providing customer and personal services. This includes customer needs assessment, meeting quality standards for services, and evaluation of customer satisfaction. **Communications and Media:** Knowledge of media production, communication, and dissemination techniques and methods. This includes alternative ways to inform and entertain via written, oral, and visual media. **Administration and Management:** Knowledge of business and management principles involved in strategic planning, resource allocation, human resources modeling, leadership technique, production methods, and coordination of people and resources. **Clerical Practices:** Knowledge of administrative and clerical procedures and systems such as word processing, managing files and records, stenography and transcription, designing forms, and other office procedures and terminology. **English Language:** Knowledge of the structure and content of the English language, including the meaning and spelling of words, rules of composition, and grammar.

Purchasing Agents, Except Wholesale, Retail, and Farm Products

◎ Education/Training Required: Bachelor's degree

◎ Annual Earnings: $47,250

◎ Growth: 11.2%

◎ Annual Job Openings: 29,000

◎ Self-Employed: 1.3%

◎ Part-Time: 5.5%

Purchase machinery, equipment, tools, parts, supplies, or services necessary for the operation of an establishment. Purchase raw or semi-finished materials for manufacturing. Purchase the highest quality merchandise at the lowest possible price and in correct amounts. Prepare purchase orders, solicit bid proposals and review requisitions for goods and services. Research and evaluate suppliers based on price, quality, selection, service, support, availability, reliability, production and distribution capabilities, and the supplier's reputation and history. Analyze price proposals, financial reports, and other data and information to determine reasonable prices. Monitor and follow applicable laws and regulations. Negotiate, or renegotiate, and administer contracts with suppliers, vendors, and other representatives. Monitor shipments to ensure that goods come in on time, and in the event of problems trace shipments and follow up undelivered goods. Confer with staff, users, and vendors to discuss defective or unacceptable goods or services and determine corrective action. Evaluate and monitor contract performance to ensure compliance with contractual obligations and to determine need for changes. Maintain and review computerized or manual records of items purchased, costs, delivery, product performance, and inventories. Review catalogs, industry periodicals, directories, trade journals, and Internet sites, and consult with other department personnel to locate necessary goods and services. Study sales records and inventory levels of current stock to develop strategic purchasing programs that facilitate employee access to supplies. Interview vendors and visit suppliers' plants and distribution centers to examine and learn about products, services and prices. Arrange the payment of duty and freight charges. Hire, train and/or supervise purchasing clerks, buyers, and expediters. Write and review product specifications, maintaining a working technical knowledge of the goods or services to be purchased. Monitor changes affecting supply and demand, tracking market conditions, price trends, or futures markets. Formulate policies and procedures for bid proposals and procurement of goods and services. **SKILLS—Time Management:** Managing one's own time and the time of others. **Negotiation:** Bringing others together and trying to reconcile differences. **Management of Personnel Resources:** Motivating, developing, and directing people as they work, identifying the best people for the job. **Persuasion:** Persuading others to change their minds or behavior. **Coordination:** Adjusting actions in relation to others' actions. **Monitoring:** Monitoring or assessing your performance or that of other individuals or organizations to make improvements or take corrective action. **Management of Financial Resources:** Determining how money will be spent to get the work done and accounting for these expenditures. **Speaking:** Talking to others to convey information effectively.

GOE—Interest Area: 14. Retail and Wholesale Sales and Service. **Work Group:** 14.05. Purchasing. **Other Jobs in This Work Group:** Wholesale and Retail Buyers, Except Farm Products. **PERSONALITY TYPE:** Enterprising. Enterprising occupations frequently involve starting up and carrying out projects. These occupations can involve leading people and making many decisions. They sometimes require risk taking and often deal with business.

EDUCATION/TRAINING PROGRAM(S)— Sales, Distribution, and Marketing Operations,

General. **RELATED KNOWLEDGE/COURSES—Clerical Practices:** Knowledge of administrative and clerical procedures and systems such as word processing, managing files and records, stenography and transcription, designing forms, and other office procedures and terminology. **Economics and Accounting:** Knowledge of economic and accounting principles and practices, the financial markets, banking, and the analysis and reporting of financial data. **Production and Processing:** Knowledge of raw materials, production processes, quality control, costs, and other techniques for maximizing the effective manufacture and distribution of goods. **Administration and Management:** Knowledge of business and management principles involved in strategic planning, resource allocation, human resources modeling, leadership technique, production methods, and coordination of people and resources. **Computers and Electronics:** Knowledge of circuit boards, processors, chips, electronic equipment, and computer hardware and software, including applications and programming. **Mathematics:** Knowledge of arithmetic, algebra, geometry, calculus, and statistics and their applications.

Purchasing Managers

- Education/Training Required: Work experience plus degree
- Annual Earnings: $67,830
- Growth: 4.8%
- Annual Job Openings: 9,000
- Self-Employed: 0.2%
- Part-Time: 2.6%

Plan, direct, or coordinate the activities of buyers, purchasing officers, and related workers involved in purchasing materials, products, and services. Maintain records of goods ordered and received. Locate vendors of materials, equipment or supplies, and interview them in order to determine product availability and terms of sales. Prepare and process requisitions and purchase orders for supplies and equipment. Control purchasing department budgets. Interview and hire staff, and oversee staff training. Review purchase order claims and contracts for conformance to company policy. Analyze market and delivery systems in order to assess present and future material availability. Develop and implement purchasing and contract management instructions, policies, and procedures. Participate in the development of specifications for equipment, products or substitute materials. Resolve vendor or contractor grievances, and claims against suppliers. Represent companies in negotiating contracts and formulating policies with suppliers. Review, evaluate, and approve specifications for issuing and awarding bids. Direct and coordinate activities of personnel engaged in buying, selling, and distributing materials, equipment, machinery, and supplies. Prepare bid awards requiring board approval. Prepare reports regarding market conditions and merchandise costs. Administer on-line purchasing systems. **SKILLS—Negotiation:** Bringing others together and trying to reconcile differences. **Management of Financial Resources:** Determining how money will be spent to get the work done and accounting for these expenditures. **Management of Material Resources:** Obtaining and seeing to the appropriate use of equipment, facilities, and materials needed to do certain work. **Operations Analysis:** Analyzing needs and product requirements to create a design. **Persuasion:** Persuading others to change their minds or behavior. **Time Management:** Managing one's own time and the time of others. **Active Learning:** Understanding the implications of new information for both current and future problem-solving and decision-making. **Coordination:** Adjusting actions in relation to others' actions.

GOE—Interest Area: 14. Retail and Wholesale Sales and Service. **Work Group:** 14.01. Managerial Work in Retail/Wholesale Sales and Service. **Other Jobs in This Work Group:** Advertising and Promotions Managers; First-Line Supervisors/Managers of Non-Retail Sales Workers; First-Line Supervisors/Managers of Retail Sales Workers; Funeral Directors; Marketing Managers; Property, Real Estate, and Community Association Managers; Sales Managers. **PERSONALITY TYPE:** Enterprising. Enterprising occupations frequently involve starting up and carrying out projects. These occupations can involve leading people and making many decisions. They sometimes require risk taking and often deal with business.

EDUCATION/TRAINING PROGRAM(S)— Purchasing, Procurement/Acquisitions and Contracts Management. **RELATED KNOWLEDGE/ COURSES—Personnel and Human Resources:** Knowledge of principles and procedures for personnel recruitment, selection, training, compensation and benefits, labor relations and negotiation, and personnel information systems. **Economics and Accounting:** Knowledge of economic and accounting principles and practices, the financial markets, banking, and the analysis and reporting of financial data. **Administration and Management:** Knowledge of business and management principles involved in strategic planning, resource allocation, human resources modeling, leadership technique, production methods, and coordination of people and resources. **Production and Processing:** Knowledge of raw materials, production processes, quality control, costs, and other techniques for maximizing the effective manufacture and distribution of goods. **Education and Training:** Knowledge of principles and methods for curriculum and training design, teaching and instruction for individuals and groups, and the measurement of training effects. **Computers and Electronics:** Knowledge of circuit boards, processors, chips, electronic equipment, and computer hardware and software, including applications and programming.

Radiation Therapists

- Education/Training Required: Associate's degree
- Annual Earnings: $55,550
- Growth: 31.6%
- Annual Job Openings: 1,000
- Self-Employed: 0%
- Part-Time: 14.2%

Provide radiation therapy to patients as prescribed by a radiologist according to established practices and standards. Duties may include reviewing prescription and diagnosis; acting as liaison with physician and supportive care personnel; preparing equipment, such as immobilization, treatment, and protection devices; and maintaining records, reports, and files. May assist in dosimetry procedures and tumor localization. Administer prescribed doses of radiation to specific body parts, using radiation therapy equipment according to established practices and standards. Position patients for treatment with accuracy according to prescription. Enter data into computer and set controls to operate and adjust equipment and regulate dosage. Follow principles of radiation protection for patient, self, and others. Maintain records, reports and files as required, including such information as radiation dosages, equipment settings and patients' reactions. Review prescription, diagnosis, patient chart, and identification. Conduct most treatment sessions independently, in accordance with the long-term treatment plan and under the general direction of the patient's physician. Check radiation therapy equipment to ensure proper operation. Observe and reassure patients during treatment and report unusual reactions to physician or turn equipment off if unexpected adverse reactions occur. Check for side effects such as skin irritation, nausea and hair loss to assess patients' reaction to treatment. Educate, prepare and reassure patients and their families by answering questions, providing physical assistance, and reinforcing physicians' advice regarding treatment reactions and post-treatment care. Calculate actual treatment dosages delivered during each session. Prepare and construct equipment, such as immobilization, treatment, and protection devices. Photograph treated area of patient and process film. Help physicians, radiation oncologists and clinical physicists to prepare physical and technical aspects of radiation treatment plans, using information about patient condition and anatomy. Train and supervise student or subordinate radiotherapy technologists. Act as liaison with physicist and supportive care personnel. Provide assistance to other health-care personnel during dosimetry procedures and tumor localization. Implement appropriate follow-up care plans. Store, sterilize, or prepare the special applicators containing the radioactive substance implanted by the physician. Assist in the preparation of sealed radioactive materials, such as cobalt, radium, cesium and isotopes, for use in radiation treatments. **SKILLS—Operation Monitoring:** Watching gauges, dials, or other indicators to make sure a machine is working properly. **Technology Design:** Generating or adapting equipment and technology to serve user needs. **Operation and Control:** Controlling operations of equipment or systems. **Time Management:** Managing one's own time and the time of others. **Instructing:** Teaching others how to do something. **Service Orientation:** Actively looking for ways to help people. **Management of Personnel Resources:** Motivating, developing, and directing people as they work, identifying the best people for the job. **Social Perceptiveness:** Being aware of others' reactions and understanding why they react as they do.

GOE—Interest Area: 08. Health Science. **Work Group:** 08.07. Medical Therapy. **Other Jobs in This Work Group:** Audiologists; Massage Therapists; Occupational Therapist Aides; Occupational Therapist Assistants; Occupational Therapists; Physical Therapist Aides; Physical Therapist Assistants; Physical Therapists; Recreational Therapists; Respiratory Therapists; Respiratory Therapy Technicians; Speech-Language Pathologists. **PERSONALITY TYPE:** Social. Social occupations frequently involve working with, communicating with, and teaching people. These occupations often involve helping or providing service to others.

EDUCATION/TRAINING PROGRAM(S)—Medical Radiologic Technology/Science—Radiation Therapist. **RELATED KNOWLEDGE/COURSES**—**Medicine and Dentistry:** Knowledge of the information and techniques needed to diagnose and treat human injuries, diseases, and deformities. This includes symptoms, treatment alternatives, drug properties and interactions, and preventive health-care measures. **Customer and Personal Service:** Knowledge of principles and processes for providing customer and personal services. This includes customer needs assessment, meeting quality standards for services, and evaluation of customer satisfaction. **Psychology:** Knowledge of human behavior and performance; individual differences in ability, personality, and interests; learning and motivation; psychological research methods; and the assessment and treatment of behavioral and affective disorders. **Biology:** Knowledge of plant and animal organisms and their tissues, cells, functions, interdependencies, and interactions with each other and the environment. **Physics:** Knowledge and prediction of physical principles and laws and their interrelationships and applications to understanding fluid, material, and atmospheric dynamics and mechanical, electrical, atomic, and subatomic structures and processes. **Mathematics:** Knowledge of arithmetic, algebra, geometry, calculus, and statistics and their applications.

Radiologic Technicians

- ◎ Education/Training Required: Associate's degree
- ◎ Annual Earnings: $41,850
- ◎ Growth: 22.9%
- ◎ Annual Job Openings: 21,000
- ◎ Self-Employed: 0.2%
- ◎ Part-Time: 17.5%

Maintain and use equipment and supplies necessary to demonstrate portions the human body on X-ray film or fluoroscopic screen for diagnostic purposes. Use beam-restrictive devices and patient-shielding techniques to minimize radiation exposure to patient and staff. Position X-ray equipment and adjust controls to set exposure factors, such as time and distance. Position patient on examining table and set up and adjust equipment to obtain optimum view of specific body area as requested by physician. Determine patients' X-ray needs by reading requests or instructions from physicians. Make exposures necessary for the requested procedures, rejecting and repeating work that does not meet established standards. Process exposed radiographs using film processors or computer generated methods. Explain procedures to patients to reduce anxieties and obtain cooperation. Perform procedures such as linear tomography, mammography, sonograms, joint and cyst aspirations, routine contrast studies, routine fluoroscopy and examinations of the head, trunk, and extremities under supervision of physician. Prepare and set up X-ray room for patient. Assure that sterile supplies, contrast materials, catheters, and other required equipment are present and in working order, requisitioning materials as necessary. Maintain records of patients examined, examinations performed, views taken, and technical factors used. Provide assistance to physicians or other technologists in the performance of more complex procedures. Monitor equipment operation and report malfunctioning equipment to supervisor. Provide students and other technologists with suggestions of additional views, alternate positioning or improved techniques to ensure the images produced are of the highest quality. Coordinate work of other technicians or technologists when procedures require more than one person. Assist with on-the-job training of new employees and students, and provide input to supervisors regarding training performance. Maintain a current file of examination protocols. Operate mobile X-ray equipment in operating room, emergency room, or at patient's bedside. Provide assistance in radiopharmaceutical administration, monitoring patients' vital signs and notifying the radiologist of any relevant changes. **SKILLS—Service Orientation:** Actively looking for ways to help people. **Science:** Using scientific rules and methods to solve problems. **Instructing:** Teaching others how to do something. **Negotiation:** Bringing others together and trying to reconcile differences. **Social Perceptiveness:** Being aware of others' reactions and understanding why they react as they do. **Active Listening:** Giving full attention to what other people are saying, taking time to understand the points being made, asking questions as appropriate, and not interrupting at inappropriate times. **Equipment Selection:** Determining the kind of tools and equipment needed to do a job. **Speaking:** Talking to others to convey information effectively. **Learning Strategies:** Selecting and using training/instructional methods and procedures appropriate for the situation when learning or teaching new things. **Coordination:** Adjusting actions in relation to others' actions.

GOE—Interest Area: 08. Health Science. **Work Group:** 08.06. Medical Technology. **Other Jobs in This Work Group:** Biological Technicians; Cardiovascular Technologists and Technicians; Diagnostic Medical Sonographers; Medical and Clinical Laboratory Technicians; Medical and Clinical Laboratory Technologists; Medical Equipment Preparers; Medical Records and Health Information Technicians; Nuclear Medicine Technologists; Opticians, Dispensing; Orthotists and Prosthetists; Radiologic Technologists. **PERSONALITY TYPE:** Realistic. Realistic occupations frequently involve work activities that include practical, hands-on problems and solutions. They often deal with plants, animals, and real-world materials like wood, tools, and machinery. Many of the occupations require working outside and do not involve a lot of paperwork or working closely with others.

EDUCATION/TRAINING PROGRAM(S)— Allied Health Diagnostic, Intervention, and Treatment Professions, Other; Medical Radiologic Technology/Science—Radiation Therapist; Radiologic Technology/Science—Radiographer. **RELAT-**

ED KNOWLEDGE/COURSES—**Clerical Practices:** Knowledge of administrative and clerical procedures and systems such as word processing, managing files and records, stenography and transcription, designing forms, and other office procedures and terminology. **Psychology:** Knowledge of human behavior and performance; individual differences in ability, personality, and interests; learning and motivation; psychological research methods; and the assessment and treatment of behavioral and affective disorders. **Medicine and Dentistry:** Knowledge of the information and techniques needed to diagnose and treat human injuries, diseases, and deformities. This includes symptoms, treatment alternatives, drug properties and interactions, and preventive health-care measures. **Customer and Personal Service:** Knowledge of principles and processes for providing customer and personal services. This includes customer needs assessment, meeting quality standards for services, and evaluation of customer satisfaction. **Physics:** Knowledge and prediction of physical principles and laws and their interrelationships and applications to understanding fluid, material, and atmospheric dynamics and mechanical, electrical, atomic, and subatomic structures and processes. **English Language:** Knowledge of the structure and content of the English language, including the meaning and spelling of words, rules of composition, and grammar.

Radiologic Technologists

- Education/Training Required: Associate's degree
- Annual Earnings: $41,850
- Growth: 22.9%
- Annual Job Openings: 21,000
- Self-Employed: 0.2%
- Part-Time: 17.5%

Take X rays and CAT scans or administer nonradioactive materials into patient's blood stream for diagnostic purposes. Includes technologists who specialize in other modalities, such as computed tomography, ultrasound, and magnetic resonance. Review and evaluate developed X rays, video tape, or computer generated information to determine if images are satisfactory for diagnostic purposes. Use radiation safety measures and protection devices to comply with government regulations and to ensure safety of patients and staff. Explain procedures and observe patients to ensure safety and comfort during scan. Operate or oversee operation of radiologic and magnetic imaging equipment to produce images of the body for diagnostic purposes. Position and immobilize patient on examining table. Position imaging equipment and adjust controls to set exposure time and distance, according to specification of examination. Key commands and data into computer to document and specify scan sequences, adjust transmitters and receivers, or photograph certain images. Monitor video display of area being scanned and adjust density or contrast to improve picture quality. Monitor patients' conditions and reactions, reporting abnormal signs to physician. Set up examination rooms, ensuring that all necessary equipment is ready. Prepare and administer oral or injected contrast media to patients. Take thorough and accurate patient medical histories. Remove and process film. Record, process and maintain patient data and treatment records, and prepare reports. Coordinate work with clerical personnel and other technologists. Demonstrate new equipment, procedures, and techniques to staff, and provide technical assistance. Provide assistance with such tasks as dressing and changing to seriously ill, injured, or disabled patients. Move ultrasound scanner over patient's body and watch pattern produced on video screen. Measure thickness of section to be radiographed, using instruments similar to measuring tapes. Operate fluoroscope to aid physician to view and guide wire or catheter through blood vessels to area of interest. Assign duties to radiologic staff to maintain patient flows and achieve production

goals. Collaborate with other medical team members, such as physicians and nurses, to conduct angiography or special vascular procedures. Perform administrative duties such as developing departmental operating budget, coordinating purchases of supplies and equipment and preparing work schedules. **SKILLS—Instructing:** Teaching others how to do something. **Social Perceptiveness:** Being aware of others' reactions and understanding why they react as they do. **Service Orientation:** Actively looking for ways to help people. **Reading Comprehension:** Understanding written sentences and paragraphs in work-related documents. **Active Listening:** Giving full attention to what other people are saying, taking time to understand the points being made, asking questions as appropriate, and not interrupting at inappropriate times. **Operation Monitoring:** Watching gauges, dials, or other indicators to make sure a machine is working properly. **Speaking:** Talking to others to convey information effectively. **Critical Thinking:** Using logic and reasoning to identify the strengths and weaknesses of alternative solutions, conclusions, or approaches to problems. **Coordination:** Adjusting actions in relation to others' actions.

GOE—Interest Area: 08. Health Science. **Work Group:** 08.06. Medical Technology. **Other Jobs in This Work Group:** Biological Technicians; Cardiovascular Technologists and Technicians; Diagnostic Medical Sonographers; Medical and Clinical Laboratory Technicians; Medical and Clinical Laboratory Technologists; Medical Equipment Preparers; Medical Records and Health Information Technicians; Nuclear Medicine Technologists; Opticians, Dispensing; Orthotists and Prosthetists; Radiologic Technicians. **PERSONALITY TYPE:** Realistic. Realistic occupations frequently involve work activities that include practical, hands-on problems and solutions. They often deal with plants, animals, and real-world materials like wood, tools, and machinery. Many of the occupations require working outside and do not involve a lot of paperwork or working closely with others.

EDUCATION/TRAINING PROGRAM(S)—Allied Health Diagnostic, Intervention, and Treatment Professions, Other; Medical Radiologic Technology/Science—Radiation Therapist; Radiologic Technology/Science—Radiographer. **RELATED KNOWLEDGE/COURSES—Medicine and Dentistry:** Knowledge of the information and techniques needed to diagnose and treat human injuries, diseases, and deformities. This includes symptoms, treatment alternatives, drug properties and interactions, and preventive health-care measures. **Customer and Personal Service:** Knowledge of principles and processes for providing customer and personal services. This includes customer needs assessment, meeting quality standards for services, and evaluation of customer satisfaction. **Psychology:** Knowledge of human behavior and performance; individual differences in ability, personality, and interests; learning and motivation; psychological research methods; and the assessment and treatment of behavioral and affective disorders. **Physics:** Knowledge and prediction of physical principles and laws and their interrelationships and applications to understanding fluid, material, and atmospheric dynamics and mechanical, electrical, atomic, and subatomic structures and processes. **Biology:** Knowledge of plant and animal organisms and their tissues, cells, functions, interdependencies, and interactions with each other and the environment. **Chemistry:** Knowledge of the chemical composition, structure, and properties of substances and of the chemical processes and transformations that they undergo. This includes uses of chemicals and their danger signs, production techniques, and disposal methods.

Recreation and Fitness Studies Teachers, Postsecondary

R

- Education/Training Required: Master's degree
- Annual Earnings: $44,180
- Growth: 38.1% for all Postsecondary Teachers
- Annual Job Openings: 216,000 for all Postsecondary Teachers
- Self-Employed: 0.3% for all Postsecondary Teachers
- Part-Time: 27.7% for all Postsecondary Teachers

Teach courses pertaining to recreation, leisure, and fitness studies, including exercise physiology and facilities management. Evaluate and grade students' class work, assignments, and papers. Prepare and deliver lectures to undergraduate and/or graduate students on topics such as anatomy, therapeutic recreation, and conditioning theory. Advise students on academic and vocational curricula, and on career issues. Compile, administer, and grade examinations, or assign this work to others. Compile bibliographies of specialized materials for outside reading assignments. Initiate, facilitate, and moderate classroom discussions. Keep abreast of developments in their field by reading current literature, talking with colleagues, and participating in professional conferences. Maintain regularly scheduled office hours in order to advise and assist students. Maintain student attendance records, grades, and other required records. Plan, evaluate, and revise curricula, course content, and course materials and methods of instruction. Prepare course materials such as syllabi, homework assignments, and handouts. Select and obtain materials and supplies such as textbooks. Supervise undergraduate and/or graduate teaching, internship, and research work. Act as advisers to student organizations. Collaborate with colleagues to address teaching and research issues. Conduct research in a particular field of knowledge, and publish findings in professional journals, books, and/or electronic media. Participate in campus and community events. Participate in student recruitment, registration, and placement activities. Perform administrative duties such as serving as department heads. Prepare students to act as sports coaches. Provide professional consulting services to government and/or industry. Serve on academic or administrative committees that deal with institutional policies, departmental matters, and academic issues. Write grant proposals to procure external research funding. **SKILLS**—No data available.

GOE—**Interest Area:** 05. Education and Training. **Work Group:** 05.03. Postsecondary and Adult Teaching and Instructing. **Other Jobs in This Work Group:** Adult Literacy, Remedial Education, and GED Teachers and Instructors; Agricultural Sciences Teachers, Postsecondary; Anthropology and Archeology Teachers, Postsecondary; Architecture Teachers, Postsecondary; Area, Ethnic, and Cultural Studies Teachers, Postsecondary; Art, Drama, and Music Teachers, Postsecondary; Atmospheric, Earth, Marine, and Space Sciences Teachers, Postsecondary; Biological Science Teachers, Postsecondary; Business Teachers, Postsecondary; Chemistry Teachers, Postsecondary; Communications Teachers, Postsecondary; Computer Science Teachers, Postsecondary; Criminal Justice and Law Enforcement Teachers, Postsecondary; Economics Teachers, Postsecondary; Education Teachers, Postsecondary; Engineering Teachers, Postsecondary; English Language and Literature Teachers, Postsecondary; Environmental Science Teachers, Postsecondary; Farm and Home Management Advisors; Foreign Language and Literature Teachers, Postsecondary; Forestry and Conservation Science Teachers, Postsecondary; Geography Teachers, Postsecondary; Graduate Teaching Assistants; Health Specialties Teachers, Postsecondary; History Teachers, Postsecondary; Home Economics Teachers, Postsecondary; Law Teachers, Postsecondary;

Library Science Teachers, Postsecondary; Mathematical Science Teachers, Postsecondary; Nursing Instructors and Teachers, Postsecondary; Philosophy and Religion Teachers, Postsecondary; Physics Teachers, Postsecondary; Political Science Teachers, Postsecondary; Psychology Teachers, Postsecondary; Self-Enrichment Education Teachers; Social Work Teachers, Postsecondary; Sociology Teachers, Postsecondary; Vocational Education Teachers, Postsecondary. **PERSONALITY TYPE:** No data available.

EDUCATION/TRAINING PROGRAM(S)—Health and Physical Education, General; Parks, Recreation and Leisure Studies; Sport and Fitness Administration/Management. **RELATED KNOWLEDGE/COURSES**—No data available.

Recreation Workers

- ◎ Education/Training Required: Bachelor's degree
- ◎ Annual Earnings: $18,950
- ◎ Growth: 20.5%
- ◎ Annual Job Openings: 56,000
- ◎ Self-Employed: 5.7%
- ◎ Part-Time: 35.6%

Conduct recreation activities with groups in public, private, or volunteer agencies or recreation facilities. Organize and promote activities, such as arts and crafts, sports, games, music, dramatics, social recreation, camping, and hobbies, taking into account the needs and interests of individual members. Enforce rules and regulations of recreational facilities in order to maintain discipline and ensure safety. Organize, lead, and promote interest in recreational activities such as arts, crafts, sports, games, camping, and hobbies. Manage the daily operations of recreational facilities. Administer first aid according to prescribed procedures, and notify emergency medical personnel when necessary. Ascertain and interpret group interests, evaluate equipment and facilities, and adapt activities to meet participant needs. Greet new arrivals to activities, introducing them to other participants, explaining facility rules, and encouraging their participation. Explain principles, techniques, and safety procedures to participants in recreational activities, and demonstrate use of materials and equipment. Evaluate recreation areas, facilities, and services in order to determine if they are producing desired results. Complete and maintain time and attendance forms and inventory lists. Confer with management in order to discuss and resolve participant complaints. Supervise and coordinate the work activities of personnel, such as training staff members and assigning work duties. Meet and collaborate with agency personnel, community organizations, and other professional personnel to plan balanced recreational programs for participants. Schedule maintenance and use of facilities. Direct special activities or events such as aquatics, gymnastics, or performing arts. Meet with staff to discuss rules, regulations, and work-related problems. Provide for entertainment and set up related decorations and equipment. Encourage participants to develop their own activities and leadership skills through group discussions. Serve as liaison between park or recreation administrators and activity instructors. Evaluate staff performance, recording evaluations on appropriate forms. Oversee the purchase, planning, design, construction, and upkeep of recreation facilities and areas. **SKILLS—Management of Personnel Resources:** Motivating, developing, and directing people as they work, identifying the best people for the job. **Service Orientation:** Actively looking for ways to help people. **Management of Financial Resources:** Determining how money will be spent to get the work done and accounting for these expenditures. **Social Perceptiveness:** Being aware of others' reactions and understanding why they react as they do. **Time Management:** Managing one's own time and the time of others. **Management of Material Resources:** Obtaining and seeing to the appropriate use of equipment, facilities, and materials needed to do certain work. **Instructing:** Teaching others how to

do something. **Coordination:** Adjusting actions in relation to others' actions.

GOE—Interest Area: 09. Hospitality, Tourism, and Recreation. **Work Group:** 09.02. Recreational Services. **Other Jobs in This Work Group:** Amusement and Recreation Attendants; Gaming and Sports Book Writers and Runners; Gaming Dealers; Locker Room, Coatroom, and Dressing Room Attendants; Motion Picture Projectionists; Slot Key Persons; Ushers, Lobby Attendants, and Ticket Takers. **PERSONALITY TYPE:** Social. Social occupations frequently involve working with, communicating with, and teaching people. These occupations often involve helping or providing service to others.

EDUCATION/TRAINING PROGRAM(S)— Health and Physical Education/Fitness, Other; Parks, Recreation and Leisure Facilities Management; Parks, Recreation and Leisure Studies; Parks, Recreation, Leisure and Fitness Studies, Other; Sport and Fitness Administration/Management. **RELATED KNOWLEDGE/COURSES—Customer and Personal Service:** Knowledge of principles and processes for providing customer and personal services. This includes customer needs assessment, meeting quality standards for services, and evaluation of customer satisfaction. **Psychology:** Knowledge of human behavior and performance; individual differences in ability, personality, and interests; learning and motivation; psychological research methods; and the assessment and treatment of behavioral and affective disorders. **Education and Training:** Knowledge of principles and methods for curriculum and training design, teaching and instruction for individuals and groups, and the measurement of training effects. **Clerical Practices:** Knowledge of administrative and clerical procedures and systems such as word processing, managing files and records, stenography and transcription, designing forms, and other office procedures and terminology. **Sales and Marketing:** Knowledge of principles and methods for showing, promoting, and selling products or services. This includes marketing strategy and tactics, product demonstration, sales techniques, and sales control systems. **Sociology and Anthropology:** Knowledge of group behavior and dynamics, societal trends and influences, human migrations, ethnicity, and cultures and their history and origins.

Registered Nurses

- ◎ Education/Training Required: Associate's degree
- ◎ Annual Earnings: $51,020
- ◎ Growth: 27.3%
- ◎ Annual Job Openings: 215,000
- ◎ Self-Employed: 1.2%
- ◎ Part-Time: 22.0%

Assess patient health problems and needs, develop and implement nursing care plans, and maintain medical records. Administer nursing care to ill, injured, convalescent, or disabled patients. May advise patients on health maintenance and disease prevention or provide case management. Licensing or registration required. Includes advance practice nurses such as: nurse practitioners, clinical nurse specialists, certified nurse midwives, and certified registered nurse anesthetists. Advanced practice nursing is practiced by RNs who have specialized formal, post-basic education and who function in highly autonomous and specialized roles. Maintain accurate, detailed reports and records. Monitor, record and report symptoms and changes in patients' conditions. Record patients' medical information and vital signs. Modify patient treatment plans as indicated by patients' responses and conditions. Consult and coordinate with health-care team members to assess, plan, implement and evaluate patient care plans. Order, interpret, and evaluate diagnostic tests to identify and assess patient's condition. Monitor all aspects of patient care, including diet and physical activity. Direct and supervise less skilled nursing/health-care personnel, or supervise a particular unit on one shift. Prepare patients for, and assist with, examinations and treatments. Observe nurses and visit patients to ensure that proper nursing care is provided. Assess the needs of individuals, families and/or communities, including assessment of individuals' home and/or work environments to identify potential health or safety problems. Instruct individuals, families and other groups on topics such as health education, disease prevention and childbirth, and develop health improvement programs. Prepare rooms, sterile instruments, equipment and supplies, and ensure that stock of supplies is maintained. Inform physician of patient's condition during anesthesia. Deliver infants and provide prenatal and postpartum care and treatment under obstetrician's supervision. Administer local, inhalation, intravenous, and other anesthetics. Provide health care, first aid, immunizations and assistance in convalescence and rehabilitation in locations such as schools, hospitals, and industry. Perform physical examinations, make tentative diagnoses, and treat patients en route to hospitals or at disaster site triage centers. Conduct specified laboratory tests. Hand items to surgeons during operations. Prescribe or recommend drugs, medical devices or other forms of treatment, such as physical therapy, inhalation therapy, or related therapeutic procedures. Direct and coordinate infection control programs, advising and consulting with specified personnel about necessary precautions. **SKILLS—Social Perceptiveness:** Being aware of others' reactions and understanding why they react as they do. **Service Orientation:** Actively looking for ways to help people. **Instructing:** Teaching others how to do something. **Time Management:** Managing one's own time and the time of others. **Critical Thinking:** Using logic and reasoning to identify the strengths and weaknesses of alternative solutions, conclusions, or approaches to problems. **Learning Strategies:** Selecting and using training/instructional methods and procedures appropriate for the situation when learning or teaching new things. **Coordination:** Adjusting actions in relation to others' actions. **Active Learning:** Understanding the implications of new information for both current and future problem-solving and decision-making. **Monitoring:** Monitoring or assessing your performance or that of other individuals or organizations to make improvements or take corrective action.

GOE—Interest Area: 08. Health Science. **Work Group:** 08.02. Medicine and Surgery. **Other Jobs in This Work Group:** Anesthesiologists; Family and General Practitioners; Internists, General; Medical Assistants; Medical Transcriptionists; Obstetricians and Gynecologists; Pediatricians, General; Pharmacists; Pharmacy Aides; Pharmacy Technicians; Physician Assistants; Psychiatrists; Surgeons; Surgical Technologists. **PERSONALITY TYPE:** Social. Social occupations frequently involve working with, communicating with, and teaching people. These occupations often involve helping or providing service to others.

EDUCATION/TRAINING PROGRAM(S)— Adult Health Nurse/Nursing; Clinical Nurse Specialist; Critical Care Nursing; Family Practice Nurse/Nurse Practitioner; Maternal/Child Health and Neonatal Nurse/Nursing; Nurse Anesthetist; Nurse Midwife/Nursing Midwifery; Nursing— Registered Nurse Training (RN, ASN, BSN, MSN); Nursing Science (MS, PhD); Nursing, Other; Occupational and Environmental Health Nursing; Pediatric Nurse/Nursing; Perioperative/Operating Room and Surgical Nurse/Nursing; Psychiatric/Mental Health Nurse/Nursing; Public Health/Community Nurse/Nursing. **RELATED KNOWLEDGE/COURSES—Psychology:** Knowledge of human behavior and performance; individual differences in ability, personality, and interests; learning and motivation; psychological research methods; and the assessment and treatment of behavioral and affective disorders. **Medicine and Dentistry:** Knowledge of the information and techniques needed to diagnose and treat human injuries, diseases, and deformities. This includes symptoms, treatment alternatives, drug properties and interactions, and preventive health-care measures. **Customer and Personal Service:** Knowledge of principles and processes for providing customer and personal services. This includes customer needs

assessment, meeting quality standards for services, and evaluation of customer satisfaction. **Therapy and Counseling:** Knowledge of principles, methods, and procedures for diagnosis, treatment, and rehabilitation of physical and mental dysfunctions and for career counseling and guidance. **Sociology and Anthropology:** Knowledge of group behavior and dynamics, societal trends and influences, human migrations, ethnicity, and cultures and their history and origins. **Philosophy and Theology:** Knowledge of different philosophical systems and religions. This includes their basic principles, values, ethics, ways of thinking, customs, and practices and their impact on human culture.

Rehabilitation Counselors

- Education/Training Required: Bachelor's degree
- Annual Earnings: $27,410
- Growth: 33.8%
- Annual Job Openings: 19,000
- Self-Employed: 4.4%
- Part-Time: 14.6%

Counsel individuals to maximize the independence and employability of persons coping with personal, social, and vocational difficulties that result from birth defects, illness, disease, accidents, or the stress of daily life. Coordinate activities for residents of care and treatment facilities. Assess client needs and design and implement rehabilitation programs that may include personal and vocational counseling, training, and job placement. Analyze information from interviews, educational and medical records, consultation with other professionals, and diagnostic evaluations, in order to assess clients' abilities, needs, and eligibility for services. Arrange for physical, mental, academic, vocational, and other evaluations to obtain information for assessing clients' needs and developing rehabilitation plans. Collaborate with clients' families to implement rehabilitation plans that include behavioral, residential, social, and/or employment goals. Confer with clients to discuss their options and goals so that rehabilitation programs and plans for accessing needed services can be developed. Confer with physicians, psychologists, occupational therapists, and other professionals, in order to develop and implement client rehabilitation programs. Develop and maintain relationships with community referral sources such as schools and community groups. Develop rehabilitation plans that fit clients' aptitudes, education levels, physical abilities, and career goals. Direct case service allocations, authorizing expenditures and payments. Maintain close contact with clients during job training and placements, in order to resolve problems and evaluate placement adequacy. Monitor and record clients' progress in order to ensure that goals and objectives are met. Prepare and maintain records and case files, including documentation such as clients' personal and eligibility information, services provided, narratives of client contacts, and relevant correspondence. Arrange for on-site job coaching or assistive devices such as specially equipped wheelchairs in order to help clients adapt to work or school environments. Collaborate with community agencies to establish facilities and programs to assist persons with disabilities. Develop diagnostic procedures for determining clients' needs. Locate barriers to client employment, such as inaccessible work sites, inflexible schedules, and transportation problems, and work with clients to develop strategies for overcoming these barriers. Participate in job development and placement programs, contacting prospective employers, placing clients in jobs, and evaluating the success of placements. **SKILLS**—No data available.

GOE—Interest Area: 10. Human Service. **Work Group:** 10.01. Counseling and Social Work. **Other Jobs in This Work Group:** Child, Family, and School Social Workers; Clinical Psychologists;

Counseling Psychologists; Marriage and Family Therapists; Medical and Public Health Social Workers; Mental Health and Substance Abuse Social Workers; Mental Health Counselors; Probation Officers and Correctional Treatment Specialists; Residential Advisors; Social and Human Service Assistants; Substance Abuse and Behavioral Disorder Counselors. **PERSONALITY TYPE:** No data available.

EDUCATION/TRAINING PROGRAM(S)—Assistive/Augmentative Technology and Rehabilitation Engineering; Vocational Rehabilitation Counseling/Counselor. **RELATED KNOWLEDGE/COURSES**—No data available.

Respiratory Therapists

- ◎ Education/Training Required: Associate's degree
- ◎ Annual Earnings: $42,050
- ◎ Growth: 34.8%
- ◎ Annual Job Openings: 10,000
- ◎ Self-Employed: 0%
- ◎ Part-Time: 15.5%

Assess, treat, and care for patients with breathing disorders. Assume primary responsibility for all respiratory care modalities, including the supervision of respiratory therapy technicians. Initiate and conduct therapeutic procedures; maintain patient records; and select, assemble, check, and operate equipment. Set up and operate devices such as mechanical ventilators, therapeutic gas administration apparatus, environmental control systems, and aerosol generators, following specified parameters of treatment. Provide emergency care, including artificial respiration, external cardiac massage and assistance with cardiopulmonary resuscitation. Determine requirements for treatment, such as type, method and duration of therapy, precautions to be taken, and medication and dosages, compatible with physicians' orders. Monitor patient's physiological responses to therapy, such as vital signs, arterial blood gases, and blood chemistry changes, and consult with physician if adverse reactions occur. Read prescription, measure arterial blood gases, and review patient information to assess patient condition. Work as part of a team of physicians, nurses and other health-care professionals to manage patient care. Enforce safety rules and ensure careful adherence to physicians' orders. Maintain charts that contain patients' pertinent identification and therapy information. Inspect, clean, test and maintain respiratory therapy equipment to ensure equipment is functioning safely and efficiently, ordering repairs when necessary. Educate patients and their families about their conditions and teach appropriate disease management techniques, such as breathing exercises and the use of medications and respiratory equipment. Explain treatment procedures to patients to gain cooperation and allay fears. Relay blood analysis results to a physician. Perform pulmonary function and adjust equipment to obtain optimum results in therapy. Perform bronchopulmonary drainage and assist or instruct patients in performance of breathing exercises. Demonstrate respiratory care procedures to trainees and other health-care personnel. Teach, train, supervise, and utilize the assistance of students, respiratory therapy technicians, and assistants. Use a variety of testing techniques to assist doctors in cardiac and pulmonary research and to diagnose disorders. Make emergency visits to resolve equipment problems. Conduct tests, such as electrocardiograms, stress testing, and lung capacity tests, to evaluate patients' cardiopulmonary functions. **SKILLS— Instructing:** Teaching others how to do something. **Science:** Using scientific rules and methods to solve problems. **Active Learning:** Understanding the implications of new information for both current and future problem-solving and decision-making. **Service Orientation:** Actively looking for ways to help people. **Time Management:** Managing one's own time and the time of others. **Reading Comprehension:** Understanding written sentences and paragraphs in work-related documents. **Trou-**

bleshooting: Determining causes of operating errors and deciding what to do about them. **Mathematics:** Using mathematics to solve problems.

GOE—Interest Area: 08. Health Science. **Work Group:** 08.07. Medical Therapy. **Other Jobs in This Work Group:** Audiologists; Massage Therapists; Occupational Therapist Aides; Occupational Therapist Assistants; Occupational Therapists; Physical Therapist Aides; Physical Therapist Assistants; Physical Therapists; Radiation Therapists; Recreational Therapists; Respiratory Therapy Technicians; Speech-Language Pathologists. **PERSONALITY TYPE:** Investigative. Investigative occupations frequently involve working with ideas and require an extensive amount of thinking. These occupations can involve searching for facts and figuring out problems mentally.

EDUCATION/TRAINING PROGRAM(S)— Respiratory Care Therapy/Therapist. **RELATED KNOWLEDGE/COURSES—Customer and Personal Service:** Knowledge of principles and processes for providing customer and personal services. This includes customer needs assessment, meeting quality standards for services, and evaluation of customer satisfaction. **Medicine and Dentistry:** Knowledge of the information and techniques needed to diagnose and treat human injuries, diseases, and deformities. This includes symptoms, treatment alternatives, drug properties and interactions, and preventive health-care measures. **Psychology:** Knowledge of human behavior and performance; individual differences in ability, personality, and interests; learning and motivation; psychological research methods; and the assessment and treatment of behavioral and affective disorders. **Biology:** Knowledge of plant and animal organisms and their tissues, cells, functions, interdependencies, and interactions with each other and the environment. **Education and Training:** Knowledge of principles and methods for curriculum and training design, teaching and instruction for individuals and groups, and the measurement of training effects. **Chemistry:** Knowledge of the chemical composition, structure, and properties of substances and of the chemical processes and transformations that they undergo. This includes uses of chemicals and their danger signs, production techniques, and disposal methods.

Sales Agents, Financial Services

◎ Education/Training Required: Bachelor's degree

◎ Annual Earnings: $62,680

◎ Growth: 13.0%

◎ Annual Job Openings: 39,000

◎ Self-Employed: 12.8%

◎ Part-Time: 6.0%

Sell financial services, such as loan, tax, and securities counseling to customers of financial institutions and business establishments. Contact prospective customers in order to present information and explain available services. Determine customers' financial services needs, and prepare proposals to sell services that address these needs. Develop prospects from current commercial customers, referral leads, and sales and trade meetings. Prepare forms or agreements to complete sales. Sell services and equipment, such as trusts, investments, and check processing services. Evaluate costs and revenue of agreements in order to determine continued profitability. Make presentations on financial services to groups in order to attract new clients. Review business trends in order to advise customers regarding expected fluctuations. **SKILLS—Persuasion:** Persuading others to change their minds or behavior. **Systems Analysis:** Determining how a system should work and how changes in conditions, operations, and the environment will affect outcomes. **Management of Financial Resources:** Determining how money will be spent to get the work done and accounting for these expenditures.

Service Orientation: Actively looking for ways to help people. **Negotiation:** Bringing others together and trying to reconcile differences. **Systems Evaluation:** Identifying measures or indicators of system performance and the actions needed to improve or correct performance relative to the goals of the system. **Active Learning:** Understanding the implications of new information for both current and future problem-solving and decision-making. **Monitoring:** Monitoring or assessing your performance or that of other individuals or organizations to make improvements or take corrective action.

GOE—Interest Area: 06. Finance and Insurance. **Work Group:** 06.05. Finance/Insurance Sales and Support. **Other Jobs in This Work Group:** Advertising Sales Agents; Insurance Sales Agents; Personal Financial Advisors; Sales Agents, Securities and Commodities. **PERSONALITY TYPE:** Enterprising. Enterprising occupations frequently involve starting up and carrying out projects. These occupations can involve leading people and making many decisions. They sometimes require risk taking and often deal with business.

EDUCATION/TRAINING PROGRAM(S)— Business and Personal/Financial Services Marketing Operations; Financial Planning and Services; Investments and Securities. **RELATED KNOWLEDGE/COURSES—Economics and Accounting:** Knowledge of economic and accounting principles and practices, the financial markets, banking, and the analysis and reporting of financial data. **Sales and Marketing:** Knowledge of principles and methods for showing, promoting, and selling products or services. This includes marketing strategy and tactics, product demonstration, sales techniques, and sales control systems. **Computers and Electronics:** Knowledge of circuit boards, processors, chips, electronic equipment, and computer hardware and software, including applications and programming. **Mathematics:** Knowledge of arithmetic, algebra, geometry, calculus, and statistics and their applications. **Law and Government:** Knowledge of laws, legal codes, court procedures, precedents, government regulations, executive orders, agency rules, and the democratic political process. **Communications and Media:** Knowledge of media production, communication, and dissemination techniques and methods. This includes alternative ways to inform and entertain via written, oral, and visual media.

Sales Agents, Securities and Commodities

- ◎ Education/Training Required: Bachelor's degree
- ◎ Annual Earnings: $62,680
- ◎ Growth: 13.0%
- ◎ Annual Job Openings: 39,000
- ◎ Self-Employed: 12.8%
- ◎ Part-Time: 6.0%

Buy and sell securities in investment and trading firms and develop and implement financial plans for individuals, businesses, and organizations. Record transactions accurately, and keep clients informed about transactions. Analyze market conditions in order to determine optimum times to execute securities transactions. Review financial periodicals, stock and bond reports, business publications and other material in order to identify potential investments for clients and to keep abreast of trends affecting market conditions. Read corporate reports and calculate ratios to determine best prospects for profit on stock purchases and to monitor client accounts. Interview clients to determine clients' assets, liabilities, cash flow, insurance coverage, tax status, and financial objectives. Review all securities transactions to ensure accuracy of information and that trades conform to regulations of governing agencies. Prepare documents needed to implement plans selected by clients. Complete sales order tickets and submit for processing of client requested transactions. Inform and advise concerned parties regarding fluctuations and securities transactions affecting plans or accounts. Prepare financial reports to monitor client or corporate finances. Identify potential clients, using advertising campaigns, mailing lists, and personal contacts. Contact prospective customers to determine customer needs, present information, and explain available services. Explain stock market terms and trading practices to clients. Offer advice on the purchase or sale of particular securities. Supply the latest price quotes on any security, as well as information on the activities and financial positions of the corporations issuing these securities. Calculate costs for billings and commissions purposes. Develop financial plans based on analysis of clients' financial status, and discuss financial options with clients. Relay buy or sell orders to securities exchanges or to firm trading departments. **SKILLS—Management of Financial Resources:** Determining how money will be spent to get the work done and accounting for these expenditures. **Systems Analysis:** Determining how a system should work and how changes in conditions, operations, and the environment will affect outcomes. **Systems Evaluation:** Identifying measures or indicators of system performance and the actions needed to improve or correct performance relative to the goals of the system. **Persuasion:** Persuading others to change their minds or behavior. **Service Orientation:** Actively looking for ways to help people. **Negotiation:** Bringing others together and trying to reconcile differences. **Active Learning:** Understanding the implications of new information for both current and future problem-solving and decision-making. **Judgment and Decision Making:** Considering the relative costs and benefits of potential actions to choose the most appropriate one.

GOE—Interest Area: 06. Finance and Insurance. **Work Group:** 06.05. Finance/Insurance Sales and Support. **Other Jobs in This Work Group:** Advertising Sales Agents; Insurance Sales Agents; Personal Financial Advisors; Sales Agents, Financial Services. **PERSONALITY TYPE:** Enterprising. Enterprising occupations frequently involve starting up and carrying out projects. These occupations can involve leading people and making many decisions. They sometimes require risk taking and often deal with business.

EDUCATION/TRAINING PROGRAM(S)— Business and Personal/Financial Services Marketing Operations; Financial Planning and Services; Investments and Securities. **RELATED KNOWL-EDGE/COURSES—Economics and Accounting:** Knowledge of economic and accounting principles and practices, the financial markets, banking, and the analysis and reporting of financial data. **Sales and Marketing:** Knowledge of principles and methods for showing, promoting, and selling products or services. This includes marketing strategy and tactics, product demonstration, sales techniques, and sales control systems. **Mathematics:** Knowledge of arithmetic, algebra, geometry, calculus, and statistics and their applications. **Computers and Electronics:** Knowledge of circuit boards, processors, chips, electronic equipment, and computer hardware and software, including applications and programming. **Customer and Personal Service:** Knowledge of principles and processes for providing customer and personal services. This includes customer needs assessment, meeting quality standards for services, and evaluation of customer satisfaction. **Personnel and Human Resources:** Knowledge of principles and procedures for personnel recruitment, selection, training, compensation and benefits, labor relations and negotiation, and personnel information systems.

Sales Engineers

- Education/Training Required: Bachelor's degree
- Annual Earnings: $68,510
- Growth: 19.9%
- Annual Job Openings: 7,000
- Self-Employed: 0.6%
- Part-Time: 0.8%

Sell business goods or services, the selling of which requires a technical background equivalent to a baccalaureate degree in engineering. Arrange for demonstrations or trial installations of equipment. Attend company training seminars to become familiar with product lines. Collaborate with sales teams to understand customer requirements, to promote the sale of company products, and to provide sales support. Confer with customers and engineers to assess equipment needs, and to determine system requirements. Create sales or service contracts for products or services. Develop sales plans to introduce products in new markets. Develop, present, or respond to proposals for specific customer requirements, including request for proposal responses and industry-specific solutions. Identify resale opportunities, and support them to achieve sales plans. Keep informed on industry news and trends, products, services, competitors, relevant information about legacy, existing, and emerging technologies, and the latest product-line developments. Plan and modify product configurations to meet customer needs. Prepare and deliver technical presentations that explain products or services to customers and prospective customers. Recommend improved materials or machinery to customers, documenting how such changes will lower costs or increase production. Research and identify potential customers for products or services. Secure and renew orders and arrange delivery. Sell products requiring extensive technical expertise and support for installation and use, such as material handling equipment, numerical-control machinery, and computer systems. Visit prospective buyers at commercial, industrial, or other establishments to show samples or catalogs, and to inform them about product pricing, availability, and advantages. Attend trade shows and seminars to promote products or to learn about industry developments. Diagnose problems with installed equipment. Document account activities, generate reports, and keep records of business transactions with customers and suppliers. Maintain sales forecasting reports. Provide information needed for the development of custom-made machinery. Provide technical and non-technical support and services to clients or other staff members regarding the use, operation, and maintenance of equipment. **SKILLS—Technology Design:** Generating or adapting equipment and technology to serve user needs. **Troubleshooting:** Determining causes of operating errors and deciding what to do about them. **Operations Analysis:** Analyzing needs and product requirements to create a design. **Persuasion:** Persuading others to change their minds or behavior. **Negotiation:** Bringing others together and trying to reconcile differences. **Management of Material Resources:** Obtaining and seeing to the appropriate use of equipment, facilities, and materials needed to do certain work. **Service Orientation:** Actively looking for ways to help people. **Speaking:** Talking to others to convey information effectively.

GOE—Interest Area: 14. Retail and Wholesale Sales and Service. **Work Group:** 14.02. Technical Sales. **Other Jobs in This Work Group:** Sales Representatives, Agricultural; Sales Representatives, Chemical and Pharmaceutical; Sales Representatives, Electrical/Electronic; Sales Representatives, Instruments; Sales Representatives, Mechanical Equipment and Supplies; Sales Representatives, Medical. **PERSONALITY TYPE:** Enterprising. Enterprising occupations frequently involve starting up and carrying out projects. These occupations can involve leading people and making many decisions. They sometimes require risk taking and often deal with business.

EDUCATION/TRAINING PROGRAM(S)— Selling Skills and Sales Operations. **RELATED KNOWLEDGE/COURSES—Sales and Marketing:** Knowledge of principles and methods for showing, promoting, and selling products or services. This includes marketing strategy and tactics, product demonstration, sales techniques, and sales control systems. **Design:** Knowledge of design techniques, tools, and principles involved in production of precision technical plans, blueprints, drawings, and models. **Engineering and Technology:** Knowledge of the practical application of engineering science and technology. This includes applying principles, techniques, procedures, and equipment

to the design and production of various goods and services. **Production and Processing:** Knowledge of raw materials, production processes, quality control, costs, and other techniques for maximizing the effective manufacture and distribution of goods. **Physics:** Knowledge and prediction of physical principles and laws and their interrelationships and applications to understanding fluid, material, and atmospheric dynamics and mechanical, electrical, atomic, and subatomic structures and processes. **Customer and Personal Service:** Knowledge of principles and processes for providing customer and personal services. This includes customer needs assessment, meeting quality standards for services, and evaluation of customer satisfaction.

Sales Managers

- Education/Training Required: Work experience plus degree
- Annual Earnings: $81,970
- Growth: 30.5%
- Annual Job Openings: 54,000
- Self-Employed: 3.0%
- Part-Time: 4.7%

Direct the actual distribution or movement of a product or service to the customer. Coordinate sales distribution by establishing sales territories, quotas, and goals and establish training programs for sales representatives. Analyze sales statistics gathered by staff to determine sales potential and inventory requirements and monitor the preferences of customers. Resolve customer complaints regarding sales and service. Monitor customer preferences to determine focus of sales efforts. Direct and coordinate activities involving sales of manufactured products, services, commodities, real estate or other subjects of sale. Determine price schedules and discount rates. Review operational records and reports to project sales and determine profitability.

Direct, coordinate, and review activities in sales and service accounting and record keeping, and in receiving and shipping operations. Confer or consult with department heads to plan advertising services and to secure information on equipment and customer specifications. Advise dealers and distributors on policies and operating procedures to ensure functional effectiveness of business. Prepare budgets and approve budget expenditures. Represent company at trade association meetings to promote products. Plan and direct staffing, training, and performance evaluations to develop and control sales and service programs. Visit franchised dealers to stimulate interest in establishment or expansion of leasing programs. Confer with potential customers regarding equipment needs and advise customers on types of equipment to purchase. Oversee regional and local sales managers and their staffs. Direct clerical staff to keep records of export correspondence, bid requests, and credit collections, and to maintain current information on tariffs, licenses, and restrictions. Direct foreign sales and service outlets of an organization. **SKILLS—Negotiation:** Bringing others together and trying to reconcile differences. **Service Orientation:** Actively looking for ways to help people. **Persuasion:** Persuading others to change their minds or behavior. **Management of Personnel Resources:** Motivating, developing, and directing people as they work, identifying the best people for the job. **Time Management:** Managing one's own time and the time of others. **Monitoring:** Monitoring or assessing your performance or that of other individuals or organizations to make improvements or take corrective action. **Instructing:** Teaching others how to do something. **Social Perceptiveness:** Being aware of others' reactions and understanding why they react as they do.

GOE—Interest Area: 14. Retail and Wholesale Sales and Service. **Work Group:** 14.01. Managerial Work in Retail/Wholesale Sales and Service. **Other Jobs in This Work Group:** Advertising and Promotions Managers; First-Line Supervisors/Managers of Non-Retail Sales Workers; First-Line Supervisors/Managers of Retail Sales Workers; Funeral Directors; Marketing Managers; Property, Real Estate, and Community Association Managers; Purchasing Managers. **PERSONALITY TYPE:** Enterprising. Enterprising occupations frequently involve starting up and carrying out projects. These occupations can involve leading people and making many decisions. They sometimes require risk taking and often deal with business.

EDUCATION/TRAINING PROGRAM(S)— Business Administration and Management, General; Business/Commerce, General; Consumer Merchandising/Retailing Management; Marketing, Other; Marketing/Marketing Management, General. **RELATED KNOWLEDGE/COURSES— Sales and Marketing:** Knowledge of principles and methods for showing, promoting, and selling products or services. This includes marketing strategy and tactics, product demonstration, sales techniques, and sales control systems. **Computers and Electronics:** Knowledge of circuit boards, processors, chips, electronic equipment, and computer hardware and software, including applications and programming. **Mathematics:** Knowledge of arithmetic, algebra, geometry, calculus, and statistics and their applications. **Customer and Personal Service:** Knowledge of principles and processes for providing customer and personal services. This includes customer needs assessment, meeting quality standards for services, and evaluation of customer satisfaction. **Administration and Management:** Knowledge of business and management principles involved in strategic planning, resource allocation, human resources modeling, leadership technique, production methods, and coordination of people and resources. **Law and Government:** Knowledge of laws, legal codes, court procedures, precedents, government regulations, executive orders, agency rules, and the democratic political process.

Secondary School Teachers, Except Special and Vocational Education

- Education/Training Required: Bachelor's degree
- Annual Earnings: $45,180
- Growth: 18.2%
- Annual Job Openings: 118,000
- Self-Employed: 0%
- Part-Time: 8.8%

Instruct students in secondary public or private schools in one or more subjects at the secondary level, such as English, mathematics, or social studies. May be designated according to subject matter specialty, such as typing instructors, commercial teachers, or English teachers. Instruct through lectures, discussions, and demonstrations in one or more subjects such as English, mathematics, or social studies. Prepare, administer, and grade tests and assignments to evaluate students' progress. Assign and grade class work and homework. Adapt teaching methods and instructional materials to meet students' varying needs and interests. Confer with other staff members to plan and schedule lessons promoting learning, following approved curricula. Confer with parents or guardians, other teachers, counselors, and administrators in order to resolve students' behavioral and academic problems. Enforce all administration policies and rules governing students. Establish and enforce rules for behavior and procedures for maintaining order among the students for whom they are responsible. Guide and counsel students with adjustment and/or academic problems, or special academic interests. Instruct and monitor students in the use and care of equipment and materials, in order to prevent injuries and damage. Maintain accurate and complete student records as required by laws, district policies, and administrative regulations. Establish clear objectives for all lessons, units, and projects, and communicate those objectives to students. Meet with other professionals to discuss individual students' needs and progress. Meet with parents and guardians to discuss their children's progress, and to determine their priorities for their children and their resource needs. Observe and evaluate students' performance, behavior, social development, and physical health. Plan and conduct activities for a balanced program of instruction, demonstration, and work time that provides students with opportunities to observe, question, and investigate. Plan and supervise class projects, field trips, visits by guest speakers, or other experiential activities, and guide students in learning from those activities. Prepare and implement remedial programs for students requiring extra help. Prepare for assigned classes, and show written evidence of preparation upon request of immediate supervisors. Prepare materials and classrooms for class activities. **SKILLS—Learning Strategies:** Selecting and using training/instructional methods and procedures appropriate for the situation when learning or teaching new things. **Instructing:** Teaching others how to do something. **Speaking:** Talking to others to convey information effectively. **Social Perceptiveness:** Being aware of others' reactions and understanding why they react as they do. **Mathematics:** Using mathematics to solve problems. **Reading Comprehension:** Understanding written sentences and paragraphs in work-related documents. **Monitoring:** Monitoring or assessing your performance or that of other individuals or organizations to make improvements or take corrective action. **Active Learning:** Understanding the implications of new information for both current and future problem-solving and decision-making.

GOE—Interest Area: 05. Education and Training. **Work Group:** 05.02. Pre-school, Elementary, and Secondary Teaching and Instructing. **Other Jobs in This Work Group:** Elementary School Teachers, Except Special Education; Kindergarten Teachers, Except Special Education; Middle School

Teachers, Except Special and Vocational Education; Preschool Teachers, Except Special Education; Special Education Teachers, Middle School; Special Education Teachers, Preschool, Kindergarten, and Elementary School; Special Education Teachers, Secondary School; Teacher Assistants; Vocational Education Teachers, Middle School; Vocational Education Teachers, Secondary School. **PERSONALITY TYPE:** Social. Social occupations frequently involve working with, communicating with, and teaching people. These occupations often involve helping or providing service to others.

EDUCATION/TRAINING PROGRAM(S)— Agricultural Teacher Education; Art Teacher Education; Biology Teacher Education; Business Teacher Education; Chemistry Teacher Education; Computer Teacher Education; Drama and Dance Teacher Education; Driver and Safety Teacher Education; English/Language Arts Teacher Education; Family and Consumer Sciences/Home Economics Teacher Education; Foreign Language Teacher Education; French Language Teacher Education; Geography Teacher Education; German Language Teacher Education; Health Occupations Teacher Education; Health Teacher Education; History Teacher Education; Junior High/Intermediate/Middle School Education and Teaching; Latin Teacher Education; Mathematics Teacher Education; Music Teacher Education; Physical Education Teaching and Coaching; Physics Teacher Education; Reading Teacher Education; Sales and Marketing Operations/Marketing and Distribution Teacher Education; Science Teacher Education/General Science Teacher Education; Secondary Education and Teaching; Social Science Teacher Education; Social Studies Teacher Education; Spanish Language Teacher Education; Speech Teacher Education; Teacher Education and Professional Development, Specific Subject Areas, Other; Teacher Education, Multiple Levels; Technology Teacher Education/Industrial Arts Teacher Education. **RELATED KNOWLEDGE/COURSES—Education and Training:** Knowledge of principles and methods for curriculum and training design, teach-

ing and instruction for individuals and groups, and the measurement of training effects. **Therapy and Counseling:** Knowledge of principles, methods, and procedures for diagnosis, treatment, and rehabilitation of physical and mental dysfunctions and for career counseling and guidance. **English Language:** Knowledge of the structure and content of the English language, including the meaning and spelling of words, rules of composition, and grammar. **History and Archeology:** Knowledge of historical events and their causes, indicators, and effects on civilizations and cultures. **Sociology and Anthropology:** Knowledge of group behavior and dynamics, societal trends and influences, human migrations, ethnicity, and cultures and their history and origins. **Geography:** Knowledge of principles and methods for describing the features of land, sea, and air masses, including their physical characteristics; locations; interrelationships; and distribution of plant, animal, and human life.

Social and Community Service Managers

- Education/Training Required: Bachelor's degree
- Annual Earnings: $46,200
- Growth: 27.7%
- Annual Job Openings: 19,000
- Self-Employed: 6.6%
- Part-Time: 10.7%

Plan, organize, or coordinate the activities of a social service program or community outreach organization. Oversee the program or organization's budget and policies regarding participant involvement, program requirements, and benefits. Work may involve directing social workers, counselors, or probation officers. Establish and maintain relationships with other agencies and organizations in community in order to meet community needs and to ensure that services are not duplicated. Prepare and maintain records and reports, such as budgets, personnel records, or training manuals. Direct activities of professional and technical staff members and volunteers. Evaluate the work of staff and volunteers in order to ensure that programs are of appropriate quality and that resources are used effectively. Establish and oversee administrative procedures to meet objectives set by boards of directors or senior management. Participate in the determination of organizational policies regarding such issues as participant eligibility, program requirements, and program benefits. Research and analyze member or community needs in order to determine program directions and goals. Speak to community groups to explain and interpret agency purposes, programs, and policies. Recruit, interview, and hire or sign up volunteers and staff. Represent organizations in relations with governmental and media institutions. Plan and administer budgets for programs, equipment and support services. Analyze proposed legislation, regulations, or rule changes in order to determine how agency services could be impacted. Act as consultants to agency staff and other community programs regarding the interpretation of program-related federal, state, and county regulations and policies. Implement and evaluate staff training programs. Direct fund-raising activities and the preparation of public relations materials. **SKILLS—Social Perceptiveness:** Being aware of others' reactions and understanding why they react as they do. **Service Orientation:** Actively looking for ways to help people. **Negotiation:** Bringing others together and trying to reconcile differences. **Management of Personnel Resources:** Motivating, developing, and directing people as they work, identifying the best people for the job. **Persuasion:** Persuading others to change their minds or behavior. **Instructing:** Teaching others how to do something. **Monitoring:** Monitoring or assessing your performance or that of other individuals or organizations to make improvements or take corrective action. **Learning Strategies:** Selecting and using training/instructional methods and procedures

appropriate for the situation when learning or teaching new things. **Time Management:** Managing one's own time and the time of others.

GOE—Interest Area: 07. Government and Public Administration. **Work Group:** 07.01. Managerial Work in Government and Public Administration. **Other Jobs in This Work Group:** Government Service Executives. **PERSONALITY TYPE:** Social. Social occupations frequently involve working with, communicating with, and teaching people. These occupations often involve helping or providing service to others.

EDUCATION/TRAINING PROGRAM(S)— Business Administration and Management, General; Business, Management, Marketing, and Related Support Services, Other; Business/Commerce, General; Community Organization and Advocacy; Entrepreneurship/Entrepreneurial Studies; Human Services, General; Non-Profit/Public/Organizational Management; Public Administration. **RELATED KNOWLEDGE/COURSES—Customer and Personal Service:** Knowledge of principles and processes for providing customer and personal services. This includes customer needs assessment, meeting quality standards for services, and evaluation of customer satisfaction. **Sociology and Anthropology:** Knowledge of group behavior and dynamics, societal trends and influences, human migrations, ethnicity, and cultures and their history and origins. **Psychology:** Knowledge of human behavior and performance; individual differences in ability, personality, and interests; learning and motivation; psychological research methods; and the assessment and treatment of behavioral and affective disorders. **Education and Training:** Knowledge of principles and methods for curriculum and training design, teaching and instruction for individuals and groups, and the measurement of training effects. **Clerical Practices:** Knowledge of administrative and clerical procedures and systems such as word processing, managing files and records, stenography and transcription, designing forms, and other office procedures and terminology. **Therapy and Counseling:** Knowledge of principles, methods, and procedures for diagnosis, treatment, and rehabilitation of physical and mental dysfunctions and for career counseling and guidance.

Social Science Research Assistants

- Education/Training Required: Associate's degree
- Annual Earnings: $48,660
- Growth: 17.5%
- Annual Job Openings: 18,000
- Self-Employed: 1.1%
- Part-Time: 20.2%

Assist social scientists in laboratory, survey, and other social research. May perform publication activities, laboratory analysis, quality control, or data management. Normally these individuals work under the direct supervision of a social scientist and assist in those activities which are more routine. Perform descriptive and multivariate statistical analyses of data, using computer software. Recruit and schedule research participants. Administer standardized tests to research subjects, and/or interview them in order to collect research data. Code data in preparation for computer entry. Conduct internet-based and library research. Develop and implement research quality control procedures. Edit and submit protocols and other required research documentation. Obtain informed consent of research subjects and/or their guardians. Prepare tables, graphs, fact sheets, and written reports summarizing research results. Prepare, manipulate, and manage extensive databases. Provide assistance in the design of survey instruments such as questionnaires. Screen potential subjects in order to determine their suitability as study participants. Track research participants, and perform any necessary followup tasks. Verify the accuracy and validity of data entered in databases; correct any errors. Allocate and manage laboratory space and resources. Design and create special programs for tasks such as statistical analysis and data entry and cleaning. Perform data entry and other clerical work as required for project completion. Perform needs assessments and/or consult with clients in order to determine the types of research and information that are required. Present research findings to groups of people. Provide assistance with the preparation of project-related reports, manuscripts, and presentations. Supervise the work of survey interviewers. Track laboratory supplies, and expenses such as participant reimbursement. Collect specimens such as blood samples, as required by research projects. **SKILLS**—No data available.

GOE—Interest Area: 15. Scientific Research, Engineering, and Mathematics. **Work Group:** 15.06. Mathematics and Data Analysis. **Other Jobs in This Work Group:** Actuaries; Mathematical Technicians; Mathematicians; Statistical Assistants; Statisticians. **PERSONALITY TYPE:** No data available.

EDUCATION/TRAINING PROGRAM(S)—Social Sciences, General. **RELATED KNOWLEDGE/COURSES**—No data available.

Social Work Teachers, Postsecondary

- Education/Training Required: Master's degree
- Annual Earnings: $51,190
- Growth: 38.1% for all Postsecondary Teachers
- Annual Job Openings: 216,000 for all Postsecondary Teachers
- Self-Employed: 0.3% for all Postsecondary Teachers
- Part-Time: 27.7% for all Postsecondary Teachers

Teach courses in social work. Evaluate and grade students' class work, assignments, and papers. Prepare and deliver lectures to undergraduate and/or graduate students on topics such as family behavior, child and adolescent mental health, and social intervention evaluation. Advise students on academic and vocational curricula, and on career issues. Compile, administer, and grade examinations, or assign this work to others. Compile bibliographies of specialized materials for outside reading assignments. Initiate, facilitate, and moderate classroom discussions. Keep abreast of developments in their field by reading current literature, talking with colleagues, and participating in professional conferences. Maintain regularly scheduled office hours in order to advise and assist students. Maintain student attendance records, grades, and other required records. Plan, evaluate, and revise curricula, course content, and course materials and methods of instruction. Prepare course materials such as syllabi, homework assignments, and handouts. Select and obtain materials and supplies such as textbooks and laboratory equipment. Supervise students' laboratory and field work. Supervise undergraduate and/or graduate teaching, internship, and research work. Act as advisers to student organizations. Collaborate with colleagues, and with community agencies, in order to address teaching and research issues. Conduct research in a particular field of knowledge, and publish findings in professional journals, books, and/or electronic media. Participate in campus and community events. Participate in student recruitment, registration, and placement activities. Perform administrative duties such as serving as department head. Provide professional consulting services to government and/or industry. Serve on academic or administrative committees that deal with institutional policies, departmental matters, and academic issues. Write grant proposals to procure external research funding. **SKILLS**—No data available.

GOE—**Interest Area:** 05. Education and Training. **Work Group:** 05.03. Postsecondary and Adult Teaching and Instructing. **Other Jobs in This Work Group:** Adult Literacy, Remedial Education, and GED Teachers and Instructors; Agricultural Sciences Teachers, Postsecondary; Anthropology and Archeology Teachers, Postsecondary; Architecture Teachers, Postsecondary; Area, Ethnic, and Cultural Studies Teachers, Postsecondary; Art, Drama, and Music Teachers, Postsecondary; Atmospheric, Earth, Marine, and Space Sciences Teachers, Postsecondary; Biological Science Teachers, Postsecondary; Business Teachers, Postsecondary; Chemistry Teachers, Postsecondary; Communications Teachers, Postsecondary; Computer Science Teachers, Postsecondary; Criminal Justice and Law Enforcement Teachers, Postsecondary; Economics Teachers, Postsecondary; Education Teachers, Postsecondary; Engineering Teachers, Postsecondary; English Language and Literature Teachers, Postsecondary; Environmental Science Teachers, Postsecondary; Farm and Home Management Advisors; Foreign Language and Literature Teachers, Postsecondary; Forestry and Conservation Science Teachers, Postsecondary; Geography Teachers, Postsecondary; Graduate Teaching Assistants; Health Specialties Teachers, Postsecondary; History Teachers, Postsecondary; Home Economics Teachers, Postsecondary; Law Teachers, Postsecondary; Library Science Teachers, Postsecondary; Mathematical Science Teachers, Postsecondary; Nursing Instructors and Teachers, Postsecondary; Philosophy and Religion Teachers, Postsecondary; Physics Teachers, Postsecondary; Political Science Teachers, Postsecondary; Psychology Teachers, Postsecondary; Recreation and Fitness Studies Teachers, Postsecondary; Self-Enrichment Education Teachers; Sociology Teachers, Postsecondary; Vocational Education Teachers, Postsecondary. **PERSONALITY TYPE:** No data available.

EDUCATION/TRAINING PROGRAM(S)—Clinical/Medical Social Work; Social Work; Teacher Education and Professional Development, Specific Subject Areas, Other. **RELATED KNOWLEDGE/COURSES**—No data available.

Sociology Teachers, Postsecondary

- Education/Training Required: Master's degree
- Annual Earnings: $53,870
- Growth: 38.1% for all Postsecondary Teachers
- Annual Job Openings: 216,000 for all Postsecondary Teachers
- Self-Employed: 0.3% for all Postsecondary Teachers
- Part-Time: 27.7% for all Postsecondary Teachers

Teach courses in sociology. Evaluate and grade students' class work, assignments, and papers. Prepare and deliver lectures to undergraduate and/or graduate students on topics such as race and ethnic relations, measurement and data collection, and workplace social relations. Advise students on academic and vocational curricula, and on career issues. Compile, administer, and grade examinations, or assign this work to others. Compile bibliographies of specialized materials for outside reading assignments. Initiate, facilitate, and moderate classroom discussions. Keep abreast of developments in their field by reading current literature, talking with colleagues, and participating in professional conferences. Maintain regularly scheduled office hours in order to advise and assist students. Maintain student attendance records, grades, and other required records. Plan, evaluate, and revise curricula, course content, and course materials and methods of instruction. Prepare course materials such as syllabi, homework assignments, and handouts. Select and obtain materials and supplies such as textbooks and laboratory equipment. Supervise students' laboratory and field work. Supervise undergraduate and/or graduate teaching, internship, and research work. Act as advisers to student organizations. Collaborate with colleagues to address teaching and research issues. Conduct research in a particular field of knowledge, and publish findings in professional journals, books, and/or electronic media. Participate in campus and community events. Participate in student recruitment, registration, and placement activities. Perform administrative duties such as serving as department head. Provide professional consulting services to government and/or industry. Serve on academic or administrative committees that deal with institutional policies, departmental matters, and academic issues. Write grant proposals to procure external research funding. **SKILLS— Instructing:** Teaching others how to do something. **Learning Strategies:** Selecting and using training/instructional methods and procedures appropriate for the situation when learning or teaching new things. **Reading Comprehension:** Understanding written sentences and paragraphs in work-related documents. **Active Learning:** Understanding the implications of new information for both current and future problem-solving and decision-making. **Speaking:** Talking to others to convey information effectively. **Writing:** Communicating effectively in writing as appropriate for the needs of the audience. **Science:** Using scientific rules and methods to solve problems. **Active Listening:** Giving full attention to what other people are saying, taking time to understand the points being made, asking questions as appropriate, and not interrupting at inappropriate times. **Critical Thinking:** Using logic and reasoning to identify the strengths and weaknesses of alternative solutions, conclusions, or approaches to problems.

GOE—Interest Area: 05. Education and Training. **Work Group:** 05.03. Postsecondary and Adult Teaching and Instructing. **Other Jobs in This Work Group:** Adult Literacy, Remedial Education, and GED Teachers and Instructors; Agricultural Sciences Teachers, Postsecondary; Anthropology and Archeology Teachers, Postsecondary; Architecture Teachers, Postsecondary; Area, Ethnic, and Cultural Studies Teachers, Postsecondary; Art, Drama, and Music Teachers, Postsecondary; Atmospheric, Earth, Marine, and Space Sciences Teachers, Postsecondary; Biological Science Teachers, Postsecondary; Business Teachers, Postsecondary; Chemistry Teachers, Postsecondary; Communications Teachers, Postsecondary; Computer Science Teachers, Postsecondary; Criminal Justice and Law Enforcement Teachers, Postsecondary; Economics Teachers, Postsecondary; Education Teachers, Postsecondary; Engineering Teachers, Postsecondary; English Language and Literature Teachers, Postsecondary; Environmental Science Teachers, Postsecondary; Farm and Home Management Advisors; Foreign Language and Literature Teachers, Postsecondary; Forestry and Conservation Science Teachers, Postsecondary; Geography Teachers, Postsecondary; Graduate Teaching Assistants; Health Specialties Teachers, Postsecondary; History Teachers, Postsecondary; Home Economics Teachers, Postsecondary; Law Teachers, Postsecondary; Library Science Teachers, Postsecondary; Mathematical Science Teachers, Postsecondary; Nursing Instructors and Teachers, Postsecondary; Philosophy and Religion Teachers, Postsecondary; Physics Teachers, Postsecondary; Political Science Teachers, Postsecondary; Psychology Teachers, Postsecondary; Recreation and Fitness Studies Teachers, Postsecondary; Self-Enrichment Education Teachers; Social Work Teachers, Postsecondary; Vocational Education Teachers, Postsecondary. **PERSONALITY TYPE:** Social. Social occupations frequently involve working with, communicating with, and teaching people. These occupations often involve helping or providing service to others.

EDUCATION/TRAINING PROGRAM(S)— Social Science Teacher Education; Sociology. **RELATED KNOWLEDGE/COURSES—Sociology and Anthropology:** Knowledge of group behavior and dynamics, societal trends and influences, human migrations, ethnicity, and cultures and their history and origins. **History and Archeology:** Knowledge of historical events and their causes, indicators, and effects on civilizations and cultures. **Education and Training:** Knowledge of principles and methods for curriculum and training design, teaching and instruction for individuals and groups, and the measurement of training effects. **Psychology:** Knowledge of human behavior and performance; individual differences in ability, personality, and interests; learning and motivation; psychological research methods; and the assessment and treatment of behavioral and affective disorders. **Economics and Accounting:** Knowledge of economic and accounting principles and practices, the financial markets, banking, and the analysis and reporting of financial data. **English Language:** Knowledge of the structure and content of the English language, including the meaning and spelling of words, rules of composition, and grammar.

Special Education Teachers, Middle School

- Education/Training Required: Bachelor's degree
- Annual Earnings: $43,260
- Growth: 30.0%
- Annual Job Openings: 59,000
- Self-Employed: 0.3%
- Part-Time: 9.3%

Teach middle school subjects to educationally and physically handicapped students. Includes teachers who specialize and work with audibly and visually handicapped students and those who teach basic academic and life processes skills to the mentally impaired. Observe and evaluate students' performance, behavior, social development, and physical health. Organize and label materials, and display students' work. Organize and supervise games and other recreational activities to promote physical, mental, and social development. Plan and conduct activities for a balanced program of instruction, demonstration, and work time that provides students with opportunities to observe, question, and investigate. Plan and supervise class projects, field trips, visits by guest speakers, or other experiential activities, and guide students in learning from those activities. Prepare for assigned classes, and show written evidence of preparation upon request of immediate supervisors. Prepare materials and classrooms for class activities. Prepare objectives and outlines for courses of study, following curriculum guidelines or requirements of states and schools. Prepare, administer, and grade tests and assignments to evaluate students' progress. Provide additional instruction in vocational areas. Provide interpretation and transcription of regular classroom materials through Braille and sign language. Develop and implement strategies to meet the needs of students with a variety of handicapping conditions. Instruct students in daily living skills required for independent maintenance and self-sufficiency, such as hygiene, safety, and food preparation. Instruct through lectures, discussions, and demonstrations in one or more subjects such as English, mathematics, or social studies. Confer with parents, administrators, testing specialists, social workers, and professionals to develop individual educational plans designed to promote students' educational, physical, and social development. Employ special educational strategies and techniques during instruction to improve the development of sensory- and perceptual-motor skills, language, cognition, and memory. Modify the general education curriculum for special-needs students based upon a variety of instructional techniques and instructional technology. Confer with other staff members to plan and schedule lessons promoting learning, following approved curricula. **SKILLS—Learning Strategies:** Selecting and using training/instructional methods and procedures appropriate for the situation when learning or teaching new things. **Social Perceptiveness:** Being aware of others' reactions and understanding why they react as they do. **Instructing:** Teaching others how to do something. **Monitoring:** Monitoring or assessing your performance or that of other individuals or organizations to make improvements or take corrective action. **Speaking:** Talking to others to convey information effectively. **Active Listening:** Giving full attention to what other peo-

ple are saying, taking time to understand the points being made, asking questions as appropriate, and not interrupting at inappropriate times. **Writing:** Communicating effectively in writing as appropriate for the needs of the audience. **Service Orientation:** Actively looking for ways to help people. **Complex Problem Solving:** Identifying complex problems and reviewing related information to develop and evaluate options and implement solutions.

GOE—Interest Area: 05. Education and Training. **Work Group:** 05.02. Pre-school, Elementary, and Secondary Teaching and Instructing. **Other Jobs in This Work Group:** Elementary School Teachers, Except Special Education; Kindergarten Teachers, Except Special Education; Middle School Teachers, Except Special and Vocational Education; Preschool Teachers, Except Special Education; Secondary School Teachers, Except Special and Vocational Education; Special Education Teachers, Preschool, Kindergarten, and Elementary School; Special Education Teachers, Secondary School; Teacher Assistants; Vocational Education Teachers, Middle School; Vocational Education Teachers, Secondary School. **PERSONALITY TYPE:** Social. Social occupations frequently involve working with, communicating with, and teaching people. These occupations often involve helping or providing service to others.

EDUCATION/TRAINING PROGRAM(S)— Special Education and Teaching, General. **RELATED KNOWLEDGE/COURSES—Therapy and Counseling:** Knowledge of principles, methods, and procedures for diagnosis, treatment, and rehabilitation of physical and mental dysfunctions and for career counseling and guidance. **Education and Training:** Knowledge of principles and methods for curriculum and training design, teaching and instruction for individuals and groups, and the measurement of training effects. **Psychology:** Knowledge of human behavior and performance; individual differences in ability, personality, and interests; learning and motivation; psychological research methods; and the assessment and treatment of behavioral and affective disorders. **Medicine and Dentistry:** Knowledge of the information and techniques needed to diagnose and treat human injuries, diseases, and deformities. This includes symptoms, treatment alternatives, drug properties and interactions, and preventive health-care measures. **English Language:** Knowledge of the structure and content of the English language, including the meaning and spelling of words, rules of composition, and grammar. **Customer and Personal Service:** Knowledge of principles and processes for providing customer and personal services. This includes customer needs assessment, meeting quality standards for services, and evaluation of customer satisfaction.

Special Education Teachers, Preschool, Kindergarten, and Elementary School

- ◉ Education/Training Required: Bachelor's degree
- ◉ Annual Earnings: $42,630
- ◉ Growth: 30.0%
- ◉ Annual Job Openings: 59,000
- ◉ Self-Employed: 0.3%
- ◉ Part-Time: 9.3%

Teach elementary and preschool school subjects to educationally and physically handicapped students. Includes teachers who specialize and work with audibly and visually handicapped students and those who teach basic academic and life processes skills to the mentally impaired. Develop and implement strategies to meet the needs of students with a variety of handicapping conditions. Instruct students in academic subjects, using a variety of techniques such as phonetics, multisensory learning, and repetition, in order to reinforce learning and to meet students' varying needs and interests. Prepare objectives and outlines for courses of study, following curriculum guidelines or requirements of states and schools. Prepare students for later grades by encouraging them to explore learning opportunities and to persevere with challenging tasks. Prepare, administer, and grade tests and assignments to evaluate students' progress. Provide interpretation and transcription of regular classroom materials through Braille and sign language. Supervise, evaluate, and plan assignments for teacher assistants and volunteers. Teach socially acceptable behavior, employing techniques such as behavior modification and positive reinforcement. Teach students personal development skills such as goal setting, independence, and self-advocacy. Administer standardized ability and achievement tests, and interpret results to determine students' strengths and areas of need. Attend professional meetings, educational conferences, and teacher training workshops in order to maintain and improve professional competence. Attend staff meetings, and serve on committees as required. Collaborate with other teachers and administrators in the development, evaluation, and revision of preschool, kindergarten, or elementary school programs. Instruct students in daily living skills required for independent maintenance and self-sufficiency, such as hygiene, safety, and food preparation. Confer with parents, administrators, testing specialists, social workers, and professionals to develop individual educational plans designed to promote students' educational, physical, and social development. Modify the general education curriculum for special-needs students based upon a variety of instructional techniques and technologies. Confer with other staff members to plan and schedule lessons promoting learning, following approved curricula. **SKILLS—Learning Strategies:** Selecting and using training/instructional methods and procedures appropriate for the situation when learning or teaching new things. **Social Perceptiveness:** Being aware of others' reactions and understanding why they react as they do. **Instructing:** Teaching others how to do something. **Monitoring:** Monitoring or assessing your performance or that of other individuals or organizations to make improvements or take corrective action. **Speaking:** Talking to others to convey information effectively. **Active Listening:** Giving full attention to what other people are saying, taking time to understand the points being made, asking questions as appropriate, and not interrupting at inappropriate times. **Writing:** Communicating effectively in writing as appropriate for the needs of the audience. **Service Orientation:** Actively looking for ways to help people. **Complex Problem Solving:** Identifying complex problems and reviewing related information to develop and evaluate options and implement solutions.

GOE—Interest Area: 05. Education and Training. **Work Group:** 05.02. Pre-school, Elementary, and Secondary Teaching and Instructing. **Other Jobs in This Work Group:** Elementary School Teachers, Except Special Education; Kindergarten Teachers, Except Special Education; Middle School Teachers, Except Special and Vocational Education; Preschool Teachers, Except Special Education; Secondary School Teachers, Except Special and Vocational Education; Special Education Teachers, Middle School; Special Education Teachers, Secondary School; Teacher Assistants; Vocational Education Teachers, Middle School; Vocational Education Teachers, Secondary School. **PERSONALITY TYPE:** Social. Social occupations frequently involve working with, communicating with, and teaching people. These occupations often involve helping or providing service to others.

EDUCATION/TRAINING PROGRAM(S)— Education/Teaching of Individuals with Autism; Education/Teaching of Individuals with Emotional Disturbances; Education/Teaching of Individuals with Hearing Impairments, Including Deafness; Education/Teaching of Individuals with Mental Retardation; Education/Teaching of Individuals with Multiple Disabilities; Education/Teaching of Individuals with Orthopedic and Other Physical Health Impairments; Education/Teaching of Individuals with Specific Learning Disabilities; Education/Teaching of Individuals with Speech or Language Impairments; Education/Teaching of Individuals with Traumatic Brain Injuries; Education/Teaching of Individuals with Vision Impairments, Including Blindness; Special Education and Teaching, General; Special Education and Teaching, Other. **RELATED KNOWLEDGE/COURSES— Therapy and Counseling:** Knowledge of principles, methods, and procedures for diagnosis, treatment, and rehabilitation of physical and mental dysfunctions and for career counseling and guidance. **Education and Training:** Knowledge of principles and methods for curriculum and training design, teaching and instruction for individuals and groups, and the measurement of training effects. **Psychology:** Knowledge of human behavior and performance; individual differences in ability, personality, and interests; learning and motivation; psychological research methods; and the assessment and treatment of behavioral and affective disorders. **Medicine and Dentistry:** Knowledge of the information and techniques needed to diagnose and treat human injuries, diseases, and deformities. This includes symptoms, treatment alternatives, drug properties and interactions, and preventive health-care measures. **English Language:** Knowledge of the structure and content of the English language, including the meaning and spelling of words, rules of composition, and grammar. **Customer and Personal Service:** Knowledge of principles and processes for providing customer and personal services. This includes customer needs assessment, meeting quality standards for services, and evaluation of customer satisfaction.

Special Education Teachers, Secondary School

- ◎ Education/Training Required: Bachelor's degree
- ◎ Annual Earnings: $44,920
- ◎ Growth: 30.0%
- ◎ Annual Job Openings: 59,000
- ◎ Self-Employed: 0.3%
- ◎ Part-Time: 9.3%

Teach secondary school subjects to educationally and physically handicapped students. Includes teachers who specialize and work with audibly and visually handicapped students and those who teach basic academic and life processes skills to the mentally impaired. Establish clear objectives for all lessons, units, and projects, and communicate those objectives to students. Guide and counsel students with adjustment and/or academic problems, or special academic interests. Instruct and monitor students in the use and care of equipment and materials, in order to prevent injuries and damage. Maintain accurate and complete student records, and prepare reports on children and activities, as required by laws, district policies, and administrative regulations. Meet with other professionals to discuss individual students' needs and progress. Meet with parents and guardians to discuss their children's progress, and to determine their priorities for their children and their resource needs. Meet with parents and guardians to provide guidance in using community resources, and to teach skills for dealing with students' impairments. Observe and evaluate students' performance, behavior, social development, and physical health. Plan and conduct activities for a balanced program of instruction, demonstration, and work time that provides students with opportunities to observe, question, and investigate. Plan and supervise class projects, field trips, visits by guest speakers, or other experiential activities, and guide students in learning from those activities. Prepare for assigned classes, and show written evidence of preparation upon request of immediate supervisors. Develop and implement strategies to meet the needs of students with a variety of handicapping conditions. Instruct students in daily living skills required for independent maintenance and self-sufficiency, such as hygiene, safety, and food preparation. Instruct through lectures, discussions, and demonstrations in one or more subjects such as English, mathematics, or social studies. Confer with parents, administrators, testing specialists, social workers, and professionals to develop individual educational plans designed to promote students' educational, physical, and social development. Modify the general education curriculum for special-needs students, based upon a variety of instructional techniques and technologies. **SKILLS—Learning Strategies:** Selecting and using training/instructional methods and procedures appropriate for the situation when learning or teaching new things. **Social Perceptiveness:** Being aware of others' reactions and understanding why they react as they do. **Instructing:** Teaching others how to do something. **Monitoring:** Monitoring or assessing your performance or that of other individuals or organizations to make improvements or take corrective action. **Speaking:** Talking to others to convey information effectively. **Active Listening:** Giving full attention to what other people are saying, taking time to understand the points being made, asking questions as appropriate, and not interrupting at inappropriate times. **Writing:** Communicating effectively in writing as appropriate for the needs of the audience. **Service Orientation:** Actively looking for ways to help people. **Complex Problem Solving:** Identifying complex problems and reviewing related information to develop and evaluate options and implement solutions.

GOE—Interest Area: 05. Education and Training. **Work Group:** 05.02. Pre-school, Elementary, and Secondary Teaching and Instructing. **Other Jobs in This Work Group:** Elementary School

Teachers, Except Special Education; Kindergarten Teachers, Except Special Education; Middle School Teachers, Except Special and Vocational Education; Preschool Teachers, Except Special Education; Secondary School Teachers, Except Special and Vocational Education; Special Education Teachers, Middle School; Special Education Teachers, Preschool, Kindergarten, and Elementary School; Teacher Assistants; Vocational Education Teachers, Middle School; Vocational Education Teachers, Secondary School. **PERSONALITY TYPE:** Social. Social occupations frequently involve working with, communicating with, and teaching people. These occupations often involve helping or providing service to others.

EDUCATION/TRAINING PROGRAM(S)— Special Education and Teaching, General. **RELATED KNOWLEDGE/COURSES—Therapy and Counseling:** Knowledge of principles, methods, and procedures for diagnosis, treatment, and rehabilitation of physical and mental dysfunctions and for career counseling and guidance. **Education and Training:** Knowledge of principles and methods for curriculum and training design, teaching and instruction for individuals and groups, and the measurement of training effects. **Psychology:** Knowledge of human behavior and performance; individual differences in ability, personality, and interests; learning and motivation; psychological research methods; and the assessment and treatment of behavioral and affective disorders. **Medicine and Dentistry:** Knowledge of the information and techniques needed to diagnose and treat human injuries, diseases, and deformities. This includes symptoms, treatment alternatives, drug properties and interactions, and preventive health-care measures. **English Language:** Knowledge of the structure and content of the English language, including the meaning and spelling of words, rules of composition, and grammar. **Customer and Personal Service:** Knowledge of principles and processes for providing customer and personal services. This includes customer needs assessment, meeting quality standards for services, and evaluation of customer satisfaction.

Speech-Language Pathologists

- Education/Training Required: Master's degree
- Annual Earnings: $50,890
- Growth: 27.2%
- Annual Job Openings: 10,000
- Self-Employed: 8.2%
- Part-Time: 28.1%

Assess and treat persons with speech, language, voice, and fluency disorders. May select alternative communication systems and teach their use. May perform research related to speech and language problems. Monitor patients' progress and adjust treatments accordingly. Evaluate hearing and speech/language test results and medical or background information to diagnose and plan treatment for speech, language, fluency, voice, and swallowing disorders. Administer hearing or speech/language evaluations, tests, or examinations to patients to collect information on type and degree of impairments, using written and oral tests and special instruments. Record information on the initial evaluation, treatment, progress, and discharge of clients. Develop and implement treatment plans for problems such as stuttering, delayed language, swallowing disorders, and inappropriate pitch or harsh voice problems, based on own assessments and recommendations of physicians, psychologists, and social workers. Develop individual or group programs in schools to deal with speech or language problems. Instruct clients in techniques for more effective communication, including sign language, lip reading, and voice improvement. Teach clients to control or strengthen tongue, jaw, face muscles, and breathing mechanisms. Develop speech exercise programs to reduce disabilities. Consult with and advise educators or medical staff on speech or hearing topics such as communication strategies and speech and language stimulation. Instruct patients and family members in strategies to cope with or avoid communication-related misunderstandings. Design, develop, and employ alternative diagnostic or communication devices and strategies. Conduct lessons and direct educational or therapeutic games to assist teachers dealing with speech problems. Refer clients to additional medical or educational services if needed. Participate in conferences or training, or publish research results, to share knowledge of new hearing or speech disorder treatment methods or technologies. Communicate with non-speaking students, using sign language or computer technology. Provide communication instruction to dialect speakers or students with limited English proficiency. Use computer applications to identify and assist with communication disabilities. **SKILLS—Instructing:** Teaching others how to do something. **Social Perceptiveness:** Being aware of others' reactions and understanding why they react as they do. **Learning Strategies:** Selecting and using training/instructional methods and procedures appropriate for the situation when learning or teaching new things. **Service Orientation:** Actively looking for ways to help people. **Time Management:** Managing one's own time and the time of others. **Active Learning:** Understanding the implications of new information for both current and future problem-solving and decision-making. **Coordination:** Adjusting actions in relation to others' actions. **Speaking:** Talking to others to convey information effectively.

GOE—Interest Area: 08. Health Science. **Work Group:** 08.07. Medical Therapy. **Other Jobs in This Work Group:** Audiologists; Massage Therapists; Occupational Therapist Aides; Occupational Therapist Assistants; Occupational Therapists; Physical Therapist Aides; Physical Therapist Assistants; Physical Therapists; Radiation Therapists; Recreational Therapists; Respiratory Therapists; Respiratory Therapy Technicians. **PERSONALITY TYPE:** Social. Social occupations frequently involve working with, communicating with, and teaching people. These occupations often involve helping or providing service to others.

EDUCATION/TRAINING PROGRAM(S)—Audiology/Audiologist and Speech-Language Pathology/Pathologist; Communication Disorders Sciences and Services, Other; Communication Disorders, General; Speech-Language Pathology/Pathologist. **RELATED KNOWLEDGE/COURSES—Therapy and Counseling:** Knowledge of principles, methods, and procedures for diagnosis, treatment, and rehabilitation of physical and mental dysfunctions and for career counseling and guidance. **Psychology:** Knowledge of human behavior and performance; individual differences in ability, personality, and interests; learning and motivation; psychological research methods; and the assessment and treatment of behavioral and affective disorders. **Education and Training:** Knowledge of principles and methods for curriculum and training design, teaching and instruction for individuals and groups, and the measurement of training effects. **English Language:** Knowledge of the structure and content of the English language, including the meaning and spelling of words, rules of composition, and grammar. **Sociology and Anthropology:** Knowledge of group behavior and dynamics, societal trends and influences, human migrations, ethnicity, and cultures and their history and origins. **Medicine and Dentistry:** Knowledge of the information and techniques needed to diagnose and treat human injuries, diseases, and deformities. This includes symptoms, treatment alternatives, drug properties and interactions, and preventive health-care measures.

Statisticians

- ◉ Education/Training Required: Master's degree
- ◉ Annual Earnings: $64,320
- ◉ Growth: 4.8%
- ◉ Annual Job Openings: 2,000
- ◉ Self-Employed: 5.7%
- ◉ Part-Time: 5.1%

Engage in the development of mathematical theory or apply statistical theory and methods to collect, organize, interpret, and summarize numerical data to provide usable information. May specialize in fields, such as bio-statistics, agricultural statistics, business statistics, economic statistics, or other fields. Adapt statistical methods in order to solve specific problems in many fields, such as economics, biology and engineering. Analyze and interpret statistical data in order to identify significant differences in relationships among sources of information. Apply sampling techniques or utilize complete enumeration bases in order to determine and define groups to be surveyed. Design research projects that apply valid scientific techniques and utilize information obtained from baselines or historical data in order to structure uncompromised and efficient analyses. Develop and test experimental designs, sampling techniques, and analytical methods. Evaluate sources of information in order to determine any limitations in terms of reliability or usability. Evaluate the statistical methods and procedures used to obtain data in order to ensure validity, applicability, efficiency, and accuracy. Examine theories, such as those of probability and inference in order to discover mathematical bases for new or improved methods of obtaining and evaluating numerical data. Identify relationships and trends in data, as well as any factors that could affect the results of research. Plan data collection methods for specific projects, and determine the types and sizes of sample groups to be used. Process large amounts of data for statistical modeling and graphic analysis, using computers. Report results of statistical analyses, including information in the form of graphs, charts, and tables. Develop an understanding of fields to which statistical methods are to be applied in order to determine whether methods and results are appropriate. Prepare data for processing by organizing information, checking for any inaccuracies, and adjusting and weighting the raw data. Supervise and provide instructions for workers collecting and tabulating data. **SKILLS—Mathematics:** Using mathematics to solve problems. **Science:** Using scientific rules and methods to solve problems. **Systems Evaluation:** Identifying measures or indicators of system performance and the actions needed to improve or correct performance relative to the goals of the system. **Active Learning:** Understanding the implications of new information for both current and future problem-solving and decision-making. **Critical Thinking:** Using logic and reasoning to identify the strengths and weaknesses of alternative solutions, conclusions, or approaches to problems. **Complex Problem Solving:** Identifying complex problems and reviewing related information to develop and evaluate options and implement solutions. **Judgment and Decision Making:** Considering the relative costs and benefits of potential actions to choose the most appropriate one. **Systems Analysis:** Determining how a system should work and how changes in conditions, operations, and the environment will affect outcomes.

GOE—Interest Area: 15. Scientific Research, Engineering, and Mathematics. **Work Group:** 15.06. Mathematics and Data Analysis. **Other Jobs in This Work Group:** Actuaries; Mathematical Technicians; Mathematicians; Social Science Research Assistants; Statistical Assistants. **PERSONALITY TYPE:** Investigative. Investigative occupations frequently involve working with ideas and require an extensive amount of thinking. These occupations can involve searching for facts and figuring out problems mentally.

EDUCATION/TRAINING PROGRAM(S)— Applied Mathematics; Biostatistics; Business Statistics; Mathematical Statistics and Probability; Mathematics, General; Statistics, General; Statistics, Other. **RELATED KNOWLEDGE/COURSES—Mathematics:** Knowledge of arithmetic, algebra, geometry, calculus, and statistics and their applications. **Computers and Electronics:** Knowledge of circuit boards, processors, chips, electronic equipment, and computer hardware and software, including applications and programming. **English Language:** Knowledge of the structure and content of the English language, including the meaning and spelling of words, rules of composition, and grammar. **Economics and Accounting:** Knowledge of economic and accounting principles and practices, the financial markets, banking, and the analysis and reporting of financial data. **Administration and Management:** Knowledge of business and management principles involved in strategic planning, resource allocation, human resources modeling, leadership technique, production methods, and coordination of people and resources. **Clerical Practices:** Knowledge of administrative and clerical procedures and systems such as word processing, managing files and records, stenography and transcription, designing forms, and other office procedures and terminology.

Substance Abuse and Behavioral Disorder Counselors

- ⚙ Education/Training Required: Master's degree
- ⚙ Annual Earnings: $31,510
- ⚙ Growth: 23.3%
- ⚙ Annual Job Openings: 10,000
- ⚙ Self-Employed: 4.5%
- ⚙ Part-Time: 14.6%

Counsel and advise individuals with alcohol, tobacco, drug, or other problems, such as gambling and eating disorders. May counsel individuals, families, or groups or engage in prevention programs. Complete and maintain accurate records and reports regarding the patients' histories and progress, services provided, and other required information. Coordinate counseling efforts with mental health professionals and other health professionals such as doctors, nurses, and social workers. Counsel clients and patients, individually and in group sessions, to assist in overcoming dependen-

cies, adjusting to life, and making changes. Develop client treatment plans based on research, clinical experience, and client histories. Interview clients, review records, and confer with other professionals in order to evaluate individuals' mental and physical condition, and to determine their suitability for participation in a specific program. Modify treatment plans to comply with changes in client status. Participate in case conferences and staff meetings. Plan and implement follow-up and aftercare programs for clients to be discharged from treatment programs. Provide clients or family members with information about addiction issues and about available services and programs, making appropriate referrals when necessary. Review and evaluate clients' progress in relation to measurable goals described in treatment and care plans. Act as liaisons between clients and medical staff. Attend training sessions in order to increase knowledge and skills. Conduct chemical dependency program orientation sessions. Confer with family members or others close to clients in order to keep them informed of treatment planning and progress. Coordinate activities with courts, probation officers, community services and other post-treatment agencies. Counsel family members to assist them in understanding, dealing with, and supporting clients or patients. Develop, implement, and evaluate public education, prevention, and health promotion programs, working in collaboration with organizations, institutions and communities. Follow progress of discharged patients in order to determine effectiveness of treatments. Instruct others in program methods, procedures, and functions. Intervene as advocate for clients or patients in order to resolve emergency problems in crisis situations. SKILLS—**Social Perceptiveness:** Being aware of others' reactions and understanding why they react as they do. **Management of Financial Resources:** Determining how money will be spent to get the work done and accounting for these expenditures. **Service Orientation:** Actively looking for ways to help people. **Management of Personnel Resources:** Motivating, developing, and directing people as they work, identifying the best people for the job. **Instructing:**

S

Teaching others how to do something. **Systems Analysis:** Determining how a system should work and how changes in conditions, operations, and the environment will affect outcomes. **Systems Evaluation:** Identifying measures or indicators of system performance and the actions needed to improve or correct performance relative to the goals of the system. **Negotiation:** Bringing others together and trying to reconcile differences.

GOE—Interest Area: 10. Human Service. **Work Group:** 10.01. Counseling and Social Work. **Other Jobs in This Work Group:** Child, Family, and School Social Workers; Clinical Psychologists; Counseling Psychologists; Marriage and Family Therapists; Medical and Public Health Social Workers; Mental Health and Substance Abuse Social Workers; Mental Health Counselors; Probation Officers and Correctional Treatment Specialists; Rehabilitation Counselors; Residential Advisors; Social and Human Service Assistants. **PERSONALITY TYPE:** Social. Social occupations frequently involve working with, communicating with, and teaching people. These occupations often involve helping or providing service to others.

EDUCATION/TRAINING PROGRAM(S)— Clinical/Medical Social Work; Mental and Social Health Services and Allied Professions, Other; Substance Abuse/Addiction Counseling. **RELATED KNOWLEDGE/COURSES—Therapy and Counseling:** Knowledge of principles, methods, and procedures for diagnosis, treatment, and rehabilitation of physical and mental dysfunctions and for career counseling and guidance. **Psychology:** Knowledge of human behavior and performance; individual differences in ability, personality, and interests; learning and motivation; psychological research methods; and the assessment and treatment of behavioral and affective disorders. **Customer and Personal Service:** Knowledge of principles and processes for providing customer and personal services. This includes customer needs assessment, meeting quality standards for services, and evaluation of customer satisfaction. **Medicine and Dentistry:** Knowledge of the information and

techniques needed to diagnose and treat human injuries, diseases, and deformities. This includes symptoms, treatment alternatives, drug properties and interactions, and preventive health-care measures. **Education and Training:** Knowledge of principles and methods for curriculum and training design, teaching and instruction for individuals and groups, and the measurement of training effects. **Communications and Media:** Knowledge of media production, communication, and dissemination techniques and methods. This includes alternative ways to inform and entertain via written, oral, and visual media.

Surgeons

- ◎ Education/Training Required: First professional degree
- ◎ Annual Earnings: More than $145,000
- ◎ Growth: 19.5%
- ◎ Annual Job Openings: 38,000
- ◎ Self-Employed: 16.9%
- ◎ Part-Time: 8.1%

Treat diseases, injuries, and deformities by invasive methods, such as manual manipulation or by using instruments and appliances. Analyze patient's medical history, medication allergies, physical condition, and examination results to verify operation's necessity and to determine best procedure. Prescribe preoperative and postoperative treatments and procedures, such as sedatives, diets, antibiotics, and preparation and treatment of the patient's operative area. Direct and coordinate activities of nurses, assistants, specialists, residents and other medical staff. Examine patient to provide information on medical condition and surgical risk. Follow established surgical techniques during the operation. Operate on patients to correct deformities, repair injuries, prevent and treat diseases, or improve or restore patients' functions. Refer patient to medical specialist or other practitioners when necessary. Conduct research to develop and test surgical techniques that can improve operating procedures and outcomes. Examine instruments, equipment, and operating room to ensure sterility. Manage surgery services, including planning, scheduling and coordination, determination of procedures, and procurement of supplies and equipment. Prepare case histories. Provide consultation and surgical assistance to other physicians and surgeons. Diagnose bodily disorders and orthopedic conditions and provide treatments, such as medicines and surgeries, in clinics, hospital wards, and operating rooms. **SKILLS—Science:** Using scientific rules and methods to solve problems. **Management of Personnel Resources:** Motivating, developing, and directing people as they work, identifying the best people for the job. **Systems Evaluation:** Identifying measures or indicators of system performance and the actions needed to improve or correct performance relative to the goals of the system. **Judgment and Decision Making:** Considering the relative costs and benefits of potential actions to choose the most appropriate one. **Systems Analysis:** Determining how a system should work and how changes in conditions, operations, and the environment will affect outcomes. **Reading Comprehension:** Understanding written sentences and paragraphs in work-related documents. **Operation and Control:** Controlling operations of equipment or systems. **Coordination:** Adjusting actions in relation to others' actions.

GOE—Interest Area: 08. Health Science. **Work Group:** 08.02. Medicine and Surgery. **Other Jobs in This Work Group:** Anesthesiologists; Family and General Practitioners; Internists, General; Medical Assistants; Medical Transcriptionists; Obstetricians and Gynecologists; Pediatricians, General; Pharmacists; Pharmacy Aides; Pharmacy Technicians; Physician Assistants; Psychiatrists; Registered Nurses; Surgical Technologists. **PERSONALITY TYPE:** Investigative. Investigative occupations frequently involve working with ideas and require an extensive amount of thinking. These occupations can involve searching for facts and figuring out problems mentally.

EDUCATION/TRAINING PROGRAM(S)— Adult Reconstructive Orthopedics (Orthopedic Surgery); Colon and Rectal Surgery; Critical Care Surgery; General Surgery; Hand Surgery; Neurological Surgery/Neurosurgery; Orthopedic Surgery of the Spine; Orthopedics/Orthopedic Surgery; Otolaryngology; Pediatric Orthopedics; Pediatric Surgery; Plastic Surgery; Sports Medicine; Thoracic Surgery; Urology; Vascular Surgery. **RELATED KNOWLEDGE/COURSES—Medicine and Dentistry:** Knowledge of the information and techniques needed to diagnose and treat human injuries, diseases, and deformities. This includes symptoms, treatment alternatives, drug properties and interactions, and preventive health-care measures. **Biology:** Knowledge of plant and animal organisms and their tissues, cells, functions, interdependencies, and interactions with each other and the environment. **Chemistry:** Knowledge of the chemical composition, structure, and properties of substances and of the chemical processes and transformations that they undergo. This includes uses of chemicals and their danger signs, production techniques, and disposal methods. **Administration and Management:** Knowledge of business and management principles involved in strategic planning, resource allocation, human resources modeling, leadership technique, production methods, and coordination of people and resources. **Therapy and Counseling:** Knowledge of principles, methods, and procedures for diagnosis, treatment, and rehabilitation of physical and mental dysfunctions and for career counseling and guidance. **Physics:** Knowledge and prediction of physical principles and laws and their interrelationships and applications to understanding fluid, material, and atmospheric dynamics and mechanical, electrical, atomic, and subatomic structures and processes. **Psychology:** Knowledge of human behavior and performance; individual differences in ability, personality, and interests; learning and motivation; psychological research methods; and the assessment and treatment of behavioral and affective disorders.

Survey Researchers

- ◎ Education/Training Required: Bachelor's degree
- ◎ Annual Earnings: $26,990
- ◎ Growth: 33.6%
- ◎ Annual Job Openings: 3,000
- ◎ Self-Employed: 9.3%
- ◎ Part-Time: 11.7%

Design or conduct surveys. May supervise interviewers who conduct the survey in person or over the telephone. May present survey results to client. Collaborate with other researchers in the planning, implementation, and evaluation of surveys. Conduct surveys and collect data, using methods such as interviews, questionnaires, focus groups, market analysis surveys, public opinion polls, literature reviews, and file reviews. Consult with clients in order to identify survey needs and any specific requirements, such as special samples. Determine and specify details of survey projects, including sources of information, procedures to be used, and the design of survey instruments and materials. Direct and review the work of staff members, including survey support staff and interviewers who gather survey data. Direct updates and changes in survey implementation and methods. Monitor and evaluate survey progress and performance, using sample disposition reports and response rate calculations. Prepare and present summaries and analyses of survey data, including tables, graphs, and fact sheets that describe survey techniques and results. Produce documentation of the questionnaire development process, data collection methods, sampling designs, and decisions related to sample statistical weighting. Support, plan, and coordinate operations for single or multiple surveys. Analyze data from surveys, old records, and/or case studies, using statistical software programs. Conduct research in order to gather information about survey topics. Hire and train recruiters and data collectors. Review, classify, and record survey data in preparation for computer analysis. Write training manuals to be used by survey interviewers. **SKILLS**—No data available.

GOE—Interest Area: 06. Finance and Insurance. **Work Group:** 06.02. Finance/Insurance Investigation and Analysis. **Other Jobs in This Work Group:** Appraisers, Real Estate; Assessors; Claims Examiners, Property and Casualty Insurance; Cost Estimators; Credit Analysts; Financial Analysts; Insurance Adjusters, Examiners, and Investigators; Insurance Appraisers, Auto Damage; Insurance Underwriters; Loan Counselors; Loan Officers; Market Research Analysts. **PERSONALITY TYPE:** No data available.

EDUCATION/TRAINING PROGRAM(S)— Applied Economics; Business/Managerial Economics; Economics, General; Marketing Research. **RELATED KNOWLEDGE/COURSES**—No data available.

Technical Writers

- ◎ Education/Training Required: Bachelor's degree
- ◎ Annual Earnings: $52,160
- ◎ Growth: 27.1%
- ◎ Annual Job Openings: 6,000
- ◎ Self-Employed: 7.3%
- ◎ Part-Time: 5.5%

Write technical materials, such as equipment manuals, appendices, or operating and maintenance instructions. May assist in layout work. Organize material and complete writing assignment according to set standards regarding order, clarity, conciseness, style, and terminology. Maintain records and files of work and revisions. Edit, standardize, or make changes to material prepared by other writers or establishment personnel. Confer with customer representatives, vendors, plant executives, or publisher to establish technical specifications and to determine subject material to be developed for publication. Review published materials and recommend revisions or changes in scope, format, content, and methods of reproduction and binding. Select photographs, drawings, sketches, diagrams, and charts to illustrate material. Study drawings, specifications, mockups, and product samples to integrate and delineate technology, operating procedure, and production sequence and detail. Interview production and engineering personnel and read journals and other material to become familiar with product technologies and production methods. Observe production, developmental, and experimental activities to determine operating procedure and detail. Arrange for typing, duplication, and distribution of material. Assist in laying out material for publication. Analyze developments in specific field to determine need for revisions in previously published materials and development of new material. Review manufacturer's and trade catalogs, drawings and other data relative to operation, maintenance, and service of equipment. Draw sketches to illustrate specified materials or assembly sequence. **SKILLS—Writing:** Communicating effectively in writing as appropriate for the needs of the audience. **Coordination:** Adjusting actions in relation to others' actions. **Active Learning:** Understanding the implications of new information for both current and future problem-solving and decision-making. **Active Listening:** Giving full attention to what other people are saying, taking time to understand the points being made, asking questions as appropriate, and not interrupting at inappropriate times. **Reading Comprehension:** Understanding written sentences and paragraphs in work-related documents. **Service Orientation:** Actively looking for ways to help people. **Technology Design:** Generating or adapting equipment and technology to serve user needs. **Speaking:** Talking to others to convey information effectively. **Learning Strategies:** Selecting and using training/instructional methods and procedures appropriate for the situation when learning or teaching new things.

GOE—Interest Area: 03. Arts and Communication. **Work Group:** 03.02. Writing and Editing. **Other Jobs in This Work Group:** Copy Writers; Creative Writers; Editors; Poets and Lyricists. **PERSONALITY TYPE:** Artistic. Artistic occupations frequently involve working with forms, designs, and patterns. They often require self-expression, and the work can be done without following a clear set of rules.

EDUCATION/TRAINING PROGRAM(S)— Business/Corporate Communications; Family and Consumer Sciences/Human Sciences Communication; Technical and Business Writing. **RELATED KNOWLEDGE/COURSES—English Language:** Knowledge of the structure and content of the English language, including the meaning and spelling of words, rules of composition, and grammar. **Clerical Practices:** Knowledge of administrative and clerical procedures and systems such as word processing, managing files and records, stenography and transcription, designing forms, and other office procedures and terminology. **Communications and Media:** Knowledge of media production, communication, and dissemination techniques and methods. This includes alternative ways to inform and entertain via written, oral, and visual media. **Computers and Electronics:** Knowledge of circuit boards, processors, chips, electronic equipment, and computer hardware and software, including applications and programming. **Education and Training:** Knowledge of principles and methods for curriculum and training design, teaching and instruction for individuals and groups, and the measurement of training effects. **Sales and Marketing:** Knowledge of principles and methods for showing, promoting, and selling products or services. This includes marketing strategy and tactics, product demonstration, sales techniques, and sales control systems.

T

Training and Development Managers

- ⊚ Education/Training Required: Work experience plus degree
- ⊚ Annual Earnings: $72,180
- ⊚ Growth: 19.4%
- ⊚ Annual Job Openings: 21,000
- ⊚ Self-Employed: 0%
- ⊚ Part-Time: 3.7%

Plan, direct, or coordinate the training and development activities and staff of an organization. Conduct orientation sessions and arrange on-the-job training for new hires. Evaluate instructor performance and the effectiveness of training programs, providing recommendations for improvement. Develop testing and evaluation procedures. Conduct or arrange for ongoing technical training and personal development classes for staff members. Confer with management and conduct surveys to identify training needs based on projected production processes, changes, and other factors. Develop and organize training manuals, multimedia visual aids, and other educational materials. Plan, develop, and provide training and staff development programs, using knowledge of the effectiveness of methods such as classroom training, demonstrations, on-the-job training, meetings, conferences, and workshops. Analyze training needs to develop new training programs or modify and improve existing programs. Review and evaluate training and apprenticeship programs for compliance with government standards. Train instructors and supervisors in techniques and skills for training and dealing with employees. Coordinate established courses with technical and professional courses provided by community schools and designate training procedures. Prepare training budget for department or organization. **SKILLS—Management of Personnel Resources:** Motivating, developing, and directing people as they work, identifying the best people for the job. **Management of Financial Resources:** Determining how money will be spent to get the work done and accounting for these expenditures. **Learning Strategies:** Selecting and using training/instructional methods and procedures appropriate for the situation when learning or teaching new things. **Negotiation:** Bringing others together and trying to reconcile differences. **Instructing:** Teaching others how to do something. **Service Orientation:** Actively looking for ways to help people. **Social Perceptiveness:** Being aware of others' reactions and understanding why they react as they do. **Persuasion:** Persuading others to change their minds or behavior.

GOE—Interest Area: 04. Business and Administration. **Work Group:** 04.01. Managerial Work in General Business. **Other Jobs in This Work Group:** Chief Executives; Compensation and Benefits Managers; General and Operations Managers; Human Resources Managers; Private Sector Executives. **PERSONALITY TYPE:** Enterprising. Enterprising occupations frequently involve starting up and carrying out projects. These occupations can involve leading people and making many decisions. They sometimes require risk taking and often deal with business.

EDUCATION/TRAINING PROGRAM(S)— Human Resources Development; Human Resources Management/Personnel Administration, General. **RELATED KNOWLEDGE/COURSES—Clerical Practices:** Knowledge of administrative and clerical procedures and systems such as word processing, managing files and records, stenography and transcription, designing forms, and other office procedures and terminology. **Personnel and Human Resources:** Knowledge of principles and procedures for personnel recruitment, selection, training, compensation and benefits, labor relations and negotiation, and personnel information systems. **Administration and Management:** Knowledge of business and management principles involved in strategic planning, resource allocation, human resources modeling, leadership technique, production methods, and coordination of people and resources. **Education and Training:** Knowledge of principles and methods for curriculum and training design, teaching and instruction for individuals and groups, and the measurement of training effects. **Psychology:** Knowledge of human behavior and performance; individual differences in ability, personality, and interests; learning and motivation; psychological research methods; and the assessment and treatment of behavioral and affective disorders. **Computers and Electronics:** Knowledge of circuit boards, processors, chips, electronic equipment, and computer hardware and software, including applications and programming.

Training and Development Specialists

- ◎ Education/Training Required: Bachelor's degree
- ◎ Annual Earnings: $44,270
- ◎ Growth: 27.9%
- ◎ Annual Job Openings: 35,000
- ◎ Self-Employed: 0.8%
- ◎ Part-Time: 7.7%

Conduct training and development programs for employees. Keep up with developments in area of expertise by reading current journals, books and magazine articles. Present information, using a variety of instructional techniques and formats such as role playing, simulations, team exercises, group discussions, videos and lectures. Schedule classes based on availability of classrooms, equipment, and instructors. Organize and develop, or obtain, training procedure manuals and guides and course materials such as handouts and visual materials. Offer specific training programs to help workers maintain or improve job skills. Monitor, evaluate and record training activities and program effectiveness. Attend meetings and seminars to obtain information for use in training programs, or to inform management of training program status. Coordinate recruitment and placement of training program participants. Evaluate training materials prepared by instructors, such as outlines, text, and handouts. Develop alternative training methods if expected improvements are not seen. Assess training needs through surveys, interviews with employees, focus groups, and/or consultation with managers, instructors or customer representatives. Screen, hire, and assign workers to positions based on qualifications. Select and assign instructors to conduct training. Devise programs to develop executive potential among employees in lower-level positions. Design, plan, organize and direct orientation and training for employees or customers of industrial or commercial establishment. Negotiate contracts with clients, including desired training outcomes, fees and expenses. Supervise instructors, evaluate instructor performance, and refer instructors to classes for skill development. Monitor training costs to ensure budget is not exceeded, and prepare budget reports to justify expenditures. Refer trainees to employer relations representatives, to locations offering job placement assistance, or to appropriate social services agencies if warranted. **SKILLS—Service Orientation:** Actively looking for ways to help people. **Instructing:** Teaching others how to do something. **Social Perceptiveness:** Being aware of others' reactions and understanding why they react as they do. **Writing:** Communicating effectively in writing as appropriate for the needs of the audience. **Persuasion:** Persuading others to change their minds or behavior. **Active Learning:** Understanding the implications of new information for both current and future problem-solving and decision-making. **Speaking:** Talking to others to convey information effectively. **Time Management:** Managing one's own time and the time of others.

GOE—Interest Area: 04. Business and Administration. **Work Group:** 04.03. Human Resources Support. **Other Jobs in This Work Group:** Compensation, Benefits, and Job Analysis Specialists; Employment Interviewers, Private or Public

Employment Service; Personnel Recruiters. **PER-SONALITY TYPE:** Social. Social occupations frequently involve working with, communicating with, and teaching people. These occupations often involve helping or providing service to others.

EDUCATION/TRAINING PROGRAM(S)— Human Resources Management/Personnel Administration, General; Organizational Behavior Studies. **RELATED KNOWLEDGE/COURSES—Customer and Personal Service:** Knowledge of principles and processes for providing customer and personal services. This includes customer needs assessment, meeting quality standards for services, and evaluation of customer satisfaction. **Psychology:** Knowledge of human behavior and performance; individual differences in ability, personality, and interests; learning and motivation; psychological research methods; and the assessment and treatment of behavioral and affective disorders. **Sociology and Anthropology:** Knowledge of group behavior and dynamics, societal trends and influences, human migrations, ethnicity, and cultures and their history and origins. **Personnel and Human Resources:** Knowledge of principles and procedures for personnel recruitment, selection, training, compensation and benefits, labor relations and negotiation, and personnel information systems. **Education and Training:** Knowledge of principles and methods for curriculum and training design, teaching and instruction for individuals and groups, and the measurement of training effects. **Clerical Practices:** Knowledge of administrative and clerical procedures and systems such as word processing, managing files and records, stenography and transcription, designing forms, and other office procedures and terminology. **Public Safety and Security:** Knowledge of relevant equipment, policies, procedures, and strategies to promote effective local, state, or national security operations for the protection of people, data, property, and institutions.

Treasurers, Controllers, and Chief Financial Officers

- Education/Training Required: Work experience plus degree
- Annual Earnings: $79,090
- Growth: 18.3%
- Annual Job Openings: 71,000
- Self-Employed: 3.1%
- Part-Time: 4.8%

Plan, direct, and coordinate the financial activities of an organization at the highest level of management. Includes financial reserve officers. Coordinate and direct the financial planning, budgeting, procurement, or investment activities of all or part of an organization. Develop internal control policies, guidelines, and procedures for activities such as budget administration, cash and credit management, and accounting. Prepare or direct preparation of financial statements, business activity reports, financial position forecasts, annual budgets, and/or reports required by regulatory agencies. Advise management on short-term and long-term financial objectives, policies, and actions. Analyze the financial details of past, present, and expected operations in order to identify development opportunities and areas where improvement is needed. Delegate authority for the receipt, disbursement, banking, protection, and custody of funds, securities, and financial instruments. Evaluate needs for procurement of funds and investment of surpluses, and make appropriate recommendations. Lead staff training and development in budgeting and financial management areas. Maintain current knowledge of organizational policies and procedures, federal and state policies and directives, and current accounting standards. Supervise employees performing financial reporting, accounting, billing, collections, payroll, and budgeting duties. Conduct or coordinate audits of company accounts and financial transactions to ensure compliance with state and federal requirements and statutes. Develop and maintain relationships with banking, insurance, and non-organizational accounting personnel in order to facilitate financial activities. Monitor and evaluate the performance of accounting and other financial staff; recommend and implement personnel actions such as promotions and dismissals. Monitor financial activities and details such as reserve levels to ensure that all legal and regulatory requirements are met. Perform tax planning work. Provide direction and assistance to other organizational units regarding accounting and budgeting policies and procedures, and efficient control and utilization of financial resources. Receive and record requests for disbursements; authorize disbursements in accordance with policies and procedures. **SKILLS—Management of Financial Resources:** Determining how money will be spent to get the work done and accounting for these expenditures. **Systems Analysis:** Determining how a system should work and how changes in conditions, operations, and the environment will affect outcomes. **Systems Evaluation:** Identifying measures or indicators of system performance and the actions needed to improve or correct performance relative to the goals of the system. **Judgment and Decision Making:** Considering the relative costs and benefits of potential actions to choose the most appropriate one. **Complex Problem Solving:** Identifying complex problems and reviewing related information to develop and evaluate options and implement solutions. **Mathematics:** Using mathematics to solve problems. **Management of Personnel Resources:** Motivating, developing, and directing people as they work, identifying the best people for the job. **Critical Thinking:** Using logic and reasoning to identify the strengths and weaknesses of alternative solutions, conclusions, or approaches to problems.

GOE—Interest Area: 06. Finance and Insurance. **Work Group:** 06.01. Managerial Work in Finance and Insurance. **Other Jobs in This Work Group:**

Financial Managers, Branch or Department. **PERSONALITY TYPE:** Enterprising. Enterprising occupations frequently involve starting up and carrying out projects. These occupations can involve leading people and making many decisions. They sometimes require risk taking and often deal with business.

EDUCATION/TRAINING PROGRAM(S)— Accounting and Business/Management; Accounting and Finance; Credit Management; Finance and Financial Management Services, Other; Finance, General; International Finance; Public Finance. **RELATED KNOWLEDGE/COURSES—Economics and Accounting:** Knowledge of economic and accounting principles and practices, the financial markets, banking, and the analysis and reporting of financial data. **Administration and Management:** Knowledge of business and management principles involved in strategic planning, resource allocation, human resources modeling, leadership technique, production methods, and coordination of people and resources. **Law and Government:** Knowledge of laws, legal codes, court procedures, precedents, government regulations, executive orders, agency rules, and the democratic political process. **Mathematics:** Knowledge of arithmetic, algebra, geometry, calculus, and statistics and their applications. **English Language:** Knowledge of the structure and content of the English language, including the meaning and spelling of words, rules of composition, and grammar. **Personnel and Human Resources:** Knowledge of principles and procedures for personnel recruitment, selection, training, compensation and benefits, labor relations and negotiation, and personnel information systems.

Urban and Regional Planners

◎ Education/Training Required: Master's degree

◎ Annual Earnings: $52,680

◎ Growth: 10.7%

◎ Annual Job Openings: 5,000

◎ Self-Employed: 2.6%

◎ Part-Time: 10.1%

Develop comprehensive plans and programs for use of land and physical facilities of local jurisdictions, such as towns, cities, counties, and metropolitan areas. Design, promote and administer government plans and policies affecting land use, zoning, public utilities, community facilities, housing, and transportation. Hold public meetings and confer with government, social scientists, lawyers, developers, the public, and special interest groups to formulate and develop land use or community plans. Recommend approval, denial or conditional approval of proposals. Determine the effects of regulatory limitations on projects. Assess the feasibility of proposals and identify necessary changes. Create, prepare, or requisition graphic and narrative reports on land use data, including land area maps overlaid with geographic variables such as population density. Advise planning officials on project feasibility, cost-effectiveness, regulatory conformance, and possible alternatives. Conduct field investigations, surveys, impact studies or other research in order to compile and analyze data on economic, social, regulatory and physical factors affecting land use. Discuss with planning officials the purpose of land use projects such as transportation, conservation, residential, commercial, industrial, and community use. Keep informed about economic and legal issues involved in zoning codes, building codes, and environmental regulations. Mediate community disputes and assist in developing alternative plans and recommendations for programs or projects. Coordi-

nate work with economic consultants and architects during the formulation of plans and the design of large pieces of infrastructure. Review and evaluate environmental impact reports pertaining to private and public planning projects and programs. Supervise and coordinate the work of urban planning technicians and technologists. Investigate property availability. **SKILLS—Persuasion:** Persuading others to change their minds or behavior. **Coordination:** Adjusting actions in relation to others' actions. **Complex Problem Solving:** Identifying complex problems and reviewing related information to develop and evaluate options and implement solutions. **Service Orientation:** Actively looking for ways to help people. **Time Management:** Managing one's own time and the time of others. **Social Perceptiveness:** Being aware of others' reactions and understanding why they react as they do. **Writing:** Communicating effectively in writing as appropriate for the needs of the audience. **Speaking:** Talking to others to convey information effectively. **Negotiation:** Bringing others together and trying to reconcile differences.

GOE—Interest Area: 07. Government and Public Administration. **Work Group:** 07.02. Public Planning. **Other Jobs in This Work Group:** City Planning Aides. **PERSONALITY TYPE:** Investigative. Investigative occupations frequently involve working with ideas and require an extensive amount of thinking. These occupations can involve searching for facts and figuring out problems mentally.

EDUCATION/TRAINING PROGRAM(S)— City/Urban, Community and Regional Planning. **RELATED KNOWLEDGE/COURSES— Design:** Knowledge of design techniques, tools, and principles involved in production of precision technical plans, blueprints, drawings, and models. **Geography:** Knowledge of principles and methods for describing the features of land, sea, and air masses, including their physical characteristics; locations; interrelationships; and distribution of plant, animal, and human life. **Customer and Personal Service:** Knowledge of principles and processes for providing customer and personal services. This includes customer needs assessment, meeting quality standards for services, and evaluation of customer satisfaction. **Building and Construction:** Knowledge of the materials, methods, and tools involved in the construction or repair of houses, buildings, or other structures such as highways and roads. **Law and Government:** Knowledge of laws, legal codes, court procedures, precedents, government regulations, executive orders, agency rules, and the democratic political process. **Clerical Practices:** Knowledge of administrative and clerical procedures and systems such as word processing, managing files and records, stenography and transcription, designing forms, and other office procedures and terminology.

Veterinarians

- Education/Training Required: First professional degree
- Annual Earnings: $65,290
- Growth: 25.1%
- Annual Job Openings: 4,000
- Self-Employed: 27.7%
- Part-Time: 10.6%

Diagnose and treat diseases and dysfunctions of animals. May engage in a particular function, such as research and development, consultation, administration, technical writing, sale or production of commercial products, or rendering of technical services to commercial firms or other organizations. Includes veterinarians who inspect livestock. Examine animals to detect and determine the nature of diseases or injuries. Treat sick or injured animals by prescribing medication, setting bones, dressing wounds, or performing surgery. Inoculate animals against various diseases such as rabies and distemper. Collect body tissue, feces, blood, urine, or other body fluids for examination and analysis. Operate diagnostic equipment such as radiographic and ultrasound equipment, and interpret the resulting images. Advise animal owners regarding sanitary measures, feeding, and general care necessary to promote health of animals. Educate the public about diseases that can be spread from animals to humans. Train and supervise workers who handle and care for animals. Provide care to a wide range of animals or specialize in a particular species, such as horses or exotic birds. Euthanize animals. Establish and conduct quarantine and testing procedures that prevent the spread of diseases to other animals or to humans, and that comply with applicable government regulations. Conduct postmortem studies and analyses to determine the causes of animals' deaths. Perform administrative duties such as scheduling appointments, accepting payments from clients, and maintaining business records. Direct the overall operations of animal hospitals, clinics, or mobile services to farms. Drive mobile clinic vans to farms so that health problems can be treated and/or prevented. Specialize in a particular type of treatment such as dentistry, pathology, nutrition, surgery, microbiology, or internal medicine. Inspect and test horses, sheep, poultry, and other animals to detect the presence of communicable diseases. Plan and execute animal nutrition and reproduction programs. Research diseases to which animals could be susceptible. Inspect animal housing facilities to determine their cleanliness and adequacy. Determine the effects of drug therapies, antibiotics, or new surgical techniques by testing them on animals. **SKILLS—Science:** Using scientific rules and methods to solve problems. **Instructing:** Teaching others how to do something. **Management of Financial Resources:** Determining how money will be spent to get the work done and accounting for these expenditures. **Reading Comprehension:** Understanding written sentences and paragraphs in work-related documents. **Active Learning:** Understanding the implications of new information for both current and future problem-solving and decision-making. **Service Orientation:** Actively looking for ways to help people. **Complex Problem Solving:** Identifying complex problems and reviewing related information to develop and evaluate options and implement solutions. **Judgment and Decision**

Making: Considering the relative costs and benefits of potential actions to choose the most appropriate one. **Time Management:** Managing one's own time and the time of others. **Management of Personnel Resources:** Motivating, developing, and directing people as they work, identifying the best people for the job.

GOE—Interest Area: 08. Health Science. **Work Group:** 08.05. Animal Care. **Other Jobs in This Work Group:** Animal Breeders; Animal Trainers; Nonfarm Animal Caretakers; Veterinary Assistants and Laboratory Animal Caretakers; Veterinary Technologists and Technicians. **PERSONALITY TYPE:** Investigative. Investigative occupations frequently involve working with ideas and require an extensive amount of thinking. These occupations can involve searching for facts and figuring out problems mentally.

EDUCATION/TRAINING PROGRAM(S)— Comparative and Laboratory Animal Medicine (Cert, MS, PhD); Laboratory Animal Medicine; Large Animal/Food Animal and Equine Surgery and Medicine (Cert, MS, PhD); Small/Companion Animal Surgery and Medicine (Cert, MS, PhD); Theriogenology; Veterinary Anatomy (Cert, MS, PhD); Veterinary Anesthesiology; Veterinary Biomedical and Clinical Sciences, Other (Cert, MS. PhD); Veterinary Dentistry; Veterinary Dermatology; Veterinary Emergency and Critical Care Medicine; Veterinary Infectious Diseases (Cert, MS, PhD); Veterinary Internal Medicine; Veterinary Medicine (DVM); Veterinary Microbiology; Veterinary Microbiology and Immunobiology (Cert, MS, PhD); Veterinary Nutrition; Veterinary Ophthalmology; Veterinary Pathology; Veterinary Pathology and Pathobiology (Cert, MS, PhD); Veterinary Physiology (Cert, MS, PhD); Veterinary Practice; Veterinary Preventive Medicine; Veterinary Preventive Medicine Epidemiology and Public Health (Cert, MS, PhD); Veterinary Radiology; Veterinary Residency Programs, Other; Veterinary Sciences/Veterinary Clinical Sciences, General (Cert, MS, PhD); Veterinary Surgery; Veterinary Toxicology; Veterinary Toxicology and Pharmacology (Cert, MS, PhD);

Zoological Medicine. **RELATED KNOWLEDGE/COURSES—Medicine and Dentistry:** Knowledge of the information and techniques needed to diagnose and treat human injuries, diseases, and deformities. This includes symptoms, treatment alternatives, drug properties and interactions, and preventive health-care measures. **Biology:** Knowledge of plant and animal organisms and their tissues, cells, functions, interdependencies, and interactions with each other and the environment. **Customer and Personal Service:** Knowledge of principles and processes for providing customer and personal services. This includes customer needs assessment, meeting quality standards for services, and evaluation of customer satisfaction. **Chemistry:** Knowledge of the chemical composition, structure, and properties of substances and of the chemical processes and transformations that they undergo. This includes uses of chemicals and their danger signs, production techniques, and disposal methods. **Sales and Marketing:** Knowledge of principles and methods for showing, promoting, and selling products or services. This includes marketing strategy and tactics, product demonstration, sales techniques, and sales control systems. **Education and Training:** Knowledge of principles and methods for curriculum and training design, teaching and instruction for individuals and groups, and the measurement of training effects.

Veterinary Technologists and Technicians

- Education/Training Required: Associate's degree
- Annual Earnings: $24,190
- Growth: 44.1%
- Annual Job Openings: 11,000
- Self-Employed: 0%
- Part-Time: 23.0%

Perform medical tests in a laboratory environment for use in the treatment and diagnosis of diseases in animals. Prepare vaccines and serums for prevention of diseases. Prepare tissue samples, take blood samples, and execute laboratory tests, such as urinalysis and blood counts. Clean and sterilize instruments and materials and maintain equipment and machines. Administer anesthesia to animals, under the direction of a veterinarian, and monitor animals' responses to anesthetics so that dosages can be adjusted. Care for and monitor the condition of animals recovering from surgery. Prepare and administer medications, vaccines, serums, and treatments, as prescribed by veterinarians. Perform laboratory tests on blood, urine, and feces, such as urinalyses and blood counts, to assist in the diagnosis and treatment of animal health problems. Administer emergency first aid, such as performing emergency resuscitation or other life saving procedures. Collect, prepare, and label samples for laboratory testing, culture, or microscopic examination. Clean and sterilize instruments, equipment, and materials. Provide veterinarians with the correct equipment and instruments, as needed. Fill prescriptions, measuring medications and labeling containers. Prepare animals for surgery, performing such tasks as shaving surgical areas. Take animals into treatment areas, and assist with physical examinations by performing such duties as obtaining temperature, pulse, and respiration data. Observe the behavior and condition of animals, and monitor their clinical symptoms. Take and develop diagnostic radiographs, using x-ray equipment. Maintain laboratory, research, and treatment records, as well as inventories of pharmaceuticals, equipment, and supplies. Give enemas and perform catheterizations, ear flushes, intravenous feedings, and gavages. Prepare treatment rooms for surgery. Maintain instruments, equipment, and machinery to ensure proper working condition. Perform dental work such as cleaning, polishing, and extracting teeth. Clean kennels, animal holding areas, surgery suites, examination rooms, and animal loading/unloading facilities to control the spread of disease. Provide information and counseling regarding issues such as animal health care, behavior problems, and nutrition. Provide assistance with animal euthanasia and the disposal of remains. Dress and suture wounds, and apply splints and other protective devices. Perform a variety of office, clerical, and accounting duties, such as reception, billing, bookkeeping, and/or selling products. **SKILLS—Instructing:** Teaching others how to do something. **Social Perceptiveness:** Being aware of others' reactions and understanding why they react as they do. **Science:** Using scientific rules and methods to solve problems. **Active Learning:** Understanding the implications of new information for both current and future problem-solving and decision-making. **Operation Monitoring:** Watching gauges, dials, or other indicators to make sure a machine is working properly. **Time Management:** Managing one's own time and the time of others. **Reading Comprehension:** Understanding written sentences and paragraphs in work-related documents. **Service Orientation:** Actively looking for ways to help people. **Equipment Maintenance:** Performing routine maintenance on equipment and determining when and what kind of maintenance is needed.

GOE—Interest Area: 08. Health Science. **Work Group:** 08.05. Animal Care. **Other Jobs in This Work Group:** Animal Breeders; Animal Trainers; Nonfarm Animal Caretakers; Veterinarians; Veterinary Assistants and Laboratory Animal Caretakers. **PERSONALITY TYPE:** No data available.

EDUCATION/TRAINING PROGRAM(S)— Veterinary/Animal Health Technology/Technician and Veterinary Assistant. **RELATED KNOWLEDGE/COURSES—Biology:** Knowledge of plant and animal organisms and their tissues, cells, functions, interdependencies, and interactions with each other and the environment. **Customer and Personal Service:** Knowledge of principles and processes for providing customer and personal services. This includes customer needs assessment, meeting quality standards for services, and evaluation of customer satisfaction. **Medicine and Dentistry:** Knowledge of the information and techniques needed to diagnose and treat human injuries, diseases, and deformities.

This includes symptoms, treatment alternatives, drug properties and interactions, and preventive health-care measures. **Chemistry:** Knowledge of the chemical composition, structure, and properties of substances and of the chemical processes and transformations that they undergo. This includes uses of chemicals and their danger signs, production techniques, and disposal methods. **Sales and Marketing:** Knowledge of principles and methods for showing, promoting, and selling products or services. This includes marketing strategy and tactics, product demonstration, sales techniques, and sales control systems. **Mathematics:** Knowledge of arithmetic, algebra, geometry, calculus, and statistics and their applications.

Vocational Education Teachers, Secondary School

- ◎ Education/Training Required: Bachelor's degree
- ◎ Annual Earnings: $45,140
- ◎ Growth: 9.0%
- ◎ Annual Job Openings: 12,000
- ◎ Self-Employed: 0%
- ◎ Part-Time: 8.8%

Teach or instruct vocational or occupational subjects at the secondary school level. Instruct students in the knowledge and skills required in a specific occupation or occupational field, using a systematic plan of lectures, discussions, audiovisual presentations, and laboratory, shop and field studies. Instruct students individually and in groups, using various teaching methods such as lectures, discussions, and demonstrations. Prepare, administer, and grade tests and assignments in order to evaluate students' progress. Assign and grade class work and homework. Confer with other staff members to

plan and schedule lessons promoting learning, following approved curricula. Confer with parents or guardians, other teachers, counselors, and administrators in order to resolve students' behavioral and academic problems. Enforce all administration policies and rules governing students. Establish and enforce rules for behavior and procedures for maintaining order among the students for whom they are responsible. Establish clear objectives for all lessons, units, and projects, and communicate those objectives to students. Guide and counsel students with adjustment and/or academic problems, or special academic interests. Instruct and monitor students the in use and care of equipment and materials, in order to prevent injury and damage. Maintain accurate and complete student records as required by law, district policy, and administrative regulations. Meet with other professionals to discuss individual students' needs and progress. Meet with parents and guardians to discuss their children's progress, and to determine their priorities for their children and their resource needs. Observe and evaluate students' performance, behavior, social development, and physical health. Place students in jobs or make referrals to job placement services. Plan and conduct activities for a balanced program of instruction, demonstration, and work time that provides students with opportunities to observe, question, and investigate. Plan and supervise class projects, field trips, visits by guest speakers or other experiential activities, and guide students in learning from those activities. Plan and supervise work-experience programs in businesses, industrial shops, and school laboratories. **SKILLS—Learning Strategies:** Selecting and using training/instructional methods and procedures appropriate for the situation when learning or teaching new things. **Instructing:** Teaching others how to do something. **Speaking:** Talking to others to convey information effectively. **Social Perceptiveness:** Being aware of others' reactions and understanding why they react as they do. **Mathematics:** Using mathematics to solve problems. **Reading Comprehension:** Understanding written sentences and paragraphs in work-related documents. **Monitoring:** Monitoring or assessing your performance or that of other individuals or organizations to make improvements or take corrective action. **Active Learning:** Understanding the implications of new information for both current and future problem-solving and decision-making.

GOE—Interest Area: 05. Education and Training. **Work Group:** 05.02. Pre-school, Elementary, and Secondary Teaching and Instructing. **Other Jobs in This Work Group:** Elementary School Teachers, Except Special Education; Kindergarten Teachers, Except Special Education; Middle School Teachers, Except Special and Vocational Education; Preschool Teachers, Except Special Education; Secondary School Teachers, Except Special and Vocational Education; Special Education Teachers, Middle School; Special Education Teachers, Preschool, Kindergarten, and Elementary School; Special Education Teachers, Secondary School; Teacher Assistants; Vocational Education Teachers, Middle School. **PERSONALITY TYPE:** Social. Social occupations frequently involve working with, communicating with, and teaching people. These occupations often involve helping or providing service to others.

EDUCATION/TRAINING PROGRAM(S)— Technology Teacher Education/Industrial Arts Teacher Education. **RELATED KNOWLEDGE/COURSES—Education and Training:** Knowledge of principles and methods for curriculum and training design, teaching and instruction for individuals and groups, and the measurement of training effects. **Therapy and Counseling:** Knowledge of principles, methods, and procedures for diagnosis, treatment, and rehabilitation of physical and mental dysfunctions and for career counseling and guidance. **English Language:** Knowledge of the structure and content of the English language, including the meaning and spelling of words, rules of composition, and grammar. **History and Archeology:** Knowledge of historical events and their causes, indicators, and effects on civilizations and cultures. **Sociology and Anthropology:** Knowledge of group behavior and dynamics, societal trends and influences, human migrations, ethnicity, and cul-

tures and their history and origins. **Geography:** Knowledge of principles and methods for describing the features of land, sea, and air masses, including their physical characteristics; locations; interrelationships; and distribution of plant, animal, and human life.

Wholesale and Retail Buyers, Except Farm Products

- Education/Training Required: Bachelor's degree
- Annual Earnings: $42,200
- Growth: 4.3%
- Annual Job Openings: 24,000
- Self-Employed: 9.9%
- Part-Time: 18.1%

Buy merchandise or commodities, other than farm products, for resale to consumers at the wholesale or retail level, including both durable and non-durable goods. Analyze past buying trends, sales records, price, and quality of merchandise to determine value and yield. Select, order, and authorize payment for merchandise according to contractual agreements. May conduct meetings with sales personnel and introduce new products. Examine, select, order, and purchase at the most favorable price merchandise consistent with quality, quantity, specification requirements and other factors. Negotiate prices, discount terms and transportation arrangements for merchandise. Analyze and monitor sales records, trends and economic conditions to anticipate consumer buying patterns and determine what the company will sell and how much inventory is needed. Interview and work closely with vendors to obtain and develop desired products. Authorize payment of invoices or return of mer-

W

chandise. Inspect merchandise or products to determine value or yield. Set or recommend mark-up rates, mark-down rates, and selling prices for merchandise. Confer with sales and purchasing personnel to obtain information about customer needs and preferences. Consult with store or merchandise managers about budget and goods to be purchased. Conduct staff meetings with sales personnel to introduce new merchandise. Manage the department for which they buy. Use computers to organize and locate inventory, and operate spreadsheet and word processing software. Train and supervise sales and clerical staff. Provide clerks with information to print on price tags, such as price, mark-ups or mark-downs, manufacturer number, season code, and style number. Determine which products should be featured in advertising, the advertising medium to be used, and when the ads should be run. Monitor competitors' sales activities by following their advertisements in newspapers and other media. **SKILLS—Management of Financial Resources:** Determining how money will be spent to get the work done and accounting for these expenditures. **Negotiation:** Bringing others together and trying to reconcile differences. **Management of Material Resources:** Obtaining and seeing to the appropriate use of equipment, facilities, and materials needed to do certain work. **Service Orientation:** Actively looking for ways to help people. **Instructing:** Teaching others how to do something. **Management of Personnel Resources:** Motivating, developing, and directing people as they work, identifying the best people for the job. **Learning Strategies:** Selecting and using training/instructional methods and procedures appropriate for the situation when learning or teaching new things. **Operations Analysis:** Analyzing needs and product requirements to create a design.

GOE—Interest Area: 14. Retail and Wholesale Sales and Service. **Work Group:** 14.05. Purchasing. **Other Jobs in This Work Group:** Purchasing Agents, Except Wholesale, Retail, and Farm Products. **PERSONALITY TYPE:** Enterprising. Enterprising occupations frequently involve starting up and carrying out projects. These occupations can involve leading people and making many decisions. They sometimes require risk taking and often deal with business.

EDUCATION/TRAINING PROGRAM(S)— Apparel and Accessories Marketing Operations; Apparel and Textile Marketing Management; Fashion Merchandising; Merchandising and Buying Operations; Sales, Distribution, and Marketing Operations, General. **RELATED KNOWLEDGE/COURSES—Sales and Marketing:** Knowledge of principles and methods for showing, promoting, and selling products or services. This includes marketing strategy and tactics, product demonstration, sales techniques, and sales control systems. **Customer and Personal Service:** Knowledge of principles and processes for providing customer and personal services. This includes customer needs assessment, meeting quality standards for services, and evaluation of customer satisfaction. **Clerical Practices:** Knowledge of administrative and clerical procedures and systems such as word processing, managing files and records, stenography and transcription, designing forms, and other office procedures and terminology. **Economics and Accounting:** Knowledge of economic and accounting principles and practices, the financial markets, banking, and the analysis and reporting of financial data. **Administration and Management:** Knowledge of business and management principles involved in strategic planning, resource allocation, human resources modeling, leadership technique, production methods, and coordination of people and resources. **Mathematics:** Knowledge of arithmetic, algebra, geometry, calculus, and statistics and their applications.

Index

A

C

D

E

Best Jobs with the Highest Percentage of College Graduates Age 55 and Over list, 38–39

Best Jobs with the Highest Percentage of Self-Employed College Graduates list, 48–49

loan officers, 18, 30, 68, 80, 92, 279–280

logisticians, 17, 27, 29, 68, 79, 280–281

M

male workers, 32, 58–64

management analysts, 16, 23, 26, 29, 38–39, 41–42, 49–52, 70, 79, 92, 281–282

managers and executives

administrative services managers, 17, 24, 28–29, 71, 79, 92, 99–100

advertising and promotions managers, 17, 23, 27, 34–37, 71, 84, 90, 102–103

agents and business managers of artists, performers, and athletes, 19, 24, 27, 33–36, 49–51, 71, 78, 93, 105–106

art directors, 19, 23, 39–40, 43, 45, 47–48, 50, 52, 71, 78, 90, 117–118

chief executives, 16, 22, 29, 38–42, 60–63, 71, 79, 145–146

compensation and benefits managers, 17, 23, 30, 71, 79, 92, 156–158

computer and information systems managers, 16, 23, 26, 29, 60–64, 70, 83, 92, 159–160

construction managers, 17, 23, 29, 48, 50, 52, 59, 61, 63, 68, 78, 92, 172–173

directors, religious activities and education, 20, 27, 31, 33, 35–38, 41–43, 46–47, 69, 83, 91, 189–190

directors—stage, motion pictures, television, and radio, 19, 48–49, 51–52, 71, 78, 90, 187–188

financial managers, branch or department, 17, 23, 29, 71, 80, 92, 232–233

gaming managers, 21, 24, 48, 50, 52, 71, 82, 93, 238–239

general and operations managers, 16, 23, 29, 60–61, 63, 71, 79, 239–241

government service executives, 17, 22, 29, 38–42, 60–63, 71, 81, 92, 244–246

human resources managers, 17, 23, 30, 71, 79, 92, 255–257

industrial production managers, 18, 23, 31, 59, 69, 84, 93, 259–260

marketing managers, 17, 23, 28, 30, 71, 84, 92, 283–285

medical and health services managers, 16, 23, 27, 30, 70, 81, 92, 294–296

natural sciences managers, 19, 23, 71, 85, 88, 309–311

private sector executives, 17, 23, 29, 38–42, 60–63, 71, 79, 92, 353–354

producers, 19, 48–49, 51–52, 71, 78, 90, 356–357

program directors, 19, 48–49, 51–52, 71, 78, 93, 358–360

property, real estate, and community association managers, 20, 30, 38, 42, 48, 52, 69, 84, 93, 360–361

public relations managers, 17, 23, 27, 71, 78, 365–367

purchasing managers, 20, 23, 71, 84, 93, 369–370

sales managers, 16, 23, 26, 29, 70, 84, 92, 385–386

work experience, 22, 37–38, 64–66, 70–71

workers

    age 20–24, 32–37

    age 55 and over, 32, 37–42

    men, 32, 58–64

    part-time, 32, 42–47

    self-employed, 32, 47–53

    women, 32, 53–58

Y–Z

young workers, 32–37